No Auto Books

Chilton

7-31-98

NISSAN 240SX/ALTIMA 1993-98 REPAIR MANUAL

P9-DMC-572

Deleted

President	Dean F. Morgantini, S.A.E.
Vice President–Finance	Barry L. Beck
Vice President–Sales	Glenn D. Potere
Executive Editor	Kevin M. G. Maher
Production Manager	Ben Greisler, S.A.E.
Project Managers	Michael Abraham, George B. Heinrich III, S.A.E., Will Kessler, A.S.E., S.A.E., Richard Schwartz
Schematics Editor	Christopher G. Ritchie
Editor	James R. Marotta

CHILTON™ Automotive Books

PUBLISHED BY **W. G. NICHOLS, INC.**

Manufactured in USA
© 1998 W. G. Nichols
1020 Andrew Drive
West Chester, PA 19380
ISBN 0-8019-8970-1
Library of Congress Catalog Card No. 98-71220
1234567890 7654321098

FINNEY CO. PUBLIC LIBRARY
605 EAST WALNUT
GARDEN CITY, KS 67846

™Chilton is a registered trademark of the Chilton Company and is licensed to W. G. Nichols, Inc.

Contents

Contents

SAFETY NOTICE

Proper service and repair procedures are vital to the safe, reliable operation of all motor vehicles, as well as the personal safety of those performing repairs. This manual outlines procedures for servicing and repairing vehicles using safe, effective methods. The procedures contain many NOTES, CAUTIONS and WARNINGS which should be followed, along with standard procedures, to eliminate the possibility of personal injury or improper service which could damage the vehicle or compromise its safety.

It is important to note that repair procedures and techniques, tools and parts for servicing motor vehicles, as well as the skill and experience of the individual performing the work, vary widely. It is not possible to anticipate all of the conceivable ways or conditions under which vehicles may be serviced, or to provide cautions as to all possible hazards that may result. Standard and accepted safety precautions and equipment should be used during cutting, grinding, chiseling, prying, or any other process that can cause material removal or projectiles.

Some procedures require the use of tools specially designed for a specific purpose. Before substituting another tool or procedure, you must be completely satisfied that neither your personal safety, nor the performance of the vehicle, will be endangered.

Although information in this manual is based on industry sources and is complete as possible at the time of publication, the possibility exists that some vehicle manufacturers made later changes which could not be included here. While striving for total accuracy, NP/Chilton cannot assume responsibility for any errors, changes or omissions that may occur in the compilation of this data.

PART NUMBERS

Part numbers listed in this reference are not recommendations by Chilton for any product brand name. They are references that can be used with interchange manuals and aftermarket supplier catalogs to locate each brand supplier's discrete part number.

SPECIAL TOOLS

Special tools are recommended by the vehicle manufacturer to perform their specific job. Use has been kept to a minimum, but, where absolutely necessary, they are referred to in the text by the part number of the tool manufacturer. These tools can be purchased, under the appropriate part number, from your local dealer or regional distributor, or an equivalent tool can be purchased locally from a tool supplier or parts outlet. Before substituting any tool for the one recommended, read the SAFETY NOTICE at the top of this page.

ACKNOWLEDGMENTS

NP/Chilton expresses appreciation to Nissan Motor Company for their generous assistance.

A special thanks to the fine companies who supported the production of this book. Hand tools, supplied by Craftsman, were used during all phases of vehicle teardown and photography. Many of the fine specialty tools used in procedures were provided courtesy of Lisle Corporation. A Rotary lift, the largest automobile lift manufacturer in the world offering the biggest variety of surface and inground lifts available, was also used.

No part of this publication may be reproduced, transmitted or stored in any form or by any means, electronic or mechanical, including photocopy, recording, or by information storage or retrieval system, without prior written permission from the publisher.

1

GENERAL INFORMATION AND MAINTENANCE

HOW TO USE THIS BOOK

Chilton's Total Car Care manual for the Nissan 240SX and Altima is intended to help you learn more about the inner workings of your vehicle while saving you money on its upkeep and operation.

The beginning of the book will likely be referred to the most, since that is where you will find information for maintenance and tune-up. The other sections deal with the more complex systems of your vehicle. Operating systems from engine through brakes are covered to the extent that the average do-it-yourselfer becomes mechanically involved. This book will not explain such things as rebuilding a differential for the simple reason that the expertise required and the investment in special tools make this task uneconomical. It will, however, give you detailed instructions to help you change your own brake pads and shoes, replace spark plugs, and perform many more jobs that can save you money, give you personal satisfaction and help you avoid expensive problems.

A secondary purpose of this book is a reference for owners who want to understand their vehicle and/or their mechanics better. In this case, no tools at all are required.

Where to Begin

Before removing any bolts, read through the entire procedure. This will give you the overall view of what tools and supplies will be required. There is nothing more frustrating than having to walk to the bus stop on Monday morning because you were short one bolt on Sunday afternoon. So read ahead and plan ahead. Each operation should be approached logically and all procedures thoroughly understood before attempting any work.

All sections contain adjustments, maintenance, removal and installation procedures, and in some cases, repair or overhaul procedures. When repair is not considered practical, we tell you how to remove the part and then how to install the new or rebuilt replacement. In this way, you at least save the labor costs. Backyard repair of some components is just not practical.

Avoiding Trouble

Many procedures in this book require you to "label and disconnect . . ." a group of lines, hoses or wires. Don't be lulled into thinking you can remember where everything goes—you won't. If you hook up vacuum or fuel lines incorrectly, the vehicle will run poorly, if at all. If you hook up electrical wiring incorrectly, you may instantly learn a very expensive lesson.

You don't need to know the official or engineering name for each hose or line. A piece of masking tape on the hose and a piece on its fitting will allow you to assign your own label such as the letter A or a short name. As long as you remember your own code, the lines can be reconnected by matching similar letters or names. Do remember that tape will dissolve in gasoline or other fluids; if a component is to be washed or cleaned, use another method of identification. A permanent felt-tipped marker can be very handy for marking metal parts. Remove any tape or paper labels after assembly.

Maintenance or Repair?

It's necessary to mention the difference between maintenance and repair. Maintenance includes routine inspections, adjustments, and replacement of parts which show signs of normal wear. Maintenance compensates for wear or deterioration. Repair implies that something has broken or is not working. A need for repair is often caused by lack of maintenance. Example: draining and refilling the automatic transmission fluid is maintenance recommended by the manufacturer at specific mileage intervals. Failure to do this can ruin the transmission/transaxle, requiring very expensive repairs. While no maintenance program can prevent items from breaking or wearing out, a general rule can be stated: MAINTENANCE IS CHEAPER THAN REPAIR.

Two basic mechanic's rules should be mentioned here. First, whenever the left side of the vehicle or engine is referred to, it is meant to specify the driver's side. Conversely, the right side of the vehicle means the passenger's side. Second, most screws and bolts are removed by turning counterclockwise, and tightened by turning clockwise.

Safety is always the most important rule. Constantly be aware of the dangers involved in working on an automobile and take the proper precautions. See the information in this section regarding SERVICING YOUR VEHICLE SAFELY and the SAFETY NOTICE on the acknowledgment page.

Avoiding the Most Common Mistakes

Pay attention to the instructions provided. There are 3 common mistakes in mechanical work:

1. Incorrect order of assembly, disassembly or adjustment. When taking something apart or putting it together, performing steps in the wrong order usually just costs you extra time; however, it CAN break something. Read the entire procedure before beginning disassembly. Perform everything in the order in which the instructions say you should, even if you can't immediately see a reason for it. When you're taking apart something that is very intricate, you might want to draw a picture of how it looks when assembled at one point in order to make sure you get everything back in its proper position. We will supply exploded views whenever possible. When making adjustments, perform them in the proper order; often, one adjustment affects another, and you cannot expect even satisfactory results unless each adjustment is made only when it cannot be changed by any other.

2. Overtorquing (or undertorquing). While it is more common for overtorquing to cause damage, undertorquing may allow a fastener to vibrate loose causing serious damage. Especially when dealing with aluminum parts, pay attention to torque specifications and utilize a torque wrench in assembly. If a torque figure is not available, remember that if you are using the right tool to perform the job, you will probably not have to strain yourself to get a fastener tight enough. The pitch of most threads is so slight that the tension you put on the wrench will be multiplied many times in actual force on what you are tightening. A good example of how critical torque is can be seen in the case of spark plug installation, especially where you are putting the plug into an aluminum cylinder head. Too little torque can fail to crush the gasket, causing leakage of combustion gases and consequent overheating of the plug and engine parts. Too much torque can damage the threads or distort the plug, changing the spark gap.

There are many commercial products available for ensuring that fasteners won't come loose, even if they are not torqued just right (a very common brand is Loctite®). If you're worried about getting something together tight enough to hold, but loose enough to avoid mechanical damage during assembly, one of these products might offer substantial insurance. Before choosing a threadlocking compound, read the label on the package and make sure the product is compatible with the materials, fluids, etc. involved.

3. Crossthreading. This occurs when a part such as a bolt is screwed into a nut or casting at the wrong angle and forced. Crossthreading is more likely to occur if access is difficult. It helps to clean and lubricate fasteners, then to start threading with the part to be installed positioned straight in. Then, start the bolt, spark plug, etc. with your fingers. If you encounter resistance, unscrew the part and start over again at a different angle until it can be inserted and turned several times without much effort. Keep in mind that many parts, especially spark plugs, have tapered threads, so that gentle turning will automatically bring the part you're threading to the proper angle, but only if you don't force it or resist a change in angle. Don't put a wrench on the part until it's been tightened a couple of turns by hand. If you suddenly encounter resistance, and the part has not seated fully, don't force it. Pull it back out to make sure it's clean and threading properly.

Always take your time and be patient; once you have some experience, working on your vehicle may well become an enjoyable hobby.

TOOLS AND EQUIPMENT

▶ **See Figures 1 thru 15**

Naturally, without the proper tools and equipment it is impossible to properly service your vehicle. It would also be virtually impossible to catalog every tool that you would need to perform all of the operations in this book. Of course, It would be unwise for the amateur to rush out and buy an expensive set of tools on the theory that he/she may need one or more of them at some time.

The best approach is to proceed slowly, gathering a good quality set of those tools that are used most frequently. Don't be misled by the low cost of bargain tools. It is far better to spend a little more for better quality. Forged wrenches, 6 or 12-point sockets and fine tooth ratchets are by far preferable to their less expensive counterparts. As any good mechanic can tell you, there are few worse experiences than trying to work on a vehicle with bad tools. Your monetary savings will be far outweighed by frustration and mangled knuckles.

Begin accumulating those tools that are used most frequently: those associated with routine maintenance and tune-up. In addition to the normal assortment of screwdrivers and pliers, you should have the following tools:

• Wrenches/sockets and combination open end/box end wrenches in sizes from ⅛–¾ in. or 3mm–19mm (depending on whether your vehicle uses standard or metric fasteners) and a ¹³⁄₁₆ in. or ⅝ in. spark plug socket (depending on plug type).

➡**If possible, buy various length socket drive extensions. Universal-joint and wobble extensions can be extremely useful, but be careful when using them, as they can change the amount of torque applied to the socket.**

• Jackstands for support.
• Oil filter wrench.
• Spout or funnel for pouring fluids.
• Grease gun for chassis lubrication (unless your vehicle is not equipped with any grease fittings—for details, please refer to information on Fluids and Lubricants, later in this section).
• Hydrometer for checking the battery (unless equipped with a sealed, maintenance-free battery).
• A container for draining oil and other fluids.
• Rags for wiping up the inevitable mess.

In addition to the above items there are several others that are not absolutely necessary, but handy to have around. These include Oil Dry® (or an equivalent oil absorbent gravel—such as cat litter) and the usual supply of lubricants, antifreeze and fluids, although these can be purchased as needed. This is a basic list for routine maintenance, but only your personal needs and desire can accurately determine your list of tools.

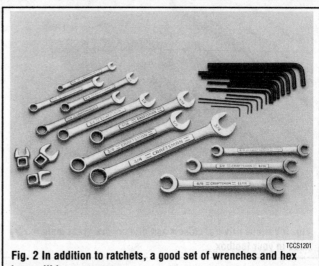

Fig. 2 In addition to ratchets, a good set of wrenches and hex keys will be necessary

Fig. 3 A hydraulic floor jack and a set of jackstands are essential for lifting and supporting the vehicle

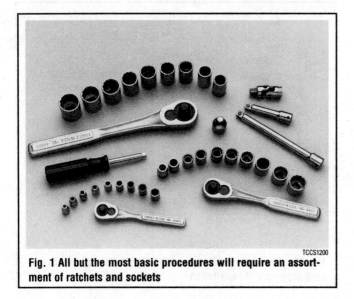

Fig. 1 All but the most basic procedures will require an assortment of ratchets and sockets

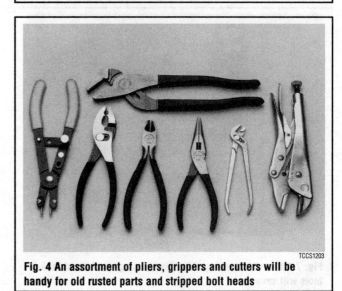

Fig. 4 An assortment of pliers, grippers and cutters will be handy for old rusted parts and stripped bolt heads

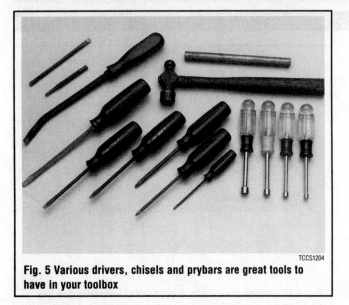

Fig. 5 Various drivers, chisels and prybars are great tools to have in your toolbox

TCCS1204

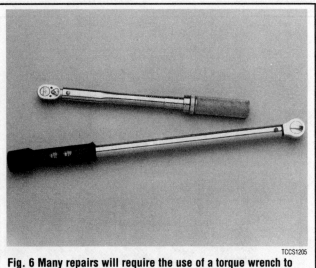

Fig. 6 Many repairs will require the use of a torque wrench to assure the components are properly fastened

TCCS1205

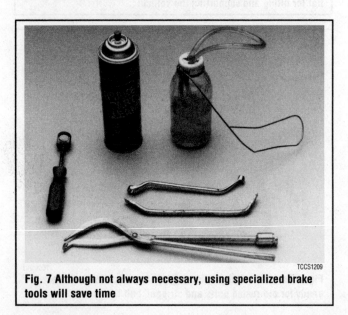

Fig. 7 Although not always necessary, using specialized brake tools will save time

TCCS1209

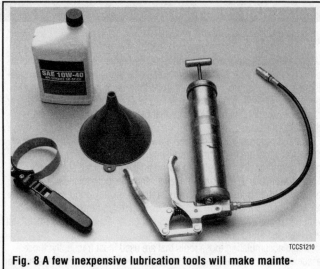
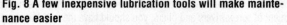

Fig. 8 A few inexpensive lubrication tools will make maintenance easier

TCCS1210

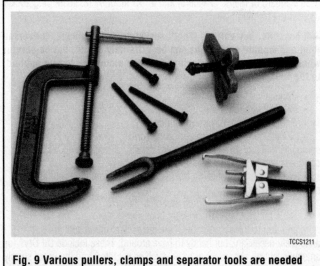
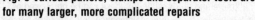

Fig. 9 Various pullers, clamps and separator tools are needed for many larger, more complicated repairs

TCCS1211

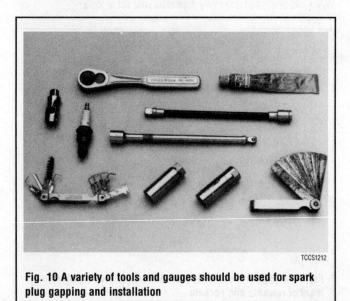

Fig. 10 A variety of tools and gauges should be used for spark plug gapping and installation

TCCS1212

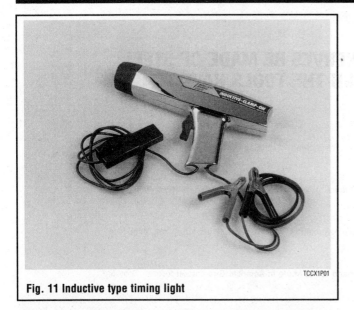

Fig. 11 **Inductive type timing light**

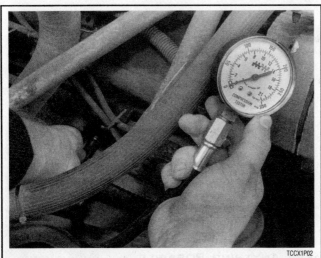

Fig. 12 **A screw-in type compression gauge is recommended for compression testing**

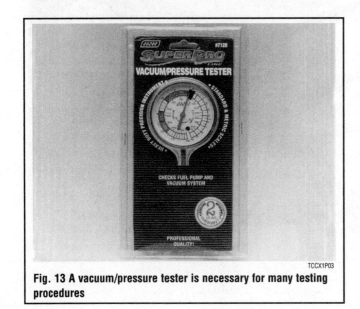

Fig. 13 **A vacuum/pressure tester is necessary for many testing procedures**

After performing a few projects on the vehicle, you'll be amazed at the other tools and non-tools on your workbench. Some useful household items are: a large turkey baster or siphon, empty coffee cans and ice trays (to store parts), ball of twine, electrical tape for wiring, small rolls of colored tape for tagging lines or hoses, markers and pens, a note pad, golf tees (for plugging vacuum lines), metal coat hangers or a roll of mechanic's wire (to hold things out of the way), dental pick or similar long, pointed probe, a strong magnet, and a small mirror (to see into recesses and under manifolds).

A more advanced set of tools, suitable for tune-up work, can be drawn up easily. While the tools are slightly more sophisticated, they need not be

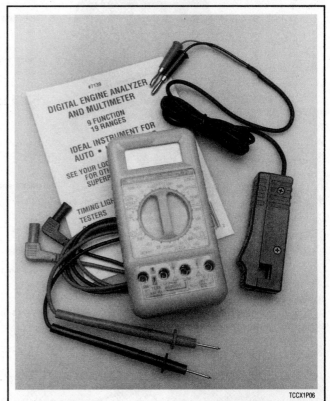

Fig. 14 **Most modern automotive multimeters incorporate many helpful features**

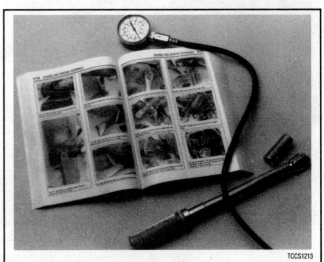

Fig. 15 **Proper information is vital, so always have a Chilton Total Car Care manual handy**

IN A SPORT THAT DEMANDS NERVES BE MADE OF STEEL, YOU CAN IMAGINE HOW TOUGH THE TOOLS HAVE TO BE.

It's pounding. Wrenching. Cranking metal against metal at 800˚.

Nothing's a more grueling test of a tool than professional racing.

That's why professional racing mechanics depend on Craftsman tools.

Over 2,200 hand tools. Made in America. Guaranteed forever. They are

the only tools tough enough to be the official tools of NASCAR, CART,

NHRA and the NASCAR Craftsman Truck Series. And of course, they are

the same tools you use to get your job done. To learn more about

Craftsman tools, or to order our products online, visit our website at

www.sears.com/craftsman.

CRAFTSMAN

MAKES ANYTHING POSSIBLE

www.sears.com/craftsman
© 1997 Sears, Roebuck and Co.

TCCA1AC1

outrageously expensive. There are several inexpensive tach/dwell meters on the market that are every bit as good for the average mechanic as a professional model. Just be sure that it goes to a least 1200–1500 rpm on the tach scale and that it works on 4, 6 and 8-cylinder engines. (If you have one or more vehicles with a diesel engine, a special tachometer is required since diesels don't use spark plug ignition systems). The key to these purchases is to make them with an eye towards adaptability and wide range. A basic list of tune-up tools could include:

- Tach/dwell meter.
- Spark plug wrench and gapping tool.
- Feeler gauges for valve or point adjustment. (Even if your vehicle does not use points or require valve adjustments, a feeler gauge is helpful for many repair/overhaul procedures).

A tachometer/dwell meter will ensure accurate tune-up work on vehicles without electronic ignition. The choice of a timing light should be made carefully. A light which works on the DC current supplied by the vehicle's battery is the best choice; it should have a xenon tube for brightness. On any vehicle with an electronic ignition system, a timing light with an inductive pickup that clamps around the No. 1 spark plug cable is preferred.

In addition to these basic tools, there are several other tools and gauges you may find useful. These include:

- Compression gauge. The screw-in type is slower to use, but eliminates the possibility of a faulty reading due to escaping pressure.
- Manifold vacuum gauge.

- 12V test light.
- A combination volt/ohmmeter
- Inductive ammeter. This is used for determining whether or not there is current in a wire. These are handy for use if a wire is broken somewhere in a wiring harness.

As a final note, you will probably find a torque wrench necessary for all but the most basic work. The beam type models are perfectly adequate, although the newer click types (breakaway) are easier to use. The click type torque wrenches tend to be more expensive. Also keep in mind that all types of torque wrenches should be periodically checked and/or recalibrated. You will have to decide for yourself which better fits your purpose.

Special Tools

Normally, the use of special factory tools is avoided for repair procedures, since these are not readily available for the do-it-yourself mechanic. When it is possible to perform the job with more commonly available tools, it will be pointed out, but occasionally, a special tool was designed to perform a specific function and should be used. Before substituting another tool, you should be convinced that neither your safety nor the performance of the vehicle will be compromised.

Special tools can usually be purchased from an automotive parts store or from your dealer. In some cases special tools may be available directly from the tool manufacturer.

SERVICING YOUR VEHICLE SAFELY

♦ See Figures 16, 17, 18 and 19

It is virtually impossible to anticipate all of the hazards involved with automotive maintenance and service, but care and common sense will prevent most accidents.

The rules of safety for mechanics range from "don't smoke around gasoline," to "use the proper tool(s) for the job." The trick to avoiding injuries is to develop safe work habits and to take every possible precaution.

Do's

- Do keep a fire extinguisher and first aid kit handy.
- Do wear safety glasses or goggles when cutting, drilling, grinding or prying, even if you have 20–20 vision. If you wear glasses for the sake of vision, wear safety goggles over your regular glasses.

- Do shield your eyes whenever you work around the battery. Batteries contain sulfuric acid. In case of contact with the eyes or skin, flush the area with water or a mixture of water and baking soda, then seek immediate medical attention.
- Do use safety stands (jackstands) for any undervehicle service. Jacks are for raising vehicles; jackstands are for making sure the vehicle stays raised until you want it to come down. Whenever the vehicle is raised, block the wheels remaining on the ground and set the parking brake.
- Do use adequate ventilation when working with any chemicals or hazardous materials. Like carbon monoxide, the asbestos dust resulting from some brake lining wear can be hazardous in sufficient quantities.
- Do disconnect the negative battery cable when working on the electrical system. The secondary ignition system contains EXTREMELY HIGH VOLTAGE. In some cases it can even exceed 50,000 volts.

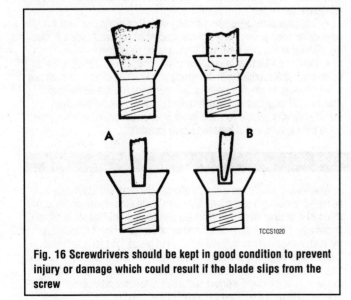

Fig. 16 Screwdrivers should be kept in good condition to prevent injury or damage which could result if the blade slips from the screw

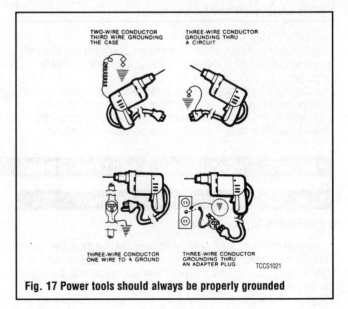

Fig. 17 Power tools should always be properly grounded

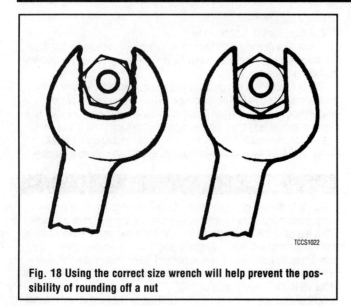

Fig. 18 Using the correct size wrench will help prevent the possibility of rounding off a nut

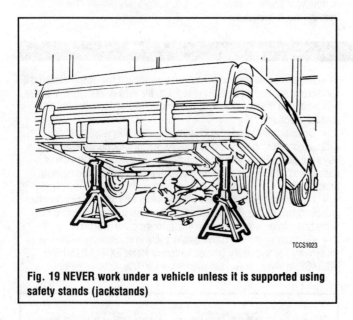

Fig. 19 NEVER work under a vehicle unless it is supported using safety stands (jackstands)

• Do follow manufacturer's directions whenever working with potentially hazardous materials. Most chemicals and fluids are poisonous if taken internally.

• Do properly maintain your tools. Loose hammerheads, mushroomed punches and chisels, frayed or poorly grounded electrical cords, excessively worn screwdrivers, spread wrenches (open end), cracked sockets, slipping ratchets, or faulty droplight sockets can cause accidents.

FASTENERS, MEASUREMENTS AND CONVERSIONS

Bolts, Nuts and Other Threaded Retainers

▶ See Figures 20, 21, 22 and 23

Although there are a great variety of fasteners found in the modern car or truck, the most commonly used retainer is the threaded fastener (nuts, bolts, screws, studs, etc). Most threaded retainers may be reused, provided that they are not damaged in use or during the repair. Some retainers (such as stretch bolts or torque prevailing nuts) are designed to deform when tightened or in use and should not be reinstalled.

• Likewise, keep your tools clean; a greasy wrench can slip off a bolt head, ruining the bolt and often harming your knuckles in the process.

• Do use the proper size and type of tool for the job at hand. Do select a wrench or socket that fits the nut or bolt. The wrench or socket should sit straight, not cocked.

• Do, when possible, pull on a wrench handle rather than push on it, and adjust your stance to prevent a fall.

• Do be sure that adjustable wrenches are tightly closed on the nut or bolt and pulled so that the force is on the side of the fixed jaw.

• Do strike squarely with a hammer; avoid glancing blows.

• Do set the parking brake and block the drive wheels if the work requires a running engine.

Don'ts

• Don't run the engine in a garage or anywhere else without proper ventilation—EVER! Carbon monoxide is poisonous; it takes a long time to leave the human body and you can build up a deadly supply of it in your system by simply breathing in a little every day. You may not realize you are slowly poisoning yourself. Always use power vents, windows, fans and/or open the garage door.

• Don't work around moving parts while wearing loose clothing. Short sleeves are much safer than long, loose sleeves. Hard-toed shoes with neoprene soles protect your toes and give a better grip on slippery surfaces. Jewelry such as watches, fancy belt buckles, beads or body adornment of any kind is not safe working around a vehicle. Long hair should be tied back under a hat or cap.

• Don't use pockets for toolboxes. A fall or bump can drive a screwdriver deep into your body. Even a rag hanging from your back pocket can wrap around a spinning shaft or fan.

• Don't smoke when working around gasoline, cleaning solvent or other flammable material.

• Don't smoke when working around the battery. When the battery is being charged, it gives off explosive hydrogen gas.

• Don't use gasoline to wash your hands; there are excellent soaps available. Gasoline contains dangerous additives which can enter the body through a cut or through your pores. Gasoline also removes all the natural oils from the skin so that bone dry hands will suck up oil and grease.

• Don't service the air conditioning system unless you are equipped with the necessary tools and training. When liquid or compressed gas refrigerant is released to atmospheric pressure it will absorb heat from whatever it contacts. This will chill or freeze anything it touches. Although refrigerant is normally non-toxic, R-12 becomes a deadly poisonous gas in the presence of an open flame. One good whiff of the vapors from burning refrigerant can be fatal.

• Don't use screwdrivers for anything other than driving screws! A screwdriver used as an prying tool can snap when you least expect it, causing injuries. At the very least, you'll ruin a good screwdriver.

• Don't use a bumper or emergency jack (that little ratchet, scissors, or pantograph jack supplied with the vehicle) for anything other than changing a flat! These jacks are only intended for emergency use out on the road; they are NOT designed as a maintenance tool. If you are serious about maintaining your vehicle yourself, invest in a hydraulic floor jack of at least a 1½ ton capacity, and at least two sturdy jackstands.

Whenever possible, we will note any special retainers which should be replaced during a procedure. But you should always inspect the condition of a retainer when it is removed and replace any that show signs of damage. Check all threads for rust or corrosion which can increase the torque necessary to achieve the desired clamp load for which that fastener was originally selected. Additionally, be sure that the driver surface of the fastener has not been compromised by rounding or other damage. In some cases a driver surface may become only partially rounded, allowing the driver to catch in only one direction. In many of these occurrences, a fastener may be installed and tightened, but the

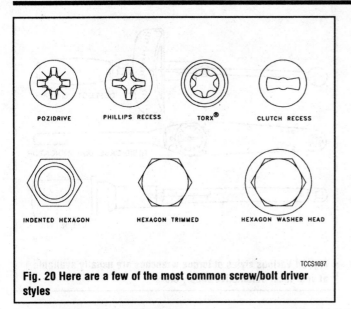

Fig. 20 Here are a few of the most common screw/bolt driver styles

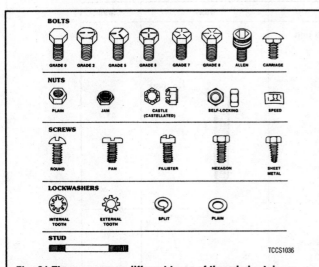

Fig. 21 There are many different types of threaded retainers found on vehicles

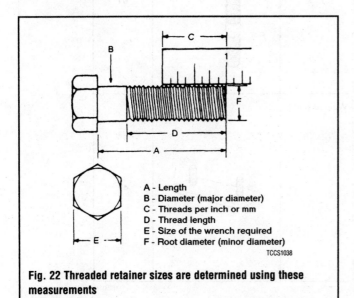

A - Length
B - Diameter (major diameter)
C - Threads per inch or mm
D - Thread length
E - Size of the wrench required
F - Root diameter (minor diameter)

TCCS1038

Fig. 22 Threaded retainer sizes are determined using these measurements

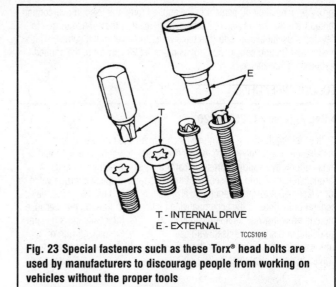

T - INTERNAL DRIVE
E - EXTERNAL

TCCS1016

Fig. 23 Special fasteners such as these Torx® head bolts are used by manufacturers to discourage people from working on vehicles without the proper tools

driver would not be able to grip and loosen the fastener again. (This could lead to frustration down the line should that component ever need to be disassembled again).

If you must replace a fastener, whether due to design or damage, you must ALWAYS be sure to use the proper replacement. In all cases, a retainer of the same design, material and strength should be used. Markings on the heads of most bolts will help determine the proper strength of the fastener. The same material, thread and pitch must be selected to assure proper installation and safe operation of the vehicle afterwards.

Thread gauges are available to help measure a bolt or stud's thread. Most automotive and hardware stores keep gauges available to help you select the proper size. In a pinch, you can use another nut or bolt for a thread gauge. If the bolt you are replacing is not too badly damaged, you can select a match by finding another bolt which will thread in its place. If you find a nut which threads properly onto the damaged bolt, then use that nut to help select the replacement bolt. If however, the bolt you are replacing is so badly damaged (broken or drilled out) that its threads cannot be used as a gauge, you might start by looking for another bolt (from the same assembly or a similar location on your vehicle) which will thread into the damaged bolt's mounting. If so, the other bolt can be used to select a nut; the nut can then be used to select the replacement bolt.

In all cases, be absolutely sure you have selected the proper replacement. Don't be shy, you can always ask the store clerk for help.

❊❊ WARNING

Be aware that when you find a bolt with damaged threads, you may also find the nut or drilled hole it was threaded into has also been damaged. If this is the case, you may have to drill and tap the hole, replace the nut or otherwise repair the threads. NEVER try to force a replacement bolt to fit into the damaged threads.

Torque

Torque is defined as the measurement of resistance to turning or rotating. It tends to twist a body about an axis of rotation. A common example of this would be tightening a threaded retainer such as a nut, bolt or screw. Measuring torque is one of the most common ways to help assure that a threaded retainer has been properly fastened.

When tightening a threaded fastener, torque is applied in three distinct areas, the head, the bearing surface and the clamp load. About 50 percent of the measured torque is used in overcoming bearing friction. This is the friction between the bearing surface of the bolt head, screw head or nut face and the base material or washer (the surface on which the fastener is rotating). Approximately 40 percent of the applied torque is used in overcoming thread friction. This leaves only about 10 percent of the applied torque to develop a useful clamp load (the force which holds a joint together). This means that friction can account for as much as 90 percent of the applied torque on a fastener.

TORQUE WRENCHES

▶ **See Figures 24, 25 and 26**

In most applications, a torque wrench can be used to assure proper installation of a fastener. Torque wrenches come in various designs and most automotive supply stores will carry a variety to suit your needs. A torque wrench should be used any time we supply a specific torque value for a fastener. A torque wrench can also be used if you are following the general guidelines in the accompanying charts. Keep in mind that because there is no worldwide standardization of fasteners, the charts are a general guideline and should be used with caution. Again, the general rule of "if you are using the right tool for the job, you should not have to strain to tighten a fastener" applies here.

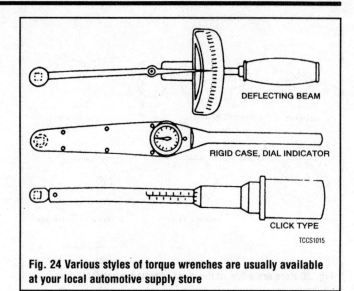

TCCS1015

Fig. 24 Various styles of torque wrenches are usually available at your local automotive supply store

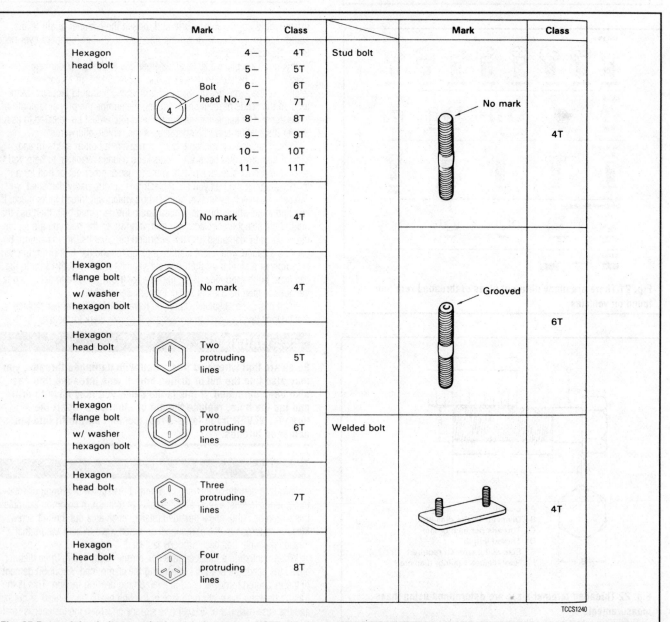

	Mark	Class		Mark	Class
Hexagon head bolt	4—	4T	Stud bolt		
	5—	5T			
	Bolt head No. 6—	6T		No mark	
	7—	7T			
	8—	8T			4T
	9—	9T			
	10—	10T			
	11—	11T			
	No mark	4T			
Hexagon flange bolt w/ washer hexagon bolt	No mark	4T		Grooved	6T
Hexagon head bolt	Two protruding lines	5T			
Hexagon flange bolt w/ washer hexagon bolt	Two protruding lines	6T	Welded bolt		
Hexagon head bolt	Three protruding lines	7T			4T
Hexagon head bolt	Four protruding lines	8T			

TCCS1240

Fig. 25 Determining bolt strength of metric fasteners—NOTE: this is a typical bolt marking system, but there is not a worldwide standard

Class	Diameter mm	Pitch mm	Specified torque					
			Hexagon head bolt			Hexagon flange bolt		
			N·m	kgf·cm	ft·lbf	N·m	kgf·cm	ft·lbf
4T	6	1	5	55	48 in.·lbf	6	60	52 in.·lbf
	8	1.25	12.5	130	9	14	145	10
	10	1.25	26	260	19	29	290	21
	12	1.25	47	480	35	53	540	39
	14	1.5	74	760	55	84	850	61
	16	1.5	115	1,150	83	—	—	—
5T	6	1	6.5	65	56 in.·lbf	7.5	75	65 in.·lbf
	8	1.25	15.5	160	12	17.5	175	13
	10	1.25	32	330	24	36	360	26
	12	1.25	59	600	43	65	670	48
	14	1.5	91	930	67	100	1,050	76
	16	1.5	140	1,400	101	—	—	—
6T	6	1	8	80	69 in.·lbf	9	90	78 in.·lbf
	8	1.25	19	195	14	21	210	15
	10	1.25	39	400	29	44	440	32
	12	1.25	71	730	53	80	810	59
	14	1.5	110	1,100	80	125	1,250	90
	16	1.5	170	1,750	127	—	—	—
7T	6	1	10.5	110	8	12	120	9
	8	1.25	25	260	19	28	290	21
	10	1.25	52	530	38	58	590	43
	12	1.25	95	970	70	105	1,050	76
	14	1.5	145	1,500	108	165	1,700	123
	16	1.5	230	2,300	166	—	—	—
8T	8	1.25	29	300	22	33	330	24
	10	1.25	61	620	45	68	690	50
	12	1.25	110	1,100	80	120	1,250	90
9T	8	1.25	34	340	25	37	380	27
	10	1.25	70	710	51	78	790	57
	12	1.25	125	1,300	94	140	1,450	105
10T	8	1.25	38	390	28	42	430	31
	10	1.25	78	800	58	88	890	64
	12	1.25	140	1,450	105	155	1,600	116
11T	8	1.25	42	430	31	47	480	35
	10	1.25	87	890	64	97	990	72
	12	1.25	155	1,600	116	175	1,800	130

TCCS1241

Fig. 26 Typical bolt torque for metric fasteners—WARNING: use only as a guide

Beam Type

◆ See Figure 27

The beam type torque wrench is one of the most popular types. It consists of a pointer attached to the head that runs the length of the flexible beam (shaft) to a scale located near the handle. As the wrench is pulled, the beam bends and the pointer indicates the torque using the scale.

Click (Breakaway) Type

◆ See Figure 28

Another popular design of torque wrench is the click type. To use the click type wrench you pre-adjust it to a torque setting. Once the torque is reached, the wrench has a reflex signaling feature that causes a momentary breakaway of the torque wrench body, sending an impulse to the operator's hand.

Pivot Head Type

◆ See Figure 29

Some torque wrenches (usually of the click type) may be equipped with a pivot head which can allow it to be used in areas of limited access. BUT, it

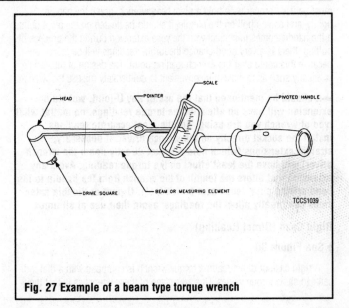

Fig. 27 Example of a beam type torque wrench

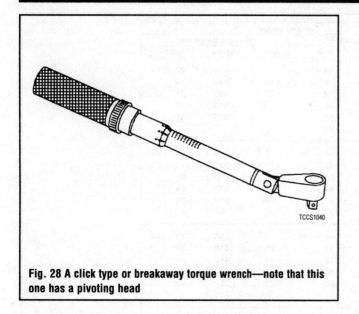

Fig. 28 A click type or breakaway torque wrench—note that this one has a pivoting head

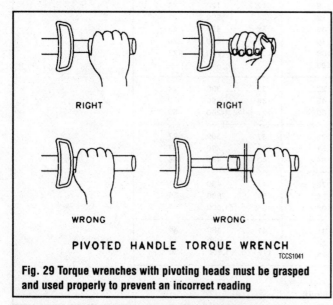

PIVOTED HANDLE TORQUE WRENCH

Fig. 29 Torque wrenches with pivoting heads must be grasped and used properly to prevent an incorrect reading

must be used properly. To hold a pivot head wrench, grasp the handle lightly, and as you pull on the handle, it should be floated on the pivot point. If the handle comes in contact with the yoke extension during the process of pulling, there is a very good chance the torque readings will be inaccurate because this could alter the wrench loading point. The design of the handle is usually such as to make it inconvenient to deliberately misuse the wrench.

➡️**It should be mentioned that the use of any U-joint, wobble or extension will have an effect on the torque readings, no matter what type of wrench you are using. For the most accurate readings, install the socket directly on the wrench driver. If necessary, straight extensions (which hold a socket directly under the wrench driver) will have the least effect on the torque reading. Avoid any extension that alters the length of the wrench from the handle to the head/driving point (such as a crow's foot). U-joint or Wobble extensions can greatly affect the readings; avoid their use at all times.**

Rigid Case (Direct Reading)

♦ See Figure 30

A rigid case or direct reading torque wrench is equipped with a dial indicator to show torque values. One advantage of these wrenches is that they

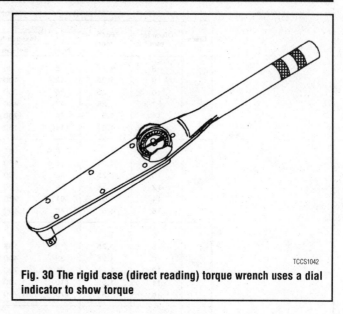

Fig. 30 The rigid case (direct reading) torque wrench uses a dial indicator to show torque

can be held at any position on the wrench without affecting accuracy. These wrenches are often preferred because they tend to be compact, easy to read and have a great degree of accuracy.

TORQUE ANGLE METERS

♦ See Figure 31

Because the frictional characteristics of each fastener or threaded hole will vary, clamp loads which are based strictly on torque will vary as well. In most applications, this variance is not significant enough to cause worry. But, in certain applications, a manufacturer's engineers may determine that more precise clamp loads are necessary (such is the case with many aluminum cylinder heads). In these cases, a torque angle method of installation would be specified. When installing fasteners which are torque angle tightened, a predetermined seating torque and standard torque wrench are usually used first to remove any compliance from the joint. The fastener is then tightened the specified additional portion of a turn measured in degrees. A torque angle gauge (mechanical protractor) is used for these applications.

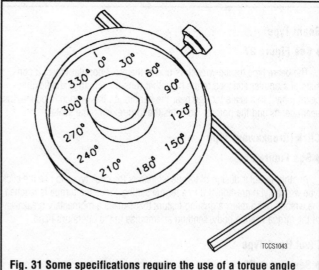

Fig. 31 Some specifications require the use of a torque angle meter (mechanical protractor)

Standard and Metric Measurements

▶ **See Figure 32**

Throughout this manual, specifications are given to help you determine the condition of various components on your vehicle, or to assist you in their installation. Some of the most common measurements include length (in. or cm/mm), torque (ft. lbs., inch lbs. or Nm) and pressure (psi, in. Hg, kPa or mm Hg). In most cases, we strive to provide the proper measurement as determined by the manufacturer's engineers.

Though, in some cases, that value may not be conveniently measured with what is available in your toolbox. Luckily, many of the measuring devices which are available today will have two scales so the Standard or Metric measurements may easily be taken. If any of the various measuring tools which are available to you do not contain the same scale as listed in the specifications, use the accompanying conversion factors to determine the proper value.

The conversion factor chart is used by taking the given specification and multiplying it by the necessary conversion factor. For instance, looking at the first line, if you have a measurement in inches such as "free-play should be 2 in." but your ruler reads only in millimeters, multiply 2 in. by the conversion factor of 25.4 to get the metric equivalent of 50.8mm. Likewise, if the specification was given only in a Metric measurement, for example in Newton Meters (Nm), then look at the center column first. If the measurement is 100 Nm, multiply it by the conversion factor of 0.738 to get 73.8 ft. lbs.

CONVERSION FACTORS

LENGTH–DISTANCE

Inches (in.)	x 25.4	= Millimeters (mm)	x .0394	= Inches
Feet (ft.)	x .305	= Meters (m)	x 3.281	= Feet
Miles	x 1.609	= Kilometers (km)	x .0621	= Miles

VOLUME

Cubic Inches (in3)	x 16.387	= Cubic Centimeters	x .061	= in3
IMP Pints (IMP pt.)	x .568	= Liters (L)	x 1.76	= IMP pt.
IMP Quarts (IMP qt.)	x 1.137	= Liters (L)	x .88	= IMP qt.
IMP Gallons (IMP gal.)	x 4.546	= Liters (L)	x .22	= IMP gal.
IMP Quarts (IMP qt.)	x 1.201	= US Quarts (US qt.)	x .833	= IMP qt.
IMP Gallons (IMP gal.)	x 1.201	= US Gallons (US gal.)	x .833	= IMP gal.
Fl. Ounces	x 29.573	= Milliliters	x .034	= Ounces
US Pints (US pt.)	x .473	= Liters (L)	x 2.113	= Pints
US Quarts (US qt.)	x .946	= Liters (L)	x 1.057	= Quarts
US Gallons (US gal.)	x 3.785	= Liters (L)	x .264	= Gallons

MASS–WEIGHT

Ounces (oz.)	x 28.35	= Grams (g)	x .035	= Ounces
Pounds (lb.)	x .454	= Kilograms (kg)	x 2.205	= Pounds

PRESSURE

Pounds Per Sq. In. (psi)	x 6.895	= Kilopascals (kPa)	x .145	= psi
Inches of Mercury (Hg)	x .4912	= psi	x 2.036	= Hg
Inches of Mercury (Hg)	x 3.377	= Kilopascals (kPa)	x .2961	= Hg
Inches of Water (H_2O)	x .07355	= Inches of Mercury	x 13.783	= H_2O
Inches of Water (H_2O)	x .03613	= psi	x 27.684	= H_2O
Inches of Water (H_2O)	x .248	= Kilopascals (kPa)	x 4.026	= H_2O

TORQUE

Pounds–Force Inches (in–lb)	x .113	= Newton Meters (N·m)	x 8.85	= in–lb
Pounds–Force Feet (ft–lb)	x 1.356	= Newton Meters (N·m)	x .738	= ft–lb

VELOCITY

Miles Per Hour (MPH)	x 1.609	= Kilometers Per Hour (KPH)	x .621	= MPH

POWER

Horsepower (Hp)	x .745	= Kilowatts	x 1.34	= Horsepower

FUEL CONSUMPTION*

Miles Per Gallon IMP (MPG)	x .354	= Kilometers Per Liter (Km/L)
Kilometers Per Liter (Km/L)	x 2.352	= IMP MPG
Miles Per Gallon US (MPG)	x .425	= Kilometers Per Liter (Km/L)
Kilometers Per Liter (Km/L)	x 2.352	= US MPG

*It is common to covert from miles per gallon (mpg) to liters/100 kilometers (1/100 km), where mpg (IMP) x 1/100 km = 282 and mpg (US) x 1/100 km = 235.

TEMPERATURE

Degree Fahrenheit (°F)	= (°C x 1.8) + 32
Degree Celsius (°C)	= (°F – 32) x .56

TCCS1044

Fig. 32 Standard and metric conversion factors chart

SERIAL NUMBER IDENTIFICATION

Vehicle

▶ **See Figures 33, 34, 35, 36 and 37**

The Vehicle Identification Number (VIN) is located at two positions on the vehicle. The first is at the top left of the dashboard, viewable through the windshield. The second location is on the firewall.

The seventeen-digit vehicle number is composed of an identification number and a six-digit vehicle serial number.

The two most important digits are the fourth and tenth. The fourth digit identifies the engine type. This will be used later in the book to identify the engines in the specification charts. The tenth digit identifies the model year.

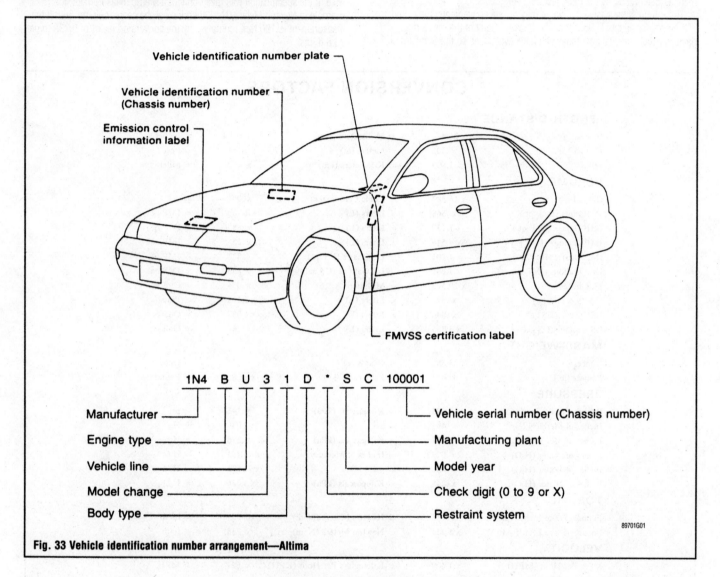

Fig. 33 Vehicle identification number arrangement—Altima

VEHICLE IDENTIFICATION CHART

Engine Code						Model Year	
Code	Liters	Cu. In. (cc)	Cyl.	Fuel Sys.	Eng. Mfg.	Code	Year
A	2.4	146 (2389)	4	MFI	Nissan	P	93
B	2.4	146 (2389)	4	MFI	Nissan	R	94
						S	95
						T	96
						V	97
						W	98

MFI - Multi-port Fuel Injection
NOTE: Code refers to the fourth digit of the vehicle identification number.

89701C01

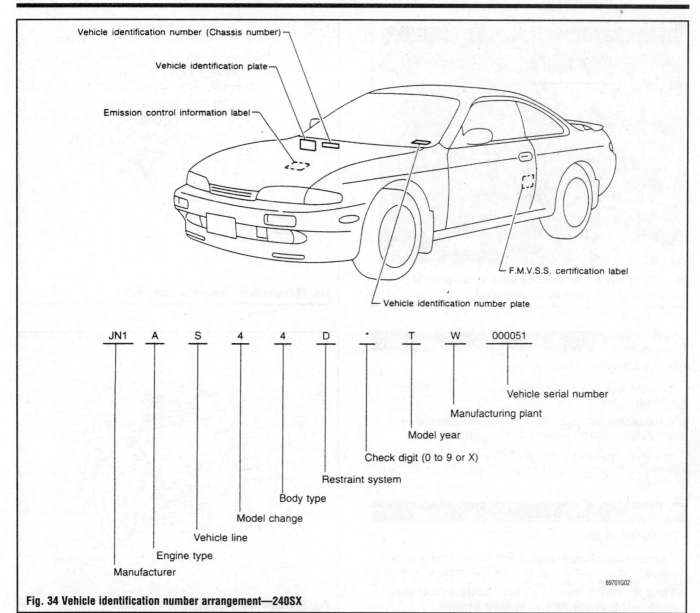

| JN1 | A | S | 4 | 4 | D | * | T | W | 000051 |

- Manufacturer
- Engine type
- Vehicle line
- Model change
- Body type
- Restraint system
- Check digit (0 to 9 or X)
- Model year
- Manufacturing plant
- Vehicle serial number

89701G02

Fig. 34 Vehicle identification number arrangement—240SX

89701P03

Fig. 35 The chassis number is located at the center of the firewall in the engine compartment

89701P04

Fig. 36 The certification label in the door jamb contains valuable information such as weight ratings, date of manufacture and VIN

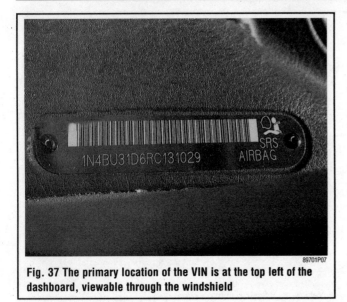

Fig. 37 The primary location of the VIN is at the top left of the dashboard, viewable through the windshield

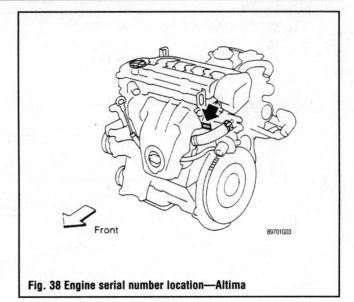

Fig. 38 Engine serial number location—Altima

Engine

▶ See Figures 38 and 39

The engine serial number is located on the exhaust side of the engine, near the bell housing.

➡It is imperative that the engine serial number be used when ordering parts or making inquiries about the engine.

Even though the Altima engine is mounted transversely and the 240SX engine is mounted longitudinally, the engine serial number is located in the same position.

Transaxle

▶ See Figures 40 and 41

The transaxle identification number is located at the bottom of the bell housing on manual transaxles or on the end of the transaxle on automatics.

➡It is imperative that the transaxle serial number be used when ordering parts or making inquiries about the transaxle.

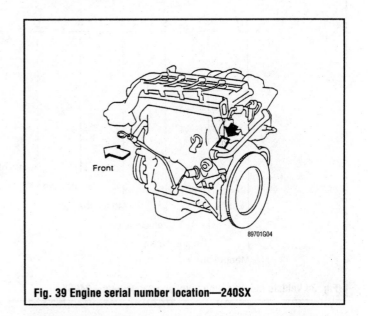

Fig. 39 Engine serial number location—240SX

ENGINE IDENTIFICATION AND SPECIFICATIONS

Year	Model	Engine ID/VIN	Engine Displacement Liters (cc)	No. of Cyl.	Engine Type	Fuel System Type	Net Horsepower @ rpm	Net Torque @ rpm (ft. lbs.)	Bore x Stroke (in.)	Com- pression Ratio	Oil Pressure @ rpm ①
1993	240SX	KA24DE	2.4 (2389)	4	DOHC	MFI	155@5600	160@4400	3.50x3.78	8.6:1	30-70@3000
	Altima	KA24DE	2.4 (2389)	4	DOHC	MFI	150@5600	154@4400	3.50x3.78	9.2:1	30-70@3000
1994	240SX	KA24DE	2.4 (2389)	4	DOHC	MFI	155@5600	160@4400	3.50x3.78	8.6:1	30-70@3000
	Altima	KA24DE	2.4 (2389)	4	DOHC	MFI	150@5600	154@4400	3.50x3.78	9.2:1	30-70@3000
1995	240SX	KA24DE	2.4 (2389)	4	DOHC	MFI	155@5600	160@4400	3.50x3.78	9.5:1	30-70@3000
	Altima	KA24DE	2.4 (2389)	4	DOHC	MFI	150@5600	154@4400	3.50x3.78	9.2:1	30-70@3000
1996	240SX	KA24DE	2.4 (2389)	4	DOHC	MFI	155@5600	160@4400	3.50x3.78	9.5:1	30-70@3000
	Altima	KA24DE	2.4 (2389)	4	DOHC	MFI	150@5600	154@4400	3.50x3.78	9.2:1	30-70@3000
1997	240SX	KA24DE	2.4 (2389)	4	DOHC	MFI	155@5600	160@4400	3.50x3.78	9.5:1	30-70@3000
	Altima	KA24DE	2.4 (2389)	4	DOHC	MFI	150@5600	154@4400	3.50x3.78	9.2:1	30-70@3000
1998	240SX	KA24DE	2.4 (2389)	4	DOHC	MFI	155@5600	160@4400	3.50x3.78	9.5:1	30-70@3000
	Altima	KA24DE	2.4 (2389)	4	DOHC	MFI	150@5600	154@4400	3.50x3.78	9.2:1	30-70@3000

MFI - Multi-port Fuel Injection
DOHC - Dual Overhead Camshaft
① 11 psi minimum @ Idle

89701C02

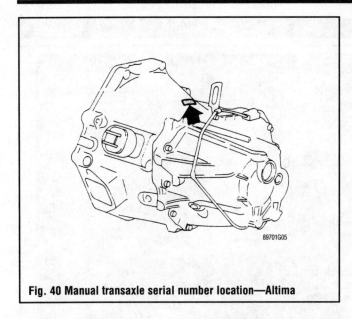

Fig. 40 Manual transaxle serial number location—Altima

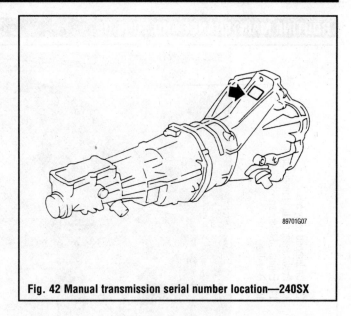

Fig. 42 Manual transmission serial number location—240SX

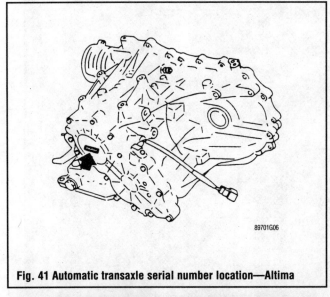

Fig. 41 Automatic transaxle serial number location—Altima

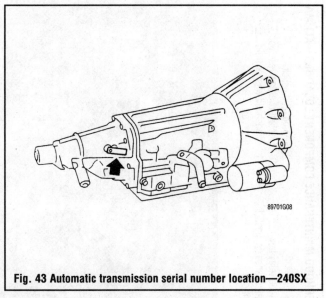

Fig. 43 Automatic transmission serial number location—240SX

Transmission

♦ **See Figures 42 and 43**

The manual transmission serial number is located on the top of the bell housing. The automatic transmission serial number is located on the passenger's side of the tail shaft.

➡It is imperative that the transmission serial number be used when ordering parts or making inquiries about the transmission.

ROUTINE MAINTENANCE AND TUNE-UP

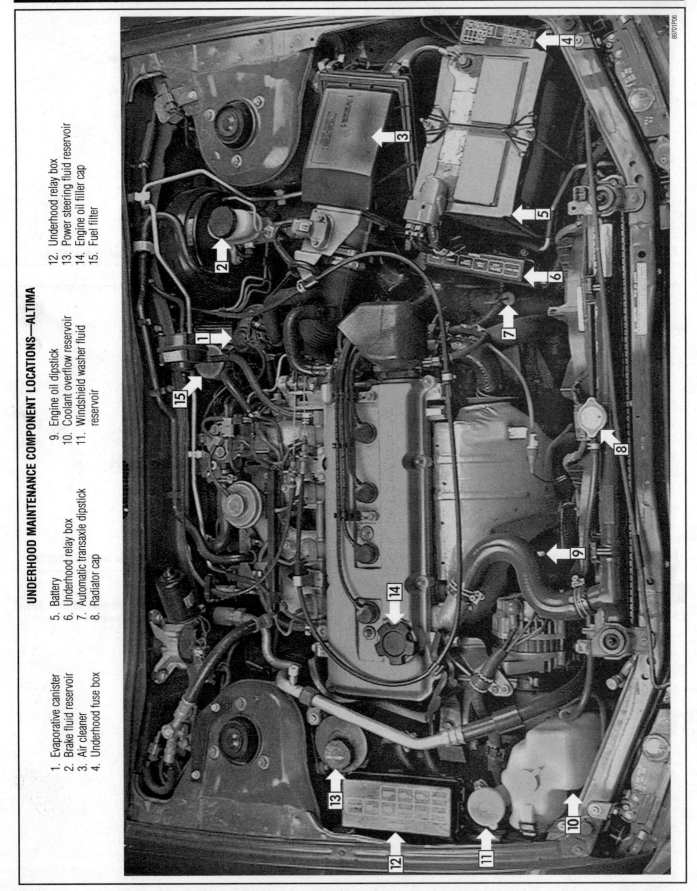

UNDERHOOD MAINTENANCE COMPONENT LOCATIONS—ALTIMA

1. Evaporative canister
2. Brake fluid reservoir
3. Air cleaner
4. Underhood fuse box
5. Battery
6. Underhood relay box
7. Automatic transaxle dipstick
8. Radiator cap
9. Engine oil dipstick
10. Coolant overflow reservoir
11. Windshield washer fluid reservoir
12. Underhood relay box
13. Power steering fluid reservoir
14. Engine oil filler cap
15. Fuel filter

89701IP06

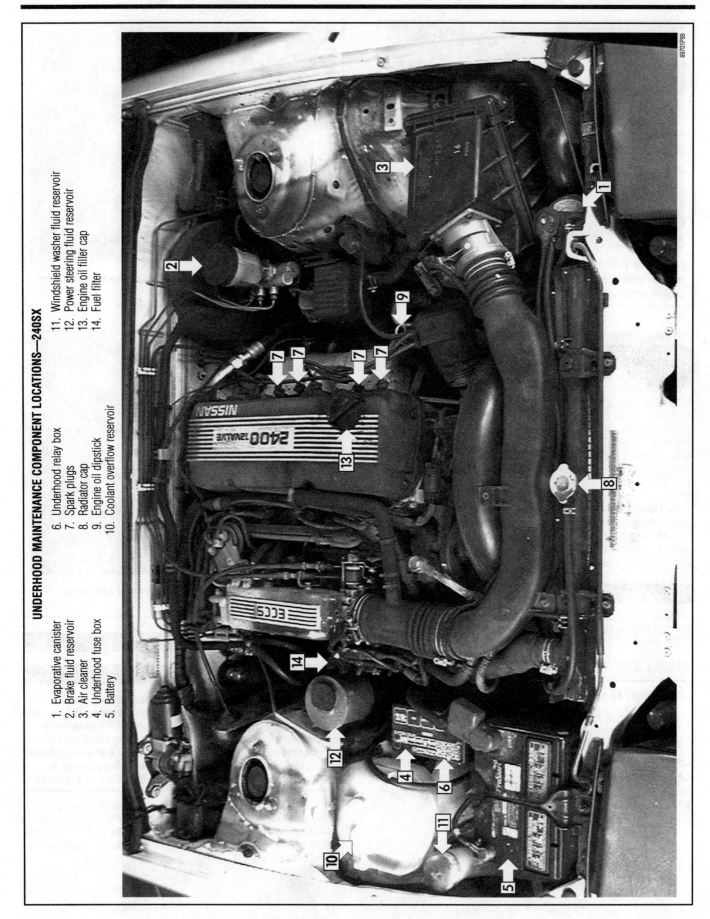

UNDERHOOD MAINTENANCE COMPONENT LOCATIONS—240SX

1. Evaporative canister
2. Brake fluid reservoir
3. Air cleaner
4. Underhood fuse box
5. Battery
6. Underhood relay box
7. Spark plugs
8. Radiator cap
9. Engine oil dipstick
10. Coolant overflow reservoir
11. Windshield washer fluid reservoir
12. Power steering fluid reservoir
13. Engine oil filler cap
14. Fuel filter

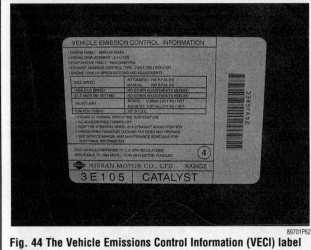

Fig. 44 The Vehicle Emissions Control Information (VECI) label contains emissions system and tune-up specifications. It is located on the underside of the hood

Fig. 45 The upper portion of the air cleaner housing is attached by four clips (arrows)

Proper maintenance and tune-up is the key to long and trouble-free vehicle life, and the work can yield its own rewards. Studies have shown that a properly tuned and maintained vehicle can achieve better gas mileage than an out-of-tune vehicle. As a conscientious owner and driver, set aside a Saturday morning, say once a month, to check or replace items which could cause major problems later. Keep your own personal log to jot down which services you performed, how much the parts cost you, the date, and the exact odometer reading at the time. Keep all receipts for such items as engine oil and filters, so that they may be referred to in case of related problems or to determine operating expenses. As a do-it-yourselfer, these receipts are the only proof you have that the required maintenance was performed. In the event of a warranty problem, these receipts will be invaluable.

The literature provided with your vehicle when it was originally delivered includes the factory recommended maintenance schedule. If you no longer have this literature, replacement copies are usually available from the dealer. A maintenance schedule is provided later in this section, in case you do not have the factory literature.

Air Cleaner (Element)

The air cleaner contains a dry paper element that keeps most dirt and dust from entering the engine. The paper element should be replaced every 30,000 miles (48,300 km).

REMOVAL & INSTALLATION

▶ **See Figures 45 and 46**

1. Release the retaining clips and remove the air cleaner cover.
2. Position the cover aside.
3. Remove the air cleaner element.

➡**Replace the element at the manufacturer's recommended intervals, or if it has become clogged. Shake any loose dirt from the air cleaner element, then shine a light through the element. If the light is not visible, replace the element with a new one.**

To install:
4. Clear the air cleaner box of debris.
5. Install the new or reusable filter element.
6. Replace the cover and fasten the clips.

Fig. 46 Release the clips, lift the air box cover and remove the air cleaner element

Fuel Filter

✳✳ CAUTION

Observe all applicable safety precautions when working around fuel. Whenever servicing the fuel system, always work in a well ventilated area. Do not allow fuel spray or vapors to come in contact with a spark or open flame. Keep a dry chemical fire extinguisher near the work area. Always keep fuel in a container specifically designed for fuel storage; also, always properly seal fuel containers to avoid the possibility of fire or explosion.

The fuel filter contains a paper element that keeps most dirt and sediment from entering the fuel system. Clean fuel is especially important on fuel injected engines, due to the small orifice size of the injectors. Even the smallest piece of dirt could clog an injector, causing serious engine performance problems.

Although the manufacturer does not give a specific inspection or replacement schedule, we at Chilton feel it is a good idea to replace the filter at 30,000 mile (48,300 km) intervals.

REMOVAL & INSTALLATION

◆ **See Figure 47**

1. Properly relieve the fuel system pressure.
2. Disconnect the negative battery cable.
3. Place shop rags over the engine, beneath the fuel hoses and filter, to prevent fuel spillage.
4. Loosen the fuel hose clamps.
5. Remove the fuel filter.

To install:

6. Position a new, high pressure type fuel filter in the engine compartment.
7. Install the fuel hoses and position the hose clamps so they are 0.12 in. (3mm) from the hose ends. Tighten the clamps.
8. Connect the negative battery cable.
9. Start the engine and check for leaks.

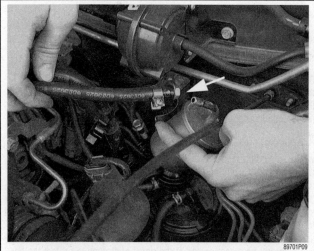

Fig. 47 The fuel filter is attached to a bracket on the firewall. Always plug fuel lines after disconnecting them from the filter

PCV Valve

Proper operation of the crankcase ventilation system is important to maintaining low emissions levels and long engine life. A malfunctioning PCV system will (1) allow blow-by gases to escape into the atmosphere, polluting the air or (2) allow blow-by gases to remain in the crankcase, contaminating the engine oil and causing the formation of sludge.

➥**For more information on the Positive Crankcase Ventilation (PCV) system, please refer to Section 4 of this manual.**

Although the manufacturer does not give a specific inspection or replacement schedule, we at Chilton feel it is a good idea to inspect/replace the PCV valve at 30,000 mile (48,300 km) intervals.

REMOVAL & INSTALLATION

Refer to the Crankcase Ventilation System coverage in Section 4 for PCV valve removal and installation.

Evaporative Canister

Proper operation of the evaporative emissions system is important to maintaining low emissions levels. A malfunctioning evaporative system will allow fuel vapors to escape into the atmosphere, polluting the atmosphere.

➥**For more information on the evaporative emissions system, please refer to Section 4 of this manual.**

Although the manufacturer does not give a specific inspection schedule, we at Chilton feel it is a good idea to inspect the evaporative canister at 30,000 mile (48,300 km) intervals.

INSPECTION

◆ **See Figures 48, 49 and 50**

Inspect all vapor hoses for tight connections. Carefully inspect hoses for damage and replace as necessary. Hoses, especially molded plastic hoses, are prone to cracking. Replace hoses as necessary.

Inspect the evaporative canister for damage. Replace canister as necessary.

Inspect the evaporative canister valves for proper operation using the procedures in Section 4 of this manual. If valves are faulty, replace the canister as an assembly.

Battery

PRECAUTIONS

Always use caution when working on or near the battery. Never allow a tool to bridge the gap between the negative and positive battery terminals. Also, be careful not to allow a tool to provide a ground between the positive cable/terminal and any metal component on the vehicle. Either of these conditions will cause a short circuit, leading to sparks and possible personal injury.

Do not smoke, have an open flame or create sparks near a battery; the gases contained in the battery are very explosive and, if ignited, could cause severe injury or death.

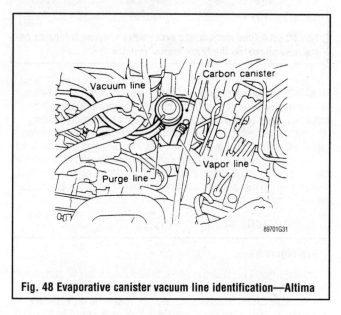

Fig. 48 Evaporative canister vacuum line identification—Altima

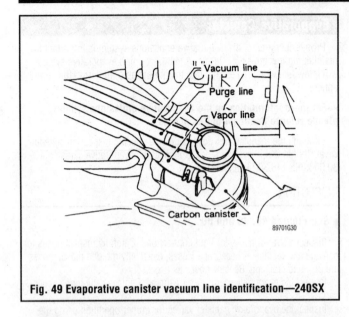

Fig. 49 Evaporative canister vacuum line identification—240SX

Fig. 50 On Altima models, the evaporative canister is located on the firewall, below the brake master cylinder

All batteries, regardless of type, should be carefully secured by a battery hold-down device. If this is not done, the battery terminals or casing may crack from stress applied to the battery during vehicle operation. A battery which is not secured may allow acid to leak out, making it discharge faster; such leaking corrosive acid can also eat away at components under the hood.

Always visually inspect the battery case for cracks, leakage and corrosion. A white corrosive substance on the battery case or on nearby components would indicate a leaking or cracked battery. If the battery is cracked, it should be replaced immediately.

GENERAL MAINTENANCE

♦ See Figure 51

A battery that is not sealed must be checked periodically for electrolyte level. You cannot add water to a sealed maintenance-free battery (though not all maintenance-free batteries are sealed); however, a sealed battery must also be checked for proper electrolyte level, as indicated by the color of the built-in hydrometer "eye."

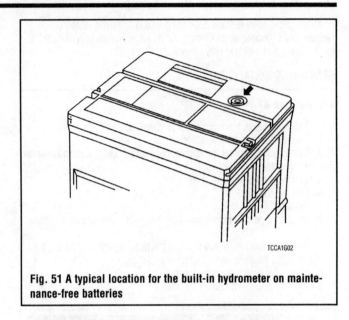

Fig. 51 A typical location for the built-in hydrometer on maintenance-free batteries

Always keep the battery cables and terminals free of corrosion. Check these components about once a year. Refer to the removal, installation and cleaning procedures outlined in this section.

Keep the top of the battery clean, as a film of dirt can help completely discharge a battery that is not used for long periods. A solution of baking soda and water may be used for cleaning, but be careful to flush this off with clear water. DO NOT let any of the solution into the filler holes. Baking soda neutralizes battery acid and will de-activate a battery cell.

Batteries in vehicles which are not operated on a regular basis can fall victim to parasitic loads (small current drains which are constantly drawing current from the battery). Normal parasitic loads may drain a battery on a vehicle that is in storage and not used for 6–8 weeks. Vehicles that have additional accessories such as a cellular phone, an alarm system or other devices that increase parasitic load may discharge a battery sooner. If the vehicle is to be stored for 6–8 weeks in a secure area and the alarm system, if present, is not necessary, the negative battery cable should be disconnected at the onset of storage to protect the battery charge.

Remember that constantly discharging and recharging will shorten battery life. Take care not to allow a battery to be needlessly discharged.

BATTERY FLUID

Check the battery electrolyte level at least once a month, or more often in hot weather or during periods of extended vehicle operation. On non-sealed batteries, the level can be checked either through the case on translucent batteries or by removing the cell caps on opaque-cased types. The electrolyte level in each cell should be kept filled to the split ring inside each cell, or the line marked on the outside of the case.

If the level is low, add only distilled water through the opening until the level is correct. Each cell is separate from the others, so each must be checked and filled individually. Distilled water should be used, because the chemicals and minerals found in most drinking water are harmful to the battery and could significantly shorten its life.

If water is added in freezing weather, the vehicle should be driven several miles to allow the water to mix with the electrolyte. Otherwise, the battery could freeze.

Although some maintenance-free batteries have removable cell caps for access to the electrolyte, the electrolyte condition and level on all sealed maintenance-free batteries must be checked using the built-in hydrometer "eye." The exact type of eye varies between battery manufacturers, but most apply a sticker to the battery itself explaining the possible readings. When in doubt, refer to the battery manufacturer's instructions to interpret battery condition using the built-in hydrometer.

→Although the readings from built-in hydrometers found in sealed batteries may vary, a green eye usually indicates a properly charged battery with sufficient fluid level. A dark eye is normally an indicator of a battery with sufficient fluid, but one which may be low in charge. And a light or yellow eye is usually an indication that electrolyte supply has dropped below the necessary level for battery (and hydrometer) operation. In this last case, sealed batteries with an insufficient electrolyte level must usually be discarded.

Checking the Specific Gravity

◗ See Figures 52, 53 and 54

A hydrometer is required to check the specific gravity on all batteries that are not maintenance-free. On batteries that are maintenance-free, the specific gravity is checked by observing the built-in hydrometer "eye" on the top of the battery case. Check with your battery's manufacturer for proper interpretation of its built-in hydrometer readings.

Fig. 52 On non-maintenance-free batteries, the fluid level can be checked through the case on translucent models; the cell caps must be removed on other models

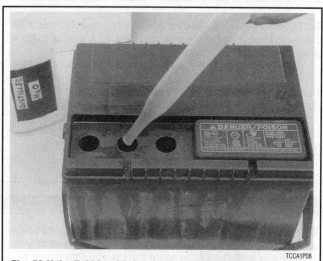

Fig. 53 If the fluid level is low, add only distilled water through the opening until the level is correct

Fig. 54 Check the specific gravity of the battery's electrolyte with a hydrometer

✷✷ CAUTION

Battery electrolyte contains sulfuric acid. If you should splash any on your skin or in your eyes, flush the affected area with plenty of clear water. If it lands in your eyes, get medical help immediately.

The fluid (sulfuric acid solution) contained in the battery cells will tell you many things about the condition of the battery. Because the cell plates must be kept submerged below the fluid level in order to operate, maintaining the fluid level is extremely important. And, because the specific gravity of the acid is an indication of electrical charge, testing the fluid can be an aid in determining if the battery must be replaced. A battery in a vehicle with a properly operating charging system should require little maintenance, but careful, periodic inspection should reveal problems before they leave you stranded.

As stated earlier, the specific gravity of a battery's electrolyte level can be used as an indication of battery charge. At least once a year, check the specific gravity of the battery. It should be between 1.20 and 1.26 on the gravity scale. Most auto supply stores carry a variety of inexpensive battery testing hydrometers. These can be used on any non-sealed battery to test the specific gravity in each cell.

The battery testing hydrometer has a squeeze bulb at one end and a nozzle at the other. Battery electrolyte is sucked into the hydrometer until the float is lifted from its seat. The specific gravity is then read by noting the position of the float. If gravity is low in one or more cells, the battery should be slowly charged and checked again to see if the gravity has come up. Generally, if after charging, the specific gravity between any two cells varies more than 50 points (0.50), the battery should be replaced, as it can no longer produce sufficient voltage to guarantee proper operation.

CABLES

◗ See Figures 55, 56, 57, 58 and 59

Once a year (or as necessary), the battery terminals and the cable clamps should be cleaned. Loosen the clamps and remove the cables, negative cable first. On batteries with posts on top, the use of a puller specially made for this purpose is recommended. These are inexpensive and available in most auto parts stores. Side terminal battery cables are secured with a small bolt.

Clean the cable clamps and the battery terminal with a wire brush, until all corrosion, grease, etc., is removed and the metal is shiny. It is especially important to clean the inside of the clamp thoroughly (an old knife is useful here), since a small deposit of foreign material or oxidation there will prevent a sound electrical connection and inhibit either starting or charging. Special tools are available for cleaning these parts, one type for conven-

Fig. 55 Maintenance is performed with household items and with special tools like this post cleaner

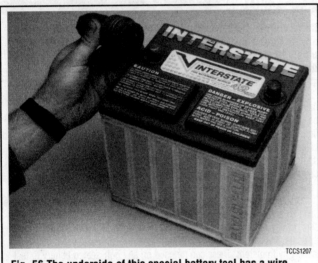

Fig. 56 The underside of this special battery tool has a wire brush to clean post terminals

Fig. 57 Place the tool over the battery posts and twist to clean until the metal is shiny

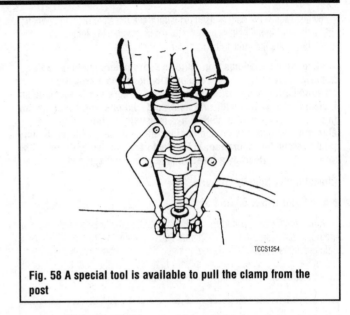

Fig. 58 A special tool is available to pull the clamp from the post

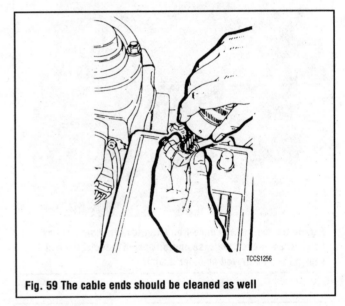

Fig. 59 The cable ends should be cleaned as well

tional top post batteries and another type for side terminal batteries. It is also a good idea to apply some dielectric grease to the terminal, as this will aid in the prevention of corrosion.

After the clamps and terminals are clean, reinstall the cables, negative cable last; DO NOT hammer the clamps onto battery posts. Tighten the clamps securely, but do not distort them. Give the clamps and terminals a thin external coating of grease after installation, to retard corrosion.

Check the cables at the same time that the terminals are cleaned. If the cable insulation is cracked or broken, or if the ends are frayed, the cable should be replaced with a new cable of the same length and gauge.

CHARGING

※※ CAUTION

The chemical reaction which takes place in all batteries generates explosive hydrogen gas. A spark can cause the battery to explode and splash acid. To avoid serious personal injury, be sure there is proper ventilation and take appropriate fire safety precautions when connecting, disconnecting, or charging a battery and when using jumper cables.

A battery should be charged at a slow rate to keep the plates inside from getting too hot. However, if some maintenance-free batteries are allowed to discharge until they are almost "dead," they may have to be charged at a high rate to bring them back to "life." Always follow the charger manufacturer's instructions on charging the battery.

REPLACEMENT

When it becomes necessary to replace the battery, select one with an amperage rating equal to or greater than the battery originally installed. Deterioration and just plain aging of the battery cables, starter motor, and associated wires makes the battery's job harder in successive years. The slow increase in electrical resistance over time makes it prudent to install a new battery with a greater capacity than the old.

Belts

INSPECTION

♦ **See Figures 60, 61, 62, 63 and 64**

Inspect the belts for signs of glazing or cracking. A glazed belt will be perfectly smooth from slippage, while a good belt will have a slight texture of fabric visible. Cracks will usually start at the inner edge of the belt and run outward. All worn or damaged drive belts should be replaced immediately. It is best to replace all drive belts at one time, as a preventive maintenance measure, during this service operation.

Nissan recommends the belts be inspected at 60,000 miles (96,600 km) and then at 15,000 miles (24,000 km) intervals.

ADJUSTMENT

♦ **See Figures 65 thru 70**

1. Drive belts should be adjusted so that deflection at the illustrated point is within specification.

➡**Do not overtension the belt, as this will cause premature belt failure.**

2. Depress the belts at the illustrated points with approximately 22 lbs of force.
3. Measure the belt deflection with a ruler.
4. If belt deflection is not within specification, adjust as follows:
   a. Loosen the adjuster lockbolt.

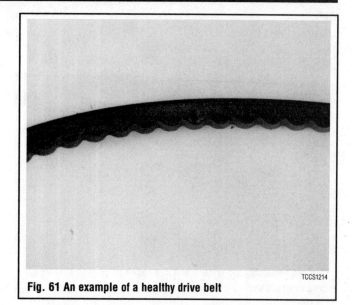
Fig. 61 An example of a healthy drive belt

Fig. 62 Deep cracks in this belt will cause flex, building up heat that will eventually lead to belt failure

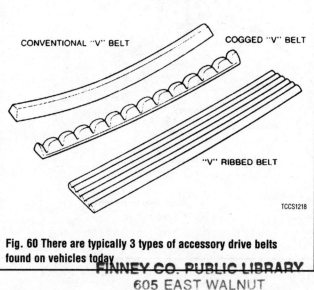
Fig. 60 There are typically 3 types of accessory drive belts found on vehicles today

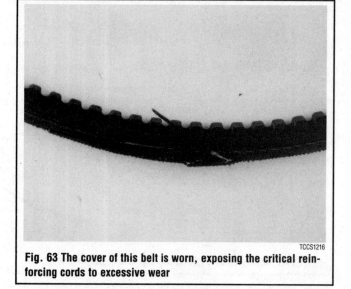
Fig. 63 The cover of this belt is worn, exposing the critical reinforcing cords to excessive wear

FINNEY CO. PUBLIC LIBRARY
605 EAST WALNUT
GARDEN CITY, KS 67846

Fig. 64 Installing too wide a belt can result in serious belt wear and/or breakage

Unit: mm (in)

	Used belt deflection		Deflection of new belt
	Limit	Deflection after adjustment	
Alternator	11 (0.43)	7 - 8 (0.28 - 0.31)	6 - 7 (0.24 - 0.28)
Air conditioner compressor	12 (0.47)	7.5 - 8.5 (0.295 - 0.335)	6.5 - 7.5 (0.256 - 0.295)
Power steering oil pump	13 (0.51)	7.5 - 8.5 (0.295 - 0.335)	6.5 - 7.5 (0.256 - 0.295)
Applied pushing force	98 N (10 kg, 22 lb)		

89701G10

Fig. 66 Drive belt deflection specifications—Altima

b. Use the appropriate adjusting bolt to loosen or tighten the drive belt tension.

c. Tighten the adjuster lockbolt to 12–14 ft. lbs. (16–19 Nm).

5. Recheck belt tension.

REMOVAL & INSTALLATION

◆ See Figures 69 and 70

➡On the Altima, the air conditioning drive belt must be removed before the water pump, power steering and alternator drive belt. On the 240SX, the water pump and power steering drive belt must be removed first, followed by the alternator drive belt and then the air conditioner drive belt.

1. Loosen the adjuster lockbolt of the appropriate tensioner, as illustrated.

2. Loosen the adjuster bolt to release tension on the drive belt.

3. Remove the drive belt from the pulleys.

To install:

4. Install a belt of the correct length on the pulleys.

5. Use the appropriate adjusting bolt to tighten the drive belt tension.

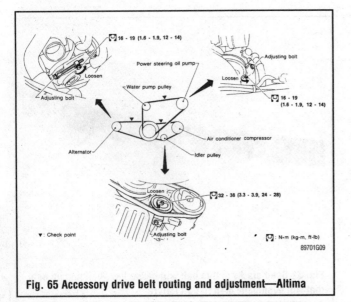

Fig. 65 Accessory drive belt routing and adjustment—Altima

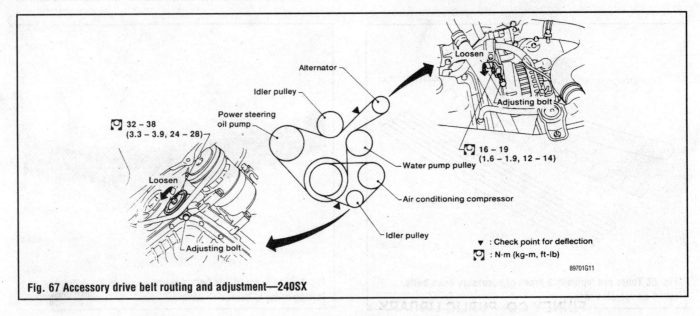

Fig. 67 Accessory drive belt routing and adjustment—240SX

	Used belt deflection		Deflection of new belt
	Limit	Deflection after adjustment	
Generator & Power steering oil pump	8 (0.31)	6 - 7 (0.24 - 0.28)	5 - 6 (0.20 - 0.24)
Air conditioning compressor	10 (0.39)	7 - 8 (0.28 - 0.31)	6 - 7 (0.24 - 0.28)
Applied pushing force	98 N (10 kg, 22 lb)		

Unit: mm (in)

89701G12

Fig. 68 Drive belt deflection specifications—240SX

89701P20

Fig. 69 Properly tension the alternator drive belt by loosening the bolts (left and right arrows), then turning the adjuster bolt (center arrow)

89701P21

Fig. 70 Adjust the A/C drive belt tension by loosening the lock-nut (upper arrow) and turning the adjuster bolt (lower arrow)

6. Check belt tension.
7. Tighten the adjuster lockbolt to 12–14 ft. lbs. (16–19 Nm).

Hoses

▶ **See Figures 71 and 72**

INSPECTION

▶ **See Figures 73, 74, 75 and 76**

Upper and lower radiator hoses, along with the heater hoses, should be checked for deterioration, leaks and loose hose clamps at least every 15,000 miles (24,000 km). It is also wise to check the hoses periodically in early spring and at the beginning of the fall or winter when you are performing other maintenance. A quick visual inspection could discover a weakened hose which might have left you stranded if it had remained unrepaired.

Whenever you are checking the hoses, make sure the engine and cooling system are cold. Visually inspect for cracking, rotting or collapsed hoses, and replace as necessary. Run your hand along the length of the hose. If a weak or swollen spot is noted when squeezing the hose wall, the hose should be replaced.

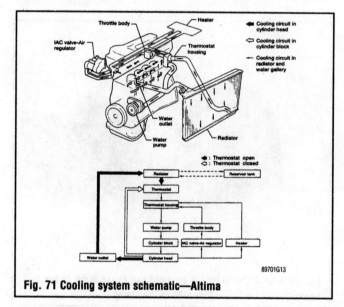

89701G13

Fig. 71 Cooling system schematic—Altima

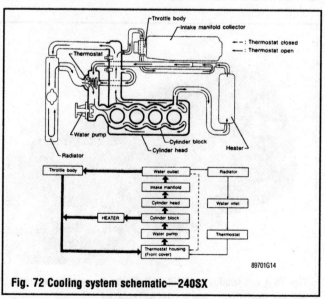

89701G14

Fig. 72 Cooling system schematic—240SX

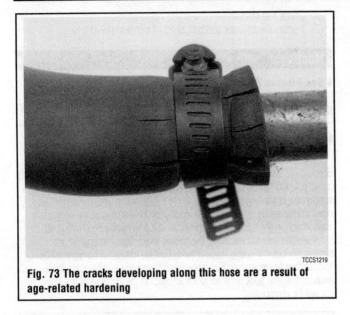

Fig. 73 The cracks developing along this hose are a result of age-related hardening

Fig. 74 A hose clamp that is too tight can cause older hoses to separate and tear on either side of the clamp

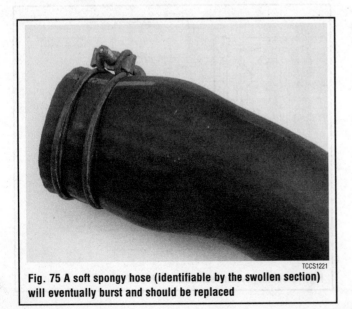

Fig. 75 A soft spongy hose (identifiable by the swollen section) will eventually burst and should be replaced

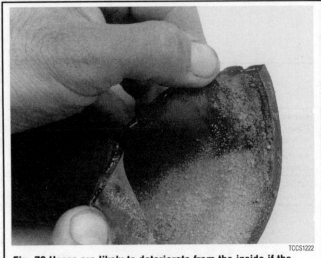

Fig. 76 Hoses are likely to deteriorate from the inside if the cooling system is not periodically flushed

REMOVAL & INSTALLATION

▶ **See Figure 77**

1. Remove the radiator pressure cap.

⁂ CAUTION

Never remove the pressure cap while the engine is running, or personal injury from scalding hot coolant or steam may result. If possible, wait until the engine has cooled to remove the pressure cap. If this is not possible, wrap a thick cloth around the pressure cap and turn it slowly to the stop. Step back while the pressure is released from the cooling system. When you are sure all the pressure has been released, use the cloth to turn and remove the cap.

2. Position a clean container under the radiator and/or engine draincock or plug, then open the drain and allow the cooling system to empty to an appropriate level. For some upper hoses, only a little coolant must be drained. To remove hoses positioned lower on the engine, such as a lower radiator hose, the entire cooling system must be emptied.

Fig. 77 If hoses are marked with an identification arrow, position this mark facing upward

❋❋ **CAUTION**

When draining coolant, keep in mind that cats and dogs are attracted by ethylene glycol antifreeze, and are quite likely to drink any that is left in an uncovered container or in puddles on the ground. This will prove fatal in sufficient quantity. Always drain coolant into a sealable container. Coolant may be reused unless it is contaminated or several years old.

3. Loosen the hose clamps at each end of the hose requiring replacement. Clamps are usually either of the spring tension type (which require pliers to squeeze the tabs and loosen) or of the screw tension type (which require screw or hex drivers to loosen). Pull the clamps back on the hose away from the connection.

4. Twist, pull and slide the hose off the fitting, taking care not to damage the neck of the component from which the hose is being removed.

➡**If the hose is stuck at the connection, do not try to insert a screwdriver or other sharp tool under the hose end in an effort to free it, as the connection and/or hose may become damaged. Heater connections especially may be easily damaged by such a procedure. If the hose is to be replaced, use a single-edged razor blade to make a slice along the portion of the hose which is stuck on the connection, perpendicular to the end of the hose. Do not cut deep so as to prevent damaging the connection. The hose can then be peeled from the connection and discarded.**

5. Clean both hose mounting connections. Inspect the condition of the hose clamps and replace them, if necessary.

To install:

6. Dip the ends of the new hose into clean engine coolant to ease installation.

7. Slide the clamps over the replacement hose, then slide the hose ends over the connections into position.

8. Position and secure the clamps at least ¼ in. (6.35mm) from the ends of the hose. Make sure they are located beyond the raised bead of the connector.

9. Close the radiator or engine drains and properly refill the cooling system with the clean drained engine coolant or a suitable mixture of ethylene glycol coolant and water.

10. If available, install a pressure tester and check for leaks. If a pressure tester is not available, run the engine until normal operating temperature is reached (allowing the system to naturally pressurize), then check for leaks.

❋❋ **CAUTION**

If you are checking for leaks with the system at normal operating temperature, BE EXTREMELY CAREFUL not to touch any moving or hot engine parts. Once temperature has been reached, shut the engine OFF, and check for leaks around the hose fittings and connections which were removed earlier.

CV-Boots

INSPECTION

◗ **See Figures 78 and 79**

The CV (Constant Velocity) boots should be checked for damage each time the oil is changed and any other time the vehicle is raised for service. These boots keep water, grime, dirt and other damaging matter from entering the CV-joints. Any of these could cause early CV-joint failure, which can be expensive to repair. Heavy grease thrown around the inside of the front wheel(s) and on the brake caliper/drum can be an indication of a torn boot. Thoroughly check the boots for missing clamps and tears. If the boot is damaged, it should be replaced immediately. Please refer to Section 7 for procedures.

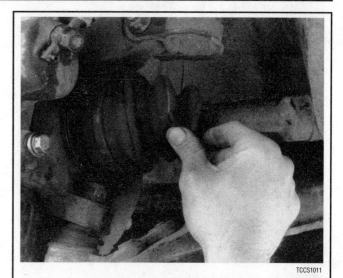

TCCS1011

Fig. 78 CV-boots must be inspected periodically for damage

TCCS1010

Fig. 79 A torn boot should be replaced immediately

Spark Plugs

◗ **See Figure 80**

A typical spark plug consists of a metal shell surrounding a ceramic insulator. A metal electrode extends downward through the center of the insulator and protrudes a small distance. Located at the end of the plug and attached to the side of the outer metal shell is the side electrode. The side electrode bends in at a 90° angle so that its tip is just past and parallel to the tip of the center electrode. The distance between these two electrodes (measured in thousandths of an inch or hundredths of a millimeter) is called the spark plug gap.

The spark plug does not produce a spark but instead provides a gap across which the current can arc. The coil produces anywhere from 20,000 to 50,000 volts (depending on the type and application) which travels through the wires to the spark plugs. The current passes along the center electrode and jumps the gap to the side electrode, and in doing so, ignites the air/fuel mixture in the combustion chamber.

Spark plugs should be replaced every 30,000 miles (48,300 km), depending on your style of driving. In normal operation plug gap increases about 0.001 in. (0.025mm) for every 2500 miles (4000 km). As the gap increases, the plug's voltage requirement also increases. It requires a greater voltage to

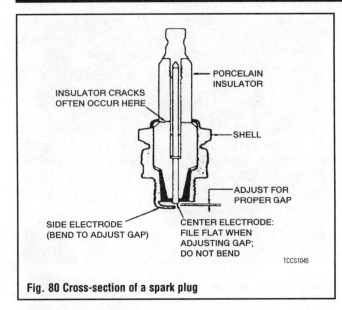

Fig. 80 Cross-section of a spark plug

Labels: PORCELAIN INSULATOR; INSULATOR CRACKS OFTEN OCCUR HERE; SHELL; ADJUST FOR PROPER GAP; SIDE ELECTRODE (BEND TO ADJUST GAP); CENTER ELECTRODE: FILE FLAT WHEN ADJUSTING GAP; DO NOT BEND — TCCS1045

jump the wider gap and about two to three times as much voltage to fire the plug at high speeds than at idle. The improved air/fuel ratio control of modern fuel injection combined with the higher voltage output of modern ignition systems will often allow an engine to run significantly longer on a set of standard spark plugs, but keep in mind that efficiency will drop as the gap widens (along with fuel economy and power).

SPARK PLUG HEAT RANGE

▶ **See Figure 81**

Spark plug heat range is the ability of the plug to dissipate heat. The longer the insulator (or the farther it extends into the engine), the hotter the plug will operate; the shorter the insulator (the closer the electrode is to the block's cooling passages) the cooler it will operate. A plug that absorbs little heat and remains too cool will quickly accumulate deposits of oil and carbon since it is not hot enough to burn them off. This leads to plug fouling and consequently to misfiring. A plug that absorbs too much heat will have no deposits but, due to the excessive heat, the electrodes will burn away quickly and might possibly lead to preignition or other ignition problems. Preignition takes place when plug tips get so hot that they glow sufficiently to ignite the air/fuel mixture before the actual spark occurs. This early ignition will usually cause a pinging during low speeds and heavy loads.

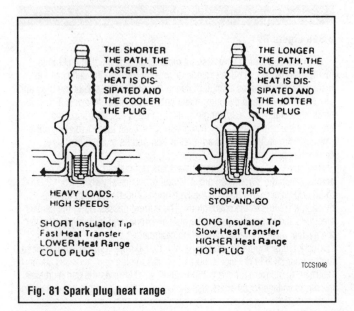

Fig. 81 Spark plug heat range

Labels: THE SHORTER THE PATH, THE FASTER THE HEAT IS DISSIPATED AND THE COOLER THE PLUG; THE LONGER THE PATH, THE SLOWER THE HEAT IS DISSIPATED AND THE HOTTER THE PLUG; HEAVY LOADS. HIGH SPEEDS; SHORT TRIP STOP-AND-GO; SHORT Insulator Tip / Fast Heat Transfer / LOWER Heat Range / COLD PLUG; LONG Insulator Tip / Slow Heat Transfer / HIGHER Heat Range / HOT PLUG — TCCS1046

The general rule of thumb for choosing the correct heat range when picking a spark plug is: if most of your driving is long distance, high speed travel, use a colder plug; if most of your driving is stop and go, use a hotter plug. Original equipment plugs are generally a good compromise between the 2 styles and most people never have the need to change their plugs from the factory-recommended heat range.

REMOVAL & INSTALLATION

▶ **See Figures 82, 83 and 84**

When you're removing spark plugs, work on one at a time. Don't start by removing the plug wires all at once, because, unless you number them, they may become mixed up. Take a minute before you begin and number the wires with tape or a marker.

1. Disconnect the negative battery cable and, if the vehicle has been run recently, allow the engine to thoroughly cool.
2. Carefully twist the spark plug wire boot to loosen it, then pull upward and remove the boot from the plug. Be sure to pull on the boot and not on the wire, otherwise the connector located inside the boot may become separated.
3. Using compressed air, blow any water or debris from the spark plug

Fig. 82 Always label the spark plug wires prior to removal

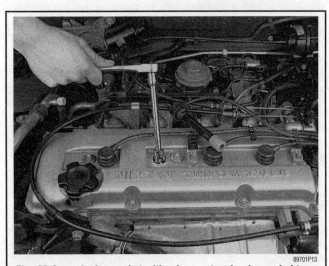

Fig. 83 A spark plug socket with a long extension is needed to reach the spark plugs on this engine

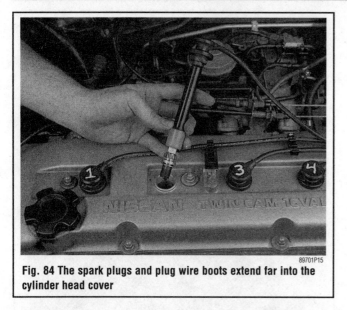

Fig. 84 The spark plugs and plug wire boots extend far into the cylinder head cover

well to assure that no harmful contaminants are allowed to enter the combustion chamber when the spark plug is removed. If compressed air is not available, use a rag or a brush to clean the area.

➡Remove the spark plugs when the engine is cold, if possible, to prevent damage to the threads. If removal of the plugs is difficult, apply a few drops of penetrating oil or silicone spray to the area around the base of the plug, and allow it a few minutes to work.

4. Using a spark plug socket that is equipped with a rubber insert to properly hold the plug, turn the spark plug counterclockwise to loosen and remove the spark plug from the bore.

❄ WARNING

Be sure not to use a flexible extension on the socket. Use of a flexible extension may allow a shear force to be applied to the plug. A shear force could break the plug off in the cylinder head, leading to costly and frustrating repairs.

To install:
5. Inspect the spark plug boot for tears or damage. If a damaged boot is found, the spark plug wire must be replaced.

6. Using a wire feeler gauge, check and adjust the spark plug gap. When using a gauge, the proper size should pass between the electrodes with a slight drag. The next larger size should not be able to pass while the next smaller size should pass freely.

7. Carefully thread the plug into the bore by hand. If resistance is felt before the plug is almost completely threaded, back the plug out and begin threading again. In small, hard to reach areas, an old spark plug wire and boot could be used as a threading tool. The boot will hold the plug while you twist the end of the wire, and the wire is supple enough to twist before it would allow the plug to crossthread.

❄ WARNING

Do not use the spark plug socket to thread the plugs. Always carefully thread the plug by hand or by using an old plug wire to prevent the possibility of crossthreading and damaging the cylinder head bore.

8. Carefully tighten the spark plug. If the plug you are installing is equipped with a crush washer, seat the plug, then tighten about ¼ turn to crush the washer. If you are installing a tapered seat plug, tighten the plug to specifications provided by the vehicle or plug manufacturer.

9. Apply a small amount of silicone dielectric compound to the end of the spark plug lead or inside the spark plug boot to prevent sticking, then install

the boot to the spark plug and push until it clicks into place. The click may be felt or heard, then gently pull back on the boot to assure proper contact.

INSPECTION & GAPPING

◆ See Figures 85 thru 95

Check the plugs for deposits and wear. If they are not going to be replaced, clean the plugs thoroughly. Remember that any kind of deposit will decrease the efficiency of the plug. Plugs can be cleaned on a spark plug cleaning machine, which can sometimes be found in service stations, or you can do an acceptable job of cleaning with a stiff brush. If the plugs are cleaned, the electrodes must be filed flat. Use an ignition points file, not an emery board or the like, which will leave deposits. The electrodes must be filed perfectly flat with sharp edges; rounded edges reduce the spark plug voltage by as much as 50%.

Check spark plug gap before installation. The ground electrode (the L-shaped one connected to the body of the plug) must be parallel to the center electrode and the specified size wire gauge (please refer to the Tune-Up Specifications chart for details) must pass between the electrodes with a slight drag.

➡NEVER adjust the gap on a used platinum type spark plug.

Always check the gap on new plugs as they are not always set correctly at the factory. Do not use a flat feeler gauge when measuring the gap on a used plug, because the reading may be inaccurate. A round-wire type gapping tool is the best way to check the gap. The correct gauge should pass through the electrode gap with a slight drag. If you're in doubt, try one size smaller and one larger. The smaller gauge should go through easily, while the larger one shouldn't go through at all. Wire gapping tools usually have a bending tool attached. Use that to adjust the side electrode until the proper distance is obtained. Absolutely never attempt to bend the center electrode. Also, be careful not to bend the side electrode too far or too often as it may weaken and break off within the engine, requiring removal of the cylinder head to retrieve it.

Fig. 85 A normally worn spark plug should have light tan or gray deposits on the firing tip

Fig. 86 A carbon fouled plug, identified by soft, sooty, black deposits, may indicate an improperly tuned vehicle. Check the air cleaner, ignition components and engine control system

Fig. 88 A physically damaged spark plug may be evidence of severe detonation in that cylinder. Watch that cylinder carefully between services, as a continued detonation will not only damage the plug, but could also damage the engine

Fig. 87 A variety of tools and gauges are needed for spark plug service

Fig. 89 Checking the spark plug gap with a feeler gauge

Fig. 90 An oil fouled spark plug indicates an engine with worn piston rings and/or bad valve seals allowing excessive oil to enter the chamber

Fig. 92 This spark plug has been left in the engine too long, as evidenced by the extreme gap—Plugs with such an extreme gap can cause misfiring and stumbling accompanied by a noticeable lack of power

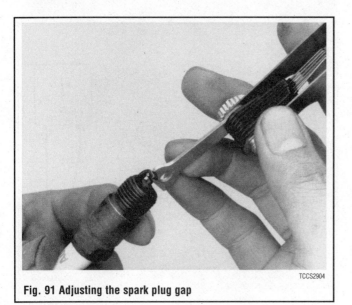

Fig. 91 Adjusting the spark plug gap

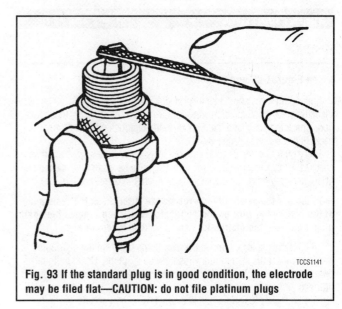

Fig. 93 If the standard plug is in good condition, the electrode may be filed flat—CAUTION: do not file platinum plugs

Fig. 94 A bridged or almost bridged spark plug, identified by a build-up between the electrodes caused by excessive carbon or oil build-up on the plug

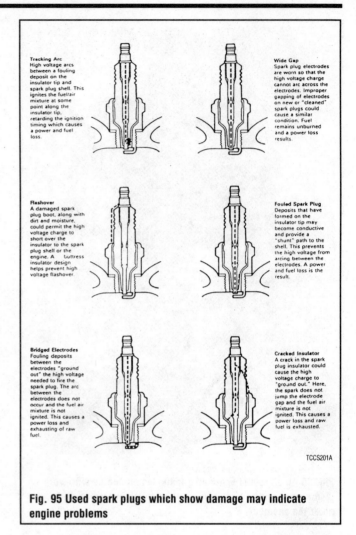

Fig. 95 Used spark plugs which show damage may indicate engine problems

Spark Plug Wires

TESTING

◆ See Figures 96 and 97

Spark plug wires should be inspected at every tune-up/safety inspection. Visually check the spark plug wires for burns, cuts or breaks in the insulation. Check the boots and the nipples on the distributor cap and/or coil pack. Replace any damaged wiring.

Every 60,000 miles (96,600 km), the resistance of the wires should be checked with an ohmmeter. Wires with excessive resistance will cause misfiring, and may make the engine difficult to start in damp weather.

➡️To isolate the cause of high resistance, first check the resistance of the spark plug wire on the distributor cap. Then remove the spark plug wire from the distributor cap and check it separately.

To check resistance, remove the distributor cap from the distributor and disconnect the spark plug wires from spark plugs. Using a digital ohmmeter, measure the resistance between the terminal inside the distributor cap and the terminal at the spark plug end of the wire. Resistance should be resistance should be between 4.15–5.61 kilohms per foot. Move each wire while testing to check for intermittent breaks. If resistance is not within specification on one or more wires, replace the entire set of wires.

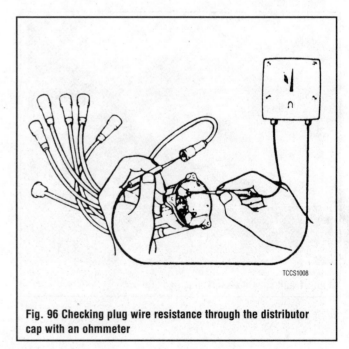

Fig. 96 Checking plug wire resistance through the distributor cap with an ohmmeter

Fig. 97 Checking individual plug wire resistance with a digital ohmmeter

Fig. 99 Remove the spark plug wires one at a time and make a note of their routing

REMOVAL & INSTALLATION

▶ **See Figures 98 and 99**

1. Label each spark plug wire and make a note of its routing.

➡ **Don't rely on wiring diagrams or sketches for spark plug wire routing. Improper arrangement of spark plug wires will induce voltage between wires, causing misfiring and surging. Be careful to arrange spark plug wires properly.**

2. Starting with the longest wire, disconnect the spark plug wire from the spark plug and then from the distributor.

To install:

3. If replacing the spark plug wires, match the old wire with an appropriately sized wire in the new set.

4. Lubricate the boots and terminals with dielectric grease and install the wire on the distributor. Make sure the wire snaps into place.

5. Route the wire in the exact path as the original and connect the wire to the spark plug.

6. Repeat the process for each remaining wire, working from the longest wire to the shortest.

Distributor Cap and Rotor

REMOVAL & INSTALLATION

▶ **See Figure 100**

1. Disconnect the negative battery cable.
2. Label and disconnect the spark plug wires from the distributor cap.

➡ **Depending on the reason for removing the distributor cap, it may make more sense to leave the spark plug wires attached. This is handy if you are testing spark plug wires, or if removal is necessary to access other components and wire play allows you to reposition the cap out of the way.**

3. Matchmark the distributor cap with the distributor housing for installation reference.

4. Remove the two attaching screws securing the cap to the distributor. Remove the cap from the distributor.

5. Remove the attaching screw from the rotor. Remove the rotor from the distributor shaft.

Fig. 98 Always label the spark plug wires prior to removal

Fig. 100 View of a dismantled distributor assembly, showing distributor rotation

To install:

6. Align and install the rotor on the distributor shaft. Tighten the attaching screw securely.

7. Align and install the distributor cap on the distributor housing. Tighten the attaching screw securely.

8. Lubricate the spark plug wire terminal ends with dielectric grease and connect the wires to their proper terminals on the distributor.

9. Connect the negative battery cable.

INSPECTION

Clean the distributor cap and rotor. Carefully check all surfaces for cracks, carbon tracks, burns or other physical damage. Make sure the carbon button is free of damage. Check the cap terminals for dirt or corrosion. Check the rotor blade and spring closely for damage. Replace components as necessary.

Ignition Timing

GENERAL INFORMATION

Ignition timing is the measurement, in degrees of crankshaft rotation, of the point at which the spark plugs fire in each of the cylinders. It is measured in degrees before or after Top Dead Center (TDC) of the compression stroke.

Ideally, the air/fuel mixture in the cylinder will be ignited by the spark plug just as the piston passes TDC of the compression stroke. If this happens, the piston will be at the beginning the power stroke just as the compressed and ignited air/fuel mixture forces the piston down and turns the crankshaft. Because it takes a fraction of a second for the spark plug to ignite the mixture in the cylinder, the spark plug must fire a little before the piston reaches TDC. Otherwise, the mixture will not be completely ignited as the piston passes TDC and the full power of the explosion will not be used by the engine.

The timing measurement is given in degrees of crankshaft rotation before the piston reaches TDC (BTDC). If the setting for the ignition timing is 20 BTDC, each spark plug must fire 20 degrees before each piston reaches TDC. This only holds true, however, when the engine is at idle speed.

As the engine speed increases, the pistons go faster. The spark plugs have to ignite the fuel even sooner if it is to be completely ignited when the piston reaches TDC. On all engines covered in this manual, spark timing changes are accomplished electronically by the Electronic Control Module (ECM) based on input from engine sensors.

If the ignition is set too far advanced, or Before Top Dead Center (BTDC), the ignition and expansion of the fuel in the cylinder will occur too soon and tend to force the piston down while it is still traveling up. This causes engine ping. On the other hand, if the ignition is set too far retarded, or After Top Dead Center (ATDC), the piston will have already started on its way down when the fuel is ignited. The piston will be forced down for only a portion of its travel, resulting in poor engine performance and lack of power.

Timing marks or scales can be found on the rim of the crankshaft pulley and the timing cover. The marks on the pulley correspond to the position of the piston in the No. 1 cylinder. A stroboscopic (dynamic) timing light is hooked onto the No. 1 cylinder spark plug wire. Every time the spark plug fires, the timing light flashes. By aiming the light at the timing marks while the engine is running, the exact position of the piston within the cylinder can be easily read (the flash of light makes the mark on the pulley appear to be standing still). Proper timing is indicated when the mark and scale are in specified alignment.

✳✳ CAUTION

When making timing adjustments with the engine running, take care not to get the timing light wires tangled in the fan blades and/or drive belts.

INSPECTION & ADJUSTMENT

◆ **See Figures 101, 102 and 103**

1. Visually inspect the air cleaner, intake hoses, ducts, EGR valve operation, electrical connections, throttle body gasket, throttle valve and throttle position sensor prior to the adjustment of the ignition timing. Correct or repair any problem as required.

2. Locate and clean the timing marks on the crankshaft pulley and the front of the engine.

3. Using chalk or white paint, color the mark on the crankshaft pulley and the mark on the scale which will indicate the correct timing when aligned with the notch on the crankshaft pulley.

4. Attach a tachometer to the engine.

5. Attach a timing light to the engine, to the No.1 cylinder's ignition wire.

➡**Check to make sure all of the wires clear the engine fan.**

6. Start the engine and allow it to reach normal operating temperatures.

7. Ensure that the engine speed is below 1000 rpm.

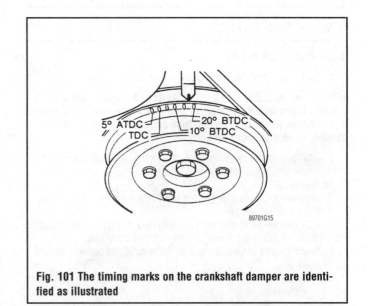

Fig. 101 The timing marks on the crankshaft damper are identified as illustrated

1. Ignition timing pointer   2. Ignition timing marks

Fig. 102 The ignition timing pointer is located on the engine front cover, while the marks are located on the crankshaft damper

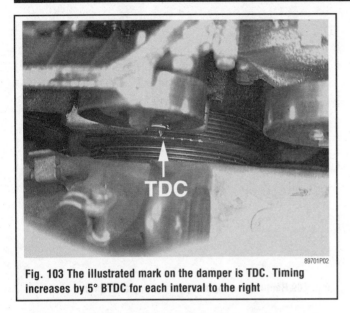

Fig. 103 The illustrated mark on the damper is TDC. Timing increases by 5° BTDC for each interval to the right

➡**Do not stand in front of the vehicle when making adjustments.**

8. Run the engine at 2000 rpm for about two minutes under a no-load condition.

➡**Make sure all of the accessories are turned off.**

9. Perform on-board engine diagnostics and repair any fault code.
10. Run the engine at 2000 rpm for about two minutes under a no-load condition.
11. Race the engine 2–3 times under no-load, then run the engine for one minute at idle.
12. Stop the engine and disconnect the throttle position sensor electrical harness. Start engine.
13. Race the engine at 2000–3000 rpm 2–3 times under no load, then run the engine at idle.
14. Check the ignition timing.
15. Aim the timing light at the timing marks. Timing should be 18–22 degrees BTDC with the transmission/transaxle in **N**.
16. As required, adjust the ignition timing to specification by turning the distributor after loosening the attaching bolts.
17. Tighten the bolt that secures the distributor and recheck the timing.
18. Check and adjust the idle speed as necessary.
19. Stop the engine and remove the timing light.

Valve Lash

INSPECTION

◆ **See Figures 104, 105 and 106**

1. Start engine and allow it to reach operating temperature.
2. Remove the cylinder head cover and all the spark plugs.
3. Set the No. 1 cylinder at TDC on its compression stroke. Align the pointer with the TDC mark on the crankshaft pulley. Check that the valve lifters on the No. 1 cylinder are loose and valve lifters on the No. 4 cylinder are tight. If not, turn the crankshaft one revolution (360 degrees) and align the pointer with the TDC mark on the crankshaft pulley.
4. Check the following valves:
• Both No. 1 intake valves.
• Both No. 1 exhaust valves.
• Both No. 2 intake valves.
• Both No. 3 exhaust valves.
5. Using a feeler gauge, measure the clearance between the valve lifter and the camshaft. Compare the measurements with the figures in the

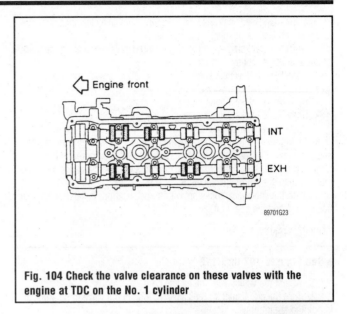

Fig. 104 Check the valve clearance on these valves with the engine at TDC on the No. 1 cylinder

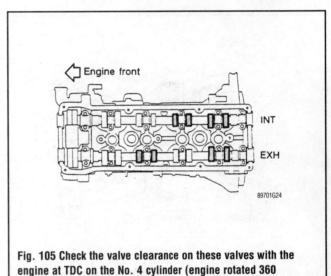

Fig. 105 Check the valve clearance on these valves with the engine at TDC on the No. 4 cylinder (engine rotated 360 degrees)

Fig. 106 Use a feeler gauge placed between the valve lifter and the camshaft to check valve lash

Engine Tune-Up Specifications Chart. Record any valve clearance measurements which are out of specification.

6. Turn the crankshaft one revolution (360 degrees) and align the mark on the crankshaft pulley with the pointer.

7. Check the following valves:
- Both No. 2 exhaust valves.
- Both No. 3 intake valves.
- Both No. 4 intake valves.
- Both No. 4 exhaust valves.

8. Using a feeler gauge, measure the clearance between the valve lifter and the camshaft. Compare the measurements with the figures in the Engine Tune-Up Specifications Chart. Record any valve clearance measurements which are out of specification.

9. If all the valve clearances are within specification, install the cylinder head cover and the spark plugs.

ADJUSTMENT

♦ **See Figures 107 thru 112**

1. Adjust the valves with the engine cold.
2. Turn the crankshaft so the camshaft lobe of the valve to be adjusted is pointed straight up.

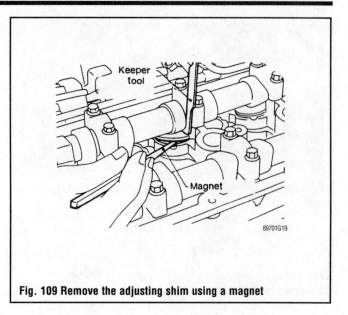

Fig. 109 Remove the adjusting shim using a magnet

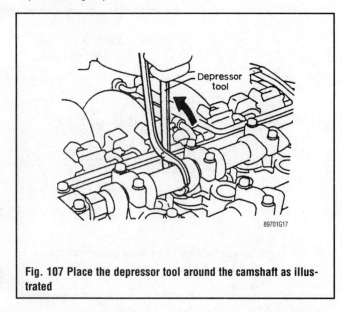

Fig. 107 Place the depressor tool around the camshaft as illustrated

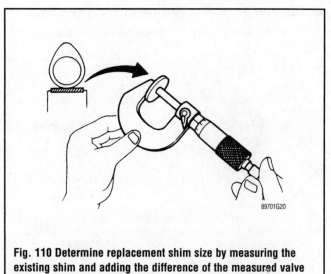

Fig. 110 Determine replacement shim size by measuring the existing shim and adding the difference of the measured valve clearance and the specified valve clearance

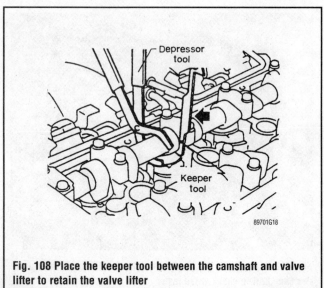

Fig. 108 Place the keeper tool between the camshaft and valve lifter to retain the valve lifter

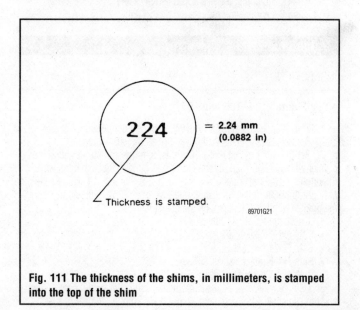

Fig. 111 The thickness of the shims, in millimeters, is stamped into the top of the shim

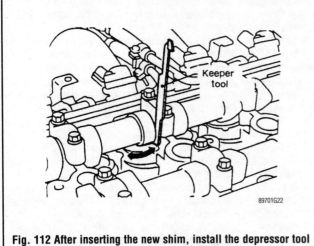

Fig. 112 After inserting the new shim, install the depressor tool and the keeper tool. Then remove the keeper tool, followed by the depressor tool, and recheck the valve clearance

3. Turn the lifter so the notch is pointed towards the center of the cylinder head; this will facilitate the shim removal process.

4. Using a depressor tool, push down on the lifter and insert a keeper tool on the edge of the lifter to keep the lifter in the depressed position.

5. Remove the depressor tool and remove the shim with a magnet.

6. Determine the replacement adjusting shim size by using the following procedures and formula:

   a. Using a micrometer determine thickness of the removed shim.

   b. Calculate the thickness of a new adjusting shim so that valve clearance is within the specified values.

- R = thickness of the removed shim.
- N = thickness of the new shim.
- M = measured valve clearance.
- Formula: $N = R + (M$—valve clearance from Engine Tune-Up Specifications Chart)

7. Shims are available in different sizes ranging from 0.0772–0.1055 in. (1.96–2.68mm), in increments of 0.0008 in. (0.02mm). The thickness is stamped on the shim; this side is always installed facing down. Select a new shim with a thickness as close as possible to the calculated value and install it in the lifter.

8. Install the new shim onto the lifter.

9. Depress the lifter and remove the keeper tool. Remove the depressor tool and recheck the valve clearance. Repeat this procedure for any other valves requiring adjustment.

10. Install the cylinder head cover and spark plugs when all valve adjustments are finished.

Idle Speed

INSPECTION & ADJUSTMENT

♦ **See Figures 113 and 114**

1. Connect a tachometer to the engine using the manufacturer's instructions.

2. Detach the throttle position sensor electrical connector. Start the engine.

3. Check the idle speed. Idle speed should be 600–700 rpm with the transmission/transaxle in **N**.

4. Race the engine at 2000–3000 rpm 2–3 times under no-load, then run the engine at idle.

5. As required, adjust the idle speed to specification by turning the distributor after loosening the attaching bolts.

6. Stop the engine and connect the throttle position sensor. Start the engine.

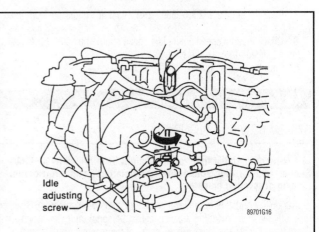

Fig. 113 If idle adjustment is necessary, place the engine control module in the correct mode, then turn the idle adjusting screw

GASOLINE ENGINE TUNE-UP SPECIFICATIONS

Year	Engine ID/VIN	Engine Displacement Liters (cc)	Spark Plugs Gap (in.)	Ignition Timing (deg.) MT	AT	Fuel Pump (psi)	Idle Speed (rpm) MT	AT	Valve Clearance In. ⑥	Ex. ⑥
1993	KA24DE ①	2.4 (2389)	0.39-0.43	18-22	18-22	⑤	650-750 ③	650-750 ③	0.012-0.015	0.013-0.016
	KA24DE ②	2.4 (2389)	0.39-0.43	18-22	18-22	⑤	650-750 ④	650-750 ④	0.012-0.015	0.013-0.016
1994	KA24DE ①	2.4 (2389)	0.39-0.43	18-22	18-22	⑤	650-750 ③	650-750 ③	0.012-0.015	0.013-0.016
	KA24DE ②	2.4 (2389)	0.39-0.43	18-22	18-22	⑤	650-750 ④	650-750 ④	0.012-0.015	0.013-0.016
1995	KA24DE ①	2.4 (2389)	0.39-0.43	18-22	18-22	⑤	650-750 ③	650-750 ③	0.013-0.016	0.013-0.016
	KA24DE ②	2.4 (2389)	0.39-0.43	18-22	18-22	⑤	650-750 ④	650-750 ④	0.012-0.015	0.013-0.016
1996	KA24DE ①	2.4 (2389)	0.39-0.43	18-22	18-22	⑤	650-750 ③	650-750 ③	0.013-0.016	0.013-0.016
	KA24DE ②	2.4 (2389)	0.39-0.43	18-22	18-22	⑤	650-750 ④	650-750 ④	0.012-0.015	0.013-0.016
1997	KA24DE ①	2.4 (2389)	0.39-0.43	18-22	18-22	⑤	650-750 ③	650-750 ③	0.013-0.016	0.013-0.016
	KA24DE ②	2.4 (2389)	0.39-0.43	18-22	18-22	⑤	650-750 ④	650-750 ④	0.012-0.015	0.013-0.016
1998	KA24DE ①	2.4 (2389)	0.39-0.43	18-22	18-22	⑤	650-750 ③	650-750 ③	0.013-0.016	0.013-0.016
	KA24DE ②	2.4 (2389)	0.39-0.43	18-22	18-22	⑤	650-750 ④	650-750 ④	0.012-0.015	0.013-0.016

NOTE: The Vehicle Emission Control Information label often reflects specifation changes made during production. Label figures must be used if they differ from those in this chart.

①   240SX
②   Altima
③   With A/C ON 950-1050 rpm
④   With A/C ON 750-850 rpm
⑤   34 psi with pressure regulator vacuum hose attached. 43 psi with pressure regulator vacuum hose disconnected.
⑥   With engine warm

89701C03

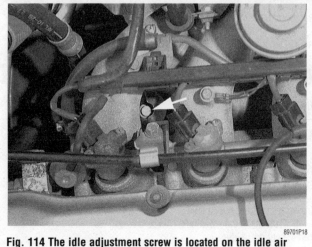

Fig. 114 The idle adjustment screw is located on the idle air control valve. The screw is visible through the intake manifold on the passenger's side

7. Race the engine at 2000–3000 rpm 2–3 times under no-load, then run the engine at idle.

8. Check the idle speed again. Idle speed should be 650–750 rpm with the transmission/transaxle in **N**.

9. Stop the engine and remove the tachometer.

Air Conditioning System

SYSTEM SERVICE & REPAIR

➡️**It is recommended that the A/C system be serviced by an EPA Section 609 certified automotive technician utilizing a refrigerant recovery/recycling machine.**

The do-it-yourselfer should not service his/her own vehicle's A/C system for many reasons, including legal concerns, personal injury, environmental damage and cost. The following are some of the reasons why you may decide not to service your own vehicle's A/C system.

According to the U.S. Clean Air Act, it is a federal crime to service or repair (involving the refrigerant) a Motor Vehicle Air Conditioning (MVAC) system for money without being EPA certified. It is also illegal to vent R-12 and R-134a refrigerants into the atmosphere. Selling or distributing A/C system refrigerant (in a container which contains less than 20 pounds of refrigerant) to any person who is not EPA 609 certified is also not allowed by law.

State and/or local laws may be more strict than the federal regulations, so be sure to check with your state and/or local authorities for further information. For further federal information on the legality of servicing your A/C system, call the EPA Stratospheric Ozone Hotline.

➡️**Federal law dictates that a fine of up to $25,000 may be leveled on people convicted of venting refrigerant into the atmosphere. Additionally, the EPA may pay up to $10,000 for information or services leading to a criminal conviction of the violation of these laws.**

When servicing an A/C system you run the risk of handling or coming in contact with refrigerant, which may result in skin or eye irritation or frostbite. Although low in toxicity (due to chemical stability), inhalation of concentrated refrigerant fumes is dangerous and can result in death; cases of fatal cardiac arrhythmia have been reported in people accidentally subjected to high levels of refrigerant. Some early symptoms include loss of concentration and drowsiness.

➡️**Generally, the limit for exposure is lower for R-134a than it is for R-12. Exceptional care must be practiced when handling R-134a.**

Also, refrigerants can decompose at high temperatures (near gas heaters or open flame), which may result in hydrofluoric acid, hydrochloric acid and phosgene (a fatal nerve gas).

R-12 refrigerant can damage the environment because it is a Chlorofluorocarbon (CFC), which has been proven to add to ozone layer depletion, leading to increasing levels of UV radiation. UV radiation has been linked with an increase in skin cancer, suppression of the human immune system, an increase in cataracts, damage to crops, damage to aquatic organisms, an increase in ground-level ozone, and increased global warming.

R-134a refrigerant is a greenhouse gas which, if allowed to vent into the atmosphere, will contribute to global warming (the Greenhouse Effect).

It is usually more economically feasible to have a certified MVAC automotive technician perform A/C system service on your vehicle. Some possible reasons for this are as follows:

• While it is illegal to service an A/C system without the proper equipment, the home mechanic would have to purchase an expensive refrigerant recovery/recycling machine to service his/her own vehicle.

• Since only a certified person may purchase refrigerant—according to the Clean Air Act, there are specific restrictions on selling or distributing A/C system refrigerant—it is legally impossible (unless certified) for the home mechanic to service his/her own vehicle. Procuring refrigerant in an illegal fashion exposes one to the risk of paying a $25,000 fine to the EPA.

R-12 Refrigerant Conversion

If your vehicle still uses R-12 refrigerant, one way to save A/C system costs down the road is to investigate the possibility of having your system converted to R-134a. The older R-12 systems can be easily converted to R-134a refrigerant by a certified automotive technician by installing a few new components and changing the system oil.

The cost of R-12 is steadily rising and will continue to increase, because it is no longer imported or manufactured in the United States. Therefore, it is often possible to have an R-12 system converted to R-134a and recharged for less than it would cost to just charge the system with R-12.

If you are interested in having your system converted, contact local automotive service stations for more details and information.

PREVENTIVE MAINTENANCE

▶ **See Figures 115 and 116**

Although the A/C system should not be serviced by the do-it-yourselfer, preventive maintenance can be practiced and A/C system inspections can be performed to help maintain the efficiency of the vehicle's A/C system. For preventive maintenance, perform the following:

• The easiest and most important preventive maintenance for your A/C

Fig. 115 A coolant tester can be used to determine the freezing and boiling levels of the coolant in your vehicle

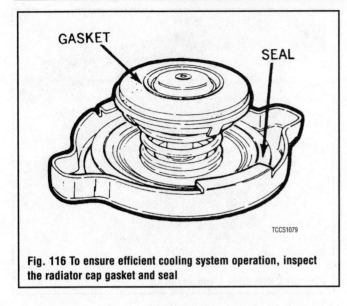

Fig. 116 To ensure efficient cooling system operation, inspect the radiator cap gasket and seal

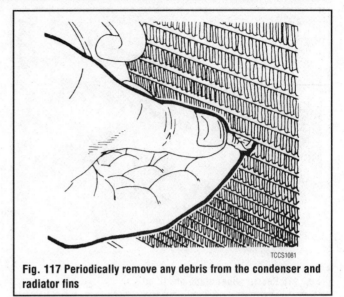

Fig. 117 Periodically remove any debris from the condenser and radiator fins

system is to be sure that it is used on a regular basis. Running the system for five minutes each month (no matter what the season) will help ensure that the seals and all internal components remain lubricated.

➡ **Some newer vehicles automatically operate the A/C system compressor whenever the windshield defroster is activated. When running, the compressor lubricates the A/C system components; therefore, the A/C system would not need to be operated each month.**

• In order to prevent heater core freeze-up during A/C operation, it is necessary to maintain proper antifreeze protection. Use a hand-held coolant tester (hydrometer) to periodically check the condition of the antifreeze in your engine's cooling system.

➡ **Antifreeze should not be used longer than the manufacturer specifies.**

• For efficient operation of an air conditioned vehicle's cooling system, the radiator cap should have a holding pressure which meets manufacturer's specifications. A cap which fails to hold these pressures should be replaced.

• Any obstruction of or damage to the condenser configuration will restrict air flow which is essential to its efficient operation. It is, therefore, a good rule to keep this unit clean and in proper physical shape.

➡ **Bug screens which are mounted in front of the condenser (unless they are original equipment) are regarded as obstructions.**

• The condensation drain tube expels any water which accumulates on the bottom of the evaporator housing into the engine compartment. If this tube is obstructed, the air conditioning performance can be restricted and condensation buildup can spill over onto the vehicle's floor.

SYSTEM INSPECTION

◆ **See Figure 117**

Although the A/C system should not be serviced by the do-it-yourselfer, preventive maintenance can be practiced and A/C system inspections can be performed to help maintain the efficiency of the vehicle's A/C system. For A/C system inspection, perform the following:

The easiest and often most important check for the air conditioning system consists of a visual inspection of the system components. Visually inspect the air conditioning system for refrigerant leaks, damaged compressor clutch, abnormal compressor drive belt tension and/or condition, plugged evaporator drain tube, blocked condenser fins, disconnected or broken wires, blown fuses, corroded connections and poor insulation.

A refrigerant leak will usually appear as an oily residue at the leakage

point in the system. The oily residue soon picks up dust or dirt particles from the surrounding air and appears greasy. Through time, this will build up and appear to be a heavy dirt impregnated grease.

For a thorough visual and operational inspection, check the following:
• Check the surface of the radiator and condenser for dirt, leaves or other material which might block air flow.
• Check for kinks in hoses and lines. Check the system for leaks.
• Make sure the drive belt is properly tensioned. When the air conditioning is operating, make sure the drive belt is free of noise or slippage.
• Make sure the blower motor operates at all appropriate positions, then check for distribution of the air from all outlets with the blower on **HIGH** or **MAX**.

➡ **Keep in mind that under conditions of high humidity, air discharged from the A/C vents may not feel as cold as expected, even if the system is working properly. This is because vaporized moisture in humid air retains heat more effectively than dry air, thereby making humid air more difficult to cool.**

• Make sure the air passage selection lever is operating correctly. Start the engine and warm it to normal operating temperature, then make sure the temperature selection lever is operating correctly.

Windshield Wipers

ELEMENT (REFILL) CARE & REPLACEMENT

◆ **See Figures 118 thru 127**

For maximum effectiveness and longest element life, the windshield and wiper blades should be kept clean. Dirt, tree sap, road tar and so on will cause streaking, smearing and blade deterioration if left on the glass. It is advisable to wash the windshield carefully with a commercial glass cleaner at least once a month. Wipe off the rubber blades with the wet rag afterwards. Do not attempt to move wipers across the windshield by hand; damage to the motor and drive mechanism will result.

To inspect and/or replace the wiper blade elements, place the wiper switch in the **LOW** speed position and the ignition switch in the **ACC** position. When the wiper blades are approximately vertical on the windshield, turn the ignition switch to **OFF**.

Examine the wiper blade elements. If they are found to be cracked, broken or torn, they should be replaced immediately. Replacement intervals will vary with usage, although ozone deterioration usually limits element life to about one year. If the wiper pattern is smeared or streaked, or if the blade chatters across the glass, the elements should be replaced. It is easiest and most sensible to replace the elements in pairs.

Fig. 118 Bosch® wiper blade and fit kit

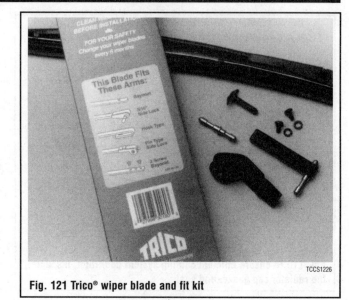

Fig. 121 Trico® wiper blade and fit kit

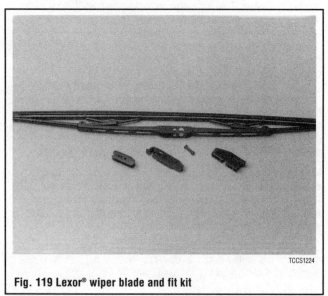

Fig. 119 Lexor® wiper blade and fit kit

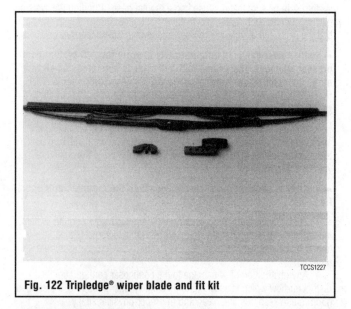

Fig. 122 Tripledge® wiper blade and fit kit

Fig. 120 Pylon® wiper blade and adaptor

Fig. 123 To remove and install a Lexor® wiper blade refill, slip out the old insert and slide in a new one

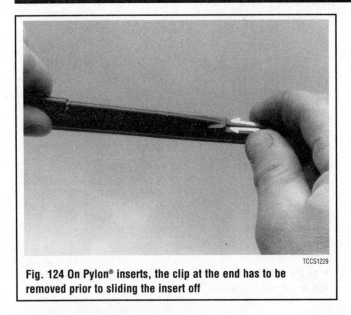

Fig. 124 On Pylon® inserts, the clip at the end has to be removed prior to sliding the insert off

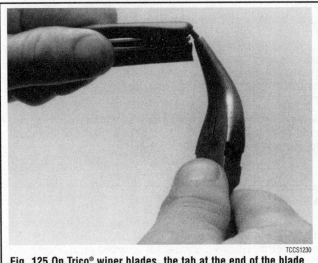

Fig. 125 On Trico® wiper blades, the tab at the end of the blade must be turned up . . .

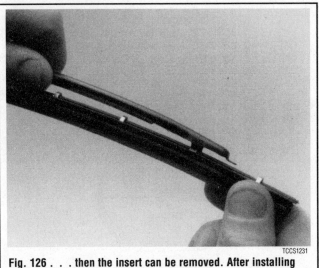

Fig. 126 . . . then the insert can be removed. After installing the replacement insert, bend the tab back

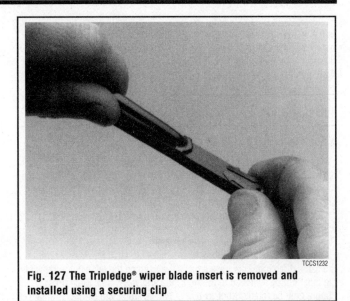

Fig. 127 The Tripledge® wiper blade insert is removed and installed using a securing clip

If your vehicle is equipped with aftermarket blades, there are several different types of refills and your vehicle might have any kind. Aftermarket blades and arms rarely use the exact same type blade or refill as the original equipment. Here are some typical aftermarket blades; not all may be available for your vehicle:

The Anco® type uses a release button that is pushed down to allow the refill to slide out of the yoke jaws. The new refill slides back into the frame and locks in place.

Some Trico® refills are removed by locating where the metal backing strip or the refill is wider. Insert a small screwdriver blade between the frame and metal backing strip. Press down to release the refill from the retaining tab.

Other types of Trico® refills have two metal tabs which are unlocked by squeezing them together. The rubber filler can then be withdrawn from the frame jaws. A new refill is installed by inserting the refill into the front frame jaws and sliding it rearward to engage the remaining frame jaws. There are usually four jaws; be certain when installing that the refill is engaged in all of them. At the end of its travel, the tabs will lock into place on the front jaws of the wiper blade frame.

Another type of refill is made from polycarbonate. The refill has a simple locking device at one end which flexes downward out of the groove into which the jaws of the holder fit, allowing easy release. By sliding the new refill through all the jaws and pushing through the slight resistance when it reaches the end of its travel, the refill will lock into position.

To replace the Tridon® refill, it is necessary to remove the wiper blade. This refill has a plastic backing strip with a notch about 1 in. (25mm) from the end. Hold the blade (frame) on a hard surface so that the frame is tightly bowed. Grip the tip of the backing strip and pull up while twisting counterclockwise. The backing strip will snap out of the retaining tab. Do this for the remaining tabs until the refill is free of the blade. The length of these refills is molded into the end and they should be replaced with identical types.

Regardless of the type of refill used, be sure to follow the part manufacturer's instructions closely. Make sure that all of the frame jaws are engaged as the refill is pushed into place and locked. If the metal blade holder and frame are allowed to touch the glass during wiper operation, the glass will be scratched.

Tires and Wheels

Common sense and good driving habits will afford maximum tire life. Fast starts, sudden stops and hard cornering are hard on tires and will shorten their useful life span. Make sure that you don't overload the vehicle or run with incorrect pressure in the tires. Both of these practices will increase tread wear.

➡For optimum tire life, keep the tires properly inflated, rotate them often and have the wheel alignment checked periodically.

Inspect your tires frequently. Be especially careful to watch for bubbles in the tread or sidewall, deep cuts or underinflation. Replace any tires with bubbles in the sidewall. If cuts are so deep that they penetrate to the cords, discard the tire. Any cut in the sidewall of a radial tire renders it unsafe. Also look for uneven tread wear patterns that may indicate the front end is out of alignment or that the tires are out of balance.

TIRE ROTATION

▶ **See Figures 128, 129 and 130**

Tires must be rotated periodically to equalize wear patterns that vary with a tire's position on the vehicle. Tires will also wear in an uneven way as the front steering/suspension system wears to the point where the alignment should be reset.

Rotating the tires will ensure maximum life for the tires as a set, so you will not have to discard a tire early due to wear on only part of the tread. Regular rotation is required to equalize wear.

When rotating "unidirectional tires," make sure that they always roll in the same direction. This means that a tire used on the left side of the vehicle must not be switched to the right side and vice-versa. Such tires should only be rotated front-to-rear or rear-to-front, while always remain-

Fig. 130 Unidirectional tires are identifiable by sidewall arrows and/or the word "rotation"

ing on the same side of the vehicle. These tires are marked on the sidewall as to the direction of rotation; observe the marks when reinstalling the tire(s).

Some styled or "mag" wheels may have different offsets front to rear. In these cases, the rear wheels must not be used up front and vice-versa. Furthermore, if these wheels are equipped with unidirectional tires, they cannot be rotated unless the tire is remounted for the proper direction of rotation.

➡ **The compact or space-saver spare is strictly for emergency use. It must never be included in the tire rotation or placed on the vehicle for everyday use.**

TIRE DESIGN

▶ **See Figure 131**

For maximum satisfaction, tires should be used in sets of four. Mixing of different types (radial, bias-belted, fiberglass belted) must be avoided. In most cases, the vehicle manufacturer has designated a type of tire on which the vehicle will perform best. Your first choice when replacing tires should be to use the same type of tire that the manufacturer recommends.

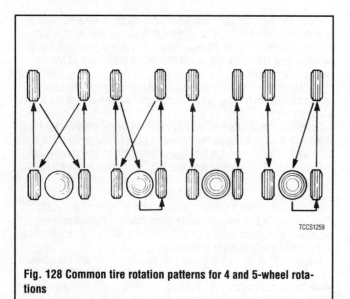

Fig. 128 Common tire rotation patterns for 4 and 5-wheel rotations

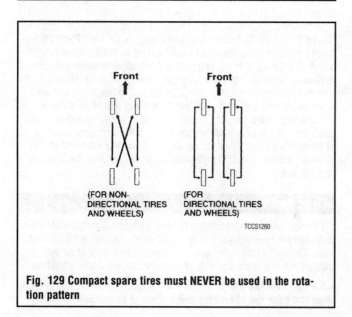

Fig. 129 Compact spare tires must NEVER be used in the rotation pattern

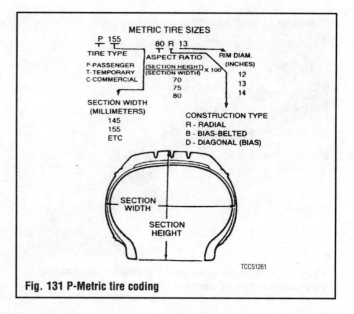

Fig. 131 P-Metric tire coding

When radial tires are used, tire sizes and wheel diameters should be selected to maintain ground clearance and tire load capacity equivalent to the original specified tire. Radial tires should always be used in sets of four.

✳✳ CAUTION

Radial tires should never be used on only the front axle.

When selecting tires, pay attention to the original size as marked on the tire. Most tires are described using an industry size code sometimes referred to as P-Metric. This allows the exact identification of the tire specifications, regardless of the manufacturer. If selecting a different tire size or brand, remember to check the installed tire for any sign of interference with the body or suspension while the vehicle is stopping, turning sharply or heavily loaded.

Snow Tires

Good radial tires can produce a big advantage in slippery weather, but in snow, a street radial tire does not have sufficient tread to provide traction and control. The small grooves of a street tire quickly pack with snow and the tire behaves like a billiard ball on a marble floor. The more open, chunky tread of a snow tire will self-clean as the tire turns, providing much better grip on snowy surfaces.

To satisfy municipalities requiring snow tires during weather emergencies, most snow tires carry either an M + S designation after the tire size stamped on the sidewall, or the designation "all-season." In general, no change in tire size is necessary when buying snow tires.

Most manufacturers strongly recommend the use of 4 snow tires on their vehicles for reasons of stability. If snow tires are fitted only to the drive wheels, the opposite end of the vehicle may become very unstable when braking or turning on slippery surfaces. This instability can lead to unpleasant endings if the driver can't counteract the slide in time.

Note that snow tires, whether 2 or 4, will affect vehicle handling in all non-snow situations. The stiffer, heavier snow tires will noticeably change the turning and braking characteristics of the vehicle. Once the snow tires are installed, you must re-learn the behavior of the vehicle and drive accordingly.

➡**Consider buying extra wheels on which to mount the snow tires. Once done, the "snow wheels" can be installed and removed as needed. This eliminates the potential damage to tires or wheels from seasonal removal and installation. Even if your vehicle has styled wheels, see if inexpensive steel wheels are available. Although the look of the vehicle will change, the expensive wheels will be protected from salt, curb hits and pothole damage.**

TIRE STORAGE

If they are mounted on wheels, store the tires at proper inflation pressure. All tires should be kept in a cool, dry place. If they are stored in the garage or basement, do not let them stand on a concrete floor; set them on strips of wood, a mat or a large stack of newspaper. Keeping them away from direct moisture is of paramount importance. Tires should not be stored upright, but in a flat position.

INFLATION & INSPECTION

▶ **See Figures 132 thru 139**

The importance of proper tire inflation cannot be overemphasized. A tire employs air as part of its structure. It is designed around the supporting strength of the air at a specified pressure. For this reason, improper inflation drastically reduces the tire's ability to perform as intended. A tire will lose some air in day-to-day use; having to add a few pounds of air periodically is not necessarily a sign of a leaking tire.

Two items should be a permanent fixture in every glove compartment: an accurate tire pressure gauge and a tread depth gauge. Check the tire pressure (including the spare) regularly with a pocket type gauge. Too often, the gauge on the end of the air hose at your corner garage is not accurate because it suffers too much abuse. Always check tire pressure when the tires are cold,

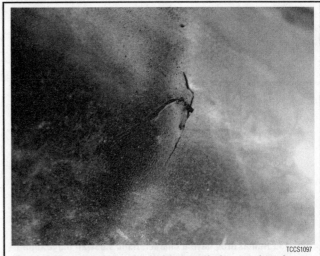

TCCS1097

Fig. 132 Tires should be checked frequently for any sign of puncture or damage

TCCS1095

Fig. 133 Tires with deep cuts, or cuts which show bulging should be replaced immediately

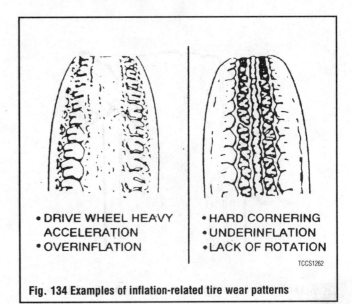

- DRIVE WHEEL HEAVY ACCELERATION
- OVERINFLATION

- HARD CORNERING
- UNDERINFLATION
- LACK OF ROTATION

TCCS1262

Fig. 134 Examples of inflation-related tire wear patterns

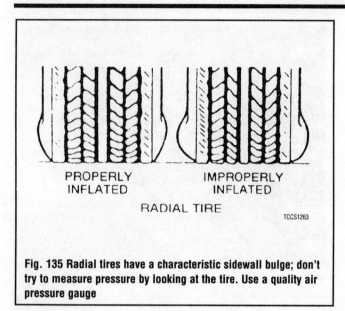

PROPERLY
INFLATED

IMPROPERLY
INFLATED

RADIAL TIRE

TCCS1263

Fig. 135 Radial tires have a characteristic sidewall bulge; don't try to measure pressure by looking at the tire. Use a quality air pressure gauge

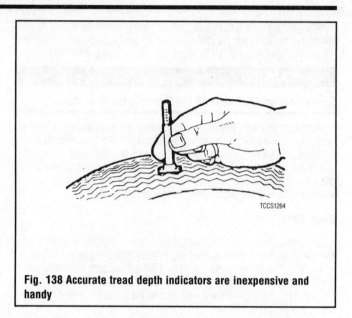

TCCS1264

Fig. 138 Accurate tread depth indicators are inexpensive and handy

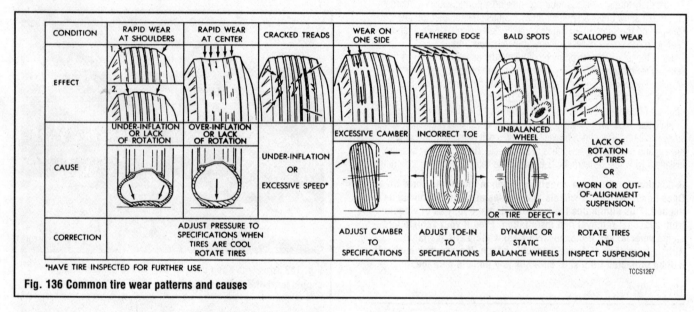

CONDITION	RAPID WEAR AT SHOULDERS	RAPID WEAR AT CENTER	CRACKED TREADS	WEAR ON ONE SIDE	FEATHERED EDGE	BALD SPOTS	SCALLOPED WEAR
EFFECT	1. 2.						
CAUSE	UNDER-INFLATION OR LACK OF ROTATION	OVER-INFLATION OR LACK OF ROTATION	UNDER-INFLATION OR EXCESSIVE SPEED*	EXCESSIVE CAMBER	INCORRECT TOE	UNBALANCED WHEEL OR TIRE DEFECT *	LACK OF ROTATION OF TIRES OR WORN OR OUT-OF-ALIGNMENT SUSPENSION.
CORRECTION		ADJUST PRESSURE TO SPECIFICATIONS WHEN TIRES ARE COOL ROTATE TIRES		ADJUST CAMBER TO SPECIFICATIONS	ADJUST TOE-IN TO SPECIFICATIONS	DYNAMIC OR STATIC BALANCE WHEELS	ROTATE TIRES AND INSPECT SUSPENSION

*HAVE TIRE INSPECTED FOR FURTHER USE.

TCCS1267

Fig. 136 Common tire wear patterns and causes

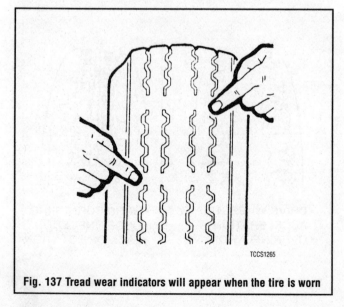

TCCS1265

Fig. 137 Tread wear indicators will appear when the tire is worn

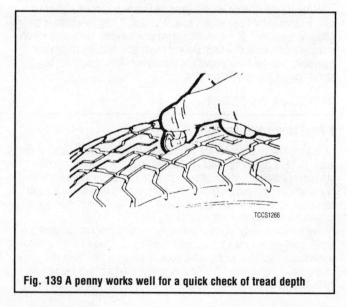

TCCS1266

Fig. 139 A penny works well for a quick check of tread depth

as pressure increases with temperature. If you must move the vehicle to check the tire inflation, do not drive more than a mile before checking. A cold tire is generally one that has not been driven for more than three hours.

A plate or sticker is normally provided somewhere in the vehicle (door post, hood, tailgate or trunk lid) which shows the proper pressure for the tires. Never counteract excessive pressure build-up by bleeding off air pressure (letting some air out). This will cause the tire to run hotter and wear quicker.

✳✳ CAUTION

Never exceed the maximum tire pressure embossed on the tire! This is the pressure to be used when the tire is at maximum loading, but it is rarely the correct pressure for everyday driving. Consult the owner's manual or the tire pressure sticker for the correct tire pressure.

Once you've maintained the correct tire pressures for several weeks, you'll be familiar with the vehicle's braking and handling personality. Slight adjustments in tire pressures can fine-tune these characteristics, but never change the cold pressure specification by more than 2 psi. A slightly softer tire pressure will give a softer ride but also yield lower fuel mileage. A slightly harder tire will give crisper dry road handling but can cause skidding on wet surfaces. Unless you're fully attuned to the vehicle, stick to the recommended inflation pressures.

All tires made since 1968 have built-in tread wear indicator bars that show up as ½ in. (13mm) wide smooth bands across the tire when $1/16$ in. (1.5mm) of tread remains. The appearance of tread wear indicators means that the tires should be replaced. In fact, many states have laws prohibiting the use of tires with less than this amount of tread.

You can check your own tread depth with an inexpensive gauge or by using a Lincoln head penny. Slip the Lincoln penny (with Lincoln's head upside-down) into several tread grooves. If you can see the top of Lincoln's head in 2 adjacent grooves, the tire has less than $1/16$ in. (1.5mm) tread left and should be replaced. You can measure snow tires in the same manner by using the "tails" side of the Lincoln penny. If you can see the top of the Lincoln memorial, it's time to replace the snow tire(s).

CARE OF SPECIAL WHEELS

If you have invested money in magnesium, aluminum alloy or sport wheels, special precautions should be taken to make sure your investment is not wasted and that your special wheels look good for the life of the vehicle.

Special wheels are easily damaged and/or scratched. Occasionally check the rims for cracking, impact damage or air leaks. If any of these are found, replace the wheel. But in order to prevent this type of damage and the costly replacement of a special wheel, observe the following precautions:

• Use extra care not to damage the wheels during removal, installation, balancing, etc. After removal of the wheels from the vehicle, place them on a mat or other protective surface. If they are to be stored for any length of time, support them on strips of wood. Never store tires and wheels upright; the tread may develop flat spots.

• When driving, watch for hazards; it doesn't take much to crack a wheel.

• When washing, use a mild soap or non-abrasive dish detergent (keeping in mind that detergent tends to remove wax). Avoid cleansers with abrasives or the use of hard brushes. There are many cleaners and polishes for special wheels.

• If possible, remove the wheels during the winter. Salt and sand used for snow removal can severely damage the finish of a wheel.

• Make certain the recommended lug nut torque is never exceeded or the wheel may crack. Never use snow chains on special wheels; severe scratching will occur.

FLUIDS AND LUBRICANTS

Fluid Disposal

Used fluids such as engine oil, transmission fluid, antifreeze and brake fluid are hazardous wastes and must be disposed of properly. Before draining any fluids, consult with your local authorities; in many areas waste oil, antifreeze, etc. is being accepted as a part of recycling programs. A number of service stations and auto parts stores are also accepting waste fluids for recycling.

Be sure of the recycling center's policies before draining any fluids, as many will not accept different fluids that have been mixed together.

Fuel and Engine Oil Recommendations

▶ **See Figures 140, 141, 142 and 143**

All Altima and 240SX models are equipped with a catalytic converter, necessitating the use of unleaded gasoline. The use of leaded gasoline will damage the catalytic converter. The engines in these vehicles are designed to use unleaded gasoline with a minimum octane rating of 87, which usually means regular unleaded.

Oil must be selected with regard to the anticipated temperatures during the period before the next oil change. Using the chart, select an oil viscosity for the lowest expected temperature, and you will be assured of easy cold starting and sufficient engine protection. The oil you pour into your engine should have an American Petroleum Institute (API) designation of SG marked on the container. For maximum fuel economy benefits, use an oil with the Roman Numeral II next to the words Energy Conserving in the API Service Symbol.

Engine

OIL LEVEL CHECK

▶ **See Figure 144**

Engine oil level should be checked every time you put fuel in the vehicle or are under the hood performing other maintenance.

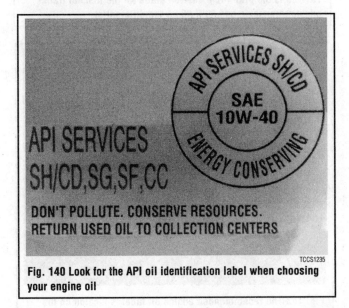

API SERVICES SH/CD,SG,SF,CC

API SERVICES SH/CD
SAE 10W-40
ENERGY CONSERVING

DON'T POLLUTE. CONSERVE RESOURCES. RETURN USED OIL TO COLLECTION CENTERS

TCCS1235

Fig. 140 Look for the API oil identification label when choosing your engine oil

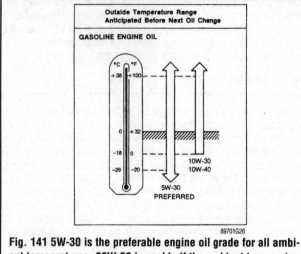

Fig. 141 5W-30 is the preferable engine oil grade for all ambient temperatures. 20W-50 is usable if the ambient temperature is above 50°F (10°C)

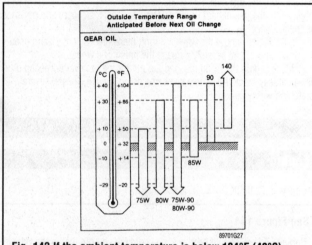

Fig. 142 If the ambient temperature is below 104°F (40°C), 75W-90 is the preferable gear oil grade for the manual transmission/transaxle and 80W-90 for the differential

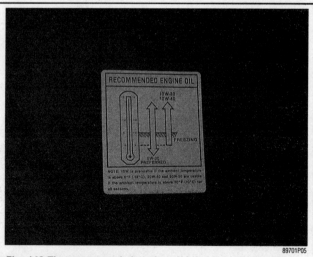

Fig. 143 The recommended engine oil label is located on the underside of the hood

Fig. 144 Correct engine oil level is between the H and L marks in the crosshatched area

❊❊ WARNING

Operating the engine without the proper amount and type of engine oil will result in severe engine damage.

1. Park the vehicle on a level surface.
2. The engine may be either hot or cold when checking oil level. However, if it is hot, wait a few minutes after the engine has been turned **OFF** to allow the oil to drain back into the crankcase. If the engine is cold, do not start it before checking the oil level.
3. Open the hood and locate the engine oil dipstick. Pull the dipstick from its tube, wipe it clean, and reinsert it. Make sure the dipstick is fully inserted.
4. Pull the dipstick from its tube again. Holding it horizontally, read the oil level. The oil should be between the **H** and **L** marks in the crosshatched area. If the oil is below the **L** mark, add oil of the proper viscosity through the capped opening on the cylinder head cover.
5. Replace the dipstick, and check the level again after adding any oil. Be careful not to overfill the crankcase. Approximately one quart of oil will raise the level from the **L** mark to the **H** mark. Excess oil will generally be consumed at an accelerated rate even if no damage to the engine seals occurs.

OIL & FILTER CHANGE

▶ **See Figures 145 thru 154**

The engine oil and filter should be changed every 7,500 miles (12,000 km) under normal service and every 3,000 miles (4,800 km) under severe service.

It is a good idea to warm the engine oil first so it will flow better. This can be accomplished by 15–20 miles (24–32 km) of highway driving. Fluid which is warmed to normal operating temperature will flow faster, drain more completely and remove more contaminants from the engine.

❊❊ CAUTION

The EPA warns that prolonged contact with used engine oil may cause a number of skin disorders, including cancer! You should make every effort to minimize your exposure to used engine oil. Protective gloves should be worn when changing the oil. Wash your hands and any other exposed skin areas as soon as possible after exposure to used engine oil. Soap and water, or waterless hand cleaner, should be used.

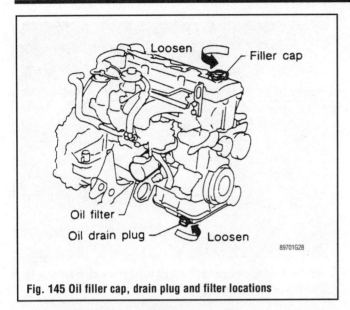

Fig. 145 Oil filler cap, drain plug and filter locations

Fig. 148 Inspect the brass drain plug washer and replace it if damaged (since a damaged washer may cause an oil leak)

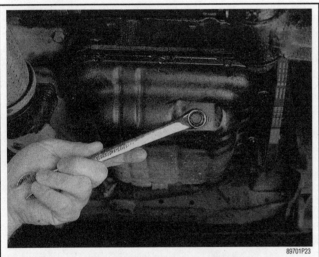

Fig. 146 Loosen the engine oil drain plug with a box end wrench. This prevents rounding the hex head on the drain plug

Fig. 149 The oil filter is located at the rear of the engine, above the right side halfshaft. The oil filter is only accessible from under the vehicle

Fig. 147 Unscrew the drain plug by hand, pushing gently inward to keep oil from running past the threads

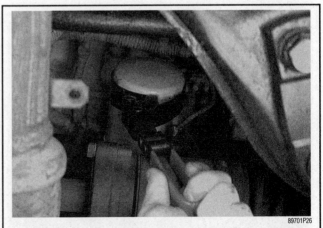

Fig. 150 Loosen the oil filter using an oil filter wrench. When tightening the filter (illustrated), rotate it approximately ¾ turn beyond the point where it makes contact (or follow any instructions which are provided on the filter or parts box)

Fig. 151 Wipe the oil filter mounting pad clean prior to installing a new oil filter

Fig. 152 Place a small amount of fresh engine oil on the oil filter gasket. This helps ensure a good seal with the engine

Fig. 153 Pour a small amount of fresh engine oil into the filter prior to installation. This prevents a lack of lubrication when the engine is initially started after the oil change

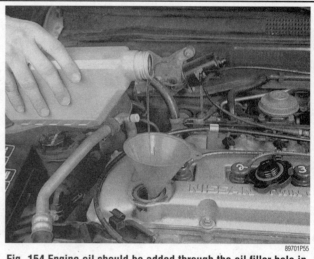

Fig. 154 Engine oil should be added through the oil filler hole in the cylinder head cover

➡The engine oil and oil filter should be changed at the recommended intervals. Though some manufacturers have at times recommended changing the filter every other oil change, we at Chilton recommend that you always change the filter with the oil. The benefit of fresh oil is quickly lost if the old filter is clogged and unable to do its job. Also, leaving the old filter in place leaves a significant amount of dirty oil in the system.

1. Raise and support the vehicle safely.
2. Make sure the oil drain plug is at the lowest point on the oil pan. If not, you may have to raise the vehicle slightly higher on one jackstand (side) than the other.
3. Before you crawl under the vehicle, take a look at where you will be working and gather all the necessary tools: such as a few wrenches or a strip of sockets, the drain pan and a clean rag. If the oil filter is more accessible from underneath the vehicle, you will also want to grab a bottle of oil, the new filter and a filter wrench at this time.
4. Position the drain pan beneath the oil pan drain plug. Keep in mind that the fast flowing oil, which will spill out as you pull the plug from the pan, will flow with enough force that it could miss the pan. Position the drain pan accordingly and be ready to move the pan more directly beneath the plug as the oil flow lessens to a trickle.
5. Loosen the drain plug with a wrench (or socket and driver), then carefully unscrew the plug with your fingers. Use a rag to shield your fingers from the heat. Push in on the plug as you unscrew it so you can feel when all of the screw threads are out of the hole (and so you will keep the oil from seeping past the threads until you are ready to remove the plug). You can then remove the plug quickly to avoid having hot oil run down your arm. This will also help assure that you have the plug in your hand, not in the bottom of a pan of hot oil.

✱✱ CAUTION

Be careful of the oil; when at operating temperature, it is hot enough to cause a severe burn.

6. Allow the oil to drain until nothing but a few drops come out of the drain hole. Check the drain plug to make sure the threads and sealing surface are not damaged. Carefully thread the plug into position and tighten it with a torque wrench to 22–29 ft. lbs. (29–39 Nm). If a torque wrench is not available, snug the drain plug and give a slight additional turn. You don't want the plug to fall out (as you would quickly become stranded), but the pan threads are EASILY stripped from overtightening (and this can be time consuming and/or costly to fix).
7. To remove the filter, you will need an oil filter wrench, since the filter may have been fitted too tightly and/or the heat from the engine may have

made it even tighter. A filter wrench can be obtained at any auto parts store and is well worth the investment.

8. Loosen the filter with the filter wrench. With a rag wrapped around the filter, unscrew the filter from the boss on the engine. Be careful of the hot oil that will run down the side of the filter. Make sure that your drain pan is under the filter before you start to remove it from the engine; should some of the hot oil happen to get on you, there will be a place to dump the filter in a hurry and the filter will usually spill a good bit of dirty oil as it is removed.

9. Wipe the base of the mounting boss with a clean, dry cloth. As applicable, partially fill the filter with fresh engine oil. This will prevent the engine from running out of oil when started. When you install the new filter, smear a small amount of fresh oil on the gasket with your finger, just enough to coat the entire contact surface. When you tighten the filter, rotate it approximately ¾ beyond the point where it makes contact (or follow any instructions which are provided on the filter or parts box).

✳✳ WARNING

Never operate the engine without engine oil, otherwise severe engine damage will result.

10. Remove the jackstands and carefully lower the vehicle, then immediately refill the engine crankcase with the proper amount of oil.

11. Refill the engine crankcase slowly, checking the level often. You may notice that it usually takes less than the amount of oil listed in the capacity chart to refill the crankcase. But, that is only until the engine is run and the oil filter is completely filled with oil. To make sure the proper level is obtained, run the engine to normal operating temperature, shut the engine **OFF**, allow the oil to drain back into the oil pan, and recheck the level. Top off the oil at this time to the FULL mark.

➡**If the vehicle is not resting on level ground, the oil level reading on the dipstick may be slightly off. Be sure to check the level only when the vehicle is sitting level.**

12. Empty your used oil into a suitable container for recycling.

Manual Transmission/Transaxle

The manual transmission/transaxle oil should be inspected every 15,000 miles (24,000 km) and replaced as necessary.

FLUID RECOMMENDATIONS

In the manual transmission, Nissan recommends the use of a 75W-90 weight gear oil meeting API specification GL-4. In the manual transaxle, Nissan recommends the use of a 80W-90 weight gear oil meeting API specification GL-4.

LEVEL CHECK

▶ See Figures 155 and 156

1. Park the vehicle on a level surface, turn the engine **OFF**, firmly apply the parking brake and block the drive wheels.

➡**Ground clearance may make access to the transmission/transaxle filler plug impossible without raising and supporting the vehicle. If the vehicle must be raised, it must be supported at four corners and level. If only the front or rear is supported, an improper fluid level will be indicated.**

2. Remove the filler plug from the side of the transmission/transaxle. The fluid level should be even with the bottom of the filler hole.

3. If additional fluid is necessary, add it through the filler hole using a siphon pump or squeeze bottle.

4. Carefully install the filler plug and tighten to 18–25 ft. lbs. (25–34 Nm) on the transmission and 14–22 ft. lbs. (20–29 Nm) on the transaxle.

➡**DO NOT overtighten the filler plug, as this can damage the transmission/transaxle.**

5. Lower the vehicle.

DRAIN & REFILL

▶ See Figures 155, 156 and 157

➡**It is a good idea to warm the gear oil first so it will flow better. This can be accomplished by 15–20 miles (24–32 km) of highway driving. Oil which is warmed to normal operating temperature will flow faster, drain more completely and remove more contaminants from the transmission/transaxle.**

✳✳ CAUTION

The EPA warns that prolonged contact with used gear oil may cause a number of skin disorders, including cancer! You should make every effort to minimize your exposure to used gear oil. Protective gloves should be worn when changing the oil. Wash your hands and any other exposed skin areas as soon as possible after exposure to used gear oil. Soap and water, or water-less hand cleaner, should be used.

1. Raise and support the vehicle safely. Remember that the vehicle must be supported level (at four points) so the proper oil level can be determined.

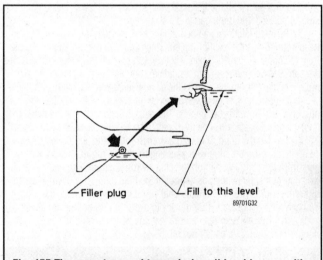

Fig. 155 The correct manual transmission oil level is even with the bottom of the filler hole

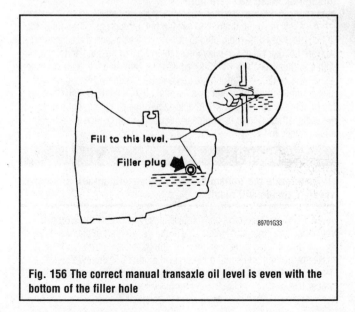

Fig. 156 The correct manual transaxle oil level is even with the bottom of the filler hole

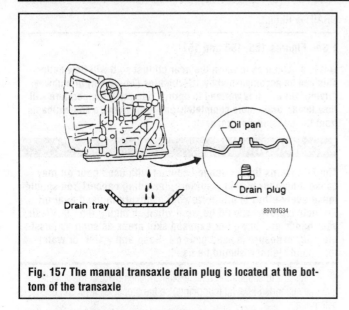

Fig. 157 The manual transaxle drain plug is located at the bottom of the transaxle

2. Before you crawl under the vehicle, take a look at where you will be working and gather all the necessary tools: such as a few wrenches or a strip of sockets, the drain pan and a clean rag.

3. Position the drain pan beneath the transmission/transaxle drain plug. Keep in mind that the fast flowing oil, which will spill out as you pull the plug from the transmission/transaxle, will flow with enough force that it could miss the pan. Position the drain pan accordingly and be ready to move the pan more directly beneath the plug as the oil flow lessens to a trickle.

4. Loosen the filler plug with a wrench (or socket and driver), then carefully unscrew the plug with your fingers. This step is performed first to ensure the transmission/transaxle can be filled with fresh oil after the used oil is drained.

5. Loosen the drain plug with a wrench (or socket and driver), then carefully unscrew the plug with your fingers. Use a rag to shield your fingers from the heat. Push in on the plug as you unscrew it so you can feel when all of the screw threads are out of the hole (and so you will keep the oil from seeping past the threads until you are ready to remove the plug). You can then remove the plug quickly to avoid having hot oil run down your arm. This will also help assure that you have the plug in your hand, not in the bottom of a pan of hot oil.

✳✳ CAUTION

Be careful of the oil; when at operating temperature, it is hot enough to cause a severe burn.

6. Allow the oil to drain until nothing but a few drops come out of the drain hole. Check the drain plug to make sure the threads and sealing surface are not damaged. Carefully thread the plug into position and tighten it with a torque wrench to 18–25 ft. lbs. (25–34 Nm) on the transmission and 14–22 ft. lbs. (20–29 Nm) on the transaxle. If a torque wrench is not available, snug the drain plug and give it a slight additional turn. You don't want the plug to fall out (as you would quickly become stranded), but the threads are easily stripped from overtightening (and this can be time consuming and/or costly to fix).

✳✳ WARNING

Never operate the transmission/transaxle without oil, otherwise severe damage will result.

7. Refill the transmission/transaxle slowly, checking the level with your finger, as illustrated, often. Due to the positioning of the filler hole, it is very difficult to see the level of oil in the transmission/transaxle. This makes overfilling and spilling the gear oil a good possibility. When the gear oil level reaches the bottom of the filler hole, the gear oil is at the proper level.

8. Check the filler plug to make sure the threads and sealing surface are not damaged. Carefully thread the plug into position and tighten it with a torque wrench to 18–25 ft. lbs. (25–34 Nm) on the transmission and 14–22 ft. lbs. (20–29 Nm) on the transaxle.

9. Remove the jackstands and carefully lower the vehicle.

10. Empty your used oil into a suitable container for recycling.

Automatic Transmission/Transaxle

The automatic transmission fluid should be inspected every 15,000 miles (24,000 km) and changed every 30,000 miles (48,300 km).

FLUID RECOMMENDATIONS

Nissan recommends the use of genuine Nissan ATF (Nissan Matic Fluid D) or equivalent automatic transmission fluid.

LEVEL CHECK

◆ **See Figures 158, 159 and 160**

It is very important to maintain the proper fluid level in an automatic transmission/transaxle. If the level is either too high or too low, poor shifting and/or internal damage are likely to occur. For this reason, a regular check of the transmission fluid level is essential.

➡**Most manufacturers specify that the transmission fluid should be checked at normal operating temperature. Drive the vehicle for 15–20 miles (24–32 km) of highway driving, allowing the transmission/transaxle to reach operating temperature. If the vehicle is driven at extended highway speeds, is driven in city traffic in hot weather, or is being used to pull a trailer, fluid temperatures will likely exceed normal operating and checking ranges. In these circumstances, give the fluid time to cool (about 30 minutes) before checking the level.**

1. Park the vehicle on a level surface, apply the parking brake and leave the engine idling. Shift the transmission/transaxle and engage each gear, then place the selector in **P**.

2. Open the hood and locate the transmission/transaxle dipstick. Wipe away any dirt in the area of the dipstick to prevent it from falling into the filler tube. Remove the dipstick, wipe it clean using a lint-free rag and reinsert it until it seats fully on the filler tube.

3. Remove the dipstick and hold it horizontally while noting the fluid level. The fluid level should be in the crosshatched area on the dipstick.

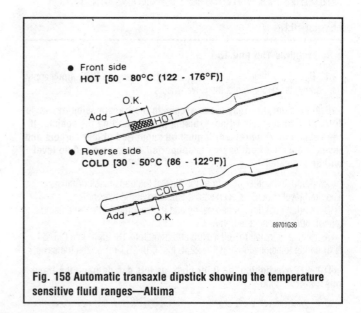

Fig. 158 Automatic transaxle dipstick showing the temperature sensitive fluid ranges—Altima

Fig. 159 The fluid level should be between the notches. Fluid level can be checked when cold . . .

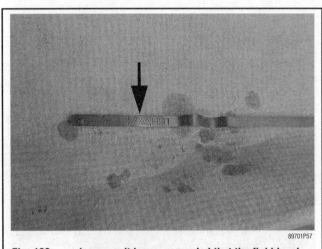

Fig. 160 . . . however, it is recommended that the fluid level be checked at normal operating temperature. When hot, the fluid level should be in the crosshatched area

➡The transmission/transaxle dipstick is labeled HOT and COLD with corresponding marked areas. If the fluid temperature is below 122°F (50°C), the COLD area should be used. If transaxle fluid temperature is above 122°F (50°C), the HOT crosshatched area should be used. For most instances, the HOT crosshatched area should be used.

4. If the level is below the crosshatched area, use a funnel and add fluid in small quantities through the dipstick filler tube. Keep the engine running while adding fluid and check the level after each small amount. Do not overfill.

➡Since the transmission fluid is added through the dipstick tube, if you check the fluid level too soon after adding fluid an incorrect reading may occur. After adding fluid, wait a few minutes to allow it to fully drain into the transmission/transaxle.

5. The fluid on the dipstick should be bright red color. If it is discolored (brown or black), or smells burnt, serious transmission/transaxle troubles, probably due to overheating, should be suspected. The transmission/transaxle should be inspected to locate the cause of the burnt fluid.

6. Replace the dipstick and make sure it is fully seated.

FLUID & FILTER SERVICE

◆ **See Figures 161 thru 173**

➡Although Nissan does not provide a specific inspection or replacement interval for the transmission/transaxle filter, we at Chilton feel that it is a good idea to service the filter at least every 30,000 miles (48,300 km) as preventive maintenance.

It is a good idea to warm the transmission fluid first so it will flow better. This can be accomplished by 15–20 miles (24–32 km) of highway driving. Fluid which is warmed to normal operating temperature will flow faster, drain more completely and remove more contaminants from the engine.

✳✳ CAUTION

The EPA warns that prolonged contact with used transmission fluid may cause a number of skin disorders, including cancer! You should make every effort to minimize your exposure to used transmission fluid. Protective gloves should be worn when changing the fluid. Wash your hands and any other exposed skin areas as soon as possible after exposure to used transmission fluid. Soap and water, or waterless hand cleaner, should be used.

Fig. 161 Loosen the transaxle pan drain plug with an appropriate size box end wrench

Fig. 162 Press against the drain plug while turning to prevent fluid from leaking past the threads

Fig. 163 Inspect the end of the drain plug for metal shavings. Clean the drain plug thoroughly prior to installation

Fig. 165 When lowering the transaxle pan, keep it level to prevent fluid from spilling. Never leave the pan hanging by just one edge, as this will bend the pan rail

Fig. 164 There are 21 bolts that attach the transaxle pan to the transaxle. Loosen all of them

Fig. 166 Once the pan is lowered from the transaxle, tilt it slightly to allow the remaining fluid to drain

➡The transmission fluid and filter should be changed at the recommended intervals. Though some manufacturers have at times recommended changing the filter every other fluid change, we at Chilton recommend that you always change the filter with the fluid. The benefit of fresh fluid is quickly lost if the old filter is clogged and unable to do its job.

1. Raise and support the vehicle safely.

2. Make sure the transmission/transaxle drain plug is at the lowest point on the pan.

3. Before you crawl under the vehicle, take a look at where you will be working and gather all the necessary tools: such as a few wrenches or a strip of sockets, an extra large drain pan and a clean rag.

4. Position the drain pan beneath the transmission/transaxle drain plug. Keep in mind that the fast flowing fluid, which will spill out as you pull the plug from the pan, will flow with enough force that it could miss the pan. Position the drain pan accordingly and be ready to move the pan more directly beneath the plug as the fluid flow lessens to a trickle.

5. Loosen the drain plug with a wrench (or socket and driver), then carefully unscrew the plug with your fingers. Use a rag to shield your fingers from the heat. Push in on the plug as you unscrew it so you can feel when all of the screw threads are out of the hole (and so you will keep the fluid from seeping past the threads until you are ready to remove the plug).

Fig. 167 There are 11 bolts and one nut that attach the transaxle oil filter to the transaxle

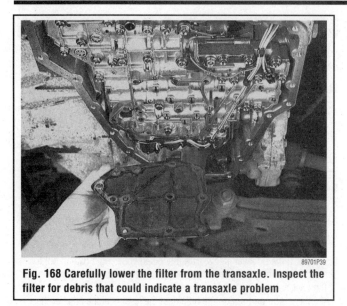

Fig. 168 Carefully lower the filter from the transaxle. Inspect the filter for debris that could indicate a transaxle problem

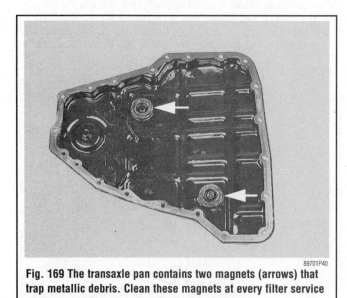

Fig. 169 The transaxle pan contains two magnets (arrows) that trap metallic debris. Clean these magnets at every filter service

Fig. 170 Thoroughly clean the old gasket material from the transaxle pan using a scraper

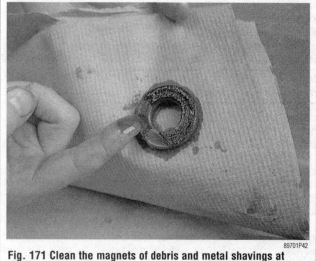

Fig. 171 Clean the magnets of debris and metal shavings at every filter service

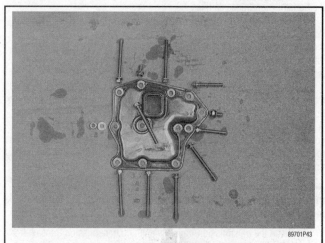

Fig. 172 Transaxle filter bolts are of various lengths. Always install bolts in their proper locations to prevent damage to the transaxle case

Fig. 173 Transaxle fluid should be added through the dipstick tube. The use of a long funnel is suggested to prevent spilling the fluid

You can then remove the plug quickly to avoid having hot fluid run down your arm. This will also help assure that you have the plug in your hand, not in the bottom of a pan of hot fluid.

❊❊ CAUTION

Be careful of the fluid; when at operating temperature, it is hot enough to cause a severe burn.

6. Allow the fluid to drain until nothing but a few drops come out of the drain hole. Check the drain plug to make sure the threads and sealing surface are not damaged. Carefully thread the plug into position and tighten it with a torque wrench to 22–29 ft. lbs. (29–39 Nm). If a torque wrench is not available, snug the drain plug and give it a slight additional turn. You don't want the plug to fall out (as you would quickly become stranded), but the pan threads are EASILY stripped from overtightening (and this can be time consuming and/or costly to fix).

7. Loosen the transmission/transaxle pan bolts evenly. Keep the pan level and carefully lower it from the transmission/transaxle. Some transmission fluid will remain in the pan. Tip the pan slightly to allow the remaining fluid to drain.

8. Loosen the filter attaching bolts. The filter tube is usually held into the transmission/transaxle with an O-ring. Make sure the O-ring comes out of the transmission/transaxle when the filter is removed. Carefully remove the transmission/transaxle filter.

9. Wipe the base of the filter mounting boss with a clean, dry cloth. When you install the new filter, smear a small amount of petroleum jelly on the O-ring with your finger, just enough to coat the entire contact surface. This will lubricate the O-ring and prevent it from getting damaged during installation of the filter.

10. Push the filter tube into the boss on the transmission/transaxle and make sure it is fully seated. Install the transmission/transaxle filter attaching bolts and tighten to 5–6 ft. lbs. (7–9 Nm).

11. Clean all the sediment out of the transmission/transaxle pan with solvent. Remove the magnets from the pan and clean them thoroughly, then return them to the pan. The magnets are used to trap any metallic particles floating in the transmission fluid.

➥Most transmission/transaxle pans and cases are made of aluminum and can be easily damaged. When removing old gasket material, take care not to gouge the aluminum.

12. Clean the transmission/transaxle pan and transmission/transaxle gasket mating surfaces of all old gasket material. After scraping all the old material off, wipe the area with a lint-free rag moistened with solvent. Allow it to dry completely.

13. Lay the new gasket on the transmission/transaxle pan and check for proper alignment. Remove the gasket, place a few dabs of adhesive on the pan and place the gasket down again. Make sure the gasket is aligned before the adhesive is dry.

14. Position the pan on the transmission/transaxle and install the pan bolts. Tighten the bolts in a crisscross pattern to 5–6 ft. lbs. (7–9 Nm).

❊❊ WARNING

Never operate the transmission/transaxle without fluid, otherwise severe damage will result.

15. Remove the jackstands and carefully lower the vehicle, then immediately refill the transmission/transaxle with the proper amount and type of fluid.

16. Refill the transmission/transaxle slowly, checking the level often. You may notice that it usually takes less than the amount of fluid listed in the Capacities chart to refill the transmission/transaxle. This is due to the torque converter being partially filled with fluid. To make sure the proper level is obtained, start the engine and shift the transmission/transaxle, engaging each gear. Then place the selector in **P**. Adjust the fluid to the proper level.

➥If the vehicle is not resting on level ground, the fluid level reading on the dipstick may be slightly off. Be sure to check the level only when the vehicle is sitting level.

17. Empty the used fluid into a suitable container for recycling.

Drive Axle

The drive axle oil on the 240SX should be inspected every 15,000 miles (24,000 km) and changed every 30,000 miles (48,300 km).

FLUID RECOMMENDATIONS

Nissan recommends the use of a 80W-90 weight gear oil meeting API specification GL-5.

LEVEL CHECK

◆ **See Figure 174**

1. Raise and support the vehicle safely.
2. With the vehicle level, remove the filler plug from the back side of the differential.
3. Drive axle oil is at the proper level if it just reaches the bottom of the filler hole. If the oil level is low, carefully insert your finger (watch out for sharp threads) into the hole and check that the oil is up to the bottom edge of the filler hole.
4. If not, add oil through the hole until the level is at the edge of the hole. Most gear oils come in a plastic squeeze bottle with a nozzle that making addition simple. You can also use a common kitchen baster. Use only the specified fluid.
5. Replace the plug and tighten to 29–43 ft. lbs. (39–59 Nm). Check for leaks.
6. Lower the vehicle.

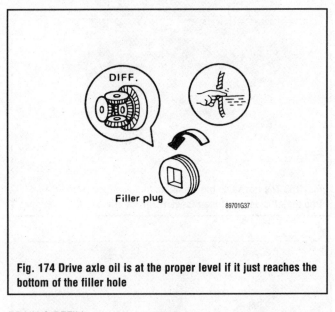

Fig. 174 Drive axle oil is at the proper level if it just reaches the bottom of the filler hole

DRAIN & REFILL

It is a good idea to warm the drive axle oil first so it will flow better. This can be accomplished by 15–20 miles (24–32 km) of highway driving. Oil which is warmed to normal operating temperature will flow faster, drain more completely and remove more contaminants from the drive axle.

❊❊ CAUTION

The EPA warns that prolonged contact with used drive axle oil may cause a number of skin disorders, including cancer! You should make every effort to minimize your exposure to used drive axle oil. Protective gloves should be worn when changing the oil. Wash your hands and any other exposed skin areas as soon as possible after exposure to used drive axle oil. Soap and water, or waterless hand cleaner should be used.

1. Raise and support the vehicle safely.
2. With the vehicle level, remove the filler plug from the back side of the differential.
3. Place a drain pan under the drain plug.
4. Remove the drain plug from the back side of the differential.
5. Allow the oil to drain from the drive axle completely.
6. Install the drain plug and tighten to 29–43 ft. lbs. (39–59 Nm).
7. Inspect the oil for contaminants. A silver haze in the oil indicates the presence of metal. Milky white oil indicates the presence of water.
8. Refill the drive axle to the proper level with the recommended grade and viscosity oil.
9. Drive axle oil is at the proper level if it just reaches the bottom of the filler hole.
10. Replace the plug and tighten to 29–43 ft. lbs. (39–59 Nm). Check for leaks.
11. Lower the vehicle.

Cooling System

◆ **See Figures 175, 176, 177 and 178**

The cooling system level should be visually inspected each time the hood is opened. Antifreeze should be replaced at 60,000 miles (96,600 km) and then every 30,000 miles (48,300 km).

If necessary, hose clamps should be checked and soft or cracked hoses replaced. Damp spots or accumulations of rust or dye near hoses, the water pump or other areas indicate areas of possible leakage. Check the surge tank cap for a worn or cracked gasket. If the cap doesn't seal properly, fluid will be lost and the engine will overheat. A worn cap should be replaced with a new one. The surge tank should be free of rust and the coolant should be free from oil. If oil is found in the coolant, the engine thermostat will not function correctly; in this case, the system must be flushed and filled with fresh coolant.

Periodically clean any debris such as leaves, paper, insects, etc. from the radiator fins. Pick the large pieces off by hand. The smaller pieces can be washed away with water pressure from a hose.

Carefully straighten any bent radiator fins with a pair of needlenose pliers. Be careful—the fins are very soft. Don't wiggle the fins back and forth too much. Straighten them once and try not to move them again.

FLUID RECOMMENDATIONS

The use of a good quality ethylene glycol based or other aluminum compatible antifreeze is recommended. It is best to add a 50/50 mix of antifreeze and water to avoid diluting the coolant in the system.

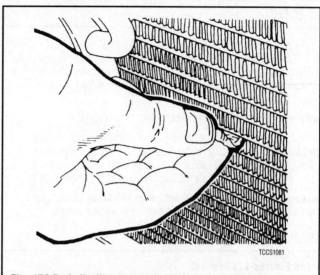

Fig. 176 Periodically remove all debris from the radiator fins

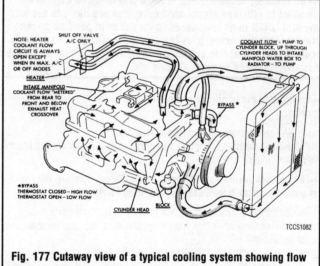

Fig. 177 Cutaway view of a typical cooling system showing flow characteristics

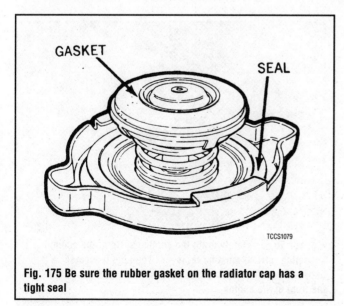

Fig. 175 Be sure the rubber gasket on the radiator cap has a tight seal

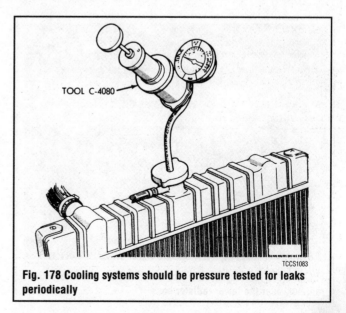

Fig. 178 Cooling systems should be pressure tested for leaks periodically

LEVEL CHECK

The coolant fluid level should be inspected at least twice a year.

1. Check the fluid level in the reserve tank to make sure the system is properly filled. Top off the cooling system using the recovery tank and its LOW and FULL markings as a guideline. If you top off the system, make a note to check it again soon.

➡**Never overfill the reserve tank.**

2. A coolant level that consistently drops is usually a sign of a small, hard to detect leak, although in the worst case it could be a sign of an internal engine leak (check the engine oil for milky white contamination). In most cases, you will be able to trace the leak to a loose fitting or damaged hose.

➡**Evaporating ethylene glycol antifreeze will leave small, white (salt-like) deposits, which can be helpful in tracing a leak.**

DRAIN, FLUSH & REFILL

◆ See Figures 179 thru 185

✳✳ CAUTION

When draining coolant, keep in mind that cats and dogs are attracted to ethylene glycol antifreeze, and are likely to drink any that is left in an uncovered container or in puddles on the ground. This will prove fatal in sufficient quantity. Always drain coolant into a sealable container. Coolant may be reused unless it is contaminated or several years old.

➡**Ensure that the engine is completely cool prior to starting this service.**

1. Remove the radiator and reserve tank caps.
2. Place a drain pan of sufficient capacity under the radiator and open the petcock (drain).

➡**The petcock is plastic and easily binds. Before opening the radiator petcock, spray it with some penetrating lubricant.**

3. When the system is completely drained, close the petcock and fill the system with a radiator cleaning fluid (clean water may also be used, but is not as efficient).
4. Idle the engine until the upper radiator hose gets hot.
5. Allow the engine to cool and drain the system again.
6. Repeat this process until the drained water is clear and free of scale.

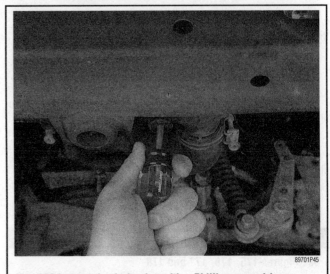
Fig. 180 Loosen the drain plug with a Phillips screwdriver

Fig. 181 Inspect the rubber washer for damage or dry rot, and replace as necessary

Fig. 179 The radiator drain is located on the driver's side of the radiator, near the lower radiator hose

Fig. 182 To completely drain the cooling system, the coolant hose plug (arrow) must be removed. The plug is located between the air conditioner compressor and oil dipstick tube, at the front of the engine

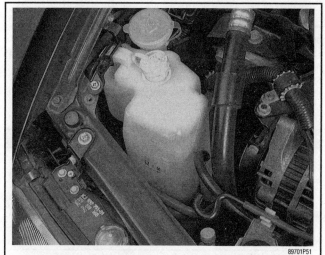

Fig. 183 The cooling system level should be kept at or below the MAX mark on the reservoir

Fig. 184 Periodic additions of coolant should be made at the reservoir . . .

Fig. 185 . . . while system refilling should be performed through the filler neck on the radiator

7. Flush the reserve tank with water and leave empty.

➡**If you decide to add the antifreeze and water separately (instead of pre-mixing them), be sure that you add a sufficient amount of antifreeze, before topping off with water.**

8. Determine the capacity of the coolant system, then properly refill the cooling system with a 50/50 mixture of fresh coolant (antifreeze and water), as follows:

    a. Fill the radiator with coolant until it reaches the radiator filler neck seat.

    b. Start the engine and allow it to idle until the thermostat opens (the upper radiator hose will become hot).

    c. Turn the engine **OFF** and refill the radiator until the coolant level is at the filler neck seat.

    d. Fill the engine coolant overflow tank with coolant to the proper mark, then install the radiator cap.

9. If available, install a pressure tester and check for leaks. If a pressure tester is not available, run the engine until normal operating temperature is reached (allowing the system to naturally pressurize), then check for leaks.

10. Check the level of protection with an antifreeze/coolant hydrometer.

Brake Master Cylinder

FLUID RECOMMENDATION

The use of fresh, uncontaminated brake fluid meeting or exceeding DOT 3 standards or equivalent is recommended.

LEVEL CHECK

▶ **See Figures 186, 187 and 188**

1. Check the level of fluid in the brake master cylinder reservoir. The fluid should be maintained between the MIN and MAX lines on the reservoir.

➡**Any sudden decrease in fluid level indicates a probable leak in the system and should be inspected immediately.**

2. Clean around the reservoir cap with a shop rag to prevent contaminating the fluid with dirt.

3. Remove the cap and add the required amount of fluid to the system.

➡**When making additions of fluid, use only fresh, uncontaminated brake fluid meeting or exceeding DOT 3 standards. Be careful not to spill any brake fluid on painted surfaces, because it will damage the paint. Do not allow the fluid container or brake fluid reservoir to**

Fig. 186 Fluid level should be maintained between the MIN and MAX marks on the brake master cylinder reservoir

Fig. 187 Always wipe the top of the master cylinder reservoir prior to removing the cap. This prevents dirt from entering the brake system

Fig. 188 Add only clean, fresh brake fluid to the reservoir. Add fluid in small amounts and never overfill the reservoir

remain open any longer than necessary; brake fluid absorbs moisture from the air, reducing its effectiveness and causing brake line corrosion.

4. Install the reservoir cap.

Clutch Master Cylinder

FLUID RECOMMENDATIONS

The use of fresh, uncontaminated brake fluid meeting or exceeding DOT 3 standards or equivalent is recommended.

LEVEL CHECK

1. Check the level of brake fluid in the clutch master cylinder reservoir. The fluid should be maintained between the MIN and MAX lines on the reservoir.

➡**Any sudden decrease in fluid level indicates a probable leak in the system and should be inspected immediately.**

2. Clean around the reservoir cap with a shop rag to prevent contaminating the fluid with dirt.

3. Remove the cap and add the required amount of fluid to the system.

➡**When making additions of fluid, use only fresh, uncontaminated brake fluid meeting or exceeding DOT 3 standards. Be careful not to spill any brake fluid on painted surfaces, because it will damage the paint. Do not allow the fluid container or clutch reservoir to remain open any longer than necessary; brake fluid absorbs moisture from the air, reducing its effectiveness and causing brake line corrosion.**

4. Install the reservoir cap.

Power Steering Pump

FLUID RECOMMENDATIONS

The use of DEXRON®II or III automatic transmission fluid or equivalent is recommended.

LEVEL CHECK

▶ **See Figures 189 and 190**

1. Park the car on a level surface.

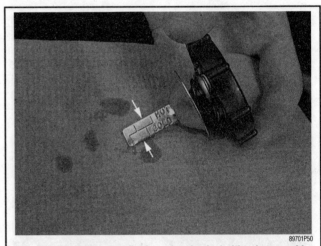

Fig. 189 Power steering fluid can be checked either hot or cold; ensure that the fluid level falls within the appropriate range (as shown by the arrows)

Fig. 190 Add fluid to the power steering reservoir if necessary

➡️**It is recommended that the power steering fluid be checked when hot. However, the power steering fluid dipstick also has marks for checking the fluid when cold.**

2. Start the engine and turn the steering wheel all the way to the left and right several times. This will raise the fluid temperature to approximately 122–176°F (50–80°C).

3. With the engine idling, check the level of fluid in the power steering pump's reservoir. The fluid should be maintained at the MAX line with the engine idling and at the MIN line with the engine off.

4. If still idling, turn the engine off. If the system requires fluid, clean around the reservoir cap with a shop rag to prevent contaminating the fluid with dirt.

5. Remove the cap and add the required amount of fluid to the system.

6. Install the reservoir cap.

Chassis Greasing

Chassis and steering components are permanently lubricated and require no periodic lubrication. Inspect the seals and boots for damage and signs of leakage. Replace damaged components as necessary.

Body Lubrication and Maintenance

LUBRICATION

▶ **See Figures 191 and 192**

To lubricate lock cylinders, apply graphite lubricant sparingly through the key slot. Insert the key and operate the lock several times to be sure that the lubricant is worked into the lock cylinder.

At least once a year, use a multi-purpose grease to lubricate the body door hinges, including the hood, fuel door and trunk/liftgate hinges and latches. The glovebox, console doors and folding seat hardware should also be lightly lubricated. Open and close the door several times to be sure that the lubricant is evenly and thoroughly distributed.

MAINTENANCE

Door and window weatherstripping should be lubricated with silicone lubricant. Flush the underbody using plain water to remove any corrosive materials picked up from the road and used for ice, snow or dust control. Make sure you thoroughly clean areas where mud and dirt may collect. If necessary, loosen sediment packed in closed areas before flushing. Clean leaves from vent and cowl areas.

To preserve the appearance of your car, it should be washed periodically with a mild soap or detergent and water solution. A detergent specifically designed for automotive use should be used to loosen dirt or grease from the vehicle. Dishwashing detergent contains degreasers which will strip the vehicles surface of wax. Only wash the vehicle when the metal feels cool and the vehicle is in the shade. Rinse the entire vehicle with water, then wash and rinse one panel at a time, beginning with the roof and upper areas. After washing is complete, rinse the vehicle one final time and dry with a soft cloth or chamois. Air drying a vehicle, by driving at highway speeds for a few miles, may quickly and easily dry a vehicle without the need for excessive elbow grease.

Periodic polishing and waxing will remove harmful deposits from the vehicles surface and protect the finish. If the finish has dulled due to age or neglect, non-abrasive cleaner may be necessary to restore the original gloss.

There are many specialized products available at your local auto parts store to care for the appearance of painted metal surfaces, plastic, chrome, wheels and tires, as well as the interior upholstery and carpeting. Be sure to follow the manufacturers' instructions before using them.

Wheel Bearings

Wheel bearings on these vehicles are of the sealed bearing type. Periodic lubrication is not required.

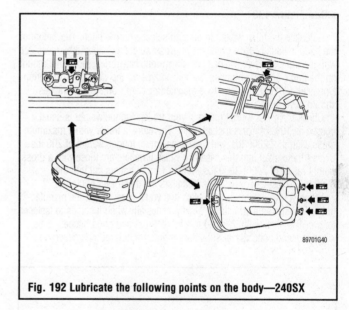

Fig. 192 Lubricate the following points on the body—240SX

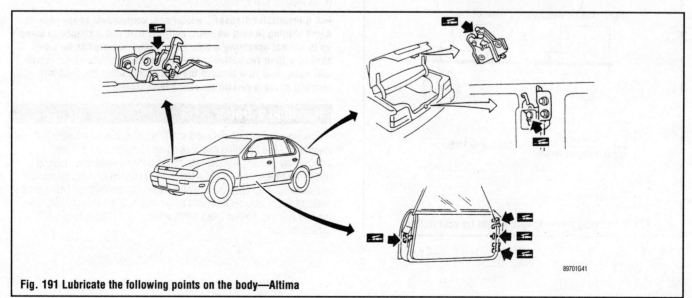

Fig. 191 Lubricate the following points on the body—Altima

TRAILER TOWING

General Recommendations

Your vehicle was primarily designed to carry passengers and cargo. It is important to remember that towing a trailer will place additional loads on your vehicles engine, drivetrain, steering, braking and other systems. However, if you decide to tow a trailer, using the proper equipment is a must.

Local laws may require specific equipment such as trailer brakes or fender mounted mirrors. Check your local laws prior to purchasing trailer equipment.

Trailer Weight

The weight of the trailer is the most important factor. A good weight-to-horsepower ratio is about 35:1, 35 lbs. of Gross Combined Weight (GCW) for every horsepower your engine develops. Multiply the engine's rated horsepower by 35 and subtract the weight of the vehicle passengers and luggage. The number remaining is the approximate maximum weight you should tow, although a numerically higher axle ratio can help compensate for heavier weight.

Hitch (Tongue) Weight

▶ See Figure 193

Calculate the hitch weight in order to select a proper hitch. The weight of the hitch is usually 10% of the trailer gross weight and should be measured with the trailer loaded. Hitches fall into various categories: those that mount on the frame and rear bumper, the bolt-on type, or the weld-on distribution type used for larger trailers. Axle mounted or clamp-on bumper hitches should never be used.

Check the gross weight rating of your trailer. Tongue weight is usually figured as 10% of gross trailer weight. Therefore, a trailer with a maximum gross weight of 2000 lbs. will have a maximum tongue weight of 200 lbs. Class I trailers fall into this category. Class II trailers are those with a gross weight rating of 2000–3000 lbs., while Class III trailers fall into the 3500–6000 lbs. category. Class IV trailers are those over 6000 lbs.

When you've determined the hitch that you'll need, follow the manufacturer's installation instructions, exactly, especially when it comes to fastener torque. The hitch will subjected to a lot of stress and good hitches come with hardened bolts. Never substitute an inferior bolt for a hardened bolt.

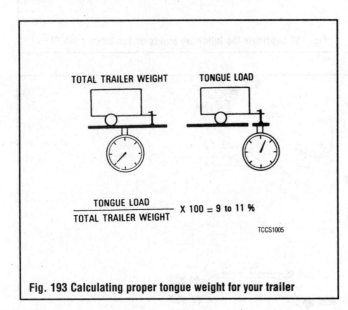

TOTAL TRAILER WEIGHT   TONGUE LOAD

$$\frac{\text{TONGUE LOAD}}{\text{TOTAL TRAILER WEIGHT}} \times 100 = 9 \text{ to } 11\%$$

TCCS1005

Fig. 193 Calculating proper tongue weight for your trailer

Drivetrain Recommendation

ENGINE

Cooling System

One of the most common, if not THE most common, problems associated with trailer towing is engine overheating. Cleaning and flushing the cooling system is good preventative maintenance. Ensure that all cooling system components are functioning properly. If your vehicle is not equipped with a factory towing package, installation of aftermarket high capacity radiators, high flow water pumps and auxiliary electric cooling fans will all help keeping your vehicle running cool.

Oil Cooler

Aftermarket engine oil coolers are helpful for prolonging engine oil life and reducing overall engine temperatures. Both of these factors increase engine life. While not absolutely necessary in towing a Class I trailer, all vehicles towing Class II and heavier trailers should be equipped with an engine oil cooler. Engine oil cooler systems usually consist of an adapter, screwed on in place of the oil filter, a remote filter mounting and a multi-tube, finned heat exchanger, which is mounted in front of the radiator or air conditioning condenser.

TRANSMISSION/TRANSAXLE

Transmission/Transaxle Cooler

An automatic transmission/transaxle is recommended for trailer towing. Modern automatics have proven reliable and, of course, easy to operate, in trailer towing. The increased load of a trailer, however, causes an increase in the temperature of the automatic transmission fluid. Heat is the worst enemy of an automatic transmission/transaxle. As the temperature of the fluid increases, the life of the fluid decreases.

It is essential, therefore, that you install an automatic transmission/transaxle cooler. The cooler, which consists of a multi-tube, finned heat exchanger, is usually installed in front of the radiator or air conditioning compressor, and hooked in-line with the transmission/transaxle cooler tank inlet line. Follow the cooler manufacturer's installation instructions.

Select a cooler of at least adequate capacity, based upon the combined gross weights of the vehicle and trailer.

➡A transmission/transaxle cooler can, sometimes, cause slow or harsh shifting in cold weather, until the fluid has a chance to come up to normal operating temperature. Some coolers can be purchased with or retrofitted with a temperature bypass valve, which will allow fluid flow through the cooler only when the fluid has reached above a certain operating temperature.

Handling a Trailer

Towing a trailer with ease and safety requires a certain amount of experience. The handling and braking characteristics of any tow vehicle may be radically changed by the added weight of a trailer. It a good idea to learn the feel of a trailer by practicing turning, stopping and backing in an open area, such as an empty parking lot. Make mental notes of space requirements and trailer response while practicing turning and braking. Follow these notes while on the road to help avoid accidents.

JUMP STARTING A DEAD BATTERY

◆ See Figure 194

Whenever a vehicle is jump started, precautions must be followed in order to prevent the possibility of personal injury. Remember that batteries contain a small amount of explosive hydrogen gas which is a by-product of battery charging. Sparks should always be avoided when working around batteries, especially when attaching jumper cables. To minimize the possibility of accidental sparks, follow the procedure carefully.

❊❊ CAUTION

NEVER hook the batteries up in a series circuit, or the entire electrical system will go up in smoke, including the starter!

Vehicles equipped with a diesel engine may utilize two 12 volt batteries. If so, the batteries are connected in a parallel circuit (positive terminal to positive terminal, negative terminal to negative terminal). Hooking the batteries up in parallel circuit increases battery cranking power without increasing total battery voltage output. Output remains at 12 volts. On the other hand, hooking two 12 volt batteries up in a series circuit (positive terminal to negative terminal, positive terminal to negative terminal) increases total battery output to 24 volts (12 volts plus 12 volts).

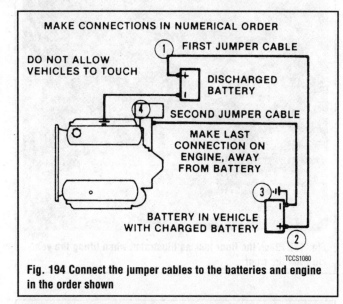

Fig. 194 Connect the jumper cables to the batteries and engine in the order shown

Jump Starting Precautions

- Be sure that both batteries are of the same voltage. Vehicles covered by this manual and most vehicles on the road today utilize a 12 volt charging system.
- Be sure that both batteries are of the same polarity (have the same terminal grounded—in most cases NEGATIVE).
- Be sure that the vehicles are not touching or a short circuit could occur.
- On serviceable batteries, be sure the vent cap holes are not obstructed.
- Do not smoke or allow sparks anywhere near the batteries.
- In cold weather, make sure the battery electrolyte is not frozen. This can occur more readily in a battery that has been in a state of discharge.
- Do not allow electrolyte to contact your skin or clothing.

Jump Starting Procedure

1. Make sure that the voltages of the 2 batteries are the same. Most batteries and charging systems are of the 12 volt variety.
2. Pull the jumping vehicle (with the good battery) into a position so the jumper cables can reach the dead battery and that vehicle's engine. Make sure that the vehicles do NOT touch.
3. Place the transmissions/transaxles of both vehicles in **Neutral** (MT) or **P** (AT), as applicable, then firmly set their parking brakes.

➡**If necessary for safety reasons, the hazard lights on both vehicles may be operated throughout the entire procedure without significantly increasing the difficulty of jumping the dead battery.**

4. Turn all lights and accessories OFF on both vehicles. Make sure the ignition switches on both vehicles are turned to the **OFF** position.
5. If so equipped, cover the battery cell caps with a rag, but do not cover the terminals.
6. Make sure the terminals on both batteries are clean and free of corrosion, or proper electrical connection will be impeded. If necessary, clean the battery terminals before proceeding.
7. Identify the positive (+) and negative (-) terminals on both batteries.
8. Connect the first jumper cable to the positive (+) terminal of the dead battery, then connect the other end of that cable to the positive (+) terminal of the booster (good) battery.
9. Connect one end of the other jumper cable to the negative (-) terminal on the booster battery and the final cable clamp to an engine bolt head, alternator bracket or other solid, metallic point on the engine with the dead battery. Try to pick a ground on the engine that is positioned away from the battery, in order to minimize the possibility of the 2 clamps touching should one loosen during the procedure. DO NOT connect this clamp to the negative (-) terminal of the bad battery.

❊❊ CAUTION

Be very careful to keep the jumper cables away from moving parts (cooling fan, belts, etc.) on both engines.

10. Check to make sure that the cables are routed away from any moving parts, then start the donor vehicle's engine. Run the engine at moderate speed for several minutes to allow the dead battery a chance to receive some initial charge.
11. With the donor vehicle's engine still running slightly above idle, try to start the vehicle with the dead battery. Crank the engine for no more than 10 seconds at a time and let the starter cool for at least 20 seconds between tries. If the vehicle does not start in 3 tries, it is likely that something else is also wrong or that the battery needs additional time to charge.
12. Once the vehicle is started, allow it to run at idle for a few seconds to make sure that it is operating properly.
13. Turn ON the headlights, heater blower and, if equipped, the rear defroster of both vehicles in order to reduce the severity of voltage spikes, and subsequent risk of damage, to the vehicles' electrical systems when the cables are disconnected. This step is especially important to any vehicle equipped with computer control modules.
14. Carefully disconnect the cables in the reverse order of connection. Start with the negative cable that is attached to the engine ground, then the negative cable on the donor battery. Disconnect the positive cable from the donor battery and, finally, disconnect the positive cable from the formerly dead battery. Be careful when disconnecting the cables from the positive terminals not to allow the alligator clips to touch any metal on either vehicle, or a short circuit and sparks will occur.

JACKING

▶ **See Figures 195 thru 200**

Your vehicle was supplied with a jack for emergency road repairs. This jack is fine for changing a flat tire, or for other short term procedures not requiring you to go beneath the vehicle. If it is used in an emergency situation, carefully follow the instructions provided either with the jack or in your owner's manual. Do not attempt to use the jack on any portions of the vehicle other than those specified by the vehicle manufacturer. Always block the diagonally opposite wheel when using a jack.

A more convenient way of jacking is the use of a garage or floor jack. You may use the floor jack at the illustrated points on the chassis of the vehicle. Bear in mind that using a jack beneath the sills of the vehicle without using the proper attachment will damage the welds.

Never place the jack under the radiator, engine or transmission/transaxle components. Severe and expensive damage will result when the jack is raised. Additionally, never jack under the floorpan or bodywork; the metal will deform.

Whenever you plan to work under the vehicle, you must support it on jackstands or ramps. Never use cinder blocks or stacks of wood to support the vehicle, even if you're only going to be under it for a few minutes. Never crawl under the vehicle when it is supported only by the tire-changing jack or other floor jack.

➡**Always position a block of wood or small rubber pad on top of the jack or jackstand to protect the lifting point's finish when lifting or supporting the vehicle.**

Small hydraulic, screw, or scissors jacks are satisfactory for raising the vehicle. Drive-on trestles or ramps are also a handy and safe way to both raise and support the vehicle. Be careful though, some ramps may be too steep to drive your vehicle onto without scraping the front bottom panels. Never support the vehicle by any suspension member (unless specifically instructed to do so by a repair manual) or by an underbody panel.

Jacking Precautions

The following safety points cannot be overemphasized:
• Always block the opposite wheel or wheels to keep the vehicle from rolling off the jack.
• When raising the front of the vehicle, firmly apply the parking brake.

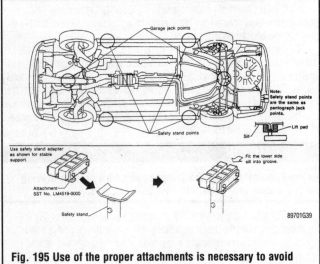

Fig. 195 Use of the proper attachments is necessary to avoid damage to the sill when lifting the vehicle

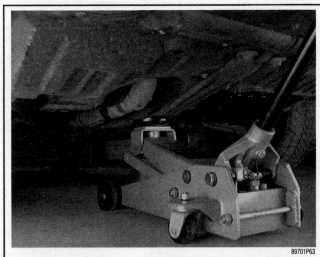

Fig. 197 Place the floor jack as illustrated when lifting the vehicle from the front

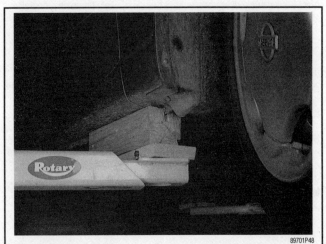

Fig. 196 To prevent the pinch welds from being damaged when raising the vehicle, adapters can be made from 4 in. x 4 in. pieces of lumber

Fig. 198 Place the jackstands as illustrated when supporting the vehicle from the front. Always use jackstands when working under the vehicle

- When the drive wheels are to remain on the ground, leave the vehicle in gear to help prevent it from rolling.
- Always use jackstands to support the vehicle when you are working

underneath. Place the stands beneath the vehicle's jacking brackets. Before climbing underneath, rock the vehicle a bit to make sure it is firmly supported.

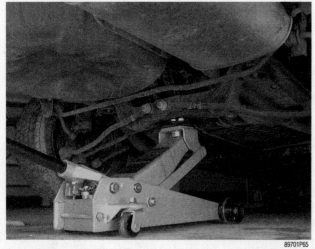

Fig. 199 Place the floor jack as illustrated when lifting the vehicle from the rear

Fig. 200 Place the jackstands as illustrated when supporting the vehicle from the rear. Always use jackstands when working under the vehicle

CAPACITIES

Year	Model	Engine ID/VIN	Engine Displacement Liters (cc)	Engine Oil with Filter	Transmission (qts.) 4-Spd	Transmission (qts.) 5-Spd	Transmission (qts.) Auto.	Transfer Case (pts.)	Drive Axle Front (pts.)	Drive Axle Rear (pts.)	Fuel Tank (gal.)	Cooling System (qts.)
1993	240SX	KA24DE	2.4 (2389)	4.00	–	2.50	8.75	–	–	2.75	16.00	7.13
	Altima	KA24DE	2.4 (2389)	4.13	–	5.00	10.00	–	–	–	16.00	8.25
1994	240SX	KA24DE	2.4 (2389)	4.00	–	2.50	8.75	–	–	2.75	16.00	7.13
	Altima	KA24DE	2.4 (2389)	4.13	–	5.00	10.00	–	–	–	16.00	8.25
1995	240SX	KA24DE	2.4 (2389)	4.00	–	2.50	8.75	–	–	2.75	16.00	7.13
	Altima	KA24DE	2.4 (2389)	4.13	–	5.00	10.00	–	–	–	16.00	8.25
1996	240SX	KA24DE	2.4 (2389)	4.00	–	2.50	8.75	–	–	2.75	16.00	7.13
	Altima	KA24DE	2.4 (2389)	4.13	–	5.00	10.00	–	–	–	16.00	8.25
1997	240SX	KA24DE	2.4 (2389)	4.00	–	2.50	8.75	–	–	2.75	16.00	7.13
	Altima	KA24DE	2.4 (2389)	4.13	–	5.00	10.00	–	–	–	16.00	8.25
1998	240SX	KA24DE	2.4 (2389)	4.00	–	2.50	8.75	–	–	2.75	16.00	7.13
	Altima	KA24DE	2.4 (2389)	4.13	–	5.00	10.00	–	–	–	16.00	8.25

89701C06

MANUFACTURER RECOMMENDED MAINTENANCE INTERVALS

89701C04

MAINTENANCE OPERATION	MAINTENANCE INTERVAL							
Perform at number of miles, kilometers or months, whichever comes first. Miles x 1,000 (km x 1,000) Months	7.5 (12) 6	15 (24) 12	22.5 (36) 18	30 (48) 24	37.5 (60) 30	45 (72) 36	52.5 (84) 42	60 (96) 48
Emission control system maintenance								
Drive belts — See NOTE (1)								I*
Air cleaner filter				[R]				[R]
Vapor lines				I*				I*
Fuel lines				I*				I*
Fuel filter — See NOTE (2)*								R*
Engine coolant — See NOTE (3)				R				R*
Engine oil	R	R	R	R	R	R	R	R
Engine oil filter (Use Nissan PREMIUM type or equivalent)		R		R		R		R
Spark plugs				[R]				[R]
Intake & exhaust valve clearance — See NOTE (4)*								
Chassis and body maintenance								
Brake lines & cables		I		I		I		I
Brake pads, discs, drums & linings		I		I		I		I
Manual & automatic transaxle oil, transmission oil, & differential gear oil		I				I		
Steering gear linkage, axle & suspension parts				I				
Exhaust system		I		I		I		I
Drive shaft boots		I		I		I		I
Air bag system — See NOTE (5)								

Abbreviations: R = Replace.   I = Inspect. Correct or replace if necessary.
[ ]: At the mileage intervals only

NOTE:
(1) After 60,000 miles (96,000 km) or 48 months, inspect every 15,000 miles (24,000 km) or 12 months.
(2) If vehicle is operated under extremely adverse weather conditions or in areas where ambient temperatures are either extremely low or extremely high, the filters might become clogged. In such an event, replace them immediately.
(3) After 60,000 miles (96,000 km) or 48 months, replace every 30,000 miles (48,000 km) or 24 months.
(4) If valve noise increases, inspect valve clearance.
(5) Inspect the air bag system 10 years after the date of manufacture noted on the certification label.
* Maintenance items and intervals with "*" are recommended by NISSAN for reliable vehicle operation. The owner need not perform such maintenance in order to maintain the emission warranty or manufacturer recall liability. Other maintenance items and intervals are required.

89701C05

MANUFACTURER RECOMMENDED SEVERE MAINTENANCE INTERVALS

MAINTENANCE INTERVAL

MAINTENANCE OPERATION	3.75	7.5	11.25	15	18.75	22.5	26.25	30	33.75	37.5	41.25	45	48.75	52.5	56.25	60
Perform at number of miles, kilometers or months, whichever comes first. — Miles x 1,000	3.75	7.5	11.25	15	18.75	22.5	26.25	30	33.75	37.5	41.25	45	48.75	52.5	56.25	60
(km x 1,000)	(6)	(12)	(18)	(24)	(30)	(36)	(42)	(48)	(54)	(60)	(66)	(72)	(78)	(84)	(90)	(96)
Months	3	6	9	12	15	18	21	24	27	30	33	36	39	42	45	48
Emission control system maintenance																
Drive belts See NOTE (1)																I*
Air cleaner filter See NOTE (2)								[R]								[R]
Vapor lines								I*								I*
Fuel lines								I*								I*
Fuel filter See NOTE (3)*																I*
Engine coolant See NOTE (4)																R*
Engine oil	R	R	R	R	R	R	R	R	R	R	R	R	R	R	R	R
Engine oil filter (Use Nissan PREMIUM type or equivalent)	R	R	R	R	R	R	R	R	R	R	R	R	R	R	R	R
Spark plugs								[R]								[R]
Intake & exhaust valve clearance See NOTE (5)*																
Chassis and body maintenance																
Brake lines & cables				I				I				I				I
Brake pads, discs, drums & linings		I		I		I		I		I		I		I		I
Manual & automatic transaxle oil, transmission oil, & differential gear oil See NOTE (6)				I				I				I				I
Steering gear & linkage, axle & suspension parts				I				I				I				I
Steering linkage ball joints & front suspension ball joints				I				I				I				I
Exhaust system				I				I				I				I
Drive shaft boots				I				I				I				I
Air bag system See NOTE (7)																

Abbreviations: R = Replace.   I = Inspect. Correct or replace if necessary.

[ ]: At the mileage intervals only

NOTE:
(1) After 60,000 miles (96,000 km) or 48 months, inspect every 15,000 miles (24,000 km) or 12 months.
(2) If operating mainly in dusty conditions, more frequent maintenance may be required.
(3) If vehicle is operated under extremely adverse weather conditions or in areas where ambient temperatures are either extremely low or extremely high, the filters might become clogged. In such an event, replace them immediately.
(4) After 60,000 miles (96,000 km) or 48 months, replace every 30,000 miles (48,000 km) or 24 months.
(5) If valve noise increases, inspect valve clearance.
(6) If towing a trailer, using a camper or a car-top carrier, or driving on rough or muddy roads, change (not just inspect) oil at every 30,000 miles (48,000 km) or 24 months.
(7) Inspect the air bag system 10 years after the date of manufacture noted on the certification label.
* Maintenance items and intervals with "*" are recommended by NISSAN for reliable vehicle operation. The owner need not perform such maintenance in order to maintain the emission warranty or manufacturer recall liability. Other maintenance items and intervals are required.

ENGLISH TO METRIC CONVERSION: MASS (WEIGHT)

Current **mass** measurement is expressed in pounds and ounces (lbs. & ozs.). The metric unit of **mass** (or weight) is the kilogram (kg). Even although this table does not show conversion of masses (weights) larger than 15 lbs, it is easy to calculate larger units by following the data immediately below.

To convert ounces (oz.) to grams (g): multiply th number of ozs. by 28
To convert grams (g) to ounces (oz.): multiply the number of grams by .035

To convert pounds (lbs.) to kilograms (kg): multiply the number of lbs. by .45
To convert kilograms (kg) to pounds (lbs.): multiply the number of kilograms by 2.2

lbs	kg	lbs	kg	oz	kg	oz	kg
0.1	0.04	0.9	0.41	0.1	0.003	0.9	0.024
0.2	0.09	1	0.4	0.2	0.005	1	0.03
0.3	0.14	2	0.9	0.3	0.008	2	0.06
0.4	0.18	3	1.4	0.4	0.011	3	0.08
0.5	0.23	4	1.8	0.5	0.014	4	0.11
0.6	0.27	5	2.3	0.6	0.017	5	0.14
0.7	0.32	10	4.5	0.7	0.020	10	0.28
0.8	0.36	15	6.8	0.8	0.023	15	0.42

ENGLISH TO METRIC CONVERSION: TEMPERATURE

To convert Fahrenheit (°F) to Celsius (°C): take number of °F and subtract 32; multiply result by 5; divide result by 9

To convert Celsius (°C) to Fahrenheit (°F): take number of °C and multiply by 9; divide result by 5; add 32 to total

Fahrenheit (F)		Celsius (C)		Fahrenheit (F)		Celsius (C)		Fahrenheit (F)		Celsius (C)	
°F	°C	°C	°F	°F	°C	°C	°F	°F	°C	°C	°F
−40	−40	−38	−36.4	80	26.7	18	64.4	215	101.7	80	176
−35	−37.2	−36	−32.8	85	29.4	20	68	220	104.4	85	185
−30	−34.4	−34	−29.2	90	32.2	22	71.6	225	107.2	90	194
−25	−31.7	−32	−25.6	95	35.0	24	75.2	230	110.0	95	202
−20	−28.9	−30	−22	100	37.8	26	78.8	235	112.8	100	212
−15	−26.1	−28	−18.4	105	40.6	28	82.4	240	115.6	105	221
−10	−23.3	−26	−14.8	110	43.3	30	86	245	118.3	110	230
−5	−20.6	−24	−11.2	115	46.1	32	89.6	250	121.1	115	239
0	−17.8	−22	−7.6	120	48.9	34	93.2	255	123.9	120	248
1	−17.2	−20	−4	125	51.7	36	96.8	260	126.6	125	257
2	−16.7	−18	−0.4	130	54.4	38	100.4	265	129.4	130	266
3	−16.1	−16	3.2	135	57.2	40	104	270	132.2	135	275
4	−15.6	−14	6.8	140	60.0	42	107.6	275	135.0	140	284
5	−15.0	−12	10.4	145	62.8	44	112.2	280	137.8	145	293
10	−12.2	−10	14	150	65.6	46	114.8	285	140.6	150	302
15	−9.4	−8	17.6	155	68.3	48	118.4	290	143.3	155	311
20	−6.7	−6	21.2	160	71.1	50	122	295	146.1	160	320
25	−3.9	−4	24.8	165	73.9	52	125.6	300	148.9	165	329
30	−1.1	−2	28.4	170	76.7	54	129.2	305	151.7	170	338
35	1.7	0	32	175	79.4	56	132.8	310	154.4	175	347
40	4.4	2	35.6	180	82.2	58	136.4	315	157.2	180	356
45	7.2	4	39.2	185	85.0	60	140	320	160.0	185	365
50	10.0	6	42.8	190	87.8	62	143.6	325	162.8	190	374
55	12.8	8	46.4	195	90.6	64	147.2	330	165.6	195	383
60	15.6	10	50	200	93.3	66	150.8	335	168.3	200	392
65	18.3	12	53.6	205	96.1	68	154.4	340	171.1	205	401
70	21.1	14	57.2	210	98.9	70	158	345	173.9	210	410
75	23.9	16	60.8	212	100.0	75	167	350	176.7	215	414

TCCS1C01

ENGLISH TO METRIC CONVERSION: LENGTH

To convert inches (ins.) to millimeters (mm): multiply number of inches by 25.4

To convert millimeters (mm) to inches (ins.): multiply number of millimeters by .04

Inches		Decimals	Milli-meters	Inches to millimeters		Inches		Decimals	Milli-meters	Inches to millimeters	
				inches	mm					inches	mm
	1/64	0.051625	0.3969	0.0001	0.00254		33/64	0.515625	13.0969	0.6	15.24
1/32		0.03125	0.7937	0.0002	0.00508	17/32		0.53125	13.4937	0.7	17.78
	3/64	0.046875	1.1906	0.0003	0.00762		35/64	0.546875	13.8906	0.8	20.32
1/16		0.0625	1.5875	0.0004	0.01016	9/16		0.5625	14.2875	0.9	22.86
	5/64	0.078125	1.9844	0.0005	0.01270		37/64	0.578125	14.6844	1	25.4
3/32		0.09375	2.3812	0.0006	0.01524	19/32		0.59375	15.0812	2	50.8
	7/64	0.109375	2.7781	0.0007	0.01778		39/64	0.609375	15.4781	3	76.2
1/8		0.125	3.1750	0.0008	0.02032	5/8		0.625	15.8750	4	101.6
	9/64	0.140625	3.5719	0.0009	0.02286		41/64	0.640625	16.2719	5	127.0
5/32		0.15625	3.9687	0.001	0.0254	21/32		0.65625	16.6687	6	152.4
	11/64	0.171875	4.3656	0.002	0.0508		43/64	0.671875	17.0656	7	177.8
3/16		0.1875	4.7625	0.003	0.0762	11/16		0.6875	17.4625	8	203.2
	13/64	0.203125	5.1594	0.004	0.1016		45/64	0.703125	17.8594	9	228.6
7/32		0.21875	5.5562	0.005	0.1270	23/32		0.71875	18.2562	10	254.0
	15/64	0.234375	5.9531	0.006	0.1524		47/64	0.734375	18.6531	11	279.4
1/4		0.25	6.3500	0.007	0.1778	3/4		0.75	19.0500	12	304.8
	17/64	0.265625	6.7469	0.008	0.2032		49/64	0.765625	19.4469	13	330.2
9/32		0.28125	7.1437	0.009	0.2286	25/32		0.78125	19.8437	14	355.6
	19/64	0.296875	7.5406	0.01	0.254		51/64	0.796875	20.2406	15	381.0
5/16		0.3125	7.9375	0.02	0.508	13/16		0.8125	20.6375	16	406.4
	21/64	0.328125	8.3344	0.03	0.762		53/64	0.828125	21.0344	17	431.8
11/32		0.34375	8.7312	0.04	1.016	27/32		0.84375	21.4312	18	457.2
	23/64	0.359375	9.1281	0.05	1.270		55/64	0.859375	21.8281	19	482.6
3/8		0.375	9.5250	0.06	1.524	7/8		0.875	22.2250	20	508.0
	25/64	0.390625	9.9219	0.07	1.778		57/64	0.890625	22.6219	21	533.4
13/32		0.40625	10.3187	0.08	2.032	29/32		0.90625	23.0187	22	558.8
	27/64	0.421875	10.7156	0.09	2.286		59/64	0.921875	23.4156	23	584.2
7/16		0.4375	11.1125	0.1	2.54	15/16		0.9375	23.8125	24	609.6
	29/64	0.453125	11.5094	0.2	5.08		61/64	0.953125	24.2094	25	635.0
15/32		0.46875	11.9062	0.3	7.62	31/32		0.96875	24.6062	26	660.4
	31/64	0.484375	12.3031	0.4	10.16		63/64	0.984375	25.0031	27	690.6
1/2		0.5	12.7000	0.5	12.70						

ENGLISH TO METRIC CONVERSION: TORQUE

To convert foot-pounds (ft. lbs.) to Newton-meters: multiply the number of ft. lbs. by 1.3

To convert inch-pounds (in. lbs.) to Newton-meters: multiply the number of in. lbs. by .11

in lbs	N-m	in lbs	N-m	in lbs	N-m	in lbs	N-m	in lbs	N-m
0.1	0.01	1	0.11	10	1.13	19	2.15	28	3.16
0.2	0.02	2	0.23	11	1.24	20	2.26	29	3.28
0.3	0.03	3	0.34	12	1.36	21	2.37	30	3.39
0.4	0.04	4	0.45	13	1.47	22	2.49	31	3.50
0.5	0.06	5	0.56	14	1.58	23	2.60	32	3.62
0.6	0.07	6	0.68	15	1.70	24	2.71	33	3.73
0.7	0.08	7	0.78	16	1.81	25	2.82	34	3.84
0.8	0.09	8	0.90	17	1.92	26	2.94	35	3.95
0.9	0.10	9	1.02	18	2.03	27	3.05	36	4.0

ENGLISH TO METRIC CONVERSION: TORQUE

Torque is now expressed as either foot-pounds (ft./lbs.) or inch-pounds (in./lbs.). The metric measurement unit for torque is the Newton-meter (Nm). This unit—the Nm—will be used for all SI metric torque references, both the present ft./lbs. and in./lbs.

ft lbs	N-m	ft lbs	N-m	ft lbs	N-m	ft lbs	N-m
0.1	0.1	33	44.7	74	100.3	115	155.9
0.2	0.3	34	46.1	75	101.7	116	157.3
0.3	0.4	35	47.4	76	103.0	117	158.6
0.4	0.5	36	48.8	77	104.4	118	160.0
0.5	0.7	37	50.7	78	105.8	119	161.3
0.6	0.8	38	51.5	79	107.1	120	162.7
0.7	1.0	39	52.9	80	108.5	121	164.0
0.8	1.1	40	54.2	81	109.8	122	165.4
0.9	1.2	41	55.6	82	111.2	123	166.8
1	1.3	42	56.9	83	112.5	124	168.1
2	2.7	43	58.3	84	113.9	125	169.5
3	4.1	44	59.7	85	115.2	126	170.8
4	5.4	45	61.0	86	116.6	127	172.2
5	6.8	46	62.4	87	118.0	128	173.5
6	8.1	47	63.7	88	119.3	129	174.9
7	9.5	48	65.1	89	120.7	130	176.2
8	10.8	49	66.4	90	122.0	131	177.6
9	12.2	50	67.8	91	123.4	132	179.0
10	13.6	51	69.2	92	124.7	133	180.3
11	14.9	52	70.5	93	126.1	134	181.7
12	16.3	53	71.9	94	127.4	135	183.0
13	17.6	54	73.2	95	128.8	136	184.4
14	18.9	55	74.6	96	130.2	137	185.7
15	20.3	56	75.9	97	131.5	138	187.1
16	21.7	57	77.3	98	132.9	139	188.5
17	23.0	58	78.6	99	134.2	140	189.8
18	24.4	59	80.0	100	135.6	141	191.2
19	25.8	60	81.4	101	136.9	142	192.5
20	27.1	61	82.7	102	138.3	143	193.9
21	28.5	62	84.1	103	139.6	144	195.2
22	29.8	63	85.4	104	141.0	145	196.6
23	31.2	64	86.8	105	142.4	146	198.0
24	32.5	65	88.1	106	143.7	147	199.3
25	33.9	66	89.5	107	145.1	148	200.7
26	35.2	67	90.8	108	146.4	149	202.0
27	36.6	68	92.2	109	147.8	150	203.4
28	38.0	69	93.6	110	149.1	151	204.7
29	39.3	70	94.9	111	150.5	152	206.1
30	40.7	71	96.3	112	151.8	153	207.4
31	42.0	72	97.6	113	153.2	154	208.8
32	43.4	73	99.0	114	154.6	155	210.2

TCCS1C03

ENGLISH TO METRIC CONVERSION: FORCE

Force is presently measured in pounds (lbs.). This type of measurement is used to measure spring pressure, specifically how many pounds it takes to compress a spring. Our present force unit (the pound) will be replaced in SI metric measurements by the Newton (N). This term will eventually see use in specifications for electric motor brush spring pressures, valve spring pressures, etc.

To convert pounds (lbs.) to Newton (N): multiply the number of lbs. by 4.45

lbs	N	lbs	N	lbs	N	oz	N
0.01	0.04	21	93.4	59	262.4	1	0.3
0.02	0.09	22	97.9	60	266.9	2	0.6
0.03	0.13	23	102.3	61	271.3	3	0.8
0.04	0.18	24	106.8	62	275.8	4	1.1
0.05	0.22	25	111.2	63	280.2	5	1.4
0.06	0.27	26	115.6	64	284.6	6	1.7
0.07	0.31	27	120.1	65	289.1	7	2.0
0.08	0.36	28	124.6	66	293.6	8	2.2
0.09	0.40	29	129.0	67	298.0	9	2.5
0.1	0.4	30	133.4	68	302.5	10	2.8
0.2	0.9	31	137.9	69	306.9	11	3.1
0.3	1.3	32	142.3	70	311.4	12	3.3
0.4	1.8	33	146.8	71	315.8	13	3.6
0.5	2.2	34	151.2	72	320.3	14	3.9
0.6	2.7	35	155.7	73	324.7	15	4.2
0.7	3.1	36	160.1	74	329.2	16	4.4
0.8	3.6	37	164.6	75	333.6	17	4.7
0.9	4.0	38	169.0	76	338.1	18	5.0
1	4.4	39	173.5	77	342.5	19	5.3
2	8.9	40	177.9	78	347.0	20	5.6
3	13.4	41	182.4	79	351.4	21	5.8
4	17.8	42	186.8	80	355.9	22	6.1
5	22.2	43	191.3	81	360.3	23	6.4
6	26.7	44	195.7	82	364.8	24	6.7
7	31.1	45	200.2	83	369.2	25	7.0
8	35.6	46	204.6	84	373.6	26	7.2
9	40.0	47	209.1	85	378.1	27	7.5
10	44.5	48	213.5	86	382.6	28	7.8
11	48.9	49	218.0	87	387.0	29	8.1
12	53.4	50	224.4	88	391.4	30	8.3
13	57.8	51	226.9	89	395.9	31	8.6
14	62.3	52	231.3	90	400.3	32	8.9
15	66.7	53	235.8	91	404.8	33	9.2
16	71.2	54	240.2	92	409.2	34	9.4
17	75.6	55	244.6	93	413.7	35	9.7
18	80.1	56	249.1	94	418.1	36	10.0
19	84.5	57	253.6	95	422.6	37	10.3
20	89.0	58	258.0	96	427.0	38	10.6

TCCS1C04

ENGLISH TO METRIC CONVERSION: LIQUID CAPACITY

Liquid or fluid capacity is presently expressed as pints, quarts or gallons, or a combination of all of these. In the metric system the liter (l) will become the basic unit. Fractions of a liter would be expressed as deciliters, centiliters, or most frequently (and commonly) as milliliters.

To convert pints (pts.) to liters (l): multiply the number of pints by .47
To convert liters (l) to pints (pts.): multiply the number of liters by 2.1
To convert quarts (qts.) to liters (l): multiply the number of quarts by .95

To convert liters (l) to quarts (qts.): multiply the number of liters by 1.06
To convert gallons (gals.) to liters (l): multiply the number of gallons by 3.8
To convert liters (l) to gallons (gals.): multiply the number of liters by .26

gals	liters	qts	liters	pts	liters
0.1	0.38	0.1	0.10	0.1	0.05
0.2	0.76	0.2	0.19	0.2	0.10
0.3	1.1	0.3	0.28	0.3	0.14
0.4	1.5	0.4	0.38	0.4	0.19
0.5	1.9	0.5	0.47	0.5	0.24
0.6	2.3	0.6	0.57	0.6	0.28
0.7	2.6	0.7	0.66	0.7	0.33
0.8	3.0	0.8	0.76	0.8	0.38
0.9	3.4	0.9	0.85	0.9	0.43
1	3.8	1	1.0	1	0.5
2	7.6	2	1.9	2	1.0
3	11.4	3	2.8	3	1.4
4	15.1	4	3.8	4	1.9
5	18.9	5	4.7	5	2.4
6	22.7	6	5.7	6	2.8
7	26.5	7	6.6	7	3.3
8	30.3	8	7.6	8	3.8
9	34.1	9	8.5	9	4.3
10	37.8	10	9.5	10	4.7
11	41.6	11	10.4	11	5.2
12	45.4	12	11.4	12	5.7
13	49.2	13	12.3	13	6.2
14	53.0	14	13.2	14	6.6
15	56.8	15	14.2	15	7.1
16	60.6	16	15.1	16	7.6
17	64.3	17	16.1	17	8.0
18	68.1	18	17.0	18	8.5
19	71.9	19	18.0	19	9.0
20	75.7	20	18.9	20	9.5
21	79.5	21	19.9	21	9.9
22	83.2	22	20.8	22	10.4
23	87.0	23	21.8	23	10.9
24	90.8	24	22.7	24	11.4
25	94.6	25	23.6	25	11.8
26	98.4	26	24.6	26	12.3
27	102.2	27	25.5	27	12.8
28	106.0	28	26.5	28	13.2
29	110.0	29	27.4	29	13.7
30	113.5	30	28.4	30	14.2

TCCS1C05

ENGLISH TO METRIC CONVERSION: PRESSURE

The basic unit of pressure measurement used today is expressed as pounds per square inch (psi). The metric unit for psi will be the kilopascal (kPa). This will apply to either fluid pressure or air pressure, and will be frequently seen in tire pressure readings, oil pressure specifications, fuel pump pressure, etc.

To convert pounds per square inch (psi) to kilopascals (kPa): multiply the number of psi by 6.89

Psi	kPa	Psi	kPa	Psi	kPa	Psi	kPa
0.1	0.7	37	255.1	82	565.4	127	875.6
0.2	1.4	38	262.0	83	572.3	128	882.5
0.3	2.1	39	268.9	84	579.2	129	889.4
0.4	2.8	40	275.8	85	586.0	130	896.3
0.5	3.4	41	282.7	86	592.9	131	903.2
0.6	4.1	42	289.6	87	599.8	132	910.1
0.7	4.8	43	296.5	88	606.7	133	917.0
0.8	5.5	44	303.4	89	613.6	134	923.9
0.9	6.2	45	310.3	90	620.5	135	930.8
1	6.9	46	317.2	91	627.4	136	937.7
2	13.8	47	324.0	92	634.3	137	944.6
3	20.7	48	331.0	93	641.2	138	951.5
4	27.6	49	337.8	94	648.1	139	958.4
5	34.5	50	344.7	95	655.0	140	965.2
6	41.4	51	351.6	96	661.9	141	972.2
7	48.3	52	358.5	97	668.8	142	979.0
8	55.2	53	365.4	98	675.7	143	985.9
9	62.1	54	372.3	99	682.6	144	992.8
10	69.0	55	379.2	100	689.5	145	999.7
11	75.8	56	386.1	101	696.4	146	1006.6
12	82.7	57	393.0	102	703.3	147	1013.5
13	89.6	58	399.9	103	710.2	148	1020.4
14	96.5	59	406.8	104	717.0	149	1027.3
15	103.4	60	413.7	105	723.9	150	1034.2
16	110.3	61	420.6	106	730.8	151	1041.1
17	117.2	62	427.5	107	737.7	152	1048.0
18	124.1	63	434.4	108	744.6	153	1054.9
19	131.0	64	441.3	109	751.5	154	1061.8
20	137.9	65	448.2	110	758.4	155	1068.7
21	144.8	66	455.0	111	765.3	156	1075.6
22	151.7	67	461.9	112	772.2	157	1082.5
23	158.6	68	468.8	113	779.1	158	1089.4
24	165.5	69	475.7	114	786.0	159	1096.3
25	172.4	70	482.6	115	792.9	160	1103.2
26	179.3	71	489.5	116	799.8	161	1110.0
27	186.2	72	496.4	117	806.7	162	1116.9
28	193.0	73	503.3	118	813.6	163	1123.8
29	200.0	74	510.2	119	820.5	164	1130.7
30	206.8	75	517.1	120	827.4	165	1137.6
31	213.7	76	524.0	121	834.3	166	1144.5
32	220.6	77	530.9	122	841.2	167	1151.4
33	227.5	78	537.8	123	848.0	168	1158.3
34	234.4	79	544.7	124	854.9	169	1165.2
35	241.3	80	551.6	125	861.8	170	1172.1
36	248.2	81	558.5	126	868.7	171	1179.0

TCCS1C06

ENGLISH TO METRIC CONVERSION: PRESSURE

The basic unit of pressure measurement used today is expressed as pounds per square inch (psi). The metric unit for psi will be the kilopascal (kPa). This will apply to either fluid pressure or air pressure, and will be frequently seen in tire pressure readings, oil pressure specifications, fuel pump pressure, etc.

To convert pounds per square inch (psi) to kilopascals (kPa): multiply the number of psi by 6.89

Psi	kPa	Psi	kPa	Psi	kPa	Psi	kPa
172	1185.9	216	1489.3	260	1792.6	304	2096.0
173	1192.8	217	1496.2	261	1799.5	305	2102.9
174	1199.7	218	1503.1	262	1806.4	306	2109.8
175	1206.6	219	1510.0	263	1813.3	307	2116.7
176	1213.5	220	1516.8	264	1820.2	308	2123.6
177	1220.4	221	1523.7	265	1827.1	309	2130.5
178	1227.3	222	1530.6	266	1834.0	310	2137.4
179	1234.2	223	1537.5	267	1840.9	311	2144.3
180	1241.0	224	1544.4	268	1847.8	312	2151.2
181	1247.9	225	1551.3	269	1854.7	313	2158.1
182	1254.8	226	1558.2	270	1861.6	314	2164.9
183	1261.7	227	1565.1	271	1868.5	315	2171.8
184	1268.6	228	1572.0	272	1875.4	316	2178.7
185	1275.5	229	1578.9	273	1882.3	317	2185.6
186	1282.4	230	1585.8	274	1889.2	318	2192.5
187	1289.3	231	1592.7	275	1896.1	319	2199.4
188	1296.2	232	1599.6	276	1903.0	320	2206.3
189	1303.1	233	1606.5	277	1909.8	321	2213.2
190	1310.0	234	1613.4	278	1916.7	322	2220.1
191	1316.9	235	1620.3	279	1923.6	323	2227.0
192	1323.8	236	1627.2	280	1930.5	324	2233.9
193	1330.7	237	1634.1	281	1937.4	325	2240.8
194	1337.6	238	1641.0	282	1944.3	326	2247.7
195	1344.5	239	1647.8	283	1951.2	327	2254.6
196	1351.4	240	1654.7	284	1958.1	328	2261.5
197	1358.3	241	1661.6	285	1965.0	329	2268.4
198	1365.2	242	1668.5	286	1971.9	330	2275.3
199	1372.0	243	1675.4	287	1978.8	331	2282.2
200	1378.9	244	1682.3	288	1985.7	332	2289.1
201	1385.8	245	1689.2	289	1992.6	333	2295.9
202	1392.7	246	1696.1	290	1999.5	334	2302.8
203	1399.6	247	1703.0	291	2006.4	335	2309.7
204	1406.5	248	1709.9	292	2013.3	336	2316.6
205	1413.4	249	1716.8	293	2020.2	337	2323.5
206	1420.3	250	1723.7	294	2027.1	338	2330.4
207	1427.2	251	1730.6	295	2034.0	339	2337.3
208	1434.1	252	1737.5	296	2040.8	240	2344.2
209	1441.0	253	1744.4	297	2047.7	341	2351.1
210	1447.9	254	1751.3	298	2054.6	342	2358.0
211	1454.8	255	1758.2	299	2061.5	343	2364.9
212	1461.7	256	1765.1	300	2068.4	344	2371.8
213	1468.7	257	1772.0	301	2075.3	345	2378.7
214	1475.5	258	1778.8	302	2082.2	346	2385.6
215	1482.4	259	1785.7	303	2089.1	347	2392.5

2

ENGINE
ELECTRICAL

DISTRIBUTOR IGNITION SYSTEM

➡For information on understanding electricity and troubleshooting electrical circuits, please refer to Section 6 of this manual.

General Information

The distributor ignition system differs from the conventional breaker points system in form only; its function is exactly the same: to supply a spark to the spark plugs at precisely the right moment to ignite the compressed air/fuel mixture in the cylinders and create mechanical movement.

Located in the distributor, in addition to the rotor, is a spoked reluctor which is pressed onto the distributor shaft. The reluctor revolves with the rotor; as it passes a pickup coil inside the distributor body, it breaks a high flux field, which occurs in the space between the reluctor and the pickup coil. The breaking of the field allows current to flow to the pickup coil. Primary ignition current is then cut off by the Electronic Control Module (ECM), allowing the magnetic field in the ignition coil to collapse, creating the spark which the distributor passes on to the spark plugs.

The ECM detects information such as the injection pulse width and camshaft position sensor signal. Responding to this information, ignition signals are transmitted to the power transistor.

Ignition timing is revised by the ECM according to internally stored data under the following conditions:

- At start-up
- During warm-up
- At idle
- During hot engine operation
- During acceleration

The knock sensor retard system is designed only for emergencies. Basic ignition timing is programmed within the anti-knocking zone, if recommended fuel is used under dry conditions. The retard system does not operate under normal driving conditions. If engine knocking occurs, the knock sensor monitors the condition. The signal is transmitted to the ECM, which retards the timing to eliminate the knocking condition.

Diagnosis and Testing

SECONDARY SPARK TEST

♦ See Figure 1

The best way to perform this procedure is to use a spark tester (available at most automotive parts stores). Two types of spark testers are commonly available:

- A Neon Bulb type tester is connected to the spark plug wire, and flashes with each ignition pulse.
- The Air Gap type tester must be adjusted to the individual spark plug gap specified for the engine. This type of tester allows the user to not only detect the presence of spark, but also the intensity (orange/yellow is weak, blue is strong).

➡If a secondary spark tester is not available, a regular spark plug may be used.

1. Disconnect a spark plug wire at the spark plug end.
2. Connect the plug wire to the spark tester and ground the tester to an appropriate location on the engine.
3. Crank the engine and check for spark at the tester.
4. If spark exists at the tester, the ignition system is functioning properly.
5. If spark does not exist at the spark plug wire, remove the distributor cap and check that the rotor is turning when the engine is cranked.
6. If the rotor is not turning, a problem exists in the engine either in the engine or the distributor.
7. If the rotor is turning, perform the spark test again using the ignition coil wire.
8. If spark does not exist at the ignition coil wire, test the ignition coil, power transistor and related wiring. Repair or replace components as necessary.

Adjustments

All adjustments in the ignition system are controlled by the ECM for optimum performance. No adjustments are possible.

Ignition Coil

TESTING

♦ See Figures 2, 3 and 4

➡Prior to testing the coil, perform a secondary spark test. If spark occurs at the spark plug, the coil is functioning properly.

1. Turn the ignition OFF.
2. Disconnect the negative battery cable.
3. Perform a visual inspection of the coil. If the coil is cracked, damaged or oil is leaking from the coil, the coil is faulty.
4. Label and disconnect the electrical harness from the ignition coil.
5. Inspect the harness connector and ignition coil terminals for dirt, corrosion or damage. Repair as necessary.

Fig. 1 A secondary spark test may be performed using a regular spark plug, attached as illustrated

Fig. 2 Testing the ignition coil primary resistance. Note that the reading on the ohmmeter is within specification

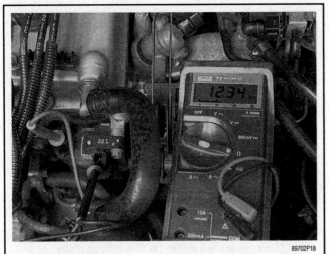

Fig. 3 Testing the ignition coil secondary resistance. Note that the reading on the ohmmeter is within specification

Fig. 5 External mount ignition coils are attached to the cylinder head using two bolts (arrows)

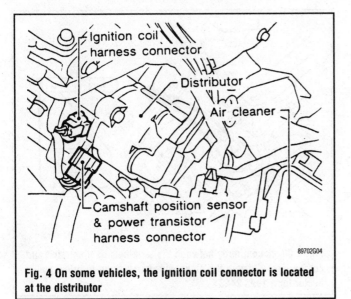

Fig. 4 On some vehicles, the ignition coil connector is located at the distributor

6. Using an ohmmeter, measure coil primary resistance between the ignition coil terminals. Resistance should be approximately 1 ohm @ 68°F (20°C).

7. Measure coil secondary resistance between the ignition coil terminals and the distributor cap high tension lead terminals. Resistance should be approximately 10 kilohms @ 68°F (20°C) on Altima and 20 kilohms @ 68°F (20°C) on 240SX.

8. If resistance is not within specification, the coil may be faulty.

REMOVAL & INSTALLATION

External Mount

♦ See Figure 5

1. Disconnect the negative battery cable.
2. Disconnect the ignition coil high tension wire.
3. Label and disconnect the coil electrical harness.
4. Remove the coil mounting bolts.
5. Carefully remove the coil.

To install:

6. Position the coil and tighten the mounting bolts securely.
7. Connect the coil electrical harness.

8. Connect the coil high tension wire.
9. Connect the negative battery cable.

Internal Mount

The internally mounted ignition coils are an integral part of the distributor assembly. If the coil is determined to be defective, the distributor should be replaced as an assembly.

Power Transistor

TESTING

Two types of power transistors are used in these vehicles. One has a two-terminal connector, while the other has a three-terminal connector. Use the appropriate test when diagnosing the power transistor on your vehicle.

➡The 1995 240SX uses a two-terminal connector. However, it is tested using the three-terminal connector procedure. The third terminal needed for the test is located on the camshaft position sensor connector. Refer to the illustration for further information.

Two-Terminal Connector

♦ See Figure 6

➡Prior to testing the power transistor, perform a secondary spark test. If spark occurs at the spark plug, the power transistor is functioning properly.

1. Turn the ignition **OFF**.
2. Disconnect the negative battery cable.
3. Perform a visual inspection of the power transistor, and replace it if damaged.
4. Label and disconnect the two-terminal electrical harness from the transistor.
5. Label and disconnect the six-terminal electrical harness from the camshaft position sensor.
6. Inspect the harness connectors and transistor terminals for dirt, corrosion or damage. Repair as necessary.
7. Using an ohmmeter, check for resistance between the connector terminals as illustrated.
8. Resistance should always exist. If resistance is zero, the power transistor may be faulty.
9. Replace the power transistor as necessary.

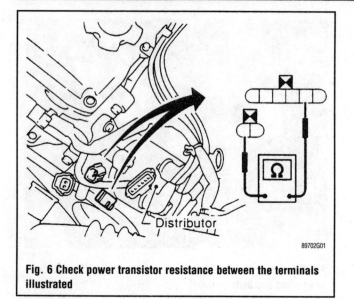

Fig. 6 Check power transistor resistance between the terminals illustrated

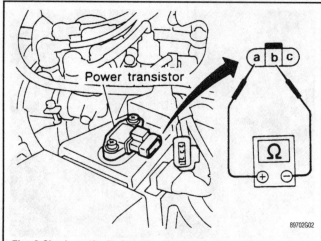

Fig. 8 Check continuity between the terminals as illustrated and compare results with the diagnosis chart—three-terminal connector for all models except 1995 240SX

Three-Terminal Connector

♦ See Figures 7, 8, 9, 10 and 11

➡Prior to testing the power transistor, perform a secondary spark test. If spark occurs at the spark plug, the power transistor is functioning properly.

1. Turn the ignition **OFF**.
2. Disconnect the negative battery cable.
3. Perform a visual inspection of the power transistor and replace if damaged.
4. Label and disconnect the electrical harness from the transistor.
5. Inspect the harness connector and transistor terminals for dirt, corrosion or damage. Repair as necessary.
6. Using an ohmmeter, check for continuity between the three terminals. Be sure to check all six probe/terminal combinations. Compare the results to the power transistor diagnosis chart.

➡Ensure that the ohmmeter leads are connected properly. Since a diode is being tested, the positive and negative leads of the ohmmeter must be placed as directed by the chart. Failure to do so will result in incorrect readings.

7. Replace the power transistor as necessary.

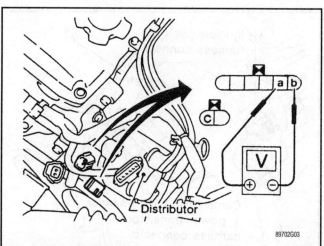

Fig. 9 Check continuity between the terminals as illustrated and compare results with the diagnosis chart—three-terminal connector for a 1995 240SX

Fig. 7 The three-terminal power transistor is located on a bracket attached to the top of the air box

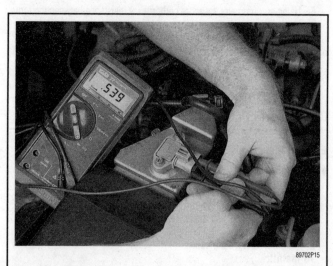

Fig. 10 A reading such as that shown qualifies as a non-infinite/non-zero reading

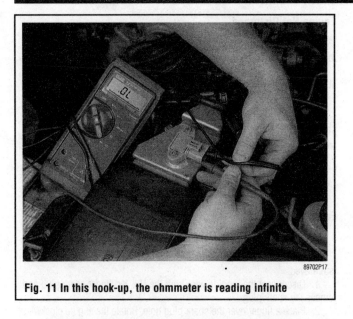

Fig. 11 In this hook-up, the ohmmeter is reading infinite

● **The digital tester must have a diode check position and be able to measure up to 20 MΩ to perform this inspection.**

⊖ terminal side / ⊕ terminal side	Terminal ⓐ		Terminal ⓑ		Terminal ⓒ	
	Resistance Ω	Result	Resistance Ω	Result	Resistance Ω	Result
Terminal ⓐ	—	—	∞	NG	∞	NG
	—	—	Not ∞ or 0	OK	Not ∞ or 0	OK
	—	—	0	NG	0	NG
Terminal ⓑ	∞	NG	—	—	∞	NG
	Not ∞ or 0	OK	—	—	Not ∞ or 0	OK
	0	NG	—	—	0	NG
Terminal ⓒ	∞	OK	∞	OK	—	—
	Not ∞ or 0	NG	Not ∞ or 0	NG	—	—
	0	NG	0	NG	—	—

NG=NOT GOOD

89702C01

● **The digital tester must have a diode check position and be able to measure up to 20 MΩ to perform this inspection.**

⊕ terminal side	⊖ terminal side					
	Terminal ⓐ		Terminal ⓑ		Terminal ⓒ	
	Resistance Ω	Result	Resistance Ω	Result	Resistance Ω	Result
Terminal ⓐ	—	—	∞	OK	∞	OK
	—	—	Not ∞ or 0	NG	Not ∞ or 0	NG
	—	—	0	NG	0	NG
Terminal ⓑ	∞	NG	—	—	∞	NG
	Not ∞ or 0	OK	—	—	Not ∞ or 0	OK
	0	NG	—	—	0	NG
Terminal ⓒ	∞	NG	∞	NG	—	—
	Not ∞ or 0	OK	Not ∞ or 0	OK	—	—
	0	NG	0	NG	—	—

∞: Infinite resistance
NG=NOT GOOD

89702C02

REMOVAL & INSTALLATION

Two-Terminal Connector

The two-terminal connector power transistor is located inside the distributor and is not serviceable separately.

Three-Terminal Connector

♦ **See Figure 12**

1. Disconnect the negative battery cable.
2. Label and disconnect the transistor electrical harness.
3. Remove the transistor mounting bolts.
4. Carefully remove the transistor.

To install:

5. Position the transistor and tighten the mounting bolts securely.
6. Connect the transistor electrical harness.
7. Connect the negative battery cable.

89702P16

Fig. 12 The three-terminal power transistor is attached to the bracket using two screws. The connector terminals are also visible in this illustration

Ignition Resistor

TESTING

1. Turn the ignition **OFF**.
2. Disconnect the negative battery cable.
3. Perform a visual inspection of the resistor and replace it if damaged.
4. Label and disconnect the two-terminal electrical harness from the resistor.
5. Inspect the harness connector and terminals for dirt, corrosion or damage. Repair as necessary.
6. Using an ohmmeter, check for resistance between the connector terminals. Resistance should be approximately 2.2 kilohms @ 68°F (20°C).
7. The resistor is faulty if resistance is not within specifications.

REMOVAL & INSTALLATION

1. Disconnect the negative battery cable.
2. Label and disconnect the resistor electrical harness.
3. Remove the resistor mounting bolts.
4. Carefully remove the resistor.

To install:

5. Position the resistor and tighten the mounting bolts securely.
6. Connect the resistor electrical harness.
7. Connect the negative battery cable.

Distributor

REMOVAL & INSTALLATION

▶ **See Figures 13 and 14**

1. Disconnect the negative battery cable.
2. Label and disconnect the distributor electrical harness.

➡**On some engines, it may be necessary to label and remove the distributor wires and cap to gain clearance to remove the distributor.**

3. Remove distributor cap and position it aside with the ignition wires still attached.
4. Matchmark the position of the rotor to the distributor housing and the distributor housing to the engine.
5. Remove the distributor hold-down bolt and clamp.
6. Remove the distributor from the engine.

To install:

➡**Before installation, inspect the distributor O-ring and drive gear for wear and/or damage. Rotate the distributor shaft to make sure it moves freely, without binding.**

Fig. 13 The distributor is removed by loosening the two attaching bolts and pulling the unit straight out of the cylinder head

Fig. 14 When the dot on the distributor tang and the slit on the collar are aligned, the rotor is positioned at the No. 1 cylinder terminal inside the distributor

Engine Not Disturbed

1. Install the distributor, aligning the distributor housing and rotor with the matchmarks made during removal.
2. Install the distributor hold-down bolt and clamp. Only snug the bolt at this time.
3. Connect the distributor electrical harness.
4. Install the distributor cap and wires.

➡**Make sure the ignition wires are securely connected to the distributor cap and spark plugs.**

5. Start the engine and adjust the ignition timing. Refer to Section 1.
6. Tighten the distributor hold-down bolt securely.
7. Recheck the initial timing and re-adjust if necessary.

Engine Disturbed

▶ **See Figure 15**

Use this procedure if the engine position is disturbed after the distributor is removed.

1. Disconnect the ignition wire from the No. 1 cylinder spark plug and remove the spark plug.
2. Place a finger over the spark plug hole. Rotate the engine clockwise until compression is felt at the spark plug hole.
3. Install the No. 1 cylinder spark plug.
4. Align the timing pointer with the Top Dead Center (TDC) mark on the crankshaft damper.
5. Rotate the distributor shaft so that the marks on the drive gear end of the shaft and the mark on the housing align as illustrated.

➡**If the distributor does not have these marks, rotate the distributor shaft so that the rotor tip is pointing to the distributor cap's No. 1 spark plug tower position.**

6. Install the distributor, making sure it seats completely on the engine. If the distributor does not seat completely, remove it and use a long, straight blade screwdriver to adjust the position of the oil pump shaft slot to the relative position of the tang on the bottom of the distributor shaft.
7. Install the distributor hold-down bolt and clamp. Only snug the bolt at this time.

➡**Ensure that the ignition wires are securely connected to the distributor cap and spark plugs.**

8. Install the distributor cap and wires.

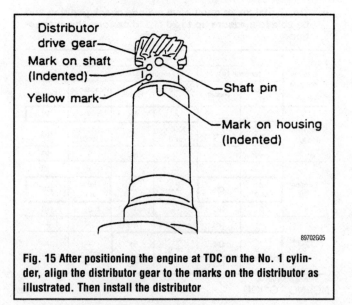

Fig. 15 After positioning the engine at TDC on the No. 1 cylinder, align the distributor gear to the marks on the distributor as illustrated. Then install the distributor

➡Ensure that the rotor tip is pointing to the distributor cap's No. 1 spark plug tower position, prior to fastening the distributor cap in place.

  9. Start the engine and adjust the ignition timing. Refer to Section 1.
  10. Tighten the distributor hold-down bolt securely.
  11. Recheck the initial timing and adjust if necessary.

FIRING ORDERS

♦ See Figures 16 and 17

➡To avoid confusion, label and remove the spark plug wires one at a time, for replacement.

If a distributor is not keyed for installation with only one orientation, it could have been removed previously and rewired. The resultant wiring

Fig. 16 2.4L Engine
Engine Firing Order: 1–3–4–2
Distributor Rotation: Counterclockwise

Crankshaft Position Sensor

Refer to Electronic Engine Controls in Section 4 for information on servicing the crankshaft position sensor.

Camshaft Position Sensor

Refer to Electronic Engine Controls in Section 4 for information on servicing the camshaft position sensor.

would hold the correct firing order, but could change the relative placement of the plug towers in relation to the engine. For this reason, it is imperative that you label all wires before disconnecting any of them. Also, before removal, compare the current wiring with the accompanying illustrations. If the current wiring does not match, make notes in your book to reflect how your engine is wired.

Fig. 17 Cylinders are numbered 1–4, starting at the accessory drive belt end of the engine

CHARGING SYSTEM

General Information

The charging system is a negative (-) ground system which consists of an alternator, regulator, charge indicator lamp, storage battery, circuit protection and wiring connecting the components.

The alternator is belt-driven from the engine. Energy is supplied from the alternator (with integral regulator) to the rotating field, through brushes, to slip-rings. The slip-rings are mounted on the rotor shaft and are connected to the field coil. This energy supplied to the rotating field from the battery is called excitation current, and is used to initially energize the field to begin the generation of electricity. Once the alternator starts to generate electricity, the excitation current comes from its own output, rather than from the battery.

The alternator produces power in the form of alternating current. The alternating current is rectified by diodes into direct current. The direct current is used to charge the battery and power the rest of the electrical system. When the ignition key is turned on, current flows from the battery, through the charging system indicator light on the instrument panel, to the voltage regulator, and to the alternator. Since the alternator is not producing any current, the alternator warning light comes on. When the engine is started, the alternator begins to produce current and turns the alternator light off.

As the alternator turns and produces current, the current is divided in two ways: charging the battery and powering the electrical components of the vehicle. Part of the current is returned to the alternator to enable it to increase its output. In this situation, the alternator is receiving current from the battery and from itself. A voltage regulator is wired into the current supply to the alternator to prevent it from receiving too much current, which would cause it to overproduce current. Conversely, if the voltage regulator does not allow the alternator to receive enough current, the battery will not be fully charged and will eventually go dead.

The battery is connected to the alternator at all times, whether the ignition key is turned on or off. If the battery were shorted to ground, the alternator would also be shorted. This would damage the alternator. To prevent this, circuit protection (usually in the form of a fuse link) is installed in the wiring between the battery and the alternator. If the battery is shorted, the circuit protection will protect the alternator.

PRECAUTIONS

  • NEVER ground or short out the alternator or regulator terminals.
  • NEVER operate the alternator with any of its or the battery's lead wires disconnected.
  • NEVER use a fast battery charger to jump start a dead battery.

- NEVER attempt to polarize an alternator.
- NEVER subject the alternator to excessive heat or dampness (for instance, steam cleaning the engine).
- NEVER use arc welding equipment on the car with the alternator connected.
- ALWAYS observe proper polarity of the battery connections; be especially careful when jump starting the car.
- ALWAYS remove the battery, or at least disconnect the ground cable, while charging.
- ALWAYS disconnect the battery ground cable while repairing or replacing an electrical component.

Alternator

TESTING

The easiest way to test the performance of the alternator is to perform a regulated voltage test.

1. Start the engine and allow it to reach operating temperature.
2. Connect a voltmeter between the positive and negative terminals of the battery.
3. Voltage should be 14.1–14.7 volts.
4. If voltage is higher or lower than specification, connect a voltmeter between the battery positive (B+) voltage output terminal of the alternator and a good engine ground.
5. Voltage should be 14.1–14.7 volts.
6. If voltage is still out of specification, a problem exists in the alternator or voltage regulator.
7. If voltage is now within specification, a problem exists in the wiring to the battery or in the battery itself.

➡Many automotive parts stores have alternator bench testers available for use by customers. An alternator bench test is the most definitive way to determine the condition of your alternator.

REMOVAL & INSTALLATION

♦ See Figures 18, 19 and 20

1. Disconnect negative battery cable.
2. On 240SX models, remove the engine undercover.
3. Loosen the adjusting bolt and remove the accessory drive belt.

Fig. 18 On Altima models, the upper radiator hose must be removed to access the alternator

Fig. 19 With the upper radiator hose removed, the alternator is easily serviced by disconnecting the electrical harnesses and removing the indicated bolts

Fig. 20 The Altima's alternator is removed from the top of the engine compartment

4. Label and disconnect the alternator's electrical harness.
5. On 240SX models, remove the cooling fan lower shroud.
6. Remove the alternator mounting bolts.
7. Carefully remove the alternator from the engine.

➡On Altima models, lift the alternator up and out of the engine compartment; on 240SX models, lower it from the underside.

To install:

8. Position the alternator on the engine.
9. Install the alternator mounting bolts and tighten to 11–15 ft. lbs. (16–20 Nm).
10. On 240SX models, install the cooling fan lower shroud.
11. Connect the electrical harness.
12. Install and properly tension the accessory drive belt.
13. On 240SX models, install the engine undercover.
14. Connect the negative battery cable.
15. Check the alternator for proper operation.

STARTING SYSTEM

General Information

The starting system includes the battery, starter motor, solenoid, ignition switch, circuit protection and wiring connecting the components. An inhibitor switch is included in the starting system to prevent the vehicle from being started with the vehicle in gear.

When the ignition key is turned to the **START** position, current flows and energizes the starter's solenoid coil. The solenoid plunger and clutch shift lever are activated, and the clutch pinion engages the ring gear on the flywheel. The switch contacts close and the starter cranks the engine until it starts.

To prevent damage caused by excessive starter armature rotation when the engine starts, the starter incorporates an over-running clutch in the pinion gear.

Starter

TESTING

The easiest way to test the performance of the starter is to perform a voltage drop test.

➡**The battery must be in good condition and fully charged prior to performing this test.**

1. Connect a voltmeter between the positive and negative terminals of the battery.
2. Turn the ignition key to the **START** position and note the voltage drop on the meter.
3. If voltage drops below 11.5 volts, there is high resistance in the starting system.
4. Check for proper connections at the battery and starter.
5. Check the resistance of the battery cables and replace as necessary.
6. If all other components in the system are functional, the starter may be faulty.

➡**Many automotive parts stores have starter bench testers available for use by customers. A starter bench test is the most definitive way to determine the condition of your starter.**

REMOVAL & INSTALLATION

240SX

1. Disconnect the negative battery cable.
2. Raise and support the vehicle safely.
3. On automatic transmission models, perform the following steps:
   a. Support the automatic transmission with a jack.
   b. Remove the 4 rear mounting bracket bolts.
   c. Slightly lower the transmission to provide clearance for the starter.
   d. Remove the automatic transmission dipstick pipe.
4. Remove the starter support bracket.
5. Label and disconnect the starter electrical harness.
6. Support the starter from under the vehicle using a jackstand.
7. Remove the starter mounting bolts.
8. Carefully lower the starter from the vehicle.
To install:
9. Position the starter on the engine and support using a jackstand.
10. Install the starter mounting bolts and tighten to 30–37 ft. lbs. (40–50 Nm).
11. Connect the starter electrical harness.

12. Install the starter support bracket.
13. On automatic transmission models, perform the following steps:
   a. Install the automatic transmission dipstick pipe.
   b. Raise the transmission and install the 4 rear mounting bracket bolts.
   c. Remove the jack supporting the automatic transmission.
14. Lower the vehicle.
15. Connect the negative battery cable.

Altima

◗ **See Figures 21, 22 and 23**

1. Disconnect the negative battery cable.
2. Raise and support the vehicle safely.
3. Remove the starter support bracket, as required.

89702P26

Fig. 21 The starter is located to the left of the oil filter housing on the engine block

89702P21

Fig. 22 The starter motor is removed from the bottom side of the engine compartment

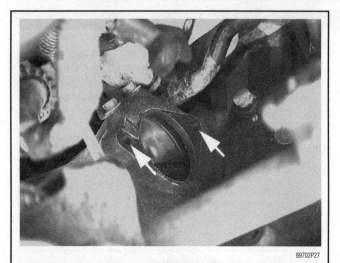

Fig. 23 When installing, be sure to align the starter's mounting bolt holes with those in the engine block

4. Label and disconnect the starter electrical harness.
5. Support the starter from beneath the vehicle using a jackstand.
6. Remove the starter mounting bolts.
7. Carefully lower the starter from the vehicle.

To install:

8. Position the starter on the engine and support it using a jackstand.
9. Install the starter mounting bolts and tighten to 30–37 ft. lbs. (40–50 Nm).
10. Connect the starter electrical harness.
11. Install the starter support bracket, as required.
12. Lower the vehicle.
13. Connect the negative battery cable.

SENDING UNITS

➥This section describes the operating principles of sending units, warning lights and gauges. Sensors which provide information to the Electronic Control Module (ECM) are covered in Section 4 of this manual.

Instrument panels contain a number of indicating devices (gauges and warning lights). These devices are composed of two separate components. One is the sending unit, mounted on the engine or other remote part of the vehicle, and the other is the actual gauge or light in the instrument panel.

Several types of sending units exist; however, most can be characterized as being either a pressure type or a resistance type. Pressure type sending units convert liquid pressure into an electrical signal which is sent to the gauge or warning light. Resistance type sending units are most often used to measure temperature and use variable resistance to control the current flow back to the indicating device. Both types of sending units are connected in series by a wire to the battery (through the ignition switch). When the ignition is turned **ON**, current flows from the battery, through the indicating device, and on to the sending unit.

Coolant Temperature Sender

TESTING

▶ **See Figure 24**

A quick way to determine if the gauge, the so-called "idiot" light, or the sending unit is faulty is to disconnect the sending unit electrical harness and ground it (if two-terminal, jumper between the terminals) with the ignition **ON**. If the gauge responds or the light illuminates, the sending unit may be faulty. Proceed with the following sending unit test.

1. Disconnect the sending unit electrical harness.
2. Remove the radiator cap and place a mechanic's thermometer in the coolant.
3. Using an ohmmeter, check the resistance between the sending unit terminals.
4. Resistance should be high (170–210 ohms) with engine coolant at 140°F (60°C) and low (47–53 ohms) with engine coolant at 212°F (100°C).

➥It is best to check resistance with the engine cool, then start the engine and watch the resistance change as the engine warms.

Fig. 24 The engine coolant temperature sensor (upper arrow) and coolant temperature gauge sender (lower arrow) are located on the passenger's side of the engine, under the intake manifold

5. If resistance does not drop as engine temperature rises, the sending unit is faulty.

REMOVAL & INSTALLATION

1. Locate the coolant temperature sending unit on the engine.
2. Disconnect the sending unit electrical harness.
3. Drain the engine coolant below the level of the switch.
4. Unfasten and remove the sending unit from the engine.
5. Coat the new sending unit with Teflon® tape or electrically conductive sealer.
6. Install the sending unit and tighten to 11–15 ft. lbs. (15–20 Nm).
7. Attach the sending unit's electrical connector.
8. Fill the engine with coolant.
9. Start the engine, allow it to reach operating temperature and check for leaks.
10. Check for proper sending unit operation.

Oil Pressure Sender

TESTING

1. Disconnect the sending unit electrical harness.
2. Using an ohmmeter, check continuity between the sending unit terminals.
3. With the engine stopped, continuity should exist.

➡**The switch inside the oil pressure sending unit closes at 10 psi or less of pressure.**

4. With the engine running, continuity should not exist.
5. If continuity does not exist as stated, the sending unit is faulty.

REMOVAL & INSTALLATION

♦ **See Figure 25**

1. Locate the oil pressure sending unit on the engine.
2. Disconnect the sending unit electrical harness.
3. Unfasten and remove the sending unit from the engine.
To install:
4. Coat the threads of the new sending unit with Teflon® tape or electrically conductive sealer.
5. Install the sending unit and tighten to 11–15 ft. lbs. (15–20 Nm).
6. Attach the sending unit's electrical connector.

89702P29

Fig. 25 The oil pressure sender is located adjacent to the oil filter. It is only accessible from below the vehicle

7. Start the engine, allow it to reach operating temperature and check for leaks.
8. Check for proper sending unit operation.

Troubleshooting Basic Starting System Problems

Problem	Cause	Solution
Starter motor rotates engine slowly	• Battery charge low or battery defective	• Charge or replace battery
	• Defective circuit between battery and starter motor	• Clean and tighten, or replace cables
	• Low load current	• Bench-test starter motor. Inspect for worn brushes and weak brush springs.
	• High load current	• Bench-test starter motor. Check engine for friction, drag or coolant in cylinders. Check ring gear-to-pinion gear clearance.
Starter motor will not rotate engine	• Battery charge low or battery defective	• Charge or replace battery
	• Faulty solenoid	• Check solenoid ground. Repair or replace as necessary.
	• Damaged drive pinion gear or ring gear	• Replace damaged gear(s)
	• Starter motor engagement weak	• Bench-test starter motor
	• Starter motor rotates slowly with high load current	• Inspect drive yoke pull-down and point gap, check for worn end bushings, check ring gear clearance
	• Engine seized	• Repair engine
Starter motor drive will not engage (solenoid known to be good)	• Defective contact point assembly	• Repair or replace contact point assembly
	• Inadequate contact point assembly ground	• Repair connection at ground screw
	• Defective hold-in coil	• Replace field winding assembly
Starter motor drive will not disengage	• Starter motor loose on flywheel housing	• Tighten mounting bolts
	• Worn drive end busing	• Replace bushing
	• Damaged ring gear teeth	• Replace ring gear or driveplate
	• Drive yoke return spring broken or missing	• Replace spring
Starter motor drive disengages prematurely	• Weak drive assembly thrust spring	• Replace drive mechanism
	• Hold-in coil defective	• Replace field winding assembly
Low load current	• Worn brushes	• Replace brushes
	• Weak brush springs	• Replace springs

TCCS2C01

Troubleshooting Basic Charging System Problems

Problem	Cause	Solution
Noisy alternator	• Loose mountings • Loose drive pulley • Worn bearings • Brush noise • Internal circuits shorted (High pitched whine)	• Tighten mounting bolts • Tighten pulley • Replace alternator • Replace alternator • Replace alternator
Squeal when starting engine or accelerating	• Glazed or loose belt	• Replace or adjust belt
Indicator light remains on or ammeter indicates discharge (engine running)	• Broken belt • Broken or disconnected wires • Internal alternator problems • Defective voltage regulator	• Install belt • Repair or connect wiring • Replace alternator • Replace voltage regulator/alternator
Car light bulbs continually burn out—battery needs water continually	• Alternator/regulator overcharging	• Replace voltage regulator/alternator
Car lights flare on acceleration	• Battery low • Internal alternator/regulator problems	• Charge or replace battery • Replace alternator/regulator
Low voltage output (alternator light flickers continually or ammeter needle wanders)	• Loose or worn belt • Dirty or corroded connections • Internal alternator/regulator problems	• Replace or adjust belt • Clean or replace connections • Replace alternator/regulator

TCCS2C02

3

ENGINE AND ENGINE OVERHAUL

ENGINE MECHANICAL

➡The engines covered in this manual are, for all intents and purposes, identical. There is one major exception—one is mounted transversely (Altima) and the other is mounted longitudinally (240SX). While many procedures on the two engines are identical, others are considerably different. Where differences occur, they will be noted.

Engine Undercover

REMOVAL & INSTALLATION

▶ **See Figures 1 and 2**

The engine undercover must be removed in order to access most components under the front of the vehicle or engine. The engine undercover is composed of four separate covers (two undercovers and two side covers), and is easily removed by loosening the attaching bolts.

89703P72

Fig. 1 Several bolts (indicated by the arrows) attach the engine undercover to the chassis

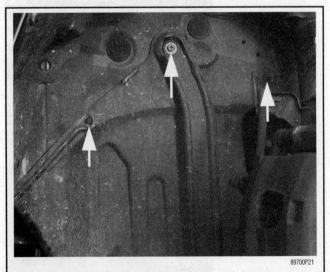

89700P21

Fig. 2 Engine undercover side skirt fastener locations

Engine

REMOVAL & INSTALLATION

In the process of removing the engine, you will come across a number of steps which call for the removal of a separate component or system, such as "disconnect the exhaust system" or "remove the radiator." In most instances, a detailed removal procedure can be found elsewhere in this manual.

It is virtually impossible to list each individual wire and hose which must be disconnected, simply because so many different model and engine combinations have been manufactured. Careful observation and common sense are the best possible approaches to any repair procedure.

Removal and installation of the engine can be made easier if you follow these basic points:

• If you have to drain any of the fluids, use a suitable container.

• Always tag any wires or hoses and, if possible, the components they came from before disconnecting them.

• Because there are so many bolts and fasteners involved, store and label the retainers from components separately in muffin pans, jars or coffee cans. This will prevent confusion during installation.

• After unbolting the transmission or transaxle, always make sure it is properly supported.

• If it is necessary to disconnect the air conditioning system, have this service performed by a qualified technician using a recovery/recycling station. If the system does not have to be disconnected, unbolt the compressor and set it aside.

• When unbolting the engine mounts, always make sure the engine is properly supported. When removing the engine, make sure that any lifting devices are properly attached to the engine. It is recommended that if your engine is supplied with lifting hooks, your lifting apparatus be attached to them.

• Lift the engine from its compartment slowly, checking that no hoses, wires or other components are still connected.

• After the engine is clear of the compartment, place it on an engine stand or workbench.

• After the engine has been removed, you can perform a partial or full teardown of the engine using the procedures outlined in this manual.

Altima

▶ **See Figure 3**

✵ CAUTION

Observe all applicable safety precautions when working around fuel. Whenever servicing the fuel system, always work in a well ventilated area. Do not allow fuel spray or vapors to come in contact with a spark or open flame. Keep a dry chemical fire extinguisher near the work area. Always keep fuel in a container specifically designed for fuel storage; also, always properly seal fuel containers to avoid the possibility of fire or explosion. The fuel system will remain under pressure after the ignition has been turned OFF.

➡The engine and transaxle must be removed as a single unit. The engine and transaxle are removed from under the vehicle.

1. Matchmark the location of the hinges on the hood and remove the hood from the vehicle.
2. Properly relieve fuel system pressure.
3. Disconnect the negative, then the positive battery cables. Remove the battery and battery tray.
4. Drain and recycle the engine coolant.
5. If equipped with an automatic transaxle, disconnect the cooler lines from the radiator.

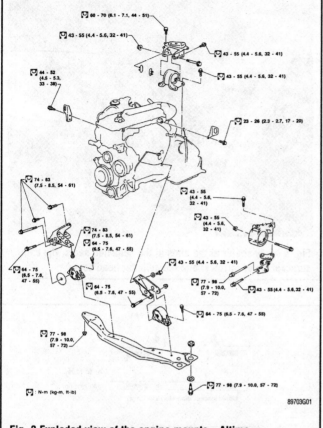

Fig. 3 Exploded view of the engine mounts—Altima

6. Remove the upper and lower hoses from the radiator and then remove the radiator assembly.

7. Disconnect the heater hoses from the engine.

8. Disconnect the throttle cable and cruise control cable (if equipped).

9. Remove the air cleaner, air box, and intake hose.

10. Disconnect the fuel feed and return hoses.

11. Label and disconnect all appropriate vacuum hoses.

12. Label and disconnect all appropriate electrical harnesses.

13. Disconnect the wiring from the starter motor.

14. If equipped, disconnect the slave cylinder from the transaxle. It is not necessary to disconnect the hydraulic hose.

15. Remove the accessory drive belts.

16. Remove the alternator, A/C compressor and power steering pump from the engine.

➡**Do not disconnect the A/C lines. Lay the A/C compressor aside in the engine compartment.**

17. Remove the right and left halfshafts from the transaxle.

18. Disconnect the exhaust pipe from the exhaust manifold.

19. Support the engine with a sling and support the transaxle with a jack.

20. Disconnect the left and right engine mounting through-bolts.

21. Remove the bolts that secure the crossmember to the vehicle and remove the crossmember.

22. Remove the front and rear engine mounts.

➡**The engine and transaxle assembly should be removed through the bottom of the vehicle. Do not attempt to remove the assembly from above.**

23. Lower the transaxle and engine assembly from the vehicle.

To install:

24. Position the engine and transaxle in the vehicle.

25. Install the front and rear engine mounts. Tighten the through-bolts to 47–55 ft. lbs. (64–75 Nm).

26. Install the right and left engine mounts. Tighten the through-bolts to 32–41 ft. lbs. (43–55 Nm).

27. Install the crossmember and tighten the mounting bolts to 57–72 ft. lbs. (77–98 Nm).

28. Remove the engine and transaxle supports.

29. The balance of installation is the reverse of the removal procedure.

30. Refill and bleed the cooling system.

31. Refill the engine with the correct grade and viscosity of engine oil. Check all the fluid levels.

32. Start the engine, bleed the cooling system, and check for leaks. Make all the necessary adjustments.

33. Install the hood.

240SX

▶ **See Figure 4**

> ❊❊❊ **CAUTION**
>
> **Observe all applicable safety precautions when working around fuel. Whenever servicing the fuel system, always work in a well ventilated area. Do not allow fuel spray or vapors to come in contact with a spark or open flame. Keep a dry chemical fire extinguisher near the work area. Always keep fuel in a container specifically designed for fuel storage; also, always properly seal fuel containers to avoid the possibility of fire or explosion. The fuel system will remain under pressure after the ignition has been turned OFF.**

1. Matchmark the location of the hinges on the hood. Unbolt and remove the hood.

2. Properly relieve fuel system pressure.

3. Disconnect the negative, then the positive battery cables. Remove the battery.

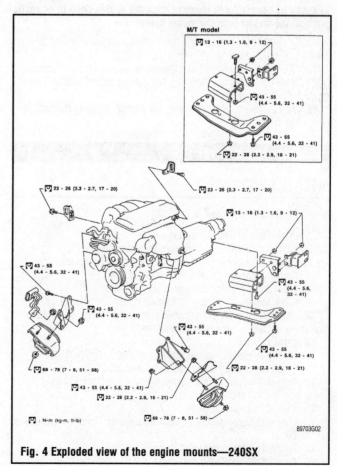

Fig. 4 Exploded view of the engine mounts—240SX

4. Remove the engine undercover.
5. Remove the transmission from the vehicle.
6. Drain and recycle the engine coolant.
7. Drain and recycle the engine oil.
8. Disconnect the automatic transmission-to-radiator cooling tubes (if applicable). Remove the radiator and radiator shroud.
9. Remove the air cleaner.
10. Remove the accessory drive belts.
11. Remove the fan and pulley.
12. Label and disconnect all appropriate vacuum lines.
13. Label and disconnect all appropriate electrical harnesses.
14. Label and disconnect the ignition wires from the spark plugs.
15. Disconnect the fuel feed and return lines.
16. Disconnect the heater hoses and throttle connections.
17. Remove the front exhaust pipe from the vehicle.

➡**Do not disconnect the A/C lines. Remove the A/C compressor and set it aside in the engine compartment.**

18. Remove the alternator, A/C compressor, and power steering pump from the engine.
19. Disconnect the power brake booster hose from the engine.
20. Attach a hoist to the lifting hooks on the engine (at either end of the cylinder head). Support the engine.
21. Remove the engine mounting nuts from both lower sides of the engine mounts.

➡**The engine assembly is removed from the top of the vehicle. When removing the engine, guide it carefully to avoid hitting parts such as the master cylinder.**

22. Remove the engine from the vehicle.

To install:

23. Position the engine in the vehicle.
24. Tighten the engine mounting nuts to 51–58 ft. lbs. (69–78 Nm).

➡**It may be necessary to lower or raise the engine hoist to correctly position the engine with the mount holes.**

25. Install the transmission and tighten the transmission mount to 16–21 ft. lbs. (22–28 Nm).
26. The balance of installation is the reverse of the removal procedure.
27. Refill the engine, transmission, and cooling system with the proper types and amounts of fluid.
28. Start the engine and run at idle until normal operating temperature is reached. Check for leaks.

Cylinder Head Cover

REMOVAL & INSTALLATION

♦ **See Figures 5, 6, 7 and 8**

1. Disconnect the negative battery cable.
2. Label and disconnect all appropriate vacuum hoses.
3. Label and disconnect all appropriate electrical harnesses.
4. Properly relieve the fuel system pressure.
5. Label and disconnect all appropriate fuel lines.
6. Label and disconnect the ignition wires from the spark plugs.
7. Unfasten the cylinder head cover bolts in the reverse order of the tightening sequence. Remove the cylinder head cover.

To install:

8. Throughly clean all gasket mating surfaces.
9. Install the cylinder head cover using new gaskets.
10. Tighten the cylinder head cover bolts to 69–95 inch lbs. (8–11Nm) using the indicated sequence.
11. Connect the ignition wires.
12. Connect all previously removed vacuum hoses, electrical harnesses and fuel lines.
13. Connect all appropriate fuel lines.
14. Connect the negative battery cable.

Fig. 5 Apply sealer at the ends of the camshaft seals, the cam sprocket cover (arrows) and the cylinder head cover

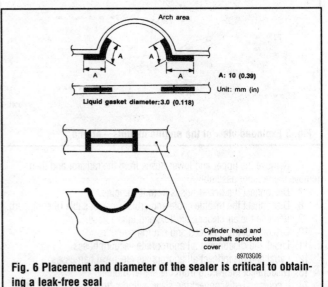

Fig. 6 Placement and diameter of the sealer is critical to obtaining a leak-free seal

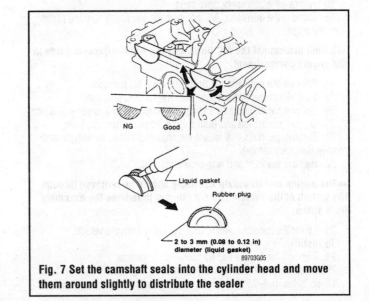
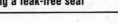

Fig. 7 Set the camshaft seals into the cylinder head and move them around slightly to distribute the sealer

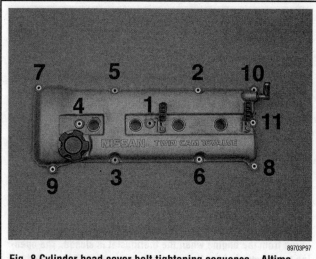

Fig. 8 Cylinder head cover bolt tightening sequence—Altima shown; 240SX similar

Thermostat

REMOVAL & INSTALLATION

▶ See Figures 9 thru 14

❄ CAUTION

Never open, service or drain the cooling system when hot; serious burns can occur from the steam and hot coolant. Also, when draining engine coolant, keep in mind that cats and dogs are attracted to ethylene glycol antifreeze and could drink any that is left in an uncovered container or in puddles on the ground. This will prove fatal in sufficient quantities. Always drain coolant into a sealable container.

1. Drain and recycle the engine coolant.
2. Remove the radiator hose from the thermostat housing.
3. Remove the bolts that secure the thermostat housing and remove the housing from the engine.
4. Remove the thermostat from the engine.

To install:

5. Throughly clean the gasket mating surfaces.

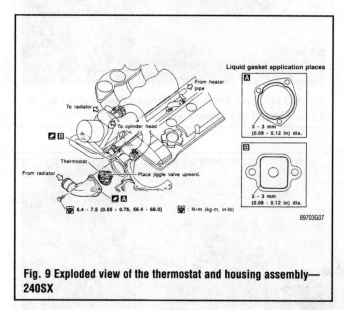

Fig. 9 Exploded view of the thermostat and housing assembly—240SX

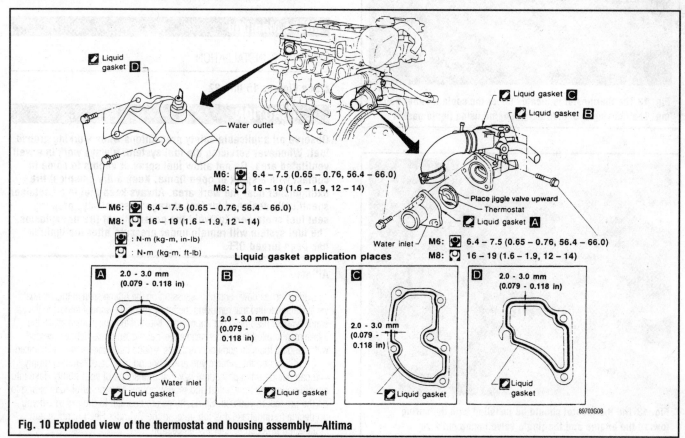

Fig. 10 Exploded view of the thermostat and housing assembly—Altima

Fig. 11 Pay special attention to alignment marks (arrow) on the hoses. These marks should usually be pointed straight up

Fig. 12 The thermostat is located under the coolant outlet housing. The housing is sealed to the engine using liquid gasket

Fig. 13 The thermostat should be installed with the spring toward the engine and the jiggle valve facing outward

Fig. 14 The thermostat jiggle valve (top arrow) allows air to purge from the engine when the thermostat is closed. The opening temperature of the thermostat (bottom arrow) is stamped into the thermostat housing

6. Apply liquid gasket to the thermostat housing, as illustrated. The gasket material should be 0.079–0.118 in. (2.0–3.0mm) wide.

7. Install the thermostat in the housing.

➡Be sure to position the thermostat with the jiggle valve to the top of the housing.

8. Position the thermostat housing on the engine and tighten the attaching bolts as follows:
- 6mm bolts—57–66 inch lbs. (6–8 Nm)
- 8mm bolts—12–14 ft. lbs. (16–19 Nm)

9. Connect the radiator hose to the thermostat housing.
10. Refill and bleed the cooling system.
11. Start the engine and check for leaks.

Intake Manifold

REMOVAL & INSTALLATION

♦ See Figures 15 thru 22

✸✸ CAUTION

Observe all applicable safety precautions when working around fuel. Whenever servicing the fuel system, always work in a well ventilated area. Do not allow fuel spray or vapors to come in contact with a spark or open flame. Keep a dry chemical fire extinguisher near the work area. Always keep fuel in a container specifically designed for fuel storage; also, always properly seal fuel containers to avoid the possibility of fire or explosion. The fuel system will remain under pressure after the ignition has been turned OFF.

Altima

During the teardown and photo session on the Altima seen in this manual, we at Chilton found that removing the intake manifold without removing the entire cylinder head is all but impossible. Most of the bolts which attach the intake manifold to the cylinder head are either hidden or cannot be accessed with standard tools. In addition, clearance around the intake manifold is limited.

Conditions on the vehicle you are servicing may be different and only you can decide if the procedure is within the scope of your ability. Take into consideration the time, effort and money you will spend prior to deciding to do the procedure yourself. Some things are best left to the experts. If you do decide to undertake this job, refer to the Cylinder Head removal and installation procedure, later in this section.

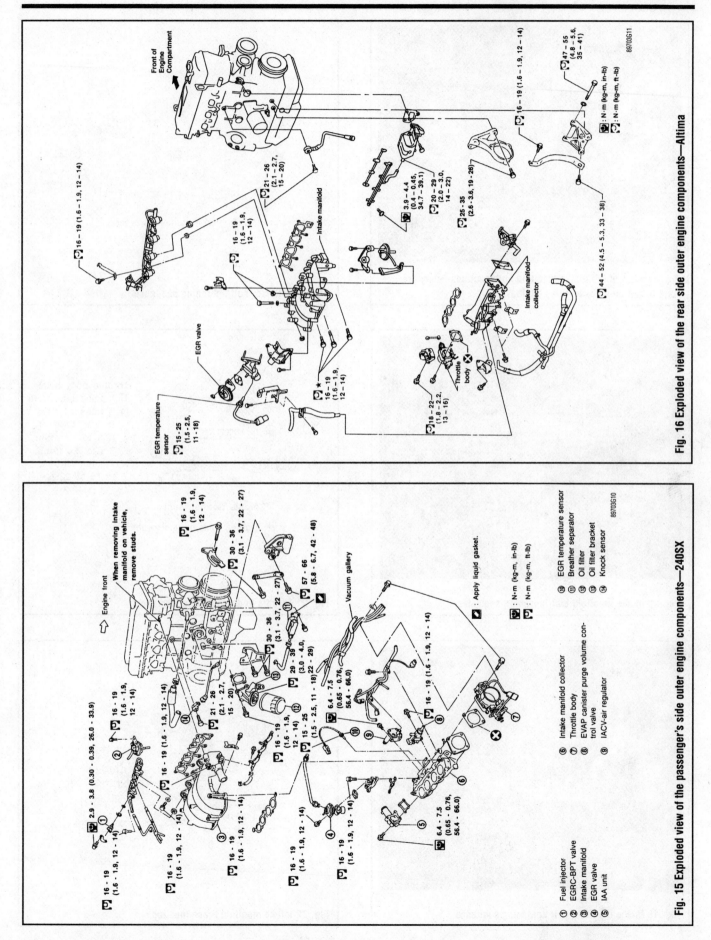

Fig. 16 Exploded view of the rear side outer engine components—Altima

Fig. 15 Exploded view of the passenger's side outer engine components—240SX

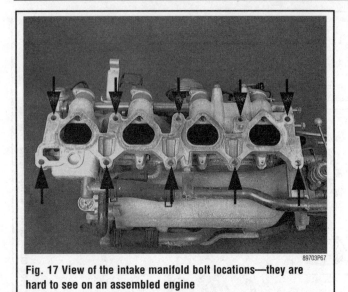

Fig. 17 View of the intake manifold bolt locations—they are hard to see on an assembled engine

Fig. 18 Intake manifold bolt loosening sequence

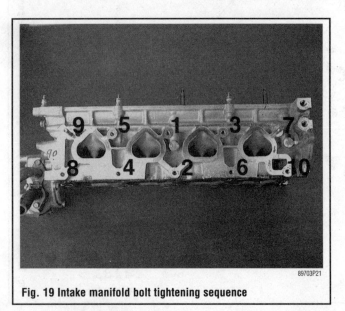

Fig. 19 Intake manifold bolt tightening sequence

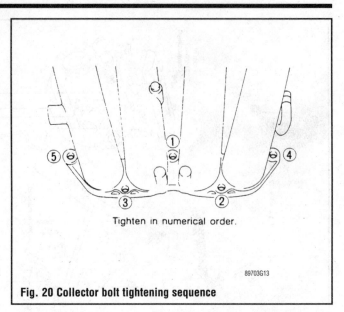

Fig. 20 Collector bolt tightening sequence

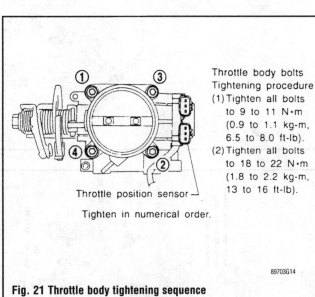

Throttle body bolts
Tightening procedure
(1) Tighten all bolts to 9 to 11 N·m (0.9 to 1.1 kg-m, 6.5 to 8.0 ft-lb).
(2) Tighten all bolts to 18 to 22 N·m (1.8 to 2.2 kg-m, 13 to 16 ft-lb).

Throttle position sensor

Tighten in numerical order.

Fig. 21 Throttle body tightening sequence

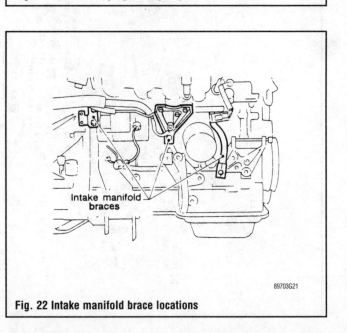

Fig. 22 Intake manifold brace locations

240SX

1. Properly relieve the fuel system pressure.
2. Disconnect the negative battery cable.
3. Drain and recycle the engine coolant.
4. Remove the air duct between the air flow meter and the throttle body.
5. Disconnect the throttle cable and the cruise control cable, if so equipped.
6. Disconnect the fuel supply and return lines from the fuel injector assembly. Plug the lines to prevent leakage.
7. Label and disconnect all appropriate electrical harnesses.
8. Label and disconnect all appropriate vacuum hoses.
9. Label and disconnect the spark plug wires from the spark plugs.
10. Remove the throttle body assembly from the intake manifold.
11. Disconnect the EGR valve tube from the exhaust manifold.
12. Remove the intake manifold mounting brackets.
13. Remove the intake manifold collector-to-intake manifold bolts/nuts in the reverse order of their tightening sequence.
14. Separate the collector from the intake manifold.
15. Remove the intake manifold-to-cylinder head bolts in the reverse order of their tightening sequence.
16. Remove the intake manifold from the engine.

To install:

17. Clean the gasket mating surfaces thoroughly.
18. Check the gasket mating surfaces for warpage and compare with the values in the applicable Specifications chart (later in this section).
19. Inspect the intake manifold/collector for damage. Repair or replace components as necessary.
20. Using new gaskets, install the intake manifold to the cylinder head and tighten the mounting bolts/nuts in the indicated sequence to 12–14 ft. lbs. (16–19 Nm).
21. Using new gaskets, install the collector to the intake manifold and tighten the mounting bolts/nuts in the illustrated sequence to 12–14 ft. lbs. (16–19 Nm).
22. Install the intake manifold mounting brackets.
23. Connect the EGR valve tube to the exhaust manifold.
24. Using a new gasket, install the throttle body and tighten the mounting bolts in a crisscross pattern to 13–16 ft. lbs. (18–22 Nm). Be sure to tighten the bolts in two progressive steps.
25. Connect the spark plug wires to the spark plugs.
26. Connect all appropriate vacuum hoses.
27. Connect all appropriate electrical harnesses.

28. Connect the fuel supply and return lines to the fuel injector assembly.
29. Connect the throttle cable and the cruise control cable, if so equipped.
30. Install the air duct between the air flow meter and the throttle body.
31. Fill and bleed the cooling system.
32. Connect the negative battery cable.

Exhaust Manifold

REMOVAL & INSTALLATION

▶ **See Figures 23 thru 33**

1. Disconnect the negative battery cable.
2. Raise and support the vehicle safely.

➡ **Before loosening the exhaust pipe retaining nuts/bolts, soak them with penetrating oil.**

3. Disconnect the exhaust pipe from the exhaust manifold.

➡ **On California models equipped with A/T and on all M/T equipped models, disconnect the exhaust pipe at the exhaust manifold collector.**

4. Label and disconnect the oxygen sensor electrical harness.
5. Remove the exhaust manifold cover.
6. Remove the EGR tube from the exhaust manifold.
7. Remove the exhaust manifold nuts/bolts in reverse order of their tightening sequence.
8. Remove the exhaust manifold from the vehicle.

To install:

9. Throughly clean all gasket mating surfaces. Check the exhaust manifold and cylinder head for flatness and compare the measurements with those in the Specifications chart, later in this section. Repair or replace components as necessary.
10. Position the exhaust manifold on the engine using new gaskets. Tighten the nuts/bolts evenly in sequence until snug. Then tighten the nuts/bolts to 27–35 ft. lbs. (37–48 Nm).
11. Position the EGR tube on the exhaust manifold and tighten the tube nuts to 29–36 ft. lbs. (39–49 Nm).
12. Install the exhaust manifold cover and the tighten bolts to 46–57 inch lbs. (5–7 Nm).

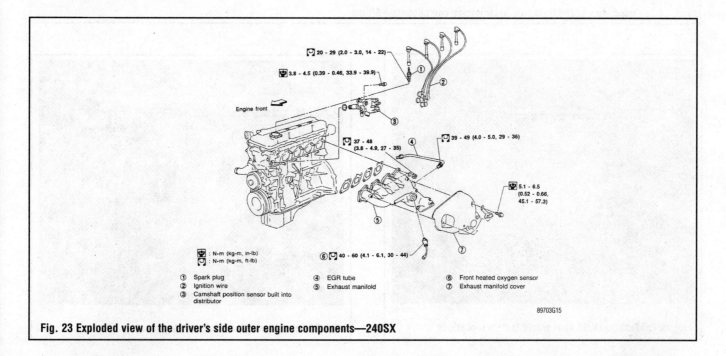

Fig. 23 Exploded view of the driver's side outer engine components—240SX

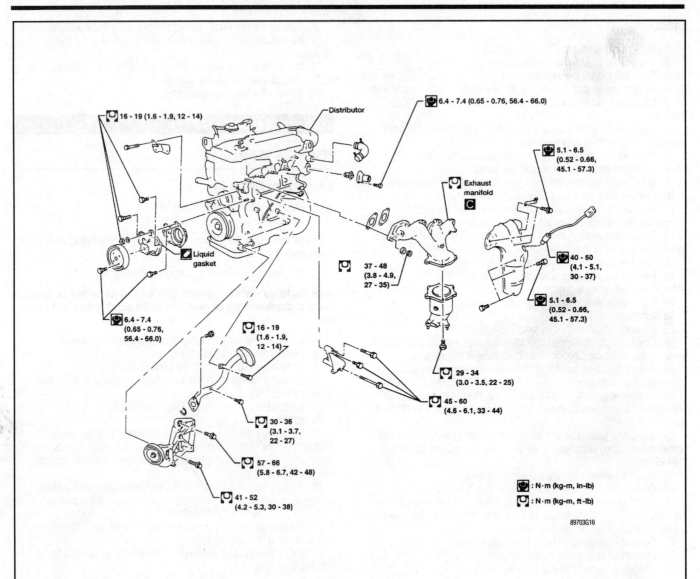

16 - 19 (1.6 - 1.9, 12 - 14)

Distributor

6.4 - 7.4 (0.65 - 0.76, 56.4 - 66.0)

5.1 - 6.5 (0.52 - 0.66, 45.1 - 57.3)

Exhaust manifold C

Liquid gasket

6.4 - 7.4 (0.65 - 0.76, 56.4 - 66.0)

37 - 48 (3.8 - 4.9, 27 - 35)

40 - 50 (4.1 - 5.1, 30 - 37)

5.1 - 6.5 (0.52 - 0.66, 45.1 - 57.3)

16 - 19 (1.6 - 1.9, 12 - 14)

29 - 34 (3.0 - 3.5, 22 - 25)

30 - 36 (3.1 - 3.7, 22 - 27)

45 - 60 (4.6 - 6.1, 33 - 44)

57 - 66 (5.8 - 6.7, 42 - 48)

41 - 52 (4.2 - 5.3, 30 - 38)

: N·m (kg-m, in-lb)

: N·m (kg-m, ft-lb)

89703G16

Fig. 24 Exploded view of the front side outer engine components—Altima

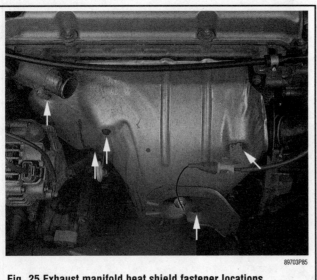

89703P85

Fig. 25 Exhaust manifold heat shield fastener locations

89703P86

Fig. 26 Exhaust manifold fastener locations

Fig. 27 Disconnect the exhaust hanger (arrow) to allow the exhaust pipe to drop away from the manifold

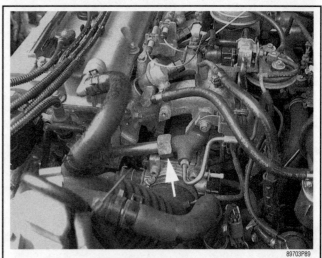

Fig. 30 Loosen the EGR tube nut (arrow) to provide enough movement to disconnect the EGR tube from the exhaust manifold

Fig. 28 The exhaust pipe is sealed to the exhaust manifold with a steel shim gasket

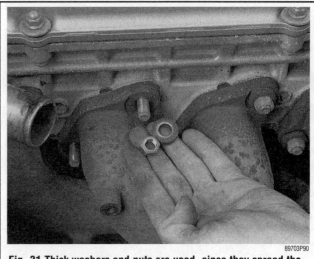

Fig. 31 Thick washers and nuts are used, since they spread the clamping load and prevent cracking of the manifold

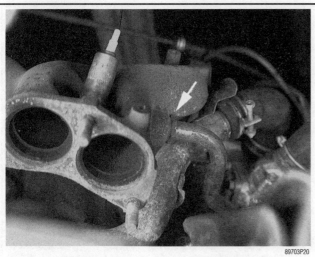

Fig. 29 The EGR tube (arrow) must be disconnected to remove the exhaust manifold

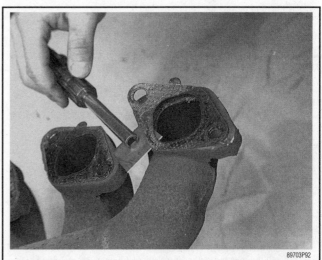

Fig. 32 Thoroughly clean all gasket material from the exhaust manifold

Fig. 33 Exhaust manifold nut tightening sequence. Loosen nuts in the reverse order

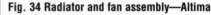
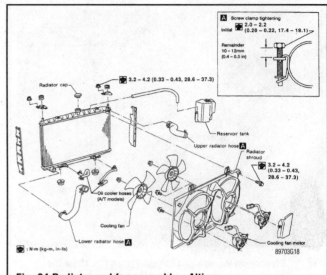

Fig. 34 Radiator and fan assembly—Altima

13. Connect the oxygen sensor electrical harness.
14. Connect the exhaust pipe to the exhaust manifold using a new gasket. Tighten the mounting nuts/bolts to 33–44 ft. lbs. (45–60 Nm).
15. Connect the negative battery cable.
16. Start the engine and check for exhaust leaks.

Radiator

✳✳ CAUTION

Never open, service or drain the radiator or cooling system when hot; serious burns can occur from the steam and hot coolant. Also, when draining engine coolant, keep in mind that cats and dogs are attracted to ethylene glycol antifreeze and could drink any that is left in an uncovered container or in puddles on the ground. This will prove fatal in sufficient quantities. Always drain coolant into a sealable container.

REMOVAL & INSTALLATION

◆ **See Figures 34 thru 42**

1. Disconnect the negative battery cable.
2. Drain and recycle the engine coolant.
3. If necessary to gain access, unbolt and set aside the power steering pump.

➡**Do not disconnect the power steering pressure hoses or drain the system.**

4. Disconnect the upper and lower radiator hoses, along with the coolant overflow reservoir hose.
5. Label and disconnect all appropriate electrical harnesses.
6. Remove the fan/shroud assembly.
7. If equipped with an automatic transaxle/transmission, disconnect and cap the oil cooling lines at the radiator.
8. Remove the radiator support brackets.
9. Remove the radiator assembly.
To install:

➡**Be sure the rubber mounting bushings are in position before the radiator is installed.**

10. Position the radiator in the vehicle.
11. Install the radiator support brackets and tighten the mounting nuts to 29–37 inch lbs. (3–4 Nm) on Altima and 34–40 inch lbs. (4–5 Nm) on 240SX.

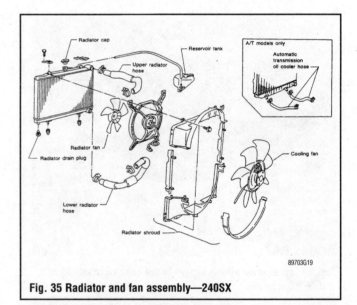

Fig. 35 Radiator and fan assembly—240SX

Fig. 36 The overflow hose fits into a clip molded into the fan shroud

Fig. 37 The radiator is mounted on the radiator support using rubber doughnuts

Fig. 38 The radiator drain (1), transaxle cooler line (2) and lower mounting posts for both the radiator (3) and engine fan (4) are visible in this picture

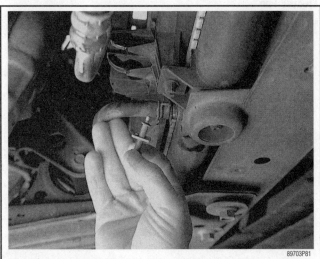

Fig. 39 Don't worry if the original equipment hose clamp comes apart during removal; it is easily reassembled

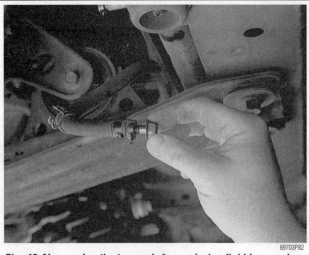

Fig. 40 Always plug the transaxle/transmission fluid hoses when removing the radiator

Fig. 41 The radiator is mounted in rubber grommets at the lower portion of the radiator support

Fig. 42 The engine fan is mounted to the radiator using studs (lower arrows) and rubber grommets at the bottom, and bolts (upper arrows) at the top

12. Install the fan motor to the shroud assembly. Tighten the fan shroud mounting bolts to 29–37 inch lbs. (3–4 Nm) on Altima and 34–40 inch lbs. (4–5 Nm) on 240SX.

13. Connect the electrical harnesses.

14. Connect the upper and lower radiator hoses, along with the coolant overflow reservoir hose.

15. Install the power steering pump, if removed.

16. Refill and bleed the cooling system.

17. Connect the negative battery cable.

18. Start the engine and check for leaks.

Cooling Fan

TESTING

Electric Fan

▶ See Figure 43

➡These vehicles use two-speed cooling fan circuits. Test the lower speed function first, then the high speed function.

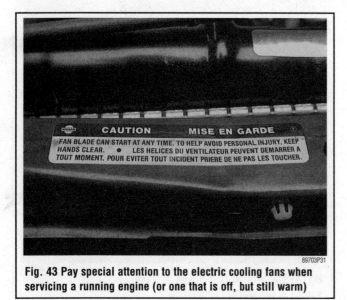

Fig. 43 Pay special attention to the electric cooling fans when servicing a running engine (or one that is off, but still warm)

LOW SPEED FUNCTION

1. Perform a complete visual inspection of all wires and components. Repair wires and replace physically damaged components as necessary.

2. Start the engine and, with the temperature lever at full COLD, turn the air conditioner and blower fan switches ON.

3. Run the engine at idle for a few minutes with the air conditioning operating and ensure that the cooling fan operates at low speed.

4. If the cooling fan does not operate at low speed, inspect the low speed cooling fan circuit.

5. Turn the ignition switch OFF and disconnect the cooling fan motor electrical harness.

6. Check continuity between terminals 1 and 5. Continuity should exist. If continuity does not exist, check for a short circuit in the harness.

7. Check continuity between terminals 4 and ground. Continuity should exist. If continuity does not exist, check for a short circuit in the harness.

8. Disconnect the ECM harness and check continuity between ECM terminals 14 and 2. Continuity should exist. If continuity does not exist, check for a short circuit in the harness.

9. Apply power and ground to the cooling fan motors. The motors should operate. If the motors do not operate properly, the cooling fans are faulty. If the motors operate properly, the cooling fan relay may be defective.

HIGH SPEED FUNCTION

1. Perform a complete visual inspection of all wires and components. Repair wires and replace physically damaged components as necessary.

2. Turn the air conditioner switch OFF.

3. Disconnect the engine coolant temperature sensor harness and attach a 150 ohm resistor (available at most electronics stores) to the harness connector terminals.

4. Start the engine. If the cooling fan does not operate at high speed, inspect the high speed cooling fan circuit.

5. Check the cooling system for leaks. Low cooling system volume may cause the coolant temperature sensor to read incorrectly. Repair leaks as necessary.

6. Check the radiator cap with a pressure tester. Replace the radiator cap as necessary.

7. Check the thermostat for proper operation. Incorrect thermostat operation affects coolant temperature sensor operation. Replace the thermostat as necessary.

8. Inspect the coolant temperature sensor for proper operation. Refer to Coolant Temperature Sensor testing in Section 4 of this manual. Replace the coolant temperature sensor as necessary.

REMOVAL & INSTALLATION

Mechanical Fan

1. Disconnect the negative battery cable.

2. Loosen the fan pulley attaching bolts, but do not remove.

3. Remove the accessory drive belts.

4. Remove the fan shroud, as necessary to gain clearance.

➡Take care to not allow the fan to contact the radiator. The radiator fins are easily damaged.

5. Remove the fan pulley attaching bolts and carefully remove the fan from the engine.

To install:

6. Install the fan pulley and hand-tighten the attaching bolts.

7. Install the fan shroud, if removed.

8. Install and tension the accessory drive belts.

9. Final-tighten the fan attaching bolts to 56–66 inch lbs. (6–8 Nm).

10. Re-tension the accessory drive belts, as necessary.

11. Connect the negative battery cable.

Electric Fan

▶ See Figures 44 and 45

1. Disconnect the negative battery cable.

2. Drain and recycle the engine coolant.

3. Disconnect the upper radiator hose from the radiator and lay it aside.

4. Label and disconnect the cooling fan electrical harnesses.

5. Remove the bolts securing the fan shroud assembly to the radiator.

6. Remove the cooling fan and shroud assembly from the vehicle.

To install:

7. Install the cooling fan and shroud assembly. Tighten the fan shroud mounting bolts to 29–37 inch lbs. (3–4 Nm) on Altima and 34–40 inch lbs. (4–5 Nm) on 240SX.

8. Install the upper radiator hose and tighten the clamp securely.

9. Refill and bleed the cooling system.

10. Connect the cooling fan electrical harnesses.

11. Connect the negative battery cable.

12. Start the engine and check for leaks.

13. Verify the operation of the cooling fans.

Fig. 44 When removing the engine fan assembly, disconnect the electrical harnesses (lower arrows) and remove the mounting bolts (upper arrows)

Fig. 46 The water pump pulley is attached by four small bolts

Fig. 45 The fan electrical harness is attached to the shroud with a special clip (arrow). Working carefully, the clip can be opened using a pick

Fig. 47 Silicone gasket sealer (arrow) is used to seal the water pump to the front cover

Water Pump

REMOVAL & INSTALLATION

Altima

▶ See Figures 46, 47 and 48

1. Disconnect the negative battery cable.
2. Drain and recycle the engine coolant.
3. Remove the upper radiator.
4. Remove the accessory drive belts from the pulleys.
5. Remove the alternator.
6. Place a floor jack beneath the engine oil pan using a piece of wood as a cushion.
7. Raise the engine slightly using a floor jack and remove the passenger's side engine mount.

➡The mounting bolts are different sizes and must be reinstalled in the correct location; therefore, it is a good idea to arrange the bolts so that they can be easily identified during installation.

Fig. 48 Water pump bolts are of various lengths. When installing the water pump, be sure the bolts are returned to their original positions

8. Unfasten the attaching bolts and remove the water pump from the engine.

To install:

9. Make sure all gasket surfaces are clean, then properly apply a continuous bead of liquid gasket to the water pump mounting surface.

10. Install the pump to the engine. Tighten the 6mm bolts to 57–66 inch lbs. (6–8 Nm) and the 8mm bolts to 12–14 ft. lbs. (16–19 Nm).

11. Install the water pump pulley and tighten the bolts to 57–66 inch lbs. (6–8 Nm).

12. Install the passenger's side engine mount.

13. Install the alternator.

14. Install the accessory drive belts on their pulleys.

15. Install the upper radiator.

16. Fill and bleed the cooling system.

17. Start the engine and check for leaks.

240SX

1. Disconnect the negative battery cable.
2. Drain and recycle the engine coolant.
3. Remove the upper radiator hose to provide working room and remove the drive belt(s) from the pulleys.
4. Remove the retaining screws and lift the fan shroud from the engine.
5. While holding the pulley, remove the nuts retaining the cooling fan and pulley to the water pump.
6. Remove the mounting bolts and remove the water pump from the engine.

To install:

7. Make sure all gasket surfaces are clean and properly apply liquid gasket to the water pump.

8. Install the water pump to the engine and tighten the bolts to 12–14 ft. lbs. (16–19 Nm).

9. Install the remaining components in the reverse order of removal.

10. Tighten the fan clutch, fan, and pulley mounting nuts to 66 inch lbs. (8 Nm).

11. Start the engine and check for leaks.

Cylinder Head

REMOVAL & INSTALLATION

♦ **See Figures 49, 50, 51, 52 and 53**

Altima

♦ **See Figures 54 thru 61**

1. Disconnect the negative battery cable.
2. Drain and recycle the engine coolant.
3. Drain and recycle the engine oil.
4. Properly relieve the fuel system pressure.
5. Disconnect the air duct from the throttle body.
6. Disconnect the intake manifold braces from the rear of the engine.
7. Remove the exhaust manifold.
8. Remove the alternator and all related brackets.
9. Remove the distributor assembly.
10. Using a block of wood, set a jack under the aluminum oil pan and remove the passenger's side engine mount.
11. Remove the cylinder head cover.
12. Remove the timing chain and camshaft sprockets.

➡**The lower timing chain should not be disengaged from the crankshaft sprocket.**

13. Remove the camshafts.

➡**The valve train components must be reassembled in their original positions. Be sure to note their locations.**

14. Loosen the cylinder head bolts in the illustrated order.

Fig. 49 Cylinder head bolt loosening sequence

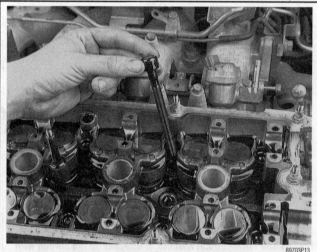

Fig. 50 Lubricate the cylinder head bolts prior to installation; this will provide a more accurate torque reading

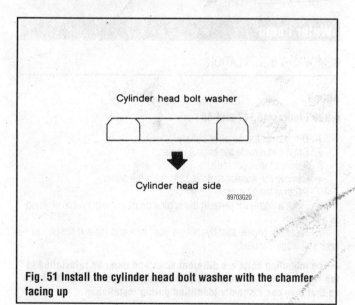

Cylinder head bolt washer

Cylinder head side

Fig. 51 Install the cylinder head bolt washer with the chamfer facing up

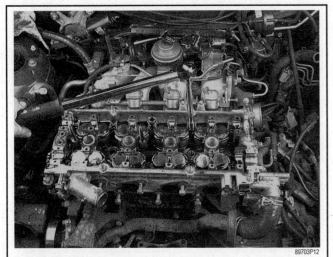

Fig. 52 Always tighten cylinder head bolts in the specified sequence, to the specified torque

Fig. 53 Cylinder head bolt tightening sequence

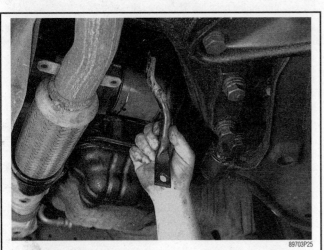

Fig. 54 One of the intake manifold braces is located on the driver's side of the engine compartment, and must be removed from beneath the vehicle

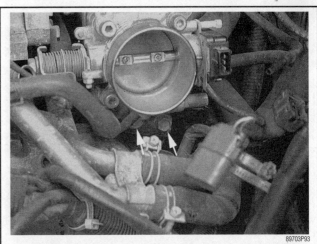

Fig. 55 The second intake manifold brace can be accessed just below the throttle body. The arrows indicate the location of the mounting bolts

Fig. 56 The bracket which surrounds the passenger's side of the cylinder head must be removed prior to removing the cylinder head

Fig. 57 The distributor is removed by loosening the two attaching bolts and pulling the unit straight out of the cylinder head

Fig. 58 Although the cylinder head and intake manifold are made of aluminum, it still takes two people to lift the assembly off the engine block

Fig. 59 Carefully inspect the cylinder head gasket for signs of damage. A leaking head gasket can cause major engine problems

Fig. 60 Thoroughly clean the engine block and cylinder head gasket mating surfaces

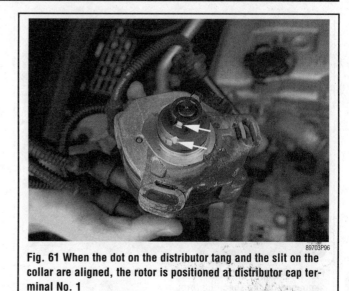

Fig. 61 When the dot on the distributor tang and the slit on the collar are aligned, the rotor is positioned at distributor cap terminal No. 1

➡A warped or cracked cylinder head could result from loosening in incorrect order. The cylinder head bolts should be loosened in two or three steps.

15. Remove the cylinder head and intake manifold as an assembly.
16. Remove the cylinder head gasket.

To install:

17. Clean the gasket mating surfaces thoroughly.
18. Inspect both the engine block and cylinder head for damage. Refer to ENGINE RECONDITIONING for further information.
19. Install a new cylinder head gasket. Ensure that the proper side of the gasket is facing up. Each gasket manufacturer will have a slightly different way of telling which side is up. Read the manufacturer's instructions carefully.
20. Install the cylinder head and temporarily tighten the cylinder head bolts. This is necessary to avoid damaging the cylinder head gasket. Be sure to install washers between the bolts and cylinder head.
21. Install the upper timing chain and cover.
22. Tighten the cylinder head bolts in the proper sequence to the following torque specifications:
   a. Tighten all the bolts to 22 ft. lbs. (29 Nm).
   b. Tighten all the bolts to 59 ft. lbs. (79 Nm).
   c. Loosen all the bolts completely.
   d. Tighten all the bolts to 18–25 ft. lbs. (25–34 Nm).
   e. Turn all the bolts 86–91 degrees clockwise.

➡If an angle wrench is not available, tighten all the bolts to 55–62 ft. lbs. (75–84 Nm).

23. Install the camshafts.
24. Install the timing chain and sprockets.
25. Install the cylinder head cover.
26. Install the passenger's side engine mount and lower the engine.
27. Install the distributor assembly.
28. Install the alternator and all related brackets.
29. Install the exhaust manifold.
30. Install the intake manifold braces.
31. Connect the air duct to the throttle body.
32. Refill and bleed the cooling system.
33. Refill the engine with the proper grade and viscosity of engine oil.
34. Connect the negative battery cable.
35. Start the engine and make the necessary adjustments.
36. Check for proper operation and leaks.

240SX

1. Disconnect the negative battery cable.
2. Drain and recycle the engine coolant.

3. Drain and recycle the engine oil.
4. Properly relieve the fuel system pressure.
5. Disconnect the air duct from the throttle body.
6. Remove the power steering pump and alternator, as necessary.
7. Disconnect the intake manifold braces.
8. Remove the intake manifold.
9. Remove the exhaust manifold.
10. Remove the distributor assembly.
11. Remove the cylinder head cover.
12. Remove the timing chain and camshaft sprockets.

➡**The lower timing chain should not be disengaged from the crankshaft sprocket.**

13. Remove the camshafts.

➡**The valve train components must be reassembled in their original positions. Be sure to note their locations.**

14. Loosen the cylinder head bolts in the illustrated order.

➡**A warped or cracked cylinder head could result from loosening in incorrect order. The cylinder head bolts should be loosened in two or three steps.**

15. Remove the cylinder head and intake manifold as an assembly.
16. Remove the cylinder head gasket.
To install:
17. Clean the gasket mating surfaces thoroughly.
18. Inspect both the engine block and cylinder head for damage. Refer to ENGINE RECONDITIONING for further information.
19. Install a new cylinder head gasket. Ensure that the proper side of the gasket is facing up. Each gasket manufacturer will have a slightly different way of telling which side is up. Read the manufacturer's instructions carefully.
20. Install the cylinder head and temporarily tighten the cylinder head bolts. This is necessary to avoid damaging the cylinder head gasket. Be sure to install washers between the bolts and cylinder head.
21. Install the upper timing chain and cover.
22. Tighten the cylinder head bolts in the proper sequence to the following torque specifications:
   a. Tighten all the bolts to 22 ft. lbs. (29 Nm).
   b. Tighten all the bolts to 59 ft. lbs. (79 Nm).
   c. Loosen all the bolts completely.
   d. Tighten all the bolts to 18–25 ft. lbs.(25–34 Nm).
   e. Turn all the bolts 86–91 degrees clockwise.

➡**If an angle wrench is not available, tighten all the bolts to 55–62 ft. lbs. (75–84 Nm).**

23. Install the timing chain and camshaft sprockets.
24. Install the cylinder head cover.
25. Install the distributor assembly.
26. Install the exhaust manifold.
27. Install the intake manifold.
28. Connect the intake manifold braces.
29. Install the power steering pump and alternator, if removed.
30. Connect the air duct to the throttle body.
31. Refill and bleed the cooling system.
32. Refill the engine with the proper grade and viscosity of engine oil.
33. Connect the negative battery cable.
34. Start the engine and make the necessary adjustments.
35. Check for proper operation and leaks.

Oil Pan

❊❊ CAUTION

The EPA warns that prolonged contact with used engine oil may cause a number of skin disorders, including cancer! You should make every effort to minimize your exposure to used engine oil.

Protective gloves should be worn when changing the oil. Wash your hands and any other exposed skin areas as soon as possible after exposure to used engine oil. Soap and water, or waterless hand cleaner, should be used.

❊❊ WARNING

Operating the engine without the proper amount and type of engine oil will result in severe engine damage.

REMOVAL & INSTALLATION

◆ **See Figures 62 and 63**

Altima

◆ **See Figures 64, 65, 66, 67 and 68**

1. Disconnect the negative battery cable.
2. Raise and support the vehicle safely.
3. Remove the engine undercover.
4. Drain and recycle the engine oil.

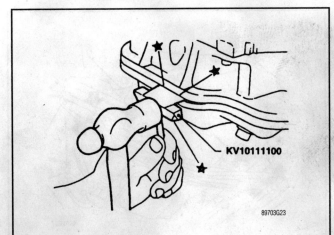

KV10111100

89703G23

Fig. 62 Insert a seal breaking tool and tap along the edges to cut through the liquid gasket. Do not use a screwdriver or scraper, as this will damage the metal

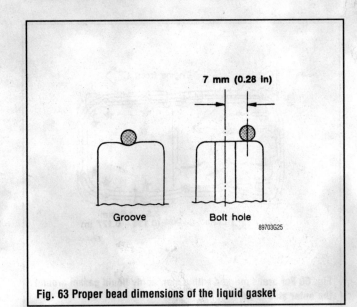

7 mm (0.28 in)

Groove   Bolt hole

89703G25

Fig. 63 Proper bead dimensions of the liquid gasket

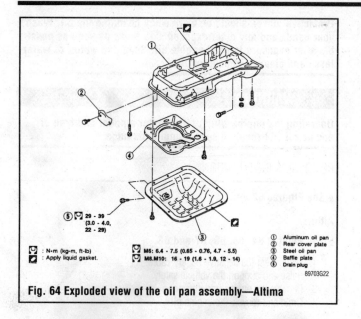

Fig. 64 Exploded view of the oil pan assembly—Altima

① Aluminum oil pan
② Rear cover plate
③ Steel oil pan
④ Baffle plate
⑤ Drain plug

⑤ 🔧 29 - 39
(3.0 - 4.0,
22 - 29)

🔧 : N·m (kg-m, ft-lb)
🔲 : Apply liquid gasket.
🔧 M6: 6.4 - 7.5 (0.65 - 0.76, 4.7 - 5.5)
🔧 M8,M10: 16 - 19 (1.6 - 1.9, 12 - 14)

89703G22

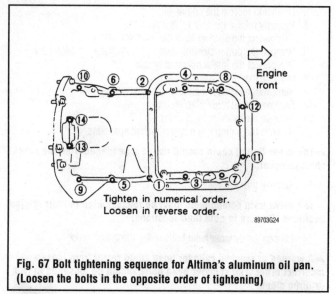

Tighten in numerical order.
Loosen in reverse order.

89703G24

Fig. 67 Bolt tightening sequence for Altima's aluminum oil pan. (Loosen the bolts in the opposite order of tightening)

89703G27

Fig. 65 Loosen the illustrated bolts to remove the center member—Altima

89703P71

Fig. 68 Bolt tightening sequence for Altima's steel oil pan. (Loosen the bolts in the opposite order of tightening)

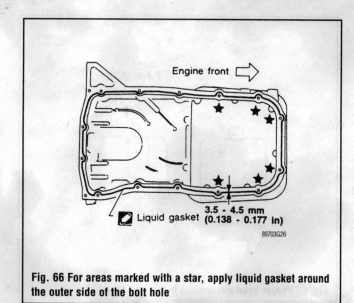

Engine front ➡

Liquid gasket

3.5 - 4.5 mm
(0.138 - 0.177 in)

89703G26

Fig. 66 For areas marked with a star, apply liquid gasket around the outer side of the bolt hole

5. Remove the bolts securing the steel oil pan to the aluminum oil pan in the reverse order of their illustrated tightening sequence.

6. Install a seal cutter between the steel oil pan and the aluminum oil pan.

7. Tapping the cutter with a hammer, slide it around the entire edge of the oil pan. Take care not to damage the aluminum oil pan.

8. Remove the steel oil pan.

9. Remove the baffle plate and oil strainer.

10. Support the transaxle with a jack and the engine with a hoist.

11. Remove the center suspension member.

12. Remove the A/C compressor and lay it aside.

➡ **Do not disconnect the A/C compressor lines.**

13. Remove the rear cover plate.

14. Remove the aluminum oil pan retaining bolts in reverse order of the illustrated tightening sequence.

15. Insert a seal cutter between the oil pan and the cylinder block.

16. Tapping the cutter with a hammer, slide it around the entire edge of the oil pan. Take care not to damage the aluminum oil pan.

17. Lower the oil pan from the cylinder block and remove it from the engine.

To install:

18. Carefully scrape the old gasket material away from the pan and cylinder block mounting surfaces, then apply a continuous bead (3.5–4.5mm) of liquid gasket around the oil pan. Install the pan within five minutes or else this step will have to be repeated.

19. Install the aluminum oil pan and tighten the mounting bolts, in the indicated sequence, to 13 ft. lbs. (17.5 Nm).

20. Install the baffle plate.

21. Install the steel oil pan, and tighten in the indicated sequence to 61 inch lbs. (7 Nm).

22. Wait 30 minutes before refilling the crankcase to allow the sealant to cure properly.

23. Install the rear cover plate.

24. Install the front suspension member.

25. Install the A/C compressor.

26. Install the center suspension member.

27. Install the engine undercover.

28. Lower the vehicle.

29. Fill the engine with the proper grade and viscosity of oil.

30. Connect the negative battery cable.

31. Start the engine and check for leaks.

240SX

♦ See Figures 69 and 70

1. Disconnect the negative battery cable.
2. Raise and support the vehicle safely.
3. Position a hoist on the engine and support the engine.
4. Drain and recycle the engine oil.
5. Disconnect the tension rod bolts at the transverse link.
6. Separate the front stabilizer bar from the side member.
7. Remove the left and right engine mounting bolts.
8. Disconnect the lower steering joint.
9. Disconnect the power steering tube bracket at the left tension rod.
10. Remove the bolts and lower the front suspension member while supporting it with a jack. It is only necessary to lower the suspension member 2.36 in. (60mm).
11. Remove the oil pan retaining bolts.
12. Insert a seal cutter between the oil pan and the cylinder block.
13. Tapping the cutter with a hammer, slide it around the entire edge of the oil pan. Do not drive the seal cutter into the oil pump or rear seal retainer portion, or the aluminum mating surface will be deformed.
14. Lower the oil pan from the cylinder block and remove it from the front side of the engine.

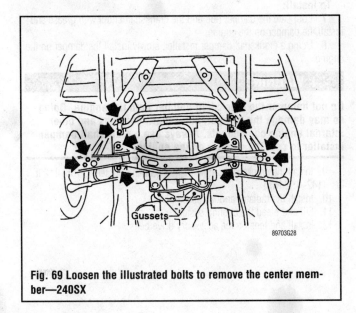

Fig. 69 Loosen the illustrated bolts to remove the center member—240SX

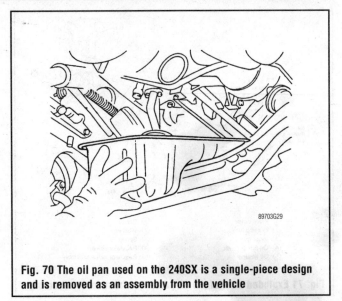

Fig. 70 The oil pan used on the 240SX is a single-piece design and is removed as an assembly from the vehicle

To install:

15. Carefully scrape the old gasket material away from the pan and cylinder block mounting surfaces, then apply a 0.138–0.177 in. (3.5–4.5mm) continuous bead of liquid gasket around the oil pan. Install the pan within 5 minutes or this step will have to be repeated.

16. Install the oil pan and tighten the mounting bolts. Start tightening the bolts from the center and work towards the ends.

17. Tighten the oil pan bolts to 57–61 inch lbs. (6.4–7.5 Nm) for 1993–94 vehicles or 12–14 ft. lbs. (16–19 Nm) for 1995–98 vehicles. Wait 30 minutes before refilling the crankcase to allow for the sealant to cure properly.

18. The remaining components are installed in the reverse order from which they were removed.

19. Fill the engine with the proper grade and viscosity of engine oil.

20. Connect the negative battery cable. Start the engine and check for leaks.

Oil Pump

REMOVAL & INSTALLATION

♦ See Figures 71 and 72

1. Disconnect the negative battery cable.
2. Drain and recycle the engine coolant.
3. Drain and recycle the engine oil.
4. Remove the cam sprocket cover.
5. Remove the front cover.

➡The oil pump assembly is mounted in the front cover.

6. Unfasten the oil pump cover and remove the gears from the front cover housing.

To install:

➡When installing the timing cover, be sure to replace the O-ring seal for the oil hole in the front cover.

7. Install the outer gear into the cavity in the front cover housing. Make sure the gears mesh properly and prime the oil pump with clean engine oil.

8. Install the oil pump cover. Tighten the retaining screws to 33–44 inch lbs. (3.7–5.0 Nm) and tighten the bolts to 12–15 inch lbs. (16–21 Nm).

9. Clean the mating surfaces thoroughly and apply a 0.079–0.118 in. (2–3mm) thick continuous bead of liquid gasket to the mating surfaces of the timing cover.

10. Install the front cover. Tighten the M6 mounting bolts to 56–66 inch lbs. (6.4–7.5 Nm) and tighten the M8 mounting bolts to 12–14 ft. lbs. (15–19 Nm).

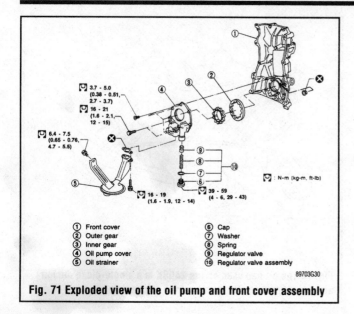

Fig. 71 Exploded view of the oil pump and front cover assembly

① Front cover
② Outer gear
③ Inner gear
④ Oil pump cover
⑤ Oil strainer
⑥ Cap
⑦ Washer
⑧ Spring
⑨ Regulator valve
⑩ Regulator valve assembly

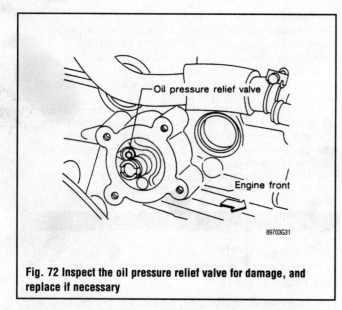

Fig. 72 Inspect the oil pressure relief valve for damage, and replace if necessary

11. Clean the mating surfaces thoroughly and apply a 0.079–0.118 in. (2–3mm) thick continuous bead of liquid gasket to the mating surfaces of the cam sprocket cover.
12. Install the cam sprocket cover. Tighten the M6 mounting bolts to 56–66 inch lbs. (6.4–7.5 Nm) and tighten the M8 mounting bolts to 12–14 ft. lbs. (15–19 Nm).
13. Refill and bleed the cooling system.
14. Refill the engine with the proper grade and viscosity of engine oil.
15. Start the engine and verify correct oil pressure.

❈❈ WARNING

If correct oil pressure does not exist, stop the engine immediately and correct the problem. Running the engine with improper oil pressure will cause severe damage.

16. Check for leaks.

Crankshaft Damper

REMOVAL & INSTALLATION

Altima

1. Remove the accessory drive belts.
2. Raise and support the vehicle safely.
3. Remove the passenger's side front wheel.
4. Remove the passenger's side engine cover.
5. Place a floor jack under the oil pan using a piece of wood as a cushion.
6. Remove the passenger's side engine mount and lower the engine slightly.
7. Remove the crankshaft damper center bolt.
8. Using a jaw type gear puller, remove the damper.
To install:
9. Lubricate the damper hub and the crankshaft snout with grease and install the damper on the engine.
10. Using a crankshaft damper installer, slowly install the damper on the engine.

❈❈ WARNING

Do not hammer the crankshaft damper onto the engine. Doing so may damage the damper, crankshaft, bearings and/or other internal engine components. Always use a crankshaft damper installer to seat the damper on the engine.

11. Install the crankshaft damper center bolt and tighten to 105–112 ft. lbs. (142–152 Nm).
12. Raise the engine and install the passenger's side engine mount.
13. Install the passenger's side engine cover.
14. Install the passenger's side front wheel.
15. Lower the vehicle safely.
16. Install and tension the accessory drive belts.

240SX

1. Raise and support the vehicle safely.
2. Drain and recycle the engine coolant.
3. Remove the radiator and engine fan assembly.
4. Remove the accessory drive belts.
5. Remove the crankshaft damper center bolt.
6. Using a jaw type gear puller, remove the damper.
To install:
7. Lubricate the damper hub and the crankshaft snout with grease and install the damper on the engine.
8. Using a crankshaft damper installer, slowly install the damper on the engine.

❈❈ WARNING

Do not hammer the crankshaft damper onto the engine. Doing so may damage the damper, crankshaft, bearings and other internal engine components. Always use a crankshaft damper installer to seat the damper on the engine.

9. Install the crankshaft damper center bolt and tighten to 105–112 ft. lbs. (142–152 Nm).
10. Install the radiator and fan assembly.
11. Fill and bleed the cooling system.
12. Install and tension the accessory drive belts.

Front Cover Seal

REMOVAL & INSTALLATION

◗ **See Figures 73, 74 and 75**

1. Remove the crankshaft damper.
2. Using a suitable tool, pry the oil seal from the front cover.

➡**When removing the oil seal, be careful not to gouge or scratch the seal bore or crankshaft surfaces.**

3. Wipe the seal bore with a clean rag.

To install:

4. Lubricate the lip of the new seal with clean engine oil.
5. Install the seal into the front cover with a suitable seal driver.

➡**Be sure to install the seal with the oil seal lip facing the engine block.**

6. Install the crankshaft damper.

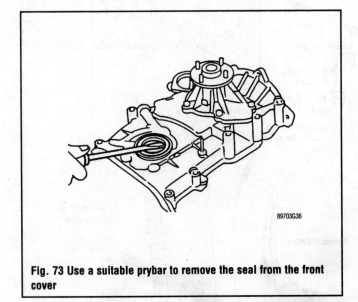

Fig. 73 Use a suitable prybar to remove the seal from the front cover

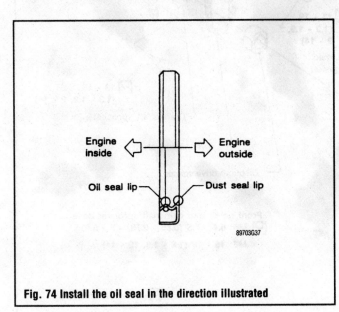

Fig. 74 Install the oil seal in the direction illustrated

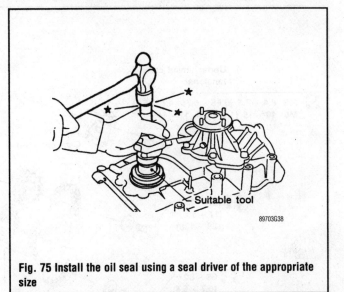

Fig. 75 Install the oil seal using a seal driver of the appropriate size

Front Cover and Camshaft Sprocket Cover

REMOVAL & INSTALLATION

◗ **See Figures 76, 77, 78 and 79**

1. Disconnect the negative battery cable.
2. Drain and recycle the engine coolant.
3. Drain and recycle the engine oil.
4. Remove the engine undercover, as required.
5. Label and disconnect all appropriate vacuum hoses, fuel lines, wires and electrical harnesses.
6. Remove the alternator and bracket, upper radiator hose, air duct, and front exhaust tube.
7. On Altima models, position a floor jack beneath the aluminum oil pan and remove the passenger's side engine mount.
8. Remove the cylinder head cover.
9. Remove the cam sprocket cover.
10. Remove the crankshaft damper.
11. Remove the front cover.

To install:

12. Apply a continuous bead of liquid gasket, as illustrated, to the front cover.
13. Install the front cover. Tighten the M6 attaching bolts to 56–66 inch lbs. (6.4–7.5 Nm). Tighten the M8 attaching bolts to 12–14 ft. lbs. (16–19 Nm).
14. Install the crankshaft damper.
15. Apply a continuous bead of liquid gasket, as illustrated, to the cam sprocket cover.
16. Install the cam sprocket cover. Tighten the M6 attaching bolts to 56–66 inch lbs. (6.4–7.5 Nm). Tighten the M8 attaching bolts to 12–14 ft. lbs. (16–19 Nm).
17. Install the cylinder head cover.
18. Install the engine undercover.
19. Refill the engine with the correct grade and viscosity of engine oil.
20. Refill and bleed the cooling system.
21. Connect the negative battery cable.

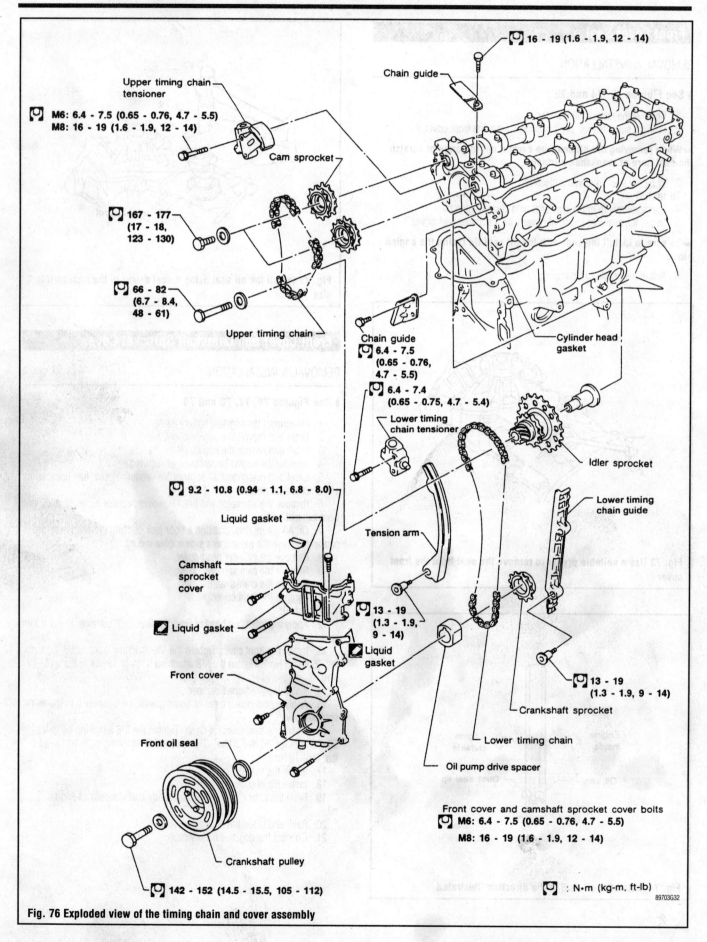

16 - 19 (1.6 - 1.9, 12 - 14)

Chain guide

Upper timing chain tensioner

M6: 6.4 - 7.5 (0.65 - 0.76, 4.7 - 5.5)
M8: 16 - 19 (1.6 - 1.9, 12 - 14)

Cam sprocket

167 - 177 (17 - 18, 123 - 130)

66 - 82 (6.7 - 8.4, 48 - 61)

Upper timing chain

Chain guide
6.4 - 7.5 (0.65 - 0.76, 4.7 - 5.5)

6.4 - 7.4 (0.65 - 0.75, 4.7 - 5.4)

Cylinder head gasket

Lower timing chain tensioner

Idler sprocket

9.2 - 10.8 (0.94 - 1.1, 6.8 - 8.0)

Lower timing chain guide

Liquid gasket

Camshaft sprocket cover

Tension arm

Liquid gasket

13 - 19 (1.3 - 1.9, 9 - 14)

Liquid gasket

Front cover

13 - 19 (1.3 - 1.9, 9 - 14)

Crankshaft sprocket

Lower timing chain

Front oil seal

Oil pump drive spacer

Crankshaft pulley

Front cover and camshaft sprocket cover bolts
M6: 6.4 - 7.5 (0.65 - 0.76, 4.7 - 5.5)
M8: 16 - 19 (1.6 - 1.9, 12 - 14)

142 - 152 (14.5 - 15.5, 105 - 112)

: N·m (kg-m, ft-lb)

89703G32

Fig. 76 Exploded view of the timing chain and cover assembly

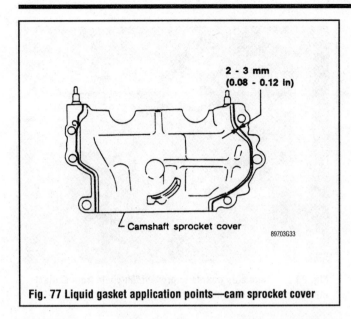

Fig. 77 Liquid gasket application points—cam sprocket cover

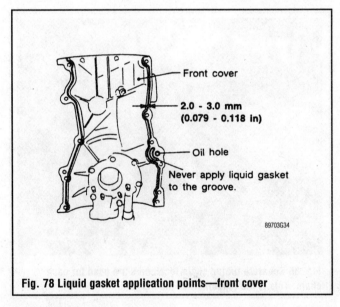

Fig. 78 Liquid gasket application points—front cover

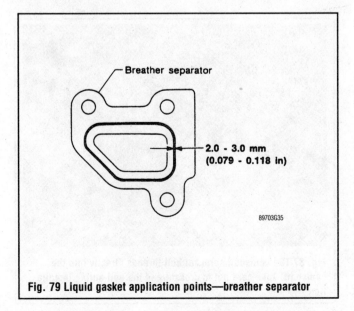

Fig. 79 Liquid gasket application points—breather separator

Timing Chain and Sprockets

REMOVAL & INSTALLATION

▶ See Figures 80 thru 94

Altima

▶ See Figures 95, 96, 97 and 98

1. Disconnect the negative battery cable.
2. Drain and recycle the engine coolant.
3. Drain and recycle the engine oil.
4. Remove the engine undercover.
5. Label and disconnect all appropriate vacuum hoses, fuel lines, wires and electrical harnesses.
6. Remove the alternator and bracket, upper radiator hose, air duct, and front exhaust tube.
7. Remove the intake manifold collector supports, intake manifold collector, and exhaust manifold.
8. Set the No. 1 piston at TDC on its compression stroke.
9. Remove the distributor.

Fig. 80 Use a small prybar to gently loosen the upper timing cover and remove it from the engine

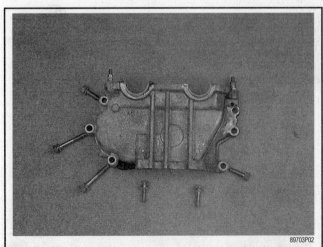

Fig. 81 The upper timing cover uses various length bolts for attachment. To avoid damage to the cylinder head, always replace bolts in their proper positions

Fig. 82 When the engine is at TDC of the compression stroke on the No. 1 cylinder, the timing marks should align as shown

Fig. 83 When removing the camshaft sprocket bolt, use a wrench to prevent the camshafts from moving

Fig. 84 The upper timing chain uses both a top guard . . .

Fig. 85 . . . and side guards to prevent the chain from contacting the covers as the chain slackens

Fig. 86 Separate timing chain tensioners are used for each chain. This is the tensioner for the top chain

Fig. 87 The camshaft sprocket bolt threads directly into the camshaft. Take care not to crossthread the bolt during installation

Fig. 88 Prior to removing the upper timing chain, be sure the alignment links (arrow), which have a dab of paint on them, are aligned with the punch marks on the camshaft sprockets

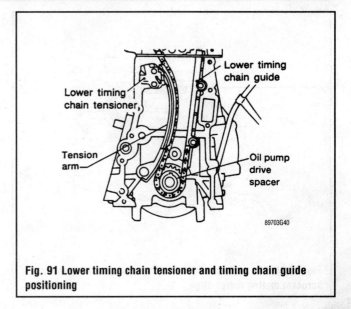

Fig. 91 Lower timing chain tensioner and timing chain guide positioning

Fig. 89 The idler sprocket is attached to the cylinder head with a single bolt. Take care not to crossthread the bolt and damage the aluminum cylinder head

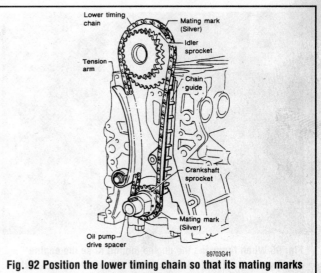

Fig. 92 Position the lower timing chain so that its mating marks align with those on the crankshaft and idler sprockets

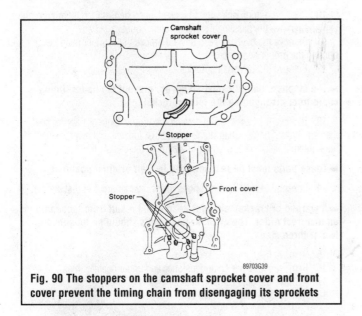

Fig. 90 The stoppers on the camshaft sprocket cover and front cover prevent the timing chain from disengaging its sprockets

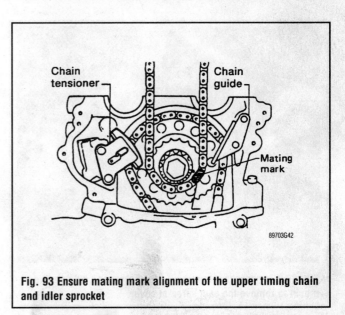

Fig. 93 Ensure mating mark alignment of the upper timing chain and idler sprocket

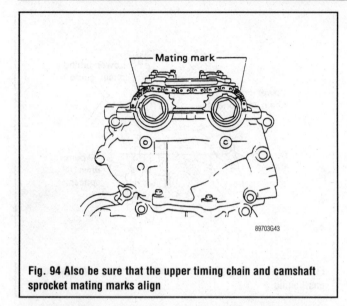

Fig. 94 Also be sure that the upper timing chain and camshaft sprocket mating marks align

Fig. 95 When removing the engine mount, raise the engine slightly using a floor jack beneath the oil pan. Protect the oil pan with a piece of wood

Fig. 96 It is necessary to remove the passenger's side engine mount to remove the cam sprocket cover

Fig. 97 Once the passenger's side engine mount is removed, access to the upper timing cover is much easier

Fig. 98 Remove the bracket to access this hidden bolt (arrow) that retains the upper timing cover

10. Position a floor jack with a block of wood beneath the aluminum oil pan and remove the passenger's side engine mount.

11. Remove the cylinder head cover. Remove the cylinder head cover bolts in the proper sequence.

12. Remove the camshaft sprockets.

➡The stoppers on the camshaft covers prevent the upper timing chain from disengaging the idler sprocket.

13. Remove the cam bearing caps in the proper sequence and remove the camshafts. The camshaft brackets must be loosened in reverse order of the tightening sequence to prevent damage to the camshaft.

➡These parts must be reassembled in their original positions.

14. Loosen the cylinder head bolts in the reverse order of installation.

➡A warped or cracked cylinder head could result from loosening in an incorrect order. The cylinder head bolts should be loosened in two or three steps.

15. Remove the cam sprocket cover.
16. Remove the upper chain tensioner and upper chain guides.
17. Remove the upper timing chain.
18. Remove the idler sprocket bolt.

➡**The stoppers on the front cover prevent the lower timing chain from disengaging the crankshaft sprocket.**

19. Remove the cylinder head and gasket.
20. Remove the oil pan.
21. Remove the crankshaft damper.
22. Remove the front cover.
23. Remove the oil pump drive spacer.
24. Remove the lower timing chain tensioner, tension arm, and lower timing chain guide.
25. Remove the lower timing chain and idler sprocket.

To install:

26. Install the crankshaft sprocket and oil pump drive spacer.

➡**Ensure that the mating marks on the crankshaft sprocket face the front of the engine.**

27. Set the No. 1 piston at TDC on its compression stroke.
28. Install the idler sprocket and lower timing chain.
29. Set the lower timing chain on the sprockets, aligning the mating marks.

➡**The mating marks on the timing chain assembly will be silver.**

30. Install the chain tension arm and chain guide.
31. Install the lower timing chain tensioner.
32. Install a new front cover oil seal.
33. Apply a continuous bead of liquid gasket, as illustrated, to the front cover.
34. Install the front cover. Tighten the M6 attaching bolts to 56–66 inch lbs. (6.4–7.5 Nm). Tighten the M8 attaching bolts to 12–14 ft. lbs. (16–19 Nm).
35. Install the crankshaft damper.
36. Install the oil strainer and oil pan.
37. When installing the front cover, install the cylinder head. Insert, but do not tighten the cylinder head bolts.

➡**Apply engine oil to the bolt threads and seat surfaces. Ensure that the washers between the bolts and cylinder head are properly positioned.**

38. Temporarily tighten the cylinder head bolts.

➡**This is necessary to avoid damaging the cylinder head gasket.**

39. Install the upper timing chain, chain tensioner and chain guide.
40. Set the upper timing chain on the idler sprocket, aligning the mating marks.
41. Apply a continuous bead of liquid gasket, as illustrated, to the cam sprocket cover.
42. Install the cam sprocket cover.

➡**Be careful not to damage the cylinder head gasket. Be careful that the upper timing chain does not slip or jump when installing the cam sprocket cover.**

43. Tighten the cylinder head bolts in the indicated sequence to the proper specification.
44. Install the camshafts and camshaft bearing caps.
45. Install the camshaft sprockets (with the chain attached).
46. Install the chain guide between both camshaft sprockets.

➡**The alignment marks on the upper portion of the timing chain should now be aligned.**

47. Install the distributor. Ensure that the No. 1 piston is set at TDC and the distributor rotor is set at No. 1 cylinder spark position.
48. Install the cylinder head cover and tighten the attaching bolts in the indicated sequence to the proper specification.
49. Install the intake manifold collector, intake manifold collector supports, and exhaust manifold.
50. Install the alternator and bracket, upper radiator hose, air duct, and front exhaust tube.
51. Connect all appropriate vacuum hoses, fuel lines, wires and electrical harnesses.

52. Install the engine undercover.
53. Refill the engine with the correct grade and viscosity of engine oil.
54. Refill and bleed the cooling system.
55. Connect the negative battery cable.
56. Start the engine and make the necessary adjustments.
57. Check for proper operation and leaks.

240SX

1. Disconnect the negative battery cable.
2. Drain and recycle the engine coolant.
3. Drain and recycle the engine oil.
4. Remove the engine undercover, as required.
5. Label and disconnect all appropriate vacuum hoses, fuel lines, wires and electrical harnesses.
6. Remove the intake and exhaust manifolds.
7. Remove the air duct, cooling fan and radiator shroud.
8. Remove the spark plugs and ignition wires.
9. Set the No. 1 piston at TDC on its compression stroke.
10. Remove the distributor.
11. Unfasten the cylinder head cover bolts in the proper sequence, then remove the cylinder head cover.
12. Remove the camshaft sprockets.

➡**The stoppers on the camshaft covers prevent the upper timing chain from disengaging the idler sprocket.**

13. Remove the camshaft bearing caps in proper sequence and remove the camshafts. The camshaft brackets must be loosened in reverse order of tightening to prevent damage to the camshaft.

➡**These parts must be reassembled in their original positions.**

14. Loosen the cylinder head bolts in the reverse order of installation.

➡**A warped or cracked cylinder head could result from loosening in incorrect order. The cylinder head bolts should be loosened in two or three steps.**

15. Remove the cam sprocket cover.
16. Remove the upper chain tensioner and upper chain guides.
17. Remove the upper timing chain.
18. Remove the idler sprocket bolt.

➡**The stoppers on the front cover prevent the lower timing chain from disengaging the crankshaft sprocket.**

19. Remove the cylinder head and gasket.
20. Remove the upper timing chain.
21. Remove the oil pan.
22. Remove the crankshaft damper.
23. Remove the front cover.
24. Remove the oil pump drive spacer.
25. Remove the lower timing chain tensioner, tension arm, and lower timing chain guide.
26. Remove the lower timing chain and idler sprocket.

To install:

27. Install the crankshaft sprocket and oil pump drive spacer.

➡**Ensure that the mating marks on the crankshaft sprocket face the front of the engine.**

28. Set the No. 1 piston at TDC on its compression stroke.
29. Install the idler sprocket and lower timing chain.
30. Set the lower timing chain on the sprockets, aligning the mating marks.

➡**The mating marks on the timing chain assembly will be silver.**

31. Install the chain tensioner arm and chain guide.
32. Install the lower timing chain tensioner.
33. Install a new front cover oil seal.
34. Apply a continuous bead of liquid gasket, as illustrated, to the front cover.

35. Install the front cover. Tighten the M6 attaching bolts to 56–66 inch lbs. (6.4–7.5 Nm). Tighten the M8 attaching bolts to 12–14 ft. lbs. (16–19 Nm).

36. Install the crankshaft damper.

37. Install the oil strainer and oil pan.

38. When installing the front cover, install the cylinder head. Insert, but do not tighten the cylinder head bolts.

➡**Apply engine oil to the bolt threads and seat surfaces. Ensure the washers between the bolts and cylinder heads are properly positioned.**

39. Temporarily tighten the cylinder head bolts.

➡**This is necessary to avoid damaging the cylinder head gasket.**

40. Install the upper timing chain, chain tensioner and chain guide.

41. Set the upper timing chain on the idler sprocket, aligning the mating marks.

42. Apply a continuous bead of liquid gasket, as illustrated, to the cam sprocket cover.

43. Install the cam sprocket cover.

➡**Be careful not to damage the cylinder head gasket. Be careful that the upper timing chain does not slip or jump when installing the cam sprocket cover.**

44. Tighten the cylinder head bolts in the indicated sequence to the proper specification.

45. Install the camshafts and camshaft bearing caps.

46. Install the camshaft sprockets (with the chain attached).

47. Install the chain guide between both camshaft sprockets.

➡**The alignment marks on the upper portion of the timing chain should now be aligned.**

48. Install the distributor. Ensure the No. 1 piston is set at TDC and the distributor rotor is set at No. 1 cylinder spark position.

49. Install the cylinder head cover and tighten the attaching bolts in the indicated sequence to the proper specification.

50. Install the spark plugs and ignition wires.

51. Install the air duct, cooling fan and radiator shroud.

52. Install the intake and exhaust manifolds.

53. Connect all appropriate vacuum hoses, fuel lines, wires and electrical harnesses.

54. Install the engine undercover, as required.

55. Refill the engine with the correct grade and viscosity of engine oil.

56. Refill and bleed the cooling system.

57. Connect the negative battery cable.

58. Start the engine and make the necessary adjustments.

59. Check for proper operation and leaks.

Camshaft, Bearings and Lifters

REMOVAL & INSTALLATION

◆ **See Figures 99, 100, 101, 102 and 103**

1. Rotate the engine so that the No. 1 cylinder is at TDC on the compression stroke.

2. Remove the distributor assembly.

3. Remove the cylinder head cover.

4. Remove the camshaft sprocket cover.

5. Remove the upper chain guides and timing chain tensioner.

6. Using a piece of mechanic's wire, secure the chain to the sprocket so the chain will not fall off during sprocket removal.

7. Hold the flats of the camshaft with a wrench, just behind the first camshaft bearing cap. Loosen and remove the camshaft sprocket bolts.

8. Remove the camshaft sprockets.

➡**The stopper on the camshaft sprocket cover prevents the timing chain from disengaging the idler sprocket.**

Fig. 99 Camshaft cap loosening sequence

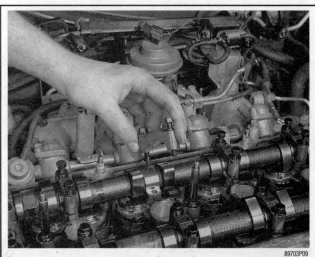

Fig. 100 Matchmark each camshaft cap, prior to removal, to ensure that they will be installed in their original positions

Fig. 101 Carefully remove the camshafts, as to not damage the bearing journals

Fig. 102 The intake and exhaust camshaft are different lengths. Note that the exhaust camshaft has slots (arrow) in one end to accept the tang from the distributor

Fig. 103 Camshaft cap tightening sequence

9. Remove the camshaft bearing caps in reverse order of the tightening sequence, then remove the camshafts.

10. Remove the valve lifter adjusting shims from the tops of the lifters.

11. Remove the valve lifters from the bores in the cylinder heads.

➡Be sure to note the location and positioning of each valve train component. Install all valve train components in their original positions.

To install:

➡When installing the valve train components, apply a coating of clean engine oil to the component.

12. Install the lifters into the lifter bores from which they were removed.

13. Install the valve shims to the lifters from which they came.

14. Install the camshafts in the same position as before removal, then install the camshaft bearing caps; tighten the cap bolts in proper sequence as follows:

    a. Tighten all bolts to 17 inch lbs. (2 Nm).

    b. Tighten all bolts to 81–104 inch lbs. (9–12 Nm).

➡When installing the timing chain and sprockets, align the marks on the sprockets with the colored links of the chain.

15. Install the camshaft sprockets (with the timing chain attached) and tighten the sprocket bolts to 123–130 ft. lbs. (167–177 Nm). Hold the flats of the camshaft with a wrench, just behind the first camshaft bearing cap while tightening.

16. Install the chain guide between both camshaft sprockets.

17. Install the camshaft sprocket cover.

18. Install the cylinder head cover.

19. Install the distributor assembly.

INSPECTION

1. Clean the camshafts with solvent and wipe dry. Remove light scuffs, scores or nicks from the camshaft machined surfaces with a smooth oil stone.

➡The camshaft(s) must be replaced if the journals are excessively worn or scored.

2. Check camshaft bores for size, taper, roundness, alignment and finish. If any of these exceed specification, install new camshaft bearings.

3. Inspect the camshaft run-out by setting the No. 1 and No. 4 journals on V-blocks and using a dial indicator. If maximum run-out of camshaft is not within specification, replace the camshaft.

4. Inspect the camshaft lobes for scoring and signs of abnormal wear. Lobe pitting in the general area of the lobe toe does not harm camshaft operation. The camshaft should not be replaced unless the lobe lift loss has exceeded specification or pitting has occurred in the lobe lift area.

5. Inspect the valve lifter and discard the entire tappet if it shows signs of pitting, scoring or excessive wear.

6. Inspect the diameter of the valve lifter and valve lifter bore, and repair or replace components as necessary.

7. Inspect all other valve train components and repair or replace as necessary.

Rear Main Seal

REMOVAL & INSTALLATION

▸ **See Figures 104, 105 and 106**

1. Remove the transmission or transaxle.

2. Remove the flywheel (flexplate).

3. Remove the oil seal retainer.

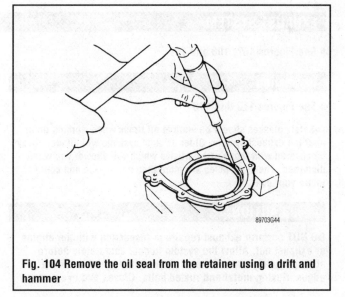

Fig. 104 Remove the oil seal from the retainer using a drift and hammer

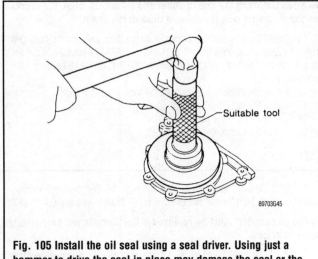

Fig. 105 Install the oil seal using a seal driver. Using just a hammer to drive the seal in place may damage the seal or the retainer

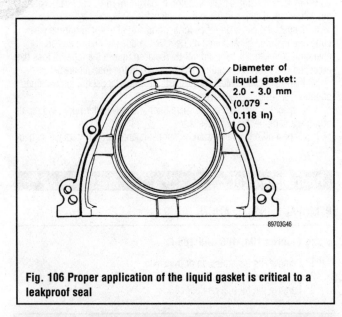

Fig. 106 Proper application of the liquid gasket is critical to a leakproof seal

4. Remove the oil seal from the retainer by tapping it out of the bore using a drift and hammer.

➡Take special care not to damage the seal bore.

To install:

5. Throughly clean all gasket mating surfaces of liquid gasket.

6. Apply engine oil to the new seal and install using an appropriately sized seal driver.

7. Apply a continuous bead of liquid gasket to the rear oil seal retainer as illustrated.

8. Install the oil seal retainer and tighten the attaching bolts to 56–66 inch lbs. (6–8 Nm).

9. Install the flywheel (flexplate).

10. Install the transmission or transaxle.

Flywheel/Flexplate

REMOVAL & INSTALLATION

The terms flywheel and flexplate are used interchangeably in this manual. Technically, a flywheel is used with a manual transmission/transaxle and a flexplate is used with an automatic transmission/transaxle.

1. Remove the transaxle or transmission from the vehicle.

2. Matchmark the flywheel to the crankshaft for installation reference.

3. Remove the flywheel (flexplate) retaining bolts.

4. Remove the flywheel (flexplate).

To install:

5. Inspect the rear main seal thoroughly. This is the time to replace a leaky seal.

6. Position the flywheel on the crankshaft and install the retaining bolts.

7. Tighten the bolts to 105–112 ft. lbs. (142–152 Nm) in a crisscross pattern.

8. Install the transaxle or transmission.

EXHAUST SYSTEM

▸ See Figures 107, 108 and 109

Inspection

▸ See Figures 110 thru 116

➡Safety glasses should be worn at all times when working on or near the exhaust system. Older exhaust systems will almost always be covered with loose rust particles which will shower you when disturbed. These particles are more than a nuisance and could injure your eye.

❊❊ CAUTION

DO NOT perform exhaust repairs or inspection with the engine or exhaust hot. Allow the system to cool completely before attempting any work. Exhaust systems are noted for sharp edges, flaking metal and rusted bolts. Gloves and eye protec-

tion are required. A healthy supply of penetrating oil and rags is highly recommended.

Your vehicle must be raised and supported safely to inspect the exhaust system properly. Placing 4 safety stands under the vehicle for support should provide enough room for you to slide under the vehicle and inspect the system completely. Start the inspection at the exhaust manifold where the header pipe is attached and work your way to the back of the vehicle. Check the complete exhaust system for open seams, holes, loose connections, or other deterioration which could permit exhaust fumes to seep into the passenger compartment. Inspect all mounting brackets and hangers for deterioration; some models may have rubber O-rings that can be overstretched and non-supportive. These components will need to be replaced if found. It has always been a practice to use a pointed tool to poke up into the exhaust system where the deterioration spots are to see whether or not they crumble. Some models may have a heat shield covering certain parts of the exhaust system; it will be necessary to remove these shields to expose the exhaust system for inspection.

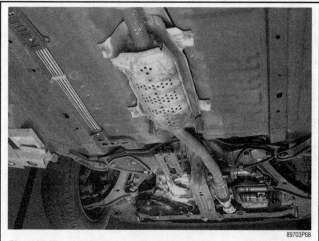

Fig. 107 The catalytic converter heat shield is a safety device. The converter produces so much heat that it can easily burn the interior components through the floor pan

Fig. 108 The rear portion of the exhaust system includes the muffler and over-the-suspension pipe

Fig. 109 The middle portion of the exhaust system includes the resonator (arrow)

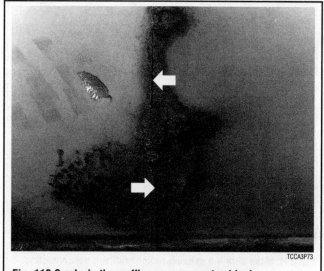

Fig. 110 Cracks in the muffler are a guaranteed leak

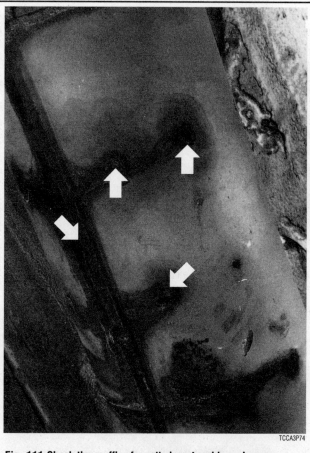

Fig. 111 Check the muffler for rotted spot welds and seams

REPLACEMENT

◆ See Figure 117

There are basically two types of exhaust systems. One is the flange type where the component ends are attached with bolts and a gasket in-between. The other exhaust system is the slip joint type. These components slip into one another using clamps to retain them together.

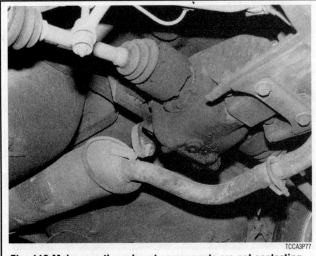
Fig. 112 Make sure the exhaust components are not contacting the body or suspension

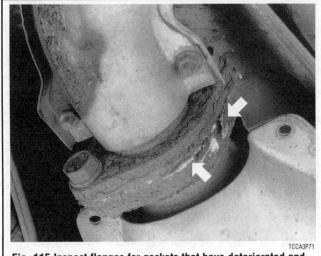
Fig. 115 Inspect flanges for gaskets that have deteriorated and need replacement

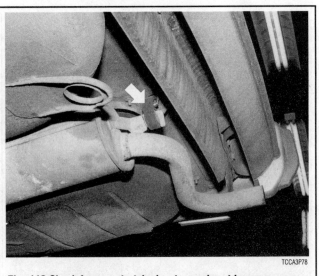
Fig. 113 Check for overstretched or torn exhaust hangers

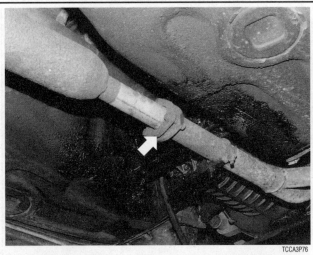
Fig. 116 Some systems, like this one, use large O-rings (donuts) in between the flanges

Fig. 114 Example of a badly deteriorated exhaust pipe

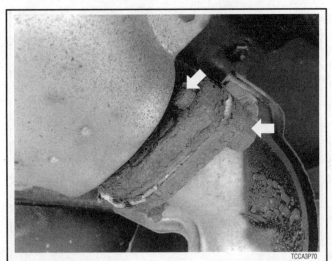
Fig. 117 Nuts and bolts will be extremely difficult to remove when deteriorated with rust

✳✳ CAUTION

Allow the exhaust system to cool sufficiently before spraying a solvent exhaust fasteners. Some solvents are highly flammable and could ignite when sprayed on hot exhaust components.

Before removing any component of the exhaust system, ALWAYS squirt a liquid rust dissolving agent onto the fasteners for ease of removal. A lot of knuckle skin will be saved by following this rule. It may even be wise to spray the fasteners and allow them to sit overnight.

Flange Type

♦ See Figure 118

✳✳ CAUTION

Do NOT perform exhaust repairs or inspection with the engine or exhaust hot. Allow the system to cool completely before attempting any work. Exhaust systems are noted for sharp edges, flaking metal and rusted bolts. Gloves and eye protection are required. A healthy supply of penetrating oil and rags is highly recommended. Never spray liquid rust dissolving agent onto a hot exhaust component.

Before removing any component on a flange type system, ALWAYS squirt

a liquid rust dissolving agent onto the fasteners for ease of removal. Start by unbolting the exhaust piece at both ends (if required). When unbolting the headpipe from the manifold, make sure that the bolts are free before trying to remove them. if you snap a stud in the exhaust manifold, the stud will have to be removed with a bolt extractor, which often means removal of the manifold itself. Next, disconnect the component from the mounting; slight twisting and turning may be required to remove the component completely from the vehicle. You may need to tap on the component with a rubber mallet to loosen the component. If all else fails, use a hacksaw to separate the parts. An oxy-acetylene cutting torch may be faster but the sparks are DANGEROUS near the fuel tank, and at the very least, accidents could happen, resulting in damage to the under-car parts, not to mention yourself.

Slip Joint Type

♦ See Figure 119

Before removing any component on the slip joint type exhaust system, ALWAYS squirt a liquid rust dissolving agent onto the fasteners for ease of removal. Start by unbolting the exhaust piece at both ends (if required). When unbolting the headpipe from the manifold, make sure that the bolts are free before trying to remove them. if you snap a stud in the exhaust manifold, the stud will have to be removed with a bolt extractor, which often means removal of the manifold itself. Next, remove the mounting U-bolts from around the exhaust pipe you are extracting from the vehicle. Don't be surprised if the U-bolts break while removing the nuts. Loosen the exhaust pipe from any mounting brackets retaining it to the floor pan and separate the components.

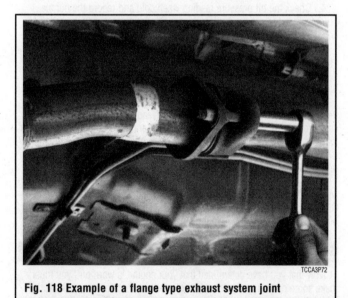

Fig. 118 Example of a flange type exhaust system joint

Fig. 119 Example of a common slip joint type system

ENGINE RECONDITIONING

Determining Engine Condition

Anything that generates heat and/or friction will eventually burn or wear out (i.e., a light bulb generates heat, therefore its life span is limited). With this in mind, a running engine generates tremendous amounts of both; friction is encountered by the moving and rotating parts inside the engine and heat is created by friction and combustion of the fuel. However, the engine has systems designed to help reduce the effects of heat and friction and provide added longevity. The oiling system reduces the amount of friction encountered by the moving parts inside the engine, while the cooling system reduces heat created by friction and combustion. If either system is not maintained, a break-down will be inevitable. Therefore, you can see how regular maintenance can affect the service life of your vehicle. If you do not drain, flush and refill your cooling system at the proper intervals, deposits will begin to accumulate in the radiator, thereby reducing the amount of

heat it can extract from the coolant. The same applies to your oil and filter; if it is not changed often enough it becomes laden with contaminates and is unable to properly lubricate the engine. This increases friction and wear.

There are a number of methods for evaluating the condition of your engine. A compression test can reveal the condition of your pistons, piston rings, cylinder bores, head gasket(s), valves and valve seats. An oil pressure test can warn you of possible engine bearing, or oil pump failures. Excessive oil consumption, evidence of oil in the engine air intake area and/or bluish smoke from the tail pipe may indicate worn piston rings, worn valve guides and/or valve seals. As a general rule, an engine that uses no more than one quart of oil every 1000 miles is in good condition. Engines that use one quart of oil or more in less than 1000 miles should first be checked for oil leaks. If any oil leaks are present, have them fixed before determining how much oil is consumed by the engine, especially if blue smoke is not visible at the tail pipe.

COMPRESSION TEST

◆ **See Figure 120**

A noticeable lack of engine power, excessive oil consumption and/or poor fuel mileage measured over an extended period are all indicators of internal engine wear. Worn piston rings, scored or worn cylinder bores, blown head gaskets, sticking or burnt valves, and worn valve seats are all possible culprits. A check of each cylinder's compression will help locate the problem.

➡ **A screw-in type compression gauge is more accurate than the type you simply hold against the spark plug hole. Although it takes slightly longer to use, it's worth the effort to obtain a more accurate reading.**

1. Make sure that the proper amount and viscosity of engine oil is in the crankcase, then ensure the battery is fully charged.
2. Warm-up the engine to normal operating temperature, then shut the engine **OFF**.
3. Disable the ignition system.
4. Label and disconnect all of the spark plug wires from the plugs.
5. Thoroughly clean the cylinder head area around the spark plug ports, then remove the spark plugs.
6. Set the throttle plate to the fully open (wide-open throttle) position. You can block the accelerator linkage open for this, or you can have an assistant fully depress the accelerator pedal.
7. Install a screw-in type compression gauge into the No. 1 spark plug hole until the fitting is snug.

❋❋ WARNING

Be careful not to crossthread the spark plug hole.

8. According to the tool manufacturer's instructions, connect a remote starting switch to the starting circuit.
9. With the ignition switch in the **OFF** position, use the remote starting switch to crank the engine through at least five compression strokes (approximately 5 seconds of cranking) and record the highest reading on the gauge.
10. Repeat the test on each cylinder, cranking the engine approximately the same number of compression strokes and/or time as the first.
11. Compare the highest readings from each cylinder to that of the others. The indicated compression pressures are considered within specifications if the lowest reading cylinder is within 75 percent of the pressure recorded for the highest reading cylinder. For example, if your highest reading cylinder pressure was 150 psi (1034 kPa), then 75 percent of that would be 113 psi (779 kPa). So the lowest reading cylinder should be no less than 113 psi (779 kPa).

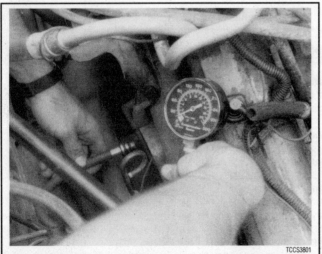

TCCS3801

Fig. 120 A screw-in type compression gauge is more accurate and easier to use without an assistant

12. If a cylinder exhibits an unusually low compression reading, pour a tablespoon of clean engine oil into the cylinder through the spark plug hole and repeat the compression test. If the compression rises after adding oil, it means that the cylinder's piston rings and/or cylinder bore are damaged or worn. If the pressure remains low, the valves may not be seating properly (a valve job is needed), or the head gasket may be blown near that cylinder. If compression in any two adjacent cylinders is low, and if the addition of oil doesn't help raise compression, there is leakage past the head gasket. Oil and coolant in the combustion chamber, combined with blue or constant white smoke from the tail pipe, are symptoms of this problem. However, don't be alarmed by the normal white smoke emitted from the tail pipe during engine warm-up or from cold weather driving. There may be evidence of water droplets on the engine dipstick and/or oil droplets in the cooling system if a head gasket is blown.

OIL PRESSURE TEST

Check for proper oil pressure at the sending unit passage with an externally mounted mechanical oil pressure gauge (as opposed to relying on a factory installed dash-mounted gauge). A tachometer may also be needed, as some specifications may require running the engine at a specific rpm.

1. With the engine cold, locate and remove the oil pressure sending unit.
2. Following the manufacturer's instructions, connect a mechanical oil pressure gauge and, if necessary, a tachometer to the engine.
3. Start the engine and allow it to idle.
4. Check the oil pressure reading when cold and record the number. You may need to run the engine at a specified rpm, so check the specifications chart located earlier in this section.
5. Run the engine until normal operating temperature is reached (upper radiator hose will feel warm).
6. Check the oil pressure reading again with the engine hot and record the number. Turn the engine **OFF**.
7. Compare your hot oil pressure reading to that given in the chart. If the reading is low, check the cold pressure reading against the chart. If the cold pressure is well above the specification, and the hot reading was lower than the specification, you may have the wrong viscosity oil in the engine. Change the oil, making sure to use the proper grade and quantity, then repeat the test.

Low oil pressure readings could be attributed to internal component wear, pump related problems, a low oil level, or oil viscosity that is too low. High oil pressure readings could be caused by an overfilled crankcase, too high of an oil viscosity or a faulty pressure relief valve.

Buy or Rebuild?

Now that you have determined that your engine is worn out, you must make some decisions. The question of whether or not an engine is worth rebuilding is largely a subjective matter and one of personal worth. Is the engine a popular one, or is it an obsolete model? Are parts available? Will it get acceptable gas mileage once it is rebuilt? Is the car it's being put into worth keeping? Would it be less expensive to buy a new engine, have your engine rebuilt by a pro, rebuild it yourself or buy a used engine from a salvage yard? Or would it be simpler and less expensive to buy another car? If you have considered all these matters and more, and have still decided to rebuild the engine, then it is time to decide how you will rebuild it.

➡ **The editors at Chilton feel that most engine machining should be performed by a professional machine shop. Don't think of it as wasting money, rather, as an assurance that the job has been done right the first time. There are many expensive and specialized tools required to perform such tasks as boring and honing an engine block or having a valve job done on a cylinder head. Even inspecting the parts requires expensive micrometers and gauges to properly measure wear and clearances. Also, a machine shop can deliver to you clean, and ready to assemble parts, saving you time and aggravation. Your maximum savings will come from performing the removal, disassembly, assembly and installation of the engine** and purchasing or renting only the tools required to perform the above tasks. Depending on the particular circumstances, you may save 40 to 60 percent of the cost doing these yourself.

A complete rebuild or overhaul of an engine involves replacing all of the moving parts (pistons, rods, crankshaft, camshaft, etc.) with new ones and machining the non-moving wearing surfaces of the block and heads. Unfortunately, this may not be cost effective. For instance, your crankshaft may have been damaged or worn, but it can be machined undersize for a minimal fee.

So, as you can see, you can replace everything inside the engine, but, it is wiser to replace only those parts which are really needed, and, if possible, repair the more expensive ones. Later in this section, we will break the engine down into its two main components: the cylinder head and the engine block. We will discuss each component, and the recommended parts to replace during a rebuild on each.

Engine Overhaul Tips

Most engine overhaul procedures are fairly standard. In addition to specific parts replacement procedures and specifications for your individual engine, this section is also a guide to acceptable rebuilding procedures. Examples of standard rebuilding practice are given and should be used along with specific details concerning your particular engine.

Competent and accurate machine shop services will ensure maximum performance, reliability and engine life. In most instances it is more profitable for the do-it-yourself mechanic to remove, clean and inspect the component, buy the necessary parts and deliver these to a shop for actual machine work.

Much of the assembly work (crankshaft, bearings, piston rods, and other components) is well within the scope of the do-it-yourself mechanic's tools and abilities. You will have to decide for yourself the depth of involvement you desire in an engine repair or rebuild.

TOOLS

The tools required for an engine overhaul or parts replacement will depend on the depth of your involvement. With a few exceptions, they will be the tools found in a mechanic's tool kit (see Section 1 of this manual). More in-depth work will require some or all of the following:
- A dial indicator (reading in thousandths) mounted on a universal base
- Micrometers and telescope gauges
- Jaw and screw-type pullers
- Scraper
- Valve spring compressor
- Ring groove cleaner
- Piston ring expander and compressor
- Ridge reamer
- Cylinder hone or glaze breaker
- Plastigage®
- Engine stand

The use of most of these tools is illustrated in this section. Many can be rented for a one-time use from a local parts jobber or tool supply house specializing in automotive work.

Occasionally, the use of special tools is called for. See the information on Special Tools and the Safety Notice in the front of this book before substituting another tool.

OVERHAUL TIPS

Aluminum has become extremely popular for use in engines, due to its low weight. Observe the following precautions when handling aluminum parts:
- Never hot tank aluminum parts (the caustic hot tank solution will eat the aluminum.
- Remove all aluminum parts (identification tag, etc.) from engine parts prior to the tanking.
- Always coat threads lightly with engine oil or anti-seize compounds before installation, to prevent seizure.

- Never overtighten bolts or spark plugs especially in aluminum threads.

When assembling the engine, any parts that will be exposed to frictional contact must be prelubed to provide lubrication at initial start-up. Any product specifically formulated for this purpose can be used, but engine oil is not recommended as a prelube in most cases.

When semi-permanent (locked, but removable) installation of bolts or nuts is desired, threads should be cleaned and coated with Loctite® or another similar, commercial non-hardening sealant.

CLEANING

♦ **See Figures 121, 122, 123 and 124**

Before the engine and its components are inspected, they must be thoroughly cleaned. You will need to remove any engine varnish, oil sludge and/or carbon deposits from all of the components to insure an accurate inspection. A crack in the engine block or cylinder head can easily become overlooked if hidden by a layer of sludge or carbon.

Most of the cleaning process can be carried out with common hand tools and readily available solvents or solutions. Carbon deposits can be chipped away using a hammer and a hard wooden chisel. Old gasket mater-

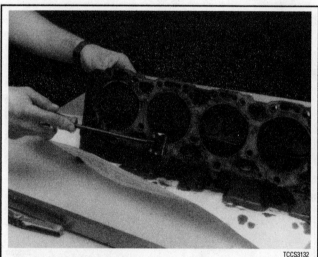

TCCS3132

Fig. 121 Use a gasket scraper to remove the old gasket material from the mating surfaces

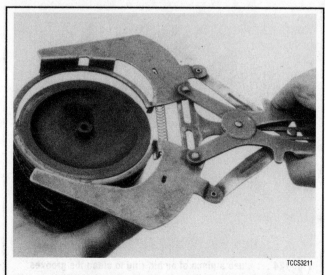

TCCS3211

Fig. 122 Use a ring expander tool to remove the piston rings

ial and varnish or sludge can usually be removed using a scraper and/or cleaning solvent. Extremely stubborn deposits may require the use of a power drill with a wire brush. If using a wire brush, use extreme care around any critical machined surfaces (such as the gasket surfaces, bearing saddles, cylinder bores, etc.). USE OF A WIRE BRUSH IS NOT RECOMMENDED ON ANY ALUMINUM COMPONENTS. Always follow any safety recommendations given by the manufacturer of the tool and/or solvent. You should always wear eye protection during any cleaning process involving scraping, chipping or spraying of solvents.

An alternative to the mess and hassle of cleaning the parts yourself is to drop them off at a local garage or machine shop. They will, more than likely, have the necessary equipment to properly clean all of the parts for a nominal fee.

✳✳ CAUTION

Always wear eye protection during any cleaning process involving scraping, chipping or spraying of solvents.

Remove any oil galley plugs, freeze plugs and/or pressed-in bearings and carefully wash and degrease all of the engine components including the fasteners and bolts. Small parts such as the valves, springs, etc.,

should be placed in a metal basket and allowed to soak. Use pipe cleaner type brushes, and clean all passageways in the components. Use a ring expander and remove the rings from the pistons. Clean the piston ring grooves with a special tool or a piece of broken ring. Scrape the carbon off of the top of the piston. You should never use a wire brush on the pistons. After preparing all of the piston assemblies in this manner, wash and degrease them again.

✳✳ WARNING

Use extreme care when cleaning around the cylinder head valve seats. A mistake or slip may cost you a new seat.

When cleaning the cylinder head, remove carbon from the combustion chamber with the valves installed. This will avoid damaging the valve seats.

REPAIRING DAMAGED THREADS

▶ **See Figures 125, 126, 127, 128 and 129**

Several methods of repairing damaged threads are available. Heli-Coil® (shown here), Keenserts® and Microdot® are among the most widely used.

Fig. 123 Clean the piston ring grooves using a ring groove cleaner tool, or . . .

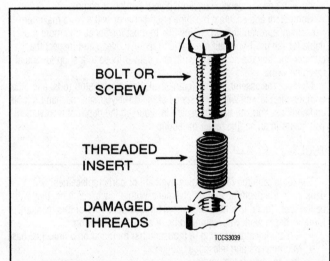

Fig. 125 Damaged bolt hole threads can be replaced with thread repair inserts

Fig. 124 . . . use a piece of an old ring to clean the grooves. Be careful, the ring can be quite sharp

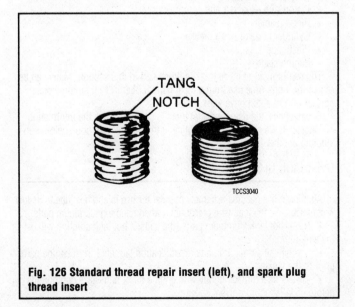

Fig. 126 Standard thread repair insert (left), and spark plug thread insert

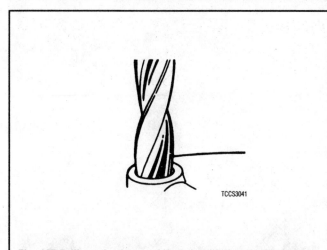

Fig. 127 Drill out the damaged threads with the specified size bit. Be sure to drill completely through the hole or to the bottom of a blind hole

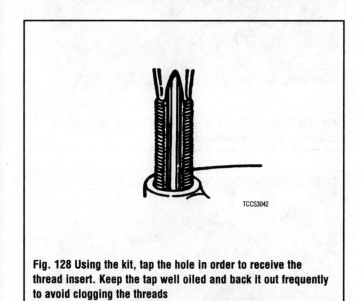

Fig. 128 Using the kit, tap the hole in order to receive the thread insert. Keep the tap well oiled and back it out frequently to avoid clogging the threads

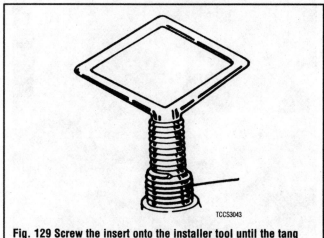

Fig. 129 Screw the insert onto the installer tool until the tang engages the slot. Thread the insert into the hole until it is ¼–½ turn below the top surface, then remove the tool and break off the tang using a punch

All involve basically the same principle—drilling out stripped threads, tapping the hole and installing a prewound insert—making welding, plugging and oversize fasteners unnecessary.

Two types of thread repair inserts are usually supplied: a standard type for most inch coarse, inch fine, metric course and metric fine thread sizes and a spark lug type to fit most spark plug port sizes. Consult the individual tool manufacturer's catalog to determine exact applications. Typical thread repair kits will contain a selection of prewound threaded inserts, a tap (corresponding to the outside diameter threads of the insert) and an installation tool. Spark plug inserts usually differ because they require a tap equipped with pilot threads and a combined reamer/tap section. Most manufacturers also supply blister-packed thread repair inserts separately in addition to a master kit containing a variety of taps and inserts plus installation tools.

Before attempting to repair a threaded hole, remove any snapped, broken or damaged bolts or studs. Penetrating oil can be used to free frozen threads. The offending item can usually be removed with locking pliers or using a screw/stud extractor. After the hole is clear, the thread can be repaired, as shown in the series of accompanying illustrations and in the kit manufacturer's instructions.

Engine Preparation

To properly rebuild an engine, you must first remove it from the vehicle, then disassemble and diagnose it. Ideally you should place your engine on an engine stand. This affords you the best access to the engine components. Follow the manufacturer's directions for using the stand with your particular engine. Remove the flywheel or flexplate before installing the engine to the stand.

Now that you have the engine on a stand, and assuming that you have drained the oil and coolant from the engine, it's time to strip it of all but the necessary components. Before you start disassembling the engine, you may want to take a moment to draw some pictures, or fabricate some labels or containers to mark the locations of various components and the bolts and/or studs which fasten them. Modern day engines use a lot of little brackets and clips which hold wiring harnesses and such, and these holders are often mounted on studs and/or bolts that can be easily mixed up. The manufacturer spent a lot of time and money designing your vehicle, and they wouldn't have wasted any of it by haphazardly placing brackets, clips or fasteners on the vehicle. If it's present when you disassemble it, put it back when you assemble, you will regret not remembering that little bracket which holds a wire harness out of the path of a rotating part.

You should begin by unbolting any accessories still attached to the engine, such as the water pump, power steering pump, alternator, etc. Then, unfasten any manifolds (intake or exhaust) which were not removed during the engine removal procedure. Finally, remove any covers remaining on the engine such as the rocker arm, front or timing cover and oil pan. Some front covers may require the vibration damper and/or crank pulley to be removed beforehand. The idea is to reduce the engine to the bare necessities (cylinder head, valve train, engine block, crankshaft, pistons and connecting rods), plus any other "in block" components such as oil pump, balance shafts and auxiliary shafts.

Finally, remove the cylinder head from the engine block and carefully place on a bench. Disassembly instructions for each component follow later in this section.

Cylinder Head

There are two basic types of cylinder heads used on today's automobiles: the Overhead Valve (OHV) and the Overhead Camshaft (OHC). The latter can also be broken down into two subgroups: the Single Overhead Camshaft (SOHC) and the Dual Overhead Camshaft (DOHC). Generally, if there is only a single camshaft on a head, it is just referred to as an OHC head. Also, an engine with a OHV cylinder head is also known as a pushrod engine.

Most cylinder heads these days are made of an aluminum alloy due to its light weight, durability and heat transfer qualities. However, cast iron was the material of choice in the past, and is still used on many vehicles today. Whether made from aluminum or iron, all cylinder heads have valves and seats. Some use two valves per cylinder, while the more hi-tech engines will utilize a multi-valve configuration using 3, 4 and even 5 valves per cylinder. When the valve contacts the seat, it does so on precision machined surfaces, which seals the combustion chamber. All cylinder heads have a valve guide for each valve. The guide centers the valve to the seat and allows it to move up and down within it. The clearance between the valve and guide can be critical. Too much clearance and the engine may consume oil, lose vacuum and/or damage the seat. Too little, and the valve can stick in the guide causing the engine to run poorly if at all, and possibly causing severe damage. The last component all cylinder heads have are valve springs. The spring holds the valve against its seat. It also returns the valve to this position when the valve has been opened by the valve train or camshaft. The spring is fastened to the valve by a retainer and valve locks (sometimes called keepers). Aluminum heads will also have a valve spring shim to keep the spring from wearing away the aluminum.

An ideal method of rebuilding the cylinder head would involve replacing all of the valves, guides, seats, springs, etc. with new ones. However, depending on how the engine was maintained, often this is not necessary. A major cause of valve, guide and seat wear is an improperly tuned engine. An engine that is running too rich, will often wash the lubricating oil out of the guide with gasoline, causing it to wear rapidly. Conversely, an engine which is running too lean will place higher combustion temperatures on the valves and seats allowing them to wear or even burn. Springs fall victim to the driving habits of the individual. A driver who often runs the engine rpm to the redline will wear out or break the springs faster then one that stays well below it. Unfortunately, mileage takes it toll on all of the parts. Generally, the valves, guides, springs and seats in a cylinder head can be machined and re-used, saving you money. However, if a valve is burnt, it may be wise to replace all of the valves, since they were all operating in the same environment. The same goes for any other component on the cylinder head. Think of it as an insurance policy against future problems related to that component.

Unfortunately, the only way to find out which components need replacing, is to disassemble and carefully check each piece. After the cylinder head is disassembled, thoroughly clean all of the components.

DISASSEMBLY

▶ **See Figures 130 and 131**

Whether it is a single or dual overhead camshaft cylinder head, the disassembly procedure is relatively unchanged. One aspect to pay attention to is careful labeling of the parts on the dual camshaft cylinder head. There will be an intake camshaft and followers as well as an exhaust camshaft and followers and they must be labeled as such. In some cases, the components are identical and could easily be installed incorrectly. DO NOT MIX THEM UP! Determining which is which is very simple; the intake camshaft and components are on the same side of the head as was the intake manifold. Conversely, the exhaust camshaft and components are on the same side of the head as was the exhaust manifold.

Cup Type Camshaft Followers

▶ **See Figures 132, 133 and 134**

Most cylinder heads with cup type camshaft followers will have the valve spring, retainer and locks recessed within the follower's bore. You will need a C-clamp style valve spring compressor tool, an OHC spring removal tool (or equivalent) and a small magnet to disassemble the head.

1. If not already removed, remove the camshaft(s) and/or followers. Mark their positions for assembly.
2. Position the cylinder head to allow use of a C-clamp style valve spring compressor tool.

➡**It is preferred to position the cylinder head gasket surface facing you with the valve springs facing the opposite direction and the head laying horizontal.**

TCCA3P54

Fig. 130 Exploded view of a valve, seal, spring, retainer and locks from an OHC cylinder head

TCCA3P62

Fig. 131 Example of a multi-valve cylinder head. Note how it has 2 intake and 2 exhaust valve ports

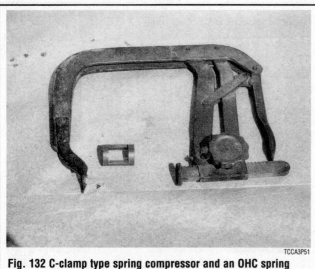

Fig. 132 C-clamp type spring compressor and an OHC spring removal tool (center) for cup type followers

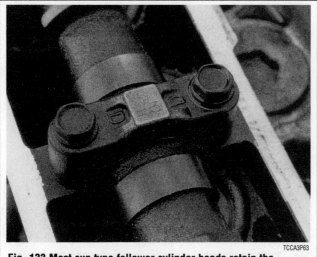

Fig. 133 Most cup type follower cylinder heads retain the camshaft using bolt-on bearing caps

Fig. 134 Position the OHC spring tool in the follower bore, then compress the spring with a C-clamp type tool

3. With the OHC spring removal adapter tool positioned inside of the follower bore, compress the valve spring using the C-clamp style valve spring compressor.

4. Remove the valve locks. A small magnetic tool or screwdriver will aid in removal.

5. Release the compressor tool and remove the spring assembly.

6. Withdraw the valve from the cylinder head.

7. If equipped, remove the valve seal.

➠Special valve seal removal tools are available. Regular or needle nose type pliers, if used with care, will work just as well. If using ordinary pliers, be sure not to damage the follower bore. The follower and its bore are machined to close tolerances and any damage to the bore will effect this relationship.

8. If equipped, remove the valve spring shim. A small magnetic tool or screwdriver will aid in removal.

9. Repeat Steps 3 through 8 until all of the valves have been removed.

Valves

▶ See Figures 135 and 136

The first thing to inspect are the valve heads. Look closely at the head, margin and face for any cracks, excessive wear or burning. The margin is the best place to look for burning. It should have a squared edge with an even width all around the diameter. When a valve burns, the margin will look melted and the edges rounded. Also inspect the valve head for any signs of tulipping. This will show as a lifting of the edges or dishing in the center of the head and will usually not occur to all of the valves. All of the heads should look the same, any that seem dished more than others are probably bad. Next, inspect the valve lock grooves and valve tips. Check for any burrs around the lock grooves, especially if you had to file them to remove the valve. Valve tips should appear flat, although slight rounding with high mileage engines is normal. Slightly worn valve tips will need to be machined flat. Last, measure the valve stem diameter with the micrometer. Measure the area that rides within the guide, especially towards the tip where most of the wear occurs. Take several measurements along its length and compare them to each other. Wear should be even along the length with little to no taper. If no minimum diameter is given in the specifications, then the stem should not read more than 0.001 in. (0.025mm) below the specification. Any valves that fail these inspections should be replaced.

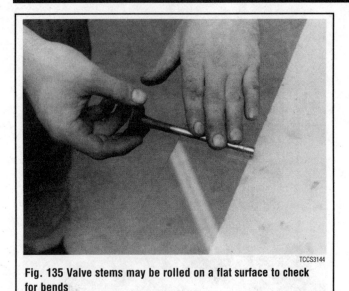

Fig. 135 Valve stems may be rolled on a flat surface to check for bends

Fig. 137 Use a caliper to check the valve spring free-length

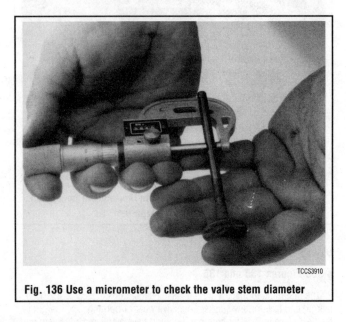

Fig. 136 Use a micrometer to check the valve stem diameter

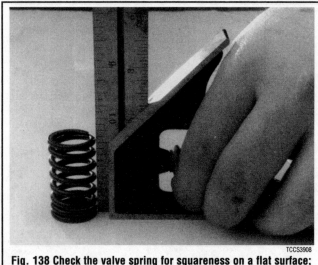

Fig. 138 Check the valve spring for squareness on a flat surface; a carpenter's square can be used

Springs, Retainers and Valve Locks

▶ See Figures 137 and 138

The first thing to check is the most obvious, broken springs. Next check the free length and squareness of each spring. If applicable, insure to distinguish between intake and exhaust springs. Use a ruler and/or carpenter's square to measure the length. A carpenter's square should be used to check the springs for squareness. If a spring pressure test gauge is available, check each springs rating and compare to the specifications chart. Check the readings against the specifications given. Any springs that fail these inspections should be replaced.

The spring retainers rarely need replacing, however they should still be checked as a precaution. Inspect the spring mating surface and the valve lock retention area for any signs of excessive wear. Also check for any signs of cracking. Replace any retainers that are questionable.

Valve locks should be inspected for excessive wear on the outside contact area as well as on the inner notched surface. Any locks which appear worn or broken and its respective valve should be replaced.

Cylinder Head

There are several things to check on the cylinder head: valve guides, seats, cylinder head surface flatness, cracks and physical damage.

VALVE GUIDES

▶ See Figure 139

Now that you know the valves are good, you can use them to check the guides, although a new valve, if available, is preferred. Before you measure anything, look at the guides carefully and inspect them for any cracks, chips or breakage. Also if the guide is a removable style (as in most aluminum heads), check them for any looseness or evidence of movement. All of the guides should appear to be at the same height from the spring seat. If any seem lower (or higher) from another, the guide has moved. Mount a dial indicator onto the spring side of the cylinder head. Lightly oil the valve stem and insert it into the cylinder head. Position the dial indicator against the valve stem near the tip and zero the gauge. Grasp the valve stem and wiggle towards and away from the dial indicator and observe the readings.

TCCS3142

Fig. 139 A dial gauge may be used to check valve stem-to-guide clearance; read the gauge while moving the valve stem

Mount the dial indicator 90 degrees from the initial point and zero the gauge and again take a reading. Compare the two readings for a out of round condition. Check the readings against the specifications given. An Inside Diameter (I.D.) gauge designed for valve guides will give you an accurate valve guide bore measurement. If the I.D. gauge is used, compare the readings with the specifications given. Any guides that fail these inspections should be replaced or machined.

VALVE SEATS

A visual inspection of the valve seats should show a slightly worn and pitted surface where the valve face contacts the seat. Inspect the seat carefully for severe pitting or cracks. Also, a seat that is badly worn will be recessed into the cylinder head. A severely worn or recessed seat may need to be replaced. All cracked seats must be replaced. A seat concentricity gauge, if available, should be used to check the seat run-out. If run-out exceeds specifications the seat must be machined (if no specification is given use 0.002 in. or 0.051mm).

CYLINDER HEAD SURFACE FLATNESS

▶ See Figures 140 and 141

After you have cleaned the gasket surface of the cylinder head of any old gasket material, check the head for flatness.

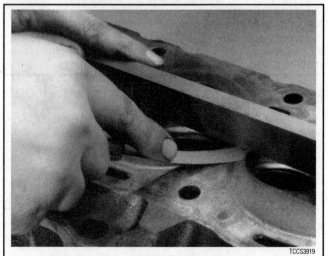

TCCS3919

Fig. 140 Check the head for flatness across the center of the head surface using a straightedge and feeler gauge

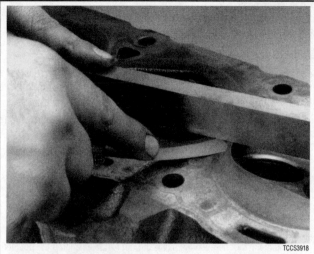

TCCS3918

Fig. 141 Checks should also be made along both diagonals of the head surface

Place a straightedge across the gasket surface. Using feeler gauges, determine the clearance at the center of the straightedge and across the cylinder head at several points. Check along the centerline and diagonally on the head surface. If the warpage exceeds 0.003 in. (0.076mm) within a 6.0 in. (15.2cm) span, or 0.006 in. (0.152mm) over the total length of the head, the cylinder head must be resurfaced. After resurfacing the heads of a V-type engine, the intake manifold flange surface should be checked, and if necessary, milled proportionally to allow for the change in its mounting position.

CRACKS AND PHYSICAL DAMAGE

Generally, cracks are limited to the combustion chamber, however, it is not uncommon for the head to crack in a spark plug hole, port, outside of the head or in the valve spring/rocker arm area. The first area to inspect is always the hottest: the exhaust seat/port area.

A visual inspection should be performed, but just because you don't see a crack does not mean it is not there. Some more reliable methods for inspecting for cracks include Magnaflux®, a magnetic process or Zyglo®, a dye penetrant. Magnaflux® is used only on ferrous metal (cast iron) heads. Zyglo® uses a spray on fluorescent mixture along with a black light to reveal the cracks. It is strongly recommended to have your cylinder head checked professionally for cracks, especially if the engine was known to have overheated and/or leaked or consumed coolant. Contact a local shop for availability and pricing of these services.

Physical damage is usually very evident. For example, a broken mounting ear from dropping the head or a bent or broken stud and/or bolt. All of these defects should be fixed or, if unrepairable, the head should be replaced.

Camshaft and Followers

Inspect the camshaft(s) and followers as described earlier in this section.

REFINISHING & REPAIRING

Many of the procedures given for refinishing and repairing the cylinder head components must be performed by a machine shop. Certain steps, if the inspected part is not worn, can be performed yourself inexpensively. However, you spent a lot of time and effort so far, why risk trying to save a couple bucks if you might have to do it all over again?

Valves

Any valves that were not replaced should be refaced and the tips ground flat. Unless you have access to a valve grinding machine, this should be done by a machine shop. If the valves are in extremely good condition, as well as the valve seats and guides, they may be lapped in without performing machine work.

It is a recommended practice to lap the valves even after machine work has been performed and/or new valves have been purchased. This insures a positive seal between the valve and seat.

LAPPING THE VALVES

→Before lapping the valves to the seats, read the rest of the cylinder head section to insure that any related parts are in acceptable enough condition to continue.

→Before any valve seat machining and/or lapping can be performed, the guides must be within factory recommended specifications.

1. Invert the cylinder head.
2. Lightly lubricate the valve stems and insert them into the cylinder head in their numbered order.
3. Raise the valve from the seat and apply a small amount of fine lapping compound to the seat.
4. Moisten the suction head of a hand-lapping tool and attach it to the head of the valve.
5. Rotate the tool between the palms of both hands, changing the position of the valve on the valve seat and lifting the tool often to prevent grooving.
6. Lap the valve until a smooth, polished circle is evident on the valve and seat.
7. Remove the tool and the valve. Wipe away all traces of the grinding compound and store the valve to maintain its lapped location.

❊❊❊ WARNING

Do not get the valves out of order after they have been lapped. They must be put back with the same valve seat they were lapped with.

Springs, Retainers and Valve Locks

There is no repair or refinishing possible with the springs, retainers and valve locks. If they are found to be worn or defective, they must be replaced with new (or known good) parts.

Cylinder Head

Most refinishing procedures dealing with the cylinder head must be performed by a machine shop. Read the sections below and review your inspection data to determine whether or not machining is necessary.

VALVE GUIDES

→If any machining or replacements are made to the valve guides, the seats must be machined.

Unless the valve guides need machining or replacing, the only service to perform is to thoroughly clean them of any dirt or oil residue.

There are only two types of valve guides used on automobile engines: the replaceable-type (all aluminum heads) and the cast-in integral-type (most cast iron heads). There are four recommended methods for repairing worn guides.
- Knurling
- Inserts
- Reaming oversize
- Replacing

Knurling is a process in which metal is displaced and raised, thereby reducing clearance, giving a true center, and providing oil control. It is the least expensive way of repairing the valve guides. However, it is not necessarily the best, and in some cases, a knurled valve guide will not stand up for more than a short time. It requires a special knurlizer and precision reaming tools to obtain proper clearances. It would not be cost effective to purchase these tools, unless you plan on rebuilding several of the same cylinder head.

Installing a guide insert involves machining the guide to accept a bronze insert. One style is the coil-type which is installed into a threaded guide. Another is the thin-walled insert where the guide is reamed oversize to accept a split-sleeve insert. After the insert is installed, a special tool is then run through the guide to expand the insert, locking it to the guide. The insert is then reamed to the standard size for proper valve clearance.

Reaming for oversize valves restores normal clearances and provides a true valve seat. Most cast-in type guides can be reamed to accept an valve with an oversize stem. The cost factor for this can become quite high as you will need to purchase the reamer and new, oversize stem valves for all guides which were reamed. Oversizes are generally 0.003 to 0.030 in. (0.076 to 0.762mm), with 0.015 in. (0.381mm) being the most common.

To replace cast-in type valve guides, they must be drilled out, then reamed to accept replacement guides. This must be done on a fixture which will allow centering and leveling off of the original valve seat or guide, otherwise a serious guide-to-seat misalignment may occur making it impossible to properly machine the seat.

Replaceable-type guides are pressed into the cylinder head. A hammer and a stepped drift or punch may be used to install and remove the guides. Before removing the guides, measure the protrusion on the spring side of the head and record it for installation. Use the stepped drift to hammer out the old guide from the combustion chamber side of the head. When installing, determine whether or not the guide also seals a water jacket in the head, and if it does, use the recommended sealing agent. If there is no water jacket, grease the valve guide and its bore. Use the stepped drift, and hammer the new guide into the cylinder head from the spring side of the cylinder head. A stack of washers the same thickness as the measured protrusion may help the installation process.

VALVE SEATS

→Before any valve seat machining can be performed, the guides must be within factory recommended specifications.

→If any machining or replacements were made to the valve guides, the seats must be machined.

If the seats are in good condition, the valves can be lapped to the seats, and the cylinder head assembled. See the valves section for instructions on lapping.

If the valve seats are worn, cracked or damaged, they must be serviced by a machine shop. The valve seat must be perfectly centered to the valve guide, which requires very accurate machining.

CYLINDER HEAD SURFACE

If the cylinder head is warped, it must be machined flat. If the warpage is extremely severe, the head may need to be replaced. In some instances, it may be possible to straighten a warped head enough to allow machining. In either case, contact a professional machine shop for service.

→Any OHC cylinder head that shows excessive warpage should have the camshaft bearing journals align bored after the cylinder head has been resurfaced.

❊❊❊ WARNING

Failure to align bore the camshaft bearing journals could result in severe engine damage including but not limited to: valve and piston damage, connecting rod damage, camshaft and/or crankshaft breakage.

CRACKS AND PHYSICAL DAMAGE

Certain cracks can be repaired in both cast iron and aluminum heads. For cast iron, a tapered threaded insert is installed along the length of the crack. Aluminum can also use the tapered inserts, however welding is the preferred method. Some physical damage can be repaired through brazing or welding. Contact a machine shop to get expert advice for your particular dilemma.

ASSEMBLY

◊ See Figure 142

The first step for any assembly job is to have a clean area in which to work. Next, thoroughly clean all of the parts and components that are to be assembled. Finally, place all of the components onto a suitable work space and, if necessary, arrange the parts to their respective positions.

Cup Type Camshaft Followers

To install the springs, retainers and valve locks on heads which have these components recessed into the camshaft follower's bore, you will need a small screwdriver-type tool, some clean white grease and a lot of patience. You will also need the C-clamp style spring compressor and the OHC tool used to disassemble the head.

1. Lightly lubricate the valve stems and insert all of the valves into the cylinder head. If possible, maintain their original locations.
2. If equipped, install any valve spring shims which were removed.
3. If equipped, install the new valve seals, keeping the following in mind:
   • If the valve seal presses over the guide, lightly lubricate the outer guide surfaces.
   • If the seal is an O-ring type, it is installed just after compressing the spring but before the valve locks.
4. Place the valve spring and retainer over the stem.
5. Position the spring compressor and the OHC tool, then compress the spring.
6. Using a small screwdriver as a spatula, fill the valve stem side of the lock with white grease. Use the excess grease on the screwdriver to fasten the lock to the driver.
7. Carefully install the valve lock, which is stuck to the end of the screwdriver, to the valve stem then press on it with the screwdriver until the grease squeezes out. The valve lock should now be stuck to the stem.
8. Repeat Steps 6 and 7 for the remaining valve lock.
9. Relieve the spring pressure slowly and insure that neither valve lock becomes dislodged by the retainer.
10. Remove the spring compressor tool.
11. Repeat Steps 2 through 10 until all of the springs have been installed.
12. Install the followers, camshaft(s) and any other components that were removed for disassembly.

Fig. 142 Once assembled, check the valve clearance and correct as needed

Engine Block

GENERAL INFORMATION

A thorough overhaul or rebuild of an engine block would include replacing the pistons, rings, bearings, timing belt/chain assembly and oil pump. For OHV engines also include a new camshaft and lifters. The block would then have the cylinders bored and honed oversize (or if using removable cylinder sleeves, new sleeves installed) and the crankshaft

would be cut undersize to provide new wearing surfaces and perfect clearances. However, your particular engine may not have everything worn out. What if only the piston rings have worn out and the clearances on everything else are still within factory specifications? Well, you could just replace the rings and put it back together, but this would be a very rare example. Chances are, if one component in your engine is worn, other components are sure to follow, and soon. At the very least, you should always replace the rings, bearings and oil pump. This is what is commonly called a "freshen up".

Cylinder Ridge Removal

Because the top piston ring does not travel to the very top of the cylinder, a ridge is built up between the end of the travel and the top of the cylinder bore.

Pushing the piston and connecting rod assembly past the ridge can be difficult, and damage to the piston ring lands could occur. If the ridge is not removed before installing a new piston or not removed at all, piston ring breakage and piston damage may occur.

➡It is always recommended that you remove any cylinder ridges before removing the piston and connecting rod assemblies. If you know that new pistons are going to be installed and the engine block will be bored oversize, you may be able to forego this step. However, some ridges may actually prevent the assemblies from being removed, necessitating its removal.

There are several different types of ridge reamers on the market, none of which are inexpensive. Unless a great deal of engine rebuilding is anticipated, borrow or rent a reamer.

1. Turn the crankshaft until the piston is at the bottom of its travel.
2. Cover the head of the piston with a rag.
3. Follow the tool manufacturers instructions and cut away the ridge, exercising extreme care to avoid cutting too deeply.
4. Remove the ridge reamer, the rag and as many of the cuttings as possible. Continue until all of the cylinder ridges have been removed.

DISASSEMBLY

♦ See Figures 143 and 144

The engine disassembly instructions following assume that you have the engine mounted on an engine stand. If not, it is easiest to disassemble the engine on a bench or the floor with it resting on the bellhousing or transmission mounting surface. You must be able to access the connecting rod fasteners and turn the crankshaft during disassembly. Also, all engine covers (timing, front, side, oil pan, whatever) should have already been

Fig. 143 Place rubber hose over the connecting rod studs to protect the crankshaft and cylinder bores from damage

removed. Engines which are seized or locked up may not be able to be completely disassembled, and a core (salvage yard) engine should be purchased.

If not done during the cylinder head removal, remove the timing chain/belt and/or gear/sprocket assembly. Remove the oil pick-up and pump assembly and, if necessary, the pump drive. If equipped, remove any balance or auxiliary shafts. If necessary, remove the cylinder ridge from the top of the bore. See the cylinder ridge removal procedure earlier in this section.

Rotate the engine over so that the crankshaft is exposed. Use a number punch or scribe and mark each connecting rod with its respective cylinder number. The cylinder closest to the front of the engine is always number 1. However, depending on the engine placement, the front of the engine could either be the flywheel or damper/pulley end. Generally the front of the engine faces the front of the vehicle. Use a number punch or scribe and also mark the main bearing caps from front to rear with the front most cap being number 1 (if there are five caps, mark them 1 through 5, front to rear).

❊❊ WARNING

Take special care when pushing the connecting rod up from the crankshaft because the sharp threads of the rod bolts/studs will score the crankshaft journal. Insure that special plastic caps are installed over them, or cut two pieces of rubber hose to do the same.

Again, rotate the engine, this time to position the number one cylinder bore (head surface) up. Turn the crankshaft until the number one piston is at the bottom of its travel, this should allow the maximum access to its connecting rod. Remove the number one connecting rods fasteners and cap

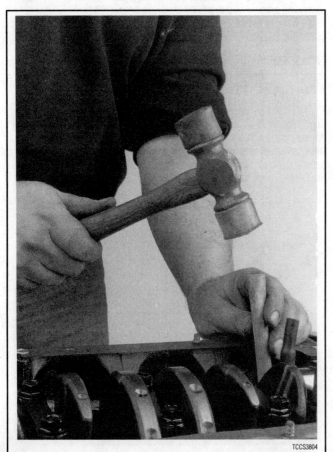

TCCS3804

Fig. 144 Carefully tap the piston out of the bore using a wooden dowel

and place two lengths of rubber hose over the rod bolts/studs to protect the crankshaft from damage. Using a sturdy wooden dowel and a hammer, push the connecting rod up about 1 in. (25mm) from the crankshaft and remove the upper bearing insert. Continue pushing or tapping the connecting rod up until the piston rings are out of the cylinder bore. Remove the piston and rod by hand, put the upper half of the bearing insert back into the rod, install the cap with its bearing insert installed, and hand-tighten the cap fasteners. If the parts are kept in order in this manner, they will not get lost and you will be able to tell which bearings came form what cylinder if any problems are discovered and diagnosis is necessary. Remove all the other piston assemblies in the same manner. On V-style engines, remove all of the pistons from one bank, then reposition the engine with the other cylinder bank head surface up, and remove that banks piston assemblies.

The only remaining component in the engine block should now be the crankshaft. Loosen the main bearing caps evenly until the fasteners can be turned by hand, then remove them and the caps. Remove the crankshaft from the engine block. Thoroughly clean all of the components.

INSPECTION

Now that the engine block and all of its components are clean, it's time to inspect them for wear and/or damage. To accurately inspect them, you will need some specialized tools:

• Two or three separate micrometers to measure the pistons and crankshaft journals
• A dial indicator
• Telescoping gauges for the cylinder bores
• A rod alignment fixture to check for bent connecting rods

If you do not have access to the proper tools, you may want to bring the components to a shop that does.

Generally, you shouldn't expect cracks in the engine block or its components unless it was known to leak, consume or mix engine fluids, it was severely overheated, or there was evidence of bad bearings and/or crankshaft damage. A visual inspection should be performed on all of the components, but just because you don't see a crack does not mean it is not there. Some more reliable methods for inspecting for cracks include Magnaflux®, a magnetic process or Zyglo®, a dye penetrant. Magnaflux® is used only on ferrous metal (cast iron). Zyglo® uses a spray on fluorescent mixture along with a black light to reveal the cracks. It is strongly recommended to have your engine block checked professionally for cracks, especially if the engine was known to have overheated and/or leaked or consumed coolant. Contact a local shop for availability and pricing of these services.

Engine Block

ENGINE BLOCK BEARING ALIGNMENT

Remove the main bearing caps and, if still installed, the main bearing inserts. Inspect all of the main bearing saddles and caps for damage, burrs or high spots. If damage is found, and it is caused from a spun main bearing, the block will need to be align-bored or, if severe enough, replacement. Any burrs or high spots should be carefully removed with a metal file.

Place a straightedge on the bearing saddles, in the engine block, along the centerline of the crankshaft. If any clearance exists between the straightedge and the saddles, the block must be align-bored.

Align-boring consists of machining the main bearing saddles and caps by means of a flycutter that runs through the bearing saddles.

DECK FLATNESS

The top of the engine block where the cylinder head mounts is called the deck. Insure that the deck surface is clean of dirt, carbon deposits and old gasket material. Place a straightedge across the surface of the deck along its centerline and, using feeler gauges, check the clearance along several points. Repeat the checking procedure with the straightedge placed along both diagonals of the deck surface. If the reading exceeds 0.003 in. (0.076mm) within a 6.0 in. (15.2cm) span, or 0.006 in. (0.152mm) over the total length of the deck, it must be machined.

CYLINDER BORES

▶ See Figure 145

The cylinder bores house the pistons and are slightly larger than the pistons themselves. A common piston-to-bore clearance is 0.0015–0.0025 in. (0.0381mm–0.0635mm). Inspect and measure the cylinder bores. The bore should be checked for out-of-roundness, taper and size. The results of this inspection will determine whether the cylinder can be used in its existing size and condition, or a rebore to the next oversize is required (or in the case of removable sleeves, have replacements installed).

The amount of cylinder wall wear is always greater at the top of the cylinder than at the bottom. This wear is known as taper. Any cylinder that has a taper of 0.0012 in. (0.305mm) or more, must be rebored. Measurements are taken at a number of positions in each cylinder: at the top, middle and bottom and at two points at each position; that is, at a point 90 degrees from the crankshaft centerline, as well as a point parallel to the crankshaft centerline. The measurements are made with either a special dial indicator or a telescopic gauge and micrometer. If the necessary precision tools to check the bore are not available, take the block to a machine shop and have them mike it. Also if you don't have the tools to check the cylinder bores, chances are you will not have the necessary devices to check the pistons, connecting rods and crankshaft. Take these components with you and save yourself an extra trip.

For our procedures, we will use a telescopic gauge and a micrometer. You will need one of each, with a measuring range which covers your cylinder bore size.

1. Position the telescopic gauge in the cylinder bore, loosen the gauges lock and allow it to expand.

➡Your first two readings will be at the top of the cylinder bore, then proceed to the middle and finally the bottom, making a total of six measurements.

2. Hold the gauge square in the bore, 90 degrees from the crankshaft centerline, and gently tighten the lock. Tilt the gauge back to remove it from the bore.

3. Measure the gauge with the micrometer and record the reading.

4. Again, hold the gauge square in the bore, this time parallel to the crankshaft centerline, and gently tighten the lock. Again, you will tilt the gauge back to remove it from the bore.

5. Measure the gauge with the micrometer and record this reading. The difference between these two readings is the out-of-round measurement of the cylinder.

6. Repeat steps 1 through 5, each time going to the next lower position, until you reach the bottom of the cylinder. Then go to the next cylinder, and continue until all of the cylinders have been measured.

The difference between these measurements will tell you all about the wear in your cylinders. The measurements which were taken 90 degrees from the crankshaft centerline will always reflect the most wear. That is because at this position is where the engine power presses the piston against the cylinder bore the hardest. This is known as thrust wear. Take your top, 90 degree measurement and compare it to your bottom, 90 degree measurement. The difference between them is the taper. When you measure your pistons, you will compare these readings to your piston sizes and determine piston-to-wall clearance.

Crankshaft

Inspect the crankshaft for visible signs of wear or damage. All of the journals should be perfectly round and smooth. Slight scores are normal for a used crankshaft, but you should hardly feel them with your fingernail. When measuring the crankshaft with a micrometer, you will take readings at the front and rear of each journal, then turn the micrometer 90 degrees and take two more readings, front and rear. The difference between the front-to-rear readings is the journal taper and the first-to-90 degree reading is the out-of-round measurement. Generally, there should be no taper or out-of-roundness found, however, up to 0.0005 in. (0.0127mm) for either can be overlooked. Also, the readings should fall within the factory specifications for journal diameters.

If the crankshaft journals fall within specifications, it is recommended that it be polished before being returned to service. Polishing the crankshaft insures that any minor burrs or high spots are smoothed, thereby reducing the chance of scoring the new bearings.

Pistons and Connecting Rods

PISTONS

▶ See Figure 146

The piston should be visually inspected for any signs of cracking or burning (caused by hot spots or detonation), and scuffing or excessive wear on the skirts. The wristpin attaches the piston to the connecting rod. The piston should move freely on the wrist pin, both sliding and pivoting. Grasp the connecting rod securely, or mount it in a vise, and try to rock the piston back and forth along the centerline of the wristpin. There should not be any excessive play evident between the piston and the pin. If there are C-clips retaining the pin in the piston then you have wrist pin bushings in the rods. There should not be any excessive play between the wrist pin and the rod bushing. Normal clearance for the wrist pin is approx. 0.001–0.002 in. (0.025mm–0.051mm).

Use a micrometer and measure the diameter of the piston, perpendicular to the wrist pin, on the skirt. Compare the reading to its original cylinder

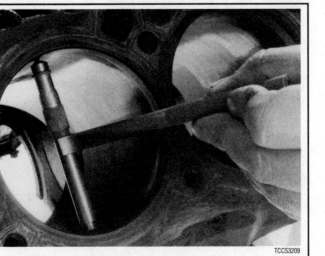

TCCS3209

Fig. 145 Use a telescoping gauge to measure the cylinder bore diameter—take several readings within the same bore

TCCS3210

Fig. 146 Measure the piston's outer diameter, perpendicular to the wrist pin, with a micrometer

measurement obtained earlier. The difference between the two readings is the piston-to-wall clearance. If the clearance is within specifications, the piston may be used as is. If the piston is out of specification, but the bore is not, you will need a new piston. If both are out of specification, you will need the cylinder rebored and oversize pistons installed. Generally if two or more pistons/bores are out of specification, it is best to rebore the entire block and purchase a complete set of oversize pistons.

CONNECTING ROD

You should have the connecting rod checked for straightness at a machine shop. If the connecting rod is bent, it will unevenly wear the bearing and piston, as well as place greater stress on these components. Any bent or twisted connecting rods must be replaced. If the rods are straight and the wrist pin clearance is within specifications, then only the bearing end of the rod need be checked. Place the connecting rod into a vice, with the bearing inserts in place, install the cap to the rod and torque the fasteners to specifications. Use a telescoping gauge and carefully measure the inside diameter of the bearings. Compare this reading to the rods original crankshaft journal diameter measurement. The difference is the oil clearance. If the oil clearance is not within specifications, install new bearings in the rod and take another measurement. If the clearance is still out of specifications, and the crankshaft is not, the rod will need to be reconditioned by a machine shop.

➡You can also use Plastigage® to check the bearing clearances. The assembling section has complete instructions on its use.

Camshaft

Inspect the camshaft and lifters/followers as described earlier in this section.

Bearings

All of the engine bearings should be visually inspected for wear and/or damage. The bearing should look evenly worn all around with no deep scores or pits. If the bearing is severely worn, scored, pitted or heat blued, then the bearing, and the components that use it, should be brought to a machine shop for inspection. Full-circle bearings (used on most camshafts, auxiliary shafts, balance shafts, etc.) require specialized tools for removal and installation, and should be brought to a machine shop for service.

Oil Pump

➡The oil pump is responsible for providing constant lubrication to the whole engine and so it is recommended that a new oil pump be installed when rebuilding the engine.

Completely disassemble the oil pump and thoroughly clean all of the components. Inspect the oil pump gears and housing for wear and/or damage. Insure that the pressure relief valve operates properly and there is no binding or sticking due to varnish or debris. If all of the parts are in proper working condition, lubricate the gears and relief valve, and assemble the pump.

REFINISHING

▶ See Figure 147

Almost all engine block refinishing must be performed by a machine shop. If the cylinders are not to be rebored, then the cylinder glaze can be removed with a ball hone. When removing cylinder glaze with a ball hone, use a light or penetrating type oil to lubricate the hone. Do not allow the hone to run dry as this may cause excessive scoring of the cylinder bores and wear on the hone. If new pistons are required, they will need to be installed to the connecting rods. This should be performed by a machine shop as the pistons must be installed in the correct relationship to the rod or engine damage can occur.

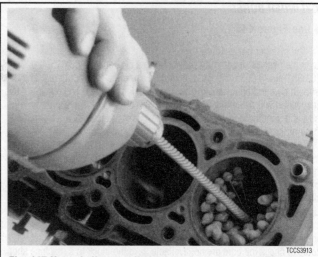
Fig. 147 Use a ball type cylinder hone to remove any glaze and provide a new surface for seating the piston rings

Pistons and Connecting Rods

▶ See Figure 148

Only pistons with the wrist pin retained by C-clips are serviceable by the home-mechanic. Press fit pistons require special presses and/or heaters to remove/install the connecting rod and should only be performed by a machine shop.

All pistons will have a mark indicating the direction to the front of the engine and the must be installed into the engine in that manner. Usually it is a notch or arrow on the top of the piston, or it may be the letter F cast or stamped into the piston.

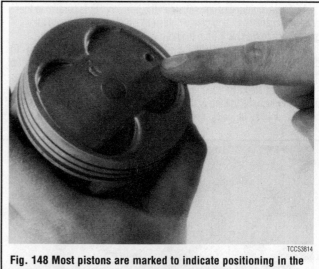
Fig. 148 Most pistons are marked to indicate positioning in the engine (usually a mark means the side facing the front)

ASSEMBLY

Before you begin assembling the engine, first give yourself a clean, dirt free work area. Next, clean every engine component again. The key to a good assembly is cleanliness.

Mount the engine block into the engine stand and wash it one last time using water and detergent (dishwashing detergent works well). While washing it, scrub the cylinder bores with a soft bristle brush and thoroughly clean all of the oil passages. Completely dry the engine and spray the entire assembly down with an anti-rust solution such as WD-40® or similar product. Take a clean lint-free rag and wipe up any excess anti-rust solution from the bores, bearing saddles, etc. Repeat the final cleaning process on the crankshaft. Replace any freeze or oil galley plugs which were removed during disassembly.

Crankshaft

▶ **See Figures 149, 150, 151 and 152**

1. Remove the main bearing inserts from the block and bearing caps.
2. If the crankshaft main bearing journals have been refinished to a definite undersize, install the correct undersize bearing. Be sure that the bearing inserts and bearing bores are clean. Foreign material under inserts will distort bearing and cause failure.
3. Place the upper main bearing inserts in bores with tang in slot.

➡ **The oil holes in the bearing inserts must be aligned with the oil holes in the cylinder block.**

4. Install the lower main bearing inserts in bearing caps.
5. Clean the mating surfaces of block and rear main bearing cap.
6. Carefully lower the crankshaft into place. Be careful not to damage bearing surfaces.
7. Check the clearance of each main bearing by using the following procedure:

   a. Place a piece of Plastigage® or its equivalent, on bearing surface across full width of bearing cap and about ¼ in. off center.

   b. Install cap and tighten bolts to specifications. Do not turn crankshaft while Plastigage® is in place.

   c. Remove the cap. Using the supplied Plastigage® scale, check width of Plastigage® at widest point to get maximum clearance. Difference between readings is taper of journal.

   d. If clearance exceeds specified limits, try a 0.001 in. or 0.002 in. undersize bearing in combination with the standard bearing. Bearing clearance must be within specified limits. If standard and 0.002 in. undersize bearing does not bring clearance within desired limits, refinish crankshaft journal, then install undersize bearings.

8. After the bearings have been fitted, apply a light coat of engine oil to the journals and bearings. Install the rear main bearing cap. Install all bearing caps except the thrust bearing cap. Be sure that main bearing caps are installed in original locations. Tighten the bearing cap bolts to specifications.

TCCS3243

Fig. 149 Apply a strip of gauging material to the bearing journal, then install and torque the cap

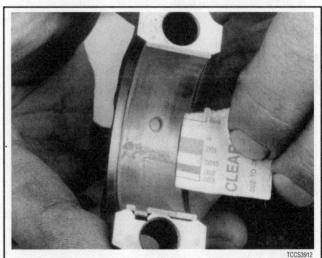

TCCS3912

Fig. 150 After the cap is removed again, use the scale supplied with the gauging material to check the clearance

TCCS3805

Fig. 151 A dial gauge may be used to check crankshaft end-play

Fig. 152 Carefully pry the crankshaft back and forth while reading the dial gauge for end-play

9. Install the thrust bearing cap with bolts finger-tight.

10. Pry the crankshaft forward against the thrust surface of upper half of bearing.

11. Hold the crankshaft forward and pry the thrust bearing cap to the rear. This aligns the thrust surfaces of both halves of the bearing.

12. Retain the forward pressure on the crankshaft. Tighten the cap bolts to specifications.

13. Measure the crankshaft end-play as follows:

    a. Mount a dial gauge to the engine block and position the tip of the gauge to read from the crankshaft end.

    b. Carefully pry the crankshaft toward the rear of the engine and hold it there while you zero the gauge.

    c. Carefully pry the crankshaft toward the front of the engine and read the gauge.

    d. Confirm that the reading is within specifications. If not, install a new thrust bearing and repeat the procedure. If the reading is still out of specifications with a new bearing, have a machine shop inspect the thrust surfaces of the crankshaft, and if possible, repair it.

14. Rotate the crankshaft so as to position the first rod journal to the bottom of its stroke.

Pistons and Connecting Rods

▶ See Figures 153, 154, 155 and 156

1. Before installing the piston/connecting rod assembly, oil the pistons, piston rings and the cylinder walls with light engine oil. Install connecting rod bolt protectors or rubber hose onto the connecting rod bolts/studs. Also perform the following:

    a. Select the proper ring set for the size cylinder bore.

    b. Position the ring in the bore in which it is going to be used.

    c. Push the ring down into the bore area where normal ring wear is not encountered.

    d. Use the head of the piston to position the ring in the bore so that the ring is square with the cylinder wall. Use caution to avoid damage to the ring or cylinder bore.

    e. Measure the gap between the ends of the ring with a feeler gauge. Ring gap in a worn cylinder is normally greater than specification. If the ring gap is greater than the specified limits, try an oversize ring set.

    f. Check the ring side clearance of the compression rings with a feeler gauge inserted between the ring and its lower land according to specification. The gauge should slide freely around the entire ring circumference without binding. Any wear that occurs will form a step at the inner portion of the lower land. If the lower lands have high steps, the piston should be replaced.

2. Unless new pistons are installed, be sure to install the pistons in the cylinders from which they were removed. The numbers on the connecting rod and bearing cap must be on the same side when installed in the cylinder bore. If a connecting rod is ever transposed from one engine or cylinder to another, new bearings should be fitted and the connecting rod should be numbered to correspond with the new cylinder number. The notch on the piston head goes toward the front of the engine.

3. Install all of the rod bearing inserts into the rods and caps.

Fig. 153 Checking the piston ring-to-ring groove side clearance using the ring and a feeler gauge

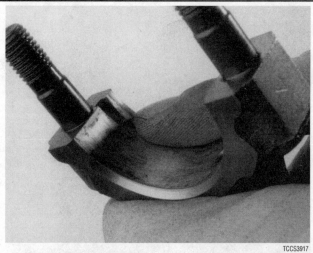
Fig. 154 The notch on the side of the bearing cap matches the tang on the bearing insert

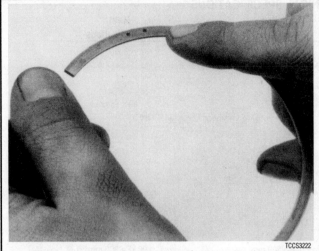

TCCS3222

Fig. 155 Most rings are marked to show which side of the ring should face up when installed to the piston

TCCS3914

Fig. 156 Install the piston and rod assembly into the block using a ring compressor and the handle of a hammer

4. Install the rings to the pistons. Install the oil control ring first, then the second compression ring and finally the top compression ring. Use a piston ring expander tool to aid in installation and to help reduce the chance of breakage.

5. Make sure the ring gaps are properly spaced around the circumference of the piston. Fit a piston ring compressor around the piston and slide the piston and connecting rod assembly down into the cylinder bore, pushing it in with the wooden hammer handle. Push the piston down until it is only slightly below the top of the cylinder bore. Guide the connecting rod onto the crankshaft bearing journal carefully, to avoid damaging the crankshaft.

6. Check the bearing clearance of all the rod bearings, fitting them to the crankshaft bearing journals. Follow the procedure in the crankshaft installation above.

7. After the bearings have been fitted, apply a light coating of assembly oil to the journals and bearings.

8. Turn the crankshaft until the appropriate bearing journal is at the bottom of its stroke, then push the piston assembly all the way down until the connecting rod bearing seats on the crankshaft journal. Be careful not to allow the bearing cap screws to strike the crankshaft bearing journals and damage them.

9. After the piston and connecting rod assemblies have been installed, check the connecting rod side clearance on each crankshaft journal.

10. Prime and install the oil pump and the oil pump intake tube.

11. Install the camshaft.
12. Install the lifters/followers into their bores.
13. Install the timing gears/chain assembly.

CYLINDER HEAD

1. Install the cylinder head using new gaskets.
2. Assemble the rest of the valve train (pushrods and rocker arms and/or shafts).

OHC Engines

CYLINDER HEAD

1. Install the cylinder head using a new gasket.
2. Install the timing sprockets/gears and the belt/chain assemblies.

Engine Covers and Components

Install the timing cover(s) and oil pan. Refer to your notes and drawings made prior to disassembly and install all of the components that were removed. Install the engine into the vehicle.

Engine Start-up and Break-in

STARTING THE ENGINE

Now that the engine is installed and every wire and hose is properly connected, go back and double check that all coolant and vacuum hoses are connected. Check that you oil drain plug is installed and properly tightened. If not already done, install a new oil filter onto the engine. Fill the crankcase with the proper amount and grade of engine oil. Fill the cooling system with a 50/50 mixture of coolant/water.

1. Connect the vehicle battery.
2. Start the engine. Keep your eye on your oil pressure indicator; if it does not indicate oil pressure within 10 seconds of starting, turn the vehicle off.

✳✳ WARNING

Damage to the engine can result if it is allowed to run with no oil pressure. Check the engine oil level to make sure that it is full. Check for any leaks and if found, repair the leaks before continuing. If there is still no indication of oil pressure, you may need to prime the system.

3. Confirm that there are no fluid leaks (oil or other).
4. Allow the engine to reach normal operating temperature (the upper radiator hose will be hot to the touch).
5. If necessary, set the ignition timing.
6. Install any remaining components such as the air cleaner (if removed for ignition timing) or body panels which were removed.

BREAKING IT IN

Make the first miles on the new engine, easy ones. Vary the speed but do not accelerate hard. Most importantly, do not lug the engine, and avoid sustained high speeds until at least 100 miles. Check the engine oil and coolant levels frequently. Expect the engine to use a little oil until the rings seat. Change the oil and filter at 500 miles, 1500 miles, then every 3000 miles past that.

KEEP IT MAINTAINED

Now that you have just gone through all of that hard work, keep yourself from doing it all over again by thoroughly maintaining it. Not that you may not have maintained it before, heck you could have had one to two hundred thousand miles on it before doing this. However, you may have bought the vehicle used, and the previous owner did not keep up on maintenance. Which is why you just went through all of that hard work. See?

2.4L (2389cc) ENGINE MECHANICAL SPECIFICATIONS

Description	English Specifications	Metric Specifications
Specifications		
Displacement	145.78 cu in.	2,389cc
Bore and stroke	3.5 x 3.78 in.	89 x 96mm
Valve arrangement	Dual Overhead Camshaft (DOHC)	
Firing order	1-3-4-2	
Number of piston rings		
Compression	2	
Oil	1	
Number of main bearings	5	
Compression ratio	9.2	
Compression pressure		
Standard	178 psi/300 rpm	1,226 kPa/300 rpm
Minimum	149 psi/300 rpm	1,030 kPa/300 rpm
Differential limit between cylinders	14 psi/300 rpm	98 kPa/300 rpm
Inspection and Adjustment		
Cylinder Head		
Head surface distortion		
Standard	Less than 0.0012 in.	Less than 0.03mm
Limit	0.004 in.	0.1mm
Nominal cylinder head height	4.972 - 4.980 in.	126.3 - 126.5mm
Limit (total amount of cylinder head resurfacing plus cylinder block resurfacing)	0.008 in.	0.2mm
Valve		
Valve head diameter		
Intake	1.437 - 1.445 in.	36.5 - 36.7mm
Exhaust	1.228 - 1.236 in.	31.2 - 31.4mm
Valve length		
Intake	3.9772 - 4.0008 in.	101.02 - 101.62mm
Exhaust	3.8787 - 3.9260 in.	98.52 - 99.72mm
Valve stem diameter		
Intake	0.2742 - 0.2748 in.	6.965 - 6.980mm
Exhaust	0.2734 - 0.2740 in.	6.945 - 6.960mm
Valve seat angle (Intake & Exhaust)	45.25° - 45.75°	
Valve margin		
Intake	0.0374 - 0.0492 in.	0.95 - 1.25mm
Exhaust	0.0453 - 0.0571 in.	1.15 - 1.45mm
Valve margin limit	More than 0.020 in.	More than 0.5mm
Valve stem end surface grinding limit	Less than 0.008 in.	Less than 0.2mm
Valve Spring		
Free height	1.8028 in.	45.79mm
Pressure		
Standard	471.7(106.1 lb) at 1.0260 in.	471.7(48.1 kg) at 26.06mm
Limit	421.31(94.73 lb) at 1.0260 in.	421.31(42.96 kg) at 26.06mm
Out-of-square	Less than 0.079 in.	Less than 2.0mm
Valve Lifter		
Valve lifter outer diameter	1.3370 - 1.3376 in.	33.960 - 33.975mm
Lifter guide inner diameter	1.3386 - 1.3394 in.	34.000 - 34.021mm
Clearance between lifter and filter guide	0.0010 - 0.0024 in.	0.025 - 0.061mm
Valve Guide		
Valve guide		
Outer diameter		
Intake & Exhaust		
Standard	0.4340 - 0.4344 in.	11.023 - 11.034mm
Service	0.4418 - 0.4423 in.	11.223 - 11.234mm

89703C01

2.4L (2389cc) ENGINE MECHANICAL SPECIFICATIONS

Description	English Specifications	Metric Specifications
Valve guide		
Inner diameter (Finished size)		
Intake & Exhaust	0.2756 - 0.2763 in.	7.000 - 7.018mm
Cylinder head valve guide hole diameter		
Intake & Exhaust		
Standard	0.4321 - 0.4329 in.	10.975 - 10.996mm
Service	0.4400 - 0.4408 in.	11.175 - 11.196mm
Interference fit of valve guide	0.0011 - 0.0023 in.	0.027 - 0.059mm
Stem-to-guide clearance		
Intake		
Standard	0.0008 - 0.0021 in.	0.020 - 0.053mm
Limit	0.0031 in.	0.08mm
Exhaust		
Standard	0.0016 - 0.0029 in.	0.040 - 0.073mm
Limit	0.004 in.	0.01mm
Valve deflection limit	0.008 in.	0.2mm
Projection length	0.524 - 0.547 in.	13.3 - 13.9mm
Valve Clearance Adjustment		
Valve clearance		
Intake	0.012 - 0.015 in.	0.31 - 0.39mm
Exhaust	0.013 - 0.016 in.	0.33 - 0.41mm
Valve Seat		
Cylinder head seat recess diameter		
Intake		
Standard	1.4764 - 1.4770 in.	37.500 - 37.516mm
Service	1.4961 - 1.4967 in.	38.000 - 38.016mm
Exhaust		
Standard	1.2677 - 1.2683 in.	32.200 - 32.216mm
Service	1.2874 - 1.2880 in.	32.700 - 32.716mm
Valve seat interference fit		
Intake & Exhaust	0.0025 - 0.0038 in.	0.064 - 0.096mm
Valve seat outer diameter		
Intake		
Standard	1.4795 - 1.4802 in.	37.580 - 37.596mm
Service	1.4992 - 1.4998 in.	38.080 - 38.096mm
Exhaust		
Standard	1.2709 - 1.2715 in.	32.280 - 32.296mm
Service	1.2905 - 1.2912 in.	32.780 - 32.796mm
Depth		
Intake	0.2437 - 0.2445 in.	6.19 - 6.21mm
Exhaust	0.240 - 0.248 in.	6.1 - 6.3mm
Height 1	0.232 - 0.236 in.	5.9 - 6.0mm
Height 2		
Intake	0.0173 - 0.0252 in.	0.44 - 0.64mm
Exhaust	0.0209 - 0.0287 in.	0.53 - 0.73mm
Cylinder Block		
Distortion		
Standard	Less than 0.0012 in.	Less than 0.03mm
Limit	0.004 in.	0.1mm
Cylinder bore		
Inner diameter		
Grade 1		
Standard	3.5039 - 3.5043 in.	89.000 - 89.010mm
Limit	0.008 in.	0.2mm
Grade 2		
Standard	3.5039 - 3.5043 in.	89.010 - 89.020mm
Limit	0.008 in.	0.2mm

89703C02

2.4L (2389cc) ENGINE MECHANICAL SPECIFICATIONS

Description	English Specifications	Metric Specifications
Grade 3		
Standard	3.5047 - 3.5051 in.	89.020 - 89.030mm
Limit	0.008 in.	0.2mm
Out-of-round (Standard)	Less than 0.0006 in.	Less than 0.015mm
Taper (Standard)	Less than 0.0004 in.	Less than 0.010mm
Difference in inner diameter between cylinders		
Standard	Less than 0.0012 in.	Less than 0.03mm
Limit	0.008 in.	0.2mm
Nomimal cylinder block height (From crankshaft center)		
Standard	9.7224 - 9.7264 in.	246.95 - 247.05mm
Limit (total amount of cylinder head resurfacing plus cylinder block resurfacing)	0.008 in.	0.2mm
Camshaft and Camshaft Bearing		
Cam Height		
Intake (Standard)	1.6699 - 1.6774 in.	42.415 - 42.605mm
Exhaust (Standard)	1.6699 - 1.6931 in.	42.415 - 43.005mm
Wear limit of cam height (Limit)	0.008 in.	0.2mm
Camshaft journal-to-bearing clearance		
Standard	0.0018 - 0.0035 in.	0.045 - 0.090mm
Limit	0.0047 in.	0.12mm
Inner diameter of camshaft bearing		
#1 journal (Standard)	1.1024 - 1.1033 in.	28.000 - 28.025mm
#2 to #5 journal (Standard)	0.9449 - 0.9459 in.	24.000 - 24.025mm
Outer diameter of camshaft journal		
#1 journal (Standard)	1.0998 - 1.1006 in.	27.935 - 27.955mm
#2 to #5 journal (Standard)	0.9423 - 0.9431 in.	23.935 - 23.955mm
Camshaft run-out (Total indicator reading)		
Standard	Less than 0.0008 in.	Less than 0.02mm
Limit	0.0016 in.	0.04mm
Camshaft end-play		
Standard	0.0028 - 0.0059 in.	0.07 - 0.15mm
Limit	0.0079 in.	0.20mm
Valve timing (Degree on crankshaft)		
a (Standard)	248	
b (Standard)	240	
c (Standard)	-1	
d (Standard)	61	
e (Standard)	8	
f (Standard)	60	
Piston, Piston Ring and Piston Pin		
Piston		
Piston skirt diameter		
Standard		
Grade No. 1	3.5027 - 3.5031 in.	88.970 - 88.980mm
Grade No. 2	3.5031 - 3.5035 in.	88.980 - 88.990mm
Grade No. 3	3.5035 - 3.5039 in.	88.990 - 89.000mm
Service (Oversize)		
0.020 in./0.5mm	3.5224 - 3.5236 in.	89.470 - 89.500mm
0.039 in./1.0mm	3.5421 - 3.5433 in.	89.970 - 90.000mm
Dimension	approx. 2.05 in.	approx. 52mm
Piston pin hole diameter	0.8263 - 0.8267 in.	20.987 - 20.999mm
Piston-to-cylinder bore clearance	0.0008 - 0.0016 in.	0.020 - 0.040mm
Piston pin		
Piston pin outer diameter (Standard)	0.8263 - 0.8268 in.	20.989 - 21.001mm
Interference fit of piston pin-to-piston pin hole (Standard)	0 - 0.0002 in.	0 - 0.004mm

89703C03

2.4L (2389cc) ENGINE MECHANICAL SPECIFICATIONS

Description	English Specifications	Metric Specifications
Piston pin-to-connecting rod bearing clearance		
Standard	0.0002 - 0.0007 in.	0.005 - 0.017mm
Limit	0.0009 in.	0.023mm
Piston ring		
Side clearance		
Top		
Standard	0.0016 - 0.0031 in.	0.040 - 0.080mm
Limit	0.004 in.	0.1mm
2nd		
Standard	0.0012 - 0.0028 in.	0.030 - 0.070mm
Limit	0.004 in.	0.1mm
Ring gap		
Top		
Standard	0.0110 - 0.0205 in.	0.28 - 0.52mm
Limit	0.039 in.	1.0mm
2nd		
Standard	0.0177 - 0.0272 in.	0.45 - 0.69mm
Limit	0.039 in.	1.0mm
Oil (rail ring)		
Standard	0.0079 - 0.0272 in.	0.20 - 0.69mm
Limit	0.039 in.	1.0mm
Connecting Rod		
Center distance (Standard)	6.4941 - 6.4980 in.	164.95 - 165.05mm
Bend per 3.94 in./100mm (Limit)	0.0059 in.	0.15mm
Torsion 3.94 in./100mm (Limit)	0.0118 in.	0.30mm
Piston pin bushing inner diameter (Standard)	0.8268 - 0.8272 in.	21.000 - 21.012mm
Connecting rod big end inner diameter - without bearing (Standard)	2.0866 - 2.0871 in.	53.000 - 53.013mm
Side Clearance		
Standard	0.008 - 0.016 in.	0.2 - 0.4mm
Limit	0.024 in.	0.6mm
Crankshaft		
Main journal diameter		
Grade No. 0	2.3609 - 2.3612 in.	59.967 - 59.975mm
Grade No. 1	2.3606 - 2.3609 in.	59.959 - 59.967mm
Grade No. 2	2.3603 - 2.3606 in.	59.951 - 59.959mm
Pin journal diameter		
Grade No. 0	1.9672 - 1.9675 in.	49.968 - 49.974mm
Grade No. 1	1.9670 - 1.9672 in.	49.962 - 49.968mm
Grade No. 2	1.9668 - 1.9670 in.	49.956 - 49.962mm
Center distance	1.8886 - 1.8917 in.	47.97 - 48.05mm
Taper of journal and pin (Standard)	Less than 0.0001 in.	Less than 0.002mm
Out-of-round of journal and pin (Standard)	Less than 0.0002 in.	Less than 0.005mm
Run-out - Total indicator reading (Standard)	Less than 0.0016 in.	Less than 0.04mm
Free end-play		
Standard	0.0020 - 0.0071 in.	0.05 - 0.18mm
Limit	0.012 in.	0.3mm
Fillet roll	More than 0.004 in.	More than 0.1mm
Bearing Clearance		
Main bearing clearance		
Standard	0.0008 - 0.0019 in.	0.020 - 0.047mm
Limit	0.004 in.	0.1mm
Connecting rod bearing clearance		
Standard	0.0004 - 0.0014 in.	0.010 - 0.035mm
Limit	0.0035 in.	0.09mm
Miscellaneous Components		
Camshaft sprocket run-out (Total indicator reading)	Less than 0.0047 in.	Less than 0.12mm
Flywheel run-out (Total indicator reading)	Less than 0.0059 in.	Less than 0.15mm
Drive plate run-out (Total indicator reading)	Less than 0.0059 in.	Less than 0.15mm

89703C04

TORQUE SPECIFICATIONS

Components	English Specification	Metric Specification
Mounts		
Altima		
Front and Rear	47–55 ft. lbs.	64–75 Nm
Right and Left	32–41 ft. lbs.	43–55 Nm
Crossmember	57–72 ft. lbs.	77–98 Nm
240SX		
Engine	51–58 ft. lbs.	69–78 Nm
Transmission	16–21 ft. lbs.	22–28 Nm
Cylinder Head Cover	69–95 inch lbs.	8–11Nm
Thermostat		
6mm Bolt	57–66 inch lbs.	6–8 Nm
8mm Bolt	12–14 ft. lbs.	16–19 Nm
Intake Manifold	12–14 ft. lbs.	16–19 Nm
Throttle Body	13–16 ft. lbs.	18–22 Nm
Exhaust Manifold		
Manifold Nuts	27–35 ft. lbs.	37–48 Nm
EGR tube	29–36 ft. lbs.	39–49 Nm
Manifold cover	46–57 inch lbs.	5–7 Nm
Exhaust pipe-to-manifold	33–44 ft. lbs.	45–60 Nm
Radiator		
Support brackets		
Altima	29–37 inch lbs.	3–4 Nm
240SX	34–40 inch lbs.	4–5 Nm
Cooling Fan		
Mechanical	56–66 inch lbs.	6–8 Nm
Electric fan shroud		
Altima	29–37 inch lbs.	3–4 Nm
240SX	34–40 inch lbs.	4–5 Nm
Water Pump		
Altima		
6mm Bolts	57–66 inch lbs.	6–8 Nm
8mm Bolts	12–14 ft. lbs.	16–19 Nm
Pulley	57–66 inch lbs.	6–8 Nm
240SX		
Pump bolts	12–14 ft. lbs.	16–19 Nm
Pulley	66 inch lbs.	8 Nm
Cylinder Head		
Step 1	22 ft. lbs.	29 Nm
Step 2	59 ft. lbs.	79 Nm
Step 3	Loosen all the bolts completely	
Step 4	18–25 ft. lbs.	25–34 Nm
Step 5	86–91° clockwise	
NOTE: If an angle wrench is not available, tighten all bolts to 55–62 ft. lbs. (75–84 Nm)		
Oil Pan		
Altima		
Aluminum pan	13 ft. lbs.	17.5 Nm
Steel pan	61 inch lbs.	7 Nm
240SX		
1993–94	57–61 inch lbs.	6.4–7.5 Nm
1995–98	12–14 ft. lbs.	16–19 Nm

89703C05

TORQUE SPECIFICATIONS

Components	English Specification	Metric Specification
Oil Pump		
Pump cover		
Screws	33–44 inch lbs.	3.7–5.0 Nm
Bolts	12–15 inch lbs.	16–21 Nm
Crankshaft Damper	105–112 ft. lbs.	142–152 Nm
Front Cover		
M6 bolts	56–66 inch lbs.	6.4–7.5 Nm
M8 bolts	12–14 ft. lbs.	15–19 Nm
Camshaft sprockets	123–130 ft. lbs.	167–177 Nm
Camshaft Caps		
Step 1	17 inch lbs.	2 Nm
Step 2	81–104 inch lbs.	9–12 Nm
Rear Main Seal	56–66 inch lbs.	6–8 Nm
Flywheel/Flexplate	105–112 ft. lbs.	142–152 Nm

89703C06

USING A VACUUM GAUGE

White needle = steady needle   *Dark needle = drifting needle*

The vacuum gauge is one of the most useful and easy-to-use diagnostic tools. It is inexpensive, easy to hook up, and provides valuable information about the condition of your engine.

Indication: Normal engine in good condition

Gauge reading: Steady, from 17–22 in./Hg.

Indication: Sticking valve or ignition miss

Gauge reading: Needle fluctuates from 15–20 in./Hg. at idle

Indication: Late ignition or valve timing, low compression, stuck throttle valve, leaking carburetor or manifold gasket.

Gauge reading: Low (15–20 in./Hg.) but steady

Indication: Improper carburetor adjustment, or minor intake leak at carburetor or manifold

NOTE: Bad fuel injector O-rings may also cause this reading.

Gauge reading: Drifting needle

Indication: Weak valve springs, worn valve stem guides, or leaky cylinder head gasket (vibrating excessively at all speeds).

NOTE: A plugged catalytic converter may also cause this reading.

Gauge reading: Needle fluctuates as engine speed increases

Indication: Burnt valve or improper valve clearance. The needle will drop when the defective valve operates.

Gauge reading: Steady needle, but drops regularly

Indication: Choked muffler or obstruction in system. Speed up the engine. Choked muffler will exhibit a slow drop of vacuum to zero.

Gauge reading: Gradual drop in reading at idle

Indication: Worn valve guides

Gauge reading: Needle vibrates excessively at idle, but steadies as engine speed increases

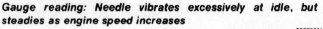

TCCS3C01

Troubleshooting Engine Mechanical Problems

Problem	Cause	Solution
External oil leaks	• Cylinder head cover RTV sealant broken or improperly seated	• Replace sealant; inspect cylinder head cover sealant flange and cylinder head sealant surface for distortion and cracks
	• Oil filler cap leaking or missing	• Replace cap
	• Oil filter gasket broken or improperly seated	• Replace oil filter
	• Oil pan side gasket broken, improperly seated or opening in RTV sealant	• Replace gasket or repair opening in sealant; inspect oil pan gasket flange for distortion
	• Oil pan front oil seal broken or improperly seated	• Replace seal; inspect timing case cover and oil pan seal flange for distortion
	• Oil pan rear oil seal broken or improperly seated	• Replace seal; inspect oil pan rear oil seal flange; inspect rear main bearing cap for cracks, plugged oil return channels, or distortion in seal groove
	• Timing case cover oil seal broken or improperly seated	• Replace seal
	• Excess oil pressure because of restricted PCV valve	• Replace PCV valve
	• Oil pan drain plug loose or has stripped threads	• Repair as necessary and tighten
	• Rear oil gallery plug loose	• Use appropriate sealant on gallery plug and tighten
	• Rear camshaft plug loose or improperly seated	• Seat camshaft plug or replace and seal, as necessary
Excessive oil consumption	• Oil level too high	• Drain oil to specified level
	• Oil with wrong viscosity being used	• Replace with specified oil
	• PCV valve stuck closed	• Replace PCV valve
	• Valve stem oil deflectors (or seals) are damaged, missing, or incorrect type	• Replace valve stem oil deflectors
	• Valve stems or valve guides worn	• Measure stem-to-guide clearance and repair as necessary
	• Poorly fitted or missing valve cover baffles	• Replace valve cover
	• Piston rings broken or missing	• Replace broken or missing rings
	• Scuffed piston	• Replace piston
	• Incorrect piston ring gap	• Measure ring gap, repair as necessary
	• Piston rings sticking or excessively loose in grooves	• Measure ring side clearance, repair as necessary
	• Compression rings installed upside down	• Repair as necessary
	• Cylinder walls worn, scored, or glazed	• Repair as necessary

TCCS3C02

Troubleshooting Engine Mechanical Problems

Problem	Cause	Solution
Excessive oil consumption (cont.)	• Piston ring gaps not properly staggered • Excessive main or connecting rod bearing clearance	• Repair as necessary • Measure bearing clearance, repair as necessary
No oil pressure	• Low oil level • Oil pressure gauge, warning lamp or sending unit inaccurate • Oil pump malfunction • Oil pressure relief valve sticking • Oil passages on pressure side of pump obstructed • Oil pickup screen or tube obstructed • Loose oil inlet tube	• Add oil to correct level • Replace oil pressure gauge or warning lamp • Replace oil pump • Remove and inspect oil pressure relief valve assembly • Inspect oil passages for obstruction • Inspect oil pickup for obstruction • Tighten or seal inlet tube
Low oil pressure	• Low oil level • Inaccurate gauge, warning lamp or sending unit • Oil excessively thin because of dilution, poor quality, or improper grade • Excessive oil temperature • Oil pressure relief spring weak or sticking • Oil inlet tube and screen assembly has restriction or air leak • Excessive oil pump clearance • Excessive main, rod, or camshaft bearing clearance	• Add oil to correct level • Replace oil pressure gauge or warning lamp • Drain and refill crankcase with recommended oil • Correct cause of overheating engine • Remove and inspect oil pressure relief valve assembly • Remove and inspect oil inlet tube and screen assembly. (Fill inlet tube with lacquer thinner to locate leaks.) • Measure clearances • Measure bearing clearances, repair as necessary
High oil pressure	• Improper oil viscosity • Oil pressure gauge or sending unit inaccurate • Oil pressure relief valve sticking closed	• Drain and refill crankcase with correct viscosity oil • Replace oil pressure gauge • Remove and inspect oil pressure relief valve assembly
Main bearing noise	• Insufficient oil supply • Main bearing clearance excessive • Bearing insert missing • Crankshaft end-play excessive • Improperly tightened main bearing cap bolts • Loose flywheel or drive plate • Loose or damaged vibration damper	• Inspect for low oil level and low oil pressure • Measure main bearing clearance, repair as necessary • Replace missing insert • Measure end-play, repair as necessary • Tighten bolts with specified torque • Tighten flywheel or drive plate attaching bolts • Repair as necessary

TCCS3C03

Troubleshooting Engine Mechanical Problems

Problem	Cause	Solution
Connecting rod bearing noise	• Insufficient oil supply	• Inspect for low oil level and low oil pressure
	• Carbon build-up on piston	• Remove carbon from piston crown
	• Bearing clearance excessive or bearing missing	• Measure clearance, repair as necessary
	• Crankshaft connecting rod journal out-of-round	• Measure journal dimensions, repair or replace as necessary
	• Misaligned connecting rod or cap	• Repair as necessary
	• Connecting rod bolts tightened improperly	• Tighten bolts with specified torque
Piston noise	• Piston-to-cylinder wall clearance excessive (scuffed piston)	• Measure clearance and examine piston
	• Cylinder walls excessively tapered or out-of-round	• Measure cylinder wall dimensions, rebore cylinder
	• Piston ring broken	• Replace all rings on piston
	• Loose or seized piston pin	• Measure piston-to-pin clearance, repair as necessary
	• Connecting rods misaligned	• Measure rod alignment, straighten or replace
	• Piston ring side clearance excessively loose or tight	• Measure ring side clearance, repair as necessary
	• Carbon build-up on piston is excessive	• Remove carbon from piston
Valve actuating component noise	• Insufficient oil supply	• Check for: (a) Low oil level (b) Low oil pressure (c) Wrong hydraulic tappets (d) Restricted oil gallery (e) Excessive tappet to bore clearance
	• Rocker arms or pivots worn	• Replace worn rocker arms or pivots
	• Foreign objects or chips in hydraulic tappets	• Clean tappets
	• Excessive tappet leak-down	• Replace valve tappet
	• Tappet face worn	• Replace tappet; inspect corresponding cam lobe for wear
	• Broken or cocked valve springs	• Properly seat cocked springs; replace broken springs
	• Stem-to-guide clearance excessive	• Measure stem-to-guide clearance, repair as required
	• Valve bent	• Replace valve
	• Loose rocker arms	• Check and repair as necessary
	• Valve seat runout excessive	• Regrind valve seat/valves
	• Missing valve lock	• Install valve lock
	• Excessive engine oil	• Correct oil level

TCCS3C04

Troubleshooting Engine Performance

Problem	Cause	Solution
Hard starting (engine cranks normally)	• Faulty engine control system component • Faulty fuel pump • Faulty fuel system component • Faulty ignition coil • Improper spark plug gap • Incorrect ignition timing • Incorrect valve timing	• Repair or replace as necessary • Replace fuel pump • Repair or replace as necessary • Test and replace as necessary • Adjust gap • Adjust timing • Check valve timing; repair as necessary
Rough idle or stalling	• Incorrect curb or fast idle speed • Incorrect ignition timing • Improper feedback system operation • Faulty EGR valve operation • Faulty PCV valve air flow • Faulty TAC vacuum motor or valve • Air leak into manifold vacuum • Faulty distributor rotor or cap • Improperly seated valves • Incorrect ignition wiring • Faulty ignition coil • Restricted air vent or idle passages • Restricted air cleaner	• Adjust curb or fast idle speed (If possible) • Adjust timing to specification • Refer to Chapter 4 • Test EGR system and replace as necessary • Test PCV valve and replace as necessary • Repair as necessary • Inspect manifold vacuum connections and repair as necessary • Replace rotor or cap (Distributor systems only) • Test cylinder compression, repair as necessary • Inspect wiring and correct as necessary • Test coil and replace as necessary • Clean passages • Clean or replace air cleaner filter element
Faulty low-speed operation	• Restricted idle air vents and passages • Restricted air cleaner • Faulty spark plugs • Dirty, corroded, or loose ignition secondary circuit wire connections • Improper feedback system operation • Faulty ignition coil high voltage wire • Faulty distributor cap	• Clean air vents and passages • Clean or replace air cleaner filter element • Clean or replace spark plugs • Clean or tighten secondary circuit wire connections • Refer to Chapter 4 • Replace ignition coil high voltage wire (Distributor systems only) • Replace cap (Distributor systems only)
Faulty acceleration	• Incorrect ignition timing • Faulty fuel system component • Faulty spark plug(s) • Improperly seated valves • Faulty ignition coil	• Adjust timing • Repair or replace as necessary • Clean or replace spark plug(s) • Test cylinder compression, repair as necessary • Test coil and replace as necessary

TCCS3C05

Troubleshooting Engine Performance

Problem	Cause	Solution
Faulty acceleration (cont.)	• Improper feedback system operation	• Refer to Chapter 4
Faulty high speed operation	• Incorrect ignition timing • Faulty advance mechanism	• Adjust timing (if possible) • Check advance mechanism and repair as necessary (Distributor systems only)
	• Low fuel pump volume • Wrong spark plug air gap or wrong plug • Partially restricted exhaust manifold, exhaust pipe, catalytic converter, muffler, or tailpipe	• Replace fuel pump • Adjust air gap or install correct plug • Eliminate restriction
	• Restricted vacuum passages • Restricted air cleaner	• Clean passages • Cleaner or replace filter element as necessary
	• Faulty distributor rotor or cap	• Replace rotor or cap (Distributor systems only)
	• Faulty ignition coil • Improperly seated valve(s)	• Test coil and replace as necessary • Test cylinder compression, repair as necessary
	• Faulty valve spring(s)	• Inspect and test valve spring tension, replace as necessary
	• Incorrect valve timing	• Check valve timing and repair as necessary
	• Intake manifold restricted	• Remove restriction or replace manifold
	• Worn distributor shaft	• Replace shaft (Distributor systems only)
	• Improper feedback system operation	• Refer to Chapter 4
Misfire at all speeds	• Faulty spark plug(s) • Faulty spark plug wire(s) • Faulty distributor cap or rotor	• Clean or relace spark plug(s) • Replace as necessary • Replace cap or rotor (Distributor systems only)
	• Faulty ignition coil • Primary ignition circuit shorted or open intermittently • Improperly seated valve(s)	• Test coil and replace as necessary • Troubleshoot primary circuit and repair as necessary • Test cylinder compression, repair as necessary
	• Faulty hydraulic tappet(s) • Improper feedback system operation • Faulty valve spring(s)	• Clean or replace tappet(s) • Refer to Chapter 4 • Inspect and test valve spring tension, repair as necessary
	• Worn camshaft lobes • Air leak into manifold	• Replace camshaft • Check manifold vacuum and repair as necessary
	• Fuel pump volume or pressure low • Blown cylinder head gasket • Intake or exhaust manifold passage(s) restricted	• Replace fuel pump • Replace gasket • Pass chain through passage(s) and repair as necessary
Power not up to normal	• Incorrect ignition timing • Faulty distributor rotor	• Adjust timing • Replace rotor (Distributor systems only)

Troubleshooting Engine Performance

Problem	Cause	Solution
Power not up to normal (cont.)	• Incorrect spark plug gap	• Adjust gap
	• Faulty fuel pump	• Replace fuel pump
	• Faulty fuel pump	• Replace fuel pump
	• Incorrect valve timing	• Check valve timing and repair as necessary
	• Faulty ignition coil	• Test coil and replace as necessary
	• Faulty ignition wires	• Test wires and replace as necessary
	• Improperly seated valves	• Test cylinder compression and repair as necessary
	• Blown cylinder head gasket	• Replace gasket
	• Leaking piston rings	• Test compression and repair as necessary
	• Improper feedback system operation	• Refer to Chapter 4
Intake backfire	• Improper ignition timing	• Adjust timing
	• Defective EGR component	• Repair as necessary
	• Defective TAC vacuum motor or valve	• Repair as necessary
Exhaust backfire	• Air leak into manifold vacuum	• Check manifold vacuum and repair as necessary
	• Faulty air injection diverter valve	• Test diverter valve and replace as necessary
	• Exhaust leak	• Locate and eliminate leak
Ping or spark knock	• Incorrect ignition timing	• Adjust timing
	• Distributor advance malfunction	• Inspect advance mechanism and repair as necessary (Distributor systems only)
	• Excessive combustion chamber deposits	• Remove with combustion chamber cleaner
	• Air leak into manifold vacuum	• Check manifold vacuum and repair as necessary
	• Excessively high compression	• Test compression and repair as necessary
	• Fuel octane rating excessively low	• Try alternate fuel source
	• Sharp edges in combustion chamber	• Grind smooth
	• EGR valve not functioning properly	• Test EGR system and replace as necessary
Surging (at cruising to top speeds)	• Low fuel pump pressure or volume	• Replace fuel pump
	• Improper PCV valve air flow	• Test PCV valve and replace as necessary
	• Air leak into manifold vacuum	• Check manifold vacuum and repair as necessary
	• Incorrect spark advance	• Test and replace as necessary
	• Restricted fuel filter	• Replace fuel filter
	• Restricted air cleaner	• Clean or replace air cleaner filter element
	• EGR valve not functioning properly	• Test EGR system and replace as necessary
	• Improper feedback system operation	• Refer to Chapter 4

Troubleshooting the Serpentine Drive Belt

Problem	Cause	Solution
Tension sheeting fabric failure (woven fabric on outside circumference of belt has cracked or separated from body of belt)	• Grooved or backside idler pulley diameters are less than minimum recommended • Tension sheeting contacting (rubbing) stationary object • Excessive heat causing woven fabric to age • Tension sheeting splice has fractured	• Replace pulley(s) not conforming to specification • Correct rubbing condition • Replace belt • Replace belt
Noise (objectional squeal, squeak, or rumble is heard or felt while drive belt is in operation)	• Belt slippage • Bearing noise • Belt misalignment • Belt-to-pulley mismatch • Driven component inducing vibration • System resonant frequency inducing vibration	• Adjust belt • Locate and repair • Align belt/pulley(s) • Install correct belt • Locate defective driven component and repair • Vary belt tension within specifications. Replace belt.
Rib chunking (one or more ribs has separated from belt body)	• Foreign objects imbedded in pulley grooves • Installation damage • Drive loads in excess of design specifications • Insufficient internal belt adhesion	• Remove foreign objects from pulley grooves • Replace belt • Adjust belt tension • Replace belt
Rib or belt wear (belt ribs contact bottom of pulley grooves)	• Pulley(s) misaligned • Mismatch of belt and pulley groove widths • Abrasive environment • Rusted pulley(s) • Sharp or jagged pulley groove tips • Rubber deteriorated	• Align pulley(s) • Replace belt • Replace belt • Clean rust from pulley(s) • Replace pulley • Replace belt
Longitudinal belt cracking (cracks between two ribs)	• Belt has mistracked from pulley groove • Pulley groove tip has worn away rubber-to-tensile member	• Replace belt • Replace belt
Belt slips	• Belt slipping because of insufficient tension • Belt or pulley subjected to substance (belt dressing, oil, ethylene glycol) that has reduced friction • Driven component bearing failure • Belt glazed and hardened from heat and excessive slippage	• Adjust tension • Replace belt and clean pulleys • Replace faulty component bearing • Replace belt
"Groove jumping" (belt does not maintain correct position on pulley, or turns over and/or runs off pulleys)	• Insufficient belt tension • Pulley(s) not within design tolerance • Foreign object(s) in grooves	• Adjust belt tension • Replace pulley(s) • Remove foreign objects from grooves

TCCS3C09

Troubleshooting the Serpentine Drive Belt

Problem	Cause	Solution
"Groove jumping" (belt does not maintain correct position on pulley, or turns over and/or runs off pulleys)	• Excessive belt speed • Pulley misalignment • Belt-to-pulley profile mismatched • Belt cordline is distorted	• Avoid excessive engine acceleration • Align pulley(s) • Install correct belt • Replace belt
Belt broken (Note: identify and correct problem before replacement belt is installed)	• Excessive tension • Tensile members damaged during belt installation • Belt turnover • Severe pulley misalignment • Bracket, pulley, or bearing failure	• Replace belt and adjust tension to specification • Replace belt • Replace belt • Align pulley(s) • Replace defective component and belt
Cord edge failure (tensile member exposed at edges of belt or separated from belt body)	• Excessive tension • Drive pulley misalignment • Belt contacting stationary object • Pulley irregularities • Improper pulley construction • Insufficient adhesion between tensile member and rubber matrix	• Adjust belt tension • Align pulley • Correct as necessary • Replace pulley • Replace pulley • Replace belt and adjust tension to specifications
Sporadic rib cracking (multiple cracks in belt ribs at random intervals)	• Ribbed pulley(s) diameter less than minimum specification • Backside bend flat pulley(s) diameter less than minimum • Excessive heat condition causing rubber to harden • Excessive belt thickness • Belt overcured • Excessive tension	• Replace pulley(s) • Replace pulley(s) • Correct heat condition as necessary • Replace belt • Replace belt • Adjust belt tension

TCCS3C10

Troubleshooting the Cooling System

Problem	Cause	Solution
High temperature gauge indication—overheating	• Coolant level low	• Replenish coolant
	• Improper fan operation	• Repair or replace as necessary
	• Radiator hose(s) collapsed	• Replace hose(s)
	• Radiator airflow blocked	• Remove restriction (bug screen, fog lamps, etc.)
	• Faulty pressure cap	• Replace pressure cap
	• Ignition timing incorrect	• Adjust ignition timing
	• Air trapped in cooling system	• Purge air
	• Heavy traffic driving	• Operate at fast idle in neutral intermittently to cool engine
		• Install proper component(s)
	• Incorrect cooling system component(s) installed	
	• Faulty thermostat	• Replace thermostat
	• Water pump shaft broken or impeller loose	• Replace water pump
	• Radiator tubes clogged	• Flush radiator
	• Cooling system clogged	• Flush system
	• Casting flash in cooling passages	• Repair or replace as necessary. Flash may be visible by removing cooling system components or removing core plugs.
	• Brakes dragging	• Repair brakes
	• Excessive engine friction	• Repair engine
	• Antifreeze concentration over 68%	• Lower antifreeze concentration percentage
	• Missing air seals	• Replace air seals
	• Faulty gauge or sending unit	• Repair or replace faulty component
	• Loss of coolant flow caused by leakage or foaming	• Repair or replace leaking component, replace coolant
	• Viscous fan drive failed	• Replace unit
Low temperature indication—undercooling	• Thermostat stuck open	• Replace thermostat
	• Faulty gauge or sending unit	• Repair or replace faulty component
Coolant loss—boilover	• Overfilled cooling system	• Reduce coolant level to proper specification
	• Quick shutdown after hard (hot) run	• Allow engine to run at fast idle prior to shutdown
	• Air in system resulting in occasional "burping" of coolant	• Purge system
	• Insufficient antifreeze allowing coolant boiling point to be too low	• Add antifreeze to raise boiling point
	• Antifreeze deteriorated because of age or contamination	• Replace coolant
	• Leaks due to loose hose clamps, loose nuts, bolts, drain plugs, faulty hoses, or defective radiator	• Pressure test system to locate source of leak(s) then repair as necessary

TCCS3C11

Troubleshooting the Cooling System (cont.)

Problem	Cause	Solution
Coolant loss—boilover	• Faulty head gasket • Cracked head, manifold, or block • Faulty radiator cap	• Replace head gasket • Replace as necessary • Replace cap
Coolant entry into crankcase or cylinder(s)	• Faulty head gasket • Crack in head, manifold or block	• Replace head gasket • Replace as necessary
Coolant recovery system inoperative	• Coolant level low • Leak in system • Pressure cap not tight or seal missing, or leaking • Pressure cap defective • Overflow tube clogged or leaking • Recovery bottle vent restricted	• Replenish coolant to FULL mark • Pressure test to isolate leak and repair as necessary • Repair as necessary • Replace cap • Repair as necessary • Remove restriction
Noise	• Fan contacting shroud • Loose water pump impeller • Glazed fan belt • Loose fan belt • Rough surface on drive pulley • Water pump bearing worn • Belt alignment	• Reposition shroud and inspect engine mounts (on electric fans inspect assembly) • Replace pump • Apply silicone or replace belt • Adjust fan belt tension • Replace pulley • Remove belt to isolate. Replace pump. • Check pulley alignment. Repair as necessary.
No coolant flow through heater core	• Restricted return inlet in water pump • Heater hose collapsed or restricted • Restricted heater core • Restricted outlet in thermostat housing • Intake manifold bypass hole in cylinder head restricted • Faulty heater control valve • Intake manifold coolant passage restricted	• Remove restriction • Remove restriction or replace hose • Remove restriction or replace core • Remove flash or restriction • Remove restriction • Replace valve • Remove restriction or replace intake manifold

NOTE: *Immediately after shutdown, the engine enters a condition known as heat soak. This is caused by the cooling system being inoperative while engine temperature is still high. If coolant temperature rises above boiling point, expansion and pressure may push some coolant out of the radiator overflow tube. If this does not occur frequently it is considered normal.*

TCCS3C12

4

DRIVEABILITY AND EMISSION CONTROLS

AIR POLLUTION

The earth's atmosphere, at or near sea level, consists approximately of 78 percent nitrogen, 21 percent oxygen and 1 percent other gases. If it were possible to remain in this state, 100 percent clean air would result. However, many varied sources allow other gases and particulates to mix with the clean air, causing our atmosphere to become unclean or polluted.

Some of these pollutants are visible while others are invisible, with each having the capability of causing distress to the eyes, ears, throat, skin and respiratory system. Should these pollutants become concentrated in a specific area and under certain conditions, death could result due to the displacement or chemical change of the oxygen content in the air. These pollutants can also cause great damage to the environment and to the many man made objects that are exposed to the elements.

To better understand the causes of air pollution, the pollutants can be categorized into 3 separate types, natural, industrial and automotive.

Natural Pollutants

Natural pollution has been present on earth since before man appeared and continues to be a factor when discussing air pollution, although it causes only a small percentage of the overall pollution problem. It is the direct result of decaying organic matter, wind born smoke and particulates from such natural events as plain and forest fires (ignited by heat or lightning), volcanic ash, sand and dust which can spread over a large area of the countryside.

Such a phenomenon of natural pollution has been seen in the form of volcanic eruptions, with the resulting plume of smoke, steam and volcanic ash blotting out the sun's rays as it spreads and rises higher into the atmosphere. As it travels into the atmosphere the upper air currents catch and carry the smoke and ash, while condensing the steam back into water vapor. As the water vapor, smoke and ash travel on their journey, the smoke dissipates into the atmosphere while the ash and moisture settle back to earth in a trail hundreds of miles long. In some cases, lives are lost and millions of dollars of property damage result.

Industrial Pollutants

Industrial pollution is caused primarily by industrial processes, the burning of coal, oil and natural gas, which in turn produce smoke and fumes. Because the burning fuels contain large amounts of sulfur, the principal ingredients of smoke and fumes are sulfur dioxide and particulate matter. This type of pollutant occurs most severely during still, damp and cool weather, such as at night. Even in its less severe form, this pollutant is not confined to just cities. Because of air movements, the pollutants move for miles over the surrounding countryside, leaving in its path a barren and unhealthy environment for all living things.

Working with Federal, State and Local mandated regulations and by carefully monitoring emissions, big business has greatly reduced the amount of pollutant introduced from its industrial sources, striving to obtain an acceptable level. Because of the mandated industrial emission clean up, many land areas and streams in and around the cities that were formerly barren of vegetation and life, have now begun to move back in the direction of nature's intended balance.

Automotive Pollutants

The third major source of air pollution is automotive emissions. The emissions from the internal combustion engines were not an appreciable problem years ago because of the small number of registered vehicles and the nation's small highway system. However, during the early 1950's, the trend of the American people was to move from the cities to the surrounding suburbs. This caused an immediate problem in transportation because the majority of suburbs were not afforded mass transit conveniences. This lack of transportation created an attractive market for the automobile manufacturers, which resulted in a dramatic increase in the number of vehicles produced and sold, along with a marked increase in highway construction

between cities and the suburbs. Multi-vehicle families emerged with a growing emphasis placed on an individual vehicle per family member. As the increase in vehicle ownership and usage occurred, so did pollutant levels in and around the cities, as suburbanites drove daily to their businesses and employment, returning at the end of the day to their homes in the suburbs.

It was noted that a smoke and fog type haze was being formed and at times, remained in suspension over the cities, taking time to dissipate. At first this "smog," derived from the words "smoke" and "fog," was thought to result from industrial pollution but it was determined that automobile emissions shared the blame. It was discovered that when normal automobile emissions were exposed to sunlight for a period of time, complex chemical reactions would take place.

It is now known that smog is a photo chemical layer which develops when certain oxides of nitrogen (NOx) and unburned hydrocarbons (HC) from automobile emissions are exposed to sunlight. Pollution was more severe when smog would become stagnant over an area in which a warm layer of air settled over the top of the cooler air mass, trapping and holding the cooler mass at ground level. The trapped cooler air would keep the emissions from being dispersed and diluted through normal air flows. This type of air stagnation was given the name "Temperature Inversion."

TEMPERATURE INVERSION

In normal weather situations, surface air is warmed by heat radiating from the earth's surface and the sun's rays. This causes it to rise upward, into the atmosphere. Upon rising it will cool through a convection type heat exchange with the cooler upper air. As warm air rises, the surface pollutants are carried upward and dissipated into the atmosphere.

When a temperature inversion occurs, we find the higher air is no longer cooler, but is warmer than the surface air, causing the cooler surface air to become trapped. This warm air blanket can extend from above ground level to a few hundred or even a few thousand feet into the air. As the surface air is trapped, so are the pollutants, causing a severe smog condition. Should this stagnant air mass extend to a few thousand feet high, enough air movement with the inversion takes place to allow the smog layer to rise above ground level but the pollutants still cannot dissipate. This inversion can remain for days over an area, with the smog level only rising or lowering from ground level to a few hundred feet high. Meanwhile, the pollutant levels increase, causing eye irritation, respiratory problems, reduced visibility, plant damage and in some cases, even disease.

This inversion phenomenon was first noted in the Los Angeles, California area. The city lies in terrain resembling a basin and with certain weather conditions, a cold air mass is held in the basin while a warmer air mass covers it like a lid.

Because this type of condition was first documented as prevalent in the Los Angeles area, this type of trapped pollution was named Los Angeles Smog, although it occurs in other areas where a large concentration of automobiles are used and the air remains stagnant for any length of time.

HEAT TRANSFER

Consider the internal combustion engine as a machine in which raw materials must be placed so a finished product comes out. As in any machine operation, a certain amount of wasted material is formed. When we relate this to the internal combustion engine, we find that through the input of air and fuel, we obtain power during the combustion process to drive the vehicle. The by-product or waste of this power is, in part, heat and exhaust gases with which we must dispose.

The heat from the combustion process can rise to over 4000°F (2204°C). The dissipation of this heat is controlled by a ram air effect, the use of cooling fans to cause air flow and a liquid coolant solution surrounding the combustion area to transfer the heat of combustion through the cylinder walls and into the coolant. The coolant is then directed to a thin-finned, multi-tubed radiator, from which the excess heat is transferred to the atmosphere by 1 of the 3 heat transfer methods, conduction, convection or radiation.

The cooling of the combustion area is an important part in the control of exhaust emissions. To understand the behavior of the combustion and transfer of its heat, consider the air/fuel charge. It is ignited and the flame front burns progressively across the combustion chamber until the burning charge reaches the cylinder walls. Some of the fuel in contact with the walls is not hot enough to burn, thereby snuffing out or quenching the combustion process. This leaves unburned fuel in the combustion chamber. This unburned fuel is then forced out of the cylinder and into the exhaust system, along with the exhaust gases.

Many attempts have been made to minimize the amount of unburned fuel in the combustion chambers due to quenching, by increasing the coolant temperature and lessening the contact area of the coolant around the combustion area. However, design limitations within the combustion chambers prevent the complete burning of the air/fuel charge, so a certain amount of the unburned fuel is still expelled into the exhaust system, regardless of modifications to the engine.

AUTOMOTIVE EMISSIONS

Before emission controls were mandated on internal combustion engines, other sources of engine pollutants were discovered along with the exhaust emissions. It was determined that engine combustion exhaust produced approximately 60 percent of the total emission pollutants, fuel evaporation from the fuel tank and carburetor vents produced 20 percent, with the final 20 percent being produced through the crankcase as a by-product of the combustion process.

Exhaust Gases

The exhaust gases emitted into the atmosphere are a combination of burned and unburned fuel. To understand the exhaust emission and its composition, we must review some basic chemistry.

When the air/fuel mixture is introduced into the engine, we are mixing air, composed of nitrogen (78 percent), oxygen (21 percent) and other gases (1 percent) with the fuel, which is 100 percent hydrocarbons (HC), in a semi-controlled ratio. As the combustion process is accomplished, power is produced to move the vehicle while the heat of combustion is transferred to the cooling system. The exhaust gases are then composed of nitrogen, a diatomic gas (N_2), the same as was introduced in the engine, carbon dioxide (CO_2), the same gas that is used in beverage carbonation, and water vapor (H_2O). The nitrogen (N_2), for the most part, passes through the engine unchanged, while the oxygen (O_2) reacts (burns) with the hydrocarbons (HC) and produces the carbon dioxide (CO_2) and the water vapors (H_2O). If this chemical process would be the only process to take place, the exhaust emissions would be harmless. However, during the combustion process, other compounds are formed which are considered dangerous. These pollutants are hydrocarbons (HC), carbon monoxide (CO), oxides of nitrogen (NOx) oxides of sulfur (SOx) and engine particulates.

HYDROCARBONS

Hydrocarbons (HC) are essentially fuel which was not burned during the combustion process or which has escaped into the atmosphere through fuel evaporation. The main sources of incomplete combustion are rich air/fuel mixtures, low engine temperatures and improper spark timing. The main sources of hydrocarbon emission through fuel evaporation on most vehicles used to be the vehicle's fuel tank and carburetor float bowl.

To reduce combustion hydrocarbon emission, engine modifications were made to minimize dead space and surface area in the combustion chamber. In addition, the air/fuel mixture was made more lean through the improved control which feedback carburetion and fuel injection offers and by the addition of external controls to aid in further combustion of the hydrocarbons outside the engine. Two such methods were the addition of air injection systems, to inject fresh air into the exhaust manifolds and the installation of catalytic converters, units that are able to burn traces of hydrocarbons without affecting the internal combustion process or fuel economy.

To control hydrocarbon emissions through fuel evaporation, modifications were made to the fuel tank to allow storage of the fuel vapors during periods of engine shut-down. Modifications were also made to the air intake system so that at specific times during engine operation, these vapors may be purged and burned by blending them with the air/fuel mixture.

CARBON MONOXIDE

Carbon monoxide is formed when not enough oxygen is present during the combustion process to convert carbon (C) to carbon dioxide (CO_2). An increase in the carbon monoxide (CO) emission is normally accompanied by an increase in the hydrocarbon (HC) emission because of the lack of oxygen to completely burn all of the fuel mixture.

Carbon monoxide (CO) also increases the rate at which the photo chemical smog is formed by speeding up the conversion of nitric oxide (NO) to nitrogen dioxide (NO_2). To accomplish this, carbon monoxide (CO) combines with oxygen (O_2) and nitric oxide (NO) to produce carbon dioxide (CO_2) and nitrogen dioxide (NO_2). ($CO + O_2 + NO = CO_2 + NO_2$).

The dangers of carbon monoxide, which is an odorless and colorless toxic gas are many. When carbon monoxide is inhaled into the lungs and passed into the blood stream, oxygen is replaced by the carbon monoxide in the red blood cells, causing a reduction in the amount of oxygen supplied to the many parts of the body. This lack of oxygen causes headaches, lack of coordination, reduced mental alertness and, should the carbon monoxide concentration be high enough, death could result.

NITROGEN

Normally, nitrogen is an inert gas. When heated to approximately 2500°F (1371°C) through the combustion process, this gas becomes active and causes an increase in the nitric oxide (NO) emission.

Oxides of nitrogen (NOx) are composed of approximately 97–98 percent nitric oxide (NO). Nitric oxide is a colorless gas but when it is passed into the atmosphere, it combines with oxygen and forms nitrogen dioxide (NO_2). The nitrogen dioxide then combines with chemically active hydrocarbons (HC) and when in the presence of sunlight, causes the formation of photochemical smog.

Ozone

To further complicate matters, some of the nitrogen dioxide (NO_2) is broken apart by the sunlight to form nitric oxide and oxygen. (NO_2 + sunlight = NO + O). This single atom of oxygen then combines with diatomic (meaning 2 atoms) oxygen (O_2) to form ozone (O_3). Ozone is one of the smells associated with smog. It has a pungent and offensive odor, irritates the eyes and lung tissues, affects the growth of plant life and causes rapid deterioration of rubber products. Ozone can be formed by sunlight as well as electrical discharge into the air.

The most common discharge area on the automobile engine is the secondary ignition electrical system, especially when inferior quality spark plug cables are used. As the surge of high voltage is routed through the secondary cable, the circuit builds up an electrical field around the wire, which acts upon the oxygen in the surrounding air to form the ozone. The faint glow along the cable with the engine running that may be visible on a dark night, is called the "corona discharge." It is the result of the electrical field passing from a high along the cable, to a low in the surrounding air, which forms the ozone gas. The combination of corona and ozone has been a major cause of cable deterioration. Recently, different and better quality insulating materials have lengthened the life of the electrical cables.

Although ozone at ground level can be harmful, ozone is beneficial to the earth's inhabitants. By having a concentrated ozone layer called the "ozonosphere," between 10 and 20 miles (16–32 km) up in the atmosphere, much of the ultra violet radiation from the sun's rays are absorbed and screened. If this ozone layer were not present, much of the earth's surface would be burned, dried and unfit for human life.

OXIDES OF SULFUR

Oxides of sulfur (SOx) were initially ignored in the exhaust system emissions, since the sulfur content of gasoline as a fuel is less than $\frac{1}{10}$ of 1 percent. Because of this small amount, it was felt that it contributed very little to the overall pollution problem. However, because of the difficulty in solving the sulfur emissions in industrial pollutions and the introduction of catalytic converter to the automobile exhaust systems, a change was mandated. The automobile exhaust system, when equipped with a catalytic converter, changes the sulfur dioxide (SO_2) into sulfur trioxide (SO_3).

When this combines with water vapors (H_2O), a sulfuric acid mist (H_2SO_4) is formed and is a very difficult pollutant to handle since it is extremely corrosive. This sulfuric acid mist that is formed, is the same mist that rises from the vents of an automobile battery when an active chemical reaction takes place within the battery cells.

When a large concentration of vehicles equipped with catalytic converters are operating in an area, this acid mist may rise and be distributed over a large ground area causing land, plant, crop, paint and building damage.

PARTICULATE MATTER

A certain amount of particulate matter is present in the burning of any fuel, with carbon constituting the largest percentage of the particulates. In gasoline, the remaining particulates are the burned remains of the various other compounds used in its manufacture. When a gasoline engine is in good internal condition, the particulate emissions are low but as the engine wears internally, the particulate emissions increase. By visually inspecting the tail pipe emissions, a determination can be made as to where an engine defect may exist. An engine with light gray or blue smoke emitting from the tail pipe normally indicates an increase in the oil consumption through burning due to internal engine wear. Black smoke would indicate a defective fuel delivery system, causing the engine to operate in a rich mode. Regardless of the color of the smoke, the internal part of the engine or the fuel delivery system should be repaired to prevent excess particulate emissions.

Diesel and turbine engines emit a darkened plume of smoke from the exhaust system because of the type of fuel used. Emission control regulations are mandated for this type of emission and more stringent measures are being used to prevent excess emission of the particulate matter. Electronic components are being introduced to control the injection of the fuel at precisely the proper time of piston travel, to achieve the optimum in fuel ignition and fuel usage. Other particulate after-burning components are being tested to achieve a cleaner emission.

Good grades of engine lubricating oils should be used, which meet the manufacturers specification. Cut-rate oils can contribute to the particulate emission problem because of their low flash or ignition temperature point. Such oils burn prematurely during the combustion process causing emission of particulate matter.

The cooling system is an important factor in the reduction of particulate matter. The optimum combustion will occur, with the cooling system operating at a temperature specified by the manufacturer. The cooling system must be maintained in the same manner as the engine oiling system, as each system is required to perform properly in order for the engine to operate efficiently for a long time.

Crankcase Emissions

Crankcase emissions are made up of water, acids, unburned fuel, oil fumes and particulates. These emissions are classified as hydrocarbons (HC) and are formed by the small amount of unburned, compressed air/fuel mixture entering the crankcase from the combustion area (between the cylinder walls and piston rings) during the compression and power strokes. The head of the compression and combustion help to form the remaining crankcase emissions.

Since the first engines, crankcase emissions were allowed into the atmosphere through a road draft tube, mounted on the lower side of the engine block. Fresh air came in through an open oil filler cap or breather. The air passed through the crankcase mixing with blow-by gases. The motion of the vehicle and the air blowing past the open end of the road draft tube caused a low pressure area (vacuum) at the end of the tube. Crankcase emissions were simply drawn out of the road draft tube into the air.

To control the crankcase emission, the road draft tube was deleted. A hose and/or tubing was routed from the crankcase to the intake manifold so the blow-by emission could be burned with the air/fuel mixture. However, it was found that intake manifold vacuum, used to draw the crankcase emissions into the manifold, would vary in strength at the wrong time and not allow the proper emission flow. A regulating valve was needed to control the flow of air through the crankcase.

Testing, showed the removal of the blow-by gases from the crankcase as quickly as possible, was most important to the longevity of the engine. Should large accumulations of blow-by gases remain and condense, dilution of the engine oil would occur to form water, soots, resins, acids and lead salts, resulting in the formation of sludge and varnishes. This condensation of the blow-by gases occurs more frequently on vehicles used in numerous starting and stopping conditions, excessive idling and when the engine is not allowed to attain normal operating temperature through short runs.

Evaporative Emissions

Gasoline fuel is a major source of pollution, before and after it is burned in the automobile engine. From the time the fuel is refined, stored, pumped and transported, again stored until it is pumped into the fuel tank of the vehicle, the gasoline gives off unburned hydrocarbons (HC) into the atmosphere. Through the redesign of storage areas and venting systems, the pollution factor was diminished, but not eliminated, from the refinery standpoint. However, the automobile still remained the primary source of vaporized, unburned hydrocarbon (HC) emissions.

Fuel pumped from an underground storage tank is cool but when exposed to a warmer ambient temperature, will expand. Before controls were mandated, an owner might fill the fuel tank with fuel from an underground storage tank and park the vehicle for some time in warm area, such as a parking lot. As the fuel would warm, it would expand and should no provisions or area be provided for the expansion, the fuel would spill out of the filler neck and onto the ground, causing hydrocarbon (HC) pollution and creating a severe fire hazard. To correct this condition, the vehicle manufacturers added overflow plumbing and/or gasoline tanks with built in expansion areas or domes.

However, this did not control the fuel vapor emission from the fuel tank. It was determined that most of the fuel evaporation occurred when the vehicle was stationary and the engine not operating. Most vehicles carry 5–25 gallons (19–95 liters) of gasoline. Should a large concentration of vehicles be parked in one area, such as a large parking lot, excessive fuel vapor emissions would take place, increasing as the temperature increases.

To prevent the vapor emission from escaping into the atmosphere, the fuel systems were designed to trap the vapors while the vehicle is stationary, by sealing the system from the atmosphere. A storage system is used to collect and hold the fuel vapors from the carburetor (if equipped) and the fuel tank when the engine is not operating. When the engine is started, the storage system is then purged of the fuel vapors, which are drawn into the engine and burned with the air/fuel mixture.

EMISSION CONTROLS

Crankcase Ventilation System

OPERATION

The crankcase ventilation system returns blow-by gas to the intake manifold. A Positive Crankcase Ventilation (PCV) valve is used to meter the gas and is located in the breather separator under the intake manifold.

During partial throttle operation of the engine, manifold vacuum is high, allowing the blow-by gas to be sucked through the PCV valve into the intake manifold. Normally, the capacity of the valve is sufficient to handle any blow-by and a small amount of ventilating air. The ventilating air is drawn from the air duct into the crankcase. The ventilating air passes through the hose connecting the air inlet tube to the cylinder head cover.

Under full throttle condition, the manifold vacuum is insufficient to draw the blow-by flow through the valve. The flow reverses, coming from the crankcase, going through the ventilating hose and into the air duct.

COMPONENT TESTING

▶ **See Figures 1 and 2**

1. Remove the PCV valve and shake it gently.
  a. If the valve rattles when shaken, connect the valve to the vacuum hose and proceed to Step 2.
  b. If the valve does not rattle, it is sticking and must be replaced.
2. Start the engine and allow it to reach normal operating temperature.
3. Check the PCV valve for vacuum by placing your finger over the end of the valve.
  a. If vacuum exists, proceed to Step 5.
  b. If vacuum does not exist, check for loose hose connections, vacuum leaks or blockage. Correct as necessary.
4. Reinstall the PCV valve.
5. With the engine running, disconnect the fresh air intake hose from the air inlet tube (which connects the air cleaner housing to the throttle body).
6. Place a stiff piece of paper over the hose end and wait 1 minute.
  a. If vacuum holds the paper in place, the system is OK; reconnect the hose.

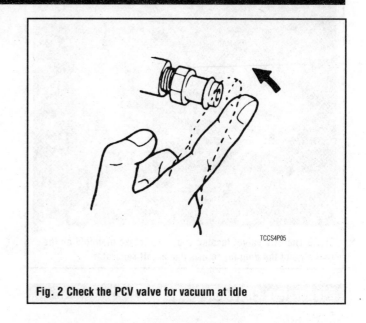

TCCS4P05

Fig. 2 Check the PCV valve for vacuum at idle

  b. If the paper is not held in place, check for loose hose connections, vacuum leaks or blockage. Correct as necessary.

REMOVAL & INSTALLATION

PCV Valve

▶ **See Figure 3**

The PCV valve is located under the intake manifold in the oil separator.
1. Disconnect the vacuum hose from the PCV valve.
2. Unscrew the PCV valve from the breather separator under the intake manifold.

To install:
3. Screw the PCV valve into the breather separator under the intake manifold.
4. Connect the vacuum hose to the PCV valve.

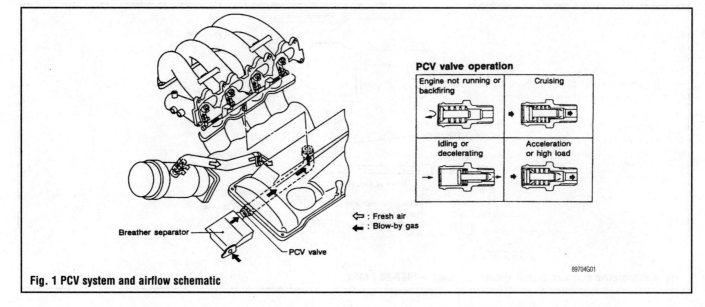

PCV valve operation

| Engine not running or backfiring | Cruising |
| Idling or decelerating | Acceleration or high load |

⇦ : Fresh air
⬅ : Blow-by gas

Breather separator

PCV valve

89704G01

Fig. 1 PCV system and airflow schematic

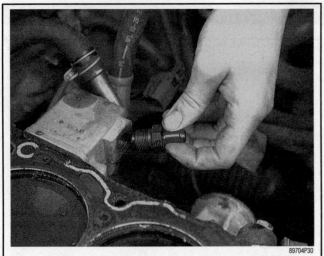

Fig. 3 The PCV valve, located under the intake manifold on the rear side of the engine, screws into an oil separator

Evaporative Emission Controls

OPERATION

▶ **See Figures 4, 5, 6 and 7**

The evaporative emission control system prevents the uncontrolled release of gasoline vapors (hydrocarbons) into the atmosphere. These vapors are produced when fuel evaporates in the sealed fuel tank..

The main component of the system is the charcoal canister. The activated charcoal in the canister absorbs and stores fuel vapors generated inside the fuel tank while the engine is inoperative. When the engine is running, the vapors are drawn through the electronically controlled purge control valve and into the intake manifold. The vapors enter the air/fuel mixture and are burned in the combustion process.

➥**Not all components are used on all vehicles.**

The purge control valve is used to time the vapor release into the intake manifold. During deceleration and idling, the purge control valve is closed and allows only a small amount of vapor to reach the intake. Under all other conditions, the valve allows vapor to be purged.

Two types of purge control valves are used: an electronic canister purge volume control valve and a purge control valve/constant purge orifice combination. The canister purge volume valve is controlled by the ECM and meters purge volume in proportion to air flow. The purge control valve/constant purge orifice combination operates mechanically. As engine speed increases and throttle vacuum rises, more vapor is purged to the intake manifold.

The canister control solenoid valve responds to signals from the ECM. When the ECM grounds the solenoid, the vacuum signal from the throttle body to the canister is cut. Generally, this is done under start-up, idling and decelerating conditions.

A fuel check valve (vacuum cut valve) is used to prevent engine vacuum from sucking fuel out of the fuel tank. The valve also functions to prevent fuel from flowing out of the fuel tank if the vehicle should roll over.

The fuel cap contains a vacuum relief valve which allows air into the fuel tank to prevent a build-up of vacuum.

The evaporative emission system canister, vacuum line and vapor hoses should be inspected every 30,000 miles (48,300 km).

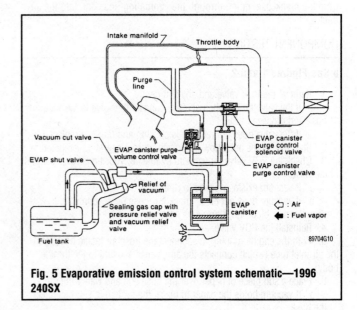

Fig. 5 Evaporative emission control system schematic—1996 240SX

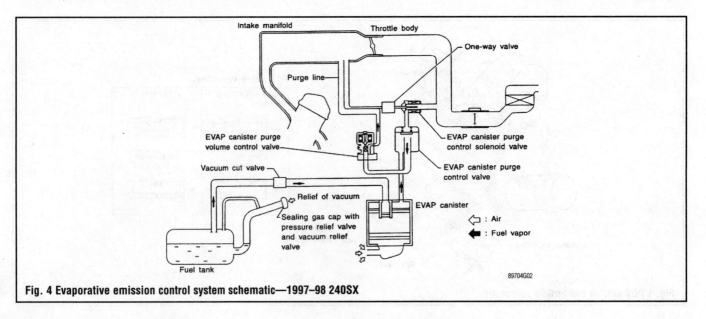

Fig. 4 Evaporative emission control system schematic—1997–98 240SX

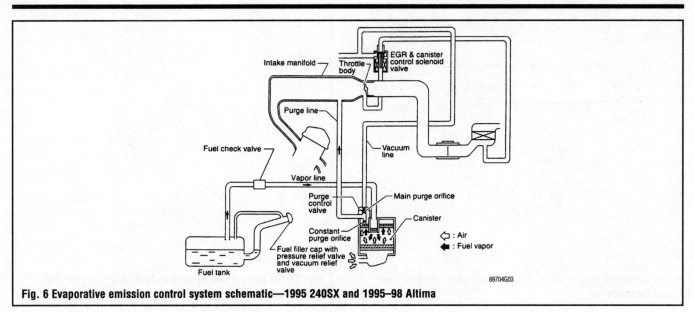

Fig. 6 Evaporative emission control system schematic—1995 240SX and 1995–98 Altima

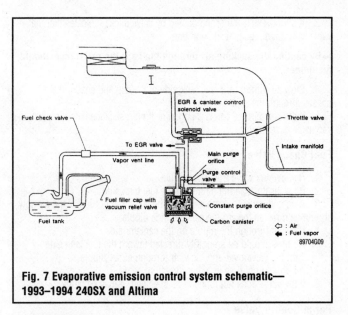

Fig. 7 Evaporative emission control system schematic—1993–1994 240SX and Altima

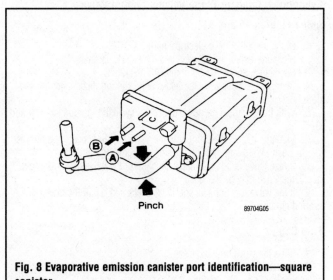

Fig. 8 Evaporative emission canister port identification—square canister

COMPONENT TESTING

Evaporative Canister

ROUND CANISTER

The round evaporative canister is a sealed component and cannot be disassembled for inspection. Visually inspect the exterior of the canister for damage and replace as necessary.

SQUARE CANISTER

♦ See Figure 8

1. Visually inspect the exterior of the canister for damage, and replace as necessary.
2. Label and disconnect all vacuum and vapor lines.
3. Inspect the lines for damage, and replace as necessary.
4. Inspect the canister for damage, and replace as necessary.
5. Pinch the fresh air vent hose.

6. Blow air in Port **A** and check that it flows freely out of Port **E**.
7. If air does not flow as specified, the canister may be defective.

Evaporative Canister Control Solenoid Valve

♦ See Figure 9

This valve may be known as the canister purge control valve on some vehicles.

1. Label and disconnect the vacuum lines and electrical harness.
2. Inspect the lines for damage, and replace as necessary.
3. Inspect the valve for damage, and replace as necessary.
4. Apply battery voltage and ground between the valve terminals.
5. Air should pass between Port **A** and Port **B**.
6. Air should not pass between Port **A** and Port **C**.
7. Remove battery voltage.
8. Air should pass between Port **A** and Port **C**.
9. Air should not pass between Port **A** and Port **B**.
10. If valve does not function as specified, it may be faulty.
11. If the valve responds as specified, check and repair power and ground circuits.

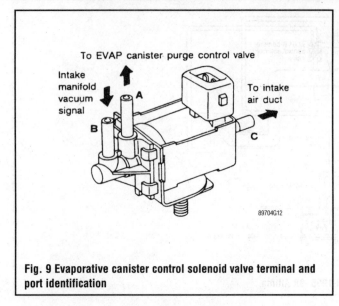

Fig. 9 Evaporative canister control solenoid valve terminal and port identification

Evaporative Canister Purge Volume Control Valve

⧫ **See Figures 10 and 11**

1. Disconnect the valve electrical harness.
2. Measure resistance between terminals, as illustrated.
3. Resistance should be 30 ohms @ 77°F (25°C).
4. Remove the valve from the intake collector and disconnect the vacuum hoses.
5. With the electrical harness connected, cycle the ignition key **ON** and **OFF**.
6. Visually inspect the plunger in the valve for movement. The plunger can be seen by looking through the side vacuum port.
7. If resistance is not within specification or the valve does not move freely, the valve may be defective.
8. If the valve functions as specified, check and repair the power and ground circuits.

Fuel Cap

1. Wipe the valve housing clean.
2. Suck air through the cap using a vacuum pump and the proper adapters supplied with the pump.

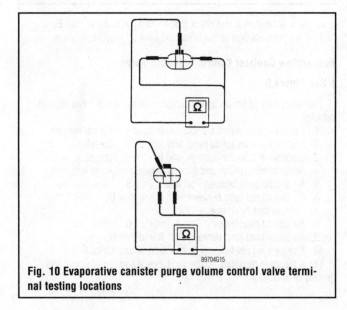

Fig. 10 Evaporative canister purge volume control valve terminal testing locations

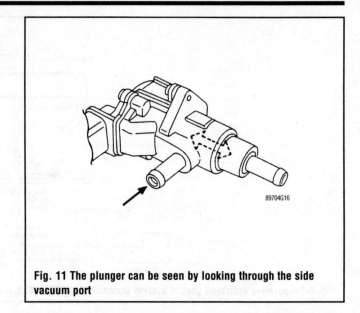

Fig. 11 The plunger can be seen by looking through the side vacuum port

3. A slight resistance accompanied by valve clicks indicates that the valve is in good mechanical condition.

➡**By continually sucking air through the cap, the resistance should disappear.**

4. Blow air through the fuel tank side of the cap and ensure that air passes through the cap.
5. If the valve in the cap is clogged or if no resistance is felt, replace the cap as an assembly.

Fuel Check Valve

1. Remove the valve from the vehicle.
2. Blow air through the nipple on the fuel tank side.
3. A considerable resistance should be felt and a portion of the air flow should be directed toward the canister side nipple.
4. Blow air through the nipple on the canister side.
5. Air flow should be smoothly directed toward the fuel tank side.
6. Turn the valve over and blow air through either nipple.
7. Air should not flow in either direction.
8. If the valve does not function as specified, it may be faulty.

Purge Control Valve

ROUND CANISTER

⧫ **See Figures 12, 13 and 14**

1. Label and disconnect all vacuum and vapor lines.
2. Inspect the lines for damage, and replace as necessary.
3. Inspect the canister for damage, and replace as necessary.
4. Blow air in Port **A** and ensure that there is no leakage.
5. Apply a 3.94–5.91 in. Hg vacuum to port **A**.
6. Cover Port **D** with your hand.
7. Blow air into Port **C** and verify that there is a free flow of air out of Port **B**.
8. If air does not flow as specified, the canister may be defective.

SQUARE CANISTER

⧫ **See Figure 15**

1. Label and disconnect all vacuum and vapor lines.
2. Inspect the lines for damage, and replace as necessary.
3. Inspect the valve for damage, and replace as necessary.
4. Plug Port **B**.

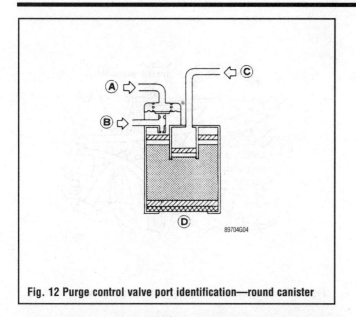

Fig. 12 Purge control valve port identification—round canister

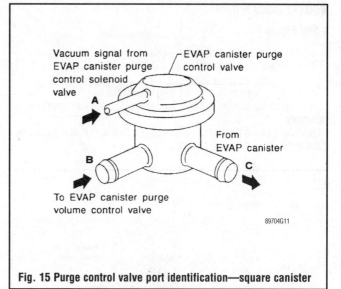

Fig. 15 Purge control valve port identification—square canister

Fig. 13 Connect a piece of vacuum hose to Port A and blow into it. If leaks are present, the valve is faulty

5. Apply an 11 psi pressure to Port **A** and hold for 15 seconds.
6. Ensure that there is no leakage.
7. Repeat the test for Port **C**.
8. If leakage occurs, the valve may be defective.

REMOVAL & INSTALLATION

Evaporative Canister

ROUND CANISTER

▶ See Figure 16

The canister is located on the firewall (Altima) or the radiator support (240SX).
1. Label and disconnect the vacuum and vapor lines.
2. Loosen the attaching bolts.
3. Carefully remove the canister from the vehicle.
4. Inspect the canister and lines for damage. Replace components as necessary.
5. Installation is the reverse of removal. Be sure to tighten the attaching bolts securely.

Fig. 14 Next, connect a vacuum pump to the valve and apply vacuum. Blow into Port C and ensure that air flows out of Port B

Fig. 16 The round canister is located on the firewall, below the fuel filter—Altima

SQUARE CANISTER

▶ **See Figure 17**

1. The canister is located on the firewall.
2. Label and disconnect the vacuum and vapor hoses.
3. Loosen the attaching bolts.
4. Carefully remove the canister from the vehicle.
5. Inspect the canister and lines for damage. Replace components as necessary.
6. Installation is the reverse of removal. Be sure to tighten the attaching bolts to 74–95 inch lbs. (8–11 Nm).

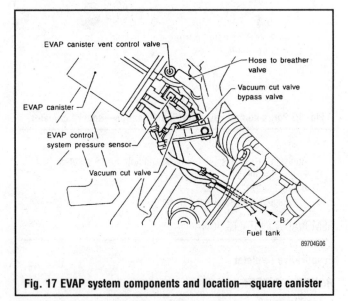

Fig. 17 EVAP system components and location—square canister

Evaporative Canister Control Solenoid Valve

The evaporative canister control solenoid valve is located on the intake manifold.

1. Label and disconnect the solenoid valve vacuum lines.
2. Loosen the solenoid valve attaching nut, then separate the valve from the intake manifold.

To install:

3. Install the solenoid valve and tighten the mounting nut to 12–14 ft. lbs. (16–19 Nm).
4. Connect the solenoid valve vacuum lines.

Evaporative Canister Purge Volume Control Valve

▶ **See Figure 18**

The evaporative canister purge volume control valve is located under the intake manifold.

1. Label and disconnect the vacuum lines and electrical harnesses.
2. Inspect the lines for damage, and replace as necessary.
3. Remove the valve from the intake collector.

To install:

4. Inspect valve for damage, and replace as necessary.
5. Install the valve on the collector.
6. Connect the vacuum lines and electrical harness.

Fuel Check Valve

The fuel check valve is located in the vapor vent line near the fuel tank.

1. Raise and support the vehicle safely.
2. Locate the valve in the vapor vent line.
3. Note the installed direction of the valve for installation reference.
4. Loosen the hose clamps and remove the valve.
5. Installation is the reverse of removal.

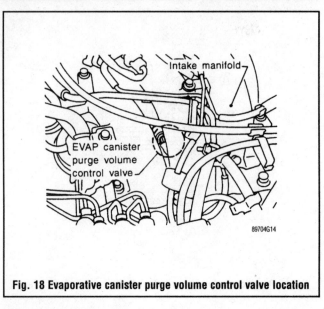

Fig. 18 Evaporative canister purge volume control valve location

Purge Control Valve

ROUND CANISTER

On round canisters, the purge control valve is an integral part of the evaporative canister. If the valve is determined to be faulty, the canister and purge control valve must be replaced as an assembly.

SQUARE CANISTER

On square canisters, the purge control valve is a separate component mounted near the canister, at the rear of the vehicle.

1. Label and disconnect the vacuum and vapor lines.
2. Inspect the lines for damage, and replace as necessary.
3. Remove the valve from the vehicle.

To install:

4. Inspect the valve for damage, and replace as necessary.
5. Install the valve on the vehicle.
6. Connect the vacuum lines.

Exhaust Gas Recirculation (EGR) System

OPERATION

The Exhaust Gas Recirculation (EGR) system cuts and controls vacuum applied to the EGR valve to suit engine operating conditions. This "cut and control" operation is accomplished through the Electronic Control Module (ECM), in conjunction with an EGR and canister control solenoid valve. When the ECM detects any of the following conditions, current flows through the solenoid valve:

- Low engine coolant temperature
- Engine starting
- High speed engine operation
- Engine idling
- Excessively high engine coolant temperature
- Mass air flow sensor malfunction

Such current flow through the solenoid valve causes port vacuum to be discharged into the atmosphere. The EGR valve and canister remain closed.

The EGR valve controls the amount of exhaust gas routed to the intake manifold. Vacuum is applied to the EGR valve in response to throttle valve opening. The vacuum controls the movement of a taper valve connected to the vacuum diaphragm of the EGR valve.

The EGR and canister control solenoid valve responds to signals from the ECM. When the ECM sends an ON (ground) signal, the coil in the solenoid valve is energized. A plunger will then move to cut the vacuum signal (from the throttle body to the EGR valve and canister purge valve). When the ECM sends an OFF signal, the vacuum signal passes through the solenoid valve. The signal then reaches the EGR valve and canister.

The EGR Backpressure Transducer (EGRC-BPT) valve monitors exhaust pressure to activate the diaphragm, controlling throttle body vacuum applied to the EGR valve. In this way, the recirculated exhaust gas is controlled in response to positioning of the EGR valve or to engine operation.

A negative temperature coefficient EGR temperature sensor is used to control EGR operation timing during warm-up and under conditions when the engine temperature is out of normal range.

SYSTEM TESTING

1. Start the engine and allow it to reach operating temperature.
2. Check for EGR valve movement while racing the engine from 2000–4000 rpm under no load.
3. The EGR valve diaphragm should lift up and down without restriction.
4. If the EGR valve does not respond as specified, perform component testing.

COMPONENT TESTING

♦ See Figure 19

EGR Valve

♦ See Figure 20

1. Label and disconnect the EGR valve vacuum hose.
2. Using a hand-held vacuum pump, slowly apply 5–10 in. Hg (17–34 kPa) of vacuum to the EGR valve nipple.
3. The EGR valve diaphragm should lift up. Release the vacuum and the EGR valve diaphragm should lower without restriction.
4. If the EGR valve does not respond as specified, remove the valve and check for obstructions. If no obstructions are found, the EGR valve may be faulty.

EGR Backpressure Transducer (EGRC-BPT) Valve

1. Label and disconnect the transducer valve's vacuum lines.
2. Plug one of the ports on top of the valve.
3. Blow into the bottom port gently while applying vacuum to the second port on top of the valve. Vacuum should hold steady and not leak.
4. Stop blowing into the bottom port and vacuum should leak out.
5. If the valve does not respond as specified, it may be faulty.

Fig. 19 The EGR valve (1), EGR backpressure transducer (2) and EGR control solenoid valve (3) are all located on the intake manifold, near the firewall

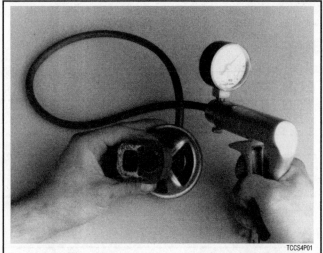

Fig. 20 The EGR function test is performed by using a vacuum pump. Watch for diaphragm movement while applying vacuum

EGR Control Solenoid Valve

♦ See Figure 21

1. Label and disconnect the solenoid valve electrical harness and vacuum lines.
2. Air should pass through Ports **A** and **B** freely.
3. Apply battery voltage and ground to the solenoid terminals.
4. Air should not pass through Ports **A** and **B** freely.
5. Air should now pass through Ports **A** and **C** freely.
6. If the valve does not respond as specified, it may be faulty.
7. If the valve responds as specified, check and repair the power and ground circuits.

Fig. 21 EGR control solenoid valve port identification

EGR Temperature Sensor

1. Disconnect the temperature sensor electrical harness and measure the resistance between the sensor terminals.
2. Resistance should be high when the sensor is cold and low when the sensor is hot.
3. Compare the cold and hot EGR temperature sensor resistance measurements with the accompanying chart.

4. If resistance is not within specifications or does not respond smoothly as temperature rises and falls, the sensor may be faulty.

5. If the sensor responds as specified, check and repair the power and ground circuits.

EGR TEMPERATURE SENSOR

EGR temperature °C (°F)	Voltage (V)	Resistance (MΩ)
0 (32)	4.81	7.9 - 9.7
50 (122)	2.82	0.57 - 0.70
100 (212)	0.8	0.08 - 0.10

89704C01

REMOVAL & INSTALLATION

▶ See Figure 22

EGR Valve

▶ See Figures 23 and 24

The EGR valve is located on the intake manifold.
1. Label and disconnect the EGR vacuum lines.
2. Loosen the EGR valve attaching nuts, then separate the valve from the intake manifold.
3. Remove and discard the EGR valve gasket.
To install:
4. Throughly clean the gasket mating surfaces on the valve and the intake manifold.
5. Install the EGR valve, along with a new gasket, and tighten the mounting nuts to 12–14 ft. lbs. (16–19 Nm).
6. Connect the EGR vacuum lines.

EGR Backpressure Transducer (EGRC-BPT) Valve

The EGR backpressure transducer valve is located on the intake manifold.
1. Label and disconnect the valve's vacuum lines.
2. Loosen the valve attaching bolts, then remove the valve from the mounting bracket.
To install:
3. Position the valve and tighten the mounting bolts to 12–14 ft. lbs. (16–19 Nm).
4. Connect the valve's vacuum lines.

Fig. 22 The EGR backpressure transducer and EGR control solenoid valve fasteners (arrows) are plainly visible

Fig. 23 The EGR valve port (arrow) allows exhaust gas to flow into the intake manifold

Fig. 24 The EGR valve gasket is made of a special, high temperature resistant material. Always replace it with a gasket made especially for EGR valves

EGR Control Solenoid Valve

▶ See Figure 25

The EGR and canister control solenoid valve is located on the intake manifold.
1. Label and disconnect the solenoid valve vacuum lines.
2. Loosen the solenoid valve attaching nut, then separate the valve from the intake manifold.
To install:
3. Install the solenoid valve and tighten the mounting nut to 12–14 ft. lbs. (16–19 Nm).
4. Connect the solenoid valve vacuum lines.

EGR Temperature Sensor

▶ See Figure 26

The EGR temperature sensor is located on the engine block, viewable through the intake manifold runners.
1. Partially drain the engine cooling system until the coolant level is below the EGR temperature sensor mounting hole.
2. Disconnect the EGR temperature sensor electrical harness.

Fig. 25 Label and disconnect the EGR control solenoid valve vacuum hoses

Fig. 26 The EGR temperature sensor (arrow) is located in the intake manifold between cylinders 3 and 4

3. Remove the sensor from the intake manifold.

To install:

4. Coat the sensor threads with Teflon® sealant.

5. Thread the sensor into the intake manifold and tighten to 11–18 ft. lbs. (15–25 Nm).

ELECTRONIC ENGINE CONTROLS

Engine Control Module (ECM)

OPERATION

The Engine Control Module (ECM) performs many functions. The module receives data from various engine sensors and computes the required fuel flow rate necessary to maintain correct air/fuel ratio throughout the entire engine operational range.

Based on the data received and information programmed into the ECM's memory, the ECM generates output signals to control relays, actuators and solenoids. The module automatically senses and compensates for any changes in altitude when driving the vehicle.

The ECM consists of a microcomputer, inspection lamps, a diagnostic mode selector, and connectors for signal input, signal output, power supply and ground. The unit is located under the center console, at the firewall on the Altima, and in the passenger's side kick panel on the 240SX.

REMOVAL & INSTALLATION

♦ See Figure 27

➥Electrostatic Discharge (ESD) can ruin sensitive electronic components. Always wear a grounding strap or discharge electricity to a good ground prior to handling any electronic components.

1. Disconnect the negative battery cable.
2. On the Altima, remove the center console.
3. On the 240SX, remove the passenger's side kick panel.
4. Label and disconnect the ECM electrical harness.
5. Remove the ECM mounting screws.
6. Carefully remove the ECM from the vehicle.

To install:

7. Position the ECM in the vehicle and tighten the mounting screws securely.
8. Connect the ECM electrical harness.
9. On the 240SX, install the passenger's side kick panel.
10. On the Altima, install the center console.

6. Connect the negative battery cable.
7. Refill the engine cooling system.
8. Start the engine and check for coolant leaks. Top off the cooling system.

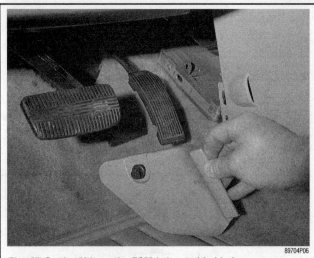

Fig. 27 On the Altima, the ECM is located behind an access panel at the front of the console

11. Connect the negative battery cable.
12. Start the vehicle and verify proper operation.
13. Read and clear the ECM trouble code memory.

Oxygen Sensor

OPERATION

The oxygen sensor supplies a signal to the ECM, which indicates a rich or lean condition during engine operation. The input data assists the computer in determining the proper air/fuel ratio. A low voltage signal from the sensor indicates too much oxygen in the exhaust (lean condition) and a high voltage signal indicates too little oxygen in the exhaust (rich condition).

Oxygen sensors are located in the exhaust system, usually in the exhaust manifold or near the catalytic converter. Heated oxygen sensors are used on some models to allow the engine to reach the closed loop state faster.

TESTING

Oxygen Sensor

The ECM contains an oxygen sensor monitor function which is used to test the oxygen sensor.

1. Locate the ECM and take note of the LED and mode switch positions.
2. Turn the ignition switch **ON**.
3. Turn the mode switch screw fully clockwise.
4. Wait at least 2 seconds.
5. Turn the mode switch screw fully counterclockwise.
6. Start the engine and allow it to reach operating temperature.
7. Run the engine at approximately 2000 rpm for 2 minutes under no load.
8. Ensure that the red LED on the ECM or the Malfunction Indicator Lamp (MIL) on the dashboard flash on and off more than 5 times every 10 seconds.
9. If the red LED on the ECM or the MIL do not function as specified, check the oxygen sensor circuit back to the ECM for continuity.
10. If continuity exists, the oxygen sensor may be faulty.

Oxygen Sensor Heater

➡**Any oxygen sensor that has been dropped from a height of more than 20 inches (51cm) may be defective.**

FRONT

▶ **See Figure 28**

1. Disconnect the sensor electrical harness.
2. Measure resistance between the outer terminals of the connector.
3. Resistance should be 2.3–4.3 ohms @ 77°F (25°C).
4. Check continuity between the center terminal and each of the outer terminals. Continuity should not exist.
5. If resistance is not as specified or continuity exists, the oxygen sensor is faulty.
6. If resistance and continuity are within specification, check and repair the circuits.

REAR

▶ **See Figures 29 and 30**

1. Disconnect the sensor electrical harness.
2. On models with a three-terminal connector, measure resistance between the two outer terminals. On models with a four-terminal connector, measure resistance between the two illustrated terminals.
3. For three-terminal connectors, the resistance should be 5.2–8.2 ohms @ 77°F (25°C). For four-terminal connectors, the resistance should be 2.3–4.3 ohms @ 77°F (25°C).
4. On models with a four-terminal connector, also check continuity between the various terminal combinations, as illustrated. Continuity should not exist.
5. If resistance is not as specified or continuity exists, the oxygen sensor is faulty.
6. If resistance and continuity are within specification, check and repair the circuits.

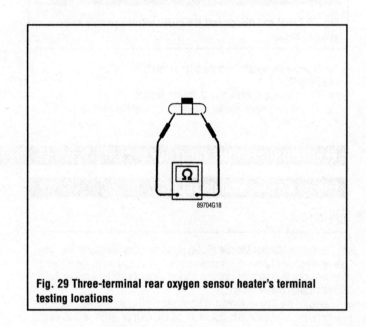

89704G18

Fig. 29 Three-terminal rear oxygen sensor heater's terminal testing locations

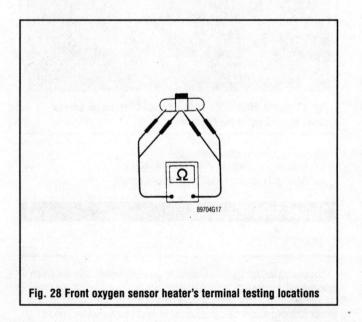

89704G17

Fig. 28 Front oxygen sensor heater's terminal testing locations

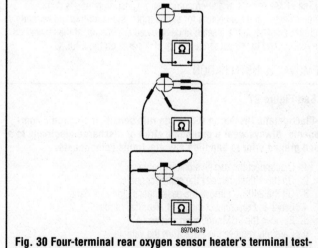

89704G19

Fig. 30 Four-terminal rear oxygen sensor heater's terminal testing locations. Check resistance (top) and continuity (middle and bottom)

REMOVAL & INSTALLATION

▶ **See Figures 31 and 32**

Oxygen sensors are located in the exhaust manifold and may also be located in the exhaust system near the catalytic converter.

1. Disconnect the negative battery cable.
2. Raise and support the vehicle safely, as required.
3. Label and disconnect the oxygen sensor electrical harness.

➡ **Lubricate the sensor threads with penetrating oil prior to removal.**

4. Remove the sensor using an box end wrench or special oxygen sensor socket.

To install:

5. Thread the sensor into the mounting boss and tighten to 30–37 ft. lbs. (40–50 Nm).

➡ **Most new oxygen sensor threads are coated with anti-seize compound. If you are reinstalling a used oxygen sensor, carefully coat the threads with anti-seize compound. Take care not to allow the oxygen sensor element to be contaminated by the compound.**

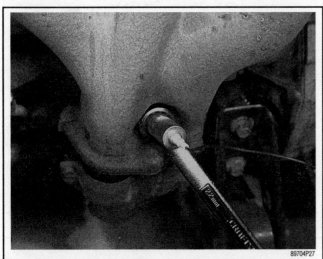

89704P27

Fig. 31 Use a box end wrench or a special oxygen sensor socket to remove the sensor from the exhaust manifold

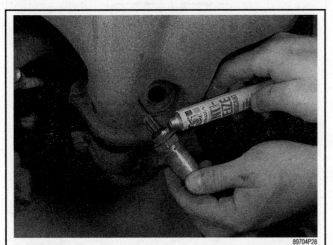

89704P28

Fig. 32 When reinstalling an old oxygen sensor, lightly coat the threads with anti-seize compound. New oxygen sensors are usually pre-coated at the factory

6. Connect the engine control electrical harness to the sensor.
7. If applicable, lower the vehicle.
8. Connect the negative battery cable.

Idle Air Control Valve-Air Regulator

OPERATION

The Idle Air Control Valve (IACV)-air regulator consists of either a wax or bimetallic spring temperature sensing mechanism and a spring. When the engine is cold, the air bypass port is open. This provides for fast idle setting while the engine heats. As the engine warms, the temperature mechanism is operated and the air bypass port closes to decrease idle speed.

TESTING

Altima

▶ **See Figure 33**

1. Remove the IACV-air regulator from the engine.
2. Immerse the IACV-air regulator in cold or hot water.
3. Insert a thermometer into the water and heat or cool it, as necessary, to reach the proper testing temperatures.
4. Check for air flow through the valve when the water temperature is approximately 68°F (20°C).
5. Almost no air should flow through the valve with the water temperature at 176°F (80°C).
6. If the IACV-air regulator does not respond as specified, it may be faulty.

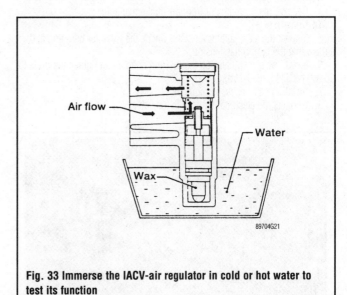

89704G21

Fig. 33 Immerse the IACV-air regulator in cold or hot water to test its function

240SX

▶ **See Figure 34**

1. Disconnect the electrical harness from the valve.
2. Remove the valve and inspect the plunger for seizing or sticking. Inspect the spring.
3. On 1993–94 models, measure the resistance between the terminals of the valve.
4. On 1995–98 models, measure the resistance between the illustrated terminals.
5. Resistance should be 70–80 ohms @ 77°F (25°C).
6. If resistance is not within specification, the valve may be faulty.
7. If resistance is within specification, check the circuits back to the ECM.

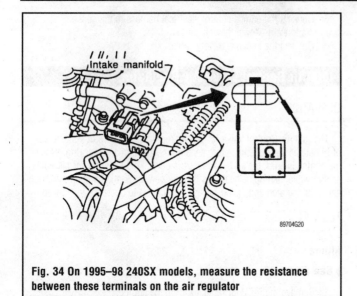

Fig. 34 On 1995–98 240SX models, measure the resistance between these terminals on the air regulator

REMOVAL & INSTALLATION

▶ **See Figure 35**

The IACV-air regulator is located at the end of the cylinder head.
1. Disconnect the electrical harness from the valve, as required.
2. Remove the air hoses, as required.
3. Remove the mounting bolts.
4. Remove the air regulator from the intake manifold.

To install:

5. Inspect the air regulator function. Check the valve for clogging and ensure that the spring has tension.
6. Install the air regulator on the intake manifold and tighten the bolts to 56–66 inch lbs. (6–7 Nm).
7. Install the air hoses, as required.
8. Connect the electrical harness to the valve.

Fig. 35 The IACV-Auxiliary Air Control (1), IACV-FICD valve (2) and IACV-air regulator (3) are located at the end of the cylinder head

Idle Air Control Valve-FICD Solenoid Valve

OPERATION

When the air conditioner is operating, the Idle Air Control Valve (IACV)-FICD solenoid valve opens to allow additional air into the engine. This will increase the idle speed to compensate for the increased load placed on the engine by the air conditioner compressor.

TESTING

▶ **See Figures 36, 37 and 38**

1. Disconnect the electrical harness from the valve.
2. Supply battery voltage and ground to the solenoid.

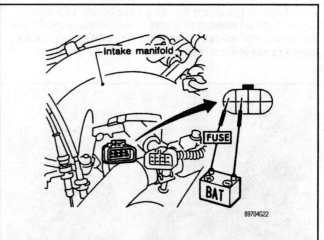

Fig. 36 IACV-FICD valve connector's testing terminal locations for 1995–96 240SX models. Other years of the 240SX use a two-terminal connector

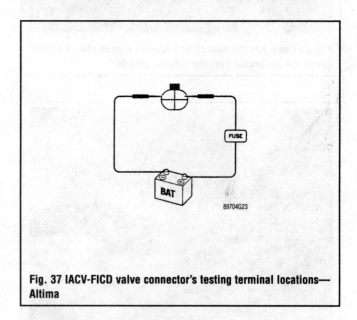

Fig. 37 IACV-FICD valve connector's testing terminal locations—Altima

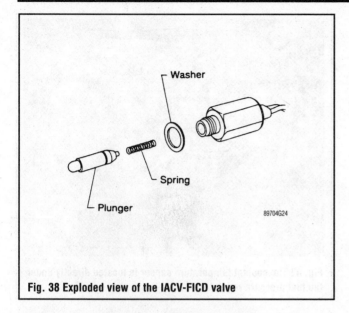

Fig. 38 Exploded view of the IACV-FICD valve

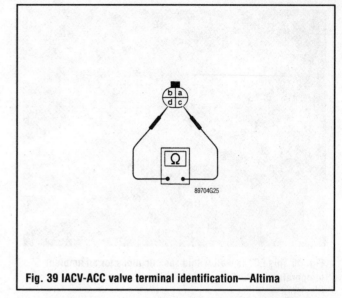

Fig. 39 IACV-ACC valve terminal identification—Altima

➡**Voltage connections for Altima and 1995–96 240SX models are illustrated. All other 240SX vehicles use a 2-terminal connector.**

3. Interrupt the circuit, then reconnect it and repeat the cycle several times. A distinct clicking noise should be heard, as battery voltage is applied and removed.

4. If clicking noise is not heard, remove the valve and inspect the plunger for seizing or sticking. Also inspect the spring.

5. If the solenoid does not function as specified, inspect the circuits back to the ECM.

REMOVAL & INSTALLATION

The idle air control valve is located on the underside of the intake manifold.

1. Disconnect the electrical harness from the valve.
2. Unscrew the valve from the IACV assembly.

To install:

3. Check the valve for clogging and ensure that the spring has tension.
4. Screw the valve into the IACV assembly. Tighten it securely.
5. Connect the electrical harness to the valve.

Idle Air Control Valve-Auxiliary Air Control

OPERATION

The Idle Air Control Valve-Auxiliary Air Control (IACV-AAC) functions by using a duty cycle (on/off/on), which is controlled by the ECM. The longer the "on" pulse, the greater the amount of air that will flow through the valve. The more air that flows through the valve, the higher the engine speed. Actual idle speed is the lowest speed at which the engine can operate steadily. This is computed by the ECM, taking into consideration various conditions such as warm-up, deceleration and engine load.

TESTING

▶ **See Figure 39**

1. Disconnect the electrical harness from the valve.
2. On 240SX models, measure the resistance between the terminals of the valve.
3. On Altima models, measure the resistance between the illustrated connector terminals.
4. Resistance should be 10 ohms @ 77°F (25°C).

5. If resistance is not within specification, the valve may be faulty.
6. If resistance is within specification, check the circuits back to the ECM.

REMOVAL & INSTALLATION

The idle air control valve is located on the underside of the intake manifold.

1. Disconnect the electrical harness from the valve.
2. Remove the valve attaching bolts.
3. Remove the valve from the assembly.

To install:

4. Install the valve on the assembly.
5. Tighten the attaching bolts securely.
6. Connect the electrical harness to the valve.

Engine Coolant Temperature Sensor

OPERATION

The Engine Coolant Temperature (ECT) sensor resistance changes in response to engine coolant temperature. The sensor resistance decreases as coolant temperature increases. This provides a reference signal to the ECM, which indicates engine coolant temperature.

TESTING

▶ **See Figure 40**

1. Disconnect the engine electrical harness from the ECT sensor.
2. Connect an ohmmeter between the ECT sensor terminals.
3. With the engine cold and the ignition switch in the **OFF** position, measure and note the ECT sensor resistance.
4. Connect the engine electrical harness to the sensor.
5. Start the engine and allow it to reach normal operating temperature.
6. Once the engine has reached normal operating temperature, turn it **OFF**.
7. Once again, disconnect the engine electrical harness from the ECT sensor.
8. Measure and note the ECT sensor resistance with the engine hot.
9. Compare the cold and hot ECT sensor resistance measurements with the accompanying chart.
10. If readings do not approximate those in the chart, the sensor may be faulty.

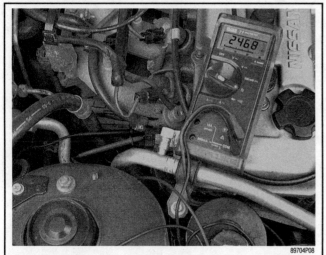

Fig. 40 This ECT is well within specifications for an ambient temperature of 70°F

ENGINE COOLANT TEMPERATURE SENSOR

Temperature °C (°F)	Resistance
20 (68)	2.1 - 2.9 kΩ
50 (122)	0.68 - 1.00 kΩ
90 (194)	0.236 - 0.260 kΩ

89704C02

REMOVAL & INSTALLATION

▶ **See Figures 41 and 42**

1. Partially drain the engine cooling system until the coolant level is below the ECT sensor mounting hole.
2. Disconnect the negative battery cable.
3. Disconnect the electrical harness from the ECT sensor.
4. Remove the coolant temperature sensor from the cylinder head.

Fig. 41 The engine coolant temperature sensor (1) and coolant temperature gauge sender (2) are located on the side of the cylinder head, under the intake manifold

Fig. 42 The coolant temperature sensor is located directly under the fuel pressure regulator

To install:
5. Coat the sensor threads with Teflon® sealant.
6. Thread the sensor into the intake manifold and tighten securely.
7. Connect the negative battery cable.
8. Refill the engine cooling system.
9. Start the engine and check for coolant leaks.
10. Top off the cooling system.

Intake Air Temperature Sensor

OPERATION

The Intake Air Temperature (IAT) sensor resistance changes in response to ambient air temperature. Sensor resistance decreases as the air temperature increases, and resistance increases as the temperature decreases. This provides a signal to the ECM, indicating the temperature of the incoming air charge.

TESTING

1. Disconnect the electrical harness from the IAT sensor.
2. Measure the resistance between the sensor terminals.
3. Compare the resistance reading with the accompanying chart.
4. If the resistance is not within specification, the IAT sensor may be faulty.
5. Connect the electrical harness to the sensor.

INTAKE AIR TEMPERATURE SENSOR

Temperature °C (°F)	Resistance
20 (68)	2.1 - 2.9 kΩ
80 (176)	0.27 - 0.38 kΩ

89704C03

REMOVAL & INSTALLATION

The intake air temperature sensor is located in the air cleaner housing.
1. Disconnect the electrical harness from the IAT sensor.
2. Remove the sensor mounting screws.

3. Remove the sensor from the air cleaner housing.

To install:

4. Install the sensor in the air cleaner housing and tighten the screws securely.

5. Connect the electrical harness to the IAT sensor.

Mass Air Flow Sensor

OPERATION

The Mass Air Flow (MAF) sensor directly measures the amount of air flowing into the engine. The sensor is mounted between the air cleaner assembly and the air cleaner outlet tube.

The sensor utilizes a hot wire sensing element to measure the amount of air entering the engine. The sensor does this by sending a signal, generated by the sensor when the incoming air cools the hot wire, to the ECM. The signal is used by the ECM to calculate the injector pulse width, which controls the air/fuel ratio in the engine.

TESTING

▶ **See Figures 43, 44, 45, 46 and 47**

1. Using a multimeter, check for voltage by backprobing the MAF sensor connector, as illustrated.

2. With the ignition switch **ON** and the engine stopped, voltage should be less than 1.0 volt.

3. With the engine idling at operating temperature, voltage should be 1.3 –1.7 volts.

4. With the engine running at approximately 4000 rpm, voltage should be approximately 4.0 volts.

➡**It is important to watch for a linear voltage rise in response to increases in engine rpm, up to about 4000 rpm.**

5. If voltage is not within specifications, check the power and ground circuits.

6. If the power and ground circuits test okay, the MAF sensor may be faulty.

REMOVAL & INSTALLATION

1. Loosen the hose clamps securing the air tube.
2. Disconnect the air tube from the MAF sensor and throttle body.
3. Label and disconnect the MAF sensor electrical harness.

Fig. 44 To backprobe the MAF sensor connector, first remove the rubber boot

Fig. 45 For this vehicle, the MAF voltage should be approximately 0.2 volts with the ignition ON. This sensor is within specifications

Fig. 43 The MAF sensor is attached to the air cleaner housing

Fig. 46 With the engine running at operating temperature, MAF voltage should be 0.85–1.35 volts. This sensor's reading is at the high side of the specification

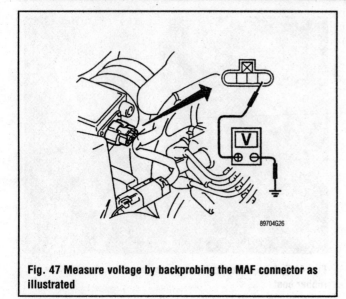

Fig. 47 Measure voltage by backprobing the MAF connector as illustrated

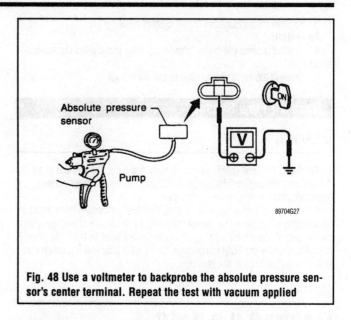

Fig. 48 Use a voltmeter to backprobe the absolute pressure sensor's center terminal. Repeat the test with vacuum applied

4. Remove the MAF sensor attaching bolts.
5. Carefully remove the MAF sensor from the air box.
To install:
6. Position the MAF sensor in the air box.
7. Install the MAF sensor attaching bolts and tighten to 13–16 ft. lbs. (18–22 Nm).
8. Connect the MAF sensor's electrical harness.
9. Connect the air tube to the MAF sensor and throttle body.
10. Tighten the hose clamps securing the air tube.

Absolute Pressure Sensor

OPERATION

The absolute pressure sensor is connected to the MAP/BARO switch solenoid valve by a hose. The sensor detects ambient barometric pressure and intake manifold pressure, and sends a voltage signal to the ECM. As pressure increases, the voltage rises. The absolute pressure sensor is not used to control the engine system. It is only used for on-board diagnosis.

TESTING

◆ **See Figure 48**

1. Remove the absolute pressure sensor with its electrical harness connected.
2. Disconnect the vacuum hose from the sensor.
3. Turn the ignition switch **ON**.
4. Backprobe the sensor connector and check output voltage, as illustrated.
5. The voltage should be 3.2–4.8 volts.
6. Connect a hand powered vacuum pump and apply a vacuum of 7.87 in. Hg (26.7 kPa).
7. Voltage should be 1.0–1.4 volts lower than the value in Step 5.
8. If voltage is not within specification or does not respond as specified, check the power and ground circuits.
9. If the power and ground circuits are okay, the sensor may be faulty.

REMOVAL & INSTALLATION

The absolute pressure sensor is mounted to the right strut tower in the engine compartment.
1. Label and disconnect the electrical harness from the sensor.
2. Label and disconnect the vacuum hose from the sensor.
3. Remove the sensor mounting screws.
4. Remove the sensor from the strut tower.
To install:
5. Install the sensor on the strut tower and tighten the screws securely.
6. Connect the vacuum hose to the sensor.
7. Connect the electrical harness to the sensor.

Manifold Absolute Pressure/Barometric Pressure Switch Solenoid Valve

OPERATION

The Manifold Absolute Pressure/Barometric pressure (BARO) switch solenoid valve allows the absolute pressure sensor to monitor either ambient barometric pressure or intake manifold pressure. The solenoid switches between two passages by duty cycle (on/off) signals from the ECM.

TESTING

◆ **See Figure 49**

1. Label and disconnect the vacuum lines and electrical harness.
2. Inspect the lines for damage, and replace as necessary.
3. Inspect the valve for damage, and replace as necessary.
4. Apply battery voltage and ground between the valve terminals.
5. Air should pass between Port **A** and Port **B**.
6. Air should not pass between Port **A** and Port **C**.
7. Remove the battery voltage.
8. Air should pass between Port **A** and Port **C**.
9. Air should not pass between Port **A** and Port **B**.
10. If the valve does not function as specified, it may be faulty.
11. If the valve responds as specified, check and repair the power and ground circuits.

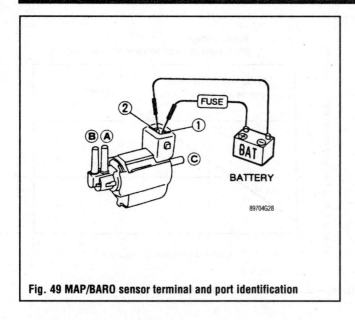

Fig. 49 MAP/BARO sensor terminal and port identification

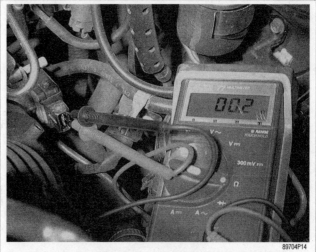

Fig. 50 Testing the TP sensor voltage with the throttle closed shows a 0.2 volt reading. This is well within specification

REMOVAL & INSTALLATION

The MAP/BARO sensor is mounted to the passenger's side strut tower in the engine compartment.
1. Label and disconnect the electrical harness from the sensor.
2. Label and disconnect the vacuum hose from the sensor.
3. Remove the sensor mounting screws.
4. Remove the sensor from the strut tower.

To install:
5. Install the sensor on the strut tower and tighten the screws securely.
6. Connect the vacuum hose to the sensor.
7. Connect the electrical harness to the sensor.

Throttle Position Sensor

OPERATION

The Throttle Position (TP) sensor is a potentiometer. It is mounted on the side of the throttle body and is connected to the throttle plate shaft. The sensor monitors throttle plate movement and position, and transmits an appropriate electrical signal to the ECM. These signals are used by the ECM to adjust the air/fuel mixture and spark timing according to engine load. The TP sensor is adjustable on some models.

Automatic transaxle/transmission TP sensors contain position switches. These switches provide a signal to the ECM when the engine is at idle and wide open throttle.

TESTING

♦ See Figures 50, 51, 52 and 53

Potentiometer

1. Disconnect the electrical harness from the sensor.
2. Check resistance between the connector terminals.
3. Resistance for 1996–98 model year vehicles should be as follows:
- Throttle closed—approximately 0.5 kilohms
- Throttle partially open—0.5–4.0 kilohms
- Throttle fully open—approximately 4.0 kilohms
4. Resistance for 1995 model year vehicles should be as follows:
- Throttle closed—approximately 1 kilohm
- Throttle partially open—1–10 kilohms
- Throttle fully open—approximately 10 kilohms

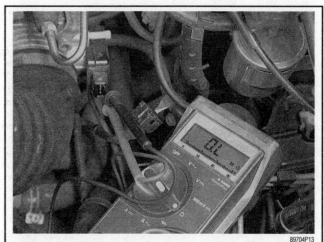

Fig. 51 This automatic transaxle equipped vehicle uses a wide open throttle switch in the TP sensor. With the throttle wide open, continuity should not exist, as indicated by the 0.L ohms reading

5. Resistance for 1993–94 model year vehicles should be as follows:
- Throttle closed—approximately 2 kilohms
- Throttle partially open—2–10 kilohms
- Throttle fully open—approximately 10 kilohms
6. Slowly rotate the throttle shaft and monitor the ohmmeter for a continuous, steady change in resistance. Any sudden jumps, or irregularities in resistance (such as jumping back and forth), indicates a malfunctioning sensor.

➡Do not perform this test on the electrical harness connector terminals, but rather on the terminals of the sensor itself.

7. If resistance is not within specification, the sensor may be faulty.
8. If resistance is within specification, check the circuits back to the ECM.
9. Connect the electrical harness to the sensor.

Position Switches

1. Disconnect the electrical harness from the sensor.
2. Check continuity between the connector terminals.
3. When the throttle is placed in the appropriate position (idle or wide open throttle), continuity should exist.

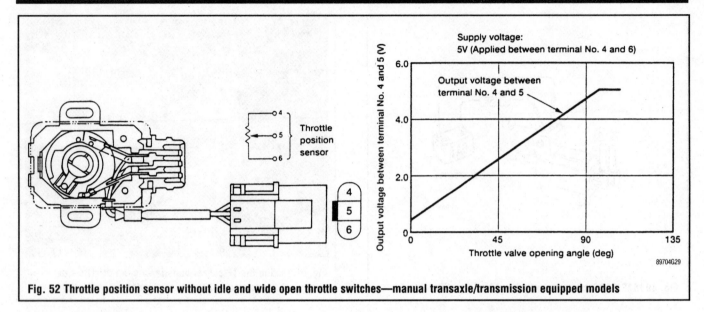

Fig. 52 Throttle position sensor without idle and wide open throttle switches—manual transaxle/transmission equipped models

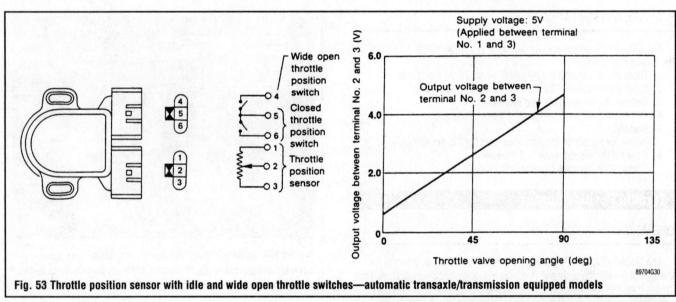

Fig. 53 Throttle position sensor with idle and wide open throttle switches—automatic transaxle/transmission equipped models

4. When the throttle is not in the idle or wide open throttle position, continuity should not exist.

➡The position switches are an integral part of the TP sensor and cannot be replaced separately. If faulty, the TP sensor must be replaced as an assembly.

5. If continuity is not as specified, the sensor is faulty.

REMOVAL & INSTALLATION

▸ **See Figure 54**

The throttle position sensor is mounted on the throttle body.
1. Label and disconnect the electrical harness from the sensor.
2. Remove the sensor mounting screws.
3. Remove the sensor from the throttle body.
To install:
4. Install the sensor on the throttle body and hand-tighten the screws.
5. Connect the electrical harness to the sensor.
6. Adjust the sensor and tighten the mounting screws securely.

Fig. 54 The throttle position sensor is located on the side of the throttle body

ADJUSTMENT

The TP sensor is adjustable on some models. To determine if your model is adjustable, simply look for adjustment slots where the mounting bolts go through the sensor. If slots exist, the sensor is adjustable. If slots do not exist, the sensor is not adjustable.

➡**Inspect the sensor carefully, as large washers may cover the adjustment slots.**

Automatic Transmission/Transaxle Models

1. Start the engine and allow it to reach operating temperature.
2. Disconnect the TP sensor and closed throttle position switch electrical harness.
3. Check continuity between the closed throttle position switch connector terminals 5 and 6.
4. Raise the engine speed to 2000 rpm, then gradually lower it.
5. Continuity should exist (the closed throttle position switch should close at approximately 1000 rpm with the transmission/transaxle in **N**.
6. If continuity is not as specified, loosen the TP sensor mounting bolts and slowly rotate the sensor.
7. Tighten the mounting bolts securely and recheck continuity.

Manual Transmission/Transaxle Models

1. Turn the ignition switch **ON**, but do not start the engine.
2. Backprobe the connector and check voltage between the center terminal and ground.
3. With the throttle closed, voltage should be 0.3–0.7 volts.
4. If voltage is not within specification, loosen the TP sensor mounting bolts and slowly rotate the sensor.
5. Tighten the mounting bolts securely and recheck the voltage.
6. Start the engine and allow it to reach operating temperature.
7. Turn the ignition switch **OFF** and wait at least 5 seconds.
8. Disconnect the TP sensor electrical harness.
9. Start the engine and wait at least 5 seconds with the transmission/transaxle in the **N** position.
10. Reconnect the TP sensor with the engine running.

Camshaft Position Sensor

OPERATION

The Camshaft Position (CMP) sensor is a basic component of the engine control system. It monitors engine speed and piston position. These input signals to the ECM are used to control fuel injection, ignition timing and other functions.

The sensor has a rotor plate and a wave forming circuit. The rotor plate has 360 slits for a 1° signal and 4 slits for a 180° signal. The wave forming circuit consists of a Light Emitting Diode (LED) and photo diode.

The rotor plate is positioned between the LED and photo diode. The LED transmits light to generate rough shaped pulses. These pulses are converted into on/off signals by the wave forming circuit and sent to the ECM.

TESTING

♦ **See Figures 55 and 56**

1. Remove the distributor assembly from the engine.
2. Disconnect the ignition wires and coil wire from the distributor.

➡**The camshaft position sensor electrical harness should remain connected.**

3. Turn the ignition switch **ON**.
4. Measure voltage between the camshaft position sensor terminals and ground, as illustrated.

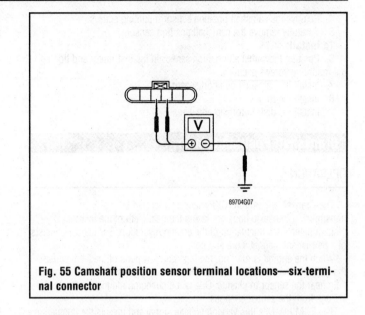

Fig. 55 Camshaft position sensor terminal locations—six-terminal connector

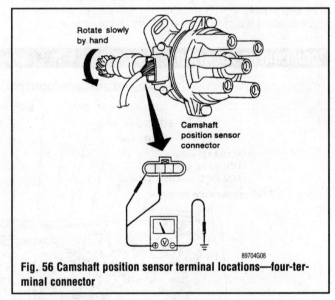

Fig. 56 Camshaft position sensor terminal locations—four-terminal connector

5. With the engine's distributor shaft rotating slowly, voltage should fluctuate between 0 and 5 volts.

➡**If the voltage signal is checked with the engine running, the normal reading will be 2.3 volts (average voltage). An oscilloscope may also be used to view the pulse signal.**

6. If voltage does not fluctuate or is not within specification, check the circuits for damage.
7. If the circuits are functional, the sensor may be faulty.
8. Install the distributor and connect the ignition and coil wires.
9. Erase stored memory codes.

REMOVAL & INSTALLATION

The camshaft position sensor is located inside the distributor. On some distributors, the camshaft position sensor is not serviceable (replacement parts may not be available separately). If the camshaft position sensor is serviceable, use the following procedure.

1. Remove the distributor cap and wires.
2. Remove the rotor.
3. Remove the camshaft position sensor cap.

4. Remove the camshaft position sensor mounting screws.
5. Carefully remove the camshaft position sensor.
To install:
6. Position the camshaft position sensor in the distributor and tighten the mounting screws securely.
7. Install the camshaft position sensor cap.
8. Install the rotor.
9. Install the distributor cap and wires.

Crankshaft Position Sensor

OPERATION

The Crankshaft Position (CKP) sensor is located on the transmission/transaxle housing, facing the gear teeth of the flywheel/flex-plate. It detects the fluctuation of the engine revolution. The sensor consists of a permanent magnet, core and coil.

When the engine is running, the high and low parts of the teeth cause the gap with the sensor to change. This changing gap causes the magnetic field near the sensor to change. Due to the changing magnetic field, the voltage from the sensor changes.

The ECM receives this varying voltage signal and detects the fluctuation of the engine revolution. This sensor is not directly used to control the engine system. It is used for the on-board diagnosis of a misfire.

TESTING

1. Remove the sensor from the engine.
2. Inspect the sensor tip. If damage to the tip is evident, replace the sensor.
3. Measure the resistance between the sensor terminals.
4. Sensor resistance should be 167–204 ohms @ 68°F (20°C) on 240SX and 432–528 ohms @ 77°F (25°C) on Altima.
5. If resistance is not within specification, the sensor may be faulty.

REMOVAL & INSTALLATION

The crankshaft position sensor is located on the transmission/transaxle housing facing the gear teeth of the flywheel/flexplate.
1. Disconnect the sensor electrical harness.
2. Remove the sensor mounting bolts.
3. Remove the sensor from the transaxle/transmission housing.
To install:
4. Install the sensor in the transaxle/transmission housing.
5. Tighten the sensor mounting bolts securely.
6. Connect the sensor electrical harness.

COMPONENT LOCATIONS

ENGINE AND EMISSION CONTROL COMPONENT LOCATIONS—240SX

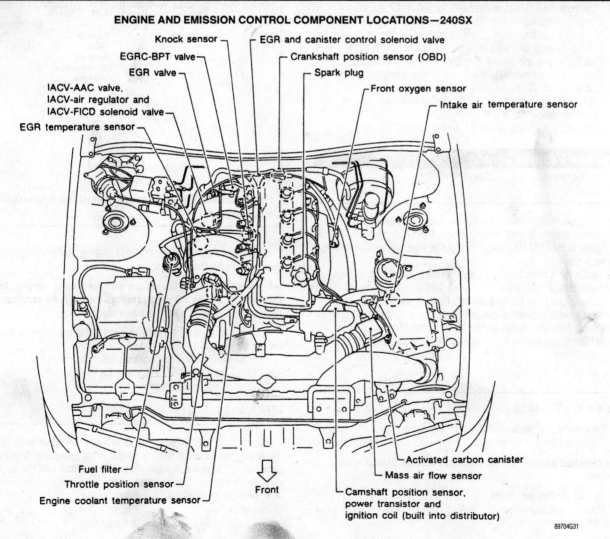

Knock sensor
EGR and canister control solenoid valve
EGRC-BPT valve
Crankshaft position sensor (OBD)
EGR valve
Spark plug
IACV-AAC valve,
IACV-air regulator and
IACV-FICD solenoid valve
Front oxygen sensor
Intake air temperature sensor
EGR temperature sensor

Fuel filter
Throttle position sensor
Engine coolant temperature sensor
Front
Activated carbon canister
Mass air flow sensor
Camshaft position sensor,
power transistor and
ignition coil (built into distributor)

89704G31

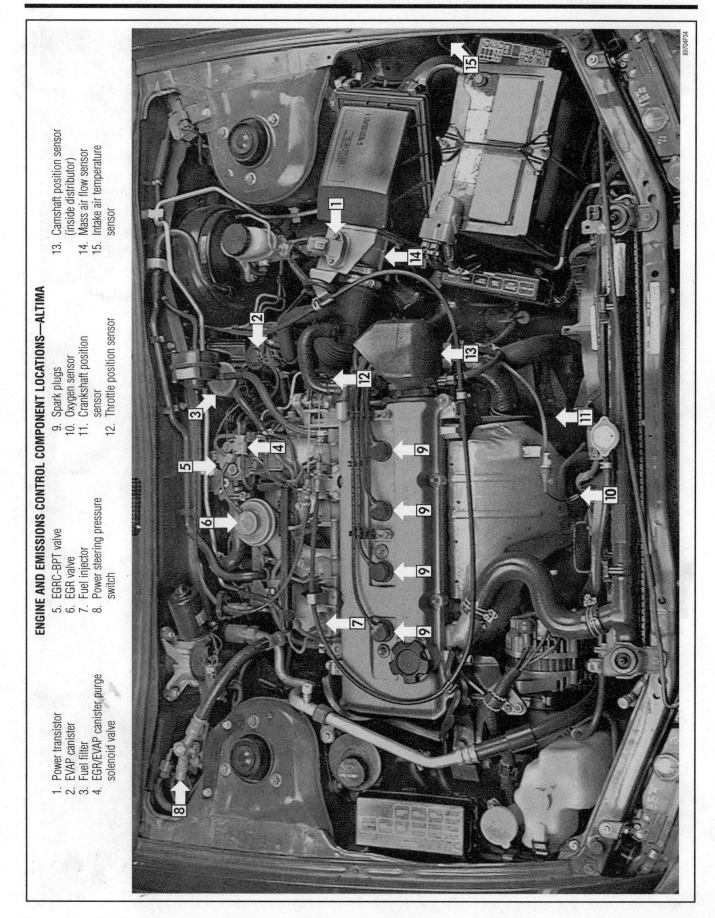

ENGINE AND EMISSIONS CONTROL COMPONENT LOCATIONS—ALTIMA

1. Power transistor
2. EVAP canister
3. Fuel filter
4. EGR/EVAP canister purge solenoid valve
5. EGRC-BPT valve
6. EGR valve
7. Fuel injector
8. Power steering pressure switch
9. Spark plugs
10. Oxygen sensor
11. Crankshaft position sensor
12. Throttle position sensor
13. Camshaft position sensor (inside distributor)
14. Mass air flow sensor
15. Intake air temperature sensor

89704P34

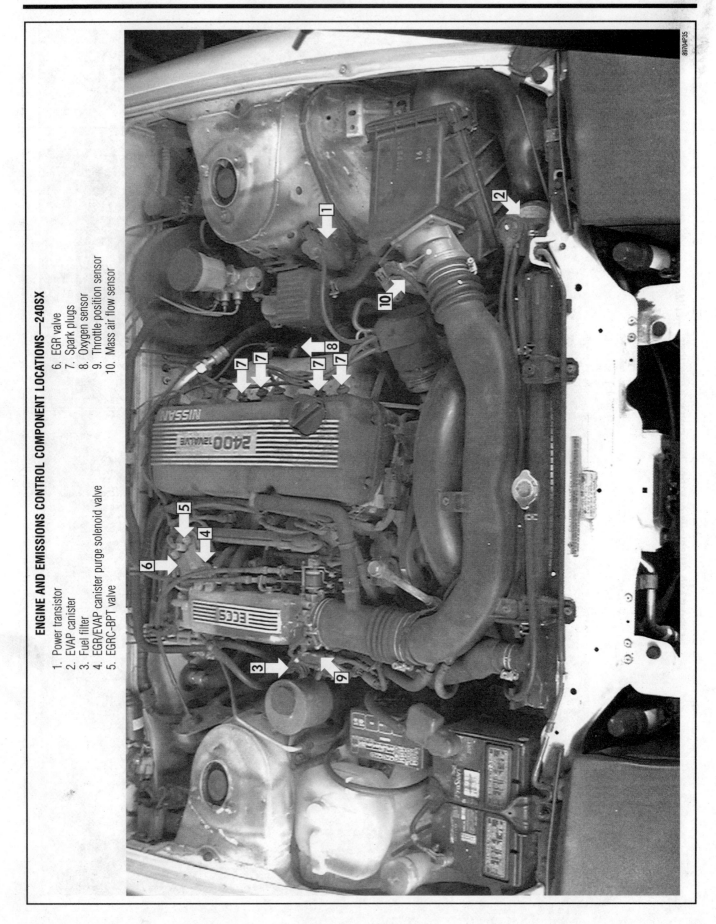

ENGINE AND EMISSIONS CONTROL COMPONENT LOCATIONS—240SX

1. Power transistor
2. EVAP canister
3. Fuel filter
4. EGR/EVAP canister purge solenoid valve
5. EGRC-BPT valve
6. EGR valve
7. Spark plugs
8. Oxygen sensor
9. Throttle position sensor
10. Mass air flow sensor

TROUBLE CODES

DIAGNOSTIC TROUBLE CODES—1993–94 (OBDII)

Diagnostic trouble code No.	Detected items	Malfunction is detected when ...	Check item (remedy)
11	Camshaft position sensor circuit	• Either 1° or 180° signal is not entered for the first few seconds during engine cranking. • Either 1° or 180° signal is not input often enough while the engine speed is higher than the specified rpm.	• Harness and connector (If harness and connector are normal, replace camshaft position sensor.)
12	Mass air flow sensor circuit	• The mass air flow sensor circuit is open or shorted. (An abnormally high or low voltage is entered.)	• Harness and connector (If harness and connector are normal, replace mass air flow sensor.)
13	Engine coolant temperature sensor circuit	• The engine coolant temperature sensor circuit is open or shorted. (An abnormally high or low output voltage is entered.)	• Harness and connector • Engine coolant temperature sensor
14	Vehicle speed sensor circuit	• The vehicle speed sensor circuit is open or shorted.	• Harness and connector • Vehicle speed sensor (pulse generator)
21	Ignition signal circuit	• The ignition signal in the primary circuit is not entered during engine cranking or running.	• Harness and connector • Power transistor unit
31	ECM	• ECM calculation function is malfunctioning.	[Replace ECM (ECCS control module).]
32	EGR function	• EGR valve does not operate. (EGR valve spring does not lift.)	• EGR valve • EGR and canister control solenoid valve
33	Oxygen sensor circuit	• The oxygen sensor circuit is open or shorted. (An abnormally high or low output voltage is entered.)	• Harness and connector • Oxygen sensor • Fuel pressure • Injectors • Intake air leaks
34	Knock sensor circuit	• The knock sensor circuit is open or shorted. (An abnormally high or low voltage is entered.)	• Harness and connector • Knock sensor
35	EGR temperature sensor circuit	• The EGR temperature sensor circuit is open or shorted. (An abnormally high or low voltage is entered.)	• Harness and connector • EGR temperature sensor
43	Throttle position sensor circuit	• The throttle position sensor circuit is open or shorted. (An abnormally high or low voltage is entered.)	• Harness and connector • Throttle position sensor
45	Injector leak	• Fuel leaks from injector.	• Injector
54	Signal circuit from A/T control unit to ECM (A/T only)	• The A/T communication line is open or shorted.	• Harness and connector
55	None	• None of the above items detected.	

89704C10

DIAGNOSTIC CODES—1995 (OBDII)

Diagnostic trouble code No. MIL	CONSULT GST	Detected items	Malfunction is detected when ...	Check Items (Possible Cause)
11	P0340	Camshaft position sensor circuit	• Either 1° or 180° signal is not detected by the ECM for the first few seconds during engine cranking. • Either 1° or 180° signal is not detected by the ECM often enough while the engine speed is higher than the specified rpm. • The relation between 1° and 180° signals is not in the normal range during the specified rpm.	• Harness or connectors (The sensor circuit is open or shorted.) • Camshaft position sensor • Starter motor • Starting system circuit (EL section) • Dead (Weak) battery
12	P0100	Mass air flow sensor circuit	• An excessively high or low voltage is entered to ECM. • Voltage sent to ECM is not practical when compared with the camshaft position sensor signal and throttle position sensor signals.	• Harness or connectors (The sensor circuit is open or shorted.) • Mass air flow sensor
13	P0115	Engine coolant temperature sensor circuit	• An excessively high or low voltage from the sensor is detected by the ECM.	• Harness or connectors (The sensor circuit is open or shorted.) • Engine coolant temperature sensor
14	P0500	Vehicle speed sensor circuit	• The almost 0 km/h (0 MPH) signal from the sensor is detected by the ECM even when vehicle is driving.	• Harness or connectors (The sensor circuit is open or shorted.) • Vehicle speed sensor
21	P1320	Ignition signal circuit	• The ignition signal in the primary circuit is not detected by the ECM during engine cranking or running.	• Harness or connectors (The ignition primary circuit is open or shorted.) • Power transistor unit • Camshaft position sensor • Camshaft position sensor circuit
25	P0505	Idle speed control function	• The idle speed control function does not operate properly.	• Harness or connectors (The valve circuit is shorted.) • IACV-AAC valve • Harness or connectors (The valve circuit is open.) • IACV-AAC valve
28	P1900	Cooling fan circuit	• Cooling fan does not operate properly. (Overheat) • Cooling system does not operate properly. (Overheat) • Engine coolant was not added to the system using the proper filling method.	• Harness or connectors. (The cooling fan circuit is open or shorted.) • Cooling fan • Radiator hose • Radiator • Radiator cap • Water pump • Thermostat
31	P0605	ECM	• ECM calculation function is malfunctioning.	• ECM (ECCS control module)
32	P0400	EGR function	• The EGR flow is excessively low or high during the specified driving condition.	• EGR valve stuck closed, open or leaking • Passage obstructed • EGR and canister control solenoid valve • Tube leaking for EGR valve vacuum • EGRC-BPT valve leaking
33	P0130	Front oxygen sensor circuit	• An excessively high voltage from the sensor is detected by the ECM. • The voltage from the sensor is constantly approx. 0.3V. • The specified maximum and minimum voltages from the sensor are not reached. • It takes more than the specified time for the sensor to respond between rich and lean.	• Harness or connectors (The sensor circuit is open or shorted.) • Front oxygen sensor • Injectors • Intake air leaks • Fuel pressure
34	P0325	Knock sensor circuit	• An excessively low or high voltage from the sensor is detected by the ECM.	• Harness or connectors (The sensor circuit is open or shorted.) • Knock sensor
35	P1401	EGR temperature sensor circuit	• An excessively low or high voltage from the sensor is detected by the ECM, even when engine coolant temperature is low or high.	• Harness or connectors (The sensor circuit is open or shorted.) • EGR temperature sensor
36	P0402	EGRC-BPT valve function	• EGRC-BPT valve does not operate properly.	• EGRC-BPT valve • Rubber tube (obstructed or misconnected)
37	P0130	Closed loop control	• The closed loop control function does not operate even when vehicle is driving in the specified condition.	• The front oxygen sensor circuit is open or shorted. • Front oxygen sensor

89704C07

DIAGNOSTIC TROUBLE CODES—1995 (OBDII) CONT.

Diagnostic trouble code No. MIL	CONSULT GST	Detected items	Malfunction is detected when ...		Check Items (Possible Cause)
41	P0110	Intake air temperature sensor circuit	• An excessively low or high voltage from the sensor is detected by the ECM. • Voltage sent to ECM is not practical when compared with the engine coolant temperature sensor signal.		• Harness or connectors (The sensor circuit is open or shorted.) • Intake air temperature sensor
43	P0120	Throttle position sensor circuit	• An excessively low or high voltage from the sensor is detected by the ECM. • Voltage sent to ECM is not practical when compared with the mass air flow sensor and camshaft position sensor signals.		• Harness or connectors (The sensor circuit is open or shorted.) • Throttle position sensor
55	(P0000)	No failure	• No malfunction related to OBD system is detected by either ECM or A/T control unit.		• No failure
65	P0304	No. 4 cylinder's misfire	(Three-way catalyst damage) The misfire occurs, which will damage three way catalyst by overheating.	(Exhaust quality deterioration) The misfire occurs, which will not damage three way catalyst but will affect emission deterioration.	• Improper spark plug • The ignition secondary circuit is open or shorted. • Insufficient compression • Incorrect fuel pressure • EGR valve • The injector circuit is open or shorted. • Injectors • Intake air leak • Lack of fuel • Magnetized flywheel (drive plate)
66	P0303	No. 3 cylinder's misfire			
67	P0302	No. 2 cylinder's misfire			
68	P0301	No. 1 cylinder's misfire			
71	P0300	Multiple cylinders' misfire			
72	P0420	Three way catalyst function	• Three way catalyst does not operate properly. • Three way catalyst does not have enough oxygen storage capacity.		• Three way catalyst • Exhaust tube • Intake air leak • Injectors • Injector leak
76	P0170	Fuel injection system function	• Fuel injection system does not operate properly. • The amount of mixture ratio compensation is excessive. (The mixture ratio is too lean or too rich.)		• Intake air leak • Front oxygen sensor • Injectors • Exhaust gas leak • Incorrect fuel pressure • Mass air flow sensor • Lack of fuel
77	P0136	Rear heated oxygen sensor circuit	• An excessively high voltage from the sensor is detected by the ECM. • The specified maximum and minimum voltages from the sensor are not reached. • It takes more than the specified time for the sensor to respond between rich and lean.		• Harness or connectors (The sensor circuit is open or shorted.) • Rear heated oxygen sensor • Fuel pressure • Injectors • Intake air leaks
82	P0335	Crankshaft position sensor (OBD) circuit	• The proper pulse signal from the sensor is not detected by the ECM while the engine is running at the specified rpm.		• Harness or connectors (The sensor circuit is open.) • Crankshaft position sensor (OBD)
84	P1605	A/T diagnosis communication line	• An incorrect signal from A/T control unit is detect-tect by the ECM.		• Harness or connectors (The communication line circuit is open or shorted.) • Dead (Weak) battery • A/T control unit
95	P1336	Crankshaft position sensor (OBD)	• The chipping of the flywheel or drive plate gear tooth (cog) is detected by the ECM.		• Harness or connectors • Crankshaft position sensor (OBD) • Flywheel (Drive plate)
98	P0125	Engine coolant temperature sensor function	• Voltage sent to ECM from the sensor is not practical, even when some time has passed after starting the engine. • Engine coolant temperature is insufficient for closed loop fuel control.		• Harness or connectors (High resistance in the sensor circuit) • Engine coolant temperature sensor • Thermostat
103	P0705	Park/Neutral position switch circuit	• The signal of the park/neutral position switch is not changed in the process of engine starting and driving.		• Harness or connectors (The switch circuit is open or shorted.) • Neutral position switch • Inhibitor switch
105	P1400	EGR and canister control solenoid valve circuit	• The improper voltage signal is detected by the ECM through the solenoid valve.		• Harness or connectors (The valve circuit is open or shorted.) • EGR and canister control solenoid valve
—	P0600	Signal circuit from A/T control unit to ECM	• ECM receives incorrect voltage from A/T control unit continuously.		• Harness or connectors (The circuit between ECM and A/T control unit is open or shorted.)

89704C08

DIAGNOSTIC TROUBLE CODES—1995 (OBDII) CONT.

Diagnostic trouble code No.		Detected items	Malfunction is detected when ...	Check Items (Possible Cause)
MIL	CONSULT GST			
111	P0705	Inhibitor switch circuit	• A/T control unit does not receive the correct voltage signal from the switch based on the gear position.	• Harness or connectors (The switch circuit is open or shorted.) • Inhibitor switch
112	P0720	Revolution sensor	• A/T control unit does not receive the proper voltage signal from the sensor.	• Harness or connectors (The sensor circuit is open or shorted.) • Revolution sensor
113	P0731	Improper shifting to 1st gear position	• A/T can not be shifted to the 1st gear position even electrical circuit is good.	• Shift solenoid valve A • Shift solenoid valve B • Overrun clutch solenoid valve • Line pressure solenoid valve • Each clutch • Hydraulic control circuit
114	P0732	Improper shifting to 2nd gear position	• A/T can not be shifted to the 2nd gear position even electrical circuit is good.	
115	P0733	Improper shifting to 3rd gear position	• A/T can not be shifted to the 3rd gear position even electrical circuit is good.	
116	P0734	Improper shifting to 4th gear position or TCC	• A/T can not be shifted to the 4th gear position or perform lock-up even electrical circuit is good.	• T/C clutch solenoid valve
118	P0750	Shift solenoid valve A	• A/T control unit detects the improper voltage drop when it tries to operate the solenoid valve.	• Harness or connectors (The solenoid circuit is open or shorted.) • Shift solenoid valve A
121	P0755	Shift solenoid valve B	• A/T control unit detects the improper voltage drop when it tries to operate the solenoid valve.	• Harness or connectors (The solenoid circuit is open or shorted.) • Shift solenoid valve B
123	P1760	Overrun clutch solenoid valve	• A/T control unit detects the improper voltage drop when it tries to operate the solenoid valve.	• Harness or connectors (The solenoid circuit is open or shorted.) • Overrun clutch solenoid valve
124	P0740	T/C clutch solenoid valve	• A/T control unit detects the improper voltage drop when it tries to operate the solenoid valve.	• Harness or connectors (The solenoid circuit is open or shorted.) • T/C clutch solenoid valve
125	P0745	Line pressure solenoid valve	• A/T control unit detects the improper voltage drop when it tries to operate the solenoid valve.	• Harness or connectors (The solenoid circuit is open or shorted.) • Line pressure solenoid valve
126	P1705	Throttle position sensor	• A/T control unit receives an excessively low or high voltage from the sensor.	• Harness or connectors (The sensor circuit is open or shorted.) • Throttle position sensor
127	P0725	Engine speed signal	• A/T control unit does not receive the proper voltage signal from the ECM	• Harness or connectors (The signal circuit is open or shorted.)
128	P0710	Fluid temperature sensor	• A/T control unit receives an excessively low or high voltage from the sensor.	• Harness or connectors (The sensor circuit is open or shorted.) • Fluid temperature sensor

89704C09

DIAGNOSTIC CODES—1996–98 (OBDII)

Diagnostic trouble code No. CONSULT GST	MIL	Detected items	Malfunction is detected when ...		Check Items (Possible Cause)
(P0000)	0505	No failure	• No malfunction related to OBD system is detected by either ECM or A/T contro unit.		• No failure
P0100	0102	Mass air flow sensor circuit	• An excessively high or low voltage is entered to ECM. • Voltage sent to ECM is not practical when compared with the camshaft position sensor signal and throttle position sensor signals.		• Harness or connectors (The sensor circuit is open or shorted.) • Mass air flow sensor
P0110	0401	Intake air temperature sensor circuit	• An excessively low or high voltage from the sensor is detected by the ECM. • Voltage sent to ECM is not practical when compared with the engine coolant temperature sensor signal.		• Harness or connectors (The sensor circuit is open or shorted.) • Intake air temperature sensor
P0115	0103	Engine coolant temperature sensor circuit	• An excessively high or low voltage from the sensor is detected by the ECM.		• Harness or connectors (The sensor circuit is open or shorted.) • Engine coolant temperature sensor
P0120	0403	Throttle position sensor circuit	• An excessively low or high voltage from the sensor is detected by the ECM. • Voltage sent to ECM is not practical when compared with the mass air flow sensor and camshaft position sensor signals.		• Harness or connectors (The sensor circuit is open or shorted.) • Throttle position sensor
P0125	0908	Engine coolant temperature sensor function	• Voltage sent to ECM from the sensor is not practical, even when some time has passed after starting the engine. • Engine coolant temperature is insufficient for closed loop fuel control.		• Harness or connectors (High resistance in the sensor circuit) • Engine coolant temperature sensor • Thermostat
P0130	0303	Front oxygen sensor 5 circuit	• An excessively high voltage from the sensor is detected by the ECM. • The voltage from the sensor is constantly approx. 0.3V. • The specified maximum and minimum voltages from the sensor are not reached. • It takes more than the specified time for the sensor to respond between rich and lean.		• Harness or connectors (The sensor circuit is open or shorted.) • Front oxygen sensor • Injectors • Intake air leaks • Fuel pressure
P0130	0307	Closed loop control	• The closed loop control function does not operate even when vehicle is driving in the specified condition.		• The front oxygen sensor circuit is open or shorted. • Front oxygen sensor
P0135	0901	Front heated oxygen sensor heater circuit	• The current amperage in the heater circuit is out of the normal range. (An improper voltage drop signal is sent to ECM through the heater.)		• Harness or connectors (The heater circuit is open or shorted.) • Front heated oxygen sensor heater
P0136	0707	Rear heated oxygen sensor circuit	• An excessively high voltage from the sensor is detected by the ECM. • The specified maximum and minimum voltages from the sensor are not reached. • It takes more than the specified time for the sensor to respond between rich and lean.		• Harness or connectors (The sensor circuit is open or shorted.) • Rear heated oxygen sensor • Fuel pressure • Injectors • Intake air leaks
P0141	0902	Rear heated oxygen sensor heater circuit	• The current amperage in the heater circuit is out of the normal range. (An improper voltage drop signal is sent to ECM through the heater.)		• Harness and connectors (The heater circuit is open or shorted.) • Front heated oxygen sensor heater
P0171	0115	Fuel injection system function	• Fuel injection system does not operate properly. • The amount of mixture ratio compensation is too large. (The mixture ratio is too lean.)		• Intake air leak • Front oxygen sensor • Injectors • Incorrect fuel pressure • Mass air flow sensor • Lack of fuel
P0172	0114	Fuel injection system function	• Fuel injection system does not operate properly. • The amount of mixture ratio compensation is too large. (The mixture ratio is too rich.)		• Front oxygen sensor • Injectors • Exhaust gas leak • Incorrect fuel pressure • Mass air flow sensor
P0300	0701	Multiple cylinders' misfire	(Three way catalyst damage) The misfire occurs, which will damage three way catalyst by overheating.	(Exhaust quality deterioration) The misfire occurs, which will not damage three way catalyst but will affect emission deterioration.	• Improper spark plug • The ignition secondary circuit is open or shorted. • Insufficient compression • Incorrect fuel pressure • EGR valve • The injector circuit is open or shorted. • Injectors • Intake air leak • Lack of fuel • Magnetized flywheel (drive plate)
P0301	0608	No. 1 cylinder's misfire			
P0302	0607	No. 2 cylinder's misfire			
P0303	0606	No. 3 cylinder's misfire			
P0304	0605	No. 4 cylinder's misfire			
P0325	0304	Knock sensor circuit	• An excessively low or high voltage from the sensor is detected by the ECM.		• Harness or connectors (The sensor circuit is open or shorted.) • Knock sensor
P0335	0802	Crankshaft position sensor (OBD) circuit	• The proper pulse signal from the sensor is not detected by the ECM while the engine is running at the specified rpm.		• Harness or connectors (The sensor circuit is open.) • Crankshaft position sensor (OBD)

89704C04

DIAGNOSTIC CODES—1996–98 (OBDII) CONT.

Diagnostic trouble code No. CONSULT GST	MIL	Detected items	Malfunction is detected when ...	Check Items (Possible Cause)
P0340	0101	Camshaft position sensor circuit	• Either 1° or 180° signal is not detected by the ECM for the first few seconds during engine cranking. • Either 1° or 180° signal is not detected by the ECM often enough while the engine speed is higher than the specified rpm. • The relation between 1° and 180° signals is not in the normal range during the specified rpm.	• Harness or connectors (The sensor circuit is open or shorted.) • Camshaft position sensor • Starter motor • Starting system circuit (EL section) • Dead (Weak) battery
P0400	0302	EGR function	• The EGR flow is excessively low or high during the specified driving condition.	• EGR valve stuck closed, open or leaking • Passage blocked • EGR valve and EVAP canister purge control solenoid valve • Tube leaking for EGR valve vacuum • EGRC-BPT valve leaking • EGR temperature sensor
P0402	0306	EGRC-BPT valve function	• EGRC-BPT valve does not operate properly.	• EGRC-BPT valve • Rubber tube (blocked or misconnected)
P0420	0702	Three way catalyst function	• Three way catalyst does not operate properly. • Three way catalyst does not have enough oxygen storage capacity.	• Three way catalyst*6 • Exhaust tube • Intake air leak • Injectors • Injector leak
P0500	0104	Vehicle speed sensor circuit	• The almost 0 km/h (0 MPH) signal from the sensor is detected by the ECM even when vehicle is driving.	• Harness or connectors (The sensor circuit is open or shorted.) • Vehicle speed sensor
P0505	0205	Idle speed control function	• The idle speed control function does not operate properly.	• Harness or connectors (The valve circuit is open.) • IACV-AAC valve • Harness or connectors (The valve circuit is shorted.) • IACV-AAC valve
P0600		Signal circuit from A/T control unit to ECM	• ECM receives incorrect voltage from A/T control unit continuously. *7 This can be detected only by "DATA MONITOR (AUTO TRIG)".	• Harness or connectors (The circuit between ECM and A/T control unit is open or shorted.)
P0605	0301	ECM	• ECM calculation function is malfunctioning.	• ECM (ECCS control module)
P0705	1003	Park/Neutral position switch circuit	• The signal of the park/neutral position switch is not changed in the process of engine starting and driving.	• Harness or connectors (The switch circuit is open or shorted.) • Neutral position switch • Inhibitor switch
P0705	1101	Inhibitor switch circuit	• A/T control unit does not receive the correct voltage signal from the switch based on the gear position.	• Harness or connectors (The switch circuit is open or shorted.) • Inhibitor switch
P0710	1208	Fluid temperature sensor	• A/T control unit receives an excessively low or high voltage from the sensor.	• Harness or connectors (The sensor circuit is open or shorted.) • Fluid temperature sensor
P0720	1102	Revolution sensor	• A/T control unit does not receive the proper voltage signal from the sensor.	• Harness or connectors (The sensor circuit is open or shorted.) • Revolution sensor
P0725	1207	Engine speed signal	• A/T control unit does not receive the proper voltage signal from the ECM.	• Harness or connectors (The signal circuit is open or shorted.)
P0731	1103	Improper shifting to 1st gear position	• A/T cannot be shifted to the 1st gear position even electrical circuit is good.	• Shift solenoid valve A • Shift solenoid valve B • Overrun clutch solenoid valve • Line pressure solenoid valve • Each clutch • Hydraulic control circuit
P0732	1104	Improper shifting to 2nd gear position	• A/T cannot be shifted to the 2nd gear position even electrical circuit is good.	
P0733	1105	Improper shifting to 3rd gear position	• A/T cannot be shifted to the 3rd gear position even electrical circuit is good.	
P0734	1106	Improper shifting to 4th gear position or TCC	• A/T cannot be shifted to the 4th gear position or perform lock-up even electrical circuit is good.	• T/C clutch solenoid valve
P0740	1204	T/C clutch solenoid valve	• A/T control unit detects the improper voltage drop when it tries to operate the solenoid valve.	• Harness or connectors (The solenoid circuit is open or shorted.) • T/C clutch solenoid valve
P0745	1205	Line pressure solenoid valve	• A/T control unit detects the improper voltage drop when it tries to operate the solenoid valve.	• Harness or connectors (The solenoid circuit is open or shorted.) • Line pressure solenoid valve
P0750	1108	Shift solenoid valve A	• A/T control unit detects the improper voltage drop when it tries to operate the solenoid valve.	• Harness or connectors (The solenoid circuit is open or shorted.) • Shift solenoid valve A
P0755	1201	Shift solenoid valve B	• A/T control unit detects the improper voltage drop when it tries to operate the solenoid valve.	• Harness or connectors (The solenoid circuit is open or shorted.) • Shift solenoid valve B

89704C05

DIAGNOSTIC CODES—1996–98 (OBDII) CONT.

Diagnostic trouble code No.		Detected items	Malfunction is detected when ...	Check Items(Possible Cause)
CONSULT GST	MIL			
P1320	0201	Ignition signal circuit	• The ignition signal in the primary circuit is not detected by the ECM during engine cranking or running.	• Harness or connectors (The ignition primary circuit is open or shorted.) • Power transistor unit • Camshaft position sensor • Camshaft position sensor circuit
P1336	0905	Crankshaft position sensor (OBD)	• The chipping of the flywheel or drive plate gear tooth (cog) is detected by the ECM.	• Harness or connectors • Crankshaft position sensor (OBD) • Flywheel (Drive plate)
P1400	1005	EGR valve and EVAP canister purge control solenoid valve circuit	• An improper voltage signal is sent to the ECM through the solenoid valve.	• Harness or connectors (The valve circuit is open or shorted.) • EGR valve and EVAP canister purge control solenoid valve
P1401	0305	EGR temperature sensor circuit	• An excessively low or high voltage from the sensor is detected by the ECM, even when engine coolant temperature is low or high.	• Harness or connectors (The sensor circuit is open or shorted.) • EGR temperature sensor
P1605	0804	A/T diagnosis communication line	• An incorrect signal from A/T control unit is detected by the ECM.	• Harness or connectors (The communication line circuit is open or shorted.) • Dead (Weak) battery • A/T control unit
P1705	1206	Throttle position sensor Throttle position switch	• A/T control unit receives an excessively low or high voltage from the sensor.	• Harness or connectors (The sensor circuit is open or shorted.) • Throttle position sensor • Throttle position switch
P1760	1203	Overrun clutch solenoid valve	• A/T control unit detects the improper voltage drop when it tries to operate the solenoid valve.	• Harness or connectors (The solenoid circuit is open or shorted.) • Overrun clutch solenoid valve
P1900	1308 (California models) 0208 (Non-California models)	Cooling fan circuit For California models For Non-California models	• Cooling fan does not operate properly. (Overheat) • Cooling system does not operate properly. (Overheat) • Engine coolant was not added to the system using the proper filling method.	• Harness or connectors. (The cooling fan circuit is open or shorted.) • Cooling fan • Radiator hose • Radiator • Radiator cap • Water pump • Thermostat

89704C06

General Information

♦ **See Figure 57**

Diagnostic trouble codes are indicated by the number of flashes from the red Light Emitting Diode (LED) on the ECM or the Malfunction Indicator Lamp (MIL) on the instrument panel.

On two and three-digit codes, the long (0.6 second) flashes indicate the number of tens digits and short (0.3 second) flashes indicate the number of single digits.

On four-digit codes, the long (0.6 second) flashes indicate the first two digits in the code and the short (0.3 second) flashes indicate the second two digits in the code.

Diagnostic Modes

The ECM is capable of outputting data in four different modes, depending on the position of the mode switch and the ignition key. Modes are switched by turning the mode screw on the side of the ECM, near the red LED. Additional modes are accessed by turning the ignition key on or off.

The ECM is located forward of the center console, behind an access panel on the Altima, and in the passenger's side kick panel on the 240SX.

With the ECM set in Mode 1 and the ignition in the **ON** position, a malfunction indicator lamp bulb check may be performed. When the engine is started, the ECM will illuminate the indicator lamps as a warning of a fault in the system.

Mode 2 is set by turning the mode selector screw fully clockwise, waiting 2 seconds and then turning the screw fully counterclockwise. With the ignition in the **ON** position, self-diagnostic results will be output as a series of lamp flashes. When the engine is started, the oxygen sensor monitor function is enabled and the red LED on the ECM is used to determine proper oxygen sensor function.

Data Link Connector (DLC)

♦ **See Figures 58, 59 and 60**

Two types of data link connectors are used on each vehicle. Each is designed to fit a specific type of tool. The data link connector for the Nissan CONSULT is located in the interior fuse panel (as illustrated). The data link connector for the Generic Scan Tool (GST) is located under the left side of the dashboard.

The data link connectors are for use with scan tools only. The terminals cannot be jumpered to read out diagnostic codes, as on some vehicles. Be sure to follow the scan tool manufacturer's instructions.

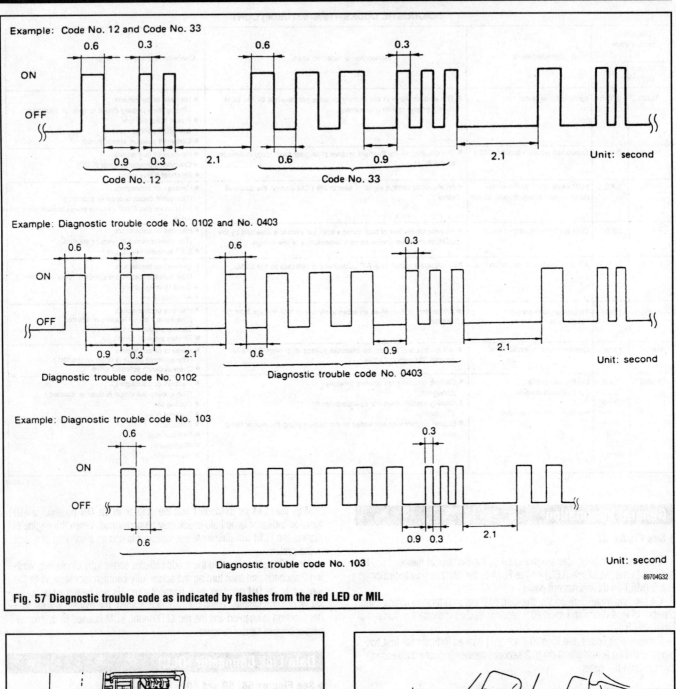

Fig. 57 Diagnostic trouble code as indicated by flashes from the red LED or MIL

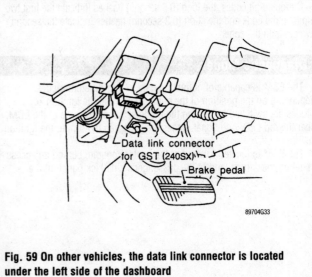

Fig. 58 On some vehicles, the data link connector is located in the fuse panel or just below the fuse panel

Fig. 59 On other vehicles, the data link connector is located under the left side of the dashboard

Fig. 60 When using a scan tool, make sure to follow all of the manufacturer's instructions carefully to ensure proper diagnosis

Fig. 61 The mode adjusting screw (top arrow) and the red LED (bottom arrow) are located on the driver's side of the ECM—Altima shown

Reading Codes

▶ **See Figure 61**

1. Remove the access cover and locate the mode adjusting screw and LED on the ECM.
2. Turn the ignition switch **ON**, but do not start the engine. Both the LED and the malfunction indicator lamp on the instrument panel should be illuminated. This is a bulb check.
3. Start the engine.

➡**Switching modes is not possible while the engine is running.**

4. If the LED or malfunction indicator lamp illuminates, there is a fault in the system.
5. Turn the mode selector screw fully clockwise. Wait 2 seconds, then turn the screw fully counterclockwise.
6. The diagnostic trouble codes will now be read from the ECM memory. They will appear as flashes of the malfunction indicator lamp, or the ECM's LED.
7. After all codes have been read, turn the mode selector screw fully clockwise to erase the codes.

➡**Turn the mode adjusting screw to the fully counterclockwise position whenever the vehicle is in use.**

8. Turn the ignition **OFF**.

➡**When the ignition switch is turned OFF during diagnosis, power to the ECM will drop after approximately 5 seconds. The diagnosis will automatically return to Mode 1 at this time.**

Clearing Codes

The easiest way to clear trouble codes is to turn the mode selector screw fully clockwise after all codes have been read.

➡**Turn the mode adjusting screw to the fully counterclockwise position whenever the vehicle is in use.**

The diagnostic memory will also be erased if the negative battery terminal is disconnected for 24 hours.

VACUUM DIAGRAMS

Following are vacuum diagrams for most of the engine and emissions package combinations covered by this manual. Because vacuum circuits will vary based on various engine and vehicle options, always refer first to the vehicle emission control information label, if present. Should the label be missing, or should the vehicle be equipped with a different engine than the vehicle's original equipment, refer to the diagrams below for the same or similar configuration.

If you wish to obtain a replacement emissions label, most manufacturers make the labels available for purchase. The labels can usually be ordered from a local dealer.

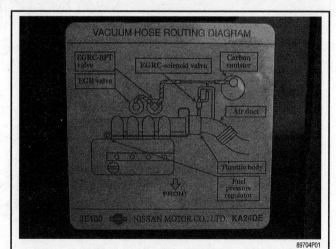

Fig. 62 An emissions system vacuum diagram sticker is normally located on the underside of the hood. This sticker may reflect mid-year production line changes

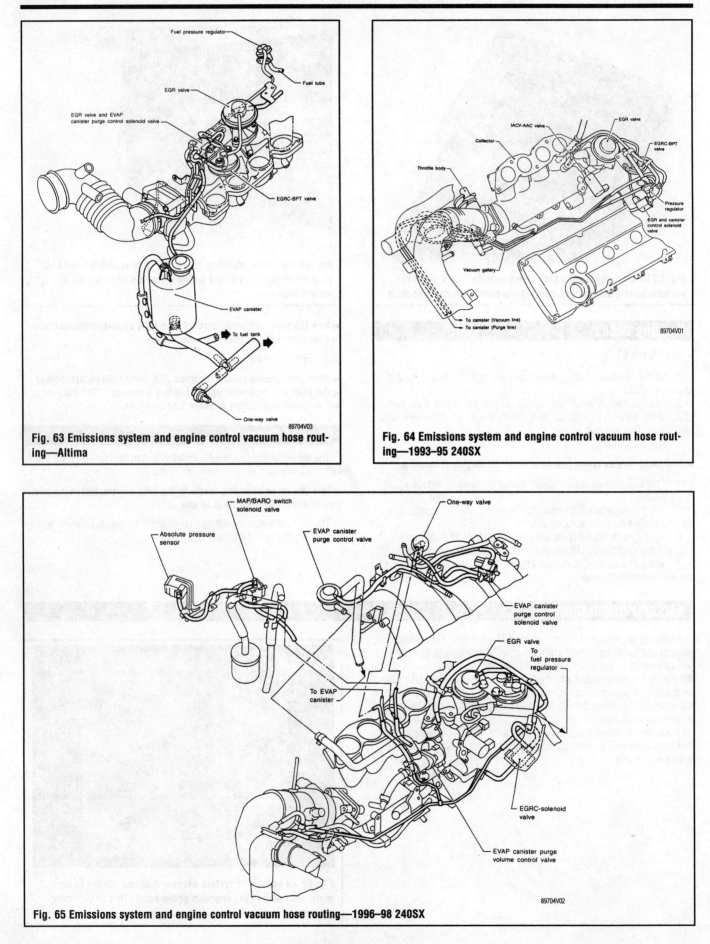

Fig. 63 Emissions system and engine control vacuum hose routing—Altima

Fig. 64 Emissions system and engine control vacuum hose routing—1993–95 240SX

Fig. 65 Emissions system and engine control vacuum hose routing—1996–98 240SX

5

FUEL SYSTEM

BASIC FUEL SYSTEM DIAGNOSIS

When there is a problem starting or driving a vehicle, two of the most important checks involve the ignition and the fuel systems. The questions most mechanics attempt to answer first, "is there spark?" and "is there fuel?" will often lead to solving most basic problems. For ignition system diagnosis and testing, please refer to the information on engine electrical components and ignition systems found earlier in this manual. If the ignition system checks out (there is spark), then you must determine if the fuel system is operating properly (is there fuel?).

GASOLINE FUEL INJECTION SYSTEM

General Information

◆ **See Figure 1**

The amount of fuel injected from the fuel injector is determined by the ECM. The ECM controls the length of time the valve remains open (injection pulse duration). The amount of fuel injected is a program value in ECM memory. The program value is preset by the engine operating conditions. These conditions are determined by input signals (for engine speed and intake air) from both the camshaft position sensor and the mass air flow sensor.

In addition, the amount of fuel injected is compensated to improve engine performance under the following various operating conditions:

Fuel is increased:
- During warm-up
- When starting the engine
- During acceleration
- During hot engine operation
- When the selector lever is changed from **N** to **D** on an automatic transaxle/transmission equipped vehicles
- During high load, high speed operation

Fuel is decreased:
- During deceleration
- During high speed operation

The mixture ratio feedback system provides the best air/fuel mixture ratio for driveability and emission control. The three-way catalyst can then better reduce CO, HC and NOx emissions. This system uses an oxygen sensor in the exhaust to determine if the engine is rich or lean. The ECM adjusts the injection pulse width according to the sensor voltage signal. This maintains the mixture ratio within the range of stoichiometric (ideal air/fuel mixture). When in mixture ratio feedback, the engine is said to be in closed loop control.

On some models, a rear oxygen sensor is located downstream of the three-way catalyst. Even if the switching characteristics of the front oxygen sensor shift, the air/fuel ratio is controlled to stoichiometric by the rear oxygen sensor.

Under the conditions below, the ECM will switch to open loop operation to maintain stabilized fuel combustion.
- Deceleration and acceleration
- High load and high engine speed operation
- Engine idling
- Malfunction of the oxygen sensor or its circuit
- Insufficient activation of the oxygen sensor or its circuit under low engine coolant temperature
- High engine coolant temperature
- After shifting from **N** to **D**
- During warm-up
- When starting the engine

The mixture ratio feedback control system monitors the mixture ratio signal transmitted from the front oxygen sensor. The feedback signal is then sent to the ECM. The ECM controls the basic mixture ratio as close to the theoretical (optimal) mixture ratio as possible. However, the basic mixture ratio is not necessarily controlled as originally designed. Both manufacturing differences and characteristic changes (such as injector clogging) during operation directly affect mixture ratio.

Accordingly, the difference between the basic and theoretical mixture ratios is monitored in this system. This is then computed in terms of injection pulse duration to automatically compensate for the difference between the two ratios.

Fuel trim refers to the feedback compensation value compared against the basic injection duration. Fuel trim includes short-term fuel trim and long-term fuel trim.

Short-term fuel trim is the short-term fuel compensation used to maintain the mixture ratio at its theoretical value. The signal from the front oxygen sensor indicates whether the mixture ratio is rich or lean, compared to the theoretical value. The signal then triggers a reduction in the fuel volume if the mixture ratio is rich, and increases the fuel volume if it is lean.

Long-term fuel trim is overall fuel compensation carried out long-term to compensate for continual deviation of the short-term trim from the central value. Such deviation will occur due to individual engine differences, wear over time, and changes in the usage environment.

Two types of fuel injection timing are used. Sequential multi-port fuel injection refers to fuel that is injected into each cylinder during each engine cycle, according to the firing order. This system is used when the engine is running.

Simultaneous multi-port fuel injection refers to fuel that is injected simultaneously into all four cylinders, twice each engine cycle. In other words, pulse signals of the same width are simultaneously transmitted from the ECM. The injectors will then receive the signals two times for each engine cycle. This system is used when the engine is being started and/or if the system is operating in the fail safe mode.

Fuel shutoff, where fuel to each cylinder is cut, occurs during deceleration or operation of the engine at excessively high speeds.

Relieving Fuel System Pressure

◆ **See Figure 2**

Always relieve the fuel system pressure prior to servicing any fuel system component.
1. Remove the fuel pump fuse.
2. Start the engine.
3. Allow the engine to run until it stalls.
4. Crank the engine for two or three seconds to release all fuel pressure.
5. Turn the ignition switch **OFF**.
6. Install the fuel pump fuse once all service has been completed.

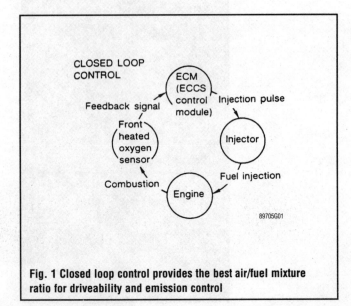

CLOSED LOOP CONTROL

Feedback signal — ECM (ECCS control module) — Injection pulse

Front heated oxygen sensor

Injector

Combustion

Fuel injection

Engine

89705G01

Fig. 1 Closed loop control provides the best air/fuel mixture ratio for driveability and emission control

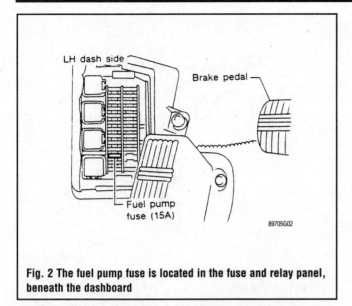

Fig. 2 The fuel pump fuse is located in the fuse and relay panel, beneath the dashboard

Fuel Pump

REMOVAL & INSTALLATION

▶ **See Figures 3, 4, 5, 6 and 7**

1. Properly relieve the fuel system pressure.
2. Remove the rear seat.
3. Remove the fuel pump cover.
4. Label and disconnect the electrical harness.
5. Label and disconnect the fuel hoses.

➡**One hose is a high pressure fuel input hose and the other is a low pressure return hose. Different hose clamps are used on each of the hoses.**

6. Matchmark the locking ring with the body for installation reference. This is to prevent overtightening of the locking ring.
7. Remove the locking ring using a special lock ring tool.

➡**It may be possible to use a large set of locking jaw pliers to loosen the lock ring. However, extreme caution must be used to not damage the plastic ring or strip the plastic threads.**

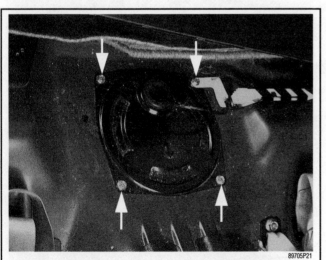

Fig. 3 The fuel pump access cover is located under the rear seat. It is secured by four screws (arrows)

Fig. 4 Fuel pump components include the locking ring (1), fuel pump assembly (2), electrical harness (3), low pressure fuel return line (4), and high pressure fuel feed line (5)

Fig. 5 The locking ring should twist off easily. If it is difficult to remove, it can be tapped around gently with a small hammer and drift

Fig. 6 The fuel pump assembly can then be lifted from the fuel tank

Fig. 7 The fuel pump assembly consists of the pump cover (1), cover gasket (2), electric fuel pump (3), and strainer (4)

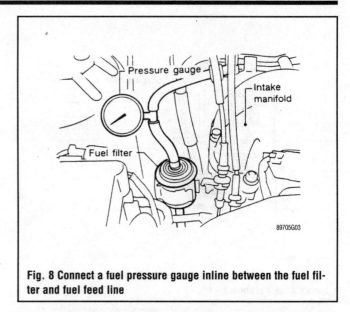

Fig. 8 Connect a fuel pressure gauge inline between the fuel filter and fuel feed line

8. Remove the fuel pump and sending unit from the fuel tank.

To install:

9. Inspect the sealing gasket and replace if damaged.
10. Install the fuel pump and sending unit in the fuel tank.
11. Install the locking ring by hand and tighten using a special lock ring tool.

➡**It may be possible to use a large set of locking jaw pliers to tighten the lock ring. However, extreme caution must be used to not damage the plastic ring or strip the plastic threads. Tighten the locking ring until the matchmarks align.**

12. Connect the fuel hoses using the proper hose clamps for the high pressure and low pressure hoses.
13. Connect the electrical harness.
14. Install the fuel pump cover.
15. Install the rear seat.

TESTING

Electrical Test

1. Remove the fuel pump inspection cover to access the fuel pump electrical harness.
2. Turn the ignition switch **OFF**.
3. Disconnect the fuel pump electrical connector.
4. Measure the resistance between the fuel pump terminals. Resistance should be 0.2–5.0 ohms @ 77°F (25°C).
5. If resistance is not within specification, the fuel pump may be faulty.
6. If the fuel pump resistance is within specification, check fuel pressure.

Pressure Test

◆ **See Figures 8 and 9**

1. Properly relieve the fuel system pressure.
2. Connect a fuel pressure gauge between the fuel filter outlet and fuel feed hose.
3. Start the engine and read the fuel pressure.

Fig. 9 Fuel pressure can be checked using an inexpensive pressure/vacuum gauge

4. Fuel pressure should be approximately 43 psi (294 kPa) a few seconds after the ignition switch is turned from **OFF** to **ON**.
5. Fuel pressure should be approximately 34 psi (235 kPa) with the engine idling.
6. Stop the engine and disconnect the fuel pressure regulator vacuum hose.
7. Plug the vacuum hose at the intake manifold and connect a hand operated vacuum pump to the pressure regulator.
8. Start the engine and note the fuel pressure as vacuum is applied and released.
9. Fuel pressure should decrease as vacuum increases.
10. If fuel pressure does not respond as specified, the fuel pressure regulator may be faulty.
11. If fuel pressure responds as specified, but fuel pressure is not within specification, the fuel pump may be faulty.

Throttle Body

REMOVAL & INSTALLATION

▶ **See Figures 10, 11, 12 and 13**

※※ CAUTION

Never smoke when working around gasoline! Avoid all sources of sparks or ignition. Gasoline vapors are EXTREMELY volatile!

1. Remove the intake duct from the throttle body.
2. Label and disconnect the vacuum hoses and the electrical harnesses.
3. Disconnect the accelerator cable.
4. Remove the four mounting bolts.
5. Remove the throttle body from the intake manifold.

To install:

6. Clean all gasket mating surfaces thoroughly.
7. Use a new gasket and position the throttle body on the intake manifold.

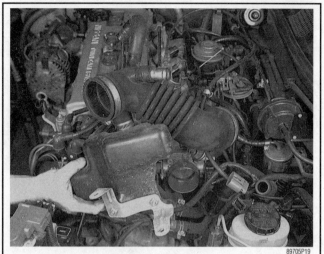

Fig. 12 The intake air tube can be removed complete with the resonator

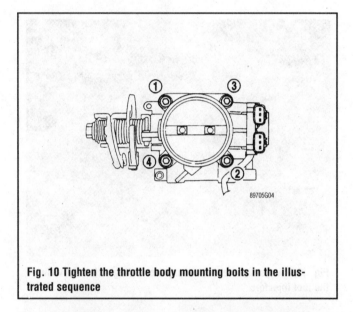

Fig. 10 Tighten the throttle body mounting bolts in the illustrated sequence

Fig. 13 Throttle body fastener locations

8. Tighten the throttle body mounting bolts to 6.5–8.0 ft. lbs. (9–11 Nm), then to 13–16 ft. lbs. (18–22 Nm) using a crisscross pattern.
9. Install and adjust the throttle cable.

➡**Check the throttle for smooth operation.**

10. Connect the electrical harnesses and vacuum hoses to the throttle body.
11. Connect the air duct to the throttle body.

Fuel Injectors

REMOVAL & INSTALLATION

▶ **See Figures 14, 15, 16, 17 and 18**

1. Properly relieve the fuel system pressure.
2. Disconnect the throttle cable and, if equipped, cruise control cable, from the throttle body.
3. Remove the throttle cable bracket from the intake manifold.
4. Label and disconnect the fuel injector electrical harnesses.
5. Disconnect and cap the fuel feed and return hoses.

Fig. 11 Label and disconnect all hoses attached to the inlet air tube

Fig. 14 Label and disconnect the fuel injector electrical harnesses

Fig. 15 The fuel injectors are retained in the intake manifold by rubber grommets

Fig. 16 The fuel injectors are retained in the fuel rail by a special cap

Fig. 17 Two O-rings (arrows) are used to provide a leakproof seal between the injector and the fuel rail

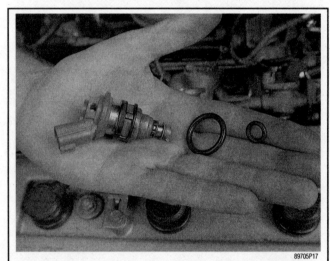

Fig. 18 Always replace the fuel injector O-rings when servicing the fuel injectors

6. Disconnect the vacuum line from the fuel pressure regulator.
7. Remove the fuel rail retaining bolts.
8. Remove the fuel rail and injector assembly from the intake manifold.
9. Remove the injector cap from the fuel rail.
10. Twist the injector slightly and pull it from the fuel rail. Repeat for the other injectors, if necessary.

➡Injectors may be very difficult to remove from the fuel rail. Take care not to damage the injector during removal.

11. Remove and discard the injector O-rings.
To install:
12. Clean the injector tailpiece and insert the injector(s) into the fuel rail with new O-rings.
13. Install the injector cap on the fuel rail and tighten the screws securely.
14. Position the injector and fuel rail assembly onto the intake manifold.
15. Tighten the fuel rail retaining bolts to 12–14 ft. lbs. (16–19 Nm).
16. Connect the vacuum line to the fuel pressure regulator.
17. Connect the fuel feed and return hoses.

18. Connect the fuel injector electrical harnesses.
19. Install the throttle cable bracket.
20. Connect and adjust the throttle and, if applicable, cruise control cables.
21. Pressurize the fuel system and check for leaks.

TESTING

♦ **See Figures 19, 20 and 21**

1. Start the engine.
2. Using a screwdriver or mechanic's stethoscope, lay the tool on the injector.
3. Place your ear against the tool and listen for a clicking sound. This sound is the injector valve opening and closing.
4. If a clicking sound is not heard, stop the engine and disconnect the injector electrical harness.
5. Install a noid light or equivalent injector harness test light on the fuel injector harness.
6. Crank the engine and check for injector signal. If signal is present, the fuel injector may be faulty.
7. If signal is present, check the fuel delivery system for proper fuel pressure.

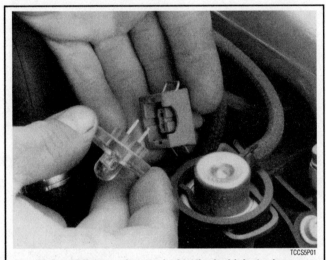

Fig. 19 A noid light can be attached to the fuel injector harness in order to test for injector pulse

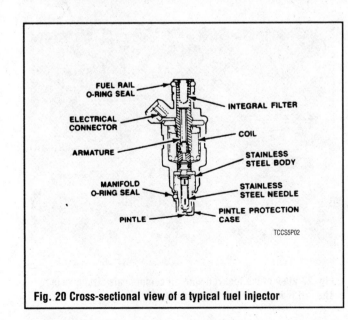

Fig. 20 Cross-sectional view of a typical fuel injector

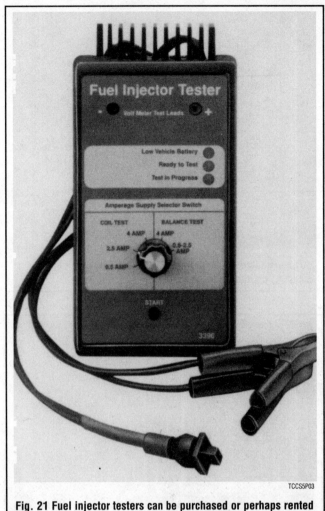

Fig. 21 Fuel injector testers can be purchased or perhaps rented

Fuel Charging Assembly

REMOVAL & INSTALLATION

♦ **See Figures 22 thru 27**

1. Properly relieve the fuel system pressure.
2. Disconnect the throttle cable and, if equipped, cruise control cable, from the throttle body.
3. Remove the throttle cable bracket from the intake manifold.
4. Label and disconnect the fuel injector electrical harnesses.
5. Disconnect and cap the fuel feed and return hoses.
6. Disconnect the vacuum line from the fuel pressure regulator.
7. Remove the fuel rail retaining bolts.
8. Remove the fuel rail and injector assembly from the intake manifold.

To install:

9. Position the injector and fuel rail assembly onto the intake manifold.
10. Tighten the fuel rail retaining bolts to 12–14 ft. lbs. (16–19 Nm).
11. Connect the vacuum line to the fuel pressure regulator.
12. Connect the fuel feed and return hoses.
13. Connect the fuel injector electrical harnesses.
14. Install the throttle cable bracket.
15. Connect and adjust the throttle and, if applicable, cruise control cables.
16. Pressurize the fuel system and check for leaks.

Fig. 22 The throttle cable bracket must be removed to gain access to the fuel rail

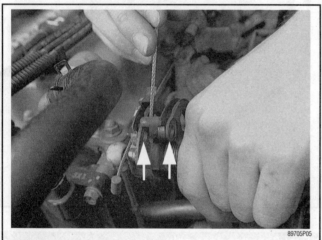

Fig. 23 To remove the throttle cable, turn the throttle shaft to its wide open position, and release the cable end from the throttle lever bore (arrows)

Fig. 24 On the Altima, the fuel feed hose is located at the driver's side of the fuel rail

Fig. 25 When removing the fuel rail, take special care not to damage the injector tips (arrow)

Fig. 26 On the Altima, the fuel return hose is located at the passenger's side of the fuel rail

Fig. 27 View of the fuel rail with all components disconnected. The rail is now ready to be removed

Fuel Pressure Regulator

REMOVAL & INSTALLATION

▶ See Figures 28, 29 and 30

1. Properly relieve the fuel system pressure.
2. Disconnect and cap the fuel return line at the regulator.
3. Disconnect the vacuum line from the regulator.
4. Remove the bolts securing the pressure regulator to the fuel rail.

➡ **Place a rag under the fuel rail to absorb any remaining fuel.**

5. Remove the regulator from the fuel rail and discard the O-ring.
   To install:
6. Install a new O-ring on the regulator and position it on the fuel rail.
7. Tighten the regulator securing bolts to 26–34 inch lbs. (3–4 Nm).
8. Connect the vacuum line to the regulator.
9. Connect the fuel return line to the regulator.
10. Pressurize the fuel system and check for leaks.

Fig. 29 Fuel pressure is controlled by a vacuum line connected to the fuel pressure regulator

Fig. 28 On the Altima, the fuel pressure regulator is attached to the passenger's side end of the fuel rail by two bolts

Fig. 30 Always use a new O-ring when installing the fuel pressure regulator

FUEL TANK

Tank Assembly

REMOVAL & INSTALLATION

▶ See Figures 31, 32, 33, 34 and 35

1. Drain the fuel from the fuel tank.
2. Properly relieve the fuel system pressure.
3. Remove the fuel pump access plate beneath the rear seat.
4. Label and disconnect the fuel hoses and electrical harness.
5. Raise and safely support the rear of the vehicle.
6. Label all fuel lines for installation reference.
7. On 240SX models, remove the exhaust center tube, driveshaft, differential carrier and rear suspension member.
8. Disconnect the fuel filler hose and vent hose.
9. Remove the fuel tank protector assembly.
10. Remove the fuel tank band retaining bolts while supporting the fuel tank with a transmission jack.
11. Slowly lower the tank assembly from the vehicle.
    To install:
12. Position the tank assembly on the vehicle.
13. Install the fuel tank retaining bands and tighten the bolts to 20–27 ft. lbs. (26–36 Nm).
14. Install the fuel tank protector assembly.
15. Connect the fuel filler hose and vent hose. Tighten the hose clamps securely.
16. On 240SX models, install the exhaust center tube, driveshaft, differential carrier and rear suspension member.
17. Lower the rear of the vehicle.
18. Connect the fuel hoses and electrical harness.
19. Install the fuel pump access plate beneath the rear seat.
20. Fill the fuel tank with a few gallons of fresh fuel.
21. Pressurize the fuel system and check for leaks.

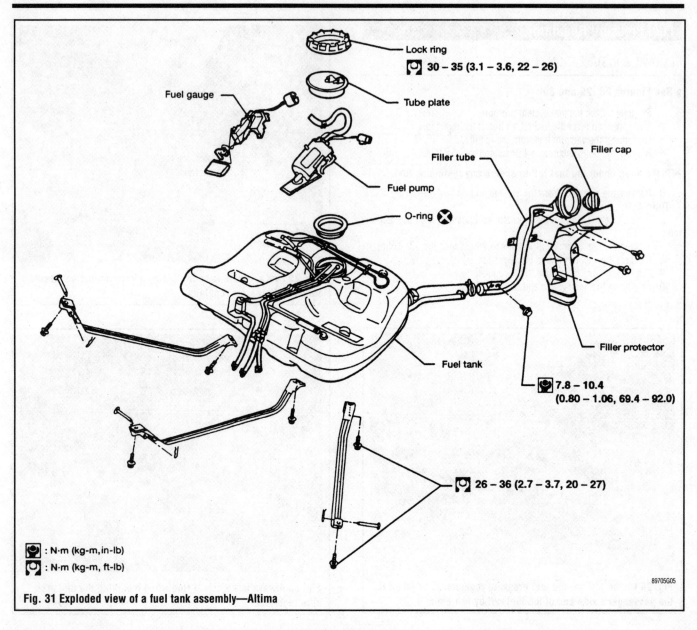

Lock ring

30 – 35 (3.1 – 3.6, 22 – 26)

Tube plate

Fuel gauge

Filler tube

Filler cap

Fuel pump

O-ring ⊗

Filler protector

Fuel tank

7.8 – 10.4
(0.80 – 1.06, 69.4 – 92.0)

26 – 36 (2.7 – 3.7, 20 – 27)

: N·m (kg-m, in-lb)

: N·m (kg-m, ft-lb)

89705G05

Fig. 31 Exploded view of a fuel tank assembly—Altima

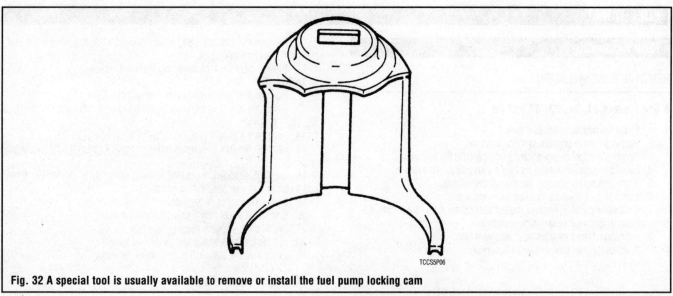

TCCS5P06

Fig. 32 A special tool is usually available to remove or install the fuel pump locking cam

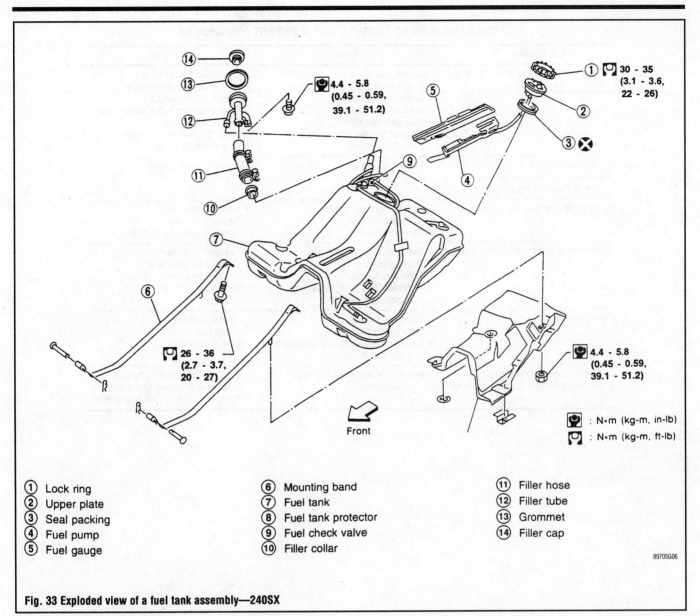

4.4 - 5.8
(0.45 - 0.59,
39.1 - 51.2)

30 - 35
(3.1 - 3.6,
22 - 26)

26 - 36
(2.7 - 3.7,
20 - 27)

4.4 - 5.8
(0.45 - 0.59,
39.1 - 51.2)

Front

: N•m (kg-m, in-lb)

: N•m (kg-m, ft-lb)

89705G06

① Lock ring	⑥ Mounting band	⑪ Filler hose
② Upper plate	⑦ Fuel tank	⑫ Filler tube
③ Seal packing	⑧ Fuel tank protector	⑬ Grommet
④ Fuel pump	⑨ Fuel check valve	⑭ Filler cap
⑤ Fuel gauge	⑩ Filler collar	

Fig. 33 Exploded view of a fuel tank assembly—240SX

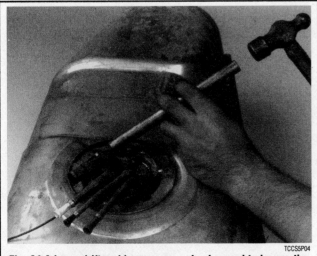

TCCS5P04

Fig. 34 A brass drift and hammer can also be used to loosen the fuel pump locking cam

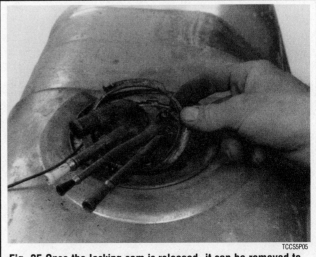

TCCS5P05

Fig. 35 Once the locking cam is released, it can be removed to free the fuel pump

Troubleshooting Basic Fuel System Problems

Problem	Cause	Solution
Engine cranks, but won't start (or is hard to start) when cold	• Empty fuel tank • Incorrect starting procedure • Defective fuel pump • No fuel in carburetor • Clogged fuel filter • Engine flooded • Defective choke	• Check for fuel in tank • Follow correct procedure • Check pump output • Check for fuel in the carburetor • Replace fuel filter • Wait 15 minutes; try again • Check choke plate
Engine cranks, but is hard to start (or does not start) when hot—(presence of fuel is assumed)	• Defective choke	• Check choke plate
Rough idle or engine runs rough	• Dirt or moisture in fuel • Clogged air filter • Faulty fuel pump	• Replace fuel filter • Replace air filter • Check fuel pump output
Engine stalls or hesitates on acceleration	• Dirt or moisture in the fuel • Dirty carburetor • Defective fuel pump • Incorrect float level, defective accelerator pump	• Replace fuel filter • Clean the carburetor • Check fuel pump output • Check carburetor
Poor gas mileage	• Clogged air filter • Dirty carburetor • Defective choke, faulty carburetor adjustment	• Replace air filter • Clean carburetor • Check carburetor
Engine is flooded (won't start accompanied by smell of raw fuel)	• Improperly adjusted choke or carburetor	• Wait 15 minutes and try again, without pumping gas pedal • If it won't start, check carburetor

TCCA5C01

6

CHASSIS ELECTRICAL

UNDERSTANDING AND TROUBLESHOOTING ELECTRICAL SYSTEMS

Basic Electrical Theory

♦ **See Figure 1**

For any 12 volt, negative ground, electrical system to operate, the electricity must travel in a complete circuit. This simply means that current (power) from the positive terminal (+) of the battery must eventually return to the negative terminal (-) of the battery. Along the way, this current will travel through wires, fuses, switches and components. If, for any reason, the flow of current through the circuit is interrupted, the component fed by that circuit will cease to function properly.

Perhaps the easiest way to visualize a circuit is to think of connecting a light bulb (with two wires attached to it) to the battery—one wire attached to the negative (-) terminal of the battery and the other wire to the positive (+) terminal. With the two wires touching the battery terminals, the circuit would be complete and the light bulb would illuminate. Electricity would follow a path from the battery to the bulb and back to the battery. It's easy to see that with longer wires on our light bulb, it could be mounted anywhere. Further, one wire could be fitted with a switch so that the light could be turned on and off.

The normal automotive circuit differs from this simple example in two ways. First, instead of having a return wire from the bulb to the battery, the current travels through the chassis of the vehicle. Since the negative (-) battery cable is attached to the chassis and the chassis is made of electrically conductive metal, the chassis of the vehicle can serve as a ground wire to complete the circuit. Secondly, most automotive circuits contain multiple components which receive power from a single circuit. This lessens the amount of wire needed to power components on the vehicle.

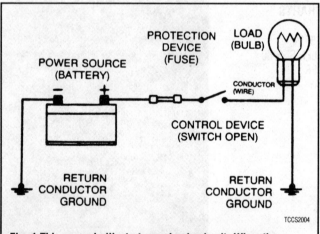

Fig. 1 This example illustrates a simple circuit. When the switch is closed, power from the positive (+) battery terminal flows through the fuse and the switch, and then to the light bulb. The light illuminates and the circuit is completed through the ground wire back to the negative (-) battery terminal. In reality, the two ground points shown in the illustration are attached to the metal chassis of the vehicle, which completes the circuit back to the battery

THE WATER ANALOGY

Electricity is the flow of electrons—hypothetical particles thought to constitute the basic "stuff" of electricity. Many people have been taught electrical theory using an analogy with water. In a comparison with water flowing through a pipe, the electrons would be the water.

The flow of electricity can be measured much like the flow of water through a pipe. The unit of measurement used is amperes, frequently abbreviated as amps (a). When connected to a circuit, an ammeter will measure the actual amount of current flowing through the circuit. When relatively few electrons flow through a circuit, the amperage is low. When many electrons flow, the amperage is high.

Just as water pressure is measured in units such as pounds per square inch (psi), electrical pressure is measured in units called volts (v). When a voltmeter is connected to a circuit, it is measuring the electrical pressure. The higher the voltage, the more current will flow through the circuit. The lower the voltage, the less current will flow.

While increasing the voltage in a circuit will increase the flow of current, the actual flow depends not only on voltage, but also on the resistance of the circuit. Resistance is the amount of force necessary to push the current through the circuit. The standard unit for measuring resistance is an ohm (W or omega). Resistance in a circuit varies depending on the amount and type of components used in the circuit. The main factors which determine resistance are:

- Material—some materials have more resistance than others. Those with high resistance are said to be insulators. Rubber is one of the best insulators available, as it allows little current to pass. Low resistance materials are said to be conductors. Copper wire is among the best conductors. Most vehicle wiring is made of copper.
- Size—the larger the wire size being used, the less resistance the wire will have. This is why components which use large amounts of electricity usually have large wires supplying current to them.
- Length—for a given thickness of wire, the longer the wire, the greater the resistance. The shorter the wire, the less the resistance. When determining the proper wire for a circuit, both size and length must be considered to design a circuit that can handle the current needs of the component.
- Temperature—with many materials, the higher the temperature, the greater the resistance. This principle is used in many of the sensors on the engine.

OHM'S LAW

The preceding definitions may lead the reader into believing that there is no relationship between current, voltage and resistance. Nothing can be further from the truth. The relationship between current, voltage and resistance can be summed up by a statement known as Ohm's law.

Voltage (E) is equal to amperage (I) times resistance (R): $E = I \times R$

Other forms of the formula are $R = E/I$ and $I = E/R$

In each of these formulas, E is the voltage in volts, I is the current in amps and R is the resistance in ohms. The basic point to remember is that as the resistance of a circuit goes up, the amount of current that flows in the circuit will go down, if voltage remains the same.

Electrical Components

POWER SOURCE

The power source for 12 volt automotive electrical systems is the battery. In most modern vehicles, the battery is a lead/acid electrochemical device consisting of six 2 volt subsections (cells) connected in series, so that the unit is capable of producing approximately 12 volts of electrical pressure. Each subsection consists of a series of positive and negative plates held a short distance apart in a solution of sulfuric acid and water.

The two types of plates are of dissimilar metals. This sets up a chemical reaction, and it is this reaction which produces current flow from the battery when its positive and negative terminals are connected to an electrical load. The power removed from the battery is replaced by the alternator, which forces electrons back through the battery, reversing the normal flow, and restoring the battery to its original chemical state.

GROUND

Two types of grounds are used in automotive electric circuits. Direct ground components are grounded through their mounting points. All other components use some sort of ground wire which is attached to the body or chassis of the vehicle. The electrical current runs through the chassis of the vehicle and returns to the battery through the ground (-) cable; if you look, you'll see that the battery ground cable connects between the battery and the body or chassis of the vehicle.

➡**It should be noted that a good percentage of electrical problems can be traced to bad grounds.**

PROTECTIVE DEVICES

♦ **See Figure 2**

It is possible for large surges of current to pass through the electrical system of your vehicle. If this surge of current were to reach the load in the circuit, it could burn it out or severely damage it. To prevent this, fuses, circuit breakers and/or fusible links are connected into the supply wires of the electrical system. These items are nothing more than a built-in weak spot in the system. When an abnormal amount of current flows through the system, these protective devices work as follows to protect the circuit:
- Fuse—when an excessive electrical current passes through a fuse, the fuse "blows" (the conductor melts) and opens the circuit, preventing the passage of current.

Fig. 2 Most vehicles use one or more fuse panels. This one is located in the driver's side kick panel

- Circuit Breaker—a circuit breaker is basically a self-repairing fuse. It will open the circuit in the same fashion as a fuse, but when the surge subsides, the circuit breaker can be reset and does not need replacement.
- Fusible Link—a fusible link (fuse link or main link) is a short length of special, Hypalon high temperature insulated wire that acts as a fuse. When an excessive electrical current passes through a fusible link, the thin gauge wire inside the link melts, creating an intentional open to protect the circuit. To repair the circuit, the link must be replaced. Some newer type fusible links are housed in plug-in modules, which are simply replaced like a fuse, while older type fusible links must be cut and spliced if they melt. Since this link is very early in the electrical path, it's the first place to look if nothing on the vehicle works, but the battery seems to be charged and is properly connected.

❋❋ CAUTION

Always replace fuses, circuit breakers and fusible links with identically rated components. Under no circumstances should a component of higher or lower amperage rating be substituted.

SWITCHES & RELAYS

♦ **See Figures 3 and 4**

Switches are used in electrical circuits to control the passage of current. The most common use is to open and close circuits between the battery and the various electric devices in the system. Switches are rated according to the amount of amperage they can handle. If a sufficient amperage rated switch is not used in a circuit, the switch could overload and cause damage.

Some electrical components which require a large amount of current to operate use a special switch called a relay. Since these circuits carry a large amount of current, the thickness of the wire in the circuit is also greater. If this large wire were connected from the load to the control switch on the dashboard, the switch would have to carry the high amperage load and the dash would be twice as large to accommodate the increased size of the wiring harness. To prevent these problems, a relay is used.

Relays are composed of a coil and a switch. These two components are linked together so that when one operates, the other operates at the same time. The large wires in the circuit are connected from the battery to one side of the relay switch and from the opposite side of the relay switch to the load. Most relays are normally open, preventing current from passing through the circuit. Additional, smaller wires are connected from the relay coil to the control switch for the circuit and from the opposite side of the relay coil to ground. When the control switch is turned on, it grounds the

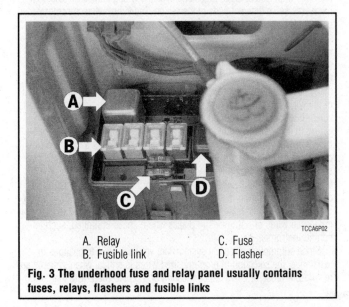

A. Relay   C. Fuse
B. Fusible link   D. Flasher

Fig. 3 The underhood fuse and relay panel usually contains fuses, relays, flashers and fusible links

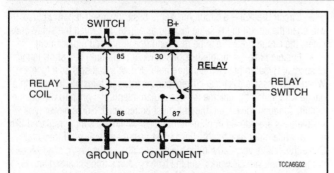

Fig. 4 Relays are composed of a coil and a switch. These two components are linked together so that when one operates, the other operates at the same time. The large wires in the circuit are connected from the battery to one side of the relay switch (B+) and from the opposite side of the relay switch to the load (component). Smaller wires are connected from the relay coil to the control switch for the circuit and from the opposite side of the relay coil to ground

smaller wire to the relay coil, causing the coil to operate. The coil pulls the relay switch closed, sending power to the component without routing it through the inside of the vehicle. Some common circuits which may use relays are the horn, headlights, starter, electric fuel pump and rear window defogger systems.

LOAD

Every complete circuit must include a "load" (something to use the electricity coming from the source). Without this load, the battery would attempt to deliver its entire power supply from one pole to another. The electricity would take a short cut to ground and cause a great amount of damage to other components in the circuit by developing a tremendous amount of heat. This condition could develop sufficient heat to melt the insulation on all the surrounding wires and reduce a multiple wire cable to a lump of plastic and copper.

WIRING & HARNESSES

The average automobile contains about ½ mile of wiring, with hundreds of individual connections. To protect the many wires from damage and to keep them from becoming a confusing tangle, they are organized into bundles, enclosed in plastic or taped together and called wiring harnesses. Different harnesses serve different parts of the vehicle. Individual wires are color coded to help trace them through a harness where sections are hidden from view.

Automotive wiring or circuit conductors can be either single strand wire, multi-strand wire or printed circuitry. Single strand wire has a solid metal core and is usually used inside such components as alternators, motors, relays and other devices. Multi-strand wire has a core made of many small strands of wire twisted together into a single conductor. Most of the wiring in an automotive electrical system is made up of multi-strand wire, either as a single conductor or grouped together in a harness. All wiring is color coded on the insulator, either as a solid color or as a colored wire with an identification stripe. A printed circuit is a thin film of copper or other conductor that is printed on an insulator backing. Occasionally, a printed circuit is sandwiched between two sheets of plastic for more protection and flexibility. A complete printed circuit, consisting of conductors, insulating material and connectors for lamps or other components is called a printed circuit board. Printed circuitry is used in place of individual wires or harnesses in places where space is limited, such as behind instrument panels.

Since automotive electrical systems are very sensitive to changes in resistance, the selection of properly sized wires is critical when systems are repaired. A loose or corroded connection or a replacement wire that is too

small for the circuit will add extra resistance and an additional voltage drop to the circuit.

The wire gauge number is an expression of the cross-section area of the conductor. The most common system for expressing wire size is the American Wire Gauge (AWG) system. As gauge number increases, area decreases and the wire becomes smaller. An 18 gauge wire is smaller than a 4 gauge wire. A wire with a higher gauge number will carry less current than a wire with a lower gauge number. Gauge wire size refers to the size of the strands of the conductor, not the size of the complete wire. It is possible, therefore, to have two wires of the same gauge with different diameters because one may have thicker insulation than the other.

12 volt automotive electrical systems generally use 10, 12, 14, 16 and 18 gauge wire. Main power distribution circuits and larger accessories usually use 10 and 12 gauge wire. Battery cables are usually 4 or 6 gauge, although 1 and 2 gauge wires are occasionally used.

It is essential to understand how a circuit works before trying to figure out why it doesn't. An electrical schematic shows the electrical current paths when a circuit is operating properly. Schematics break the entire electrical system down into individual circuits. In a schematic, no attempt is made to represent wiring and components as they physically appear on the vehicle; switches and other components are shown as simply as possible. Face views of harness connectors show the cavity or terminal locations in all multi-pin connectors to help locate test points.

CONNECTORS

▶ **See Figures 5 and 6**

Three types of connectors are commonly used in automotive applications—weatherproof, molded and hard shell.

• Weatherproof—these connectors are most commonly used in the engine compartment or where the connector is exposed to the elements. Terminals are protected against moisture and dirt by sealing rings which provide a weathertight seal. All repairs require the use of a special terminal and the tool required to service it. Unlike standard blade type terminals, these weatherproof terminals cannot be straightened once they are bent. Make certain that the connectors are properly seated and all of the sealing rings are in place when connecting leads.

• Molded—these connectors require complete replacement of the connector if found to be defective. This means splicing a new connector assembly into the harness. All splices should be soldered to insure proper contact. Use care when probing the connections or replacing terminals in them, as it is possible to create a short circuit between opposite terminals. If this happens to the wrong terminal pair, it is possible to damage certain

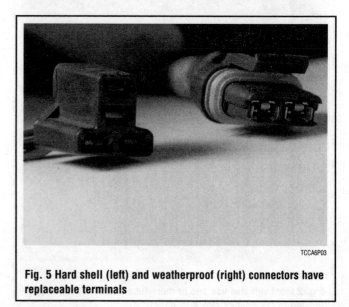

Fig. 5 Hard shell (left) and weatherproof (right) connectors have replaceable terminals

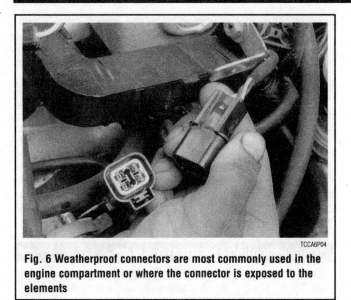

Fig. 6 Weatherproof connectors are most commonly used in the engine compartment or where the connector is exposed to the elements

components. Always use jumper wires between connectors for circuit checking and NEVER probe through weatherproof seals.
• Hard Shell—unlike molded connectors, the terminal contacts in hard-shell connectors can be replaced. Replacement usually involves the use of a special terminal removal tool that depresses the locking tangs (barbs) on the connector terminal and allows the connector to be removed from the rear of the shell. The connector shell should be replaced if it shows any evidence of burning, melting, cracks, or breaks. Replace individual terminals that are burnt, corroded, distorted or loose.

Test Equipment

Pinpointing the exact cause of trouble in an electrical circuit is most times accomplished by the use of special test equipment. The following describes different types of commonly used test equipment and briefly explains how to use them in diagnosis. In addition to the information covered below, the tool manufacturer's instructions booklet (provided with the tester) should be read and clearly understood before attempting any test procedures.

JUMPER WIRES

✳✳ CAUTION

Never use jumper wires made from a thinner gauge wire than the circuit being tested. If the jumper wire is of too small a gauge, it may overheat and possibly melt. Never use jumpers to bypass high resistance loads in a circuit. Bypassing resistances, in effect, creates a short circuit. This may, in turn, cause damage and fire. Jumper wires should only be used to bypass lengths of wire.

Jumper wires are simple, yet extremely valuable, pieces of test equipment. They are basically test wires which are used to bypass sections of a circuit. Although jumper wires can be purchased, they are usually fabricated from lengths of standard automotive wire and whatever type of connector (alligator clip, spade connector or pin connector) that is required for the particular application being tested. In cramped, hard-to-reach areas, it is advisable to have insulated boots over the jumper wire terminals in order to prevent accidental grounding. It is also advisable to include a standard automotive fuse in any jumper wire. This is commonly referred to as a "fused jumper". By inserting an in-line fuse holder between a set of test leads, a fused jumper wire can be used for bypassing open circuits. Use a 5 amp fuse to provide protection against voltage spikes.

Jumper wires are used primarily to locate open electrical circuits, on either the ground (-) side of the circuit or on the power (+) side. If an electrical component fails to operate, connect the jumper wire between the component and a good ground. If the component operates only with the jumper installed, the ground circuit is open. If the ground circuit is good, but the component does not operate, the circuit between the power feed and component may be open. By moving the jumper wire successively back from the component toward the power source, you can isolate the area of the circuit where the open is located. When the component stops functioning, or the power is cut off, the open is in the segment of wire between the jumper and the point previously tested.

You can sometimes connect the jumper wire directly from the battery to the "hot" terminal of the component, but first make sure the component uses 12 volts in operation. Some electrical components, such as fuel injectors, are designed to operate on about 4 volts, and running 12 volts directly to these components will cause damage.

TEST LIGHTS

▶ See Figure 7

The test light is used to check circuits and components while electrical current is flowing through them. It is used for voltage and ground tests. To use a 12 volt test light, connect the ground clip to a good ground and probe wherever necessary with the pick. The test light will illuminate when voltage is detected. This does not necessarily mean that 12 volts (or any particular amount of voltage) is present; it only means that some voltage is present. It is advisable before using the test light to touch its ground clip and probe across the battery posts or terminals to make sure the light is operating properly.

✳✳ WARNING

Do not use a test light to probe electronic ignition spark plug or coil wires. Never use a pick-type test light to probe wiring on computer controlled systems unless specifically instructed to do so. Any wire insulation that is pierced by the test light probe should be taped and sealed with silicone after testing.

Like the jumper wire, the 12 volt test light is used to isolate opens in circuits. But, whereas the jumper wire is used to bypass the open to operate the load, the 12 volt test light is used to locate the presence of voltage in a circuit. If the test light illuminates, there is power up to that point in the circuit; if the test light does not illuminate, there is an open circuit (no power). Move the test light in successive steps back toward the power source until

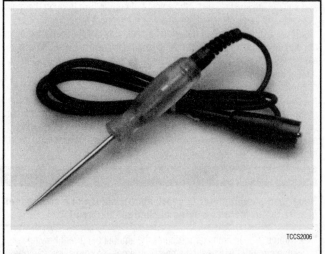

Fig. 7 A 12 volt test light is used to detect the presence of voltage in a circuit

the light in the handle illuminates. The open is between the probe and a point which was previously probed.

The self-powered test light is similar in design to the 12 volt test light, but contains a 1.5 volt penlight battery in the handle. It is most often used in place of a multimeter to check for open or short circuits when power is isolated from the circuit (continuity test).

The battery in a self-powered test light does not provide much current. A weak battery may not provide enough power to illuminate the test light even when a complete circuit is made (especially if there is high resistance in the circuit). Always make sure that the test battery is strong. To check the battery, briefly touch the ground clip to the probe; if the light glows brightly, the battery is strong enough for testing.

➡**A self-powered test light should not be used on any computer controlled system or component. The small amount of electricity transmitted by the test light is enough to damage many electronic automotive components.**

MULTIMETERS

Multimeters are an extremely useful tool for troubleshooting electrical problems. They can be purchased in either analog or digital form and have a price range to suit any budget. A multimeter is a voltmeter, ammeter and ohmmeter (along with other features) combined into one instrument. It is often used when testing solid state circuits because of its high input impedance (usually 10 megaohms or more). A brief description of the multimeter main test functions follows:

• Voltmeter—the voltmeter is used to measure voltage at any point in a circuit, or to measure the voltage drop across any part of a circuit. Voltmeters usually have various scales and a selector switch to allow the reading of different voltage ranges. The voltmeter has a positive and a negative lead. To avoid damage to the meter, always connect the negative lead to the negative (-) side of the circuit (to ground or nearest the ground side of the circuit) and connect the positive lead to the positive (+) side of the circuit (to the power source or the nearest power source). Note that the negative voltmeter lead will always be black and that the positive voltmeter will always be some color other than black (usually red).

• Ohmmeter—the ohmmeter is designed to read resistance (measured in ohms) in a circuit or component. All ohmmeters will have a selector switch which permits the measurement of different ranges of resistance (usually the selector switch allows the multiplication of the meter reading by 10, 100, 1,000 and 10,000). Since the meters are powered by an internal battery, the ohmmeter can be used as a self-powered test light. When the ohmmeter is connected, current from the ohmmeter flows through the circuit or component being tested. Since the ohmmeter's internal resistance and voltage are known values, the amount of current flow through the meter depends on the resistance of the circuit or component being tested. The ohmmeter can also be used to perform a continuity test for suspected open circuits. In using the meter for making continuity checks, do not be concerned with the actual resistance readings. Zero resistance, or any ohm reading, indicates continuity in the circuit. Infinite resistance indicates an opening in the circuit. A high resistance reading where there should be none indicates a problem in the circuit. Checks for short circuits are made in the same manner as checks for open circuits, except that the circuit must be isolated from both power and normal ground. Infinite resistance indicates no continuity to ground, while zero resistance indicates a dead short to ground.

✳✳✳ WARNING

Never use an ohmmeter to check the resistance of a component or wire while there is voltage applied to the circuit.

• Ammeter—an ammeter measures the amount of current flowing through a circuit in units called amperes or amps. At normal operating voltage, most circuits have a characteristic amount of amperes, called "current draw" which can be measured using an ammeter. By referring to a specified current draw rating, then measuring the amperes and comparing the two values, one can determine what is happening within the circuit to aid in diagnosis. An open circuit, for example, will not allow any current to flow, so the ammeter reading will be zero. A damaged component or circuit will have an increased current draw, so the reading will be high. The ammeter is always connected in series with the circuit being tested. All of the current that normally flows through the circuit must also flow through the ammeter; if there is any other path for the current to follow, the ammeter reading will not be accurate. The ammeter itself has very little resistance to current flow and, therefore, will not affect the circuit, but it will measure current draw only when the circuit is closed and electricity is flowing. Excessive current draw can blow fuses and drain the battery, while a reduced current draw can cause motors to run slowly, lights to dim and other components to not operate properly.

Troubleshooting Electrical Systems

When diagnosing a specific problem, organized troubleshooting is a must. The complexity of a modern automotive vehicle demands that you approach any problem in a logical, organized manner. There are certain troubleshooting techniques which are standard:

• Establish when the problem occurs. Does the problem appear only under certain conditions? Were there any noises, odors or other unusual symptoms?

• Isolate the problem area. To do this, make some simple tests and observations, then eliminate the systems that are working properly. Check for obvious problems, such as broken wires and loose or dirty connections. Always check the obvious before assuming something complicated is the cause.

• Test for problems systematically to determine the cause once the problem area is isolated. Are all the components functioning properly? Is there power going to electrical switches and motors. Performing careful, systematic checks will often turn up most causes on the first inspection, without wasting time checking components that have little or no relationship to the problem.

• Test all repairs after the work is done to make sure that the problem is fixed. Some causes can be traced to more than one component, so a careful verification of repair work is important in order to pick up additional malfunctions that may cause a problem to reappear or a different problem to arise. A blown fuse, for example, is a simple problem that may require more than another fuse to repair. If you don't look for a problem that caused a fuse to blow, a shorted wire (for example) may go undetected.

Experience has shown that most problems tend to be the result of a fairly simple and obvious cause, such as loose or corroded connectors, bad grounds or damaged wire insulation which causes a short. This makes careful visual inspection of components during testing essential to quick and accurate troubleshooting.

Testing

OPEN CIRCUITS

◗ **See Figure 8**

1. Isolate the circuit from power and ground.
2. Connect the self-powered test light or ohmmeter ground clip to a good ground and probe sections of the circuit sequentially.
3. If the light is out or there is infinite resistance, the open is between the probe and the circuit ground.
4. If the light is on or the meter shows continuity, the open is between the probe and end of the circuit toward the power source.

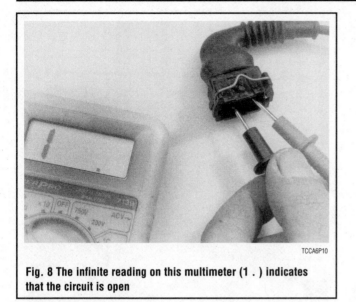

Fig. 8 The infinite reading on this multimeter (1 .) indicates that the circuit is open

SHORT CIRCUITS

➡Never use a self-powered test light to perform checks for opens or shorts when power is applied to the electrical system under test. The 12 volt vehicle power will quickly burn out the light bulb in the test light.

1. Isolate the circuit from power and ground.
2. Connect the self-powered test light or ohmmeter ground clip to a good ground and probe any easy-to-reach test point in the circuit.
3. If the light comes on or there is continuity, there is a short somewhere in the circuit.
4. To isolate the short, probe a test point at either end of the isolated circuit (the light should be on or the meter should indicate continuity).
5. Leave the test light probe engaged and sequentially open connectors or switches, remove parts, etc. until the light goes out or continuity is broken.
6. When the light goes out, the short is between the last two circuit components which were opened.

VOLTAGE

▶ See Figures 9 and 10

This test determines voltage available from the battery and should be the first step in any electrical troubleshooting procedure. Many electrical problems, especially on computer controlled systems, can be caused by a low state of charge in the battery. Excessive corrosion at the battery cable terminals can cause poor contact that will prevent proper charging and full battery current flow.

1. Set the voltmeter selector switch to the 20V position.
2. Connect the multimeter negative lead to the battery's negative (-) post or terminal and the positive lead to the battery's positive (+) post or terminal.
3. Turn the ignition switch **ON** to provide a load.
4. A well charged battery should register over 12 volts. If the meter reads below 11.5 volts, the battery power may be insufficient to operate the electrical system properly.

VOLTAGE DROP

▶ See Figure 11

When current flows through a load, the voltage beyond the load drops. This voltage drop is due to the resistance created by the load and also by small resistances created by corrosion at the connectors and damaged insulation on the wires. The maximum allowable voltage drop under load is critical, especially if there is more than one load in the circuit, since all voltage drops are cumulative.

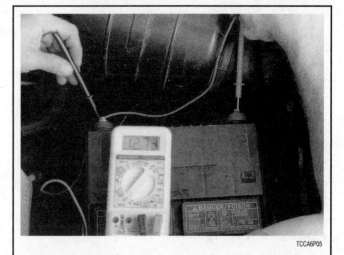

Fig. 9 Using a multimeter to check battery voltage. This battery is fully charged

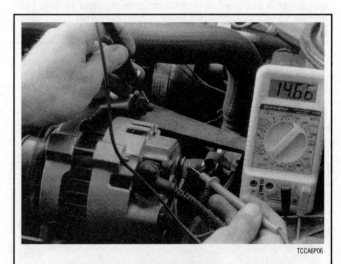

Fig. 10 Testing voltage output between the alternator's BAT terminal and ground. This voltage reading is normal

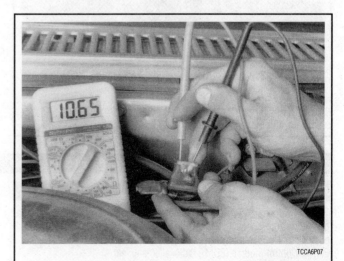

Fig. 11 This voltage drop test revealed high resistance (low voltage) in the circuit

1. Set the voltmeter selector switch to the 20 volt position.
2. Connect the multimeter negative lead to a good ground.
3. Operate the circuit and check the voltage prior to the first component (load).
4. There should be little or no voltage drop in the circuit prior to the first component. If a voltage drop exists, the wire or connectors in the circuit are suspect.
5. While operating the first component in the circuit, probe the ground side of the component with the positive meter lead and observe the voltage readings. A small voltage drop should be noticed. This voltage drop is caused by the resistance of the component.
6. Repeat the test for each component (load) down the circuit.
7. If a large voltage drop is noticed, the preceding component, wire or connector is suspect.

RESISTANCE

▶ See Figures 12 and 13

❉❉ WARNING

Never use an ohmmeter with power applied to the circuit. The ohmmeter is designed to operate on its own power supply. The normal 12 volt automotive electrical system current could damage the meter!

1. Isolate the circuit from the vehicle's power source.
2. Ensure that the ignition key is **OFF** when disconnecting any components or the battery.
3. Where necessary, also isolate at least one side of the circuit to be checked, in order to avoid reading parallel resistances. Parallel circuit resistances will always give a lower reading than the actual resistance of either of the branches.

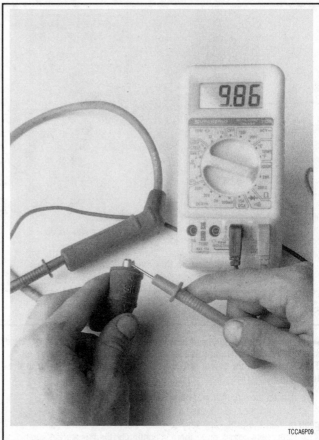

Fig. 13 Spark plug wires can be checked for excessive resistance using an ohmmeter

4. Connect the meter leads to both sides of the circuit (wire or component) and read the actual measured ohms on the meter scale. Make sure the selector switch is set to the proper ohm scale for the circuit being tested, to avoid misreading the ohmmeter test value.

Wire and Connector Repair

Almost anyone can replace damaged wires, as long as the proper tools and parts are available. Automotive wire and terminals are available to fit almost any need. Even the specialized weatherproof, molded and hard shell connectors are now available from aftermarket suppliers.

Be sure the ends of all the wires are fitted with the proper terminal hardware and connectors. Wrapping a wire around a stud is never a permanent solution and will only cause trouble later. Replace wires one at a time to avoid confusion. Always route wires exactly the same as the factory.

➡**If connector repair is necessary, only attempt it if you have the proper tools. Weatherproof and hard shell connectors require special tools to release the pins inside the connector. Attempting to repair these connectors with conventional hand tools will damage them.**

Fig. 12 Checking the resistance of a coolant temperature sensor with an ohmmeter. Reading is 1.04 kilohms

BATTERY CABLES

Disconnecting the Cables

When working on any electrical component on the vehicle, it is always a good idea to disconnect the negative (–) battery cable. This will prevent potential damage to many sensitive electrical components such as the Engine Control Module (ECM), radio, alternator, etc.

➡**Any time you disengage the battery cables, it is recommended that you disconnect the negative (–) battery cable first. This will prevent your accidentally grounding the positive (+) terminal to the body of the vehicle when disconnecting it, thereby preventing damage to the above mentioned components.**

Before you disconnect the cable(s), first turn the ignition to the **OFF** position. This will prevent a draw on the battery which could cause arcing (electricity trying to ground itself to the body of a vehicle, just like a spark plug jumping the gap) and, of course, damaging some components such as the alternator diodes.

AIR BAGS (SUPPLEMENTAL RESTRAINT SYSTEM)

General Information

▶ See Figures 14 and 15

A Supplemental Restraint System (SRS), more commonly known as air bags, is installed in all 1994 and later vehicles. The system is designed to protect the driver and, on some vehicles, the front seat passenger from serious injury when the vehicle is involved in a frontal collision.

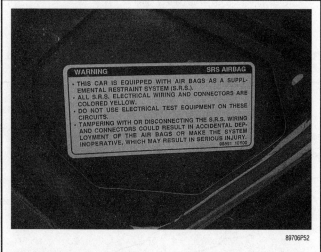

89706P52

Fig. 14 All vehicles equipped with air bags will carry this label under the hood

89706P53

Fig. 15 The front air bag sensor is located next to the hood latch. Extreme caution should be exercised when working around this sensor

When the battery cable(s) are reconnected (negative cable last), be sure to check that your lights, windshield wipers and other electrically operated safety components are all working correctly. If your vehicle contains an Electronically Tuned Radio (ETR), don't forget to also reset your radio stations. Ditto for the clock.

The system consists of an air bag mounted in the steering wheel, a control unit and various sensors. Those vehicles with front seat passenger protection also contain an air bag mounted above the glove box on the dashboard.

✳✳ CAUTION

Air bag sensors are mounted behind the grille and under the console. Extreme caution should be exercised when working in these areas.

SERVICE PRECAUTIONS

- Do not use a circuit tester to check SRS function.
- Before servicing the SRS, turn the ignition **OFF**, disconnect both the negative, then the positive battery cables and wait at least 10 minutes.
- Replace the air bag module if it has been dropped or sustained any impact.
- Do not expose the air bag module to temperature exceeding 194°F (90°C).
- Do not allow oil, grease or water to come in contact with the air bag module.
- The diagnosis and senor units must always be mounted with the arrow pointing toward the front of the vehicle.
- Check the diagnosis and sensor units for damage, deformities or rust prior to installation, and replace as required.
- The spiral cable in the steering wheel must be aligned with the neutral position, since its rotations are limited. Do not attempt to turn the steering wheel or column after the steering wheel has been removed.
- Handle air bags with extreme caution. Always place them with the pad side facing upward.
- Do not use old bolts after their removal from any SRS parts. Always install SRS parts with new bolts of the proper type and strength.
- In the event of air bag inflation, the front instrument panel assembly should be replaced.

DISARMING THE SYSTEM

Before servicing the SRS, turn the ignition **OFF**, and disconnect the negative, then positive battery cables, and wait at least 10 minutes.

➡It is still possible for the air bag to deploy for up to 10 minutes after the cables are removed. Therefore, do not work on any air bag system connectors or wires until at least 10 minutes have passed.

ARMING THE SYSTEM

Connect the positive, then the negative battery cables. Turn the ignition switch **ON** and wait for the air bag warning lamp on the instrument panel to illuminate. The warning lamp will turn off after approximately 7 seconds if no malfunctions are present. If the warning lamp does not function as stated, the SRS system should be inspected by a qualified technician.

HEATING & AIR CONDITIONING

Blower Motor

REMOVAL & INSTALLATION

▶ **See Figures 16 and 17**

The blower motor is located under the passenger's side of the dashboard, attached to the bottom of the intake unit.

1. Disconnect the negative battery cable.
2. Remove the glove box, as required.
3. Disconnect the blower motor electrical harness.
4. Disconnect the blower motor cooling tube, as required.
5. Remove the screws that attach the blower motor to the heater unit.
6. Remove the blower motor from the car.

To install:

7. Inspect the blower wheel for damage, and replace it as necessary. Replace the blower motor mounting seal.
8. Position the blower motor on the heater unit and install the screws. Center the unit in the opening and tighten the screws securely.

9. If applicable, attach the blower motor cooling tube.
10. Connect the blower motor electrical harness.
11. If applicable, install the glove box.
12. Connect the negative battery cable.
13. Check the blower for proper operation at all speeds.

Heater Core

REMOVAL & INSTALLATION

➡ **Factory "Removal and Installation" procedures were not available at the time this manual was published. The following procedure should be used as a guide. Refer to the exploded view of the heater system and modify the service steps as necessary.**

1. Disconnect the negative battery cable.
2. Set the TEMP lever to the HOT position.
3. Drain and recycle the engine coolant.
4. Disconnect the heater hoses from the heater unit.
5. At this point, the manufacturer suggests you remove the front seats.

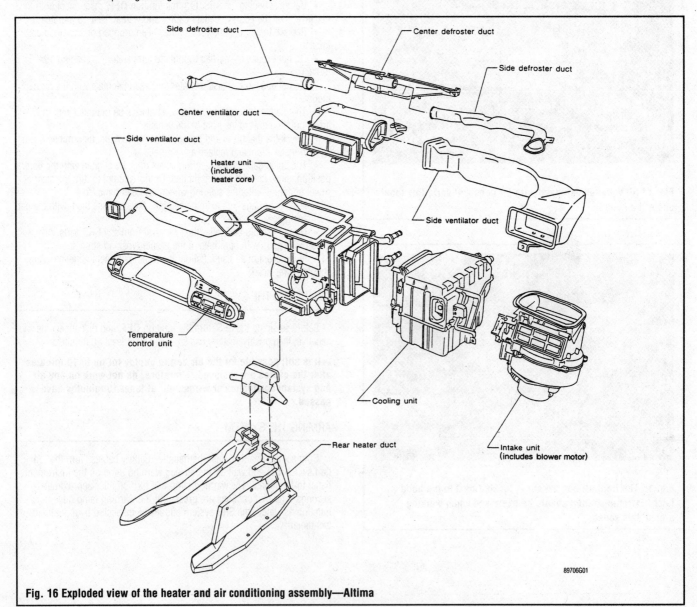

89706G01

Fig. 16 Exploded view of the heater and air conditioning assembly—Altima

To do this, remove the plastic covers over the ends of the seat runners, both front and back, to expose the seat mounting bolts. Remove the bolts and remove the seats.

6. Remove the console box and the floor carpets.

7. Remove the instrument panel lower covers from both the driver's and passenger's sides of the car. Remove the lower cluster lids.

8. Remove the left-hand side ventilator duct.

9. Remove the radio, sound balancer and stereo cassette deck, if equipped.

10. Remove the instrument panel stay.

11. Remove the rear heater duct from the floor of the vehicle.

12. Remove the center ventilator duct.

13. Remove the left and right-hand side air guides from the lower heater outlets.

14. Label and disconnect the electrical harness.

15. Remove the screws at the bottom sides of the heater unit and the screw at the top of the unit.

16. Remove the unit, together with the heater control assembly.

➡**On late model vehicles, the heater control cables and control assembly may have to be removed before the heater unit is removed. Always mark control cables before removing them to ensure correct adjustment and proper operation.**

To install:

17. Install the heater unit, together with the heater control assembly.

18. Install the screws at the bottom sides of the heater unit and the screw at the top of the unit.

19. Connect the electrical harness.

20. Install the left and right-hand side air guides on the lower heater outlets.

21. Install the center ventilator duct.

22. Position the rear heater duct on the floor of the vehicle.

23. Install the instrument panel stay.

24. Install the radio, sound balancer and stereo cassette deck, if equipped.

25. Install the left-hand side ventilator duct.

26. Install the instrument panel lower covers. Install the lower cluster lids.

27. Install the console and the floor carpets.

28. Install the front seats.

29. Connect the heater hoses to the heater unit.

30. Connect the negative battery cable.

31. Refill and bleed the engine with coolant.

32. Check for leaks. Adjust the coolant level as necessary.

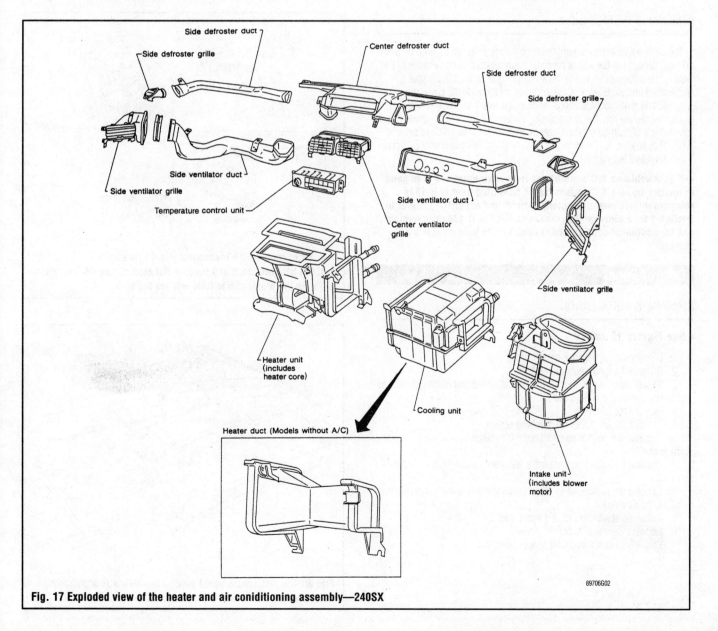

Fig. 17 Exploded view of the heater and air coniditioning assembly—240SX

89706G02

Heater Water Control Valve

REMOVAL & INSTALLATION

▶ **See Figure 18**

1. Drain and recycle the engine coolant.
2. Disconnect the control cable from the valve and lay it aside.
3. Disconnect the heater hoses from the valve.

➡**Some coolant will remain in the hoses, so place a pan under the vehicle to catch any spills.**

4. Remove the control valve from the vehicle.

To install:

5. Position the control valve in the vehicle.
6. Connect the heater hoses to the valve.
7. Connect the control cable to the valve.
8. Refill and bleed the engine with coolant.
9. Check for leaks. Adjust the coolant level as necessary.

Air Conditioning Components

REMOVAL & INSTALLATION

Repair or service of air conditioning components is not covered by this manual, because of the risk of personal injury or death, and because of the legal ramifications of servicing these components without the proper EPA certification and experience. Cost, personal injury or death, environmental damage, and legal considerations (such as the fact that it is a federal crime to vent refrigerant into the atmosphere), dictate that the A/C components on your vehicle should be serviced only by a Motor Vehicle Air Conditioning (MVAC) or Mobile Air Conditioning Society (MACS) trained, and EPA certified automotive technicians.

➡**If your vehicle's A/C system uses R-12 refrigerant and is in need of recharging, the A/C system can be converted over to R-134a refrigerant (less environmentally harmful and expensive). Refer to Section 1 for additional information on R-12 to R-134a conversions, and for additional considerations dealing with your vehicle's A/C system.**

Control Panel

REMOVAL & INSTALLATION

▶ **See Figures 19 and 20**

1. Disconnect the negative battery cable.
2. Remove the instrument cluster trim.
3. Slowly pull the trim piece from the dashboard and reach behind it to disconnect the electrical harnesses.
4. Remove the trim panel.
5. Remove the control panel attaching screws.
6. Separate the control panel from the trim panel.

To install:

7. Position the control panel on the trim panel and tighten the screws securely.
8. Connect the control panel electrical connectors and position the trim panel on the dashboard.
9. Install the instrument cluster trim panel.
10. Connect the negative battery cable.
11. Check the control panel for proper operation.

Fig. 18 The heater control valve is located at the rear, center of the engine compartment

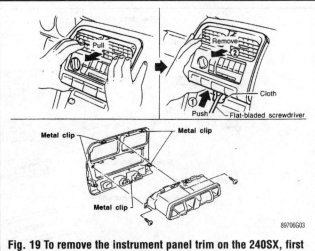

Fig. 19 To remove the instrument panel trim on the 240SX, first pull the trim rearward and insert a flat bladed screwdriver. Push down on the metal clip to fully release the trim

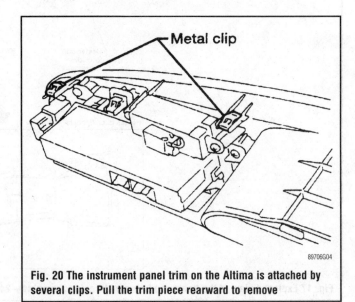

Fig. 20 The instrument panel trim on the Altima is attached by several clips. Pull the trim piece rearward to remove

CRUISE CONTROL

▶ See Figures 21, 22, 23 and 24

Nissan refers to their cruise control as the Automatic Speed Control Device (ASCD) system. The ASCD system maintains a desired speed of the vehicle under normal driving conditions. The cruise control system's main parts are the control switches, control unit, actuator, speed sensor, vacuum pump, vacuum pump relay, vacuum switch, electrical release switches and electrical harness.

➡The use of the speed control is not recommended when driving conditions do not permit maintaining a constant speed, such as in heavy traffic or on roads that are winding, icy, snow covered or slippery.

Fig. 21 The cruise control vacuum pump is located at the rear, driver's side of the engine compartment

Fig. 23 The two bottom vacuum pump fasteners are accessed through the fender well

Fig. 22 Cruise control vacuum pump fastener locations

Fig. 24 Two main components of the cruise control system are the vacuum pump (right) and vacuum actuator (left)

CRUISE CONTROL TROUBLESHOOTING

Problem	Possible Cause
Will not hold proper speed	Incorrect cable adjustment
	Binding throttle linkage
	Leaking vacuum servo diaphragm
	Leaking vacuum tank
	Faulty vacuum or vent valve
	Faulty stepper motor
	Faulty transducer
	Faulty speed sensor
	Faulty cruise control module
Cruise intermittently cuts out	Clutch or brake switch adjustment too tight
	Short or open in the cruise control circuit
	Faulty transducer
	Faulty cruise control module
Vehicle surges	Kinked speedometer cable or casing
	Binding throttle linkage
	Faulty speed sensor
	Faulty cruise control module
Cruise control inoperative	Blown fuse
	Short or open in the cruise control circuit
	Faulty brake or clutch switch
	Leaking vacuum circuit
	Faulty cruise control switch
	Faulty stepper motor
	Faulty transducer
	Faulty speed sensor
	Faulty cruise control module

Note: Use this chart as a guide. Not all systems will use the components listed.

TCCA6C01

ENTERTAINMENT SYSTEMS

Radio

REMOVAL & INSTALLATION

▶ **See Figure 25**

1. Disconnect the negative battery cable.
2. Remove the dashboard trim panel that surrounds the radio.
3. Remove the four screws securing the radio.
4. Carefully pull the radio from the dashboard.

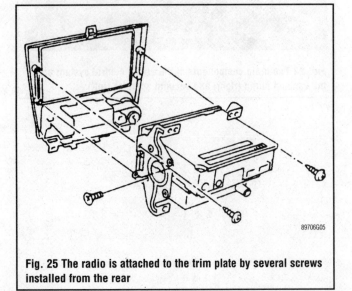

89706G05

Fig. 25 The radio is attached to the trim plate by several screws installed from the rear

5. Label and disconnect the electrical harnesses and antenna wire.
6. Remove the radio from the vehicle.

To install:

7. Connect the electrical harnesses and antenna wire.
8. Carefully position the radio in the dashboard.
9. Install the four radio attaching screws and tighten securely.
10. Install the trim panel that surrounds the radio.
11. Connect the negative battery cable.

Speakers

REMOVAL & INSTALLATION

Front

▶ **See Figure 26**

1. Disconnect the negative battery cable.
2. Remove the front door panel.
3. Remove the four speaker attaching screws.

➡ **Take care not to damage the speaker cone.**

4. Pull the speaker from the plastic housing.
5. Depress the clip and disconnect the electrical harness.

To install:

6. Connect the speaker electrical harness.
7. Position the speaker in the plastic housing.
8. Install and tighten the four speaker attaching screws.

➡ **Hand-tighten the screws only. Overtightening can damage the plastic housing.**

9. Install the front door panel.
10. Connect the negative battery cable.

Fig. 26 The front speaker is retained in a plastic housing by four screws. Depress the clip (arrow) to disconnect the speaker electrical harness

Rear

♦ See Figures 27, 28, 29 and 30

➡The speaker grilles on this vehicle are attached to the package shelf from the underside by four screws. The package shelf must be removed to remove the speaker grilles.

1. Disconnect the negative battery cable.
2. Remove the rear seat.
3. Remove the package shelf.
4. Remove the four speaker attaching screws.

➡Take care not to damage the speaker cone.

5. Pull the speaker from the plastic housing.
6. Depress the clip and disconnect the electrical harness.

To install:

7. Connect the speaker electrical harness.
8. Position the speaker, then install and tighten the four speaker attaching screws.
9. Install the package shelf.
10. Install the rear seat.
11. Connect the negative battery cable.

Fig. 28 Close up view of the "Christmas tree" type clip used to attach the package shelf cover

Fig. 29 The rear speakers are attached to the package shelf with four screws (arrows)

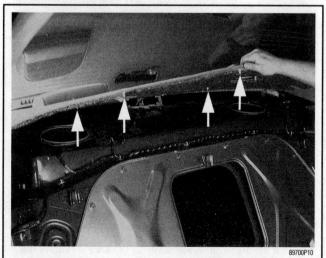

Fig. 27 The package shelf cover is attached by four clips (arrows). Gently pry up on the cover to release the clips

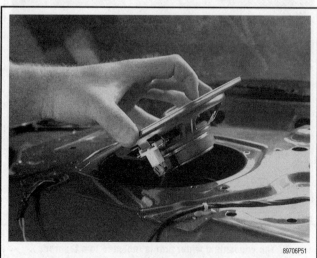

Fig. 30 Carefully lift the speaker from the package shelf. Take care not to damage the speaker's paper cone

WINDSHIELD WIPERS AND WASHERS

Windshield Wiper Blade and Arm

REMOVAL & INSTALLATION

♦ See Figures 31, 32, 33 and 34

➥On most models, the wiper arms are of different lengths. Label the wiper arms when removing to ensure that they are installed in their correct positions on the vehicle.

1. Use a small screwdriver to pry up the cap covering the wiper arm pivot nut.
2. Remove the wiper arm pivot nut.
3. Matchmark the wiper arm and the pivot stud for installation reference.
4. Use a battery post puller or equivalent tool to extract the wiper arm from the pivot shaft.

➥The wiper arm pivot shaft is splined and tapered. Considerable force may be needed to remove the wiper arm from the stud.

Work carefully and use the proper tools to avoid damage to the vehicle.

5. Remove the wiper blade and arm assembly from the vehicle.
To install:
6. Align the matchmarks on the pivot shaft and wiper arm.
7. If matchmarks were not made, proceed as follows:
   a. Position the wiper arms so they are approximately horizontal.
   b. Measure the distance between the bottom edge of the windsheild and the center of the wiper blade.
   c. Adjust the wiper arms until the measured distance is 0.71–1.30 in. (18–33mm) for the driver's side arm and 0.67–1.26 in. (17–32mm) for the passenger's side arm.
   d. Install the wiper arm on the pivot stud and ensure that the splines engage fully.
8. Install the wiper arm and pivot shaft nut. Tighten the nut to 34–45 inch lbs. (4–5 Nm).
9. Install the pivot nut cap.

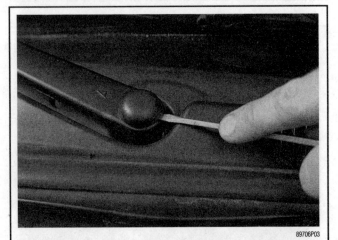

Fig. 31 The windshield wiper arm retaining nuts are hidden behind plastic covers. Pry the covers up gently to avoid damaging them

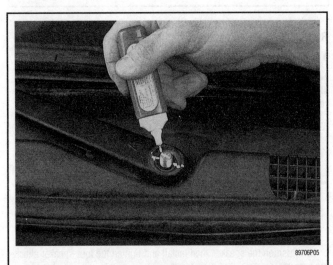

Fig. 33 To ensure that the windshield wipers are returned to their correct positions, always matchmark the wiper arm to the stud

Fig. 32 The windshield wiper arm is mounted to a tapered, splined stud, and is secured by a nut

Fig. 34 A battery terminal puller comes in handy to remove the windshield wiper arm from the stud

Windshield Wiper Motor

REMOVAL & INSTALLATION

▶ **See Figures 35 thru 43**

1. Disconnect the negative battery cable.
2. Remove the wiper arm assemblies.
3. Remove the cowl cover. The cowl cover is attached by plastic rivets, a screw in the center position and weatherstripping clips along the edge.
4. Remove the panel on the cowl to access the wiper linkage at the motor.
5. Remove the wiper motor retaining bolts.
6. Disconnect the wiper arm linkage at the ball socket by prying the linkage from the wiper motor lever arm.
7. Disconnect the wiper motor electrical harness.
8. Remove the wiper motor from the vehicle.

To install:

9. Position the wiper motor in the vehicle.
10. Connect the wiper motor electrical harness.
11. Connect the wiper arm linkage at the ball socket by snapping the socket in place over the ball.

Fig. 37 . . . a screw in the center position . . .

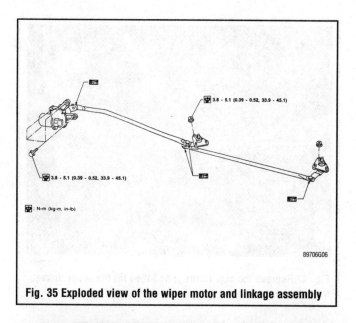

Fig. 35 Exploded view of the wiper motor and linkage assembly

Fig. 38 . . . and the weatherstripping clips along the edge

Fig. 36 The cowl cover is attached by plastic rivets . . .

Fig. 39 The windshield wiper motor lever is hidden behind an access panel on the cowl

Fig. 40 The windshield wiper motor is secured to the cowl by four bolts (arrows)

Fig. 42 When replacing the wiper motor, the lever must be transferred. Always matchmark the lever to the motor shaft

1. Ball   2. Socket

Fig. 41 The wiper motor lever connects to the wiper linkage using a ball and socket

Fig. 43 Remove the nuts (arrows) and then lift the wiper linkage from the cowl

12. Install the wiper motor retaining bolts and tighten to 33–45 inch lbs. (4–5 Nm).

13. Install the wiper linkage panel on the cowl and tighten the screws securely.

14. Install the cowl cover.

15. Install the wiper arm assemblies.

16. Connect the negative battery cable.

Windshield Washer Motor

REMOVAL & INSTALLATION

The windshield washer motor is either mounted to or contained in the washer reservoir.

1. Label and disconnect the washer motor electrical harness.
2. Label and disconnect the washer motor hoses.

➡ Position a drain pan under the washer reservoir to catch any washer fluid which leaks out.

3. Remove the washer reservoir from the vehicle.
4. Remove the washer pump from the reservoir.

To install:

5. Install the washer pump on the reservoir.
6. Install the washer reservoir in the vehicle.
7. Connect the washer motor hoses.
8. Connect the washer motor electrical harness.

INSTRUMENTS AND SWITCHES

Instrument Cluster

REMOVAL & INSTALLATION

▶ **See Figures 44 and 45**

1. Disarm the Supplemental Restraint System (SRS) and remove the air bag from the steering wheel.
2. Remove the steering wheel.

3. Remove the kick plate and dashboard side finisher on the driver's side.
4. Remove the instrument panel lower panel on the driver's side.
5. Remove the dashboard lower reinforcement panel.
6. Remove the steering column covers, spiral cable and combination switch.
7. Unfasten the cluster lid. Pull the cluster lid toward you, reach behind it and disconnect the electrical harnesses.
8. Unfasten the instrument cluster. Pull the instrument cluster toward you, reach behind it and disconnect the speedometer cable, as required.

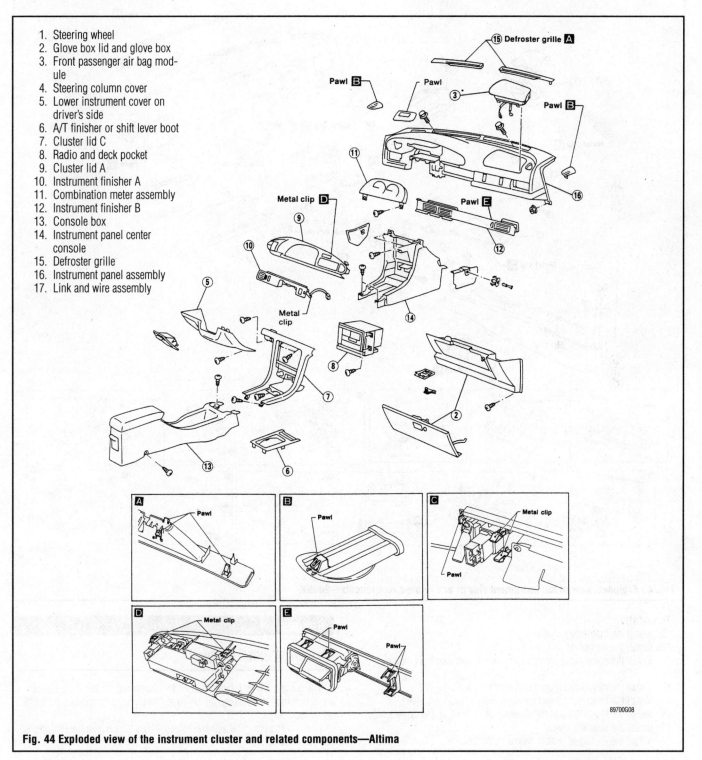

1. Steering wheel
2. Glove box lid and glove box
3. Front passenger air bag module
4. Steering column cover
5. Lower instrument cover on driver's side
6. A/T finisher or shift lever boot
7. Cluster lid C
8. Radio and deck pocket
9. Cluster lid A
10. Instrument finisher A
11. Combination meter assembly
12. Instrument finisher B
13. Console box
14. Instrument panel center console
15. Defroster grille
16. Instrument panel assembly
17. Link and wire assembly

Fig. 44 Exploded view of the instrument cluster and related components—Altima

89700G08

1. Steering column cover and combination switch
2. A/T finisher or M/T shift lever boots
3. Instrument lower cover on driver side
4. Instrument lower reinforcement
5. Cluster lid A
6. Combination meter
7. Center ventilation assembly
8. Cluster lid C and audio
9. A/C or heater control
10. Glove box assembly
11. Console box
12. Instrument side finisher
13. Defroster grille
14. Front pillar garnish
15. Instrument panel and pads

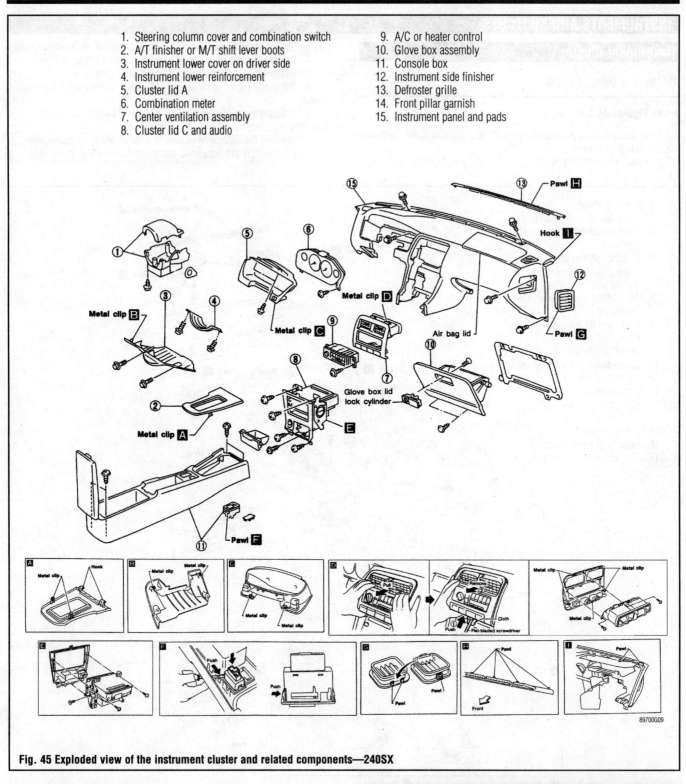

Fig. 45 Exploded view of the instrument cluster and related components—240SX

To install:
9. Install the instrument cluster.
10. Install the cluster lid.
11. Install the spiral cable, combination switch and steering column covers.
12. Install the dashboard lower reinforcement panel.
13. Install the instrument panel lower panel on the driver's side.
14. Install the kick plate and dashboard side finisher on the driver's side.
15. Install the steering wheel.
16. Install the air bag assembly, then arm the SRS.

Gauges

REMOVAL & INSTALLATION

The gauges are an integral part of the instrument cluster. If the gauges are determined to be faulty, the entire instrument cluster must be replaced as an assembly.

Check with your local authorities about laws concerning the replacement of speedometers.

LIGHTING

▶ **See Figure 46**

Headlights

REMOVAL & INSTALLATION

Sealed Beam Headlights

▶ **See Figure 47**

➡**If headlamps do not open on the 240SX, first check the fusible link for the headlight motor. Also check the retractor switch. If the headlamps do not retract, check the retractor control relay.**

1. Open the headlamp.
2. Disconnect the negative battery cable.
3. Unbolt and remove the finisher.
4. Remove the headlamp lid.
5. Remove the bulb retaining ring.
6. Unplug and remove the headlamp bulb.

To install:

7. Installation is the reverse of removal.

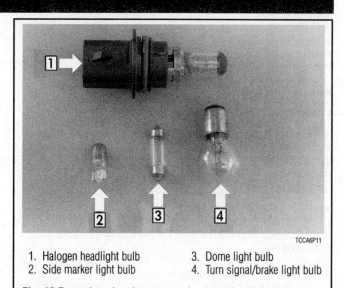

TCCA6P11

1. Halogen headlight bulb
2. Side marker light bulb
3. Dome light bulb
4. Turn signal/brake light bulb

Fig. 46 Examples of various types of automotive light bulbs

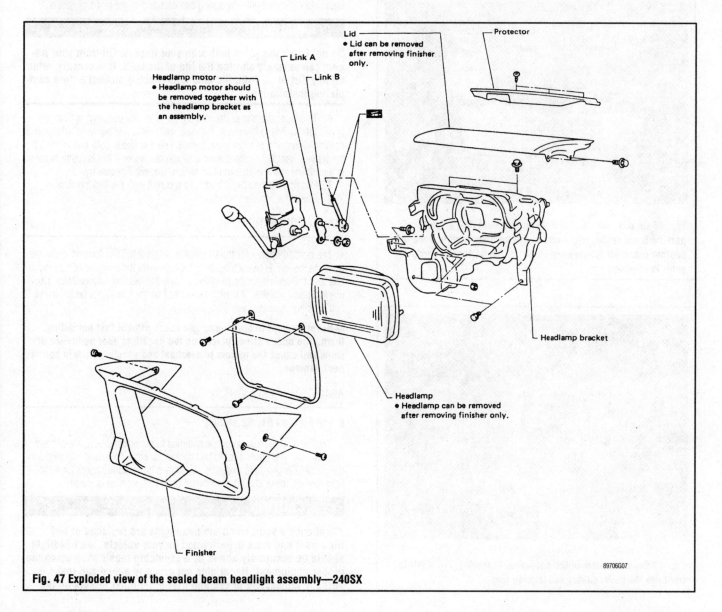

Fig. 47 Exploded view of the sealed beam headlight assembly—240SX

89706G07

8. Be sure to seat the rubber cap containing the electrical connector firmly, so that the lip makes contact with the headlamp body.

9. Adjust the headlamp lid so it is flush with the hood and fender, and so the lid joint is equal on all sides. This is done by adjusting the lid mounting screws while open. Close the headlamp by operating the manual knob on the headlamp motor.

Halogen Headlight Bulbs

♦ **See Figures 48, 49 and 50**

➡This procedure only applies to replaceable halogen headlight bulbs (such as Nos. 9004 and 9005); it does not pertain to sealed beam units.

1. Open the vehicle's hood and secure it in an upright position.
2. Unfasten the locking ring which secures the bulb and socket assembly, then withdraw the assembly rearward.
3. If necessary, gently pry the socket's retaining clip over the projection on the bulb (use care not to break the clip.) Pull the bulb from the socket.

To install:

4. Before installing a light bulb into the socket, ensure that all electrical contact surfaces are free of corrosion or dirt.

Fig. 48 On this vehicle, the headlamp socket (left arrow) and parking lamp socket (right arrow) are both accessible once the coolant reservoir (passenger's side) or the battery (driver's side) is removed

Fig. 49 Exploded view of the headlamp assembly. From left to right are the bulb, gasket and locking ring

Fig. 50 The headlamp bulb is retained in the headlamp cover by a spring clip (arrow)

5. Line up the replacement headlight bulb with the socket. Firmly push the bulb onto the socket until the spring clip latches over the bulb's projection.

✳✳ WARNING

Do not touch the glass bulb with your fingers. Oil from your fingers can severely shorten the life of the bulb. If necessary, wipe off any dirt or oil from the bulb with rubbing alcohol before completing installation.

6. To ensure that the replacement bulb functions properly, activate the applicable switch to illuminate the bulb which was just replaced. (If this is a combination low and high beam bulb, be sure to check both intensities.) If the replacement light bulb does not illuminate, either it too is faulty or there is a problem in the bulb circuit or switch. Correct if necessary.
7. Position the headlight bulb and secure it with the locking ring.
8. Close the vehicle's hood.

MANUAL OPERATION

The manual opener for the headlights on the 240SX is located under the hood, to the inside of each headlight. Disconnect the negative battery cable and turn the opener knobs to raise or lower the headlight assemblies. During inclement weather, it is recommended that the headlights be left in the "up" position to keep them from freezing closed.

➡Never attempt to open headlight doors without first defrosting them. The undue stress placed on the headlight door by the ice or snow will cause the motors to overheat and possibly sustain permanent damage.

AIMING THE HEADLIGHTS

♦ **See Figures 51, 52 and 53**

The headlights must be properly aimed to provide the best, safest road illumination. The lights should be checked for proper aim and adjusted as necessary. Certain state and local authorities have requirements for headlight aiming; these should be checked before adjustment is made.

✳✳ CAUTION

About once a year, when the headlights are replaced or any time front end work is performed on your vehicle, the headlight should be accurately aimed by a reputable repair shop using the proper equipment. Headlights not properly aimed can make it virtually impossible to see and may blind other drivers on the

road, possibly causing an accident. Note that the following procedure is a temporary fix, until you can take your vehicle to a repair shop for a proper adjustment.

Headlight adjustment may be temporarily made using a wall, as described below, or on the rear of another vehicle. When adjusted, the lights should not glare in oncoming car or truck windshields, nor should they illuminate the passenger compartment of vehicles driving in front of you. These adjustments are rough and should always be fine-tuned by a repair shop which is equipped with headlight aiming tools. Improper adjustments may be both dangerous and illegal.

For most of the vehicles covered by this manual, horizontal and vertical aiming of each sealed beam unit is provided by two adjusting screws, which move the retaining ring and adjusting plate against the tension of a coil spring. There is no adjustment for focus; this is done during headlight manufacturing.

➡Because the composite headlight assembly is bolted into position, no adjustment should be necessary or possible. Some applications, however, may be bolted to an adjuster plate or may be retained by adjusting screws. If so, follow this procedure when adjusting the lights, BUT always have the adjustment checked by a reputable shop.

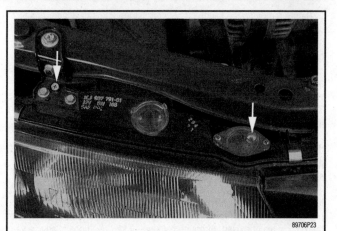

Fig. 51 The headlamp buckets contain bubble levels to make headlamp aiming easier. Up/down adjustment is made using the left adjuster (left arrow) and side/side using the right adjuster (right arrow)

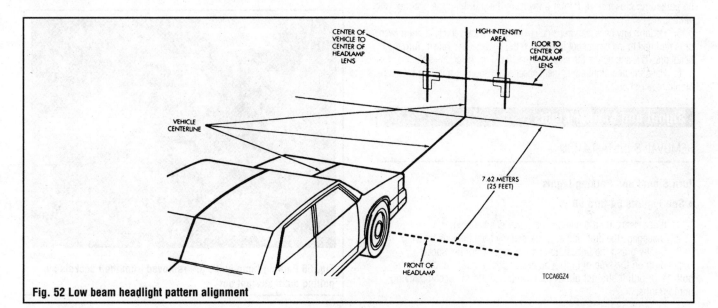

Fig. 52 Low beam headlight pattern alignment

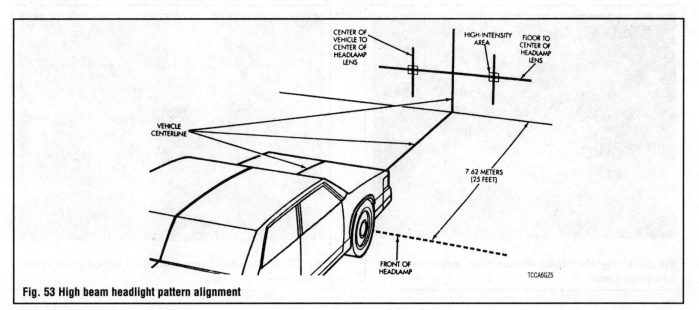

Fig. 53 High beam headlight pattern alignment

Before removing the headlight bulb or disturbing the headlamp in any way, note the current settings in order to ease headlight adjustment upon reassembly. If the high or low beam setting of the old lamp still works, this can be done using the wall of a garage or a building:

1. Park the vehicle on a level surface, with the fuel tank about ½ full and with the vehicle empty of all extra cargo (unless normally carried). The vehicle should be facing a wall which is no less than 6 feet (1.8m) high and 12 feet (3.7m) wide. The front of the vehicle should be about 25 feet (7.7m) from the wall.

2. If aiming is to be performed outdoors, it is advisable to wait until dusk in order to properly see the headlight beams on the wall. If done in a garage, darken the area around the wall as much as possible by closing shades or hanging cloth over the windows.

3. Turn the headlights **ON** and mark the wall at the center of each light's low beam, then switch on the brights and mark the center of each light's high beam. A short length of masking tape which is visible from the front of the vehicle may be used. Although marking all four positions is advisable, marking one position from each light should be sufficient.

4. If neither beam on one side is working, and if another like-sized vehicle is available, park the second one in the exact spot where the vehicle was and mark the beams using the same-side light. Then, switch the vehicles so the one to be aimed is back in the original spot. It must be parked no closer to or farther away from the wall than the second vehicle.

5. Perform any necessary repairs, but make sure the vehicle is not moved, or is returned to the exact spot from which the lights were marked. Turn the headlights **ON** and adjust the beams to match the marks on the wall.

6. Have the headlight adjustment checked as soon as possible by a reputable repair shop.

Signal and Marker Lights

REMOVAL & INSTALLATION

Turn Signal and Parking Lights

♦ See Figures 54 thru 60

1. If necessary, unfasten and remove the lens housing.
2. Disengage the bulb and socket assembly from the lens housing.
3. Gently grasp the light bulb and remove it from the socket. Depending on the type of bulb, you must either depress and twist the bulb ⅛ or pull it straight out of its socket. Refer to the accompanying photographs.

Fig. 55 Remove the socket by twisting ¼ turn counterclockwise, then depress and twist the bulb ⅛ turn

Fig. 56 Parking lamp bulbs are removed from their sockets by pulling them straight out

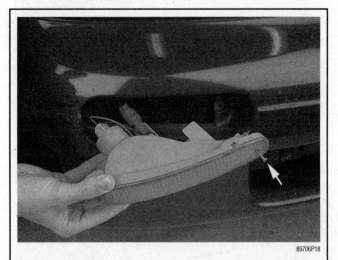

Fig. 54 Turn signal lights are attached to the bumper assembly by a single screw

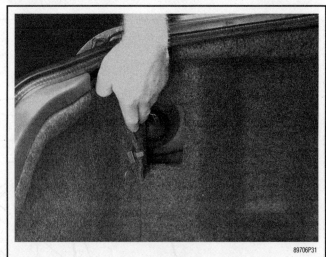

Fig. 57 The rear parking lamp is accessed through a door in the trunk liner

Fig. 58 Remove the rubber moisture resistant boot

Fig. 59 When installing the moisture resistant boot, be sure to maintain the proper orientation, as marked

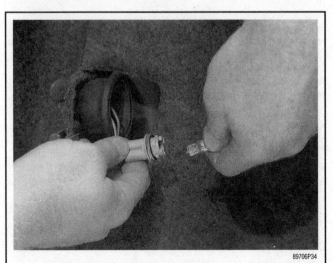

Fig. 60 To remove the rear parking lamp bulb, pull it straight out of the socket

To install:

4. Before installing the light bulb into the socket, ensure that all electrical contact surfaces are free of corrosion or dirt.

5. Line up the base of the light bulb with the socket, then insert the light bulb into the socket until it is fully seated. If the (turn signal) bulb has pins on its base, be sure that they are properly oriented.

6. To ensure that the replacement bulb functions properly, activate the applicable switch to illuminate the bulb which was just replaced. If the replacement light bulb does not illuminate, either it too is faulty or there is a problem in the bulb circuit or switch. Correct as necessary.

7. Install the socket and bulb assembly into the lens housing.

8. If applicable, position and reattach the lens housing.

Side Marker Lights

◆ **See Figure 61**

1. Disengage the bulb and socket assembly from the lens housing.
2. Gently grasp the light bulb and pull it straight out of the socket.

To install:

3. Before installing the light bulb into the socket, ensure that all electrical contact surfaces are free of corrosion or dirt.

4. Line up the base of the light bulb with the socket, then insert the light bulb into the socket until it is fully seated.

5. To ensure that the replacement bulb functions properly, activate the applicable switch to illuminate the bulb which was just replaced. If the replacement light bulb does not illuminate, either it too is faulty or there is a problem in the bulb circuit or switch. Correct as necessary.

6. Install the socket and bulb assembly into the lens housing.

Fig. 61 The marker lights are removed by depressing the tab (arrow) with a thin bladed tool. Take care not to scratch the paint

Tail and Brake Lights

◆ **See Figures 62, 63, 64, 65 and 66**

1. Depending on the vehicle and bulb application, either unscrew and remove the lens or disengage the bulb and socket assembly from the rear of the lens housing.

2. To remove a light bulb with retaining pins from its socket, grasp the bulb, then gently depress and twist it 1/8 turn counterclockwise, and pull it from the socket.

To install:

3. Before installing a light bulb into the socket, ensure that all electrical contact surfaces are free of corrosion or dirt.

Fig. 62 The trunk liner is attached using small plastic rivets

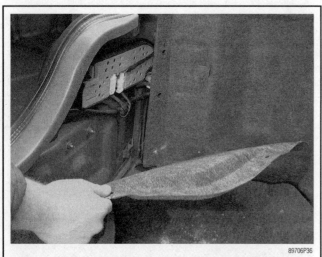

Fig. 63 Remove the rivets and fold back the liner to reveal the tail light housing

Fig. 64 Depress the clip and pull the back of the lens housing away to reveal the lamps

Fig. 65 Four individual bulbs make up the tail lamp assembly

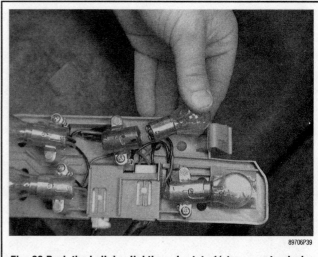

Fig. 66 Push the bulb in slightly and rotate ⅛ turn counterclockwise to remove

➡Before installing the light bulb, note the positions of the two retaining pins on the bulb. They will likely be at different heights on the bulb, to ensure that the bulb is installed correctly. If, when installing the bulb, it does not turn easily, do not force it. Remove the bulb and rotate it 180 degrees from its former position, then reinsert it into the bulb socket.

4. Insert the light bulb into the socket and, while depressing the bulb, twist it ⅛ turn clockwise until the two pins on the light bulb are properly engaged in the socket.

5. To ensure that the replacement bulb functions properly, activate the applicable switch to illuminate the bulb which was just replaced. If the replacement light bulb does not illuminate, either it too is faulty or there is a problem in the bulb circuit or switch. Correct if necessary.

6. If applicable, install the socket and bulb assembly into the rear of the lens housing; otherwise, install the lens over the bulb.

Dome Light

▶ See Figure 67

1. Using a small prytool, carefully remove the cover lens from the lamp assembly.

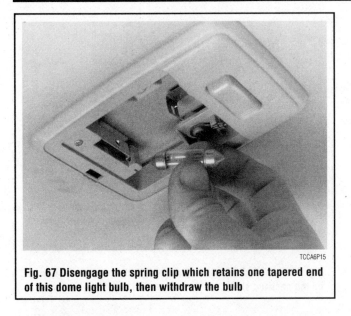

Fig. 67 Disengage the spring clip which retains one tapered end of this dome light bulb, then withdraw the bulb

2. Remove the bulb from its retaining clip contacts. If the bulb has tapered ends, gently depress the spring clip/metal contact and disengage the light bulb, then pull it free of the two metal con-tacts.

To install:

3. Before installing the light bulb into the metal contacts, ensure that all electrical conducting surfaces are free of corrosion or dirt.

4. Position the bulb between the two metal contacts. If the contacts have small holes, be sure that the tapered ends of the bulb are situated in them.

5. To ensure that the replacement bulb functions properly, activate the applicable switch to illuminate the bulb which was just replaced. If the replacement light bulb does not illuminate, either it is faulty or there is a problem in the bulb circuit or switch. Correct as necessary.

6. Install the cover lens until its retaining tabs are properly engaged.

Trunk, License Plate and High-Mount Brake Lights

◆ **See Figures 68 thru 77**

Refer to the appropriate illustrations for removal and installation procedures.

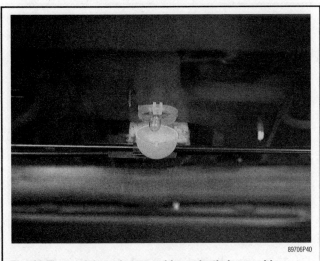

Fig. 68 The trunk lamp is covered by a plastic lens and is located under the package shelf

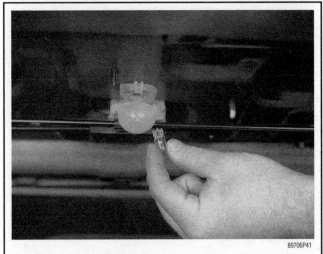

Fig. 69 To remove the trunk lamp, simply pull it straight out of the socket

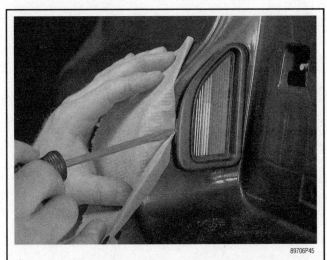

Fig. 70 Use a shop rag to protect the paint when prying the license plate lens from the body

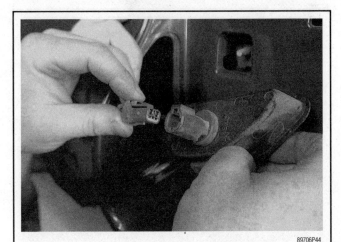

Fig. 71 The license plate lamp is easily disconnected from the electrical harness by depressing the locking tab and unplugging the connector

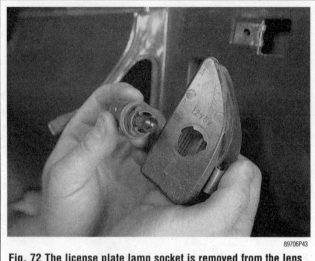

Fig. 72 The license plate lamp socket is removed from the lens with a ¼ turn counterclockwise and a slight pull

Fig. 73 To remove the license plate lamp, simply pull it straight out of the socket

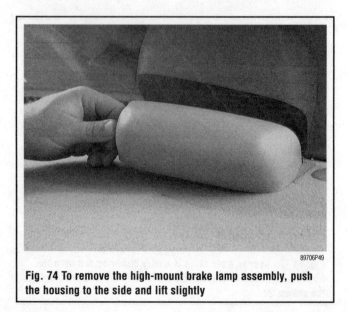

Fig. 74 To remove the high-mount brake lamp assembly, push the housing to the side and lift slightly

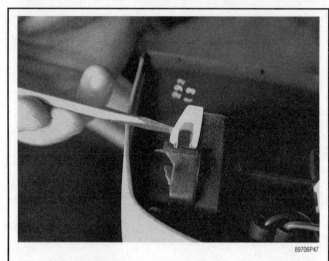

Fig. 75 This clip holds the high-mount brake lamp to the bracket on the package shelf

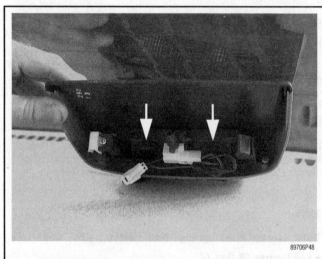

Fig. 76 The high-mount brake lamp housing contains two bulb and socket assemblies (arrows)

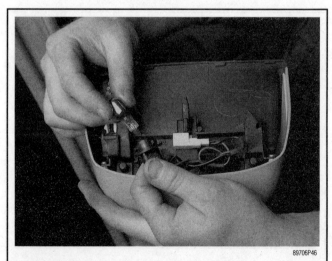

Fig. 77 To remove the high-mount brake lamp bulb, twist and remove the socket, then pull the bulb straight out

Fog/Driving Lights

REMOVAL & INSTALLATION

▶ **See Figure 78**

1. Remove the fasteners attaching the fog lamp to the bumper.
2. Remove the fasteners for the engine undercover, then pull down the cover slightly.
3. Disconnect the fog light electrical harness.
4. Remove the fog light assembly from the bumper.
5. Turn the fog light bulb housing counterclockwise.
6. Remove the bulb from the assembly.

❊❊ WARNING

Do not touch the glass bulb with your fingers. Oil from your fingers can severely shorten the life of the bulb. If necessary, wipe off any dirt or oil from the bulb with rubbing alcohol before completing installation.

To install:
7. Installation is the reverse of removal.
8. Tighten all fasteners securely.
9. Check the fog lights for proper operation.

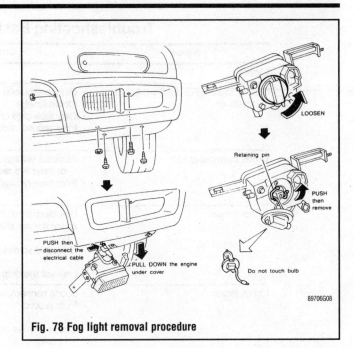

89706G08

Fig. 78 Fog light removal procedure

Bulb Specifications

Item	Wattage (W)
Headlamp	
Inside	65
Outside	60/55
Front fog lamp	55
Front turn signal lamp	27
Clearance lamp	8
Front side marker lamp	3.8
Rear side marker lamp	3.8
Rear combination lamp	
Turn signal lamp	27
Stop/Tail lamp	27/8
Back-up lamp	27
License plate lamp	5
High-mounted stop lamp	5

89706C01

Troubleshooting Basic Lighting Problems

Problem	Cause	Solution
Lights		
One or more lights don't work, but others do	• Defective bulb(s) • Blown fuse(s) • Dirty fuse clips or light sockets • Poor ground circuit	• Replace bulb(s) • Replace fuse(s) • Clean connections • Run ground wire from light socket housing to car frame
Lights burn out quickly	• Incorrect voltage regulator setting or defective regulator • Poor battery/alternator connections	• Replace voltage regulator • Check battery/alternator connections
Lights go dim	• Low/discharged battery • Alternator not charging • Corroded sockets or connections • Low voltage output	• Check battery • Check drive belt tension; repair or replace alternator • Clean bulb and socket contacts and connections • Replace voltage regulator
Lights flicker	• Loose connection • Poor ground • Circuit breaker operating (short circuit)	• Tighten all connections • Run ground wire from light housing to car frame • Check connections and look for bare wires
Lights "flare"—Some flare is normal on acceleration—if excessive, see "Lights Burn Out Quickly"	• High voltage setting	• Replace voltage regulator
Lights glare—approaching drivers are blinded	• Lights adjusted too high • Rear springs or shocks sagging • Rear tires soft	• Have headlights aimed • Check rear springs/shocks • Check/correct rear tire pressure
Turn Signals		
Turn signals don't work in either direction	• Blown fuse • Defective flasher • Loose connection	• Replace fuse • Replace flasher • Check/tighten all connections
Right (or left) turn signal only won't work	• Bulb burned out • Right (or left) indicator bulb burned out • Short circuit	• Replace bulb • Check/replace indicator bulb • Check/repair wiring
Flasher rate too slow or too fast	• Incorrect wattage bulb • Incorrect flasher	• Flasher bulb • Replace flasher (use a variable load flasher if you pull a trailer)
Indicator lights do not flash (burn steadily)	• Burned out bulb • Defective flasher	• Replace bulb • Replace flasher
Indicator lights do not light at all	• Burned out indicator bulb • Defective flasher	• Replace indicator bulb • Replace flasher

TCCA6C02A

TRAILER WIRING

Wiring the vehicle for towing is fairly easy. There are a number of good wiring kits available and these should be used, rather than trying to design your own.

All trailers will need brake lights and turn signals, as well as tail lights and side marker lights. Most areas require extra marker lights for overwide trailers. Also, most areas have recently required back-up lights for trailers, and most trailer manufacturers have been building trailers with back-up lights for several years.

Additionally, some Class I, most Class II and just about all Class III trailers will have electric brakes. Add to this number an accessories wire, to operate trailer internal equipment or to charge the trailer's battery, and you can have as many as seven wires in the harness.

Determine the equipment on your trailer and buy the wiring kit necessary. The kit will contain all the wires needed, plus a plug adapter set which includes the female plug, mounted on the bumper or hitch, and the male plug, wired into, or plugged into the trailer harness.

When installing the kit, follow the manufacturer's instructions. The color coding of the wires is usually standard throughout the industry. One point to note: some domestic vehicles, and most imported vehicles, have separate turn signals. On most domestic vehicles, the brake lights and rear turn signals operate with the same bulb. For those vehicles without separate turn signals, you can purchase an isolation unit so that the brake lights won't blink whenever the turn signals are operated.

One, final point: the best kits are those with a spring loaded cover on the vehicle mounted socket. This cover prevents dirt and moisture from corroding the terminals. Never let the vehicle socket hang loosely; always mount it securely to the bumper or hitch.

CIRCUIT PROTECTION

Fuses

REPLACEMENT

Fuses are located either in the engine compartment or passenger compartment fuse and relay panels. If a fuse blows, a single component or single circuit will not function properly.

1. Remove the fuse and relay panel cover.
2. Inspect the fuses to determine which is faulty.
3. Unplug and discard the fuse.
4. Inspect the panel terminals and clean if corroded. If any terminals are damaged, replace the terminals.
5. Plug in a new fuse of the same amperage rating.

✳✳ WARNING

Never exceed the amperage rating of a blown fuse. If the replacement fuse also blows, check for a problem in the circuit.

6. Check for proper operation of the affected component or circuit.

Maxi-Fuses (Fusible Links)

Maxi-fuses are located in the engine compartment relay box. If a maxi-fuse blows, an entire circuit or several circuits will not function properly.

REPLACEMENT

1. Remove the fuse and relay box cover.
2. Inspect the fusible links to determine which is faulty.

3. Unplug and discard the fusible link.
4. Inspect the box terminals and clean if corroded. If any terminals are damaged, replace the terminals.
5. Plug in a new fusible link of the same amperage rating.

✳✳ WARNING

Never exceed the amperage rating of a blown maxi-fuse. If the replacement fuse also blows, check for a problem in the circuit(s).

6. Check for proper operation of the affected circuit(s).

Flashers

The flashers are located in the passenger compartment fuse and relay box. If the turn signals operate in only one direction, a bulb is probably burned out. If they do not operate in either direction, a bulb on each side may be burned out, or the flasher may be defective.

REPLACEMENT

1. Remove the passenger compartment fuse and relay box cover, noting which position the flasher unit occupies.
2. Unplug and discard the flasher.
3. Inspect the box terminals and clean if corroded. If any terminals are damaged, replace the terminals.
4. Plug in a new flasher of the same type.
5. Operate the turn signals and hazard lights. Check for proper operation.

Engine Compartment Relay Locations—Early Model Altima

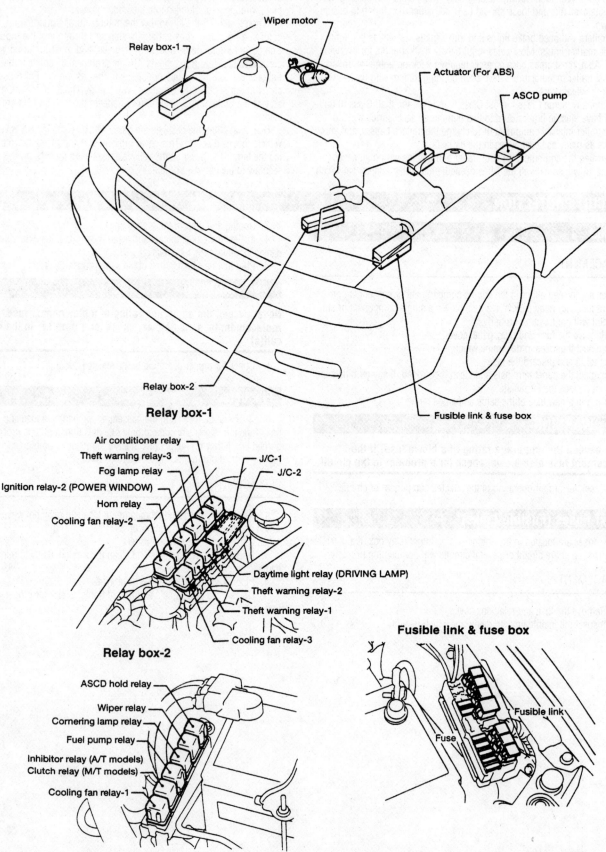

Wiper motor

Relay box-1

Actuator (For ABS)

ASCD pump

Relay box-2

Relay box-1

Fusible link & fuse box

Air conditioner relay

Theft warning relay-3

Fog lamp relay

Ignition relay-2 (POWER WINDOW)

Horn relay

Cooling fan relay-2

J/C-1

J/C-2

Daytime light relay (DRIVING LAMP)

Theft warning relay-2

Theft warning relay-1

Cooling fan relay-3

Relay box-2

ASCD hold relay

Wiper relay

Cornering lamp relay

Fuel pump relay

Inhibitor relay (A/T models)

Clutch relay (M/T models)

Cooling fan relay-1

Fusible link & fuse box

Fusible link

Fuse

89706C02

Passenger Compartment Relay Locations—Early Model Altima

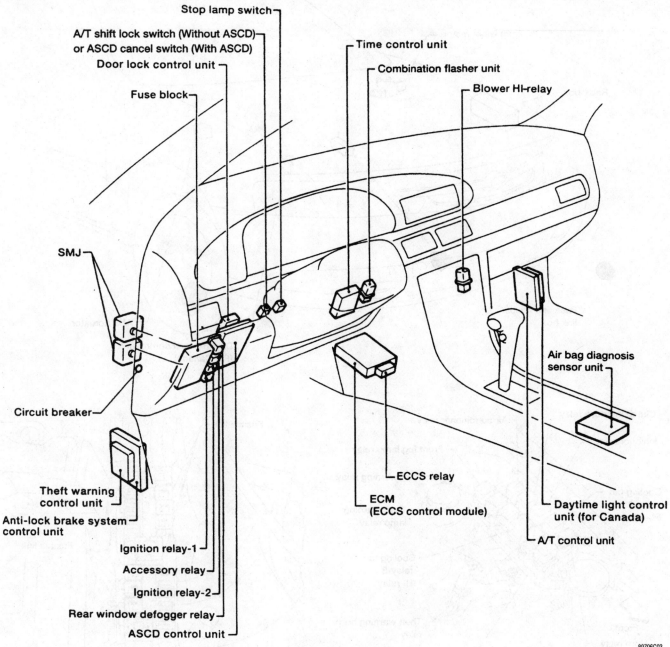

Stop lamp switch

A/T shift lock switch (Without ASCD) or ASCD cancel switch (With ASCD)

Door lock control unit

Fuse block

Time control unit

Combination flasher unit

Blower HI-relay

SMJ

Circuit breaker

Air bag diagnosis sensor unit

Theft warning control unit

Anti-lock brake system control unit

Ignition relay-1

Accessory relay

Ignition relay-2

Rear window defogger relay

ASCD control unit

ECCS relay

ECM (ECCS control module)

Daytime light control unit (for Canada)

A/T control unit

89706C03

Engine Compartment Relay Locations—Late Model Altima

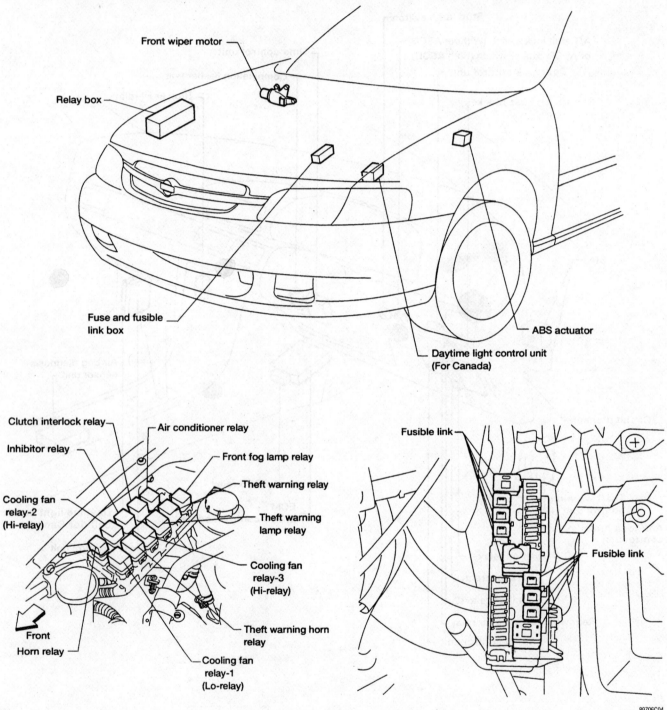

Front wiper motor

Relay box

Fuse and fusible link box

Daytime light control unit (For Canada)

ABS actuator

Clutch interlock relay

Inhibitor relay

Air conditioner relay

Front fog lamp relay

Theft warning relay

Cooling fan relay-2 (Hi-relay)

Theft warning lamp relay

Cooling fan relay-3 (Hi-relay)

Theft warning horn relay

Front

Horn relay

Cooling fan relay-1 (Lo-relay)

Fusible link

Fusible link

89706C04

Passenger Compartment Relay Locations—Late Model Altima

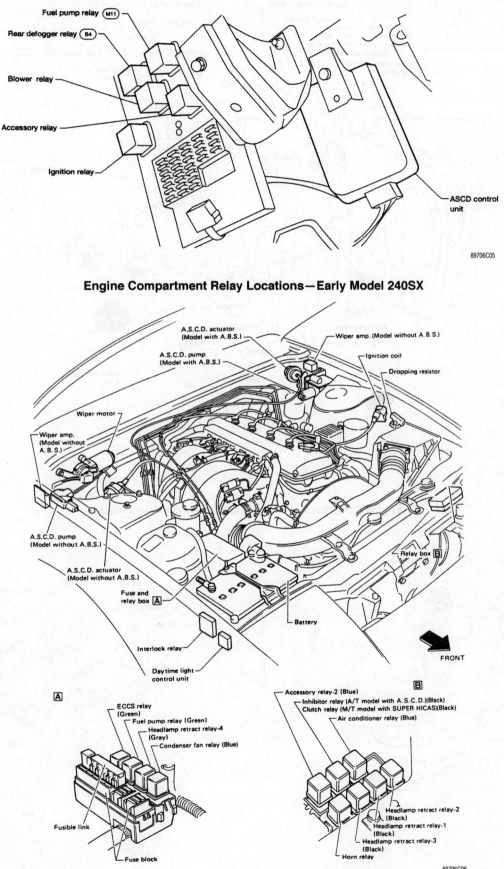

Fuel pump relay (M11)
Rear defogger relay (B4)
Blower relay
Accessory relay
Ignition relay
ASCD control unit

89706C05

Engine Compartment Relay Locations—Early Model 240SX

A.S.C.D. actuator (Model with A.B.S.)
A.S.C.D. pump (Model with A.B.S.)
Wiper amp. (Model without A.B.S.)
Ignition coil
Dropping resistor
Wiper motor
Wiper amp. (Model without A.B.S.)
A.S.C.D. pump (Model without A.B.S.)
A.S.C.D. actuator (Model without A.B.S.)
Fuse and relay box A
Battery
Relay box B
Interlock relay
Daytime light control unit
FRONT

A
ECCS relay (Green)
Fuel pump relay (Green)
Headlamp retract relay-4 (Gray)
Condenser fan relay (Blue)
Fusible link
Fuse block

B
Accessory relay-2 (Blue)
Inhibitor relay (A/T model with A.S.C.D.)(Black)
Clutch relay (M/T model with SUPER HICAS)(Black)
Air conditioner relay (Blue)
Headlamp retract relay-2 (Black)
Headlamp retract relay-1 (Black)
Headlamp retract relay-3 (Black)
Horn relay

89706C06

Passenger Compartment Relay Locations—Early Model 240SX

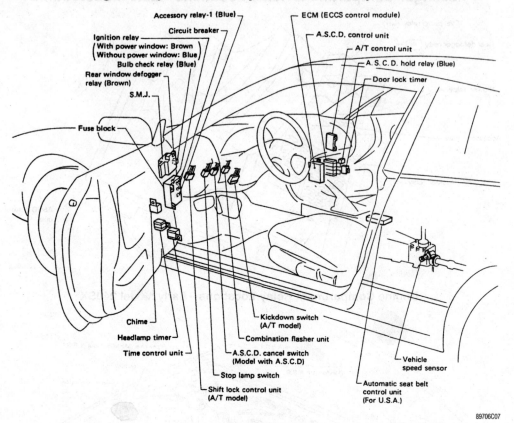

Accessory relay-1 (Blue)
Circuit breaker
ECM (ECCS control module)
A.S.C.D. control unit
A/T control unit
Ignition relay
(With power window: Brown)
(Without power window: Blue)
Bulb check relay (Blue)
A.S.C.D. hold relay (Blue)
Rear window defogger relay (Brown)
Door lock timer
S.M.J.
Fuse block
Chime
Kickdown switch (A/T model)
Headlamp timer
Combination flasher unit
Time control unit
A.S.C.D. cancel switch (Model with A.S.C.D)
Vehicle speed sensor
Stop lamp switch
Shift lock control unit (A/T model)
Automatic seat belt control unit (For U.S.A.)

89706C07

Engine Compartment Relay Locations—Late Model 240SX

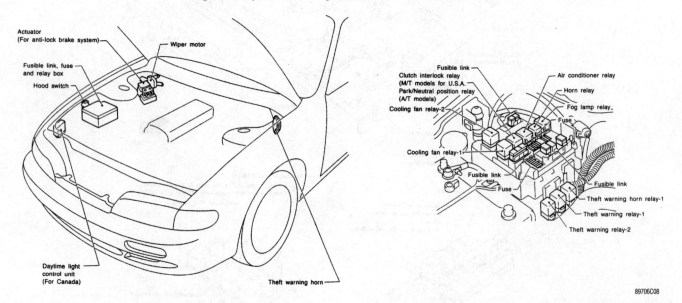

Actuator (For anti-lock brake system)
Wiper motor
Fusible link, fuse and relay box
Hood switch
Fusible link
Clutch interlock relay (M/T models for U.S.A.)
Park/Neutral position relay (A/T models)
Air conditioner relay
Horn relay
Fog lamp relay
Cooling fan relay-2
Fuse
Cooling fan relay-1
Fusible link
Fuse
Fusible link
Theft warning horn relay-1
Theft warning relay-1
Daytime light control unit (For Canada)
Theft warning horn
Theft warning relay-2

89706C08

Passenger Compartment Relay Locations—Late Model 240SX

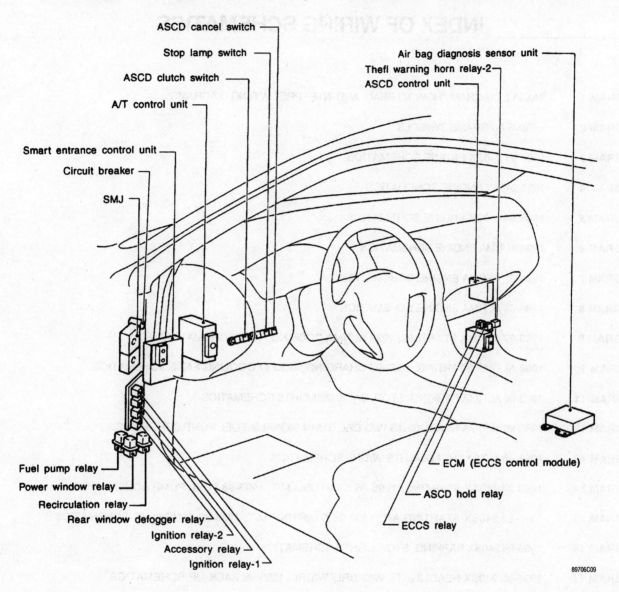

ASCD cancel switch

Stop lamp switch

ASCD clutch switch

A/T control unit

Smart entrance control unit

Circuit breaker

SMJ

Air bag diagnosis sensor unit

Thefl warning horn relay-2

ASCD control unit

Fuel pump relay

Power window relay

Recirculation relay

Rear window defogger relay

Ignition relay-2

Accessory relay

Ignition relay-1

ECM (ECCS control module)

ASCD hold relay

ECCS relay

89706C09

INDEX OF WIRING SCHEMATICS

89706W01

SAMPLE DIAGRAM: HOW TO READ & INTERPRET WIRING DIAGRAMS

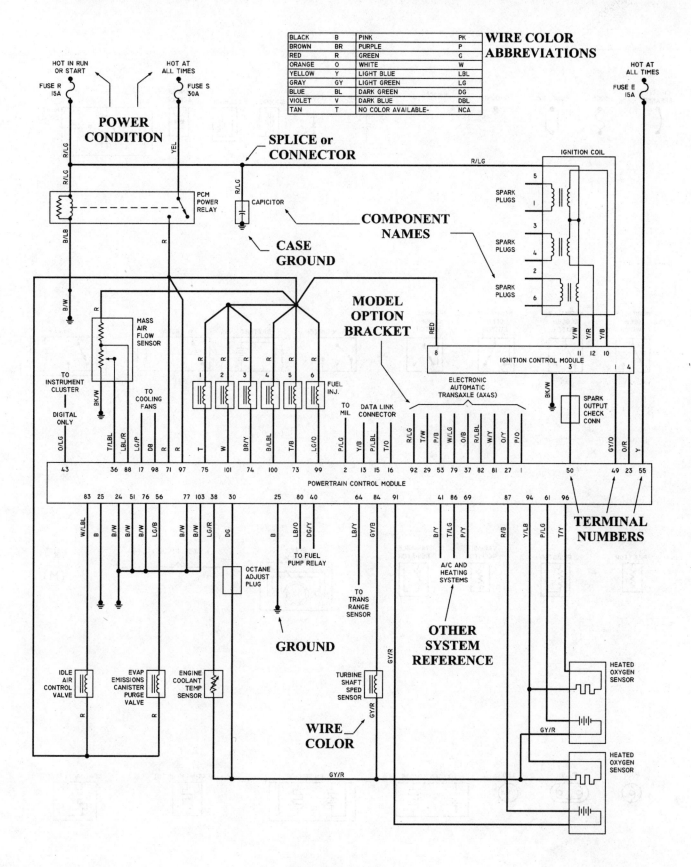

DIAGRAM 1

TCCA6W01

WIRING DIAGRAM SYMBOLS

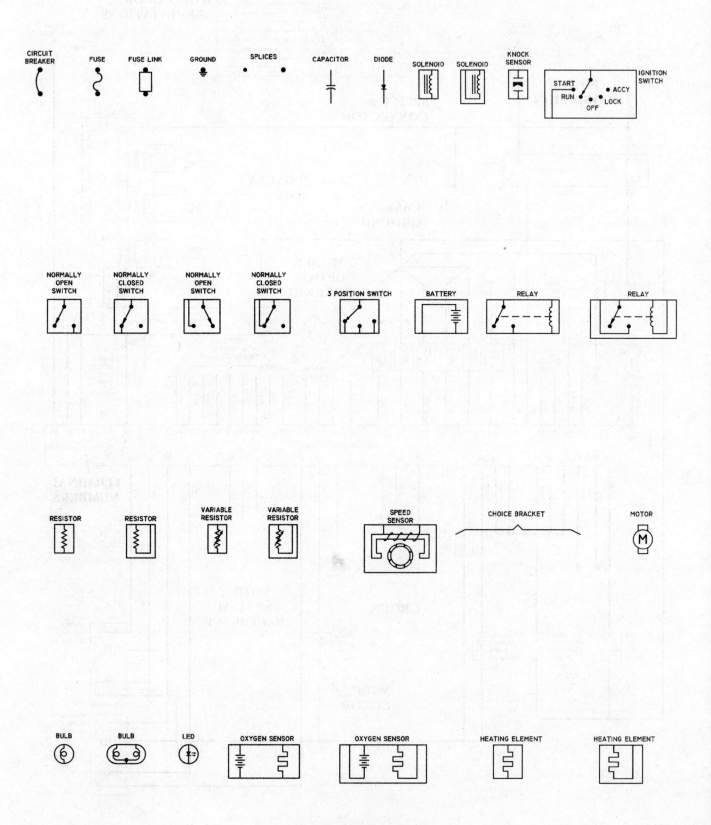

DIAGRAM 2

TCCA6W02

1996-98 240SX Engine Schematics

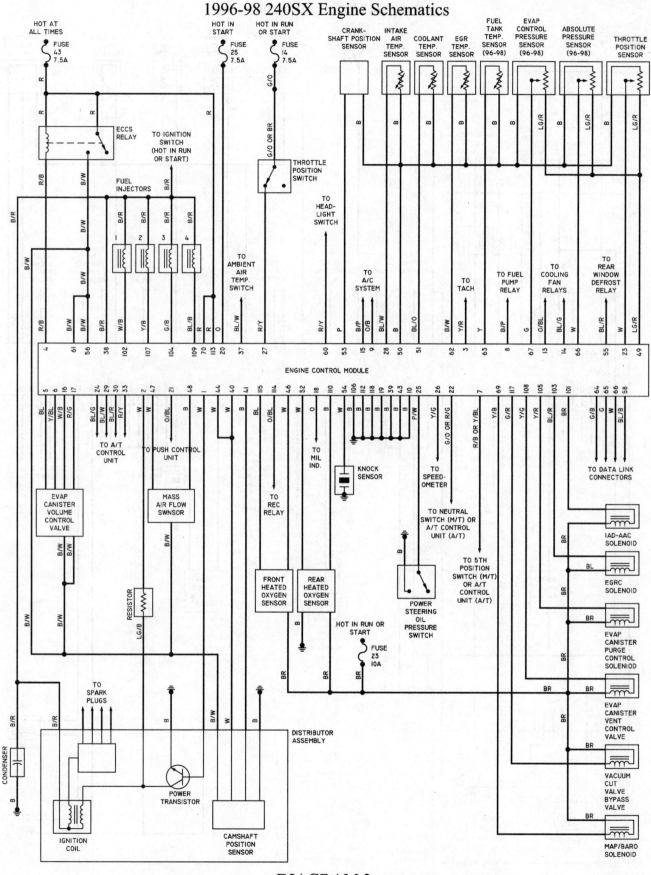

DIAGRAM 3

89706E01

1995 240SX Engine Schematics

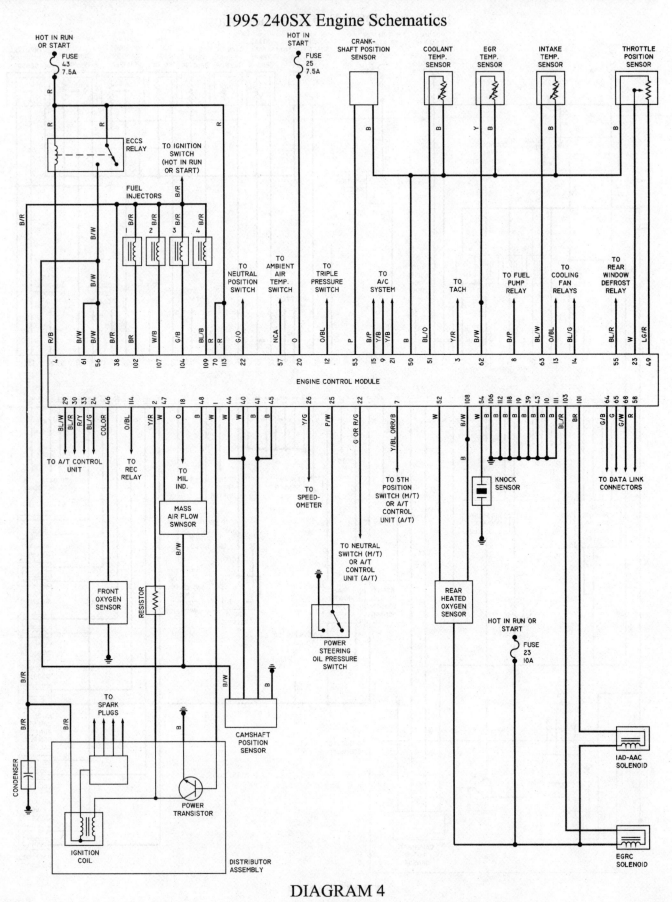

DIAGRAM 4

89706E04

1993-94 240SX Engine Schematics

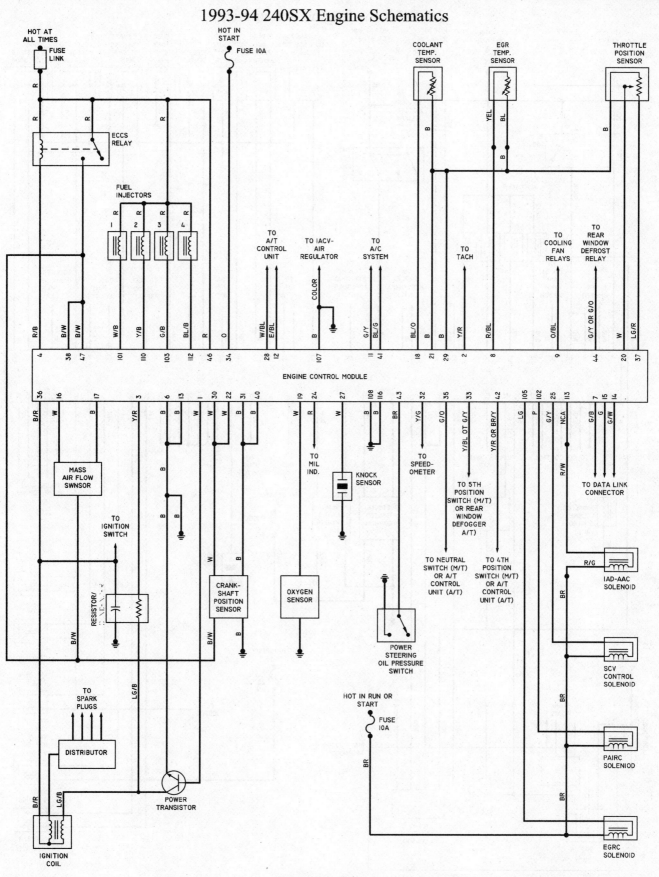

DIAGRAM 5

89706E02

1998 Altima Engine Schematics

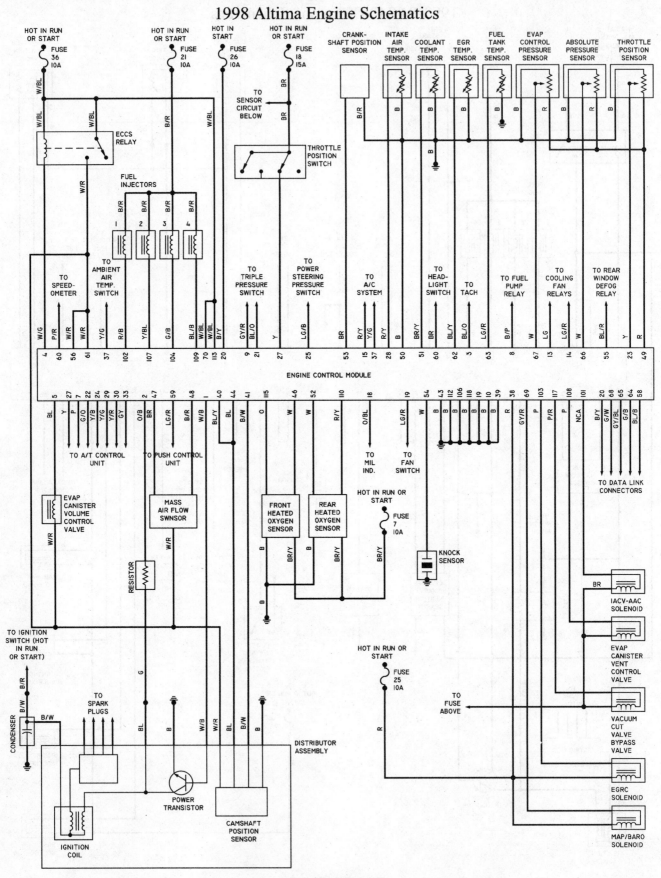

DIAGRAM 6

89706E03

1995-97 Altima Engine Schematics

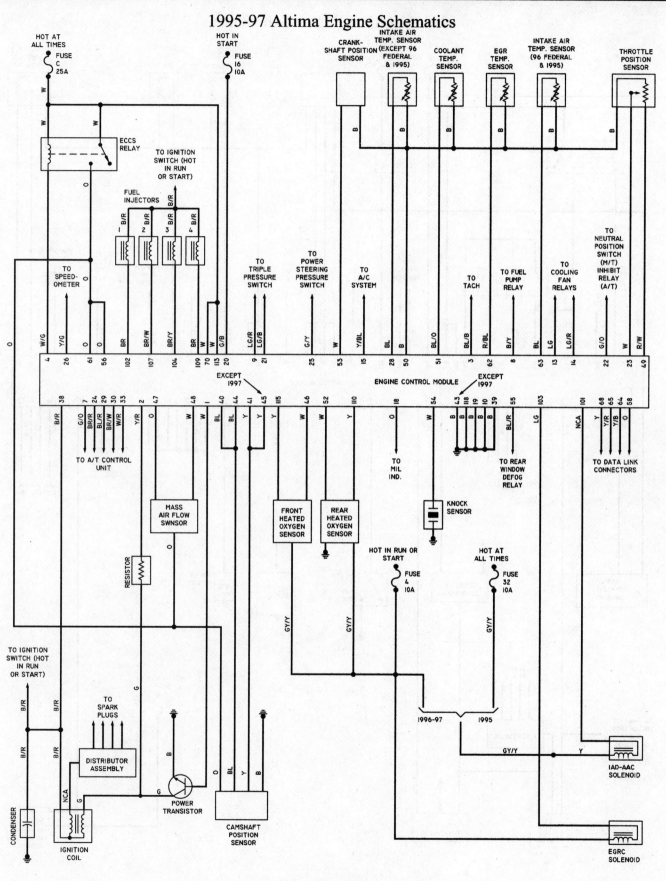

DIAGRAM 7

89706E05

1993-94 Altima Engine Schematics

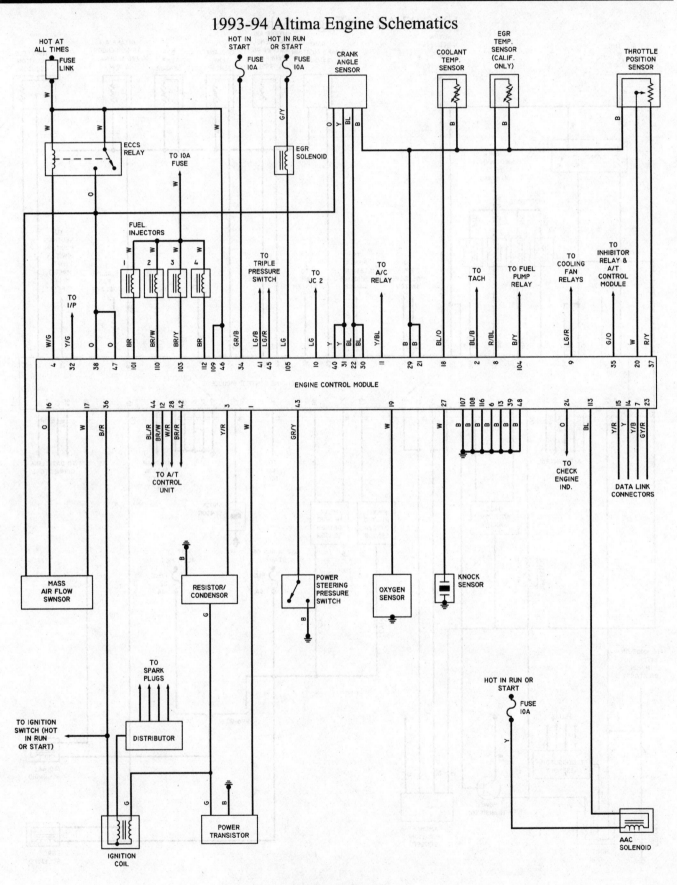

DIAGRAM 8

89706E06

1993-98 Altima Chassis Schematics

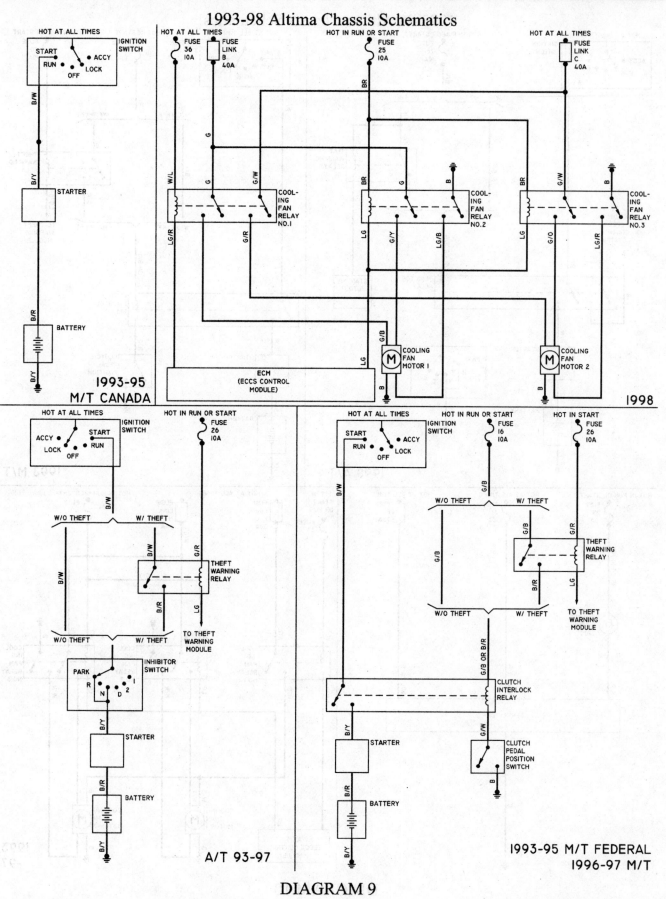

1993-95
M/T CANADA

1998

A/T 93-97

1993-95 M/T FEDERAL
1996-97 M/T

DIAGRAM 9

89706B01

1993-98 Altima Chassis Schematics

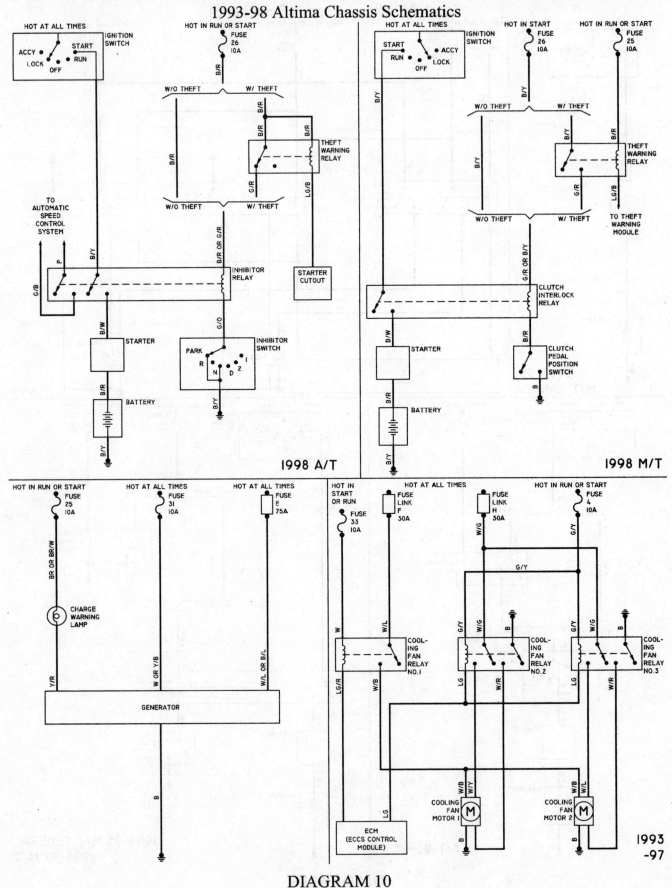

1998 A/T

1998 M/T

1993 -97

DIAGRAM 10

89706B02

1993-98 Altima Chassis Schematics

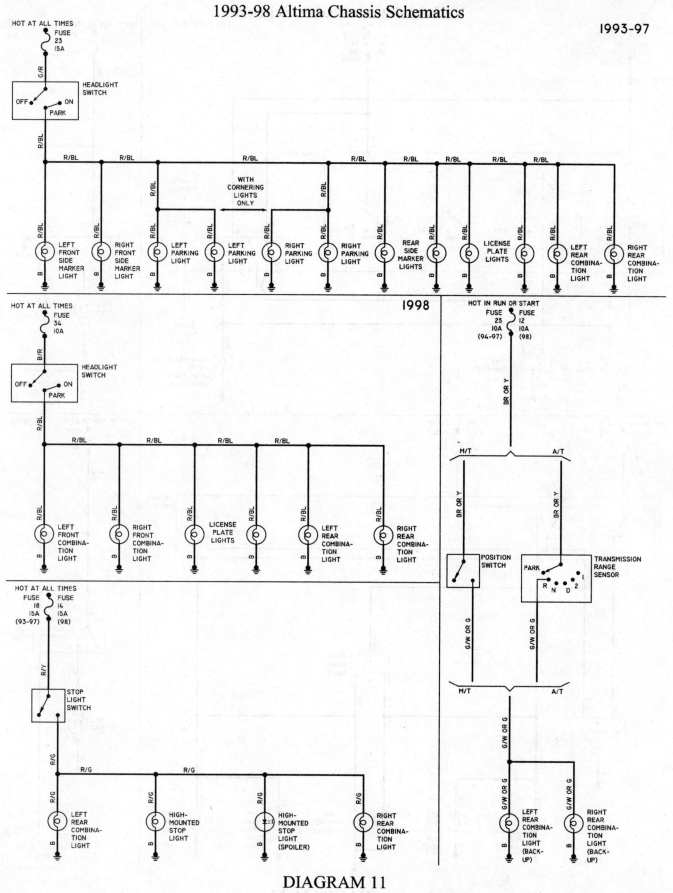

DIAGRAM 11

89706B03

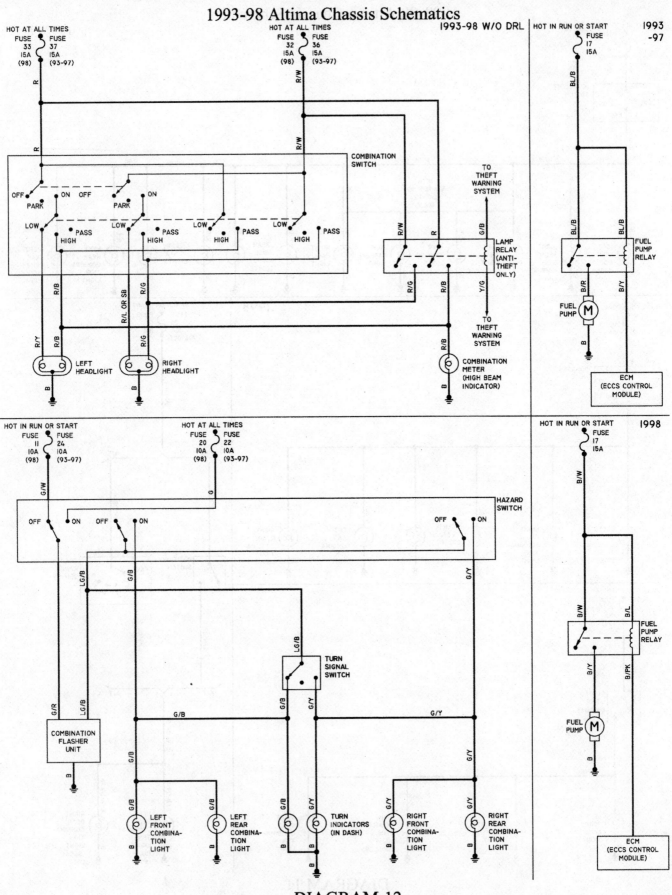

1993-98 Altima Chassis Schematics

DIAGRAM 12

89706B04

1993-98 Altima Chassis Schematics

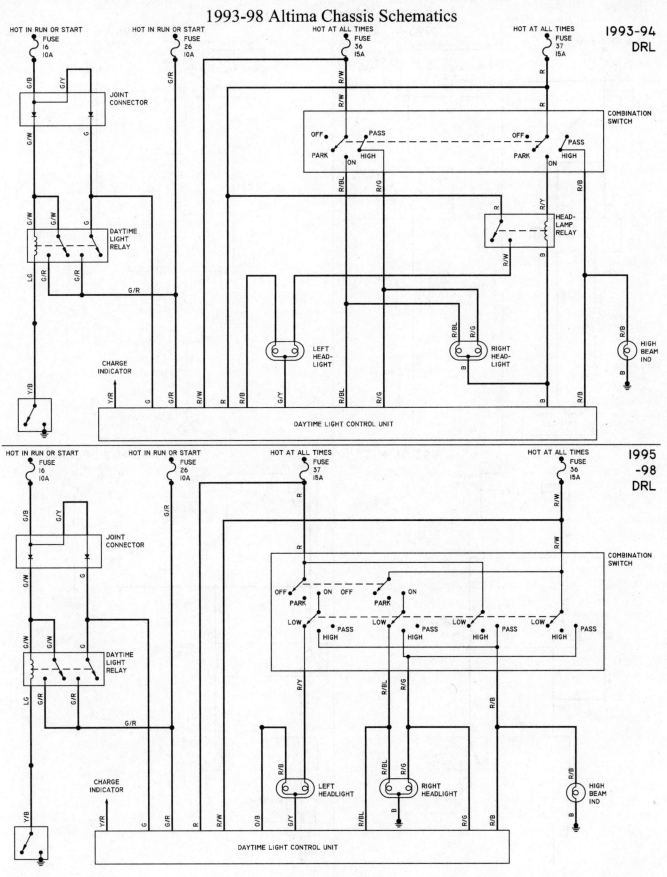

DIAGRAM 13

89706B05

1993-98 240SX Chassis Schematics

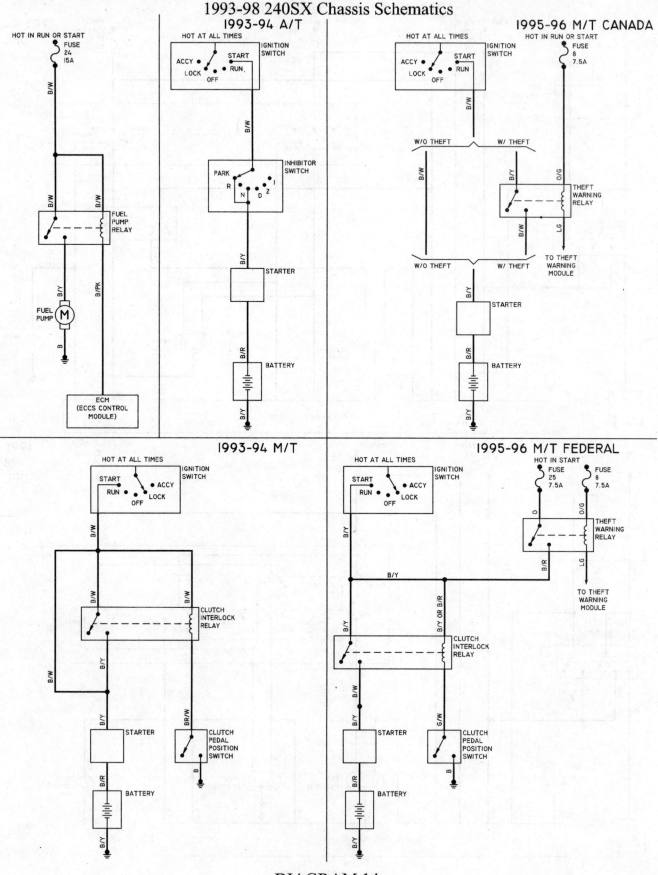

DIAGRAM 14

89706B06

1993-98 240SX Chassis Schematics

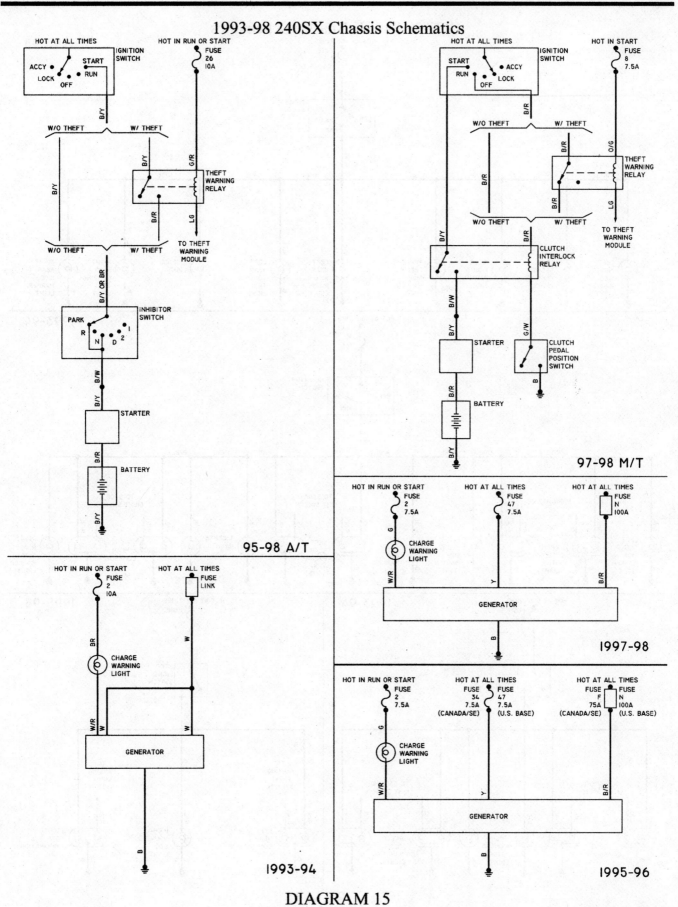

DIAGRAM 15

89706B07

1993-98 240SX Chassis Schematics

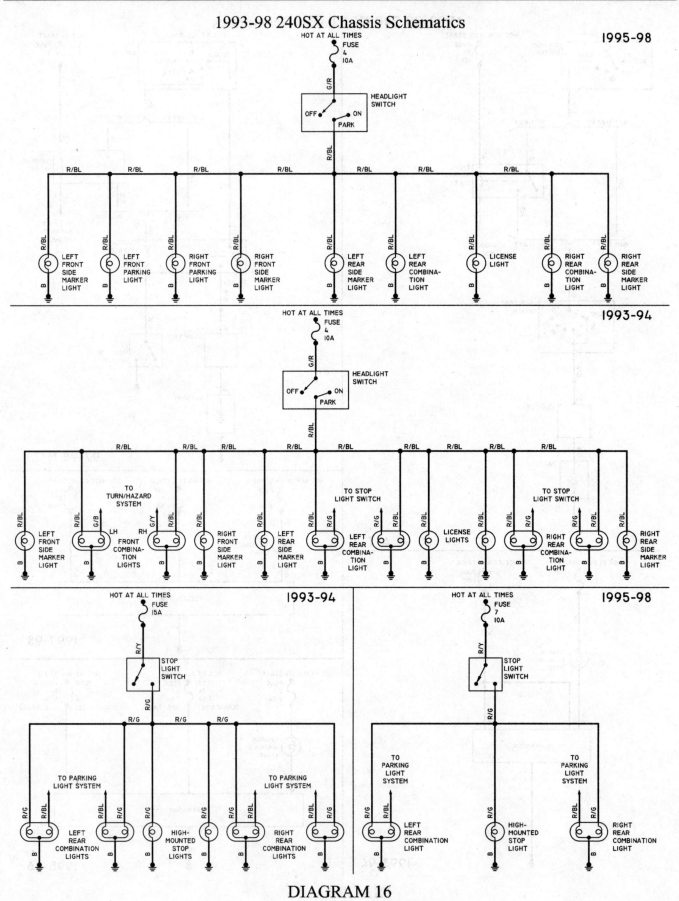

DIAGRAM 16

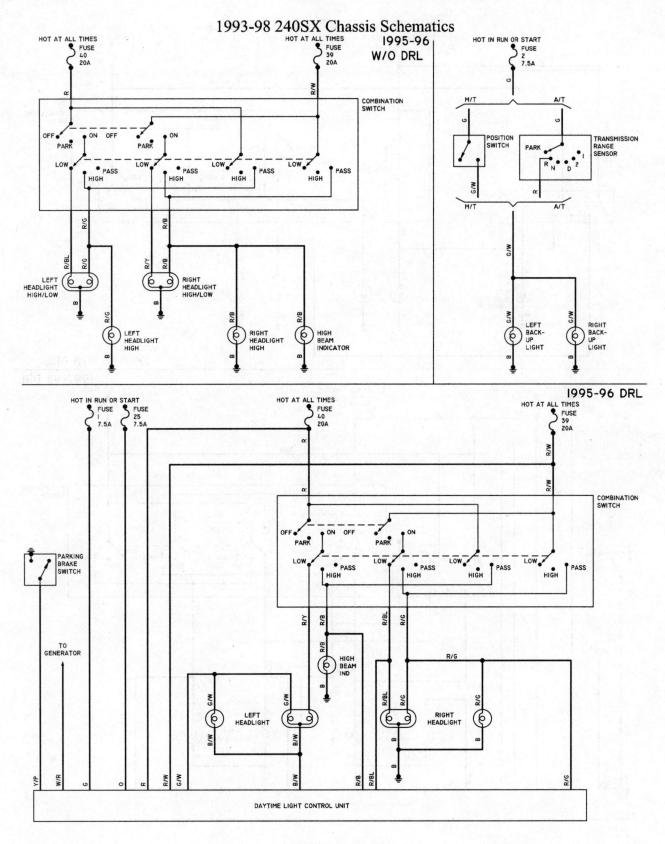

1993-98 240SX Chassis Schematics

DIAGRAM 17

89706B09

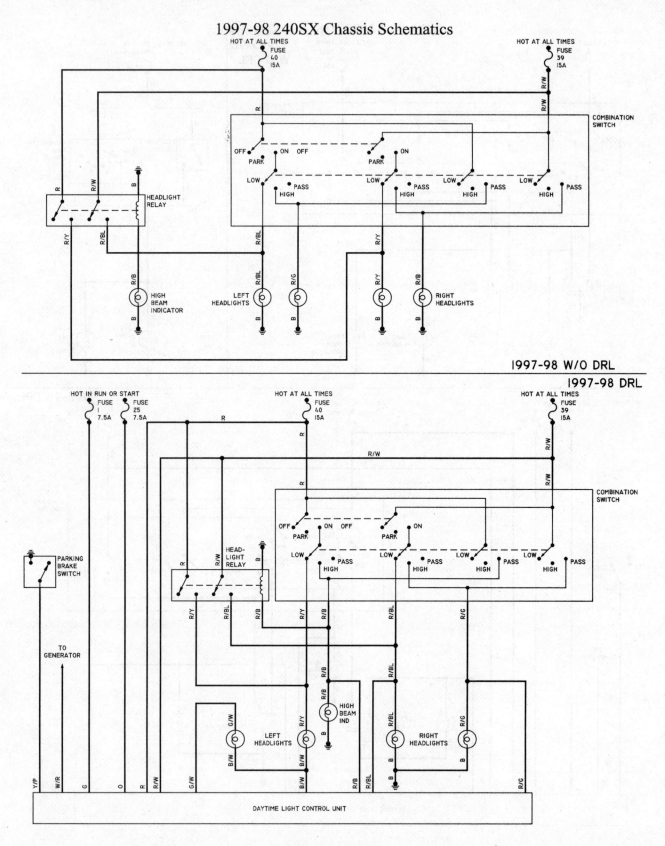

1997-98 240SX Chassis Schematics

DIAGRAM 18

89706B10

1993-98 240SX Chassis Schematics

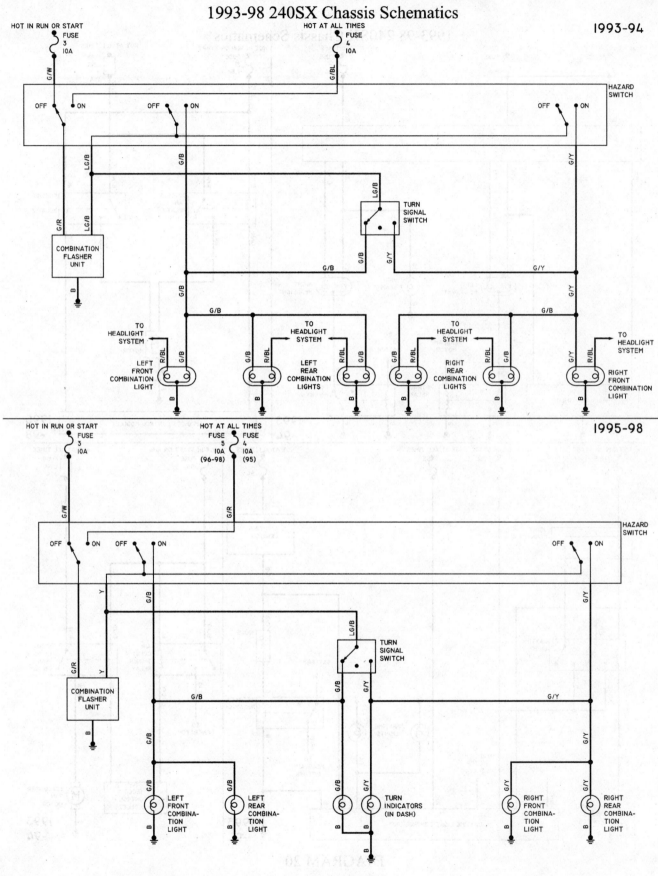

DIAGRAM 19

89706B11

1993-98 240SX Chassis Schematics

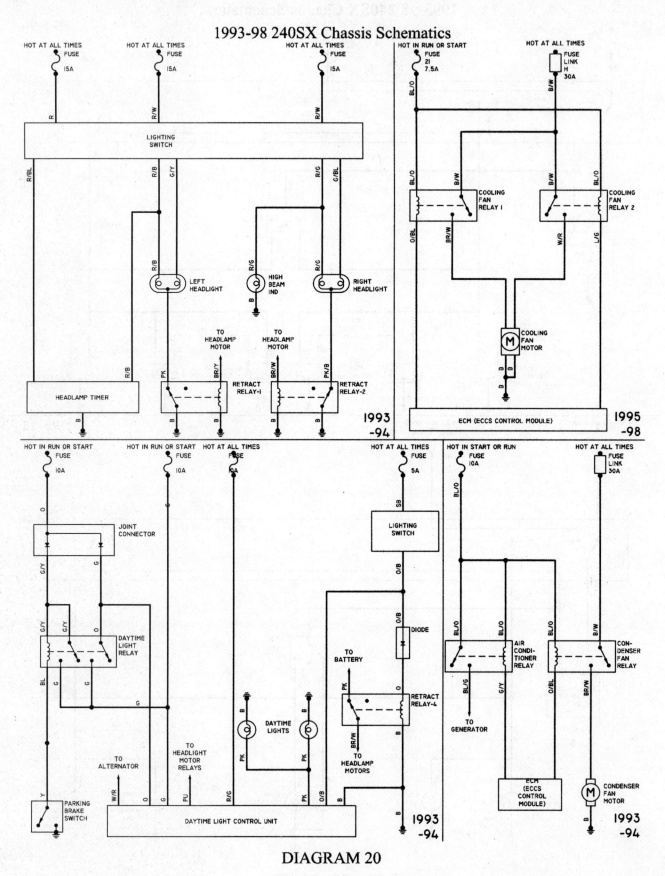

DIAGRAM 20

89706B12

7

DRIVE TRAIN

MANUAL TRANSMISSION

Understanding the Manual Transmission

Because of the way an internal combustion engine breathes, it can produce torque (or twisting force) only within a narrow speed range. Most overhead valve pushrod engines must turn at about 2500 rpm to produce their peak torque. Often by 4500 rpm, they are producing so little torque that continued increases in engine speed produce no power increases.

The torque peak on overhead camshaft engines is, generally, much higher, but much narrower.

The manual transmission and clutch are employed to vary the relationship between engine RPM and the speed of the wheels so that adequate power can be produced under all circumstances. The clutch allows engine torque to be applied to the transmission input shaft gradually, due to mechanical slippage. The vehicle can, consequently, be started smoothly from a full stop.

The transmission changes the ratio between the rotating speeds of the engine and the wheels by the use of gears. 4-speed or 5-speed transmissions are most common. The lower gears allow full engine power to be applied to the rear wheels during acceleration at low speeds.

The clutch driveplate is a thin disc, the center of which is splined to the transmission input shaft. Both sides of the disc are covered with a layer of material which is similar to brake lining and which is capable of allowing slippage without roughness or excessive noise.

The clutch cover is bolted to the engine driveplate and incorporates a diaphragm spring which provides the pressure to engage the clutch. The cover also houses the pressure plate. When the clutch pedal is released, the driven disc is sandwiched between the pressure plate and the smooth surface of the driveplate, thus forcing the disc to turn at the same speed as the engine crankshaft.

The transmission contains a mainshaft which passes all the way through the transmission, from the clutch to the driveshaft. This shaft is separated at one point, so that front and rear portions can turn at different speeds.

Power is transmitted by a countershaft in the lower gears and reverse. The gears of the countershaft mesh with gears on the mainshaft, allowing power to be carried from one to the other. Countershaft gears are often integral with that shaft, while several of the mainshaft gears can either rotate independently of the shaft or be locked to it. Shifting from one gear to the next causes one of the gears to be freed from rotating with the shaft and locks another to it. Gears are locked and unlocked by internal dog clutches which slide between the center of the gear and the shaft. The forward gears usually employ synchronizers; friction members which smoothly bring gear and shaft to the same speed before the toothed dog clutches are engaged.

Adjustments

The manual transmission used in these vehicles is equipped with an integral linkage system. No adjustment are necessary or possible.

Shift Lever

REMOVAL & INSTALLATION

▶ **See Figure 1**

1. Unscrew the shift lever knob and remove.
2. Remove the shift lever trim panel.
3. Remove the hole cover and the upper boot.
4. Remove the lower boot retainers. Remove the lower boot.

➡**Take care to not damage or rip the boots.**

5. Remove the snaprings that retain the shift lever in the transmission unit.
6. Lift the shift lever from the transmission.

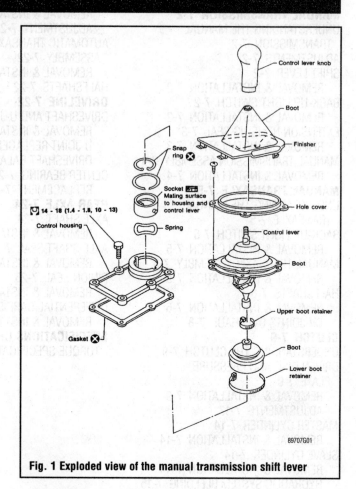

Fig. 1 Exploded view of the manual transmission shift lever

To install:

7. Position the shift lever in the transmission and secure it with the snaprings.
8. Install the lower boot and secure with the retainers.
9. Install the upper boot and the hole cover.
10. Install the shift lever trim panel.
11. Screw on the shift lever knob.

Back-up Light Switch

REMOVAL & INSTALLATION

▶ **See Figure 2**

The reverse lamp switch is located on the passenger's side of the transmission, near the bell housing.

1. Raise and safely support the vehicle.
2. Disconnect the switch electrical harness.
3. Unscrew the switch from the transmission.

➡**When removing the switch, place a drain pan beneath the transmission to catch the fluid.**

To install:

4. Screw the switch into the transmission and tighten to 14–22 ft. lbs. (20–29 Nm).
5. Connect the switch electrical harness.
6. Lower the vehicle.

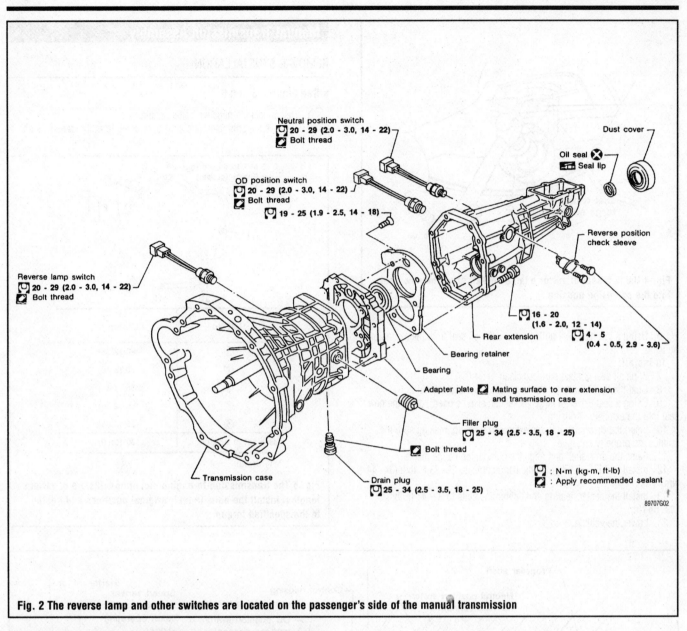

Neutral position switch
🔧 20 - 29 (2.0 - 3.0, 14 - 22)
🔩 Bolt thread

OD position switch
🔧 20 - 29 (2.0 - 3.0, 14 - 22)
🔩 Bolt thread

🔧 19 - 25 (1.9 - 2.5, 14 - 18)

Reverse lamp switch
🔧 20 - 29 (2.0 - 3.0, 14 - 22)
🔩 Bolt thread

Dust cover

Oil seal ⊗
▭ Seal lip

Reverse position check sleeve

🔧 16 - 20
(1.6 - 2.0, 12 - 14)

🔧 4 - 5
(0.4 - 0.5, 2.9 - 3.6)

Rear extension

Bearing retainer

Bearing

Adapter plate 🔩 Mating surface to rear extension and transmission case

Filler plug
🔧 25 - 34 (2.5 - 3.5, 18 - 25)

🔩 Bolt thread

Transmission case

Drain plug
🔧 25 - 34 (2.5 - 3.5, 18 - 25)

🔧 : N•m (kg-m, ft-lb)
🔩 : Apply recommended sealant

89707G02

Fig. 2 The reverse lamp and other switches are located on the passenger's side of the manual transmission

Extension Housing Seal

REMOVAL & INSTALLATION

▶ See Figures 3 and 4

The driveshaft used in these vehicles is a two-piece design with a center bearing. It should only be necessary to remove the front portion of the driveshaft to perform this procedure. However, the center bearing may have to be removed to allow clearance.

1. Raise and safely support the vehicle.
2. Matchmark the driveshaft and differential companion flanges.

➡ If the driveshaft is not installed in the correct position, it may cause a serious vibration.

3. Remove the center bearing and mounting brackets from the cross-member, as required.
4. Loosen the companion flange bolts and lower the driveshaft from the differential.
5. Carefully withdraw the driveshaft from the transmission. Plug the extension opening to prevent leakage.

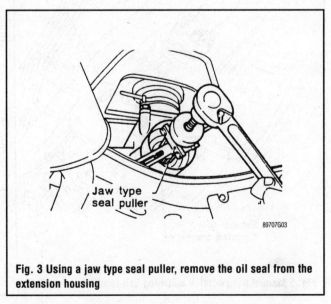

Jaw type seal puller

89707G03

Fig. 3 Using a jaw type seal puller, remove the oil seal from the extension housing

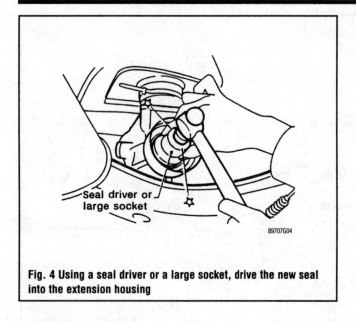

Fig. 4 Using a seal driver or a large socket, drive the new seal into the extension housing

6. Using a jaw type seal puller, remove the oil seal from the extension housing.

To install:

7. Wipe all seal contact surfaces clean.

8. Coat the lip of the new seal with clean transmission fluid.

9. Using a seal driver (a large socket can also be used), drive the new seal into the extension housing.

10. Insert the driveshaft into the extension housing, making sure the splines are properly engaged.

11. Raise the driveshaft and align the companion flange marks.

12. Install and EVENLY tighten the flange bolts to 29–33 ft. lbs. (34–44 Nm).

13. Install the center bearing and tighten the bolts to 32–41 ft. lbs. (43–55 Nm).

14. Lower the vehicle.

Manual Transmission Assembly

REMOVAL & INSTALLATION

▶ **See Figures 5 and 6**

1. Disconnect the negative battery cable.
2. Remove the shift lever and control housing from the transmission.

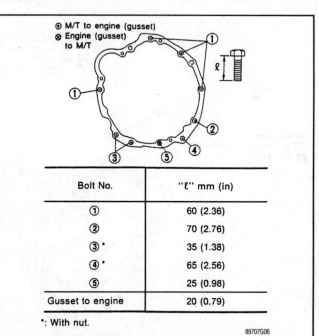

Bolt No.	"ℓ" mm (in)
①	60 (2.36)
②	70 (2.76)
③ *	35 (1.38)
④ *	65 (2.56)
⑤	25 (0.98)
Gusset to engine	20 (0.79)

*: With nut.

Fig. 6 The transmission-to-engine mounting bolts are of various lengths. Install the bolts in their original positions and tighten to the specified torque

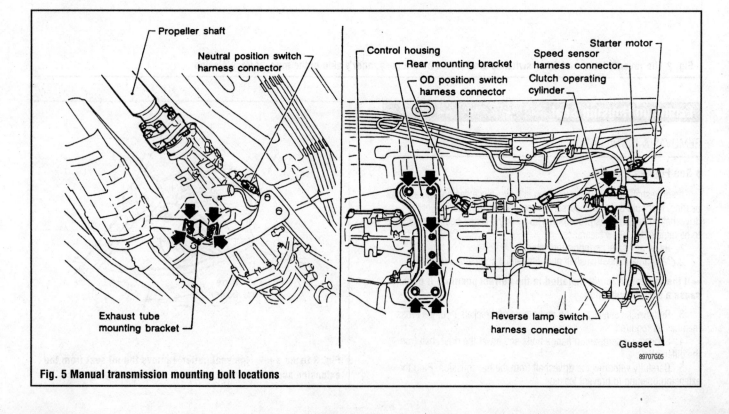

Fig. 5 Manual transmission mounting bolt locations

3. Remove the crankshaft position sensor from the upper side of the transmission case.

4. Remove the clutch operating cylinder.

5. Label and disconnect the electrical harnesses.

6. Remove the starter motor.

7. Remove the driveshaft and plug the rear of the transmission to prevent fluid loss.

➡**Take care to not damage the spline, sleeve yoke or rear oil seal when removing the propeller shaft.**

8. Remove the engine and transmission gussets.

9. Remove the exhaust pipe mounting bracket.

10. Support the transmission with a suitable jack.

11. Remove the rear transmission mounting bracket.

12. Lower the transmission as much as possible without putting undue stress on other components.

13. Remove the transmission-to-engine attaching bolts.

14. Pull the transmission back and away from the engine, then lower it from the vehicle.

To install:

15. Position the transmission on the engine and install the transmission-to-engine attaching bolts. Tighten the bolts as follows:

    a. Tighten bolts labeled No. 1 and 2 to 29–36 ft. lbs. (39–49 Nm).

    b. Tighten all other bolts to 22–29 ft. lbs. (29–39 Nm).

➡**Bolts are of varying lengths. Install the bolts in their proper positions.**

16. The remainder of the installation procedure is the reverse of removal.

MANUAL TRANSAXLE

Understanding the Manual Transaxle

Because of the way an internal combustion engine breathes, it can produce torque, or twisting force, only within a narrow speed range. Most modern, overhead valve pushrod engines must turn at about 2500 rpm to produce their peak torque. By 4500 rpm they are producing so little torque that continued increases in engine speed produce no power increases. The torque peak on overhead camshaft engines is generally much higher, but much narrower.

The manual transaxle and clutch are employed to vary the relationship between engine speed and the speed of the wheels so that adequate engine power can be produced under all circumstances. The clutch allows engine torque to be applied to the transaxle input shaft gradually, due to mechanical slippage. Consequently, the vehicle may be started smoothly from a full stop. The transaxle changes the ratio between the rotating speeds of the engine and the wheels by the use of gears. The gear ratios allow full engine power to be applied to the wheels during acceleration at low speeds and at highway/passing speeds.

In a front wheel drive transaxle, power is usually transmitted from the input shaft to a mainshaft or output shaft located slightly beneath and to the side of the input shaft. The gears of the mainshaft mesh with gears on the input shaft, allowing power to be carried from one to the other. All forward gears are in constant mesh and are free from rotating with the shaft unless the synchronizer and clutch is engaged. Shifting from one gear to the next causes one of the gears to be freed from rotating with the shaft and locks another to it. Gears are locked and unlocked by internal dog clutches which slide between the center of the gear and the shaft. The forward gears employ synchronizers; friction members which smoothly bring gear and shaft to the same speed before the toothed dog clutches are engaged.

Back-up Light Switch

REMOVAL & INSTALLATION

▶ **See Figure 7**

The back-up lamp/neutral position switch is located at the bottom of the transaxle. The switch connector is located at the top of the transaxle, with the wire running down the side of the case.

1. Raise and safely support the vehicle.

2. Disconnect the switch electrical harness.

➡**Before removing the switch, place a drain pan beneath the transaxle to catch dripping fluid.**

3. Unfasten the screw and remove the switch from the transaxle.

To install:

4. Position the switch in the transaxle and tighten its attaching bolt to 24–36 inch lbs. (3–4 Nm).

5. Connect the switch electrical harness.

6. Lower the vehicle.

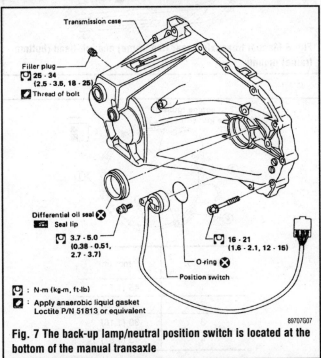

Fig. 7 The back-up lamp/neutral position switch is located at the bottom of the manual transaxle

Manual Transaxle Assembly

REMOVAL & INSTALLATION

▶ **See Figures 8 and 9**

1. Disconnect the negative, then the positive battery cables.

2. Remove the battery and battery bracket.

3. Remove the air cleaner box and mass air flow sensor.

4. Remove the air duct.

5. Remove the clutch operating cylinder from the transaxle.

6. Disconnect the back-up lamp switch harness connector.

7. Remove the starter.

8. Remove the crankshaft position sensor.

➡**Take care not to damage the sensor tip.**

9. Remove the shift control rod.

10. Drain and recycle the gear oil from the transaxle.

➡**Take note of the condition of the oil as it is draining. Milky oil (which shows up as streaks of white) indicates the presence of moisture. Silvery streaks in the oil indicate the presence of metal. If either condition exists, serious problems may exist inside the transaxle.**

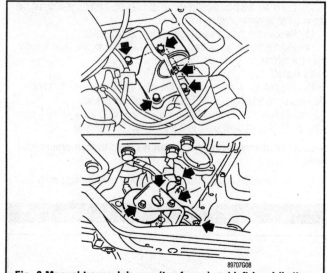

Fig. 8 Manual transaxle's rear (top frame) and left-hand (bottom frame) mounts

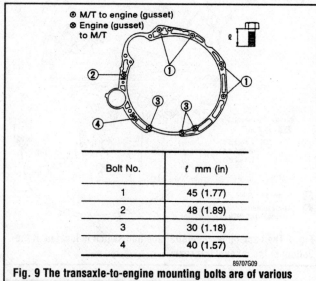

⊕ M/T to engine (gusset)
⊗ Engine (gusset) to M/T

Bolt No.	ℓ mm (in)
1	45 (1.77)
2	48 (1.89)
3	30 (1.18)
4	40 (1.57)

Fig. 9 The transaxle-to-engine mounting bolts are of various lengths. Install the bolts in their original positions and tighten to the specified torque

11. Remove the halfshafts.
12. Support the engine by placing a jack beneath the oil pan. Use a piece of wood between the jack and oil pan as a cushion.
13. Remove the rear and left-hand transaxle mounts.
14. Raise the jack to access the lower housing bolts.
15. Remove the lower housing bolts and lower the jack.
16. Remove the upper housing bolts.
17. Pull the transaxle away from the engine and lower it from the vehicle carefully.
To install:
18. Position the transaxle on the engine and install the transaxle-to-engine attaching bolts. Tighten the bolts as follows:
   a. Tighten bolts labeled No. 1 and 2 to 29–36 ft. lbs. (39–49 Nm).
   b. Tighten all other bolts to 22–30 ft. lbs. (30–40 Nm).

➡**Bolts are of varying lengths. Install the bolts in their proper positions.**

19. The remainder of the installation procedure is the reverse of removal.

Halfshafts

REMOVAL & INSTALLATION

◆ **See Figures 10 thru 17**

1. Raise and safely support the vehicle.
2. Remove the wheel.
3. Remove the wheel bearing locknut.

➡**The brake caliper need not be removed to perform this service. Do not twist or stretch the brake hose when moving components.**

4. Remove the cotter pin and nut securing the lower ball joint to the knuckle.
5. Strike the knuckle with a hammer and pull down the transverse link to separate the lower ball joint from the knuckle.
6. Disconnect the tie rod ball joint.
7. Separate the halfshaft from the knuckle by tapping it lightly. If it is hard to remove, a halfshaft removal tool can be mounted on the wheel studs to press the halfshaft from the hub.

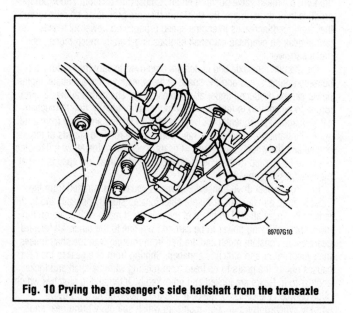

Fig. 10 Prying the passenger's side halfshaft from the transaxle

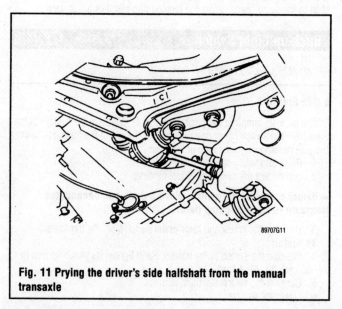

Fig. 11 Prying the driver's side halfshaft from the manual transaxle

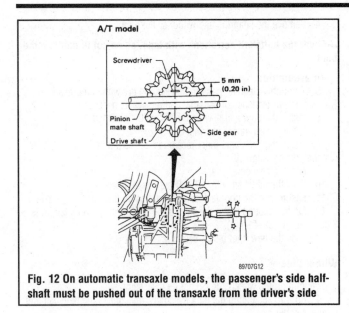

Fig. 12 On automatic transaxle models, the passenger's side half-shaft must be pushed out of the transaxle from the driver's side

Fig. 15 The halfshaft must be pried from the transaxle case as illustrated. Take care not to damage the seal (arrow)

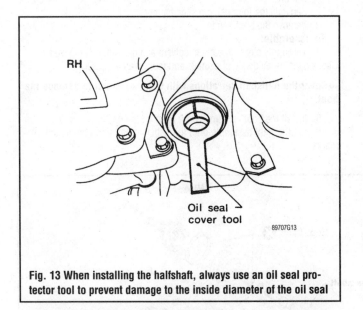

Fig. 13 When installing the halfshaft, always use an oil seal protector tool to prevent damage to the inside diameter of the oil seal

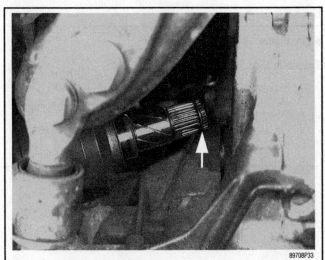

Fig. 16 The halfshaft is retained in the transaxle by a circlip (arrow)

Fig. 14 The splined portion (arrow) of the halfshaft fits into the hub

Fig. 17 Carefully remove the halfshaft from the vehicle. Do not allow the CV-joints to overextend

➡**When removing the halfshafts, cover the boots to prevent damaging them.**

8. Remove the halfshafts from the transaxle by gently prying them from the housing.

To install:

9. Using an oil seal cover tool to protect the inner diameter of the oil seal, install the halfshafts.

10. Properly align the serrations and then withdraw the oil seal cover tool.

11. Push on the halfshaft to press the circlip on the halfshaft into the groove on the side gear.

12. After inserting the halfshaft, attempt to gently pull the halfshaft out of the transaxle. If it pulls out, the circlip is not properly meshed with the side gear.

13. Connect the tie rod ball joint.

14. Attach the lower ball joint and steering knuckle.

15. Install the nut and cotter pin securing the lower ball joint to the knuckle.

16. Install the wheel bearing locknut. Tighten the locknut to 174–231 ft. lbs. (235–314 Nm).

17. Install the wheel.

18. Lower the vehicle.

CV-JOINTS OVERHAUL

♦ **See Figure 18**

Transaxle Side

1. Remove the boot bands.

2. Matchmark the slide joint housing and inner race, prior to separating the joint assembly.

3. Pry off the snaping and remove the ball cage, inner race and balls as a unit.

4. Remove the snaping and withdraw the boot.

➡**Cover the halfshaft serrations with tape, so as not to damage the boot.**

To assemble:

5. Throughly clean all parts in solvent and dry with compressed air. Check parts for evidence of damage, and replace as necessary.

6. Install the boot and new boot band on the halfshaft.

7. Install a new inner snaping.

8. Install the ball cage, inner race and balls as a unit. Ensure that the matchmarks are aligned.

9. Install a new outer snaping.

10. Pack the halfshaft with 5.0–6.0 ounces of grease.

11. Ensure that the boot is properly installed on the halfshaft groove.

12. Set the boot so that it does not swell or deform when its length is 3.82–3.90 in. (97–99mm).

13. Lock the new boot bands securely.

Wheel Side

The joint on the wheel side cannot be disassembled.

1. Prior to separating the joint assembly, matchmark the halfshaft and joint assembly.

2. Separate the joint using a slide hammer.

3. Remove the boot bands.

To assemble:

4. Throughly clean all parts in solvent and dry with compressed air. Check parts for evidence of damage and replace as necessary.

➡**Cover the halfshaft serrations with tape, so as not to damage the boot.**

5. Install the boot and small boot band on the halfshaft.

6. Set the joint assembly onto the halfshaft and align the matchmarks.

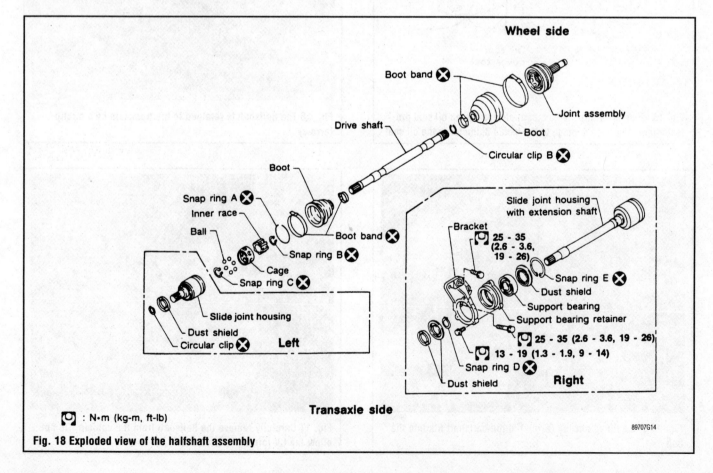

Fig. 18 Exploded view of the halfshaft assembly

89707G14

7. Attach the joint assembly to the halfshaft by lightly tapping the serrated end with a plastic hammer.

➡**Using a metal hammer may damage the threads on the end of the joint.**

8. Pack the halfshaft with 3.5–4.0 ounces of grease.
9. Ensure that the boot is properly installed on the halfshaft groove.
10. Set the boot so that it does not swell or deform when its length is 3.327–3.406 in. (84.5–86.5mm).
11. Lock the new boot bands securely.

Support Bearing

1. Remove the dust shield.
2. Remove the snapring.

3. Press the support bearing assembly off the halfshaft using a hydraulic press and the appropriate adapters.
4. Separate the support bearing from the retainer using a bearing driver.

To assemble:

5. Throughly clean all parts in solvent and dry with compressed air. Check the parts for evidence of damage.
6. Ensure that the wheel bearing rolls freely and is free from noise, cracks, pitting and wear.
7. Check the support bearing bracket for cracks, and replace as necessary.
8. Install the bearing into the retainer using a bearing driver.
9. Press the halfshaft into the bearing using a hydraulic press.
10. Install the new snapring.
11. Install the new dust shield.

CLUTCH

Understanding the Clutch

❊❊ CAUTION

The clutch driven disc may contain asbestos, which has been determined to be a cancer causing agent. Never clean clutch surfaces with compressed air! Avoid inhaling any dust from any clutch surface! When cleaning clutch surfaces, use a commercially available brake cleaning fluid.

The purpose of the clutch is to disconnect and connect engine power at the transaxle/transmission. A vehicle at rest requires a lot of engine torque to get all that weight moving. An internal combustion engine does not develop a high starting torque (unlike steam engines) so it must be allowed to operate without any load until it builds up enough torque to move the vehicle. Torque increases with engine rpm. The clutch allows the engine to build up torque by physically disconnecting the engine from the transaxle/transmission, relieving the engine of any load or resistance.

The transfer of engine power to the transaxle/transmission (the load) must be smooth and gradual; if it weren't, drive line components would wear out or break quickly. This gradual power transfer is made possible by gradually releasing the clutch pedal. The clutch disc and pressure plate are the connecting link between the engine and transaxle/transmission. When the clutch pedal is released, the disc and plate contact each other (the clutch is engaged) physically joining the engine and transaxle/transmission. When the pedal is pushed inward, the disc and plate separate (the clutch is disengaged) disconnecting the engine from the transaxle/transmission.

Most clutches utilize a single plate, dry friction disc with a diaphragm-style spring pressure plate. The clutch disc has a splined hub which attaches the disc to the input shaft. The disc has friction material where it contacts the driveplate and pressure plate. Torsion springs on the disc help absorb engine torque pulses. The pressure plate applies pressure to the clutch disc, holding it tight against the surface of the driveplate. The clutch operating mechanism consists of a release bearing, fork and cylinder assembly.

There is a circular diaphragm spring within the pressure plate cover (transaxle/transmission side). In a relaxed state (when the clutch pedal is fully released) this spring is convex; that is, it is dished outward toward the transmission. Pushing in the clutch pedal actuates the attached linkage. Connected to the other end of this is the throw out fork, which hold the throw out bearing. When the clutch pedal is depressed, the clutch linkage pushes the fork and bearing forward to contact the diaphragm spring of the pressure plate. The outer edges of the spring are secured to the pressure plate and are pivoted on rings so that when the center of the spring is compressed by the throw out bearing, the outer edges bow outward and, by so doing, pull the pressure plate in the same direction—away from the clutch disc. This action separates the disc from the plate, disengaging the clutch and allowing the transaxle/transmission to be shifted into another gear. A coil type clutch return spring attached to the clutch pedal arm permits full

release of the pedal. Releasing the pedal pulls the throw out bearing away from the diaphragm spring resulting in a reversal of spring position. As bearing pressure is gradually released from the spring center, the outer edges of the spring bow outward, pushing the pressure plate into closer contact with the clutch disc. As the disc and plate move closer together, friction between the two increases and slippage is reduced until, when full spring pressure is applied (by fully releasing the pedal) the speed of the disc and plate are the same. This stops all slipping, creating a direct connection between the plate and disc which results in the transfer of power from the engine to the transaxle/transmission. The clutch disc is now rotating with the pressure plate at engine speed and, because it is splined to the transaxle/transmission shaft, the shaft now turns at the same engine speed.

The release fork and actuating linkage transfer pedal motion to the release bearing. In the engaged position (pedal released) the diaphragm spring holds the pressure plate against the clutch disc, so engine torque is transmitted to the input shaft. When the clutch pedal is depressed, the release bearing pushes the diaphragm spring center toward the driveplate. The diaphragm spring pivots the fulcrum, relieving the load on the pressure plate. Steel spring straps riveted to the clutch cover lift the pressure plate from the clutch disc, disengaging the engine drive from the transaxle/transmission and enabling the gears to be changed.

The clutch is operating properly if:

1. It will stall the engine when released with the vehicle held stationary.
2. The shift lever can be moved freely between 1st and reverse gears when the vehicle is stationary and the clutch disengaged.

Driven Disc and Pressure Plate

REMOVAL & INSTALLATION

◆ **See Figures 19 thru 35**

1. Remove the transmission/transaxle from the engine.
2. Insert a clutch alignment tool all the way into the clutch disc hub. This must be done to support the weight of the clutch disc during removal.
3. Matchmark the clutch assembly-to-driveplate relationship for installation reference.
4. Loosen the pressure plate bolts in sequence, a turn at a time.
5. Remove the pressure plate and clutch disc.

To install:

6. Inspect all components and replace as necessary.

➡**The clutch cover and pressure plate are balanced as an assembly. If replacement of either part becomes necessary, replace all components as an assembly (clutch disc, pressure plate and release bearing).**

7. Lubricate the transaxle/transmission splines with grease.
8. Install the disc on the splines and slide it back and forth a few times. Remove the disc and remove any excess grease.

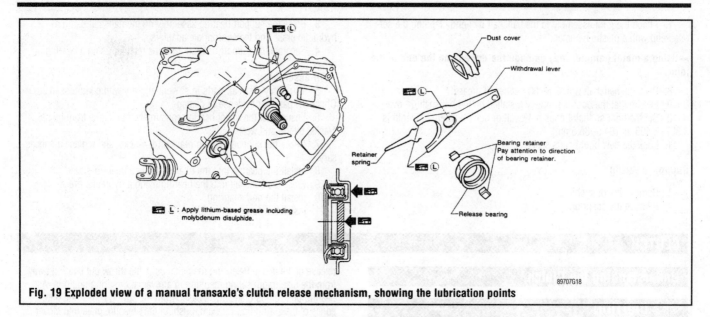

Fig. 19 Exploded view of a manual transaxle's clutch release mechanism, showing the lubrication points

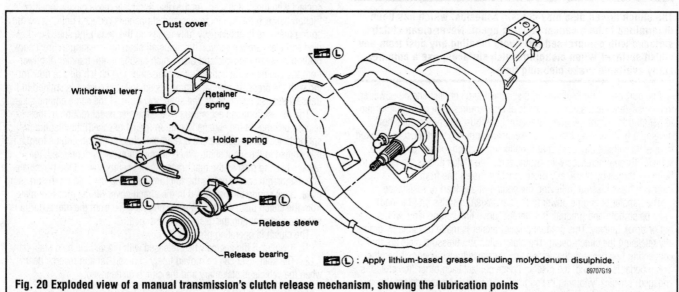

Fig. 20 Exploded view of a manual transmission's clutch release mechanism, showing the lubrication points

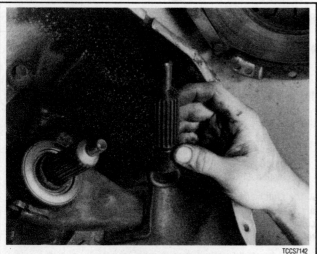

Fig. 21 Typical clutch alignment tool; note how the splines match the transmission's input shaft

Fig. 22 Loosen and remove the clutch and pressure plate bolts evenly, a little at a time . . .

TCCS7118

Fig. 23 . . . then carefully remove the clutch and pressure plate assembly from the driveplate

TCCS7122

Fig. 26 . . . then remove the driveplate from the crankshaft in order to replace it or have it machined

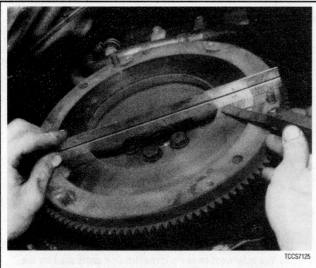

TCCS7125

Fig. 24 Check across the driveplate surface; it should be flat

TCCS7123

Fig. 27 Upon installation, it is usually a good idea to apply a threadlocking compound to the driveplate bolts

TCCS7121

Fig. 25 If necessary, lock the driveplate in place and remove the retaining bolts . . .

TCCS7126

Fig. 28 Check the pressure plate for excessive wear

Fig. 29 Be sure that the driveplate surface is clean, before installing the clutch

Fig. 30 Install a clutch alignment arbor, to align the clutch assembly during installation

Fig. 31 Clutch plate and pressure plate installed with the alignment arbor in place

Fig. 32 The pressure plate-to-driveplate bolt holes should align

Fig. 33 You may want to use a threadlocking compound on the clutch assembly bolts

Fig. 34 Install the clutch assembly bolts and tighten in steps, using an X pattern

Fig. 35 Be sure to use a torque wrench to tighten all bolts

➡️**Be sure no grease contacts the disc or pressure plate.**

9. Remove the release mechanism from the transmission/transaxle housing.

10. Lubricate the bearing sleeve inside groove, the contact point of the withdrawal lever and bearing sleeve, the contact surface of the lever ball pin and the lever with a lithium based molybdenum disulfide grease.

11. Install the clutch disc on the alignment tool.

12. Install the pressure plate and evenly tighten the bolts to 16–22 ft. lbs. (22–29 Nm).

13. Remove the clutch alignment tool.

14. Install the transmission/transaxle.

15. Bleed the clutch hydraulic system and adjust the clutch pedal.

ADJUSTMENTS

Pedal Height

▶ **See Figure 36**

1. Loosen the locknut and adjust the pedal height by means of the pedal stopper or cruise control cancel switch.

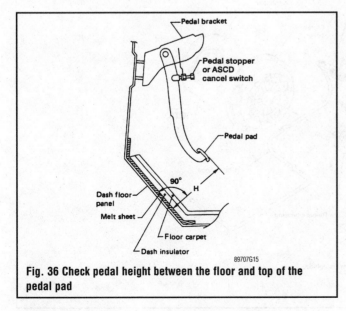

Fig. 36 Check pedal height between the floor and top of the pedal pad

2. Pedal height should be 6.61–7.01 in. (168–178mm) on Altima, and 7.56–7.95 in. (192–202mm) on 240SX between the floor and the top of the pedal pad.

3. Tighten the pedal stopper to 12–16 ft. lbs. (16–22 Nm) or the cruise control switch to 9–11 ft. lbs. (12–15 Nm).

Free-Play

▶ **See Figure 37**

1. Loosen the locknut and adjust the pedal free-play by means of the master cylinder pushrod.

2. Pedal free-play should be 0.35–0.63 in. (9–16mm) on Altima, and 0.039–0.118 in. (1–3mm) on 240SX between the floor and the top of the pedal pad.

3. Tighten the locknut securely.

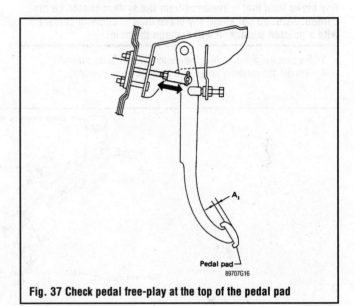

Fig. 37 Check pedal free-play at the top of the pedal pad

Clutch Interlock Switch

▶ **See Figure 38**

1. Loosen the locknut and adjust the clearance between the stopper rubber and the clutch interlock switch threads.

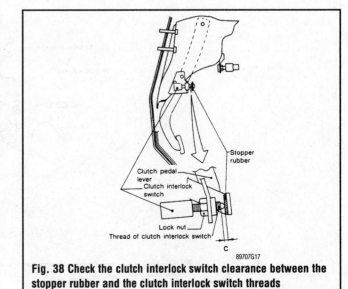

Fig. 38 Check the clutch interlock switch clearance between the stopper rubber and the clutch interlock switch threads

2. Clearance should be 0.004–0.039 in. (0.1–1.0mm) on Altima and 0.012–0.039 in. (0.3–1.0mm) on 240SX.

3. Tighten the locknut securely.

Master Cylinder

▶ See Figure 39

REMOVAL & INSTALLATION

1. Disconnect the clutch pedal arm from the pushrod clevis.
2. Disconnect and cap the hydraulic line at the clutch master cylinder.

✳✳ WARNING

Any brake fluid that is removed from the system should be discarded. Also, do not allow any brake fluid to come in contact with a painted surface; it will damage the paint.

3. Remove the nuts attaching the master cylinder to the firewall.
4. Remove the master cylinder from the engine compartment.

To install:

5. Install the master cylinder and tighten the attaching nuts to 5–8 ft. lbs. (8–11 Nm).

6. Connect the clutch hydraulic line to the master cylinder. Tighten the fitting securely.

7. Connect the clutch pedal arm to the pushrod clevis.

8. Bleed the clutch hydraulic system.

Slave Cylinder

REMOVAL & INSTALLATION

1. Raise and safely support the vehicle.
2. Disconnect and cap the hydraulic line at the slave cylinder.
3. Remove the nuts attaching the slave cylinder to the transmission/transaxle.
4. Remove the slave cylinder.

To install:

5. Install the slave cylinder and tighten the attaching nuts to 22–30 ft. lbs. (30–40 Nm).

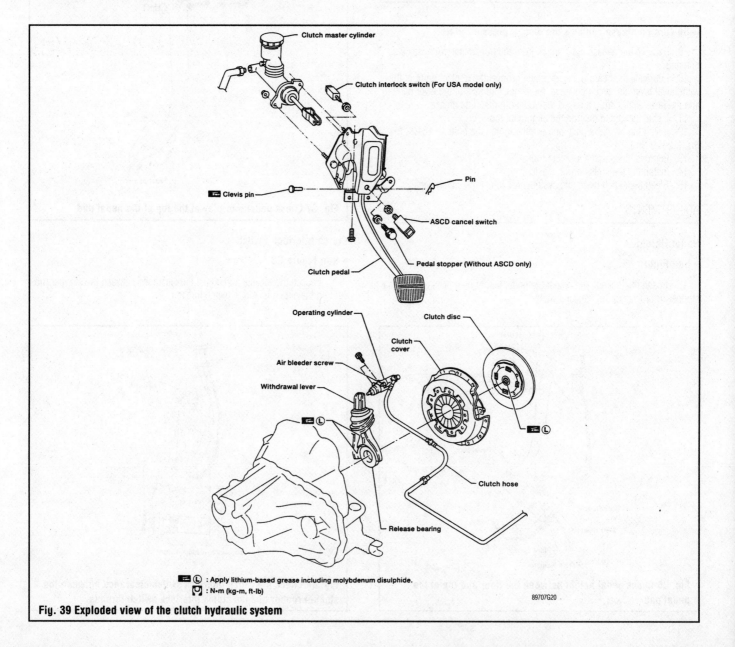

Fig. 39 Exploded view of the clutch hydraulic system

89707G20

6. Connect the clutch hydraulic line to the slave cylinder. Tighten the fitting securely.

7. Bleed the clutch hydraulic system.

HYDRAULIC SYSTEM BLEEDING

⁂ CAUTION

Brake fluid contains polyglycol ethers and polyglycols. Avoid contact with the eyes and wash your hands thoroughly after handling brake fluid. If you do get brake fluid in your eyes, flush your eyes with clean, running water for 15 minutes. If eye irritation persists, or if you have taken brake fluid internally, IMMEDIATELY seek medical assistance.

⁂ WARNING

Clean, high quality brake fluid is essential to the safe and proper operation of the clutch hydraulic system. You should always buy the highest quality brake fluid that is available. If the clutch hydraulic system becomes contaminated, drain and flush the system, then refill the master cylinder with new fluid.

AUTOMATIC TRANSMISSION

Understanding the Automatic Transmission

The automatic transmission allows engine torque and power to be transmitted to the rear wheels within a narrow range of engine operating speeds. It will allow the engine to turn fast enough to produce plenty of power and torque at very low speeds, while keeping it at a sensible rpm at high vehicle speeds (and it does this job without driver assistance). The transmission uses a light fluid as the medium for the transmission of power. This fluid also works in the operation of various hydraulic control circuits and as a lubricant. Because the transmission fluid performs all of these functions, trouble within the unit can easily travel from one part to another. For this reason, and because of the complexity and unusual operating principles of the transmission, a very sound understanding of the basic principles of operation will simplify troubleshooting.

TORQUE CONVERTER

◆ See Figure 40

The torque converter replaces the conventional clutch. It has three functions:

1. It allows the engine to idle with the vehicle at a standstill, even with the transmission in gear.

2. It allows the transmission to shift from range-to-range smoothly, without requiring that the driver close the throttle during the shift.

3. It multiplies engine torque to an increasing extent as vehicle speed drops and throttle opening is increased. This has the effect of making the transmission more responsive and reduces the amount of shifting required.

The torque converter is a metal case which is shaped like a sphere that has been flattened on opposite sides. It is bolted to the rear end of the engine's crankshaft. Generally, the entire metal case rotates at engine speed and serves as the engine's driveplate.

The case contains three sets of blades. One set is attached directly to the case. This set forms the torus or pump. Another set is directly connected to the output shaft, and forms the turbine. The third set is mounted on a hub which, in turn, is mounted on a stationary shaft through a one-way clutch. This third set is known as the stator.

A pump, which is driven by the converter hub at engine speed, keeps the torque converter full of transmission fluid at all times. Fluid flows continuously through the unit to provide cooling.

Under low speed acceleration, the torque converter functions as follows: The torus is turning faster than the turbine. It picks up fluid at the center of the converter and, through centrifugal force, slings it outward. Since the outer edge of the converter moves faster than the portions at the center, the fluid picks up speed.

The fluid then enters the outer edge of the turbine blades. It then travels back toward the center of the converter case along the turbine blades. In impinging upon the turbine blades, the fluid loses the energy picked up in the torus.

If the fluid was now returned directly into the torus, both halves of the converter would have to turn at approximately the same speed at all times, and torque input and output would both be the same.

In flowing through the torus and turbine, the fluid picks up two types of flow, or flow in two separate directions. It flows through the turbine blades, and it spins with the engine. The stator, whose blades are stationary when the vehicle is being accelerated at low speeds, converts one type of flow into another. Instead of allowing the fluid to flow straight back into the torus, the stator's curved blades turn the fluid almost 90° toward the direction of rotation of the engine. Thus the fluid does not flow as fast toward the torus, but is already spinning when the torus picks it up. This has the effect of allowing the torus to turn much faster than the turbine. This difference in

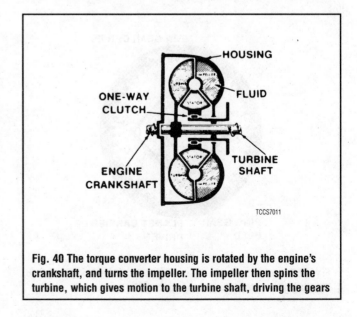

Fig. 40 The torque converter housing is rotated by the engine's crankshaft, and turns the impeller. The impeller then spins the turbine, which gives motion to the turbine shaft, driving the gears

---

Never reuse any brake fluid. Any brake fluid that is removed from the system should be discarded. Also, do not allow any brake fluid to come in contact with a painted surface; it will damage the paint.

1. Check the level of fluid in the clutch master cylinder reservoir and fill to the specified level. During the bleeding process, continue to check and replenish the reservoir to prevent the fluid level from getting lower than ½ the specified level.

2. Remove the dust cap from the bleeder screw on the clutch slave cylinder and connect a clear tube to the bleeder screw. Insert the other end of the tube into a clean, clear plastic or glass container half filled with brake fluid.

3. Pump the clutch pedal SLOWLY several times.

4. Hold the clutch pedal down and loosen the bleeder screw.

5. Tighten the bleeder screw and release the clutch pedal gradually.

6. Repeat until all evidence of air bubbles completely disappears from the brake fluid being pumped out through the tube.

7. When the air is completely removed, securely tighten the bleeder screw and replace the dust cap.

8. Check the level of fluid in the clutch master cylinder reservoir and fill as necessary.

9. Depress the clutch pedal several times to check the operation of the clutch hydraulic system. Check for leaks.

speed may be compared to the difference in speed between the smaller and larger gears in any gear train. The result is that engine power output is higher, and engine torque is multiplied.

As the speed of the turbine increases, the fluid spins faster and faster in the direction of engine rotation. As a result, the ability of the stator to redirect the fluid flow is reduced. Under cruising conditions, the stator is eventually forced to rotate on its one-way clutch in the direction of engine rotation. Under these conditions, the torque converter begins to behave almost like a solid shaft, with the torus and turbine speeds being almost equal.

PLANETARY GEARBOX

▶ **See Figures 41, 42 and 43**

The ability of the torque converter to multiply engine torque is limited. Also, the unit tends to be more efficient when the turbine is rotating at relatively high speeds. Therefore, a planetary gearbox is used to carry the power output of the turbine to the driveshaft.

Planetary gears function very similarly to conventional transmission gears. However, their construction is different in that three elements make up one gear system, and, in that all three elements are different from one

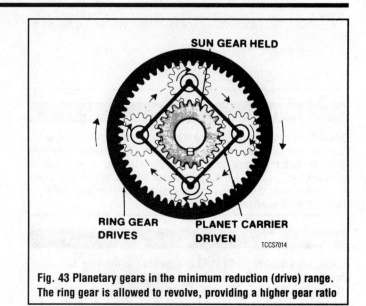

Fig. 43 Planetary gears in the minimum reduction (drive) range. The ring gear is allowed to revolve, providing a higher gear ratio

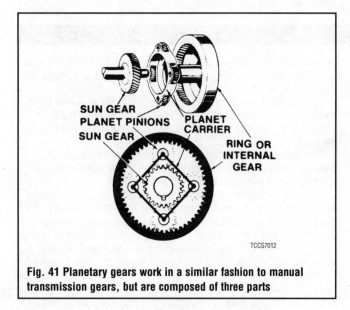

Fig. 41 Planetary gears work in a similar fashion to manual transmission gears, but are composed of three parts

another. The three elements are: an outer gear that is shaped like a hoop, with teeth cut into the inner surface; a sun gear, mounted on a shaft and located at the very center of the outer gear; and a set of three planet gears, held by pins in a ring-like planet carrier, meshing with both the sun gear and the outer gear. Either the outer gear or the sun gear may be held stationary, providing more than one possible torque multiplication factor for each set of gears. Also, if all three gears are forced to rotate at the same speed, the gearset forms, in effect, a solid shaft.

Most automatics use the planetary gears to provide various reductions ratios. Bands and clutches are used to hold various portions of the gearsets to the transmission case or to the shaft on which they are mounted. Shifting is accomplished, then, by changing the portion of each planetary gearset which is held to the transmission case or to the shaft.

SERVOS & ACCUMULATORS

▶ **See Figure 44**

The servos are hydraulic pistons and cylinders. They resemble the hydraulic actuators used on many other machines, such as bulldozers. Hydraulic fluid enters the cylinder, under pressure, and forces the piston to move to engage the band or clutches.

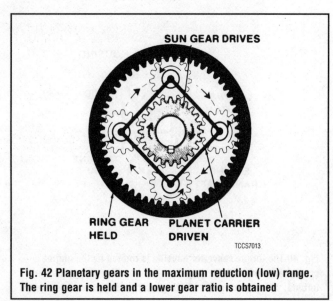

Fig. 42 Planetary gears in the maximum reduction (low) range. The ring gear is held and a lower gear ratio is obtained

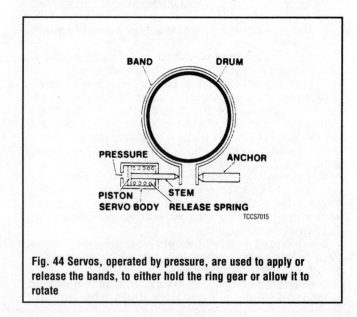

Fig. 44 Servos, operated by pressure, are used to apply or release the bands, to either hold the ring gear or allow it to rotate

The accumulators are used to cushion the engagement of the servos. The transmission fluid must pass through the accumulator on the way to the servo. The accumulator housing contains a thin piston which is sprung away from the discharge passage of the accumulator. When fluid passes through the accumulator on the way to the servo, it must move the piston against spring pressure, and this action smoothes out the action of the servo.

HYDRAULIC CONTROL SYSTEM

The hydraulic pressure used to operate the servos comes from the main transmission oil pump. This fluid is channeled to the various servos through the shift valves. There is generally a manual shift valve which is operated by the transmission selector lever and an automatic shift valve for each automatic upshift the transmission provides.

➡**Many new transmissions are electronically controlled. On these models, electrical solenoids are used to better control the hydraulic fluid. Usually, the solenoids are regulated by an electronic control module.**

There are two pressures which affect the operation of these valves. One is the governor pressure which is effected by vehicle speed. The other is the modulator pressure which is effected by intake manifold vacuum or throttle position. Governor pressure rises with an increase in vehicle speed, and modulator pressure rises as the throttle is opened wider. By responding to these two pressures, the shift valves cause the upshift points to be delayed with increased throttle opening to make the best use of the engine's power output.

Most transmissions also make use of an auxiliary circuit for downshifting. This circuit may be actuated by the throttle linkage the vacuum line which actuates the modulator, by a cable or by a solenoid. It applies pressure to a special downshift surface on the shift valve or valves.

The transmission modulator also governs the line pressure, used to actuate the servos. In this way, the clutches and bands will be actuated with a force matching the torque output of the engine.

Neutral Safety Switch

REMOVAL & INSTALLATION

◆ See Figure 45

The switch unit is bolted to the transmission case, behind the transmission shift lever. The switch prevents the engine from being started in any transmission position except **P** or **N**. It also controls the back-up lights.

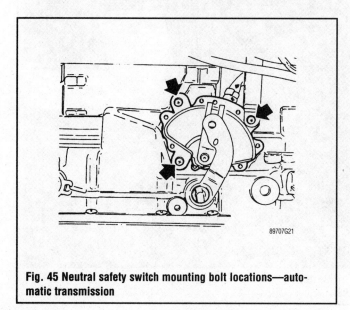

Fig. 45 Neutral safety switch mounting bolt locations—automatic transmission

1. Raise and safely support the vehicle.
2. Disconnect the manual control linkage from the manual shaft.
3. Remove the switch attaching bolts.
4. Remove the switch from the transmission.
To install:
5. Install the switch on the transmission and hand-tighten the attaching bolts.
6. Adjust the switch and tighten the bolts securely.
7. Connect the manual control linkage to the manual shaft.
8. Adjust the manual control linkage as necessary.
9. Lower the vehicle.

ADJUSTMENT

◆ See Figure 46

1. Place the transmission selector lever in **N**.
2. Loosen the attaching bolts.
3. With an aligning pin (2.0mm diameter) installed in the switch, move the switch until the pin falls into the hole in the rotor.
4. Tighten the attaching bolts securely.
5. Ensure that the engine will start only in **P** or **N**.
6. Ensure that the back-up lights go on only in **R**.

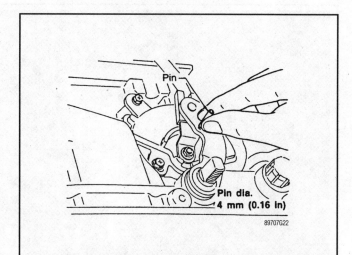

Fig. 46 Insert the adjusting pin into both the neutral safety switch and the manual shaft—automatic transmission

Back-up Light Switch

REMOVAL & INSTALLATION

Refer to the Neutral Safety Switch service procedures, as this switch also controls the back-up lights.

Extension Housing Seal

REMOVAL & INSTALLATION

1. Raise the vehicle and support it safely.
2. Matchmark the driveshaft (if the driveshaft is not installed in the correct position, it may cause a vibration) and differential companion flanges.
3. Loosen the companion flange bolts and lower the driveshaft from the differential.
4. Carefully withdraw the driveshaft from the transmission. Plug the extension opening to prevent leakage.

5. Using the proper tool, remove the oil seal from the extension.

To install:

6. Wipe all seal contact surfaces clean. Coat the lip of the new seal with clean transmission fluid.

7. Using the proper drift tool, drive the new seal into the extension housing.

8. Insert the driveshaft into the extension housing, making sure the splines are properly engaged.

9. Install the driveshaft.

10. Lower the vehicle.

Automatic Transmission Assembly

REMOVAL & INSTALLATION

▶ **See Figures 47, 48 and 49**

1. Disconnect the negative battery cable.
2. Raise and safely support the vehicle.
3. Label and disconnect the transmission electrical harness.
4. Disconnect and cap the transmission cooler lines.

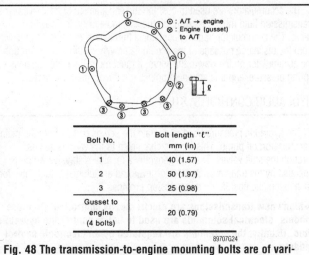

⊚ : A/T → engine
⊗ : Engine (gusset) to A/T

Bolt No.	Bolt length "ℓ" mm (in)
1	40 (1.57)
2	50 (1.97)
3	25 (0.98)
Gusset to engine (4 bolts)	20 (0.79)

89707G24

Fig. 48 The transmission-to-engine mounting bolts are of various lengths. Install the bolts in their original positions and tighten to the specified torque

89708P44

Fig. 47 View of the automatic transmission from under the vehicle—240SX

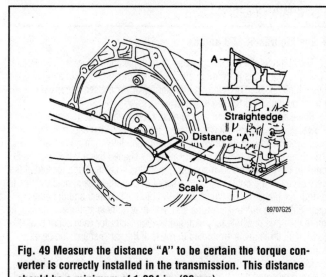

Fig. 49 Measure the distance "A" to be certain the torque converter is correctly installed in the transmission. This distance should be a minimum of 1.024 in. (26mm)

5. Remove the control linkage from the selector lever.
6. Remove the driveshaft.

➡**Insert a plug into the rear oil seal after removing the driveshaft. Take care to not damage the spline, sleeve yoke and rear oil seal when removing the driveshaft.**

7. Remove the heat insulator from the catalytic converter.
8. Remove the exhaust pipe bracket and separate the rear exhaust pipe from the converter.
9. Remove the starter motor.
10. Remove the gussets and end plate.
11. Remove the bolt securing the torque converter to the driveplate. Turn the crankshaft to gain access to subsequent bolts.
12. Support the transmission with a jack.
13. Remove the rear transmission mounting bracket.
14. Lower the transmission as much as possible without damaging other components.
15. Remove the transmission-to-engine attaching bolts.
16. Pull the transmission back and away from the engine, then lower it from the vehicle.
To install:
17. Check the driveplate run-out. Maximum allowable run-out is 0.020 in. (0.5 mm). Replace the driveplate as necessary.
18. As required, install the torque converter in the transmission. The torque converter is correctly installed when the distance between the bell housing and the converter boss is at least 1.024 in. (26mm), as illustrated.

19. Position the transmission on the engine and install the transmission-to-engine attaching bolts. Tighten the bolts as follows:
   a. Tighten bolts labeled No. 1 and 2 to 29–36 ft. lbs. (39–49 Nm).
   b. Tighten all other bolts to 22–29 ft. lbs. (29–39 Nm).

➡**Bolts are of varying lengths. Install the bolts in their proper positions.**

20. The remainder of the installation procedure is the reverse of removal.

ADJUSTMENTS

◆ **See Figure 50**

If the detents cannot be felt or the pointer indicator is improperly aligned while shifting from the **P** range to range **1**, the linkage should be adjusted.

➡**If the vehicle has an automatic transmission interlock system, the system will prevent the transmission selector from being shifted from the P position unless the brake pedal is depressed.**

1. Place the shifter in the **P** position.
2. Loosen the locknuts.
3. Tighten the outer locknut **X** until it touches the trunnion, pulling the selector lever toward the **R** range side without pushing the button.
4. Back off the outer locknut **X** ¼–½ turn, then tighten the inner locknut **Y** to 5–11 ft. lbs. (8–15 Nm).
5. Move the selector lever from **P** to **1**. Make sure it moves smoothly.

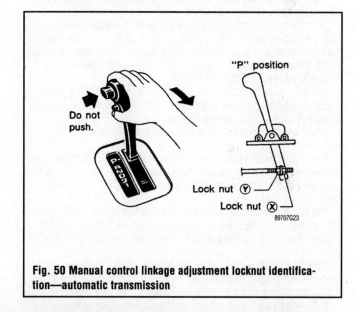

Fig. 50 Manual control linkage adjustment locknut identification—automatic transmission

AUTOMATIC TRANSAXLE

Understanding the Automatic Transaxle

The automatic transaxle allows engine torque and power to be transmitted to the front wheels within a narrow range of engine operating speeds. It will allow the engine to turn fast enough to produce plenty of power and torque at very low speeds, while keeping it at a sensible rpm at high vehicle speeds (and it does this job without driver assistance). The transaxle uses a light fluid as the medium for the transmission of power. This fluid also works in the operation of various hydraulic control circuits and as a lubricant. Because the transaxle fluid performs all of these functions, trouble within the unit can easily travel from one part to another. For this reason, and because of the complexity and unusual operating principles of the transaxle, a very sound understanding of the basic principles of operation will simplify troubleshooting.

TORQUE CONVERTER

◆ **See Figure 51**

The torque converter replaces the conventional clutch. It has three functions:

1. It allows the engine to idle with the vehicle at a standstill, even with the transaxle in gear.
2. It allows the transaxle to shift from range-to-range smoothly, without requiring that the driver close the throttle during the shift.
3. It multiplies engine torque to an increasing extent as vehicle speed drops and throttle opening is increased. This has the effect of making the transaxle more responsive and reduces the amount of shifting required.

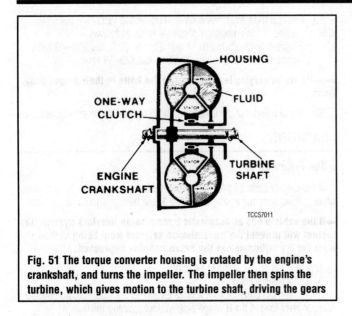

Fig. 51 The torque converter housing is rotated by the engine's crankshaft, and turns the impeller. The impeller then spins the turbine, which gives motion to the turbine shaft, driving the gears

The torque converter is a metal case which is shaped like a sphere that has been flattened on opposite sides. It is bolted to the rear end of the engine's crankshaft. Generally, the entire metal case rotates at engine speed and serves as the engine's driveplate.

The case contains three sets of blades. One set is attached directly to the case. This set forms the torus or pump. Another set is directly connected to the output shaft, and forms the turbine. The third set is mounted on a hub which, in turn, is mounted on a stationary shaft through a one-way clutch. This third set is known as the stator.

A pump, which is driven by the converter hub at engine speed, keeps the torque converter full of transmission fluid at all times. Fluid flows continuously through the unit to provide cooling.

Under low speed acceleration, the torque converter functions as follows:

The torus is turning faster than the turbine. It picks up fluid at the center of the converter and, through centrifugal force, slings it outward. Since the outer edge of the converter moves faster than the portions at the center, the fluid picks up speed.

The fluid then enters the outer edge of the turbine blades. It then travels back toward the center of the converter case along the turbine blades. In impinging upon the turbine blades, the fluid loses the energy picked up in the torus.

If the fluid was now returned directly into the torus, both halves of the converter would have to turn at approximately the same speed at all times, and torque input and output would both be the same.

In flowing through the torus and turbine, the fluid picks up two types of flow, or flow in two separate directions. It flows through the turbine blades, and it spins with the engine. The stator, whose blades are stationary when the vehicle is being accelerated at low speeds, converts one type of flow into another. Instead of allowing the fluid to flow straight back into the torus, the stator's curved blades turn the fluid almost 90° toward the direction of rotation of the engine. Thus the fluid does not flow as fast toward the torus, but is already spinning when the torus picks it up. This has the effect of allowing the torus to turn much faster than the turbine. This difference in speed may be compared to the difference in speed between the smaller and larger gears in any gear train. The result is that engine power output is higher, and engine torque is multiplied.

As the speed of the turbine increases, the fluid spins faster and faster in the direction of engine rotation. As a result, the ability of the stator to redirect the fluid flow is reduced. Under cruising conditions, the stator is eventually forced to rotate on its one-way clutch in the direction of engine rotation. Under these conditions, the torque converter begins to behave almost like a solid shaft, with the torus and turbine speeds being almost equal.

PLANETARY GEARBOX

◆ See Figures 52, 53 and 54

The ability of the torque converter to multiply engine torque is limited. Also, the unit tends to be more efficient when the turbine is rotating at relatively high speeds. Therefore, a planetary gearbox is used to carry the power output of the turbine to the driveshaft.

Planetary gears function very similarly to conventional transaxle gears. However, their construction is different in that three elements make up one gear system, and, in that all three elements are different from one another. The three elements are: an outer gear that is shaped like a hoop, with teeth cut into the inner surface; a sun gear, mounted on a shaft and located at the very center of the outer gear; and a set of three planet gears, held by pins in a ring-like planet carrier, meshing with both the sun gear and the outer gear. Either the outer gear or the sun gear may be held stationary, providing more than one possible torque multiplication factor for each set of gears. Also, if all three gears are forced to rotate at the same speed, the gearset forms, in effect, a solid shaft.

Most automatics use the planetary gears to provide various reductions ratios. Bands and clutches are used to hold various portions of the gearsets

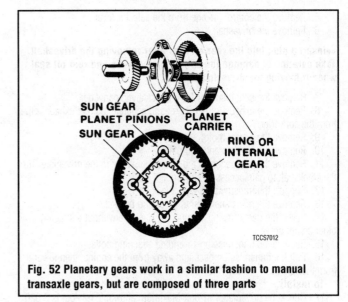

Fig. 52 Planetary gears work in a similar fashion to manual transaxle gears, but are composed of three parts

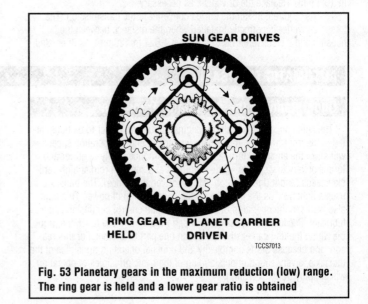

Fig. 53 Planetary gears in the maximum reduction (low) range. The ring gear is held and a lower gear ratio is obtained

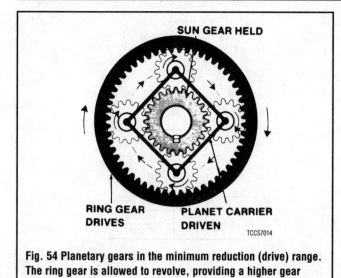

Fig. 54 Planetary gears in the minimum reduction (drive) range. The ring gear is allowed to revolve, providing a higher gear ratio

to the transaxle case or to the shaft on which they are mounted. Shifting is accomplished, then, by changing the portion of each planetary gearset which is held to the transaxle case or to the shaft.

SERVOS & ACCUMULATORS

▶ See Figure 55

The servos are hydraulic pistons and cylinders. They resemble the hydraulic actuators used on many other machines, such as bulldozers. Hydraulic fluid enters the cylinder, under pressure, and forces the piston to move to engage the band or clutches.

The accumulators are used to cushion the engagement of the servos. The transmission fluid must pass through the accumulator on the way to the servo. The accumulator housing contains a thin piston which is sprung away from the discharge passage of the accumulator. When fluid passes through the accumulator on the way to the servo, it must move the piston against spring pressure, and this action smoothes out the action of the servo.

HYDRAULIC CONTROL SYSTEM

The hydraulic pressure used to operate the servos comes from the main transaxle oil pump. This fluid is channeled to the various servos through

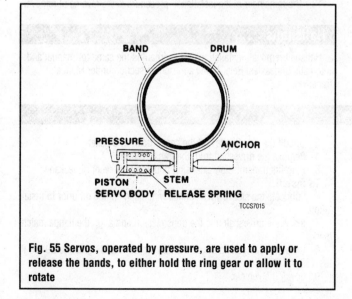

Fig. 55 Servos, operated by pressure, are used to apply or release the bands, to either hold the ring gear or allow it to rotate

the shift valves. There is generally a manual shift valve which is operated by the transaxle selector lever and an automatic shift valve for each automatic upshift the transaxle provides.

→**Many new transaxles are electronically controlled. On these models, electrical solenoids are used to better control the hydraulic fluid. Usually, the solenoids are regulated by an electronic control module.**

There are two pressures which affect the operation of these valves. One is the governor pressure which is effected by vehicle speed. The other is the modulator pressure which is effected by intake manifold vacuum or throttle position. Governor pressure rises with an increase in vehicle speed, and modulator pressure rises as the throttle is opened wider. By responding to these two pressures, the shift valves cause the upshift points to be delayed with increased throttle opening to make the best use of the engine's power output.

Most transaxles also make use of an auxiliary circuit for downshifting. This circuit may be actuated by the throttle linkage the vacuum line which actuates the modulator, by a cable or by a solenoid. It applies pressure to a special downshift surface on the shift valve or valves.

The transaxle modulator also governs the line pressure, used to actuate the servos. In this way, the clutches and bands will be actuated with a force matching the torque output of the engine.

Neutral Safety Switch

REMOVAL & INSTALLATION

▶ See Figure 56

The switch unit is bolted to the transaxle case, behind the shift lever. The switch prevents the engine from being started in any transaxle position except **P** or **N**. It also controls the back-up lights.

1. Raise and safely support the vehicle.
2. Disconnect the manual control linkage from the manual shaft.
3. Remove the switch attaching bolts.
4. Remove the switch from the transaxle.

To install:

5. Mount the switch on the transaxle and hand-tighten the attaching bolts.
6. Adjust the switch and tighten the bolts securely.
7. Connect the manual control linkage to the manual shaft.
8. Adjust the manual control linkage as necessary.
9. Lower the vehicle.

Fig. 56 Neutral safety switch mounting bolt locations—automatic transaxle

ADJUSTMENT

▶ **See Figure 57**

1. Place the transaxle selector lever in **N**.
2. Loosen the attaching bolts.
3. Insert a 0.16 in. (4mm) diameter aligning pin into the switch, then move the switch until the pin falls into the hole in the rotor.
4. Tighten the attaching bolts securely.
5. Ensure that the engine will start only in **P** or **N**.
6. Ensure that the back-up lights go on only in **R**.

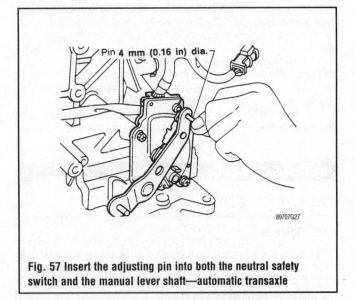

Fig. 57 Insert the adjusting pin into both the neutral safety switch and the manual lever shaft—automatic transaxle

Automatic Transaxle Assembly

REMOVAL & INSTALLATION

▶ **See Figure 58**

1. Disconnect the negative, then the positive battery cables.
2. Remove the battery and battery bracket.
3. Remove the air cleaner box and mass air flow sensor.
4. Label and disconnect the transaxle electrical harnesses.
5. Remove the crankshaft position sensor.
6. Remove the passenger's side mounting bracket from the vehicle.
7. Disconnect the control cable at the transaxle.
8. Drain and recycle the transmission fluid.

➡**Take note of the condition of the fluid as it is draining. Milky fluid (which shows up as streaks of white) indicates the presence of**

DRIVELINE

Driveshaft and U-Joints

REMOVAL & INSTALLATION

▶ **See Figure 59**

The 240SX uses a driveshaft with three U-joints and a center support bearing. The driveshaft is balanced as an assembly.
1. Raise and safely support the vehicle.
2. Matchmark the flanges on the driveshaft and differential for installation reference; this will help maintain driveline balance.

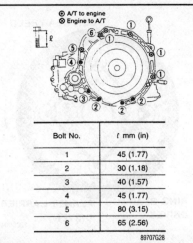

Bolt No.	ℓ mm (in)
1	45 (1.77)
2	30 (1.18)
3	40 (1.57)
4	45 (1.77)
5	80 (3.15)
6	65 (2.56)

89707G28

Fig. 58 Transaxle-to-engine mounting bolts are of various lengths. Install the bolts in their original positions and tighten to the specified torque

moisture. Silvery streaks in the fluid indicate the presence of metal. If either condition exists, serious problems may exist inside the transaxle.

9. Remove the halfshafts.
10. Disconnect and cap the oil cooler pipes.
11. Remove the starter motor.
12. Support the engine by placing a jack beneath the oil pan. Use a piece of wood between the jack and oil pan as a cushion.
13. Remove the center member.
14. Remove the rear plate cover and disconnect the torque converter from the driveplate.
15. Remove the transaxle-to-engine bolts.
16. Pull the transaxle away from the engine and lower it from the vehicle carefully.

To install:

17. Position the transaxle to the engine and install the transaxle-to-engine attaching bolts. Tighten the bolts as follows:
   a. Tighten bolts labeled No. 1 to 29–36 ft. lbs. (39–49 Nm).
   b. Tighten bolts labeled No. 2, 3, 5 and 6 to 22–27 ft. lbs. (30–36 Nm).
   c. Tighten bolt labeled No. 4 to 22–27 ft. lbs. (30–36 Nm).

➡**Bolts are of varying lengths. Install the bolts in their proper positions.**

18. The remainder of the installation procedure is the reverse of removal.

Halfshafts

Halfshaft removal, installation and overhaul is the same for manual and automatic transaxles. Refer to the appropriate section under Manual Transaxle.

3. Unbolt the rear flange and the center bearing bracket.
4. Remove the driveshaft from the transmission.
5. Plug the transmission extension housing to prevent oil leakage.
To install:
6. Lubricate the sleeve yoke splines with clean engine oil prior to installation.
7. Insert the driveshaft into the transmission and align the flange matchmarks.
8. Install the flange and the center bearing bolts and tighten to 29–33 ft. lbs. (39–44 Nm).
9. Lower the vehicle.

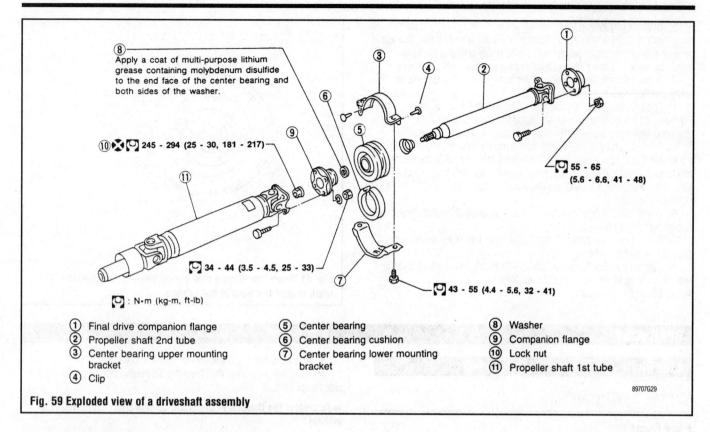

Apply a coat of multi-purpose lithium grease containing molybdenum disulfide to the end face of the center bearing and both sides of the washer.

⑩ ✕ 🔧 245 - 294 (25 - 30, 181 - 217)

🔧 55 - 65 (5.6 - 6.6, 41 - 48)

🔧 34 - 44 (3.5 - 4.5, 25 - 33)

🔧 43 - 55 (4.4 - 5.6, 32 - 41)

🔧 : N•m (kg-m, ft-lb)

① Final drive companion flange
② Propeller shaft 2nd tube
③ Center bearing upper mounting bracket
④ Clip
⑤ Center bearing
⑥ Center bearing cushion
⑦ Center bearing lower mounting bracket
⑧ Washer
⑨ Companion flange
⑩ Lock nut
⑪ Propeller shaft 1st tube

89707G29

Fig. 59 Exploded view of a driveshaft assembly

U-JOINT REPLACEMENT

1. Mark the relationship of all components for reassembly.
2. Remove the snaprings. On early units, the snaprings are seated in the yokes. On later units, the snaprings seat in the needle bearing races.
3. Tap the yoke with a brass or rubber mallet to release one bearing cap. Be careful not to lose the needle rollers.
4. Remove the other bearing caps.
5. Remove the U-joint spiders from the yokes.

To assemble:

➧U-joint spiders must be replaced if their bearing journals are worn more than 0.006 in. (0.15mm) from their original diameter.

6. Place the needle rollers in the races and hold them in place with grease.
7. Put the spiders into place in their yokes.
8. Replace all seals and bearing caps.
9. Tap the races into position and secure them with snaprings.

➧On later model vehicles with snaprings seated in the needle bearing races, different thicknesses of snaprings are available for U-joint adjustment. The play should not exceed 0.007 in. (0.02mm).

10. Inspect the U-joint assembly. Spline backlash should not exceed 0.019 in. (0.5mm) and driveshaft run-out should not exceed 0.024 in (0.6mm).

DRIVESHAFT BALANCING

◆ **See Figure 60**

To check and correct an unbalanced driveshaft, proceed as follows:
1. Remove the undercoating and other foreign material which could upset shaft balance. Road test the vehicle.
2. If vibration is noted, disconnect the driveshaft at the differential carrier companion flange, then rotate the companion flange 90, 180 or 270 degrees and reconnect the driveshaft.
3. Roadtest the vehicle; if vibration still exists, replace the driveshaft assembly. Note that the driveshaft should be free of dents or cracks and run-out should not exceed 0.024 in. (0.6mm).

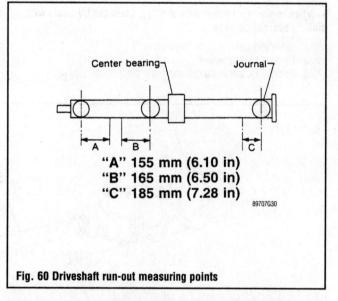

"A" 155 mm (6.10 in)
"B" 165 mm (6.50 in)
"C" 185 mm (7.28 in)

89707G30

Fig. 60 Driveshaft run-out measuring points

Center Bearing

REMOVAL & INSTALLATION

◆ **See Figure 61**

The center bearing is a sealed unit, which must be replaced as an assembly if defective.
1. Remove the driveshaft assembly.
2. Matchmark the flanges behind the center yoke for installation reference.
3. Matchmark the front driveshaft with the mark made on the flanges.
4. Remove the bolts and separate the shafts.

5. Devise a way to hold the driveshaft while unbolting the companion flange from the front driveshaft. Do not place the front driveshaft tube in a vise, because chances are it will get crushed. The best way is to grip the flange somehow while loosening the nut. It will require some strength to remove.

6. Press the companion flange off the front driveshaft and press the center bearing from its mount.

7. The new bearing is already lubricated. Install it into the mount, making sure that the seals and so on are facing the same way as when removed. Also make sure the "F" mark is facing the front of the vehicle.

8. Slide the companion flange onto the front driveshaft, aligning the marks made during removal. Install the washer and locknut. If the washer and locknut are separate pieces, tighten them to 145–175 ft. lbs. (106–129 Nm). If the washer and locknut are one piece, tighten it to 180–217 ft. lbs. (132–160 Nm).

9. Check that the bearing rotates freely around the driveshaft. Stake the nut (always use a new nut).

10. Connect the companion flange to the other half of the driveshaft, aligning the matchmarks.

11. Tighten the front flange bolts to 25–33 ft. lbs. (34–44 Nm) and the rear flange bolts to 41–48 ft. lbs. (55–65 Nm).

12. Install the driveshaft.

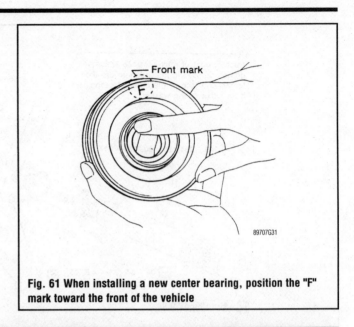

Fig. 61 When installing a new center bearing, position the "F" mark toward the front of the vehicle

REAR AXLE

Axle Shaft

REMOVAL & INSTALLATION

♦ See Figure 62

➡When removing the rear axle shaft(s), cover the CV-boots with cloth to prevent damage.

1. Raise and safely support the vehicle.
2. Remove the rear wheel.
3. Remove the adjusting cap and cotter pin from the axle nut.

4. Apply the parking brake and remove the axle nut.
5. Disconnect the axle shaft from the differential side by removing the side flange bolts.

➡To protect the threads of the shaft, temporarily install the axle locknut.

6. Grasp the axle shaft at the center and extract it from the wheel hub. This may be done by prying it with a prybar or by tapping it with a wooden block and mallet.
    To install:
7. Insert the shaft into the wheel hub and temporarily install the axle locknut.

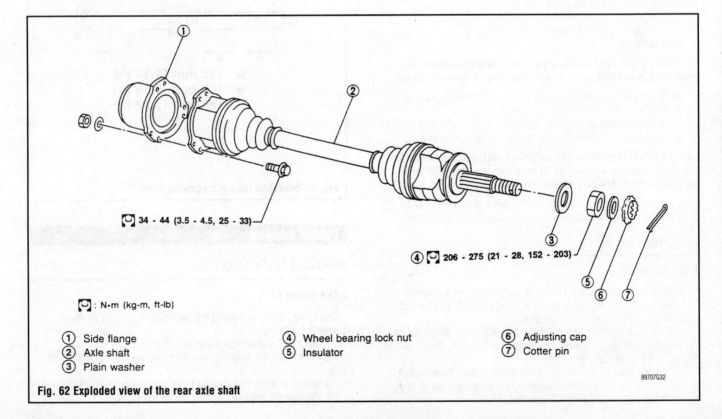

34 - 44 (3.5 - 4.5, 25 - 33)

④ 206 - 275 (21 - 28, 152 - 203)

: N·m (kg-m, ft-lb)

① Side flange
② Axle shaft
③ Plain washer
④ Wheel bearing lock nut
⑤ Insulator
⑥ Adjusting cap
⑦ Cotter pin

Fig. 62 Exploded view of the rear axle shaft

➡️Take care not to damage the oil seal on either end of the axle shaft.

8. Connect the axle shaft to the differential and install the flange bolts. Tighten the flange bolts to 25–33 ft. lbs. (34–44 Nm).

9. Apply the parking brake and tighten the axle locknut to152–203 ft. lbs. (206–275 Nm).

10. Install a new cotter pin and adjusting cap.
11. Install the rear wheel.
12. Lower the vehicle.

Axle Shaft Seal

REMOVAL & INSTALLATION

▶ **See Figure 63**

1. Remove the axle shaft.
2. Matchmark the side flange, then remove it using a suitable puller.
3. Remove the oil seal.

To install:

4. Apply multi-purpose grease to the sealing lips of the oil seal. Press the oil seal into the carrier.
5. Install the side flange with special tool J39352, or equivalent.
6. Install the axle shaft. Check the fluid level.

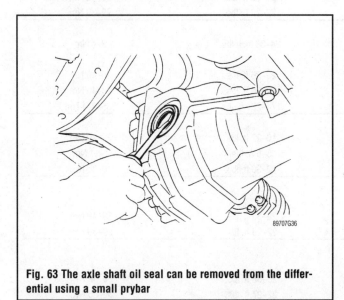

Fig. 63 The axle shaft oil seal can be removed from the differential using a small prybar

Pinion Seal

REMOVAL & INSTALLATION

▶ **See Figures 64, 65 and 66**

1. Remove the driveshaft.
2. Loosen the drive pinion nut. A companion flange holding tool can be manufactured from a piece of steel.
3. Matchmark and remove the companion flange, using a jaw type puller.
4. Remove the front oil seal from the differential carrier.

To install:

5. Apply multi-purpose grease to the sealing lips of the oil seal.
6. Press the front oil seal into the carrier using a seal driver.
7. Install the companion flange and drive pinion nut.
8. Tighten the drive pinion nut to 137–217 ft. lbs. (186–294 Nm).
9. Install the driveshaft.

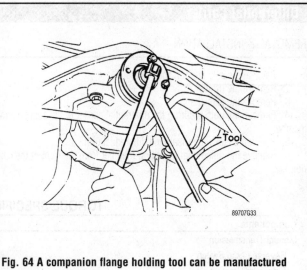

Fig. 64 A companion flange holding tool can be manufactured from a piece of steel

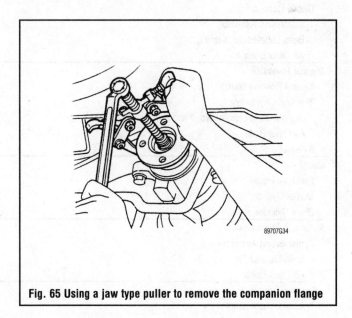

Fig. 65 Using a jaw type puller to remove the companion flange

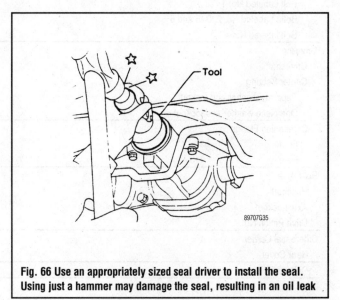

Fig. 66 Use an appropriately sized seal driver to install the seal. Using just a hammer may damage the seal, resulting in an oil leak

Differential Carrier

REMOVAL & INSTALLATION

1. Raise and safely support the vehicle.
2. Remove the driveshaft.
3. Remove the axle shafts.
4. Remove the nuts securing the differential carrier to the suspension members.
5. Position a jack underneath the differential unit.
6. Remove the differential mounting member from the front of the carrier.

7. Move the differential forward, together with the jack.
8. Remove the rear cover stud bolts from the suspension member.
9. Lower the differential carrier using the jack.

To install:

10. Position the differential carrier in the vehicle using the jack.
11. Install the rear cover stud bolts and tighten to 72–87 ft. lbs. (98–118 Nm).
12. Move the differential rearward, together with the jack.
13. Install the differential mounting member on the front of the carrier and tighten to 72–87 ft. lbs. (98–118 Nm).
14. Install the axle shafts.
15. Install the driveshaft.
16. Lower the vehicle.

TORQUE SPECIFICATIONS

Components	English Specification	Metric Specification
Manual Transmission		
Reverse Lamp Switch	14–22 ft. lbs.	20–29 Nm
Extension Housing Seal		
Flange Bolts	29–33 ft. lbs.	34–44 Nm
Center Bearing Bolts	32–41 ft. lbs.	43–55 Nm
Transmission Assembly		
Bolts Labeled No. 1 and 2	29–36 ft. lbs.	39–49 Nm
All Other Bolts	22–29 ft. lbs.	29–39 Nm
Manual Transaxle		
Neutral Position Switch	24–36 inch lbs.	3–4 Nm
Transaxle Assembly		
Tighten Bolts Labeled No. 1 and 2	29–36 ft. lbs.	39–49 Nm
All Other Bolts	22–30 ft. lbs.	30–40 Nm
Axle Nut	174–231 ft. lbs.	235–314 Nm
Clutch		
Pressure Plate	16–22 ft. lbs.	22–29 Nm
Master Cylinder	5–8 ft. lbs.	8–11 Nm
Slave Cylinder	22–30 ft. lbs.	30–40 Nm
Automatic Transmission		
Transmission Assembly		
Bolts Labeled No. 1 and 2	29–36 ft. lbs.	39–49 Nm
All Other Bolts	22–29 ft. lbs.	29–39 Nm
Automatic Transaxle		
Transaxle Assembly		
Bolt Labeled No. 1	29–36 ft. lbs.	39–49 Nm
Bolts Labeled No. 2, 3, 5 and 6	22–27 ft. lbs.	30–36 Nm
Bolt labeled No. 4	22–27 ft. lbs.	30–36 Nm
Driveline		
Driveshaft	29–33 ft. lbs.	39–44 Nm
Center Bearing		
Separate washer and locknut	145–175 ft. lbs.	106–129 Nm
One piece washer and locknut	180–217 ft. lbs.	132–160 Nm
Companion Flange		
Front	25–33 ft. lbs.	34–44 Nm
Rear	41–48 ft. lbs.	55–65 Nm
Rear Axle		
Halfshaft	25–33 ft. lbs.	34–44 Nm
Axle Locknut	152–203 ft. lbs.	206–275 Nm
Drive Pinion Nut	137–217 ft. lbs.	186–294 Nm
Differential Carrier		
Rear Cover	72–87 ft. lbs.	98–118 Nm
Differential Mount	72–87 ft. lbs.	98–118 Nm

8

SUSPENSION AND STEERING

WHEELS

Wheels

REMOVAL & INSTALLATION

▶ See Figures 1 thru 7

1. Park the vehicle on a level surface.
2. Remove the jack, tire iron and, if necessary, the spare tire from their storage compartments.
3. Check the owner's manual or refer to Section 1 of this manual for the jacking points on your vehicle. Then, place the jack in the proper position.
4. If equipped with lug nut trim caps, remove them by either unscrewing or pulling them off the lug nuts, as appropriate. Consult the owner's manual, if necessary.

5. If equipped with a wheel cover or hub cap, insert the tapered end of the tire iron in the groove and pry off the cover.
6. Apply the parking brake and block the diagonally opposite wheel with a wheel chock or two.

➡ Wheel chocks may be purchased at your local auto parts store, or a block of wood cut into wedges may be used. If possible, keep one or two of the chocks in your tire storage compartment, in case any of the tires has to be removed on the side of the road.

7. If equipped with an automatic transmission/transaxle, place the selector lever in **P** or Park; with a manual transmission/transaxle, place the shifter in Reverse.
8. With the tires still on the ground, use the tire iron/wrench to break the lug nuts loose.

Fig. 1 Place the jack at the proper lifting point on your vehicle

Fig. 3 With the vehicle still on the ground, break the lug nuts loose using the wrench end of the tire iron

Fig. 2 Before jacking the vehicle, block the diagonally opposite wheel with one or, preferably, two chocks

Fig. 4 After the lug nuts have been loosened, raise the vehicle using the jack until the tire is clear of the ground

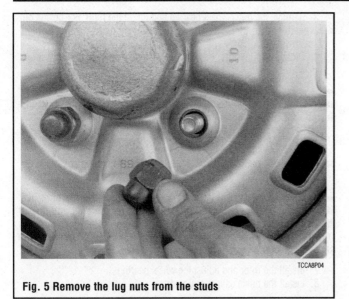

Fig. 5 Remove the lug nuts from the studs

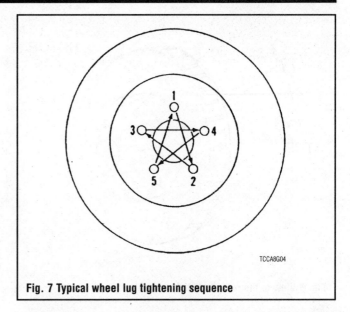

Fig. 7 Typical wheel lug tightening sequence

15. Using a torque wrench, tighten the lug nuts in a crisscross pattern to 72–86 ft. lbs. (98–117 Nm). Check your owner's manual or refer to Section 1 of this manual for the proper tightening sequence.

✳✳ WARNING

Do not overtighten the lug nuts, as this may cause the wheel studs to stretch or the brake disc (rotor) to warp.

16. If so equipped, install the wheel cover or hub cap. Make sure the valve stem protrudes through the proper opening before tapping the wheel cover into position.
17. If equipped, install the lug nut trim caps by pushing them or screwing them on, as applicable.
18. Remove the jack from under the vehicle, and place the jack and tire iron/wrench in their storage compartments. Remove the wheel chock(s).
19. If you have removed a flat or damaged tire, place it in the storage compartment of the vehicle and take it to your local repair station to have it fixed or replaced as soon as possible.

INSPECTION

Inspect the tires for lacerations, puncture marks, nails and other sharp objects. Repair or replace as necessary. Also check the tires for tread wear and air pressure as outlined in Section 1 of this manual.

Check the wheel assemblies for dents, cracks, rust and metal fatigue. Repair or replace as necessary.

Wheel Lug Studs

REPLACEMENT

With Disc Brakes

◗ See Figures 8, 9 and 10

1. Raise and support the appropriate end of the vehicle safely using jackstands, then remove the wheel.
2. Remove the brake pads and caliper. Support the caliper aside using wire or a coat hanger. For details, please refer to Section 9 of this manual.

Fig. 6 Remove the wheel and tire assembly from the vehicle

➡️**If a nut is stuck, never use heat to loosen it or damage to the wheel and bearings may occur. If the nuts are seized, one or two heavy hammer blows directly on the end of the bolt usually loosens the rust. Be careful, as continued pounding will likely damage the brake drum or rotor.**

9. Using the jack, raise the vehicle until the tire is clear of the ground. Support the vehicle safely using jackstands.
10. Remove the lug nuts, then remove the tire and wheel assembly.
To install:
11. Make sure the wheel and hub mating surfaces, as well as the wheel lug studs, are clean and free of all foreign material. Always remove rust from the wheel mounting surface and the brake rotor or drum. Failure to do so may cause the lug nuts to loosen in service.
12. Install the tire and wheel assembly and hand-tighten the lug nuts.
13. Using the tire wrench, tighten all the lug nuts, in a crisscross pattern, until they are snug.
14. Raise the vehicle and withdraw the jackstand, then lower the vehicle.

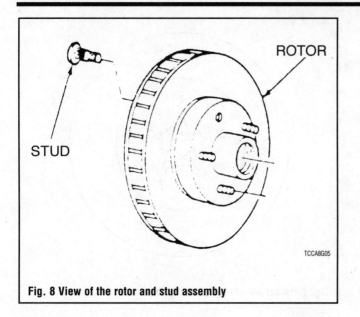

Fig. 8 View of the rotor and stud assembly

3. Remove the outer wheel bearing and lift off the rotor. For details on wheel bearing removal, installation and adjustment, please refer to Section 1 of this manual.

4. Properly support the rotor using press bars, then drive the stud out using an arbor press.

➡ **If a press is not available, CAREFULLY drive the old stud out using a blunt drift. MAKE SURE the rotor is properly and evenly supported or it may be damaged.**

To install:

5. Clean the stud hole with a wire brush and start the new stud with a hammer and drift pin. Do not use any lubricant or thread sealer.

6. Finish installing the stud with the press.

➡ **If a press is not available, start the lug stud through the bore in the hub, then position about 4 flat washers over the stud and thread the lug nut. Hold the hub/rotor while tightening the lug nut, and the stud should be drawn into position. MAKE SURE THE STUD IS FULLY SEATED, then remove the lug nut and washers.**

7. Install the rotor and adjust the wheel bearings.

8. Install the brake caliper and pads.

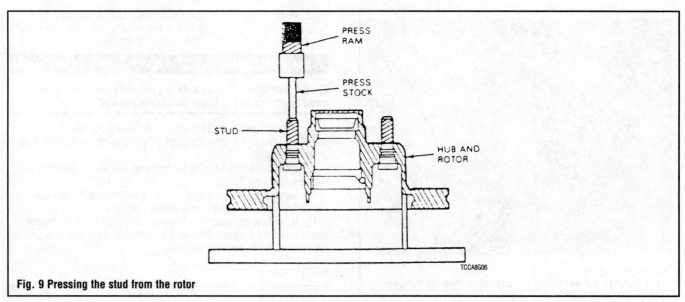

Fig. 9 Pressing the stud from the rotor

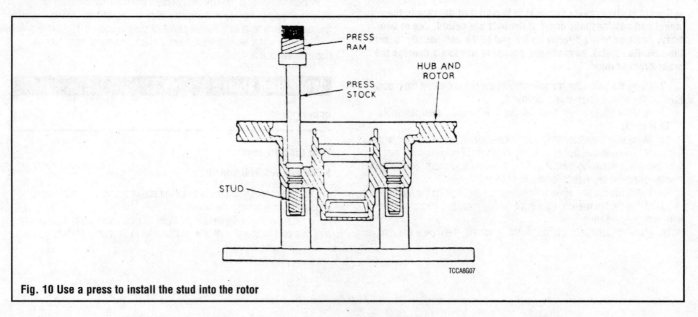

Fig. 10 Use a press to install the stud into the rotor

9. Install the wheel, then remove the jackstands and carefully lower the vehicle.

10. Tighten the lug nuts to the proper torque.

With Drum Brakes

◆ See Figures 11, 12 and 13

1. Raise the vehicle and safely support it with jackstands, then remove the wheel.

2. Remove the brake drum.

3. If necessary to provide clearance, remove the brake shoes, as outlined in Section 9 of this manual.

4. Using a large C-clamp and socket, press the stud from the axle flange.

5. Coat the serrated part of the stud with liquid soap and place it into the hole.

To install:

6. Position about 4 flat washers over the stud and thread the lug nut. Hold the flange while tightening the lug nut, and the stud should be drawn into position. MAKE SURE THE STUD IS FULLY SEATED, then remove the lug nut and washers.

7. If applicable, install the brake shoes.

8. Install the brake drum.

9. Install the wheel, then remove the jackstands and carefully lower the vehicle.

10. Tighten the lug nuts to the proper torque.

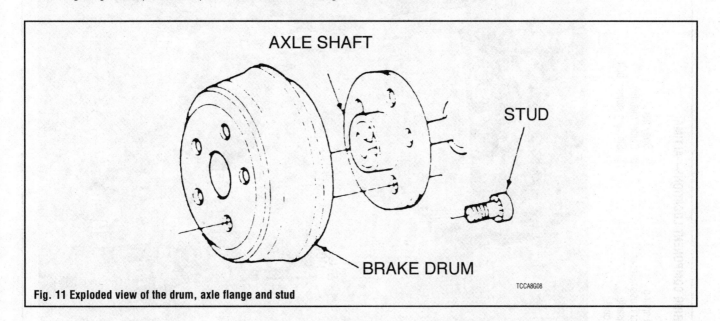

Fig. 11 Exploded view of the drum, axle flange and stud

TCCA8G08

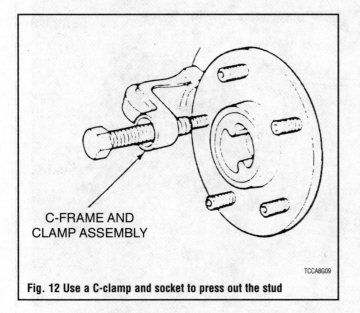

Fig. 12 Use a C-clamp and socket to press out the stud

TCCA8G09

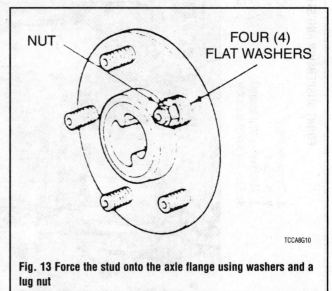

Fig. 13 Force the stud onto the axle flange using washers and a lug nut

TCCA8G10

FRONT SUSPENSION

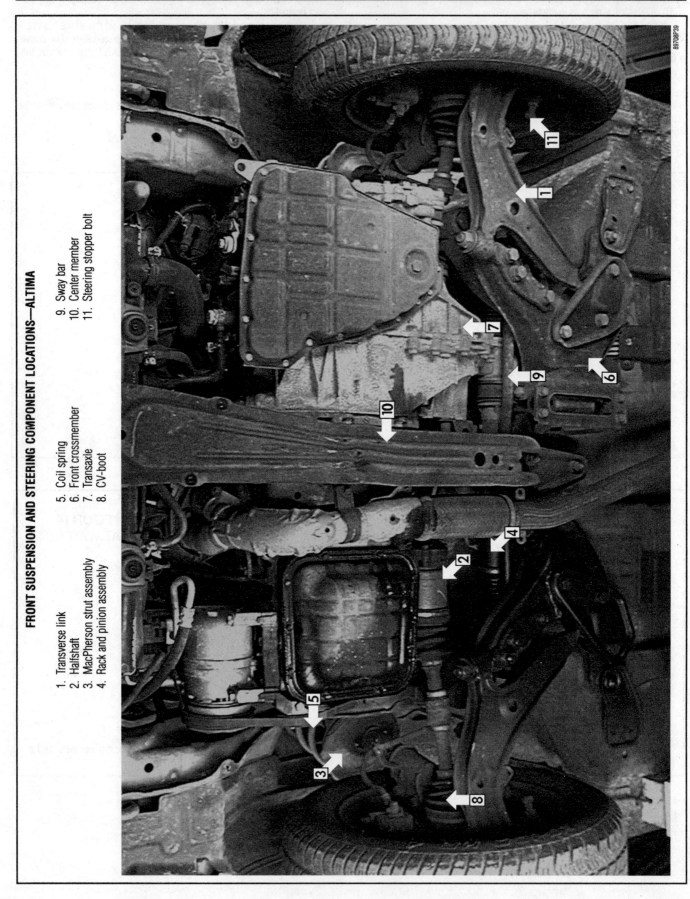

FRONT SUSPENSION AND STEERING COMPONENT LOCATIONS—ALTIMA

1. Transverse link
2. Halfshaft
3. MacPherson strut assembly
4. Rack and pinion assembly
5. Coil spring
6. Front crossmember
7. Transaxle
8. CV-boot
9. Sway bar
10. Center member
11. Steering stopper bolt

89708P29

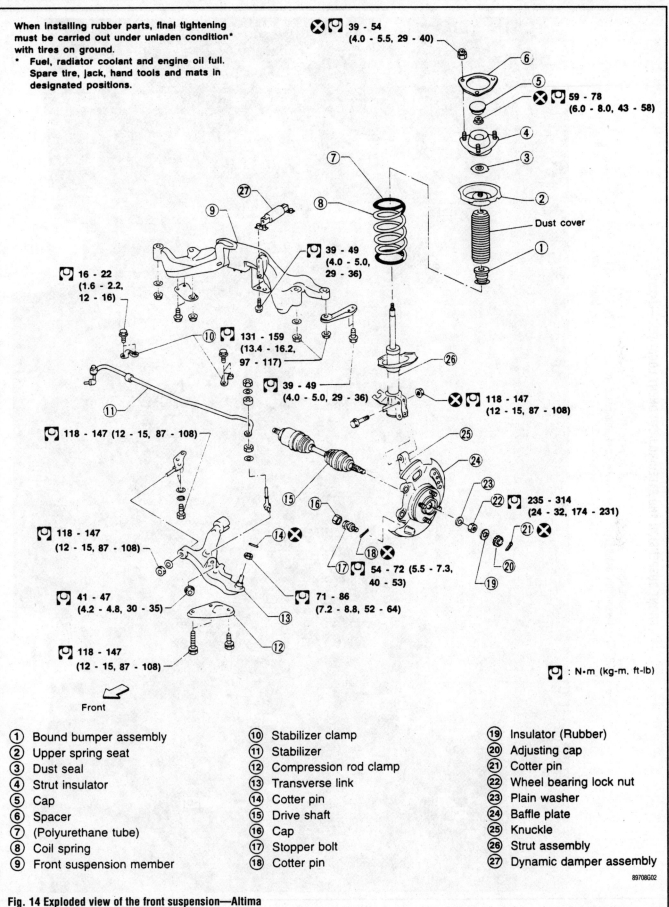

When installing rubber parts, final tightening must be carried out under unladen condition* with tires on ground.
* Fuel, radiator coolant and engine oil full. Spare tire, jack, hand tools and mats in designated positions.

39 - 54 (4.0 - 5.5, 29 - 40)

59 - 78 (6.0 - 8.0, 43 - 58)

Dust cover

16 - 22 (1.6 - 2.2, 12 - 16)

39 - 49 (4.0 - 5.0, 29 - 36)

131 - 159 (13.4 - 16.2, 97 - 117)

39 - 49 (4.0 - 5.0, 29 - 36)

118 - 147 (12 - 15, 87 - 108)

118 - 147 (12 - 15, 87 - 108)

235 - 314 (24 - 32, 174 - 231)

118 - 147 (12 - 15, 87 - 108)

54 - 72 (5.5 - 7.3, 40 - 53)

41 - 47 (4.2 - 4.8, 30 - 35)

71 - 86 (7.2 - 8.8, 52 - 64)

118 - 147 (12 - 15, 87 - 108)

: N•m (kg-m, ft-lb)

Front

① Bound bumper assembly	⑩ Stabilizer clamp	⑲ Insulator (Rubber)
② Upper spring seat	⑪ Stabilizer	⑳ Adjusting cap
③ Dust seal	⑫ Compression rod clamp	㉑ Cotter pin
④ Strut insulator	⑬ Transverse link	㉒ Wheel bearing lock nut
⑤ Cap	⑭ Cotter pin	㉓ Plain washer
⑥ Spacer	⑮ Drive shaft	㉔ Baffle plate
⑦ (Polyurethane tube)	⑯ Cap	㉕ Knuckle
⑧ Coil spring	⑰ Stopper bolt	㉖ Strut assembly
⑨ Front suspension member	⑱ Cotter pin	㉗ Dynamic damper assembly

89708G02

Fig. 14 Exploded view of the front suspension—Altima

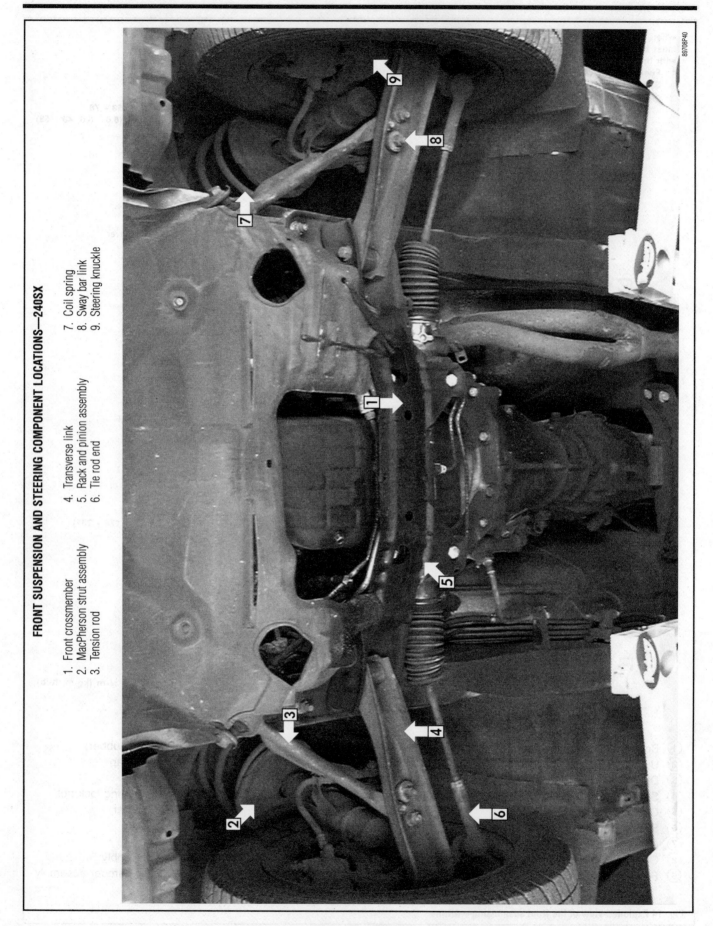

FRONT SUSPENSION AND STEERING COMPONENT LOCATIONS—240SX

1. Front crossmember
2. MacPherson strut assembly
3. Tension rod
4. Transverse link
5. Rack and pinion assembly
6. Tie rod end
7. Coil spring
8. Sway bar link
9. Steering knuckle

When installing rubber parts, final tightening must be carried out under unladen condition* with tires on ground.

* Fuel, radiator coolant and engine oil full. Spare tire, jack, hand tools and mats in designated positions.

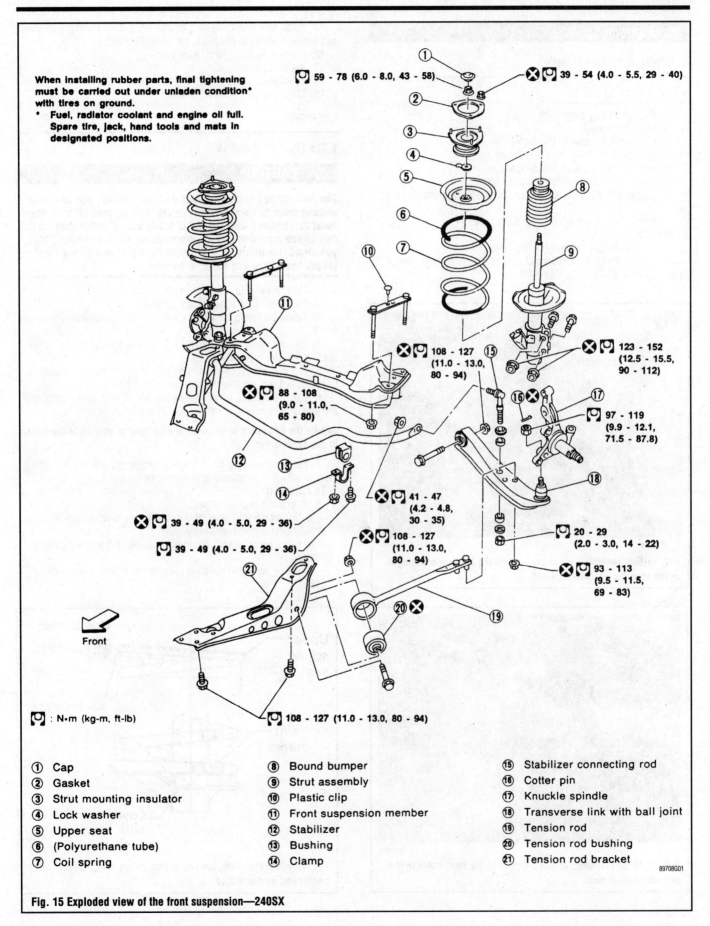

59 - 78 (6.0 - 8.0, 43 - 58)

39 - 54 (4.0 - 5.5, 29 - 40)

123 - 152 (12.5 - 15.5, 90 - 112)

108 - 127 (11.0 - 13.0, 80 - 94)

88 - 108 (9.0 - 11.0, 65 - 80)

97 - 119 (9.9 - 12.1, 71.5 - 87.8)

41 - 47 (4.2 - 4.8, 30 - 35)

39 - 49 (4.0 - 5.0, 29 - 36)

39 - 49 (4.0 - 5.0, 29 - 36)

108 - 127 (11.0 - 13.0, 80 - 94)

20 - 29 (2.0 - 3.0, 14 - 22)

93 - 113 (9.5 - 11.5, 69 - 83)

Front

: N·m (kg-m, ft-lb)

108 - 127 (11.0 - 13.0, 80 - 94)

① Cap	⑧ Bound bumper	⑮ Stabilizer connecting rod
② Gasket	⑨ Strut assembly	⑯ Cotter pin
③ Strut mounting insulator	⑩ Plastic clip	⑰ Knuckle spindle
④ Lock washer	⑪ Front suspension member	⑱ Transverse link with ball joint
⑤ Upper seat	⑫ Stabilizer	⑲ Tension rod
⑥ (Polyurethane tube)	⑬ Bushing	⑳ Tension rod bushing
⑦ Coil spring	⑭ Clamp	㉑ Tension rod bracket

89708G01

Fig. 15 Exploded view of the front suspension—240SX

MacPherson Struts

REMOVAL & INSTALLATION

♦ **See Figures 16 and 17**

1. Raise and safely support the vehicle.
2. Remove the wheel.
3. Matchmark the strut-to-steering knuckle location.
4. Disconnect the brake hose from the strut.
5. Support the transverse link using a jack.
6. Remove the strut-to-steering knuckle bolts.
7. Support the strut assembly and remove the 3 upper strut-to-body nuts.
8. Remove the strut assembly from the vehicle.

To install:

9. Position the strut assembly in the vehicle.
10. Support the strut assembly and install the 3 upper strut-to-body nuts. Tighten to 29–40 ft. lbs. (39–54 Nm).

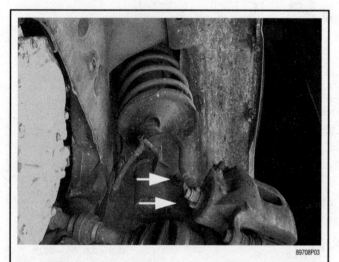

Fig. 16 The front strut assembly is removed by disconnecting it at the steering knuckle (arrows)

89708P03

Fig. 17 Three fasteners attach the strut to the strut tower in the engine compartment

89708P30

11. Install new strut-to-steering knuckle bolts. Align the matchmarks and tighten the bolts to 87–108 ft. lbs. (118–147 Nm).
12. Connect the brake hose to the strut.
13. Install the wheel.
14. Lower the vehicle.
15. Check the front wheel alignment.

OVERHAUL

♦ **See Figures 18 and 19**

❋❋ CAUTION

The coil springs are under considerable tension, and can exert enough force to cause serious injury. Coil springs on all models must be removed with the aid of a coil spring compressor. If you don't have one, don't try to improvise by using something else; you could risk injury. Disassemble the struts using only the proper tools, and use extreme caution.

1. Remove the strut from the vehicle.
2. Secure the strut assembly in a vise.
3. Attach the spring compressor to the spring, leaving the top few coils free.
4. Remove the dust cap from the top of the strut to expose the center nut, if a dust cap is provided.
5. Compress the spring just far enough to permit the strut insulator to be turned by hand. Remove the self-locking center nut.
6. Remove the strut insulator, strut bearing, oil seal, upper spring seat and bound bumper rubber from the top of the strut.

➡**Note the sequence of removal and be sure to assemble the parts in the same order.**

7. Remove the spring with the spring compressor still attached. You are now left with the replaceable portion of the strut.

To assemble:

8. Inspect the strut as follows:
   a. Inspect the strut assembly for smooth operation through its full stroke, both compression and extension.
   b. Check for oil leakage occurring on the welded or gland packing portion.
   c. Check the piston rod for cracks, deformation or other damage.

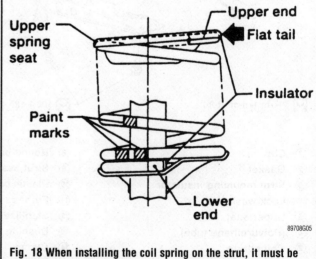

Fig. 18 When installing the coil spring on the strut, it must be positioned as illustrated

89708G05

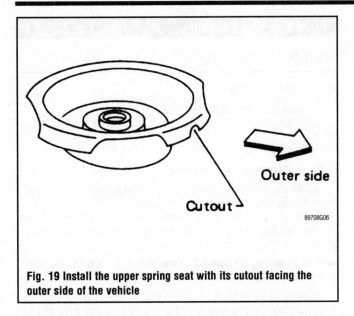

Fig. 19 Install the upper spring seat with its cutout facing the outer side of the vehicle

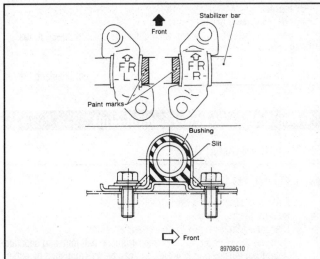

Fig. 20 Position the stabilizer bar and bushing as illustrated when installing

d. Check the strut mounting insulator cemented rubber-to- metal portion for separation or cracks.

e. Check the thrust bearing parts for abnormal wear, noise or excessive rattle in an axial direction.

f. Check the spring and insulator for cracks, deformation or other damage.

9. Reassemble the strut in the reverse order of disassembly.

10. When installing the coil on the strut, it must be positioned so that the flat tail is on top and the paint marks are as illustrated.

11. Install the upper spring seat with its cutout facing the outer side of the vehicle, in line with the strut-to-knuckle attachment points.

12. Replace the strut lower mounting nuts.

13. Tighten the strut rod nut to 43–58 ft. lbs. (59–78 Nm).

Lower Ball Joint

INSPECTION

1. Inspect the ball joint for play when disconnected from the steering knuckle. If the ball joint stud is worn, hard to swing, or if play in an axial direction is excessive, the ball joint is defective.

- Swinging force "A" should be 2–12 lbs. (8–55 N).
- Turning torque "B" should be 4–30 inch lbs. (0.5–3 Nm).
- Vertical end-play should be 0 in. (0mm).

2. Replace the transverse link assembly if the ball joint is defective.

3. Inspect the dust cover for damage and replace as necessary.

REMOVAL & INSTALLATION

The lower ball joint is an integral part of the transverse link. If the ball joint is defective, replace the transverse link as an assembly.

Sway (Stabilizer) Bar

REMOVAL & INSTALLATION

♦ See Figures 20, 21 and 22

1. Raise and support the vehicle safely.
2. Disconnect the sway bar links from the sway bar.
3. Remove the sway bar brackets.
4. Remove the sway bar.

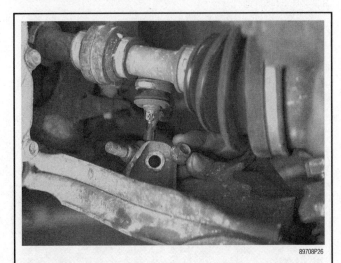

Fig. 21 The front sway bar link connects the sway bar to the transverse link

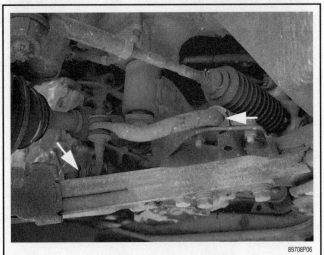

Fig. 22 The front sway bar is attached between the chassis (right arrow) and the transverse link (left arrow)

To install:

5. Install the sway bar.

6. Install the sway bar brackets and tighten the bolts to 30–36 ft. lbs. (40–49 Nm).

7. Lower the vehicle.

8. With the vehicle at ride height, connect the sway bar links and tighten the nuts to 12–16 ft. lbs. (16–22 Nm).

Transverse Link (Lower Control Arm)

REMOVAL & INSTALLATION

♦ **See Figures 14, 15 and 23**

1. Raise and support the vehicle safely.

2. Remove the front wheel.

3. Disconnect the sway bar from the transverse link.

4. Remove the cotter pin and castle nut from the ball joint and separate the ball joint from the steering knuckle. This can be accomplished by either striking the knuckle with a hammer or using a ball joint separator tool.

5. Remove the nuts and bolts connecting the transverse link to the suspension member.

6. Remove the transverse link from the vehicle.

To install:

7. Position the transverse link in the vehicle.

8. Temporarily tighten the nuts and/or bolts securing the transverse link to the chassis.

9. Install the ball joint in the steering knuckle and tighten the ball joint nut to 52–64 ft. lbs. (71–86 Nm).

10. Connect the sway bar to the transverse link.

11. Install the front wheel.

12. Lower the vehicle.

13. Tighten the transverse link attaching bolts/nuts to 87–108 ft. lbs. (118–147 Nm) once the vehicle is at ride height.

89708P05

Fig. 23 Remove the bolts and nut (arrows) to disconnect the transverse link from the chassis—Altima shown

TRANSVERSE LINK BUSHING REPLACEMENT

The bushings are an integral part of the transverse link. If the bushings are defective, replace the transverse link as an assembly.

Front Hub and Knuckle

REMOVAL & INSTALLATION

♦ **See Figures 24 thru 31**

1. Raise and safely support the vehicle.

2. Disconnect the ABS wheel sensor from the knuckle and set it aside.

3. Remove the axle locknut.

➡**Do not disconnect the brake hose.**

4. Remove the brake caliper assembly and rotor. Suspend the caliper out of the way using a piece of mechanic's wire.

5. Remove the cotter pin and loosen the tie rod end ball joint retaining nut. Separate the tie rod end from the steering knuckle using a ball joint puller.

➡**When removing the halfshaft, cover the CV-boots with shop rags to prevent damaging them.**

6. Separate the halfshaft from the knuckle by lightly tapping it using a plastic hammer. If the halfshaft is hard to remove, a jaw type puller may be used to force the shaft through the hub.

7. Loosen the lower ball joint attaching nut and separate the ball joint from the knuckle. This can be accomplished by either striking the knuckle with a hammer or using a ball joint separator tool.

8. Disconnect the steering knuckle from the transverse link.

9. Remove the strut lower mounting bolts.

10. Remove the knuckle from the vehicle.

To install:

11. Position the knuckle on the vehicle.

12. Install new strut lower mounting bolts.

13. Attach the steering knuckle to the transverse link, and fasten the lower ball joint to the steering knuckle. Install a new cotter pin.

14. Insert the halfshaft into the knuckle and hub assembly.

15. Attach the tie rod end to the steering knuckle, and fasten the ball joint. Install a new cotter pin.

16. Install the brake caliper assembly and rotor.

17. Install the axle locknut and tighten to 174–231 ft. lbs. (235–314 Nm).

18. Connect the ABS wheel sensor to the knuckle.

19. Lower the vehicle.

Front Wheel Bearings

REMOVAL & INSTALLATION

♦ **See Figure 32**

The wheel bearings do not usually require maintenance. If a bearing growls during operation, drags or turns roughly when the hub is turned by hand, replace the wheel bearing assembly. Always replace races when wheel bearings are replaced.

➡**The use of a hydraulic press and appropriate adapters is necessary to perform this procedure.**

1. Remove the steering knuckle from the vehicle.

2. Press out the hub and inner race.

3. Remove the bearing inner race and then the outer grease seal.

4. Remove the inner grease seal.

5. Remove the inner and outer snaprings.

6. Press out the bearing outer race.

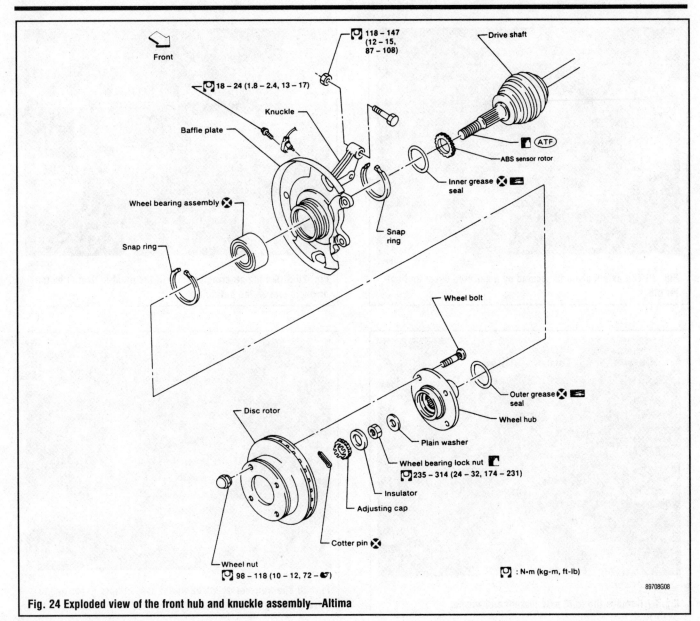

Fig. 24 Exploded view of the front hub and knuckle assembly—Altima

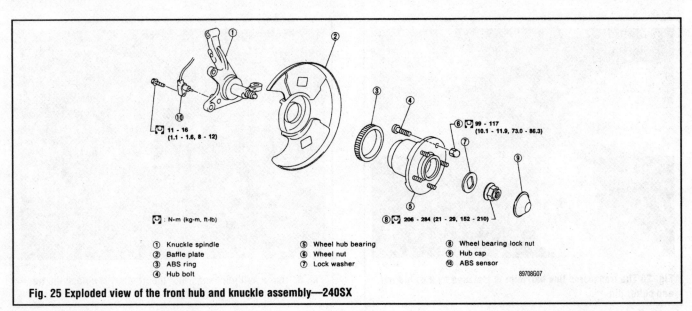

① Knuckle spindle
② Baffle plate
③ ABS ring
④ Hub bolt
⑤ Wheel hub bearing
⑥ Wheel nut
⑦ Lock washer
⑧ Wheel bearing lock nut
⑨ Hub cap
⑩ ABS sensor

Fig. 25 Exploded view of the front hub and knuckle assembly—240SX

Fig. 26 The axle locknut is secured by a serrated cover and cotter pin

Fig. 27 Remove the front axle locknut and washer

Fig. 28 The transverse link ball joint is fastened by a castle nut and cotter pin

Fig. 29 Strike the steering knuckle at the point indicated by the arrow to loosen the ball joint

Fig. 30 The transverse link ball joint uses a taper fit (arrow) to ensure a snug fit in the steering knuckle

Fig. 31 Use a ball joint separator tool (puller) to detach the tie rod end's ball joint from the knuckle

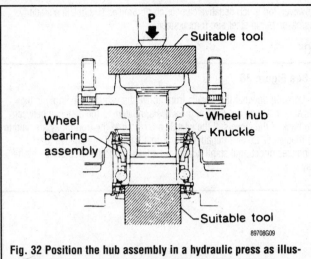

Fig. 32 Position the hub assembly in a hydraulic press as illustrated to install the wheel bearing. (Turn the hub over to remove the bearing)

Fig. 33 The stopper bolt is adjusted when setting the front wheel turning angle during wheel alignment

To assemble:

7. Inspect the wheel hub and knuckle for cracks. Also check the snapring for wear or cracks. Replace components as necessary.

8. Install the inner snapring into the groove of the knuckle.

➡**Do not press the inner race of the wheel bearing assembly. Do not apply oil or grease to the mating surfaces of the wheel bearing outer race and knuckle.**

9. Press the new wheel bearing assembly into the knuckle.
10. Install the outer snapring into the groove of the knuckle.
11. Pack the grease seal lips with multi-purpose grease.
12. Install the inner and outer grease seals.
13. Press the wheel hub into the knuckle.
14. Install the steering knuckle on the vehicle.

Wheel Alignment

▶ **See Figure 33**

If the tires are worn unevenly, if the vehicle is not stable on the highway, or if the handling seems uneven in spirited driving, the wheel alignment should be checked. If an alignment problem is suspected, first check for improper tire inflation and other possible causes. These can be worn suspension or steering components, accident damage or even unmatched tires. If any worn or damaged components are found, they must be replaced before the wheels can be properly aligned. Wheel alignment requires very expensive equipment and involves minute adjustments which must be accurate; it should only be performed by a trained technician. Take your vehicle to a properly equipped shop.

Following is a description of the alignment angles which are adjustable on most vehicles and how they affect vehicle handling. Although these angles can apply to both the front and rear wheels, usually only the front suspension is adjustable.

CASTER

▶ **See Figure 34**

Looking at a vehicle from the side, caster angle describes the steering axis rather than a wheel angle. The steering knuckle is attached to a control arm or strut at the top and a control arm at the bottom. The wheel pivots around the line between these points to steer the vehicle. When the upper point is tilted back, this is described as positive caster. Having a positive caster tends to make the wheels self-centering, increasing directional stability. Excessive

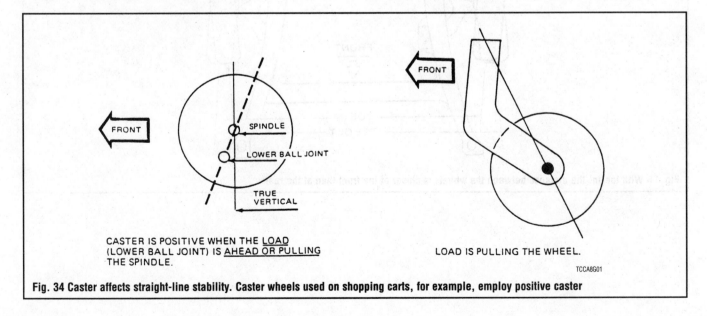

Fig. 34 Caster affects straight-line stability. Caster wheels used on shopping carts, for example, employ positive caster

positive caster makes the wheels hard to steer, while an uneven caster will cause a pull to one side. Overloading the vehicle or sagging rear springs will affect caster, as will raising the rear of the vehicle. If the rear of the vehicle is lower than normal, the caster becomes more positive.

CAMBER

▶ **See Figure 35**

Looking from the front of the vehicle, camber is the inward or outward tilt of the top of wheels. When the tops of the wheels are tilted in, this is negative camber; if they are tilted out, it is positive. In a turn, a slight amount of negative camber helps maximize contact of the tire with the road.

However, too much negative camber compromises straight-line stability, increases bump steer and torque steer.

TOE

▶ **See Figure 36**

Looking down at the wheels from above the vehicle, toe angle is the distance between the front of the wheels, relative to the distance between the back of the wheels. If the wheels are closer at the front, they are said to be toed-in or to have negative toe. A small amount of negative toe enhances directional stability and provides a smoother ride on the highway.

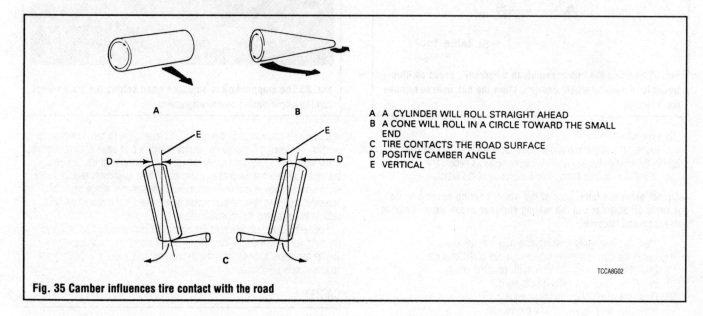

A A CYLINDER WILL ROLL STRAIGHT AHEAD
B A CONE WILL ROLL IN A CIRCLE TOWARD THE SMALL END
C TIRE CONTACTS THE ROAD SURFACE
D POSITIVE CAMBER ANGLE
E VERTICAL

TCCA8G02

Fig. 35 Camber influences tire contact with the road

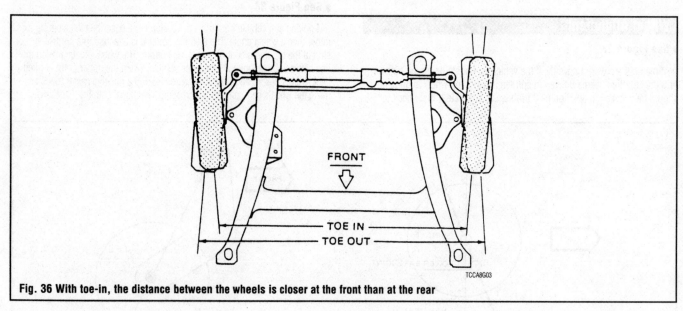

FRONT

TOE IN
TOE OUT

TCCA8G03

Fig. 36 With toe-in, the distance between the wheels is closer at the front than at the rear

REAR SUSPENSION

REAR SUSPENSION COMPONENT LOCATIONS—ALTIMA

1. Rear suspension member
2. MacPherson strut assembly
3. Sway bar
4. Radius link
5. Front parallel link
6. Rear parallel link
7. Toe adjuster
8. Knuckle
9. Sway bar bushing

89708P38

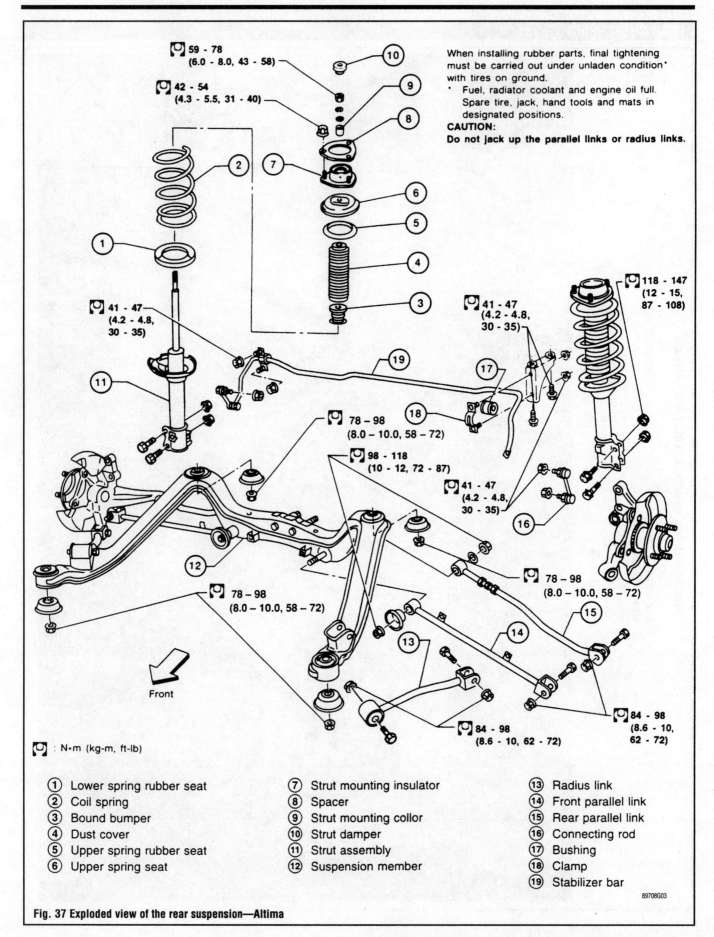

When installing rubber parts, final tightening must be carried out under unladen condition* with tires on ground.
* Fuel, radiator coolant and engine oil full. Spare tire, jack, hand tools and mats in designated positions.

CAUTION:
Do not jack up the parallel links or radius links.

59 - 78 (6.0 - 8.0, 43 - 58)

42 - 54 (4.3 - 5.5, 31 - 40)

41 - 47 (4.2 - 4.8, 30 - 35)

118 - 147 (12 - 15, 87 - 108)

41 - 47 (4.2 - 4.8, 30 - 35)

78 - 98 (8.0 - 10.0, 58 - 72)

98 - 118 (10 - 12, 72 - 87)

41 - 47 (4.2 - 4.8, 30 - 35)

78 - 98 (8.0 - 10.0, 58 - 72)

78 - 98 (8.0 - 10.0, 58 - 72)

84 - 98 (8.6 - 10, 62 - 72)

84 - 98 (8.6 - 10, 62 - 72)

Front

: N·m (kg-m, ft-lb)

1. Lower spring rubber seat
2. Coil spring
3. Bound bumper
4. Dust cover
5. Upper spring rubber seat
6. Upper spring seat
7. Strut mounting insulator
8. Spacer
9. Strut mounting collor
10. Strut damper
11. Strut assembly
12. Suspension member
13. Radius link
14. Front parallel link
15. Rear parallel link
16. Connecting rod
17. Bushing
18. Clamp
19. Stabilizer bar

89708G03

Fig. 37 Exploded view of the rear suspension—Altima

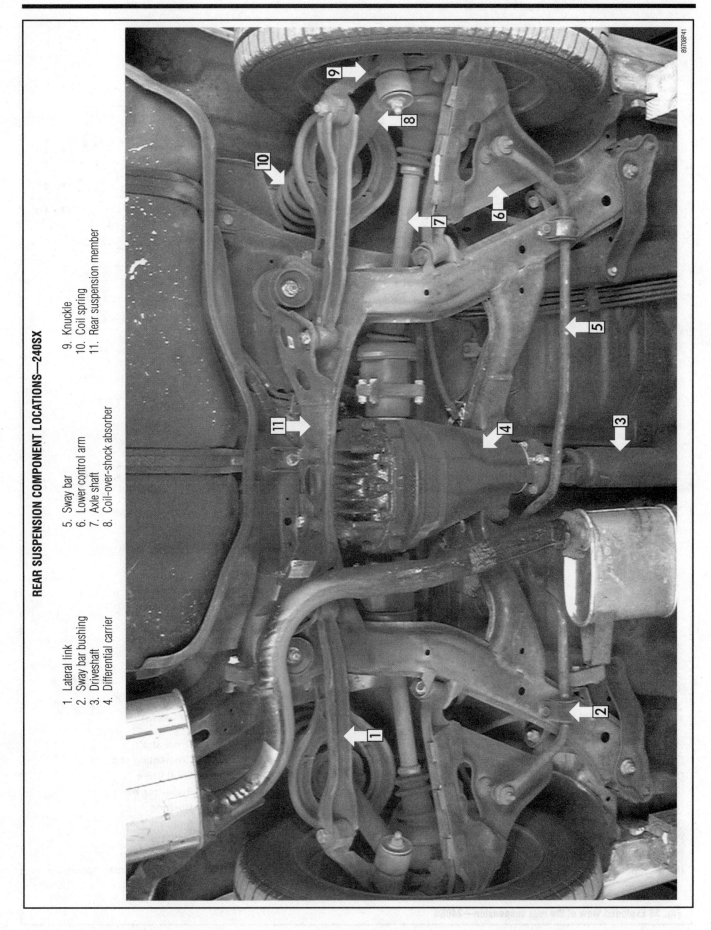

REAR SUSPENSION COMPONENT LOCATIONS—240SX

1. Lateral link
2. Sway bar bushing
3. Driveshaft
4. Differential carrier
5. Sway bar
6. Lower control arm
7. Axle shaft
8. Coil-over-shock absorber
9. Knuckle
10. Coil spring
11. Rear suspension member

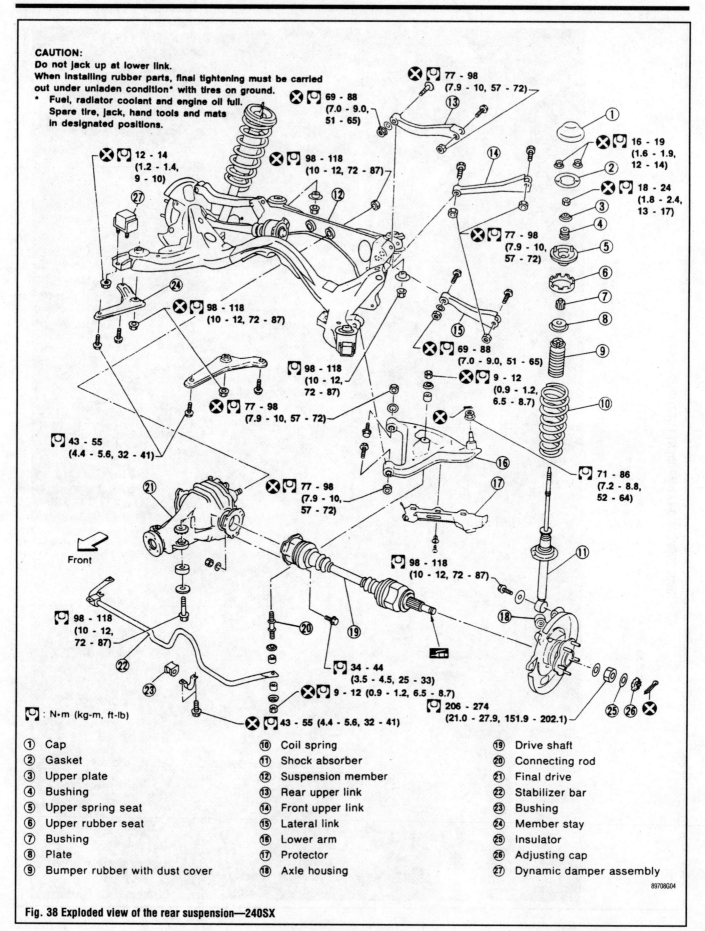

CAUTION:
Do not jack up at lower link.
When installing rubber parts, final tightening must be carried out under unladen condition* with tires on ground.
* Fuel, radiator coolant and engine oil full.
  Spare tire, jack, hand tools and mats in designated positions.

77 - 98
(7.9 - 10, 57 - 72)

69 - 88
(7.0 - 9.0, 51 - 65)

12 - 14
(1.2 - 1.4, 9 - 10)

98 - 118
(10 - 12, 72 - 87)

16 - 19
(1.6 - 1.9, 12 - 14)

18 - 24
(1.8 - 2.4, 13 - 17)

77 - 98
(7.9 - 10, 57 - 72)

98 - 118
(10 - 12, 72 - 87)

69 - 88
(7.0 - 9.0, 51 - 65)

98 - 118
(10 - 12, 72 - 87)

9 - 12
(0.9 - 1.2, 6.5 - 8.7)

77 - 98
(7.9 - 10, 57 - 72)

43 - 55
(4.4 - 5.6, 32 - 41)

71 - 86
(7.2 - 8.8, 52 - 64)

Front

77 - 98
(7.9 - 10, 57 - 72)

98 - 118
(10 - 12, 72 - 87)

98 - 118
(10 - 12, 72 - 87)

34 - 44
(3.5 - 4.5, 25 - 33)

9 - 12 (0.9 - 1.2, 6.5 - 8.7)

206 - 274
(21.0 - 27.9, 151.9 - 202.1)

43 - 55 (4.4 - 5.6, 32 - 41)

: N·m (kg-m, ft-lb)

① Cap
② Gasket
③ Upper plate
④ Bushing
⑤ Upper spring seat
⑥ Upper rubber seat
⑦ Bushing
⑧ Plate
⑨ Bumper rubber with dust cover
⑩ Coil spring
⑪ Shock absorber
⑫ Suspension member
⑬ Rear upper link
⑭ Front upper link
⑮ Lateral link
⑯ Lower arm
⑰ Protector
⑱ Axle housing
⑲ Drive shaft
⑳ Connecting rod
㉑ Final drive
㉒ Stabilizer bar
㉓ Bushing
㉔ Member stay
㉕ Insulator
㉖ Adjusting cap
㉗ Dynamic damper assembly

89708G04

Fig. 38 Exploded view of the rear suspension—240SX

MacPherson Struts

REMOVAL & INSTALLATION

▶ **See Figures 39, 40 and 41**

The 240SX uses a coil-over-shock absorber assembly that looks much like a MacPherson strut. It is removed, installed and overhauled in much the same manner.

1. Remove the rear seat and package shelf to gain access to the upper strut attaching nuts.
2. Remove the upper strut attaching nuts.
3. Raise and safely support the vehicle.
4. Remove the wheel.
5. Matchmark the strut-to-steering knuckle location.
6. Disconnect the brake hose from the strut.
7. Remove the strut-to-knuckle bolts.
8. Remove the strut assembly from the vehicle.

Fig. 39 The top of the rear strut is covered by a plastic cap. Remove the cap to reveal the three upper strut fasteners

Fig. 40 The three nuts (arrows) attach the top of the rear strut to the strut tower

Fig. 41 The two bolts (arrows) attach the bottom of the rear strut to the wheel knuckle

To install:

9. Position the strut assembly in the vehicle.
10. Install new strut-to-knuckle bolts. Align the matchmarks and tighten the bolts to 87–108 ft. lbs. (118–147 Nm).
11. Connect the brake hose to the strut.
12. Install the wheel.
13. Lower the vehicle.
14. Install the 3 upper strut-to-body nuts. Tighten to 29–40 ft. lbs. (39–54 Nm).
15. Check the rear wheel alignment.

OVERHAUL

For details on MacPherson Strut overhaul, refer to the procedure under the Front Suspension portion of this section.

Control Arms/Links

REMOVAL & INSTALLATION

▶ **See Figures 42, 43, 44, 45 and 46**

Altima

The Altima's rear suspension uses (on each side) a radius link, a front parallel link and a rear parallel link. Each component is attached to the knuckle assembly at one end and the rear suspension member (or chassis) at the other end. The following procedure can be used to remove and install all components.

1. Raise and safely support the vehicle.
2. Remove the wheel.
3. Before removing the rear parallel link retaining bolts, matchmark them to retain the toe setting.
4. Remove the link retaining bolts.
5. Remove the link from the vehicle.

To install:

6. Position the link in the vehicle and install the link retaining bolts. Hand-tighten the bolts.

➡**When installing the rear parallel link, pay special attention to the matchmarks made during removal.**

Fig. 42 The front parallel link is attached to the steering knuckle and rear suspension member (arrows)

Fig. 45 The rear suspension member is attached to the body at four points (arrows) with rubber bushings

Fig. 43 The strut (1), rear parallel link (2), front parallel link (3), and radius link (4) are all connected to the knuckle

Fig. 46 To remove the rear parallel link, loosen and remove the bolts (arrows). The rear toe setting will need to be checked after assembly

7. Install the wheel.
8. Lower the vehicle.

➥Final tightening of the link mounting bolts should take place with the wheels on the ground and the vehicle at normal ride height.

9. Tighten the front and rear parallel link-to-chassis bolts to 72–87 ft. lbs. (98–118 Nm).
10. Tighten all other bolts to 62–72 ft. lbs. (84–98 Nm).
11. Check the rear wheel alignment.

240SX

The rear suspension on the 240SX uses (on each side) a lower arm, lateral link, front upper link and rear upper link. Each component is attached to the knuckle assembly at one end and the rear suspension member (or chassis) at the other end.

LATERAL AND UPPER LINKS

1. Raise and safely support the vehicle.
2. Remove the wheel.
3. Before removing the link retaining bolts, matchmark them to retain the camber and toe settings.

Fig. 44 The radius link is attached to the rear suspension member and knuckle (arrows)

4. Remove the link retaining bolts.
5. Remove the link from the vehicle.

To install:

6. Position the link in the vehicle and install the link retaining bolts. Hand-tighten the bolts.

➡**When installing the link, pay special attention to the matchmarks made during removal.**

7. Install the wheel.
8. Lower the vehicle.

➡**Final tightening of the link mounting bolts should take place with the wheels on the ground and the vehicle at normal ride height.**

9. Tighten all bolts except the lateral link-to-chassis bolt to 57–72 ft. lbs. (77–98 Nm).
10. Tighten the lateral link-to-chassis bolt to 51–65 ft. lbs. (69–88 Nm).
11. Check the rear wheel alignment.

LOWER ARM

1. Raise and support the vehicle safely.
2. Remove the rear wheel.
3. Disconnect the sway bar from the lower arm.
4. Remove the cotter pin and castle nut from the ball joint and separate the ball joint from the knuckle. This can be accomplished either by striking the knuckle with a hammer or by using a ball joint separator tool.
5. Remove the nuts and bolts connecting the lower arm to the suspension member.
6. Remove the lower arm from the vehicle.

To install:

7. Position the lower arm in the vehicle.
8. Temporarily tighten the nuts and/or bolts securing the lower arm to the chassis.
9. Install the ball joint in the knuckle and tighten the ball joint nut to 52–64 ft. lbs. (71–86 Nm). Install a new cotter pin.
10. Connect the sway bar to the lower arm link.
11. Install the rear wheel.
12. Lower the vehicle.

➡**Final tightening of the link mounting bolts should take place with the wheels on the ground and the vehicle at normal ride height.**

13. Tighten the lower arm attaching bolts/nuts to 57–72 ft. lbs. (77–98 Nm).

Sway Bar

REMOVAL & INSTALLATION

▶ **See Figures 20, 47 and 48**

On the Altima, the sway bar is attached to the lower portion of the strut. On the 240SX, the sway bar is attached to the lower arm. Even though the attachment points are different, the sway bar still functions and is serviced in the same manner.
1. Raise and support the vehicle safely.
2. Disconnect the sway bar links from the sway bar.
3. Remove the sway bar brackets.
4. Remove the sway bar.

To install:

5. Position the sway bar.
6. Install the sway bar brackets and tighten the bolts to 30–35 ft. lbs. (41–47 Nm) on the Altima or 32–41 ft. lbs. (43–55 Nm) on the 240SX.

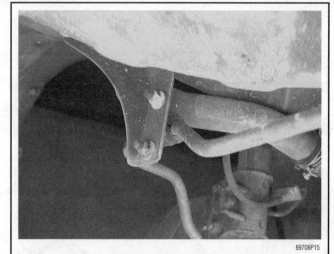

Fig. 47 The rear sway bar is attached to the chassis using a rubber bushing. The bushing is held in place by a bracket

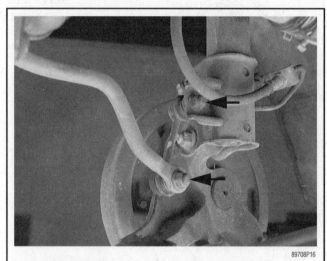

Fig. 48 On Altima models, a sway bar link attaches the sway bar to the strut (arrows)

7. Lower the vehicle.
8. With the vehicle at ride height, connect the sway bar links and tighten the nuts to 30–35 ft. lbs. (41–47 Nm) on the Altima or 78–104 inch lbs. (9–12 Nm) on the 240SX.

Rear Hub and Bearing

REMOVAL & INSTALLATION

Altima

▶ **See Figures 49, 50 and 51**

The wheel bearing is an integral part of the hub assembly and is not serviced separately. The wheel bearing does not usually require maintenance. If the bearing growls during operation, drags or turns roughly when the hub is turned by hand, replace the hub assembly.

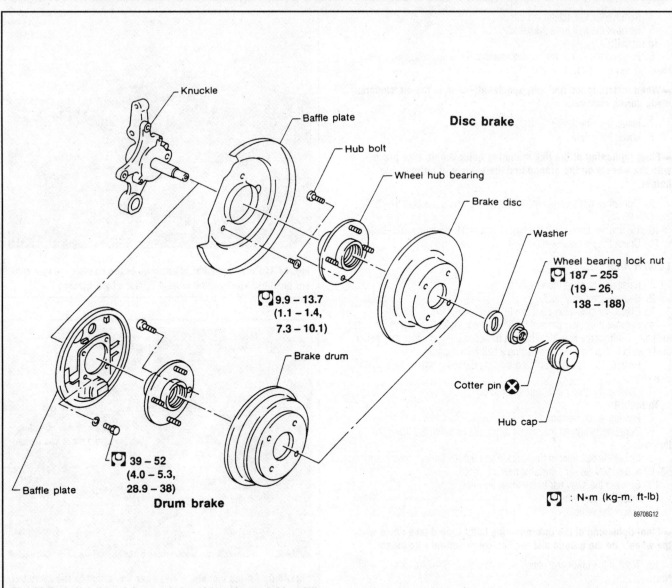

Disc brake

— Knuckle
— Baffle plate
— Hub bolt
— Wheel hub bearing
— Brake disc
— Washer
— Wheel bearing lock nut
187 – 255
(19 – 26,
138 – 188)

9.9 – 13.7
(1.1 – 1.4,
7.3 – 10.1)

— Brake drum

Cotter pin

Hub cap

39 – 52
(4.0 – 5.3,
28.9 – 38)
— Baffle plate
Drum brake

: N•m (kg-m, ft-lb)

89708G12

Fig. 49 Exploded view of the rear hub and knuckle assembly—Altima

89708P02

Fig. 50 The rear hub is attached to the stub axle with a washer and nut. The cotter pin prevents the nut from loosening

89708P20

Fig. 51 The rear hub spins on a sealed bearing. No periodic maintenance of this bearing is necessary

1. Raise and support the vehicle safely.
2. Remove the rear wheel.
3. Remove the hub cap.
4. Remove the cotter pin. Unfasten and remove the wheel bearing locknut and washer.
5. Remove the brake rotor or brake drum.
6. Remove the rear wheel hub and bearing assembly from the spindle.

To install:

7. Position the rear wheel hub on the spindle.
8. Install the spindle washer and locknut, then loosely tighten the nut.
9. Install the brake rotor or brake drum.
10. Tighten the wheel bearing locknut to 137–188 ft. lbs. (186–255 Nm).
11. Install a new cotter pin, then attach the hub cap.
12. Check wheel bearing axial end-play. End-play should be 0.0020 in. (0.05mm) or less.
13. Install the rear wheel.
14. Lower the vehicle.

240SX

♦ **See Figures 52 and 53**

The wheel bearing does not usually require maintenance. If the bearing growls during operation, drags or turns roughly when the hub is turned by hand, replace the bearing.

➡**The use of a hydraulic press and appropriate adapters is necessary to perform this procedure.**

1. Raise and support the vehicle safely.
2. Remove the rear wheel.
3. Remove the hub cap.
4. Remove the cotter pin, followed by the serrated nut cover. Unfasten and remove the wheel bearing locknut and washer.

➡**When removing the axle shaft, cover the CV-boots with shop rags to prevent damaging them.**

5. Separate the axle shaft from the knuckle by lightly tapping it using a plastic hammer. If the shaft is hard to remove, a jaw type puller may be used to force the shaft through the hub.
6. Remove the brake rotor or brake drum.
7. Remove the knuckle.
8. Remove the wheel bearing flange and hub from the knuckle.
9. Using a hydraulic press and appropriate adapters, separate the hub from the wheel bearing.

To install:

10. Press the hub into the new bearing assembly.
11. Position the wheel bearing flange and hub to the knuckle.

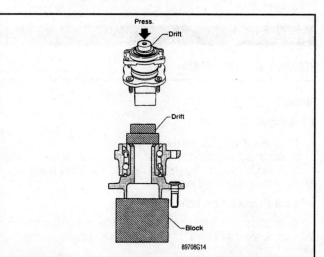

Fig. 53 Position the hub assembly in a hydraulic press as illustrated to install the wheel bearing. (Turn the hub over to remove the bearing)

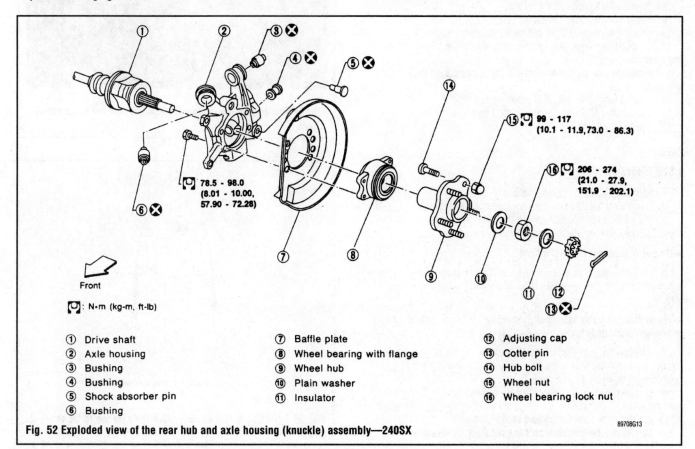

Front

[icon]: N·m (kg-m, ft-lb)

① Drive shaft
② Axle housing
③ Bushing
④ Bushing
⑤ Shock absorber pin
⑥ Bushing
⑦ Baffle plate
⑧ Wheel bearing with flange
⑨ Wheel hub
⑩ Plain washer
⑪ Insulator
⑫ Adjusting cap
⑬ Cotter pin
⑭ Hub bolt
⑮ Wheel nut
⑯ Wheel bearing lock nut

Fig. 52 Exploded view of the rear hub and axle housing (knuckle) assembly—240SX

12. Tighten the flange attaching nuts to 58–72 ft. lbs. (78–98 Nm).
13. Install the knuckle.
14. Install the spindle washer and locknut, then loosely tighten the nut.
15. Install the brake rotor or brake drum.
16. Tighten the wheel bearing locknut to 152–203 ft. lbs. (206–275 Nm).
17. Install the serrated nut cover and a new cotter pin.
18. Install the hub cap.
19. Check wheel bearing axial end-play. End-play should be 0.0020 in. (0.05mm) or less.
20. Install the rear wheel.
21. Lower the vehicle.

Rear Knuckle

REMOVAL & INSTALLATION

Altima

▶ **See Figure 49**

1. Raise and safely support the vehicle.
2. Disconnect the ABS wheel sensor from the knuckle and set it aside.
3. Pry off the hub cap, then remove the cotter pin. Unfasten and remove the axle locknut and washer.

➡**Do not disconnect the brake hose.**

4. On disc brake equipped vehicles, remove the brake caliper assembly and rotor. Suspend the caliper out of the way using a piece of mechanic's wire.
5. Disconnect the parallel links and radius link from the knuckle.
6. Remove the strut lower mounting bolts.
7. Remove the knuckle from the vehicle.

To install:
8. Position the knuckle on the vehicle.
9. Install new strut lower mounting bolts.
10. Connect the parallel links and radius link to the knuckle.
11. On disc brake equipped vehicles, install the brake caliper assembly and rotor.
12. Install the axle washer and locknut. Be sure to tighten the locknut to specifications.
13. Install a new cotter pin, then attach the hub cap.
14. Connect the ABS wheel sensor to the knuckle.
15. Lower the vehicle.

240SX

▶ **See Figure 52**

1. Raise and safely support the vehicle.
2. Disconnect the ABS wheel sensor from the knuckle and set it aside.
3. Pry off the hub cap, then remove the cotter pin and serrated nut cover. Unfasten and remove the axle locknut and washer.

➡**Do not disconnect the brake hose.**

4. On disc brake equipped vehicles, remove the brake caliper assembly and rotor. Suspend the caliper out of the way using a piece of mechanic's wire.

➡**When removing the axle shaft, cover the CV-boots with shop rags to prevent damaging them.**

5. Separate the axle shaft from the knuckle by lightly tapping it using a plastic hammer. If the shaft is hard to remove, a jaw type puller may be used to force the shaft through the hub.
6. Loosen the lower ball joint attaching nut and separate the ball joint from the knuckle. This can be accomplished either by striking the knuckle with a hammer or by using a ball joint separator tool.
7. Disconnect the knuckle from the upper links and lateral link.

8. Remove the strut lower mounting bolts.
9. Remove the knuckle from the vehicle.

To install:
10. Position the knuckle on the vehicle.
11. Install new strut lower mounting bolts.
12. Connect the knuckle to the upper links and lateral link.
13. Connect the lower ball joint to the knuckle.
14. Insert the axle shaft into the knuckle and hub assembly.
15. If applicable, install the brake caliper assembly and rotor.
16. Install the axle washer and locknut. Tighten the locknut to specifications.
17. Install the serrated nut cover, followed by a new cotter pin. Attach the hub cap.
18. Connect the ABS wheel sensor to the knuckle.
19. Lower the vehicle.

Wheel Alignment

▶ **See Figures 54 and 55**

Rear wheel alignment is possible on all vehicles covered in this manual. The individual angles and settings are identical to a front wheel alignment. Refer to front wheel alignment in this section for more information.

89708P11

Fig. 54 These adjusters (arrows) allow the rear toe to be set—Altima

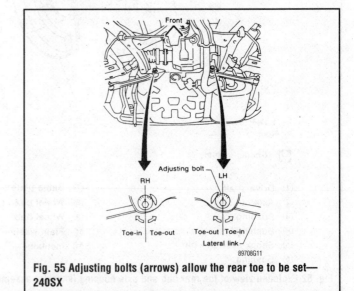

89708G11

Fig. 55 Adjusting bolts (arrows) allow the rear toe to be set—240SX

STEERING

Steering Wheel

REMOVAL & INSTALLATION

❄ CAUTION

The models covered by this manual may be equipped with a Supplemental Restraint System (SRS), which uses an air bag. Whenever working near any of the SRS components, such as the impact sensors, the air bag module, steering column and instrument panel, disable the SRS, as described in Section 6.

Altima

1. Disable the air bag system by disconnecting the negative battery cable and waiting at least 10 minutes, prior to starting this procedure.

➡**The air bag module mounting bolts are coated with a special bonding agent. Replace with new bolts whenever they are removed.**

2. Remove the air bag left and right retaining bolts and remove the air bag assembly.

❄ CAUTION

Always carry an air bag assembly with the bag and trim cover away from your body. Store the assembly facing upward; never place the assembly face down on any surface.

3. Remove the steering wheel hold-down nut.
4. Verify that the wheels are in the straight-ahead position. Make a matchmark on the steering shaft and a matching one on the steering wheel.
5. Remove the steering wheel with the proper pulling tool.
To install:
6. Install the steering wheel, being careful to align the matchmarks.
7. Install the steering wheel hold-down nut.
8. Tighten the hold-down nut to 25–29 ft. lbs. (33–39 Nm).
9. With the front wheels raised off the floor, verify that the steering wheel turns freely and an equal number of turns to the left and to the right from center.
10. Install the air bag and tighten the mounting bolts to 11–18 ft. lbs. (15–25 Nm).
11. Enable the air bag system.
12. Connect the negative battery cable.

240SX

1. Disable the air bag system by disconnecting the negative battery cable and waiting at least 10 minutes, prior to starting this procedure.
2. Remove the access cover on the side of the steering wheel.
3. Remove and discard the special bolt from the side of the steering column.
4. Remove the steering wheel pad/air bag module assembly from the steering wheel.

❄ CAUTION

Always carry an air bag assembly with the bag and trim cover away from your body. Store the assembly facing upward; never place the assembly face down on any surface.

5. Matchmark the steering wheel to the steering column shaft.
6. Remove the steering wheel hold-down nut.
7. Remove the steering wheel with a suitable puller tool.
To install:
8. Install the steering wheel and align the matchmark located on the steering column shaft.
9. Install the steering wheel hold-down nut.

10. Tighten the nut to 22–29 ft. lbs. (29–39 Nm).
11. Install the steering wheel pad/air bag module.
12. Install a new steering wheel pad/air bag module assembly securing bolt and tighten the bolt to 11–18 ft. lbs. (15–25 Nm).
13. Install the access cover to the side of the steering column.
14. Connect the negative battery cable and enable the air bag system.

Combination Switch

REMOVAL & INSTALLATION

❄ CAUTION

The models covered by this manual may be equipped with a Supplemental Restraint System (SRS), which uses an air bag. Whenever working near any of the SRS components, such as the impact sensors, the air bag module, steering column and instrument panel, disable the SRS, as described in Section 6.

1. Disable the air bag system by disconnecting the negative battery cable and waiting at least 10 minutes, prior to starting this procedure.
2. Remove the steering wheel.
3. Remove the steering column covers.

➡**At this point, the individual switch assemblies can be removed without removing the combination switch base assembly. To service an individual switch/stalk assembly, disconnect the electrical lead and remove the two stalk-to-base mounting screws. If the switch base must be removed, proceed with the remainder of the removal procedure.**

4. Disconnect the electrical harness from the switch.
5. Remove the retaining screws, push down on the base of the switch with moderate pressure, then twist the switch and pull it from the steering wheel shaft.
To install:
6. Install the switch on the steering shaft and tighten the retaining screws.

➡**Many vehicles have turn signal switches with a tab that must fit into a hole in the steering shaft. This fit is necessary in order for the system to return the switch to the neutral position after the turn has been made. Be sure to align the tab and the hole when installing the combination switch.**

7. Connect the electrical harness to the switch.
8. Install the steering column covers.
9. Install the steering wheel.
10. Connect the negative battery cable.
11. Check the switch functions for proper operation.

Ignition Switch and Lock Cylinder

REMOVAL & INSTALLATION

The steering lock/ignition switch/warning buzzer switch assembly is attached to the steering column by special bolts whose heads shear off upon installation. The bolts must be drilled out to remove the assembly or be removed with an appropriate tool. The bolts may also be removed with a hammer and chisel by notching the bolts and tapping them counterclockwise with the hammer and chisel.

➡**The ignition switch or warning switch can be replaced without removing the steering lock assembly. The ignition switch is on the back of the assembly and the warning switch is on the side.**

❊❊ CAUTION

The models covered by this manual may be equipped with a Supplemental Restraint System (SRS), which uses an air bag. Whenever working near any of the SRS components, such as the impact sensors, the air bag module, steering column and instrument panel, disable the SRS, as described in Section 6.

1. Disable the air bag system by disconnecting the negative battery cable and waiting at least 10 minutes, prior to starting this procedure.
2. Remove the steering column covers.
3. Remove the steering wheel.
4. Remove the spiral cable assembly.
5. Remove the combination switch from the steering column.
6. Remove the steering column support nuts and lower the steering column.
7. Disconnect the ignition switch wiring.
8. Remove the bolts that secure the steering lock and remove the steering lock assembly.

To install:

9. Install the steering lock assembly and secure with new shear type bolts.
10. Connect the ignition switch wiring harness.
11. Raise the steering column and secure with mounting nuts. Tighten the mounting nuts to 11–14 ft. lbs. (15–19 Nm).
12. Install the spiral cable assembly.
13. Install the combination switch.
14. Install the steering column covers.
15. Install the steering wheel.
16. Connect the negative battery cable.

Tie Rod Ends

REMOVAL & INSTALLATION

▶ **See Figures 56, 57, 58, 59 and 60**

1. Raise and support the vehicle safely.
2. Remove the front wheel(s).
3. Remove the castle nut's cotter pin, then remove the castle nut.
4. Detach the tie rod end from the steering knuckle with a ball joint remover tool.
5. Loosen the tie rod locknut.
6. Count the exact number of exposed threads on the tie rod ends and unscrew the tie rod end.

Fig. 57 The tie rod end is attached to the tie rod and steering knuckle (arrows)

Fig. 58 The tie rod end's ball joint is a taper fit (arrow) into the steering knuckle

Fig. 56 The tie rod end's castle nut is secured by a cotter pin

Fig. 59 Use a backup wrench to hold the tie rod steady when loosening the locknut

89708P37

Fig. 60 Count the number of turns it takes to fully remove the tie rod end

To install:

7. Lubricate the tie rod threads and screw the tie rod ends into place so that the previously noted number of threads are visible with the locknut tightened to 58–72 ft. lbs. (78–98 Nm).

8. Insert the tie rod end's ball joint stud into the steering knuckle and tighten the castle nut to 22–36 ft. lbs. (29–49 Nm). Install a new cotter pin.

9. Install the front wheel(s).

10. Lower the vehicle.

11. Check the wheel alignment.

Rack and Pinion

REMOVAL & INSTALLATION

❊❊ CAUTION

The models covered by this manual may be equipped with a Supplemental Restraint System (SRS), which uses an air bag. Whenever working near any of the SRS components, such as the impact sensors, the air bag module, steering column and instrument panel, disable the SRS, as described in Section 6.

1. Disable the air bag system by disconnecting the negative battery cable and waiting at least 10 minutes, prior to starting this procedure.

2. Raise and safely support the vehicle.

3. Matchmark the rack and pinion to the steering shaft.

4. Remove the bolt securing the lower steering column shaft to the rack and pinion assembly.

5. If equipped with power steering, disconnect and cap the hoses from the power steering pump at the rack and pinion assembly.

6. Remove the cotter pins and castle nuts from the tie rod ends.

7. Using a ball joint separator tool, detach the tie rod ends from the steering knuckle.

8. Remove the front exhaust pipe mounting nuts and bolts.

9. Remove the front exhaust pipe from the vehicle.

10. If necessary (and applicable), disconnect the control cable or linkage from the transmission and position it out of the way.

11. Unfasten the mounting bolts/nuts, then remove the rack and pinion assembly from the vehicle.

➥**Use care when separating the steering column joint.**

To install:

12. Inspect the rack and pinion mounting bushings, and replace as necessary.

➥**When installing the lower steering joint to the rack and pinion, make sure that the wheels are pointing straight-ahead and that the steering column joint slot is aligned.**

13. Align the steering column-to-the rack and pinion assembly matchmark, and position the rack in the vehicle.

14. Be sure to properly install the mounting bushings and hand-tighten the mounting nuts or bolts.

15. Tighten the rack mounting bolts/nuts to 65–80 ft. lbs. (88–108 Nm) on 240SX or 54–72 ft. lbs. (73–97 Nm) on Altima.

16. Install the pinch bolt on the steering column shaft to 17–22 ft. lbs. (24–29 Nm).

17. Attach the tie rod ends to the steering knuckles.

18. If removed, connect the control cable or linkage to the transmission.

19. Using new gaskets, install the front exhaust pipe assembly.

20. If equipped with power steering, connect the power steering pump hoses to the rack.

21. Lower the vehicle.

22. Connect the negative battery cable.

23. Start the engine, then fill and bleed the power steering system.

24. Check the front end alignment.

Power Steering Pump

REMOVAL & INSTALLATION

1. Disconnect the negative battery cable.

2. Place a drain pan under the vehicle to catch any power steering fluid that is spilled.

3. Label, disconnect and plug the power steering hoses.

4. Remove the drive belt from the air conditioning compressor, if equipped.

5. Loosen the accessory drive belt tension and remove the belt.

6. Unfasten and remove the power steering pump from the engine.

To install:

7. Position the power steering pump on the engine and install the mounting bolts. Tighten the bolts to 42–48 ft. lbs. (57–66 Nm).

8. Using new O-rings, connect the power steering hoses to the steering pump.

9. Install and tighten the hose clamp on the return hose. Tighten the banjo bolt on the pressure side to 36–51 ft. lbs. (49–69 Nm).

10. Connect the negative battery cable.

11. Start the engine, then fill and bleed the power steering system.

BLEEDING

1. Raise and support the front of the vehicle safely.

2. Check and add fluid to the reservoir, if necessary.

3. Turn the steering wheel quickly (all the way), right and left, just touching the stops. Continue turning the steering wheel until the fluid level in the reservoir no longer decreases.

4. Check the fluid level, and add fluid as required.

5. Start the engine and continue turning the steering wheel from right to left, lightly touching the stops until the fluid level in the reservoir no longer decreases.

6. Stop the engine and check the fluid level; add fluid as required.

➥**When bleeding the system, make sure the temperature of the fluid reaches 140–176°F (60–80°C).**

7. Repeat the steps until all of the air is bled from the system.

8. If the air cannot be bled from the system, turn and hold the steering wheel at each stop for at least 5 seconds, but never more than 15 seconds.

TORQUE SPECIFICATIONS

Components	English Specification	Metric Specification
Wheels		
Lug nuts	72–86 ft. lbs.	98–117 Nm
Front Suspension		
Front Strut		
Upper strut nuts	29–40 ft. lbs.	39–54 Nm
Strut-to-steering knuckle	87–108 ft. lbs.	118–147 Nm
Strut rod nut	43–58 ft. lbs.	59–78 Nm
Sway Bar		
Sway bar brackets	30–36 ft. lbs.	40–49 Nm
Sway bar link nuts	12–16 ft. lbs.	16–22 Nm
Lower Arm		
Ball joint nut	52–64 ft. lbs.	71–86 Nm
Transverse Link	87–108 ft. lbs.	118–147 Nm
Axle locknut	174–231 ft. lbs.	235–314 Nm
Rear Suspension		
Rear Strut		
Strut-to-knuckle bolts	87–108 ft. lbs.	118–147 Nm
Upper strut-to-body nuts	29–40 ft. lbs.	39–54 Nm
Strut rod nut	43–58 ft. lbs.	59–78 Nm
Control Arms/links		
Altima		
Front and rear parallel link-to-chassis bolts	72–87 ft. lbs.	98–118 Nm
All other bolts	62–72 ft. lbs.	84–98 Nm
240SX		
Lateral link-to-chassis bolt	57–72 ft. lbs.	77–98 Nm
Sway Bar		
Bracket		
Altima	30–35 ft. lbs.	41–47 Nm
240SX	32–41 ft. lbs.	43–55 Nm
Links		
Altima	30–35 ft. lbs.	41–47 Nm
240SX	78–104 ft. lbs.	9–12 Nm
Rear Hub		
Locknut		
Altima	137–188 ft. lbs.	186–255 Nm
240SX	152–203 ft. lbs.	206–275 Nm
Steering		
Steering Wheel Nut		
240SX	22–29 ft. lbs.	29–39 Nm.
Altima	25–29 ft. lbs.	33–39 Nm.
Air Bag Module	11–18 ft. lbs.	15–25 Nm
Steering Column	11–14 ft. lbs.	15–19 Nm
Tie Rod		
Locknut	58–72 ft. lbs.	78–98 Nm
Castle Nut	22–36 ft. lbs.	29–49 Nm
Rack and Pinion		
Rack mounting bolts/nuts		
240SX	65–80 ft. lbs.	88–108 Nm
Altima	54–72 ft. lbs.	73–97 Nm
Pinch bolt	17–22 ft. lbs.	24–29 Nm
Power Steering		
Pump Mounting	42–48 ft. lbs.	57–66 Nm
Pressure Hose	36–51 ft. lbs.	49–69 Nm

89708C01

9

BRAKES

BRAKE OPERATING SYSTEM

Basic Operating Principles

Hydraulic systems are used to actuate the brakes of all modern automobiles. The system transports the power required to force the frictional surfaces of the braking system together from the pedal to the individual brake units at each wheel. A hydraulic system is used for two reasons.

First, fluid under pressure can be carried to all parts of an automobile by small pipes and flexible hoses without taking up a significant amount of room or posing routing problems.

Second, a great mechanical advantage can be given to the brake pedal end of the system, and the foot pressure required to actuate the brakes can be reduced by making the surface area of the master cylinder pistons smaller than that of any of the pistons in the wheel cylinders or calipers.

The master cylinder consists of a fluid reservoir along with a double cylinder and piston assembly. Double type master cylinders are designed to separate the front and rear braking systems hydraulically in case of a leak. The master cylinder coverts mechanical motion from the pedal into hydraulic pressure within the lines. This pressure is translated back into mechanical motion at the wheels by either the wheel cylinder (drum brakes) or the caliper (disc brakes).

Steel lines carry the brake fluid to a point on the vehicle's frame near each of the vehicle's wheels. The fluid is then carried to the calipers and wheel cylinders by flexible tubes in order to allow for suspension and steering movements.

In drum brake systems, each wheel cylinder contains two pistons, one at either end, which push outward in opposite directions and force the brake shoe into contact with the drum.

In disc brake systems, the cylinders are part of the calipers. At least one cylinder in each caliper is used to force the brake pads against the disc.

All pistons employ some type of seal, usually made of rubber, to minimize fluid leakage. A rubber dust boot seals the outer end of the cylinder against dust and dirt. The boot fits around the outer end of the piston on disc brake calipers, and around the brake actuating rod on wheel cylinders.

The hydraulic system operates as follows: When at rest, the entire system, from the piston(s) in the master cylinder to those in the wheel cylinders or calipers, is full of brake fluid. Upon application of the brake pedal, fluid trapped in front of the master cylinder piston(s) is forced through the lines to the wheel cylinders. Here, it forces the pistons outward, in the case of drum brakes, and inward toward the disc, in the case of disc brakes. The motion of the pistons is opposed by return springs mounted outside the cylinders in drum brakes, and by spring seals, in disc brakes.

Upon release of the brake pedal, a spring located inside the master cylinder immediately returns the master cylinder pistons to the normal position. The pistons contain check valves and the master cylinder has compensating ports drilled in it. These are uncovered as the pistons reach their normal position. The piston check valves allow fluid to flow toward the wheel cylinders or calipers as the pistons withdraw. Then, as the return springs force the brake pads or shoes into the released position, the excess fluid reservoir through the compensating ports. It is during the time the pedal is in the released position that any fluid that has leaked out of the system will be replaced through the compensating ports.

Dual circuit master cylinders employ two pistons, located one behind the other, in the same cylinder. The primary piston is actuated directly by mechanical linkage from the brake pedal through the power booster. The secondary piston is actuated by fluid trapped between the two pistons. If a leak develops in front of the secondary piston, it moves forward until it bottoms against the front of the master cylinder, and the fluid trapped between the pistons will operate the rear brakes. If the rear brakes develop a leak, the primary piston will move forward until direct contact with the secondary piston takes place, and it will force the secondary piston to actuate the front brakes. In either case, the brake pedal moves farther when the brakes are applied, and less braking power is available.

All dual circuit systems use a switch to warn the driver when only half of the brake system is operational. This switch is usually located in a valve body which is mounted on the firewall or the frame below the master cylinder. A hydraulic piston receives pressure from both circuits, each circuit's pressure being applied to one end of the piston. When the pressures are in balance, the piston remains stationary. When one circuit has a leak, however, the greater pressure in that circuit during application of the brakes will push the piston to one side, closing the switch and activating the brake warning light.

In disc brake systems, this valve body also contains a metering valve and, in some cases, a proportioning valve. The metering valve keeps pressure from traveling to the disc brakes on the front wheels until the brake shoes on the rear wheels have contacted the drums, ensuring that the front brakes will never be used alone. The proportioning valve controls the pressure to the rear brakes to lessen the chance of rear wheel lock-up during very hard braking.

Warning lights may be tested by depressing the brake pedal and holding it while opening one of the wheel cylinder bleeder screws. If this does not cause the light to go on, substitute a new lamp, make continuity checks, and, finally, replace the switch as necessary.

The hydraulic system may be checked for leaks by applying pressure to the pedal gradually and steadily. If the pedal sinks very slowly to the floor, the system has a leak. This is not to be confused with a springy or spongy feel due to the compression of air within the lines. If the system leaks, there will be a gradual change in the position of the pedal with a constant pressure.

Check for leaks along all lines and at wheel cylinders. If no external leaks are apparent, the problem is inside the master cylinder.

DISC BRAKES

Instead of the traditional expanding brakes that press outward against a circular drum, disc brake systems utilize a disc (rotor) with brake pads positioned on either side of it. An easily-seen analogy is the hand brake arrangement on a bicycle. The pads squeeze onto the rim of the bike wheel, slowing its motion. Automobile disc brakes use the identical principle but apply the braking effort to a separate disc instead of the wheel.

The disc (rotor) is a casting, usually equipped with cooling fins between the two braking surfaces. This enables air to circulate between the braking surfaces making them less sensitive to heat buildup and more resistant to fade. Dirt and water do not drastically affect braking action since contaminants are thrown off by the centrifugal action of the rotor or scraped off the by the pads. Also, the equal clamping action of the two brake pads tends to ensure uniform, straight line stops. Disc brakes are inherently self-adjusting. There are three general types of disc brake:
1. A fixed caliper.
2. A floating caliper.
3. A sliding caliper.

The fixed caliper design uses two pistons mounted on either side of the rotor (in each side of the caliper). The caliper is mounted rigidly and does not move.

The sliding and floating designs are quite similar. In fact, these two types are often lumped together. In both designs, the pad on the inside of the rotor is moved into contact with the rotor by hydraulic force. The caliper, which is not held in a fixed position, moves slightly, bringing the outside pad into contact with the rotor. There are various methods of attaching floating calipers. Some pivot at the bottom or top, and some slide on mounting bolts. In any event, the end result is the same.

DRUM BRAKES

Drum brakes employ two brake shoes mounted on a stationary backing plate. These shoes are positioned inside a circular drum which rotates with the wheel assembly. The shoes are held in place by springs. This allows them to slide toward the drums (when they are applied) while keeping the linings and drums in alignment. The shoes are actuated by a wheel cylinder which is mounted at the top of the backing plate. When the brakes are applied, hydraulic pressure forces the wheel cylinder's actuating links outward. Since these links bear directly against the top of the brake shoes, the tops of the shoes are then forced against the inner side of the drum. This action forces the bottoms of the two shoes to contact the brake drum by rotating the entire assembly slightly (known as servo action). When pressure within the wheel cylinder is relaxed, return springs pull the shoes back away from the drum.

Most modern drum brakes are designed to self-adjust themselves during application when the vehicle is moving in reverse. This motion causes both shoes to rotate very slightly with the drum, rocking an adjusting lever, thereby causing rotation of the adjusting screw. Some drum brake systems are designed to self-adjust during application whenever the brakes are applied. This on-board adjustment system reduces the need for maintenance adjustments and keeps both the brake function and pedal feel satisfactory.

Brake Light Switch

REMOVAL & INSTALLATION

▶ See Figure 1

The brake light (stop lamp) switch is located on the brake pedal assembly.

1. Disconnect the negative battery cable.
2. Disconnect the electrical harness at the switch.
3. Loosen the switch locknut.
4. Remove the switch.

To install:

5. Install and adjust the switch.
6. Tighten the switch locknut.
7. Connect the electrical harness at the switch.
8. Connect the negative battery cable.

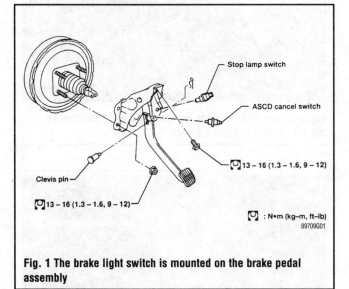

Fig. 1 The brake light switch is mounted on the brake pedal assembly

ADJUSTMENT

▶ See Figure 2

1. Adjust the clearance between the brake pedal and the stop lamp switch or Automatic Speed Control Device (ASCD) switch, by loosening the locknut and adjusting the switch.

2. The clearance should be approximately 0.012–0.039 in. (0.30–1.00mm) between the switch threads and the brake pedal.

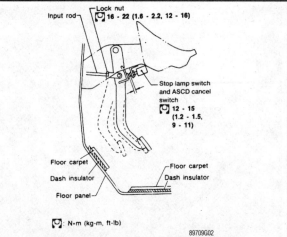

Fig. 2 The brake light switch is adjusted so the clearance between the switch threads and the brake pedal assembly is within specification

Master Cylinder

REMOVAL & INSTALLATION

▶ See Figures 3 thru 11

1. Disconnect the negative battery cable.

2. Label and disconnect the brake fluid level sensor electrical harness from the reservoir.

3. Clean the outside of the master cylinder thoroughly, particularly around the cap and fluid lines.

4. Disconnect and cap the brake fluid lines to prevent dirt from entering the system.

5. Remove the master cylinder mounting nuts and lift the master cylinder from the brake booster.

To install:

➡**Vehicles with adjustable pushrods will have an adjustable clevis with a locknut at the brake pedal connection under the dashboard.**

Fig. 3 Disconnect the brake lines (arrows) from the master cylinder

Fig. 4 The master cylinder is mounted on two studs protruding from the firewall

Fig. 5 Always use a flare nut wrench when tightening or loosening the brake tube fittings

Fig. 6 The master cylinder uses a brake fluid level sensor. The connector (arrow) is located at the side of the reservoir

Fig. 7 All brake tubes use double flare connections for a leakproof seal

Fig. 8 Master cylinder ports are identified as controlling the front (F) or rear (R) brake circuits

Fig. 9 The brake fluid reservoir is attached to the master cylinder using rubber grommets (arrows)

Fig. 10 The master cylinder pushrod length must be checked with vacuum applied to the brake booster

Fig. 11 A vacuum pump comes in handy to siphon brake fluid from the reservoir

6. On vehicles equipped with an adjustable pushrod, adjust the pushrod length.

  a. Apply approximately 19 in. Hg of vacuum to the brake booster using a hand operated vacuum pump.

  b. Measure the output rod length from the end of the rod to the front face of the booster, as illustrated.

  c. The dimension of the rod should be 0.4045–0.4144 in. (10.275–10.525mm).

7. Bench bleed the master cylinder assembly prior to installation.

8. Install the master cylinder and tighten the mounting nuts to 9–11 ft. lbs. (12–15 Nm).

9. Connect the brake lines and tighten to 11–13 ft. lbs. (15–18 Nm).

10. Fill the brake system with fresh, clean fluid.

11. Bleed the brake system.

12. Connect the negative battery cable.

13. Connect the brake fluid level sensor electrical harness.

14. Check for fluid leaks and verify proper brake system operation.

Power Brake Booster

Virtually all modern vehicles use a vacuum assisted power brake system to multiply the braking force and reduce pedal effort. Since vacuum is

always available when the engine is operating, the system is simple and efficient. A vacuum diaphragm is located on the front of the master cylinder and assists the driver in applying the brakes, reducing both the effort and travel he must put into moving the brake pedal.

The vacuum diaphragm housing is normally connected to the intake manifold by a vacuum hose. A check valve is placed at the point where the hose enters the diaphragm housing, so that during periods of low manifold vacuum, braking assist will not be lost.

Depressing the brake pedal closes off the vacuum source and allows atmospheric pressure to enter on one side of the diaphragm. This causes the master cylinder pistons to move and apply the brakes. When the brake pedal is released, vacuum is applied to both sides of the diaphragm and springs return the diaphragm and master cylinder pistons to the released position.

If the vacuum supply fails, the brake pedal rod will contact the end of the master cylinder actuator rod and the system will apply the brakes without any power assistance. The driver will notice that much higher pedal effort is needed to stop the car and that the pedal feels harder than usual.

TESTING

Vacuum Leak Test

1. Operate the engine at idle without touching the brake pedal for at least one minute.

2. Turn off the engine and wait one minute.

3. Test for the presence of assist vacuum by depressing the brake pedal and releasing it several times. If vacuum is present in the system, light application will produce less and less pedal travel. If there is no vacuum, air is leaking into the system.

System Operation Test

1. With the engine **OFF**, pump the brake pedal until the supply vacuum is entirely gone.

2. Put light, steady pressure on the brake pedal.

3. Start the engine and let it idle. If the system is operating correctly, the brake pedal should fall toward the floor if constant pressure is maintained.

Power brake systems may be tested for hydraulic leaks just as ordinary systems are tested.

REMOVAL & INSTALLATION

▶ **See Figures 12 and 13**

➡**Make sure all vacuum lines and connectors are in good condition. A small vacuum leak will cause a big problem in the power brake system.**

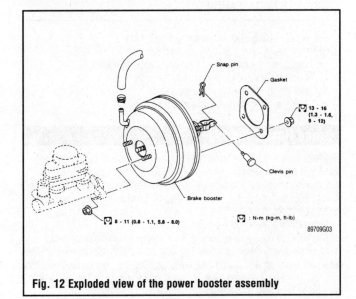

Fig. 12 Exploded view of the power booster assembly

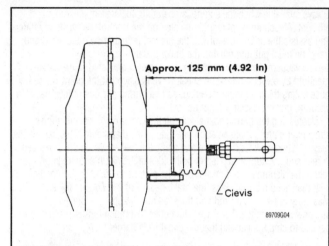

Fig. 13 On vehicles with an adjustable pushrod, adjust the rod so that the measurement between the booster and centerline of the clevis hole is 4.92 in. (125mm)

1. Disconnect the negative battery cable.
2. Remove the master cylinder from the brake booster with the brake lines still connected.
3. Disconnect the vacuum lines from the booster.
4. Disconnect the booster pushrod at the pedal clevis.
5. Remove the booster mounting nuts from under the dashboard.
6. Lift the booster from the engine compartment.

To install:

7. On vehicles with an adjustable pushrod, adjust the brake booster rod so the measurement between the booster and the centerline of the clevis hole is 4.92 in. (125mm).
8. Install the brake booster assembly and tighten the attaching nuts to 9–12 ft. lbs. (13–16 Nm).
9. Adjust the master cylinder pushrod and install the master cylinder assembly.
10. Connect the booster pushrod to the pedal clevis.
11. Connect the vacuum lines to the brake booster.
12. Connect the negative battery cable.
13. Start the engine and check for proper brake operation.

Proportioning Valve

REMOVAL & INSTALLATION

The proportioning valve is located at the end of the brake master cylinder. Proportioning valves are only used on vehicles without ABS.

1. Disconnect the brake line to the proportioning valve.
2. Unscrew the valve from the master cylinder.
3. Installation is the reverse of removal.
4. Bleed the brake system and check for leaks.

Brake Hoses and Pipes

Metal lines and rubber brake hoses should be checked frequently for leaks and external damage. Metal lines are particularly prone to crushing and kinking under the vehicle. Any such deformation can restrict the proper flow of fluid and, therefore, impair braking at the wheels. Rubber hoses should be checked for cracking or scraping; such damage can create a weak spot in the hose and it could fail under pressure.

Any time the lines are removed or disconnected, extreme cleanliness must be observed. Clean all joints and connections before disassembly (use a stiff bristle brush and clean brake fluid); be sure to plug the lines and ports as soon as they are opened. New lines and hoses should be flushed clean with brake fluid before installation to remove any contamination.

REMOVAL & INSTALLATION

▶ See Figures 14, 15, 16, 17 and 18

1. Disconnect the negative battery cable.
2. Raise and safely support the vehicle on jackstands.
3. Remove any wheel and tire assemblies necessary for access to the particular line you are removing.
4. Thoroughly clean the surrounding area at the joints to be disconnected.
5. Place a suitable catch pan under the joint to be disconnected.
6. Using two wrenches (one to hold the joint and one to turn the fitting), disconnect the hose or line to be replaced.
7. Disconnect the other end of the line or hose, moving the drain pan if necessary. Always use a back-up wrench to avoid damaging the fitting.
8. Disconnect any retaining clips or brackets holding the line and remove the line from the vehicle.

➡️If the brake system is to remain open for more time than it takes to swap lines, tape or plug each remaining clip and port to keep contaminants out and fluid in.

To install:

9. Install the new line or hose, starting with the end farthest from the master cylinder. Connect the other end, then confirm that both fittings are

Fig. 14 The front brake hose is attached to the strut using a spring clip

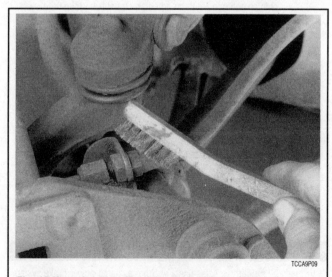

Fig. 15 Use a brush to clean the fittings of any debris

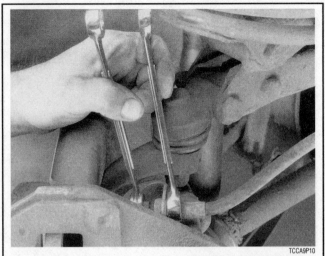

Fig. 16 Use two wrenches to loosen the fitting. If available, use flare nut type wrenches

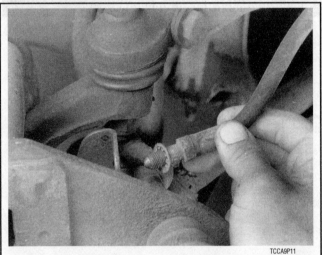

Fig. 17 Any gaskets/crush washers should be replaced with new ones during installation

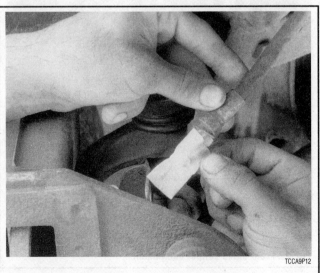

Fig. 18 Tape or plug the line to prevent contamination

correctly threaded and turn smoothly using finger pressure. Make sure the new line will not rub against any other part. Brake lines must be at least ½ in. (13mm) from the steering column and other moving parts. Any protective shielding or insulators must be reinstalled in the original location.

✳ WARNING

Make sure the hose is NOT kinked or touching any part of the frame or suspension after installation. These conditions may cause the hose to fail prematurely.

10. Using two wrenches as before, tighten each fitting.
11. Install any retaining clips or brackets on the lines.
12. If removed, install the wheel and tire assemblies, then carefully lower the vehicle to the ground.
13. Refill the brake master cylinder reservoir with clean, fresh brake fluid, meeting DOT 3 specifications. Properly bleed the brake system.
14. Connect the negative battery cable.

Bleeding the Brake System

▶ See Figures 19, 20 and 21

✳ WARNING

Clean, high quality brake fluid is essential to the safe and proper operation of the brake system. You should always buy the highest quality brake fluid that is available. If the brake fluid becomes contaminated, drain and flush the system, then refill the master cylinder with new fluid. Never reuse any brake fluid. Any brake fluid that is removed from the system should be discarded.

When any part of the hydraulic system has been disconnected for repair or replacement, air may get into the lines and cause a spongy pedal action (because air can be compressed and brake fluid cannot). To correct this condition, it is necessary to bleed the hydraulic system to be sure all air is purged.

When bleeding the brake system, bleed one component at a time, beginning at the one with the longest hydraulic line (farthest from the master cylinder). ALWAYS keep the master cylinder reservoir filled with fresh brake fluid during the bleeding operation. Never use brake fluid that has been drained from the hydraulic system, no matter how clean it is.

1. Clean all dirt from around the master cylinder fill cap, remove the cap and fill the master cylinder with brake fluid until the level is within ¼ in. (6mm) of the top edge of the reservoir.

Fig. 19 The brake system can be bled using a vacuum type bleeder

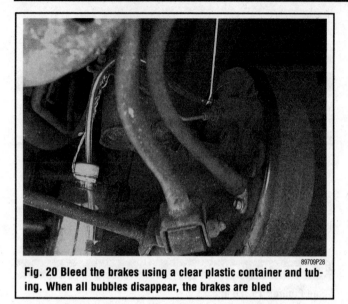

Fig. 20 Bleed the brakes using a clear plastic container and tubing. When all bubbles disappear, the brakes are bled

Fig. 21 Loosen the bleeder screw using a line wrench. This will prevent the fitting from rounding off

2. Clean the bleeder screws. The bleeder screws are located on the back of the brake backing plate (drum brakes) and on the top of the brake calipers (disc brakes). Some master cylinders and other brake components such as ABS modulators have bleeders located on them also.

3. Attach a length of rubber hose over the bleeder screw and place the other end of the hose in a glass jar, submerged in brake fluid.

4. Open the bleeder screw ½–¾ turn. Have an assistant slowly depress the brake pedal.

5. Close the bleeder screw and tell your assistant to allow the brake pedal to return slowly. Continue this process to purge all air from the system.

6. When bubbles cease to appear at the end of the bleeder hose, close the bleeder screw and remove the hose. Tighten the bleeder screw to 61–87 inch lbs.(7–9 Nm).

7. Check the master cylinder fluid level and add fluid accordingly. Do this after bleeding each component.

8. Repeat the bleeding operation at the remaining components, ending with the one closet to the master cylinder.

9. Fill the master cylinder reservoir to the proper level.

Master Cylinder Bench Bleeding

When replacing the master cylinder, it is a good idea to bleed the cylinder prior to installing it on the vehicle. This makes the system bleeding operation much easier.

1. Place the master cylinder in a vise.

2. Connect 2 lines to the fluid outlet orifices and place them into the reservoir.

➡**Master cylinder bleeding kits are available from automotive stores.**

3. Fill the reservoir with clean, fresh brake fluid.

4. Using a wooden dowel, depress the pushrod slowly, allowing the pistons to return.

5. Do this several times until the air bubbles in the brake fluid are gone.

6. Remove the bleeding tubes from the master cylinder, plug the outlets and install the master cylinder.

DISC BRAKES

♦ **See Figures 22, 23 and 24**

✳✳ CAUTION

Older brake pads or shoes may contain asbestos, which has been determined to be a cancer causing agent. Never clean the brake surfaces with compressed air! Avoid inhaling any dust from any brake surface! When cleaning brake surfaces, use a commercially available brake cleaning fluid.

Brake Pads

REMOVAL & INSTALLATION

♦ **See Figures 25 thru 34**

1. Remove the brake master cylinder reservoir cap.

2. Siphon and recycle approximately half the fluid from the reservoir.

3. Raise and support the vehicle safely.

4. Remove the wheels.

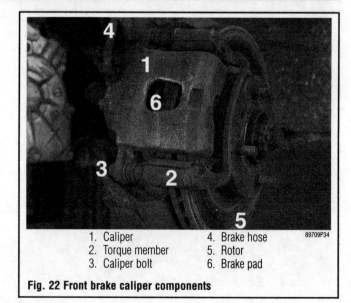

1. Caliper
2. Torque member
3. Caliper bolt
4. Brake hose
5. Rotor
6. Brake pad

Fig. 22 Front brake caliper components

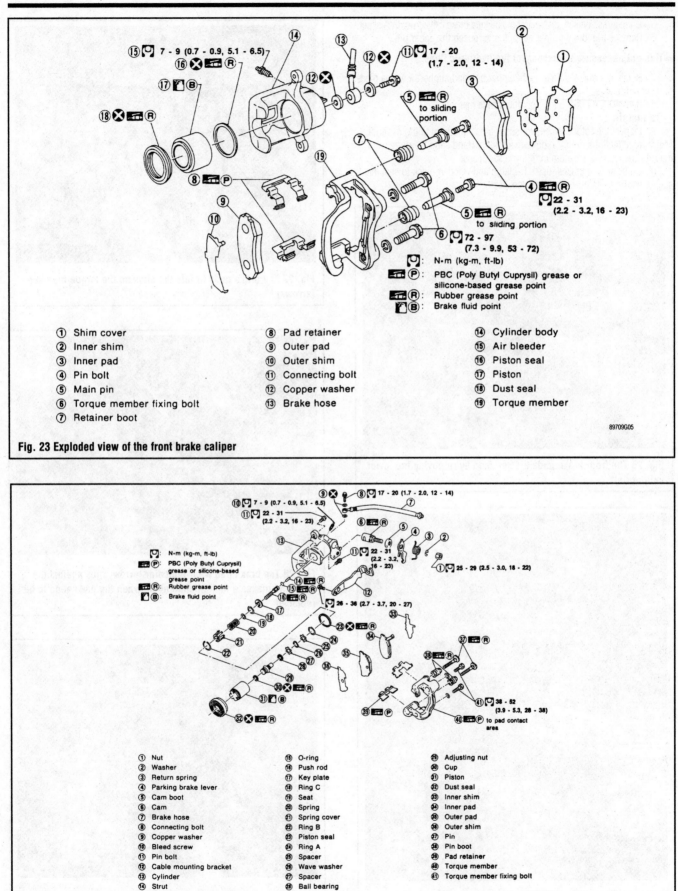

Fig. 23 Exploded view of the front brake caliper

① Shim cover	⑧ Pad retainer	⑭ Cylinder body
② Inner shim	⑨ Outer pad	⑮ Air bleeder
③ Inner pad	⑩ Outer shim	⑯ Piston seal
④ Pin bolt	⑪ Connecting bolt	⑰ Piston
⑤ Main pin	⑫ Copper washer	⑱ Dust seal
⑥ Torque member fixing bolt	⑬ Brake hose	⑲ Torque member
⑦ Retainer boot		

89709G05

Fig. 24 Exploded view of the rear brake caliper

① Nut	⑮ O-ring	㉙ Adjusting nut
② Washer	⑯ Push rod	㉚ Cup
③ Return spring	⑰ Key plate	㉛ Piston
④ Parking brake lever	⑱ Ring C	㉜ Dust seal
⑤ Cam boot	⑲ Seat	㉝ Inner shim
⑥ Cam	⑳ Spring	㉞ Inner pad
⑦ Brake hose	㉑ Spring cover	㉟ Outer pad
⑧ Connecting bolt	㉒ Ring B	㊱ Outer shim
⑨ Copper washer	㉓ Piston seal	㊲ Pin
⑩ Bleed screw	㉔ Ring A	㊳ Pin boot
⑪ Pin bolt	㉕ Spacer	㊴ Pad retainer
⑫ Cable mounting bracket	㉖ Wave washer	㊵ Torque member
⑬ Cylinder	㉗ Spacer	㊶ Torque member fixing bolt
⑭ Strut	㉘ Ball bearing	

89709G06

5. On rear disc brakes, disconnect the parking brake cable from the caliper.

6. Remove the lower caliper pin bolt and loosen the upper pin.

➡**It is not necessary to disconnect the hydraulic lines.**

7. Rotate the brake caliper on the upper bolt and support it with a piece of mechanic's wire.

8. Remove the brake pads from the torque member.

To install:

9. Inspect the rotor surfaces for scoring or buildup of lining material. Minor imperfections do not require machining. Hand sand the glaze from the rotor using 150 grit aluminum oxide sandpaper.

10. On front disc brakes, use a C-clamp and wooden block to seat the caliper piston in its bore, as illustrated.

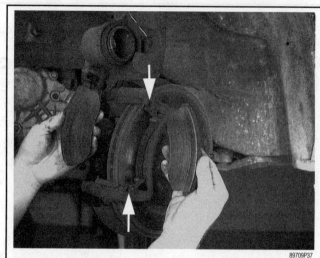

Fig. 27 The brake pads fit into the slots on the torque member (arrows)

Fig. 25 The front brake pads are serviced by removing the lower caliper bolt . . .

Fig. 28 The brake pad wear indicator (arrow) rubs against the rotor and makes a high pitched noise when the pads need to be replaced

Fig. 26 . . . and rotating the caliper upward. Support the caliper using a piece of wire

Fig. 29 Lubricate the pad retainers with a silicone based grease at the points indicated (arrows)

Fig. 30 The main caliper pin (arrow) should be inspected each time the front brakes are serviced

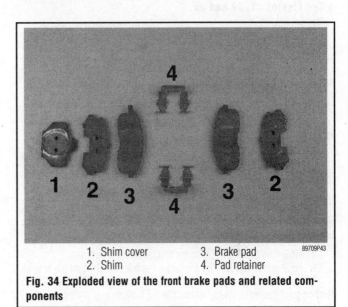

Fig. 33 Pad shims are used to prevent brake pads from vibrating in the caliper. Such harmonic vibration is the cause of most brake squeal

Fig. 31 On front brakes, use a large C-clamp to press the piston back into the caliper

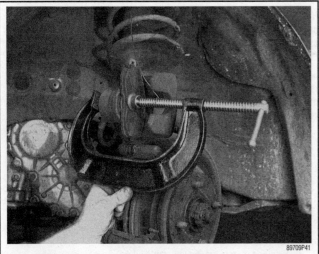

1. Shim cover
2. Shim
3. Brake pad
4. Pad retainer

Fig. 34 Exploded view of the front brake pads and related components

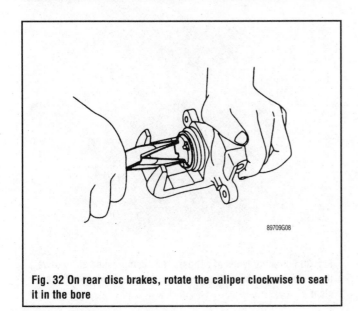

Fig. 32 On rear disc brakes, rotate the caliper clockwise to seat it in the bore

11. On rear disc brakes, rotate the caliper piston clockwise to seat it in its bore.

➡Seating the piston must be done to provide clearance for the disc brake caliper to fit over the rotor with new brake pads.

12. Remove all built-up rust from the inside of the brake caliper pad contact area.

13. Install the brake pads, with the pad retainers, into the brake caliper torque member.

14. Rotate the brake caliper into position on the torque member.

15. Install the brake caliper pin bolt and tighten to 16–23 ft. lbs. (22–31 Nm).

16. Connect the parking brake cable to the caliper.

➡Failure to tighten the lug nuts to the proper torque in a star pattern may result in damage to the brake rotor.

17. Install the wheel and tighten the lug nuts properly.

18. Lower the vehicle.

19. Fill the master cylinder reservoir with fresh, clean brake fluid and install the cap.

20. Pump the brake pedal to seat the brake pads.

21. Bleed the brake system as necessary.

INSPECTION

➡**Brake pad lining thickness can be checked without removing the pads from the caliper.**

1. Inspect the brake pads for wear using a ruler or Vernier caliper. If the lining is thinner than specification, or there is evidence of the lining being contaminated by brake fluid or oil, replace all brake pad assemblies (a complete axle set).

2. When replacing pads, always check the surface of the rotors for scoring or wear. The rotors should be removed for resurfacing if badly scored.

➡**The Brake Specifications chart in this section contains the manufacturer's specified pad wear limit. However, this measurement may disagree with your state inspection laws. Always abide by your state inspection law specifications if they disagree with the manufacturer's specifications.**

Brake Caliper

REMOVAL & INSTALLATION

♦ **See Figures 31, 32 and 35**

1. Siphon and recycle approximately half the fluid from the reservoir.
2. Raise and support the vehicle safely.
3. Remove the wheels.
4. On rear disc brakes, disconnect the parking brake cable from the caliper.
5. Disconnect and cap the brake hose.
6. Remove the torque member mounting bolts.
7. Remove the caliper with the torque member attached from the knuckle.

To install:

8. On front disc brakes, use a C-clamp and wooden block to seat the caliper piston in its bore, as shown.
9. On rear disc brakes, rotate the caliper piston clockwise to seat it in its bore, as illustrated.

➡**Seating the piston must be done to provide clearance for the disc brake caliper to fit over the rotor with new brake pads.**

10. Install the brake pads, with the pad retainers, if removed.
11. Position the caliper with the torque member attached on the knuckle.
12. Install the torque member bolts and tighten to 53–72 ft. lbs. (72–97 Nm) on front brakes or 28–38 ft. lbs. (38–52 Nm) on rear brakes.

13. Connect the brake hose and tighten the banjo bolt to 12–14 ft. lbs. (17–20 Nm).
14. On rear disc brakes, connect the parking brake cable to the caliper.

➡**Failure to tighten the lug nuts to the proper torque in a star pattern may result in damage to the brake rotor.**

15. Install the wheel and tighten the lug nuts properly.
16. Lower the vehicle.
17. Fill the master cylinder reservoir with fresh fluid and install the cap.
18. Pump the brake pedal to seat the brake pads.
19. Bleed the brake system.

OVERHAUL

♦ **See Figures 36 thru 43**

➡**Some vehicles may be equipped with dual piston calipers. The procedure to overhaul the caliper is essentially the same with the exception of multiple pistons, O-rings and dust boots.**

1. Remove the caliper from the vehicle and place on a clean workbench.

❋ CAUTION

NEVER place your fingers in front of the pistons in an attempt to catch or protect the pistons when applying compressed air. This could result in personal injury!

➡**Depending upon the vehicle, there are two different ways to remove the piston from the caliper. Refer to the brake pad replacement procedure to make sure you have the correct procedure for your vehicle.**

2. The first method is as follows:
   a. Stuff a shop towel or a block of wood into the caliper to catch the piston.
   b. Remove the caliper piston using compressed air applied to the caliper inlet hole. Inspect the piston for scoring, nicks, corrosion and/or worn or damaged chrome plating. The piston must be replaced if any of these conditions are found.
3. For the second method, you must rotate the piston to retract it from the caliper.
4. If equipped, remove the anti-rattle clip.
5. Use a prytool to remove the caliper boot, being careful not to scratch the housing bore.

Fig. 35 Never allow the caliper to hang by the brake hose. Always suspend the caliper with a piece of wire

89709P13

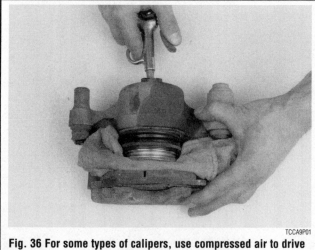

TCCA9P01

Fig. 36 For some types of calipers, use compressed air to drive the piston out of the caliper, but make sure to keep your fingers clear

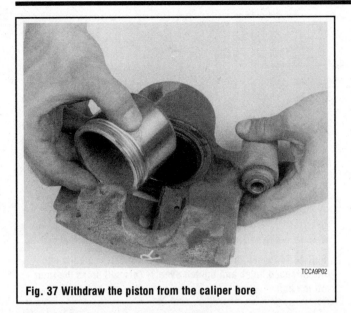

Fig. 37 Withdraw the piston from the caliper bore

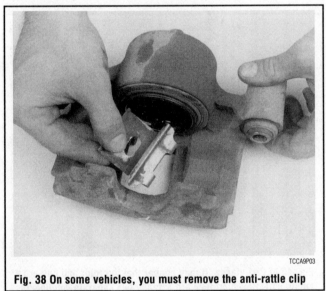

Fig. 38 On some vehicles, you must remove the anti-rattle clip

Fig. 39 Use a prytool to carefully pry around the edge of the boot . . .

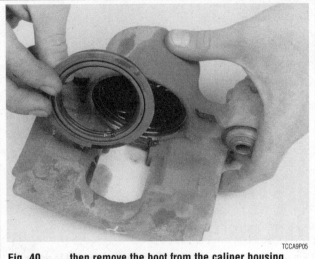

Fig. 40 . . . then remove the boot from the caliper housing, taking care not to score or damage the bore

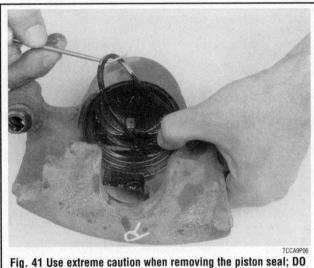

Fig. 41 Use extreme caution when removing the piston seal; DO NOT scratch the caliper bore

6. Remove the piston seals from the groove in the caliper bore.

7. Carefully loosen the brake bleeder valve cap and valve from the caliper housing.

8. Inspect the caliper bores, pistons and mounting threads for scoring or excessive wear.

9. Use crocus cloth to polish out light corrosion from the piston and bore.

10. Clean all parts with denatured alcohol and dry with compressed air.

To assemble:

11. Lubricate and install the bleeder valve and cap.

12. Install the new seals into the caliper bore grooves, making sure they are not twisted.

13. Lubricate the piston bore.

14. Install the pistons and boots into the bores of the calipers and push to the bottom of the bores.

15. Use a suitable driving tool to seat the boots in the housing.

16. Install the caliper in the vehicle.

17. Install the wheel and tire assembly, then carefully lower the vehicle.

18. Properly bleed the brake system.

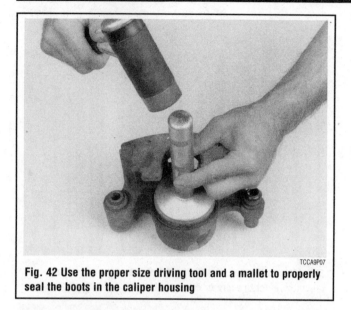

Fig. 42 Use the proper size driving tool and a mallet to properly seal the boots in the caliper housing

Fig. 44 To loosen the rotor from the hub, insert two bolts into the threaded holes and tighten evenly. This will press the rotor off the hub

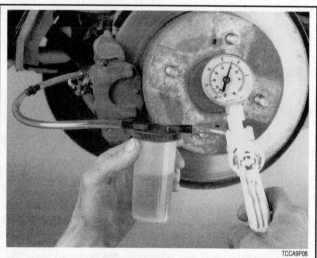

Fig. 43 There are tools, such as this Mighty-Vac, available to assist in proper brake system bleeding

Fig. 45 At first glance, it may appear that the rotor and hub are a single unit. However, they are actually two separate components

Brake Disc (Rotor)

REMOVAL & INSTALLATION

♦ **See Figures 44, 45, 46 and 47**

1. Remove the brake master cylinder reservoir cap.
2. Siphon and recycle approximately half the fluid from the reservoir.
3. Raise and support the vehicle safely.
4. Remove the wheel(s).
5. Remove the caliper.
6. On front rotors, insert two bolts into the threaded holes and tighten evenly to loosen the rotor from the hub. This will press the rotor off the hub.
7. Rear rotors are a slip fit onto the hub. Simply pull the rotor off the hub.

To install:

8. Use a wire brush to clean the hub mounting surfaces, then apply a coating of anti-seize compound to the hub. This prevents the rotor from rusting to the hub.
9. Install the rotor on the hub.
10. Position the caliper with the torque member attached on the knuckle.
11. Install the torque member bolts and tighten to 53–72 ft. lbs. (72–97 Nm) on front brakes or 28–38 ft. lbs. (38–52 Nm) on rear brakes.

Fig. 46 Use a wire brush to clean the hub mounting surfaces . . .

Fig. 47 . . . then apply a coating of anti-seize compound to the hub. This prevents the rotor from rusting to the hub

➡**Failure to tighten the lug nuts to the proper torque in a star pattern may result in damage to the brake rotor.**

12. Install the wheel and tighten the lug nuts properly.
13. Lower the vehicle.
14. Fill the master cylinder reservoir with fresh, clean brake fluid and install the cap.
15. Pump the brake pedal to seat the brake pads.
16. Bleed the brake system.

INSPECTION

Using a brake rotor micrometer or Vernier caliper, measure the rotor thickness in several places around the rotor.

Mount a magnetic base dial indicator to the strut and zero the indicator stylus on the face of the rotor. Turn the rotor 360 degrees by hand and record the run-out.

➡**On rear rotors, attach the dial indicator using the lug nuts to hold it flush to the hub during run-out measurement.**

Compare measurements to the Brake Specifications chart. If the thickness and run-out are not within specifications, replace the rotor.

DRUM BRAKES

⬧ See Figure 48

✻✻ CAUTION

Older brake pads or shoes may contain asbestos, which has been determined to be a cancer causing agent. Never clean the brake surfaces with compressed air! Avoid inhaling any dust from any brake surface! When cleaning brake surfaces, use a commercially available brake cleaning fluid.

Brake Drum

REMOVAL & INSTALLATION

⬧ See Figures 49, 50 and 51

1. Raise and support the vehicle safely.
2. Remove the wheels.

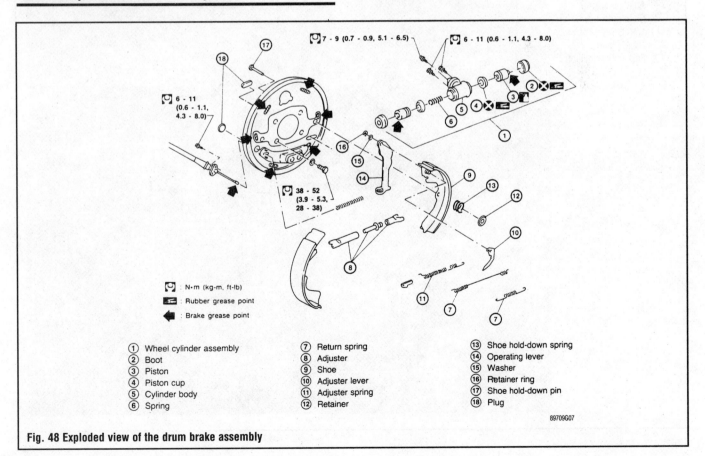

7 - 9 (0.7 - 0.9, 5.1 - 6.5)

6 - 11 (0.6 - 1.1, 4.3 - 8.0)

6 - 11 (0.6 - 1.1, 4.3 - 8.0)

38 - 52 (3.9 - 5.3, 28 - 38)

: N·m (kg-m, ft-lb)

: Rubber grease point

: Brake grease point

① Wheel cylinder assembly	⑦ Return spring	⑬ Shoe hold-down spring
② Boot	⑧ Adjuster	⑭ Operating lever
③ Piston	⑨ Shoe	⑮ Washer
④ Piston cup	⑩ Adjuster lever	⑯ Retainer ring
⑤ Cylinder body	⑪ Adjuster spring	⑰ Shoe hold-down pin
⑥ Spring	⑫ Retainer	⑱ Plug

Fig. 48 Exploded view of the drum brake assembly

DRUM BRAKE COMPONENTS

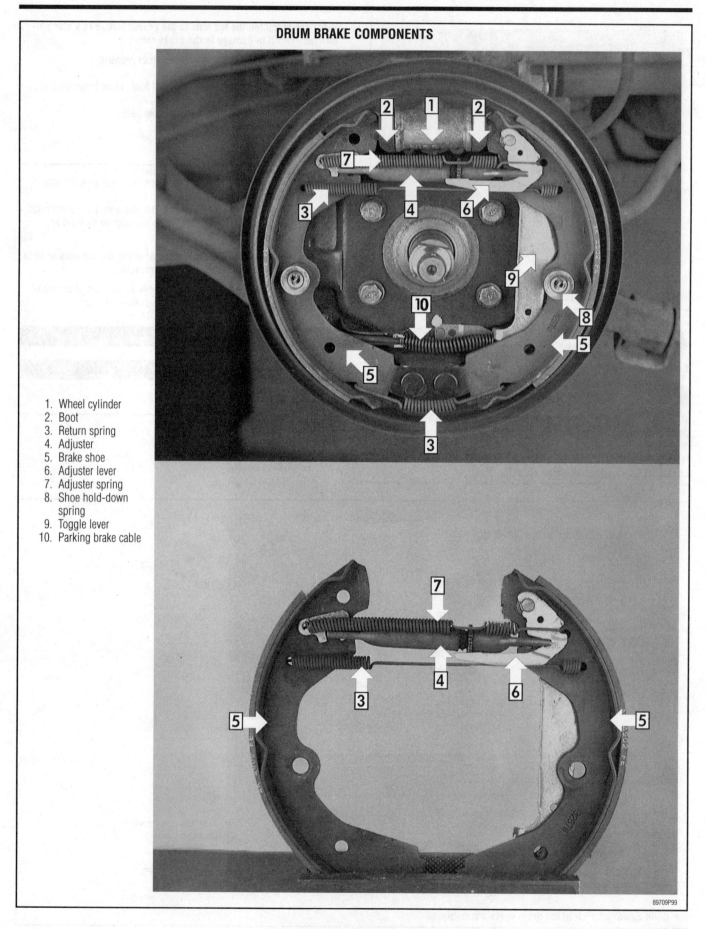

1. Wheel cylinder
2. Boot
3. Return spring
4. Adjuster
5. Brake shoe
6. Adjuster lever
7. Adjuster spring
8. Shoe hold-down
   spring
9. Toggle lever
10. Parking brake cable

89709P99

Fig. 49 Most brake drums will have the maximum safe diameter stamped or embossed into the drum. Never exceed this diameter when machining the drum

Fig. 50 This backing plate has the brake pad dimensions stamped into it. Such information may be needed when ordering replacement brake pads

Fig. 51 To loosen the drum from the hub, insert two bolts into the threaded holes and tighten evenly. This will press the drum off the hub

3. Insert two bolts into the threaded holes and tighten evenly to loosen the drum from the hub. This will press the drum off the hub.
4. Remove the drum from the hub.
To install:
5. Use a wire brush to clean the hub mounting surfaces, then apply a coating of anti-seize compound to the hub. This prevents the drum from rusting to the hub.
6. Install the drum on the hub.

➡**Failure to tighten the lug nuts to the proper torque in a star pattern may result in damage to the brake drum.**

7. Install the wheel and tighten the lug nuts properly.
8. Lower the vehicle.

INSPECTION

Using a brake drum inside micrometer or Vernier caliper, measure the inside diameter in several places around the drum.

Compare measurements to the Brake Specifications chart. If the inside diameter is not within specifications, replace the drum.

Check that there are no cracks or chips in the braking surface. Excessive bluing indicates overheating and a replacement drum is needed.

The drum can be machined to remove minor damage and to establish a rounded braking surface on a warped drum. Never exceed the maximum oversize of the drum when machining the braking surface. The maximum inside diameter is stamped on the drum.

Brake Shoes

INSPECTION

1. Inspect the brake shoes for wear using a ruler or Vernier caliper. If the lining is thinner than specification or there is evidence of the lining being contaminated by brake fluid or oil, replace all brake shoe assemblies (a complete axle set).
2. When replacing shoes, always check the surface of the drums for scoring or wear. The drums should be removed for resurfacing if badly scored.

➡**The Brake Specifications chart in this section contains the manufacturer's specified shoe wear limit. However, this measurement may disagree with your state inspection laws. Always abide by your state inspection law specifications if they disagree with the manufacturer's specifications.**

REMOVAL & INSTALLATION

♦ **See Figures 52, 53, 54, 55 and 56**

1. Raise the vehicle and remove the rear wheels.
2. Release the parking brake.
3. Remove the brake drum.
4. Remove the return springs, adjuster assembly, hold-down springs, and brake shoes.

➡**The brake shoes can be removed as an assembly by removing the hold-down springs and releasing the parking brake cable. This allows the brake shoe assembly to be disassembled off the vehicle.**

5. Disconnect the parking brake cable from the brake shoe.
To install:
6. Clean the backing plate. A very thin film of lithium grease may be applied to the pivot points at the ends of the brake shoes. Grease the shoe locating buttons on the backing plate, also. Be careful not to get grease on the linings or drum.
7. Inspect the wheel cylinder for leaks and replace as necessary.
8. Inspect the brake drums, and machine or replace as necessary.
9. Reconnect the parking brake cable.

Fig. 52 Always use a brake cleaning fluid to clean brake dust from the components prior to servicing

Fig. 53 The brake shoe retainers are removed using pliers. A special brake shoe retainer tool is also available

Fig. 54 The brake shoe retainer assemblies include a retainer, spring and stud

Fig. 55 A shoe return spring keeps the bottom of the brake shoes together

Fig. 56 Disconnect the parking brake cable from the brake shoe by pulling back the spring and releasing the cable from the toggle lever

10. Hook the return springs into the new shoes. The return spring ends should be between the shoes and the backing plate. The longer return spring must be adjacent to the wheel cylinder.

11. Install the adjuster assembly between the brake shoes. (Rotate the nut until the adjuster rod is at its shortest point.) Place one shoe in the adjuster and piston slots, then pry the other shoe into position. Install the hold-down springs and reconnect the return springs.

12. Install the brake drums and wheels.

13. Adjust the brakes.

14. Bleed the hydraulic system, if necessary.

15. Apply the parking brake and ensure that the brake shoes do not drag once the parking brake is released.

ADJUSTMENTS

The drum brakes are self-adjusting and require a manual adjustment only after the brake shoes have been replaced, or when the length of the adjusting screw has been changed while performing some other service.

1. Raise and support the vehicle safely.

2. Remove the rubber plug from the adjusting slot on the backing plate.

3. Insert a brake adjustment tool into the slot and engage the lowest possible tooth on the starwheel. Move the end of the brake spoon down-

ward to move the starwheel upward and expand the adjusting screw. Repeat this operation until the brakes lock the wheels.

4. Insert a small screwdriver or piece of firm wire (coat hanger wire) into the adjusting slot and push the automatic adjusting lever out and free of the starwheel on the adjusting screw, and hold it there.

5. Engage the topmost tooth possible on the starwheel with the brake adjusting spoon. Move the end of the adjusting spoon upward to move the adjusting screw starwheel downward and contract the adjusting screw. Back off the adjusting screw starwheel until the wheel spins freely with a minimum of drag. Keep track of the number of turns that the starwheel is backed off, or the number of strokes taken with the brake adjusting spoon.

6. Repeat this operation for the other side. When backing off the brakes on the other side, the starwheel adjuster must be backed off the same number of turns to prevent side-to-side brake pull.

7. Install the wheel and tire assemblies, then lower the vehicle.

8. When the brakes are adjusted, make several stops while backing the vehicle to equalize the brakes on both of the wheels.

Wheel Cylinder

REMOVAL & INSTALLATION

◆ **See Figures 57, 58, 59 and 60**

1. Raise and safely support the vehicle.
2. Remove the wheel(s).
3. Remove the brake drum.
4. Remove the brake shoe assembly.
5. Disconnect and cap the flare nut and the brake line from the wheel cylinder.
6. Remove the wheel cylinder-to-backing plate bolts.
7. Remove the wheel cylinder.

➡**If the wheel cylinder is difficult to remove, tap it with a soft hammer to release it from the backing plate.**

To install:

8. Install the wheel cylinder assembly to the backing plate and tighten the bolts to 60–72 inch lbs. (6–9 Nm).
9. Connect the brake line.
10. Install the brake shoe assembly.
11. Install the brake drum.
12. Install the wheel(s).
13. Bleed the brake system.
14. Adjust the rear brakes as necessary.

Fig. 58 Note that the bleeder screw is missing in this photo. It was removed to prevent damaging it while loosening the brake line fitting

Fig. 59 The wheel cylinder bolts are accessed from the rear of the backing plate

Fig. 57 The wheel cylinder (arrow) is located at the top of the brake backing plate, and provides force to press the brake shoes against the drum

Fig. 60 The wheel cylinder fits into a special cutout on the backing plate

OVERHAUL

▶ **See Figures 61 thru 70**

Wheel cylinder overhaul kits may be available, but often at little or no savings over a new or reconditioned wheel cylinder. It often makes sense with these components to substitute a new or reconditioned part instead of attempting an overhaul.

If no replacement is available, or you would prefer to overhaul your wheel cylinders, the following procedure may be used. When rebuilding and installing wheel cylinders, avoid getting any contaminants into the system. Always use clean, new, high quality brake fluid. If dirty or improper fluid has been used, it will be necessary to drain the entire system, flush the system with the proper brake fluid, replace all rubber components, then refill and bleed the system.

1. Remove the wheel cylinder from the vehicle and place on a clean workbench.

2. Remove and discard the old rubber boots, then withdraw the pistons. Piston cylinders are equipped with seals and a spring assembly, all located behind the pistons in the cylinder bore.

3. Remove the remaining inner components, seals and spring assembly. Compressed air may be useful in removing these components. If no compressed air is available, be VERY careful not to score the wheel cylinder bore when removing parts from it. Discard all components for which replacements were supplied in the rebuild kit.

4. Wash the cylinder and metal parts in denatured alcohol or clean brake fluid.

❊❊❊ WARNING

Never use a mineral-based solvent such as gasoline, kerosene or paint thinner for cleaning purposes. These solvents will swell rubber components and quickly deteriorate them.

5. Allow the parts to air dry or use compressed air. Do not use rags for cleaning, since lint will remain in the cylinder bore.

6. Inspect the pistons and replace if they show scratches.

7. Lubricate the cylinder bore and seals using clean brake fluid.

8. Position the spring assembly.

9. Install the inner seals, then the pistons.

10. Insert the new boots into the counterbores by hand. Do not lubricate the boots.

11. Install the wheel cylinder.

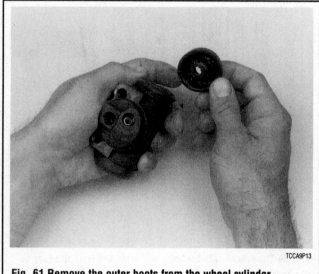

Fig. 61 Remove the outer boots from the wheel cylinder

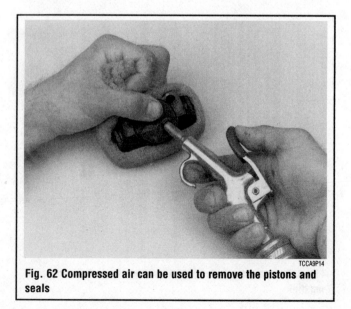

Fig. 62 Compressed air can be used to remove the pistons and seals

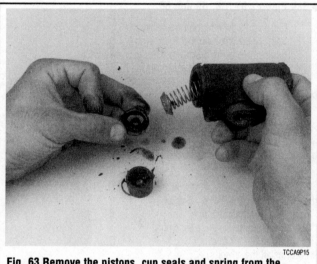

Fig. 63 Remove the pistons, cup seals and spring from the cylinder

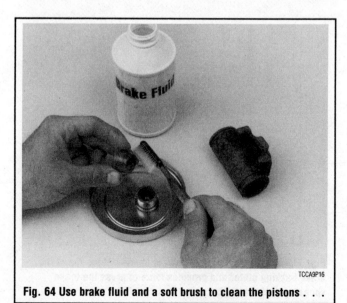

Fig. 64 Use brake fluid and a soft brush to clean the pistons . . .

Fig. 65 . . . and the bore of the wheel cylinder

Fig. 66 Once cleaned and inspected, the wheel cylinder is ready for assembly

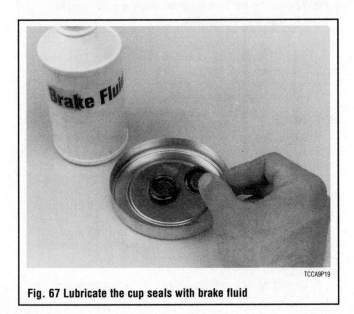

Fig. 67 Lubricate the cup seals with brake fluid

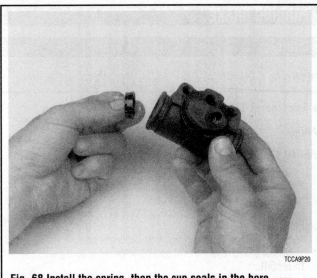

Fig. 68 Install the spring, then the cup seals in the bore

Fig. 69 Lightly lubricate the pistons, then install them

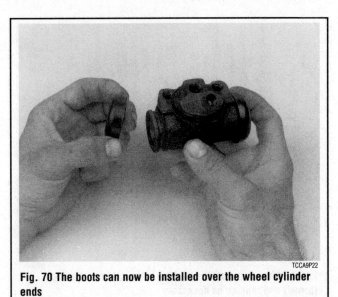

Fig. 70 The boots can now be installed over the wheel cylinder ends

PARKING BRAKE

Cable(s)

REMOVAL & INSTALLATION

♦ **See Figures 71, 72, 73 and 74**

Altima

FRONT CABLE

1. Remove the center console assembly.
2. Loosen and remove the parking brake cable adjusting nut at the base of the parking brake lever.
3. From under the vehicle, disconnect the parking brake cables at the equalizer.
4. Unbolt the parking brake lever from the center console.
5. Unbolt and remove the front parking brake cable from the vehicle.
To install:
6. Install the front parking brake cable into the parking brake lever and start the adjusting nut on the front cable.

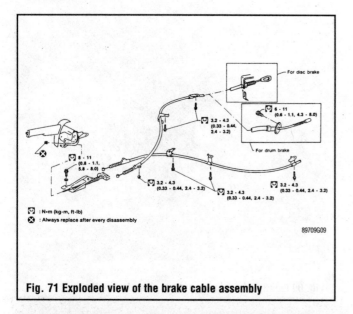

Fig. 71 Exploded view of the brake cable assembly

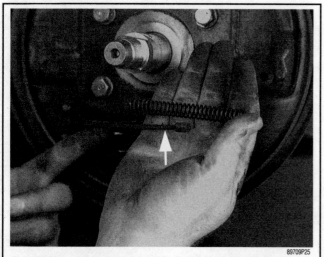

Fig. 72 Always inspect the parking brake cable for fraying (arrow) and replace as necessary

Fig. 73 The parking brake cable is attached to the backing plate by two bolts (arrows)

Fig. 74 Once the bolts are removed, pull the parking brake cable through the backing plate

7. Install the lever and cable assembly into the vehicle. Tighten the mounting bolts to 9–12 ft. lbs. (13–16 Nm).
8. From under the vehicle, connect the parking brake cables at the equalizer.
9. Install the center console assembly.

REAR CABLE

1. Remove the rear wheel and the brake drum or disc assembly.
2. At the cable adjuster, loosen the adjusting nut, then separate the rear cable from the equalizer.
3. On rear drum brakes, remove the brake shoes from the backing plate, then separate the rear cable from the toggle lever.
4. On rear disc brakes, remove the cable retainer and the cable end from the toggle lever.
5. Remove the bolts that secure the cable to the vehicle underbody.
6. Pull the cable through the backing plate and remove it from the vehicle.
To install:
7. Connect the cable to the toggle lever and tighten the cable retainer nut on the backing plate to 9–12 ft. lbs. (13–16 Nm).

8. Install the bolts that secure the cable to the vehicle underbody and tighten the bolt to 45–57 inch lbs. (5.1–6.5 Nm).

9. At the cable equalizer, connect the parking brake cable and tighten the bolt or mounting nut to 9–12 ft. lbs. (13–16 Nm).

10. Install the brake drum or disc and wheel assembly.

11. Adjust the parking brake cable.

240SX

FRONT CABLE

1. Remove the parking brake console box.

2. Fully loosen the parking brake cable adjustment at the base of the parking brake lever, and remove the adjusting nut.

3. Disconnect the parking brake cables from the equalizer.

4. If necessary, remove the front seat.

5. Disconnect the warning lamp switch plate connector.

6. Using a chisel and hammer, break the clinched portion of the control lever at the front cable.

7. Remove the bolts that secure the front cable to the floor and remove the front cable.

To install:

8. Thread the front cable into the parking brake lever and start the adjusting nut by hand.

9. Reinstall the front cable through the floor and secure with mounting bolts.

10. Connect the warning lamp switch plate connector.

11. If removed, install the front seat.

12. Connect the parking brake cables to the equalizer.

13. Install the parking brake console box.

14. Adjust the parking brake assembly.

REAR CABLE

1. Back off the adjusting nut in the base of the parking brake lever to loosen the cable tension.

2. Working from underneath the vehicle, disconnect the cable at the equalizer.

3. Remove the cable support bracket mounting bolts.

4. Disconnect the cable from the rear brakes.

5. Remove the lock plate clips from the parking brake cable guides.

➡**Matchmark the cable position to the guide brackets for reference during installation.**

6. Remove the cable from the vehicle.

To install:

7. Connect the cable to the rear brakes and install the lock plate.

8. Connect the cable to the equalizer.

9. Connect the cable support brackets.

10. Adjust the cable.

ADJUSTMENT

Altima

➡**Make sure the rear brakes are properly adjusted prior to adjusting the parking brake.**

1. Pull the parking brake lever with 44 lbs. (196 N) of force and note the number of notches moved.

2. The parking brake lever should raise 7–8 notches.

3. Locate the parking brake adjuster at the base of the lever and rotate the adjuster nut on the threaded rod to obtain the proper parking brake lever adjustment.

4. Bend the parking brake warning lamp switch plate so that the brake warning light comes on when the parking brake lever is pulled up one notch. The brake light should turn off when the lever is fully released.

240SX

1. Raise the parking brake lever 4 to 5 notches.

2. Insert an offset box end wrench or ratchet and socket assembly into the opening in the control lever, and loosen the self-lock adjusting nut. Remove the wrench and push the lever completely down.

3. Depress the brake pedal about five times. This will automatically set the rear caliper in the proper position.

➡**Use 44 lbs. (196 N) of force to raise the lever for adjustment purposes.**

4. Adjust the parking brake cable until the proper stroke is achieved. The proper stroke is 6 to 8 notches for 1993–94 vehicles or 7 to 9 notches for 1995–98 vehicles. When the parking brake lever is pulled the specific number of notches, the rear wheels should not turn. When the parking brake lever is released, the rear wheels should turn freely.

5. Bend the parking brake warning lamp switch plate so that the brake warning light comes on when the parking brake lever is pulled up one notch. The brake light should be extinguished when the lever is pushed completely down.

6. After the proper stroke is achieved, tighten the adjusting nut.

ANTI-LOCK BRAKE SYSTEM

General Information

▶ **See Figures 75 and 76**

The Anti-Lock Brake System (ABS) is designed to prevent locked wheel skidding during hard braking or during braking on slippery surfaces. The front wheels of a vehicle cannot apply steering force if they are locked and sliding; the vehicle will continue in its previous direction of travel. The anti-lock brake systems found on these vehicles hold the wheels just below the point of locking, thereby allowing some steering response and preventing the rear of the vehicle from sliding sideways while braking.

There are conditions for which ABS provides no benefit. Hydroplaning is possible when the tires ride on a film of water, losing contact with the paved surface. This renders the vehicle totally uncontrollable until road contact is regained. Extreme steering maneuvers at high speed, or cornering beyond the limits of tire adhesion, can result in skidding which is independent of vehicle braking.

Under normal braking conditions, ABS functions in the same manner as a standard brake system. The system is merely a combination of electrical and hydraulic components, working together, to control the flow of brake fluid to the wheels when necessary.

The ABS control unit is the electronic brain of the system, receiving and interpreting speed signals from the speed sensors. The control unit will enter anti-lock mode when it senses impending wheel lock at any wheel, and immediately control the brake line pressure to the affected wheel.

The actuator assembly is separate from the master cylinder and booster. It contains the wheel circuit valves used to control brake fluid pressure to each wheel circuit.

The wheel speed sensors monitor decelerating wheel speed and provide data to the control module.

The Altima uses a four-channel ABS system with independent wheel speed sensors/controls at each wheel. The 240SX uses a three-channel system with a single wheel speed sensor for the rear wheels (located on the differential) and independent wheel speed sensors/controls for each of the front wheels.

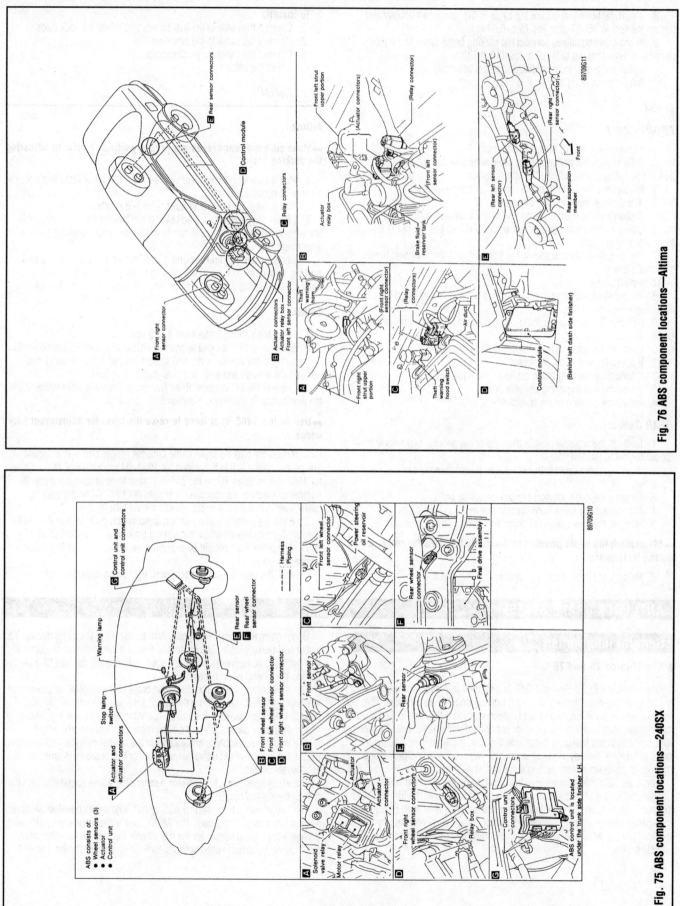

Fig. 76 ABS component locations—Altima

Fig. 75 ABS component locations—240SX

PRECAUTIONS

- Certain components within the Anti-lock Brake System (ABS) are not intended to be serviced or repaired individually. Only those components with removal and installation procedures should be serviced.
- Do not use rubber hoses or other parts not specifically identified for an ABS system. When using repair kits, replace all parts included in the kit. Partial or incorrect repair may lead to functional problems and require the replacement of components.
- Lubricate rubber parts with clean, fresh brake fluid to ease assembly. Do not use lubricated shop air to clean parts; damage to rubber components may result.
- Use only specified brake fluid from an unopened container.
- If any hydraulic component or line is removed or replaced, it may be necessary to bleed the entire system.
- A clean repair area is essential. Always clean the reservoir and cap thoroughly before removing the cap. The slightest amount of dirt in the fluid may plug an orifice and impair the system function. Perform repairs after components have been thoroughly cleaned; use only denatured alcohol to clean components. Do not allow ABS components to come into contact with any substance containing mineral oil; this includes used shop rags.
- The ABS control unit is a microprocessor similar to other computer units in the vehicle. Ensure that the ignition switch is **OFF** before removing or installing controller harnesses. Avoid static electricity discharge at or near the controller.
- If any arc welding is to be done on the vehicle, the control unit should be unplugged before welding operations begin.

Reading Codes

▶ See Figure 77

On Altima, drive the vehicle over 20 mph (32 km/h) for at least one minute. Turn the ignition **OFF** and ground the **L** terminal of the data link connector under the dashboard. The codes will appear as flashes of the ABS lamp on the dashboard.

➡Do not press the brake pedal while reading codes.

On 240SX, drive the vehicle over 20 mph (32 km/h) for at least one minute. With the engine running, inspect the LED on the control unit. The codes will appear as flashes of the LED.

Clearing Codes

On Altima, clear the codes by grounding and ungrounding the **L** terminal of the data link connector under the dashboard three times within 12.5 seconds. Each ground should last more than one second. The ABS warning lamp on the dashboard will go out after the erasing operation has been completed.

On 240SX, clear the codes by disconnecting the negative battery cable for at least one minute.

Wheel Sensor

TESTING

1. Unfasten the wheel sensor electrical connector.
2. Measure the resistance between the sensor terminals. Resistance should be 0.6–3.3 kilohms on 240SX or 1.0–1.25 kilohms on Altima.
3. If resistance is not within specification, the sensor may be faulty.
4. If resistance is within specification, check and repair circuits back to the control module.

REMOVAL & INSTALLATION

▶ See Figure 78

On the Altima, wheel sensors are located at each wheel, mounted to the knuckle. On 240SX, the front wheel sensors are located at each wheel, mounted to the knuckle. The rear wheel sensor is located at the differential housing, mounted near the driveshaft.

1. Raise and safely support the vehicle.
2. Unfasten the sensor electrical connector.
3. Remove the sensor mounting bolt.
4. Carefully remove the sensor.
5. Installation is the reverse of removal.
6. Tighten the mounting bolts to 13–17 ft. lbs. (18–24 Nm) for all sensors except front ones on the 240SX. Tighten the 240SX front sensor bolts to 8–12 ft. lbs. (11–16 Nm).

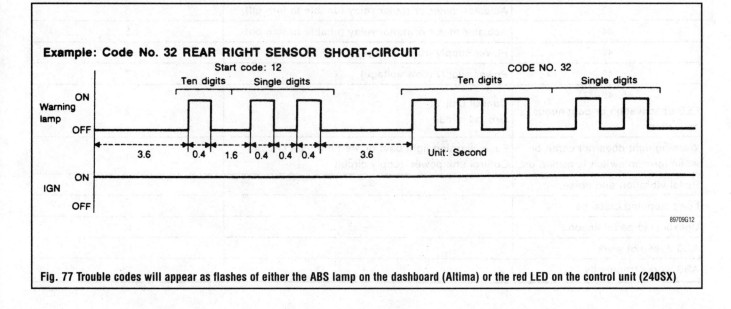

Example: Code No. 32 REAR RIGHT SENSOR SHORT-CIRCUIT

89709G12

Fig. 77 Trouble codes will appear as flashes of either the ABS lamp on the dashboard (Altima) or the red LED on the control unit (240SX)

ABS MALFUNCTION CODE/SYMPTOM CHART—240SX

Code No. (No. of LED flashes)	Malfunctioning part and circuit	Diagnostic procedure
01	Front right sensor (open-circuit)	4
02	Front left sensor (open-circuit)	4
03	Rear sensor (open-circuit)	4
05	Front right sensor (short-circuit)	4
06	Front left sensor (short-circuit)	4
07	Rear sensor (short-circuit)	4
11	Actuator front right inlet solenoid valve (open-circuit)	3
12	Actuator front left inlet solenoid valve (open-circuit)	3
13	Actuator rear inlet solenoid valve (open-circuit)	3
15	Actuator front right outlet solenoid valve (open-circuit)	3
16	Actuator front left outlet solenoid valve (open-circuit)	3
17	Actuator rear outlet solenoid valve (open-circuit)	3
21	Actuator front right inlet solenoid valve (short-circuit)	3
22	Actuator front left inlet solenoid valve (short-circuit)	3
23	Actuator rear inlet solenoid valve (short-circuit)	3
25	Actuator front right outlet solenoid valve (short-circuit)	3
26	Actuator front left outlet solenoid valve (short-circuit)	3
27	Actuator rear outlet solenoid valve (short-circuit)	3
41	Solenoid valve relay circuit (unable to turn off)	6
42	Solenoid valve relay circuit (unable to turn on)	6
43	Actuator motor or motor relay (unable to turn off)	5
44	Actuator motor or motor relay (unable to turn on)	5
47	Power supply (High voltage)	7
48	Power supply (Low voltage)	7
45, 46, 77 LED deactivation or continuous activation	Control unit Ground circuit	2
Warning light does not come on when ignition switch is turned on.	Fuse, warning light bulb or warning light circuit Control unit power supply circuit	1
Pedal vibration and noise	—	9
Long stopping distance	—	10
Unexpected pedal action	—	11
ABS does not work.	—	12
ABS works frequently.	—	13

89709C02

Code No. (No. of LED flashes)		Malfunctioning part	Diagnostic procedure
45		Actuator front left outlet solenoid valve	1
46		Actuator front left inlet solenoid valve	1
41		Actuator front right outlet solenoid valve	1
42		Actuator front right inlet solenoid valve	1
51		Actuator rear right outlet solenoid valve	1
52		Actuator rear right inlet solenoid valve	1
55		Actuator rear left outlet solenoid valve	1
56		Actuator rear left inlet solenoid valve	1
25	*1	Front left sensor (open-circuit)	2
26	*1	Front left sensor (short-circuit)	2
21	*1	Front right sensor (open-circuit)	2
22	*1	Front right sensor (short-circuit)	2
35	*1	Rear left sensor (open-circuit)	2
36	*1	Rear left sensor (short-circuit)	2
31	*1	Rear right sensor (open-circuit)	2
32	*1	Rear right sensor (short-circuit)	2
18	*1	Sensor rotor	2
61	*3	Actuator motor or motor relay	3
63		Solenoid valve relay	4
57	*2	Power supply (Low voltage)	5
71		Control unit	6
Warning lamp stays on when ignition switch is turned ON.		Control unit power supply circuit Warning lamp bulb circuit Control unit or control unit connector Solenoid valve relay stuck Power supply for solenoid valve relay coil	13
Warning lamp stays on during self-diagnosis.		Control unit	—
Warning lamp does not come on when ignition switch is turned ON.		Fuse, warning lamp bulb or warning lamp circuit Control unit	12
Warning lamp does not come on during self-diagnosis.		Control unit	—
Pedal vibration and noise		—	11
Long stopping distance		—	9
Unexpected pedal action		—	8
ABS does not work.		—	10
ABS works frequently.		—	7

*1: If one or more wheels spin on a rough or slippery road for 40 seconds or more, the ABS warning lamp will illuminate. This does not indicate a malfunction. Only in the case of the short-circuit (Code Nos. 26, 22, 32, and 36), after repair the ABS warning lamp also illuminates when the ignition switch is turned ON. In this case, drive the vehicle at speeds greater than 30 km/h (19 MPH) for approximately 1 minute as specified in "SELF-DIAGNOSIS PROCEDURE", BR-48. Check to ensure that the ABS warning lamp goes out while the vehicle is being driven.

*2: The trouble code "57", which refers to a low power supply voltage, does not indicate that the ABS control unit is malfunctioning. Do not replace the ABS control unit with a new one.

*3: The trouble code "61" can sometimes appear when the ABS motor is not properly grounded. If it appears, be sure to check the condition of the ABS motor ground circuit connection.

89709C03

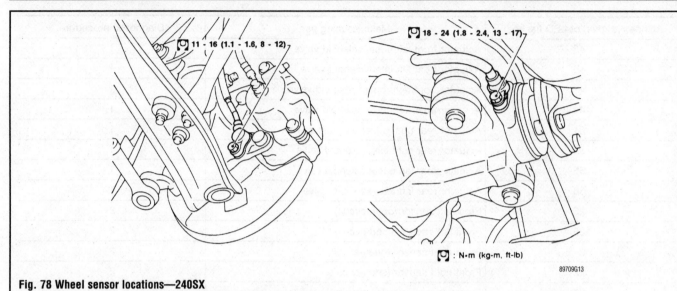

Fig. 78 Wheel sensor locations—240SX

Sensor Rotor

TESTING

1. Inspect the sensor rotor for physical damage.
2. Measure the rotor-to-sensor clearance using a non-magnetic feeler gauge. Clearance should be 0.0108–0.0295 in. (0.274–0.749mm) on front rotors and 0.0138–0.0246 in. (0.350–0.625mm) on rear rotors.
3. If clearance is not within specification, replace the damaged or worn components.

REMOVAL & INSTALLATION

▶ **See Figure 79**

1. Raise and safely support the vehicle.
2. Remove the wheel.
3. Remove the wheel hub.
4. Using a hydraulic press and appropriate adapters, remove the sensor rotor from the hub.

To install:

5. Install the sensor rotor with the lip facing upward and press into place.
6. Install the wheel hub.
7. Install the wheel.
8. Lower the vehicle.

Actuator

REMOVAL & INSTALLATION

▶ **See Figure 80**

The actuator is located in the engine compartment.
1. Disconnect the negative battery cable.
2. Drain and recycle the brake fluid.
3. Matchmark the brake lines leading to the actuator for installation reference.
4. Label and disconnect the actuator electrical harness.
5. Disconnect and cap the brake lines leading to the actuator.

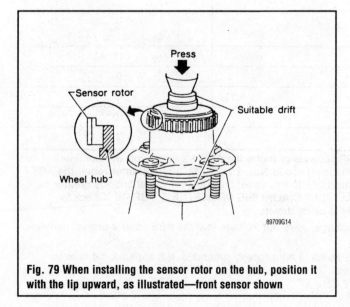

Fig. 79 When installing the sensor rotor on the hub, position it with the lip upward, as illustrated—front sensor shown

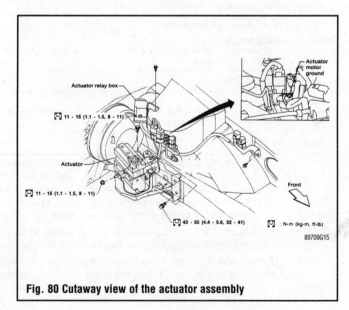

Fig. 80 Cutaway view of the actuator assembly

6. Remove the actuator mounting bolts.
7. Remove the actuator.
To install:
8. Install the actuator and tighten the mounting bolts to 12–13 ft. lbs. (16–18 Nm).
9. Position the brake lines leading to the actuator so that the match-marks align.
10. Connect the brake lines.
11. Fasten the actuator electrical harness.
12. Connect the negative battery cable.
13. Fill the brake system with fresh, clean brake fluid.
14. Bleed the brake system.

ABS Control Module

TESTING

There is no practical way to test the ABS control module in the field. If a preliminary check of all power and ground circuits yields normal results, and all components connected to the control module are functioning properly, the ABS control module may be faulty.

REMOVAL & INSTALLATION

The ABS control module is located under the driver's side of the dashboard on Altima, and at the driver's side of the trunk, behind a filler panel on the 240SX.

1. Disconnect the negative battery cable.
2. Label and disconnect the ABS electric harnesses.
3. Remove the control module mounting screws.
4. Remove the control module.
To install:
5. Install the control module and tighten the mounting screws securely.
6. Connect the ABS electric harnesses.
7. Connect the negative battery cable.

Bleeding the ABS System

All Nissan vehicles equipped with an Anti-lock Brake System (ABS) utilize a low-pressure system. Special depressurization procedures are, therefore, NOT necessary prior to servicing the ABS brakes on vehicles so-equipped.

The bleeding procedures for vehicles with conventional braking systems and those with ABS are similar. (Refer to the bleeding procedure, earlier in this section.) **However, the order in which bleeding should be performed is different.** On ABS equipped vehicles, bleed the brakes in the following order: left rear, right rear, left front and right front.

BRAKE SPECIFICATIONS
All measurements in inches unless noted

Year	Model	Master Cylinder Bore	Brake Disc Original Thickness	Brake Disc Minimum Thickness	Brake Disc Maximum Runout	Brake Drum Diameter Original Inside Diameter	Brake Drum Diameter Max. Wear Limit	Brake Drum Diameter Maximum Machine Diameter	Minimum Lining Thickness Front	Minimum Lining Thickness Rear
1993	240SX	0.8750 ②	NA	④	0.003	–	–	–	0.079	0.059
	Altima	0.9375 ③	NA	⑤	0.003	9.000	–	9.060	0.079	0.059 ①
1994	240SX	0.8750 ②	NA	④	0.003	–	–	–	0.079	0.059
	Altima	0.9375 ③	NA	⑤	0.003	9.000	–	9.060	0.079	0.059 ①
1995	240SX	0.8750 ②	NA	④	0.003	–	–	–	0.079	0.059
	Altima	0.9375 ③	NA	⑤	0.003	9.000	–	9.060	0.079	0.059 ①
1996	240SX	0.8750 ②	NA	④	0.003	–	–	–	0.079	0.059
	Altima	0.9375 ③	NA	⑤	0.003	9.000	–	9.060	0.079	0.059 ①
1997	240SX	0.8750 ②	NA	⑥	0.003	–	–	–	0.079	0.059
	Altima	0.9375 ③	NA	⑤	0.003	9.000	–	9.060	0.079	0.059 ①
1998	240SX	0.8750 ②	NA	⑥	0.003	–	–	–	0.079	0.059
	Altima	0.9375 ③	NA	⑤	0.003	9.000	–	9.060	0.079	0.059 ①

① Disc Brake: 0.079
② Optional: 0.9375
③ With ABS: 1.000
④ Front with ABS: 0.787
  Front without ABS: .709
  Rear: 0.315
⑤ Front: 0.787

89709C01

Troubleshooting the Brake System

Problem	Cause	Solution
Low brake pedal (excessive pedal travel required for braking action.)	• Excessive clearance between rear linings and drums caused by inoperative automatic adjusters	• Make 10 to 15 alternate forward and reverse brake stops to adjust brakes. If brake pedal does not come up, repair or replace adjuster parts as necessary.
	• Worn rear brakelining	• Inspect and replace lining if worn beyond minimum thickness specification
	• Bent, distorted brakeshoes, front or rear	• Replace brakeshoes in axle sets
	• Air in hydraulic system	• Remove air from system. Refer to Brake Bleeding.
Low brake pedal (pedal may go to floor with steady pressure applied.)	• Fluid leak in hydraulic system	• Fill master cylinder to fill line; have helper apply brakes and check calipers, wheel cylinders, differential valve tubes, hoses and fittings for leaks. Repair or replace as necessary.
	• Air in hydraulic system	• Remove air from system. Refer to Brake Bleeding.
	• Incorrect or non-recommended brake fluid (fluid evaporates at below normal temp).	• Flush hydraulic system with clean brake fluid. Refill with correct-type fluid.
	• Master cylinder piston seals worn, or master cylinder bore is scored, worn or corroded	• Repair or replace master cylinder
Low brake pedal (pedal goes to floor on first application—o.k. on subsequent applications.)	• Disc brake pads sticking on abutment surfaces of anchor plate. Caused by a build-up of dirt, rust, or corrosion on abutment surfaces	• Clean abutment surfaces
Fading brake pedal (pedal height decreases with steady pressure applied.)	• Fluid leak in hydraulic system	• Fill master cylinder reservoirs to fill mark, have helper apply brakes, check calipers, wheel cylinders, differential valve, tubes, hoses, and fittings for fluid leaks. Repair or replace parts as necessary.
	• Master cylinder piston seals worn, or master cylinder bore is scored, worn or corroded	• Repair or replace master cylinder
Decreasing brake pedal travel (pedal travel required for braking action decreases and may be accompanied by a hard pedal.)	• Caliper or wheel cylinder pistons sticking or seized	• Repair or replace the calipers, or wheel cylinders
	• Master cylinder compensator ports blocked (preventing fluid return to reservoirs) or pistons sticking or seized in master cylinder bore	• Repair or replace the master cylinder
	• Power brake unit binding internally	• Test unit according to the following procedure: (a) Shift transmission into neutral and start engine (b) Increase engine speed to 1500 rpm, close throttle and fully depress brake pedal (c) Slow release brake pedal and stop engine (d) Have helper remove vacuum check valve and hose from power unit. Observe for backward movement of brake pedal. (e) If the pedal moves backward, the power unit has an internal bind—replace power unit

TCCA9C01

Troubleshooting the Brake System (cont.)

Problem	Cause	Solution
Spongy brake pedal (pedal has abnormally soft, springy, spongy feel when depressed.)	• Air in hydraulic system • Brakeshoes bent or distorted • Brakelining not yet seated with drums and rotors • Rear drum brakes not properly adjusted	• Remove air from system. Refer to Brake Bleeding. • Replace brakeshoes • Burnish brakes • Adjust brakes
Hard brake pedal (excessive pedal pressure required to stop vehicle. May be accompanied by brake fade.)	• Loose or leaking power brake unit vacuum hose • Incorrect or poor quality brakelining • Bent, broken, distorted brakeshoes • Calipers binding or dragging on mounting pins. Rear brakeshoes dragging on support plate.	• Tighten connections or replace leaking hose • Replace with lining in axle sets • Replace brakeshoes • Replace mounting pins and bushings. Clean rust or burrs from rear brake support plate ledges and lubricate ledges with molydisulfide grease. **NOTE:** If ledges are deeply grooved or scored, do not attempt to sand or grind them smooth—replace support plate.
	• Caliper, wheel cylinder, or master cylinder pistons sticking or seized • Power brake unit vacuum check valve malfunction	• Repair or replace parts as necessary • Test valve according to the following procedure: (a) Start engine, increase engine speed to 1500 rpm, close throttle and immediately stop engine (b) Wait at least 90 seconds then depress brake pedal (c) If brakes are not vacuum assisted for 2 or more applications, check valve is faulty
	• Power brake unit has internal bind	• Test unit according to the following procedure: (a) With engine stopped, apply brakes several times to exhaust all vacuum in system (b) Shift transmission into neutral, depress brake pedal and start engine (c) If pedal height decreases with foot pressure and less pressure is required to hold pedal in applied position, power unit vacuum system is operating normally. Test power unit. If power unit exhibits a bind condition, replace the power unit.
	• Master cylinder compensator ports (at bottom of reservoirs) blocked by dirt, scale, rust, or have small burrs (blocked ports prevent fluid return to reservoirs). • Brake hoses, tubes, fittings clogged or restricted • Brake fluid contaminated with improper fluids (motor oil, transmission fluid, causing rubber components to swell and stick in bores • Low engine vacuum	• Repair or replace master cylinder **CAUTION:** Do not attempt to clean blocked ports with wire, pencils, or similar implements. Use compressed air only. • Use compressed air to check or unclog parts. Replace any damaged parts. • Replace all rubber components, combination valve and hoses. Flush entire brake system with DOT 3 brake fluid or equivalent. • Adjust or repair engine

TCCA9C02

Troubleshooting the Brake System (cont.)

Problem	Cause	Solution
Grabbing brakes (severe reaction to brake pedal pressure.)	• Brakelining(s) contaminated by grease or brake fluid	• Determine and correct cause of contamination and replace brakeshoes in axle sets
	• Parking brake cables incorrectly adjusted or seized	• Adjust cables. Replace seized cables.
	• Incorrect brakelining or lining loose on brakeshoes	• Replace brakeshoes in axle sets
	• Caliper anchor plate bolts loose	• Tighten bolts
	• Rear brakeshoes binding on support plate ledges	• Clean and lubricate ledges. Replace support plate(s) if ledges are deeply grooved. Do not attempt to smooth ledges by grinding.
	• Incorrect or missing power brake reaction disc	• Install correct disc
	• Rear brake support plates loose	• Tighten mounting bolts
Dragging brakes (slow or incomplete release of brakes)	• Brake pedal binding at pivot	• Loosen and lubricate
	• Power brake unit has internal bind	• Inspect for internal bind. Replace unit if internal bind exists.
	• Parking brake cables incorrrectly adjusted or seized	• Adjust cables. Replace seized cables.
	• Rear brakeshoe return springs weak or broken	• Replace return springs. Replace brakeshoe if necessary in axle sets.
	• Automatic adjusters malfunctioning	• Repair or replace adjuster parts as required
	• Caliper, wheel cylinder or master cylinder pistons sticking or seized	• Repair or replace parts as necessary
	• Master cylinder compensating ports blocked (fluid does not return to reservoirs).	• Use compressed air to clear ports. Do not use wire, pencils, or similar objects to open blocked ports.
Vehicle moves to one side when brakes are applied	• Incorrect front tire pressure	• Inflate to recommended cold (reduced load) inflation pressure
	• Worn or damaged wheel bearings	• Replace worn or damaged bearings
	• Brakelining on one side contaminated	• Determine and correct cause of contamination and replace brakelining in axle sets
	• Brakeshoes on one side bent, distorted, or lining loose on shoe	• Replace brakeshoes in axle sets
	• Support plate bent or loose on one side	• Tighten or replace support plate
	• Brakelining not yet seated with drums or rotors	• Burnish brakelining
	• Caliper anchor plate loose on one side	• Tighten anchor plate bolts
	• Caliper piston sticking or seized	• Repair or replace caliper
	• Brakelinings water soaked	• Drive vehicle with brakes lightly applied to dry linings
	• Loose suspension component attaching or mounting bolts	• Tighten suspension bolts. Replace worn suspension components.
	• Brake combination valve failure	• Replace combination valve
Chatter or shudder when brakes are applied (pedal pulsation and roughness may also occur.)	• Brakeshoes distorted, bent, contaminated, or worn	• Replace brakeshoes in axle sets
	• Caliper anchor plate or support plate loose	• Tighten mounting bolts
	• Excessive thickness variation of rotor(s)	• Refinish or replace rotors in axle sets

TCCA9C03

10

BODY AND TRIM

EXTERIOR

Doors

REMOVAL & INSTALLATION

❈❈ WARNING

To prevent damage to the vehicle, two people should perform this procedure.

1. Open the door and support it under its center using a floor jack.
2. Matchmark the door hinge for installation reference.
3. Label and disconnect the electrical harnesses.
4. Remove the door hinge-to-body attaching bolts and washers.
5. Carefully remove the door from the vehicle.
   To install:
6. Position the door on the vehicle, carefully aligning the matchmarks made during removal.
7. Tighten the attaching bolts to 15–21 ft. lbs. (21–28 Nm).
8. Carefully close the door to check for proper alignment.
9. Readjust the door hinges as necessary.
10. Once the door is properly aligned, adjust the door lock (striker).

ADJUSTMENT

1. Determine which hinge bolts must be loosened to move the door in the desired direction.
2. Matchmark the hinge to the door as a starting reference.
3. Loosen the hinge bolts just enough to permit movement of the door with a padded prybar, but not loose enough to permit the door to move on its own.
4. Move the door the distance estimated to obtain the desired fit.
5. Tighten the door hinge-to-body bolts to 15–21 ft. lbs. (21–28 Nm).
6. Check the door to ensure that it closes properly and that there is no binding or interference with the adjacent panel.
7. Repeat the operation until the desired fit is obtained.
8. Check the door lock (striker) alignment for proper door closing, and adjust as necessary.

Hood

REMOVAL & INSTALLATION

❈❈ WARNING

To prevent damage to the vehicle, two people should perform this procedure.

1. Open and support the hood.
2. Matchmark the hood hinges to the hood for installation reference.
3. Note the spacing between the front fender and hood for alignment reference.
4. Protect the body with a cover to prevent damage to the paint.
5. Remove the hood hinge-to-hood attaching bolts.

➡**Take care not to let the hood slip when the bolts are removed.**

6. Remove the hood from the vehicle.
   To install:
7. Position the hood on the vehicle and hand-tighten the retaining bolts.

8. Align the matchmarks and tighten the hood hinge bolts to 12–14 ft. lbs. (16–19 Nm) on Altima or 15–20 ft. lbs. (21–26 Nm) on 240SX models.
9. Carefully lower the hood to check for proper alignment.
10. Adjust the hood alignment as necessary.

ALIGNMENT

◆ See Figures 1 and 2

1. The hood can be adjusted fore-and-aft and side-to-side by loosening the hood hinge retaining bolts.
2. Reposition the hood as required and tighten the hood hinge bolts to 12–14 ft. lbs. (16–19 Nm) on Altima or 15–20 ft. lbs. (21–26 Nm) on 240SX models.
3. To raise or lower the hood in relation to the fenders, add spacers between the hood and hinges.
4. Check the hood lock (striker) alignment for proper hood closing, and adjust as necessary.

Trunk Lid

REMOVAL & INSTALLATION

◆ See Figures 3 and 4

❈❈ WARNING

To prevent damage to the vehicle, two people should perform this procedure.

1. Open and support the trunk lid.
2. Matchmark the trunk lid hinges to the trunk lid for installation reference.
3. Note the spacing between the rear fender and trunk lid for alignment reference.
4. Protect the body with a cover to prevent damage to the paint.
5. Remove the trunk lid-to-hinge bolts.

➡**Take care not to let the trunk lid slip when the bolts are removed.**

6. Remove the trunk lid from the vehicle.
   To install:
7. Position the trunk lid on the vehicle and hand-tighten the retaining bolts.
8. Align the matchmarks and tighten the trunk lid bolts to 12–14 ft. lbs. (16–19 Nm).
9. Carefully lower the trunk lid to check for proper alignment.
10. Adjust the trunk lid alignment as necessary.

ALIGNMENT

◆ See Figures 3 and 4

1. The trunk lid can be adjusted fore-and-aft and side-to-side by loosening the trunk lid bolts.
2. Reposition the trunk lid as required and tighten the trunk lid bolts to 12–14 ft. lbs. (16–19 Nm).
3. To raise or lower the trunk lid in relation to the fenders, add spacers between the trunk lid and hinges.
4. Check the trunk lid lock (striker) alignment for proper trunk lid closing, and adjust as necessary.

Hood lock adjustment
- Adjust hood so that hood primary lock meshes at a position 1 to 1.5 mm (0.039 to 0.059 in) lower than fender.
- After hood lock adjustment, adjust bumper rubber.
- When securing hood lock, ensure it does not tilt. Striker must be positioned at the center of hood primary lock.
- After adjustment, ensure that hood primary and secondary lock operate properly.

Hood lock secondary latch hooking length

More than 5.0 mm (0.197 in)

Hood

Secondary latch

Bumper rubber adjustment
- Adjust so that hood is aligned with fender. At that time deflection is approx. 2 mm (0.08 in).
  [Bumper rubber free height is approx. 13 mm (0.51 in)]

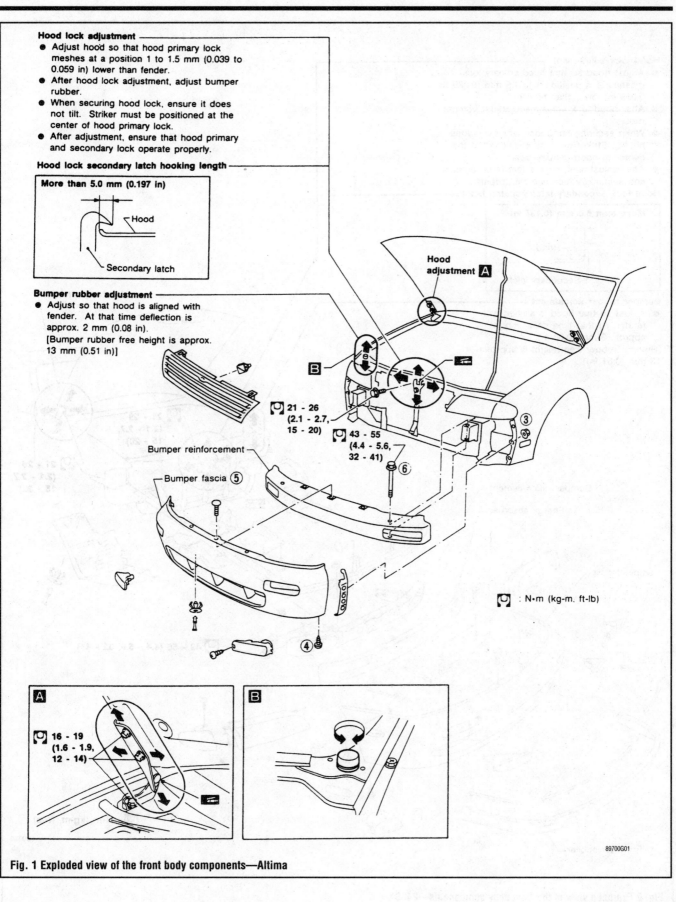

Hood adjustment Ⓐ

B

21 - 26 (2.1 - 2.7, 15 - 20)

43 - 55 (4.4 - 5.6, 32 - 41)

Bumper reinforcement

Bumper fascia ⑤

③

⑥

④

: N·m (kg-m, ft-lb)

Ⓐ
16 - 19 (1.6 - 1.9, 12 - 14)

Ⓑ

89700G01

Fig. 1 Exploded view of the front body components—Altima

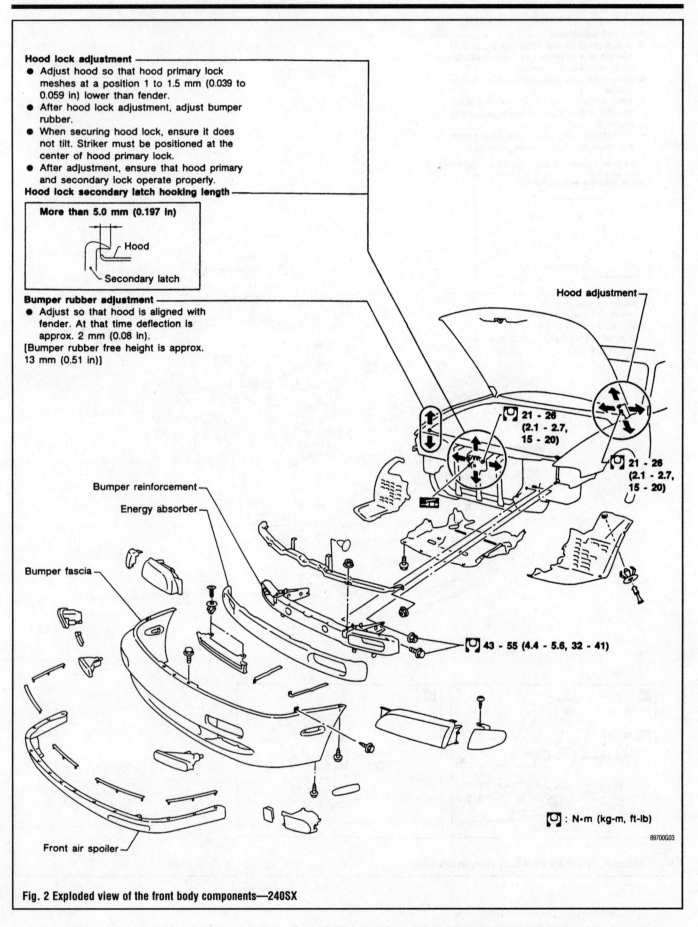

Hood lock adjustment
- Adjust hood so that hood primary lock meshes at a position 1 to 1.5 mm (0.039 to 0.059 in) lower than fender.
- After hood lock adjustment, adjust bumper rubber.
- When securing hood lock, ensure it does not tilt. Striker must be positioned at the center of hood primary lock.
- After adjustment, ensure that hood primary and secondary lock operate properly.

Hood lock secondary latch hooking length

More than 5.0 mm (0.197 in)
- Hood
- Secondary latch

Bumper rubber adjustment
- Adjust so that hood is aligned with fender. At that time deflection is approx. 2 mm (0.08 in).
[Bumper rubber free height is approx. 13 mm (0.51 in)]

Hood adjustment

21 - 26 (2.1 - 2.7, 15 - 20)

21 - 26 (2.1 - 2.7, 15 - 20)

Bumper reinforcement

Energy absorber

Bumper fascia

43 - 55 (4.4 - 5.6, 32 - 41)

Front air spoiler

: N·m (kg-m, ft-lb)

89700G03

Fig. 2 Exploded view of the front body components—240SX

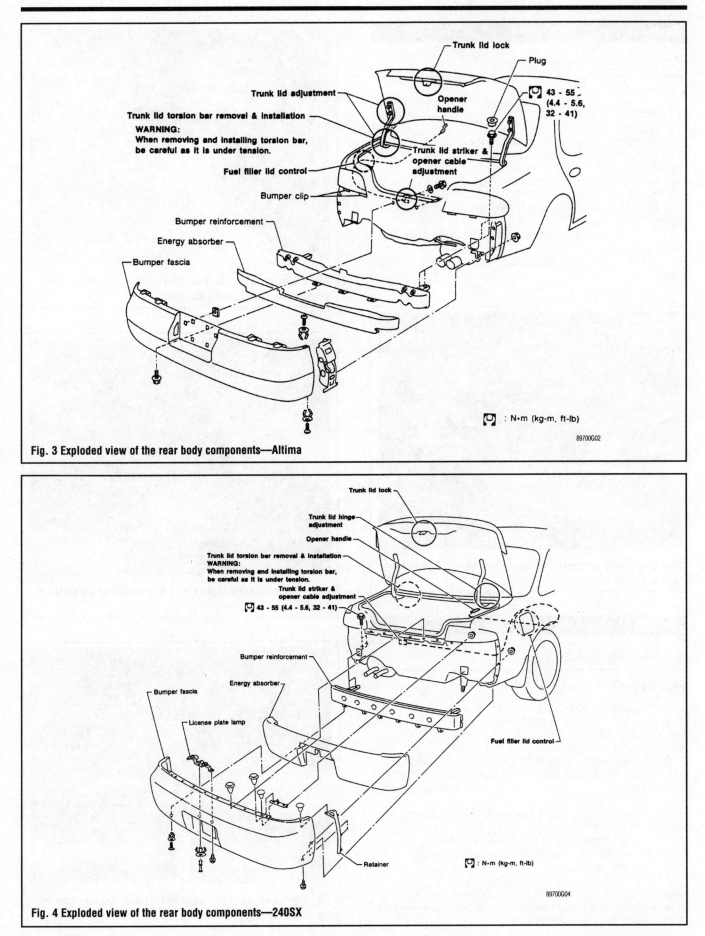

Fig. 3 Exploded view of the rear body components—Altima

Fig. 4 Exploded view of the rear body components—240SX

Grille

REMOVAL & INSTALLATION

▶ **See Figure 5**

1. Open and support the hood.
2. Locate the grille attaching clips.
3. Using a long, straight bladed screwdriver, reach in through the grille and rotate the attaching clips ¼ turn. This will align the square head of the clip with the square hole in the grille.
4. Carefully remove the grille from the vehicle.

To install:

5. Remove any clips still left in the holes on the body and properly position them in the grille.
6. Position the grille on the body and align all the attaching clips with their respective holes.
7. Carefully push the grille into position, making sure all attaching clips engage properly.

Fig. 5 The grille is attached to the radiator support by 5 quarter-turn fasteners (arrows)

Outside Mirrors

REMOVAL & INSTALLATION

▶ **See Figures 6, 7, 8 and 9**

1. Disconnect the negative battery cable.
2. Remove the interior door panel.
3. Carefully pry up the plastic cover.
4. Remove the sail trim panel.
5. On power mirrors, disconnect the mirror electrical harness.
6. Remove the mirror attaching screws, then carefully pull the mirror from the door.

To install:

7. Position the mirror on the vehicle, making sure the rubber molding around the mirror is installed correctly.
8. Install the mirror attaching screws and tighten securely.
9. On power mirrors, connect the mirror electrical harness.
10. Install the sail trim panel.
11. Position the plastic cover and push into place to engage the tangs.
12. Install the interior door panel.
13. Connect the negative battery cable.

Fig. 6 After removing the inner door panel, use a small screwdriver to pry up the plastic trim cover

Fig. 7 The door panel hooks onto a clip (arrow) on the sail trim panel

Fig. 8 Unfasten the three screws which attach the side view mirror to the door . . .

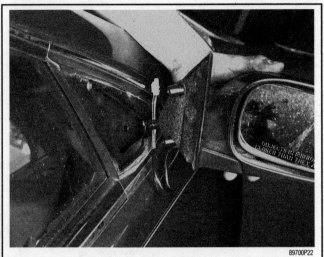

Fig. 9 . . . then lift the side view mirror away from the door after freeing it from the weatherstripping

Antenna

➡On some vehicles, the antenna is impregnated in the rear window glass. On these vehicles, the antenna can be repaired using an antenna repair kit.

REPLACEMENT

Fixed Mast

1. Remove the antenna mast.
2. Remove the antenna nut and base.
3. Disconnect the antenna cable at the antenna.
4. Remove the mounting bolt at the bottom of the antenna.
5. Remove the antenna through the trunk.
6. Installation is the reverse of removal.
7. Tighten the mounting bolt securely.

Power Antenna

MOTOR

1. Remove the antenna nut and base.
2. Disconnect the antenna cable at the antenna.
3. Remove the mounting bolts at the bottom of the power unit.
4. Remove the power unit through the trunk.
5. Installation is the reverse of removal.
6. Tighten the mounting bolts securely.

ROD

1. Remove the antenna nut and base.
2. Remove the antenna rod while raising it by operating the antenna motor.

To install:
3. Lower the antenna rod by operating the antenna motor.
4. Insert the gear section of the antenna rope into place with it facing toward the antenna motor.
5. As soon as rope is wound onto the antenna motor, stop the motor.

6. Insert the antenna rod lower end into the antenna motor pipe.
7. Retract the antenna rod completely by operating the antenna motor.
8. Install the antenna nut and base.

Fenders

REMOVAL & INSTALLATION

1. Remove the front bumper.
2. Remove the headlamp lens assembly.
3. Remove the front wheel inner splash shield.
4. Remove the rocker panel trim, as necessary.
5. Remove the hood, as necessary.
6. Locate and remove the fender mounting bolts and clips.
7. Carefully remove the fender from the vehicle.
8. Installation is the reverse of removal.
9. Carefully align the fender to allow proper clearance to open the front door.

Power Sunroof

REMOVAL & INSTALLATION

♦ **See Figure 10**

1. Tilt up the sunroof lid.
2. Remove the lid side trim.
3. Remove the lid bolts and the lid assembly.
4. Remove the rear drain mount screws and the drain.
5. Remove the shade assembly holders from the sunroof frame.
6. Remove the shade assembly.
7. Remove the sunroof switch, interior accessories and headliner.
8. Remove the switch bracket.
9. Remove the motor assembly, spacer and clip.
10. Remove the wind deflector mount holders from the sunroof frame.
11. Remove the wind deflector.
12. Disconnect the drain hose.
13. Remove the sunroof brackets.
14. Remove the sunroof frame assembly.
15. Remove the link and wire assemblies.

To install:
16. Tilt up the sunroof lid.
17. Install the link and wire assemblies.
18. Install the sunroof frame assembly.
19. Install the sunroof brackets.
20. Connect the drain hose.
21. Install the wind deflector.
22. Install the wind deflector mount holders on the sunroof frame.
23. Install the motor assembly, spacer and clip.
24. Install the switch bracket.
25. Install the sunroof switch, interior accessories and headliner.
26. Install the shade assembly.
27. Install the shade assembly holders on the sunroof frame.
28. Install the rear drain mount screws and the drain.
29. Install the lid bolts and the lid assembly.
30. Install the lid side trim.

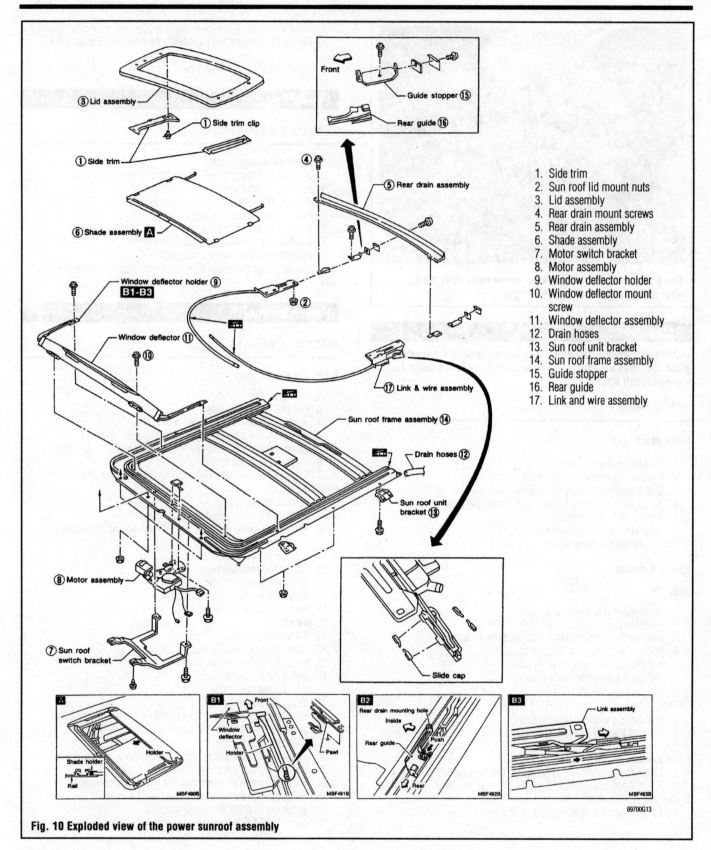

1. Side trim
2. Sun roof lid mount nuts
3. Lid assembly
4. Rear drain mount screws
5. Rear drain assembly
6. Shade assembly
7. Motor switch bracket
8. Motor assembly
9. Window deflector holder
10. Window deflector mount screw
11. Window deflector assembly
12. Drain hoses
13. Sun roof unit bracket
14. Sun roof frame assembly
15. Guide stopper
16. Rear guide
17. Link and wire assembly

Fig. 10 Exploded view of the power sunroof assembly

INTERIOR

Instrument Panel

REMOVAL & INSTALLATION

♦ **See Figures 11 and 12**

1. Disconnect the negative battery cable.
2. Disable the air bag and remove it from the steering wheel.

⁂ CAUTION

Be sure to place the air bag module on a flat surface with the pad side facing upward. In the event of accidental deployment, this will minimize the chance of injury.

3. Remove the steering wheel.
4. Remove the kick plate and dashbaord side finisher on the driver's side.

1. Steering wheel
2. Glove box lid and glove box
3. Front passenger air bag module
4. Steering column cover
5. Lower instrument cover on driver's side
6. A/T finisher or shift lever boot
7. Cluster lid C
8. Radio and deck pocket
9. Cluster lid A
10. Instrument finisher A
11. Combination meter assembly
12. Instrument finisher B
13. Console box
14. Instrument panel center console
15. Defroster grille
16. Instrument panel assembly
17. Link and wire assembly

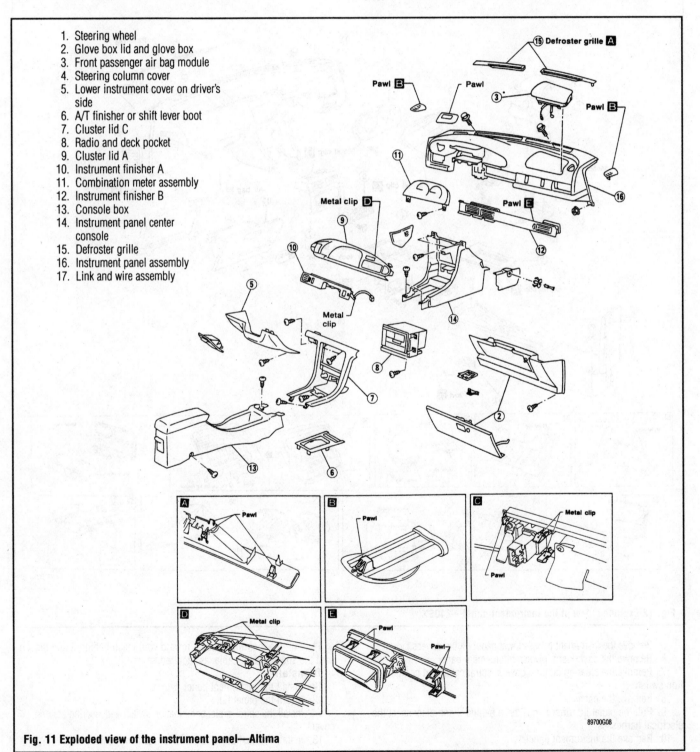

89700G08

Fig. 11 Exploded view of the instrument panel—Altima

1. Steering column cover and combination switch
2. A/T finisher or M/T shift lever boots
3. Instrument lower cover on driver side
4. Instrument lower reinforcement
5. Cluster lid A
6. Combination meter
7. Center ventilation assembly
8. Cluster lid C and audio

9. A/C or heater control
10. Glove box assembly
11. Console box
12. Instrument side finisher
13. Defroster grille
14. Front pillar garnish
15. Instrument panel and pads

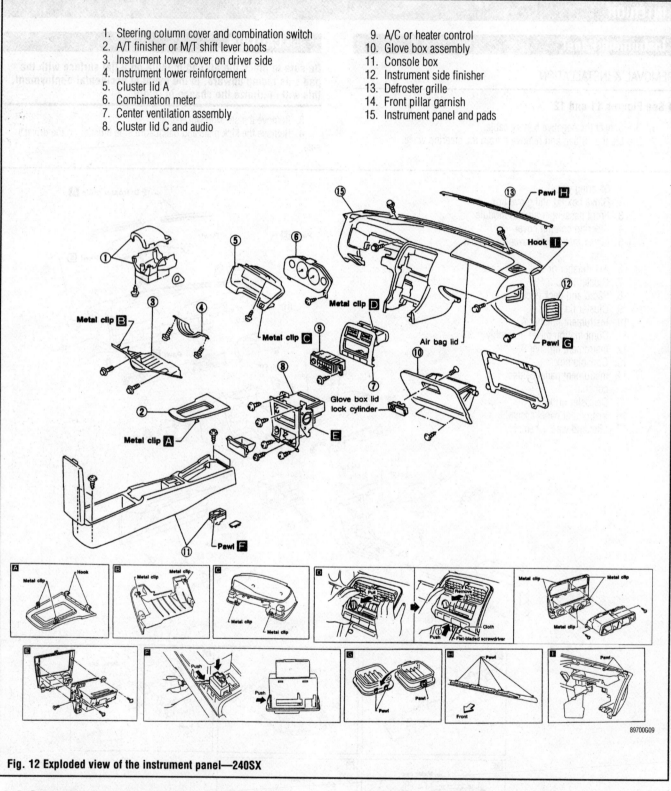

Fig. 12 Exploded view of the instrument panel—240SX

5. Remove the instrument panel's lower panel on the driver's side.
6. Remove the dashboard lower reinforcement panel.
7. Remove the steering column covers, spiral cable and combination switch.
8. Remove the panel lid.
9. Pull the panel lid toward you, reach behind it and disconnect the electrical harnesses.
10. Remove the instrument panel.

11. Pull the instrument panel toward you, reach behind it and disconnect the speedometer cable, as required.
To install:
12. Install the instrument panel.
13. Install the panel lid.
14. Install the spiral cable, combination switch and steering column covers.
15. Install the dashboard lower reinforcement panel.

16. Install the instrument panel's lower panel on the driver's side.
17. Install the kick plate and dashboard side finisher on the driver's side.
18. Install the steering wheel.
19. Install the air bag assembly.
20. Enable the air bag system.
21. Connect the negative battery cable.

Console

REMOVAL & INSTALLATION

1. Unsnap and remove the A/T finisher or M/T boot.
2. Remove the cluster lid, as required to gain clearance.
3. Remove the center console attaching screws.
4. Lift the console slightly and disconnect the electrical harnesses.
5. Carefully lift the center console from the vehicle.
To install:
6. Position the center console in the vehicle.
7. Install and securely tighten all attaching screws.
8. Install the cluster lid.
9. Install the A/T finisher or M/T boot.

Door Panels

REMOVAL & INSTALLATION

▶ **See Figures 13 thru 19**

1. Open the door fully.
2. Remove the inside handle escutcheon.
3. Remove the pull handle.
4. If so equipped, remove the power window switch trim and switch assembly.
5. If applicable, disconnect the switch assembly wiring harness.

➡**The door panel is held in place by several clips. Use a door panel clip removal tool to avoid damaging the clips, door panel or door.**

6. Carefully pry the door panel from the door.
7. Lift the door panel straight up to release it from the lip at the top of the door.
To install:
8. Replace any damaged clips.

Fig. 14 Rear door panel fastener locations

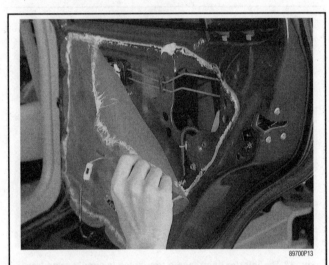

Fig. 15 A plastic moisture barrier prevents condensation from damaging the interior door panel

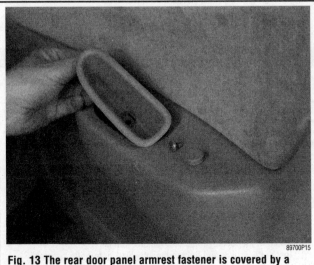

Fig. 13 The rear door panel armrest fastener is covered by a trim plug

Fig. 16 A special caulking is used to keep the moisture barrier in place

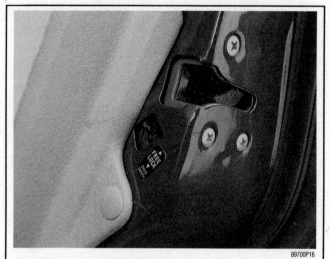

89700P16

Fig. 17 The child safety lock lever is located on the rear doors, near the door lock mechanism

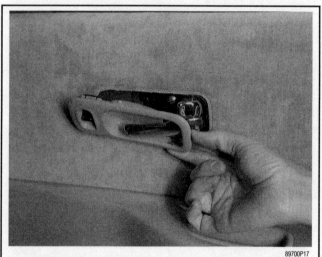

89700P17

Fig. 18 The interior door handle trim piece is simply pried from the door panel

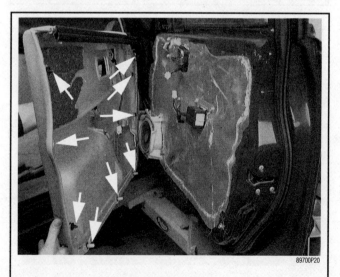

89700P20

Fig. 19 Front door panel fastener locations

9. Position the door panel on the door frame and ensure that the panel fits over the lip at the top of the door.

10. Align the clips with the holes in the door and, using your fist, tap the door panel into place.

11. Connect the switch assembly wiring harness, if so equipped.

12. If applicable, install the power window switch trim and switch assembly.

13. Install the pull handle.

14. Install the inside handle escutcheon.

Door Locks

REMOVAL & INSTALLATION

➡When a lock cylinder is replaced, all the door lock cylinders should be replaced in a set, or have a qualified locksmith rekey the replacement door lock cylinder. This will eliminate carrying an extra key which will only fit one lock.

Lock Cylinders

1. Remove the door panel and moisture barrier.

2. Disconnect the lock cylinder from the rod by turning the resin clip.

3. Loosen the nuts attaching the outside door handle and remove the outside door handle.

4. Remove the lock cylinder by removing the retaining clip.

To install:

5. Install the lock cylinder and clip on the door handle.

6. Install the outside door handle.

7. Connect the rod to the lock cylinder and securely fasten the resin clip.

8. Install the moisture barrier and door panel.

Power Door Lock Actuators

1. Disconnect the negative battery cable.

2. Remove the door panel and moisture barrier.

3. Unfasten the actuator's electrical connector.

4. Disconnect the required linkage rods.

5. Remove the actuator assembly retaining screws.

6. Remove the actuator from the door.

To install:

7. Install the actuator in the door and tighten the retaining screws securely.

8. Connect the required linkage rods.

9. Fasten the actuator's electrical connector.

10. Install the moisture barrier and door panel.

11. Connect the negative battery cable.

Trunk Lock

REMOVAL & INSTALLATION

➡When a lock cylinder is replaced, all the door lock cylinders should be replaced in a set, or have a qualified locksmith rekey the replacement door lock cylinder. This will eliminate carrying an extra key which will only fit one lock.

1. Remove the interior trim, as required.

2. Loosen the nuts/bolts attaching the striker to the trunk lid.

3. Remove the striker.

4. Withdraw the lock cylinder after removing the retaining clip.

To install:

5. Position the lock cylinder and install the retaining clip.

6. Install the striker and tighten the attaching nuts/bolts securely.

7. Install the interior trim, as required.

Electric Window Motor and Regulator

REMOVAL & INSTALLATION

▶ **See Figures 20, 21, 22, 23 and 24**

1. Ensure that the window is fully closed.
2. Disconnect the negative battery cable.
3. Open the door fully.
4. Remove the inner door panel and moisture barrier.

5. Disconnect the electric window motor harness.
6. Remove the electric window motor and regulator, using the illustrations as a guide.

To install:

7. Install the electric window motor and regulator. Tighten the attaching bolts to the illustrated specifications.
8. Connect the electric window motor harness.
9. Connect the negative battery cable.
10. Operate the window to ensure proper functioning.
11. Adjust the window regulator mechanism, as required.
12. Install the moisture barrier and inner door panel.

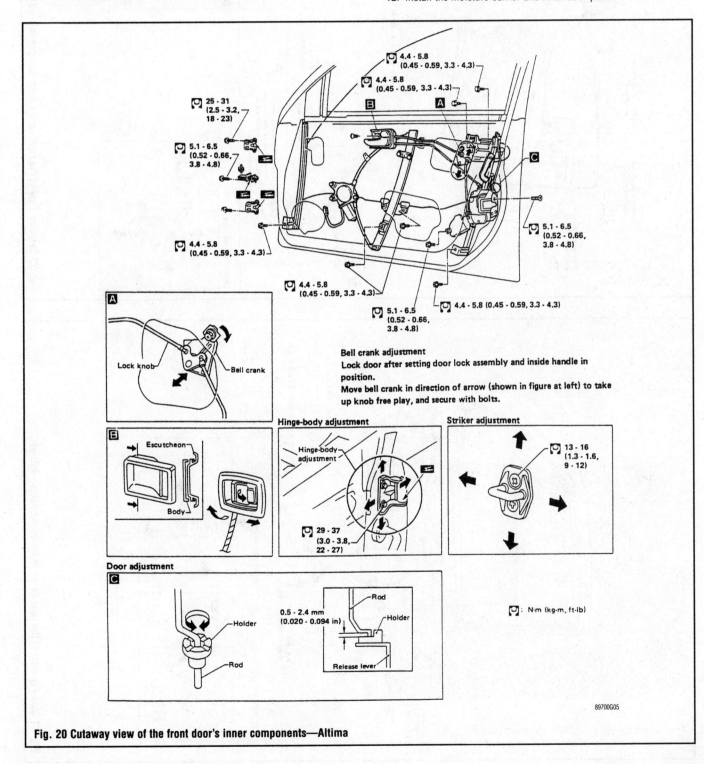

89700G05

Fig. 20 Cutaway view of the front door's inner components—Altima

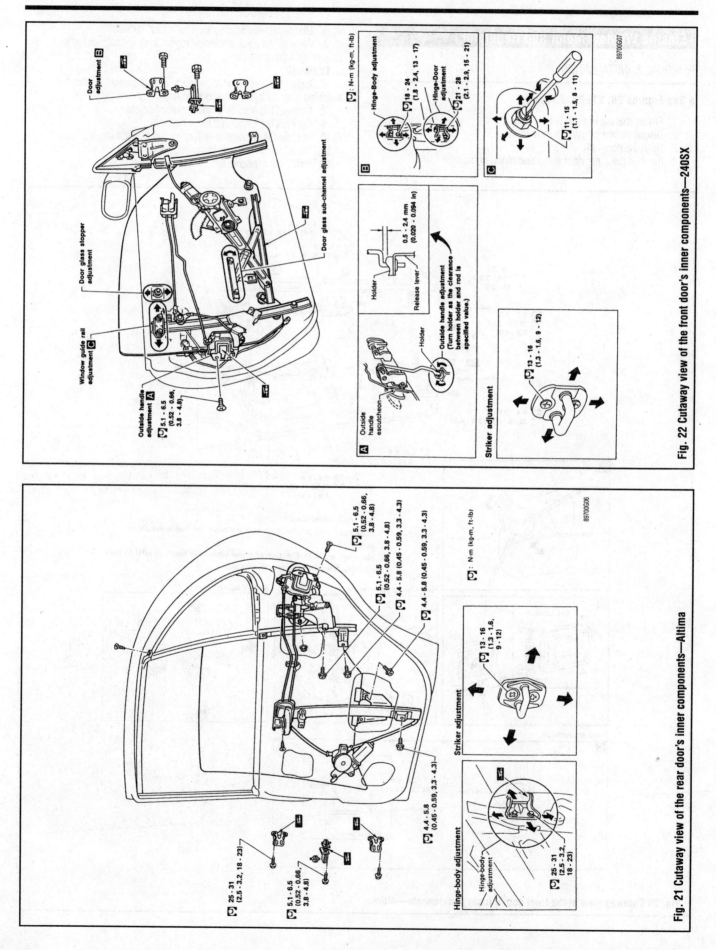

Fig. 22 Cutaway view of the front door's inner components—240SX

Fig. 21 Cutaway view of the rear door's inner components—Altima

Fig. 23 The white arrows indicate power window motor attaching bolts, while the black arrows indicate window regulator attaching bolts—front door (Altima shown)

Fig. 24 The white arrows indicate power window motor attaching bolts, while the black arrows indicate window regulator attaching bolts—rear door

Windshield and Fixed Glass

REMOVAL & INSTALLATION

If your windshield, or other fixed window, is cracked or chipped, you may decide to replace it with a new one yourself. However, there are two main reasons why replacement windshields and other window glass should be installed only by a professional automotive glass technician: safety and cost.

The most important reason a professional should install automotive glass is for safety. The glass in the vehicle, especially the windshield, is designed with safety in mind in case of a collision. The windshield is specially manufactured from two panes of specially-tempered glass with a thin layer of transparent plastic between them. This construction allows the glass to "give" in the event that a part of your body hits the windshield during the collision, and prevents the glass from shattering, which could cause lacerations, blinding and other harm to passengers of the vehicle. The other fixed windows are designed to be tempered so that if they break during a collision, they shatter in such a way that there are no large pointed glass pieces. The professional automotive glass technician knows how to install the glass in a vehicle so that it will function optimally during a collision. Without the proper experience, knowledge and tools, installing a piece of automotive glass yourself could lead to additional harm if an accident should ever occur.

Cost is also a factor when deciding to install automotive glass yourself. Performing this could cost you much more than a professional may charge for the same job. Since the windshield is designed to break under stress, an often life saving characteristic, windshields tend to break VERY easily when an inexperienced person attempts to install one. Do-it-yourselfers buying two, three or even four windshields from a salvage yard because they have broken them during installation are common stories. Also, since the automotive glass is designed to prevent the outside elements from entering your vehicle, improper installation can lead to water and air leaks. Annoying whining noises at highway speeds from air leaks or inside body panel rusting from water leaks can add to your stress level and subtract from your wallet. After buying two or three windshields, installing them and ending up with a leak that produces a noise while driving and water damage during rainstorms, the cost of having a professional do it correctly the first time may be much more alluring. We here at Chilton, therefore, advise that you have a professional automotive glass technician service any broken glass on your vehicle.

WINDSHIELD CHIP REPAIR

◆ **See Figures 25 thru 39**

➡**Check with your state and local authorities on the laws for state safety inspection. Some states or municipalities may not allow chip repair as a viable option for correcting stone damage to your windshield.**

Although severely cracked or damaged windshields must be replaced, there is something that you can do to prolong or even prevent the need for replacement of a chipped windshield. There are many companies which offer windshield chip repair products, such as Loctite's® Bullseye™ windshield repair kit. These kits usually consist of a syringe, pedestal and a sealing

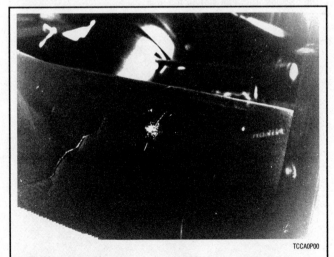

Fig. 25 Small chips on your windshield can be fixed with an aftermarket repair kit, such as the one from Loctite®

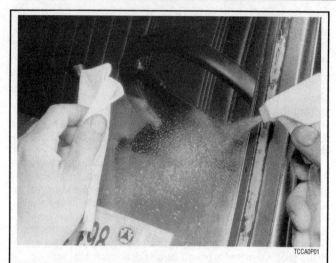

Fig. 26 To repair a chip, clean the windshield with glass cleaner and dry it completely

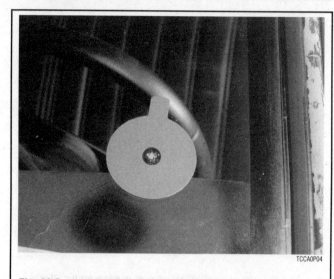

Fig. 29 Be sure that the tab points upward on the windshield

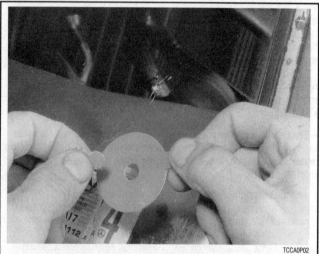

Fig. 27 Remove the center from the adhesive disc and peel off the backing from one side of the disc . . .

Fig. 30 Peel the backing off the exposed side of the adhesive disc . . .

Fig. 28 . . . then press it on the windshield so that the chip is centered in the hole

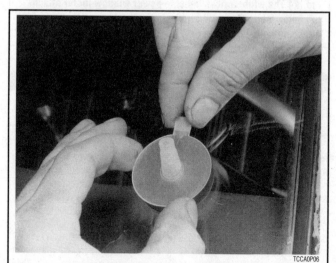

Fig. 31 . . . then position the plastic pedestal on the adhesive disc, ensuring that the tabs are aligned

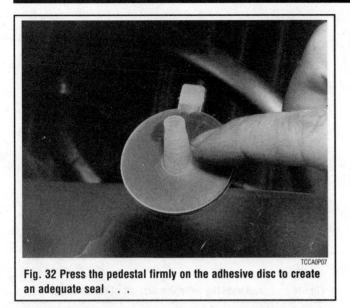

Fig. 32 Press the pedestal firmly on the adhesive disc to create an adequate seal . . .

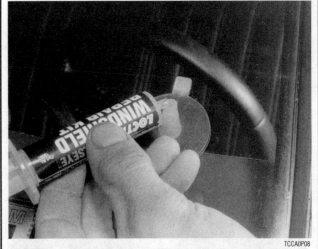

Fig. 33 . . . then install the applicator syringe nipple in the pedestal's hole

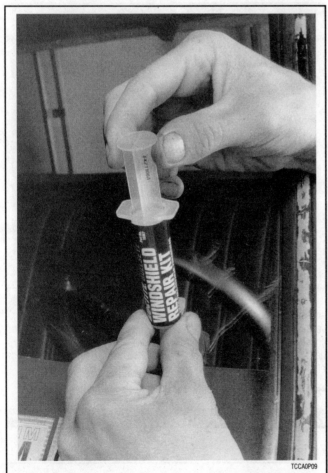

Fig. 34 Hold the syringe with one hand while pulling the plunger back with the other hand

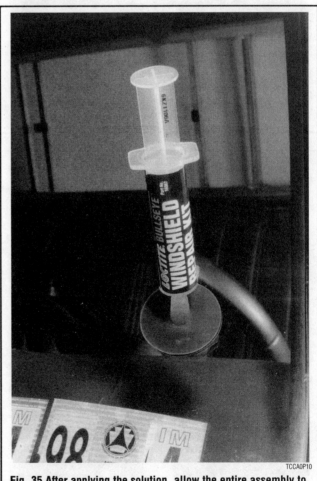

Fig. 35 After applying the solution, allow the entire assembly to sit until it has set completely

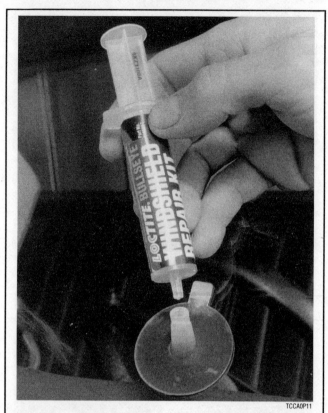

Fig. 36 After the solution has set, remove the syringe from the pedestal . . .

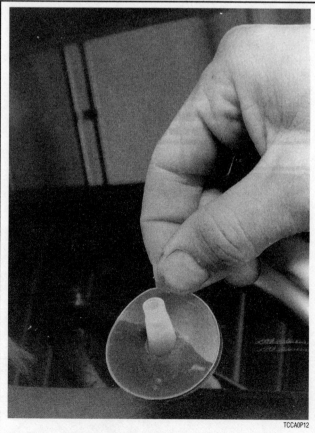

Fig. 37 . . . then peel the pedestal off of the adhesive disc . . .

Fig. 38 . . . and peel the adhesive disc off of the windshield

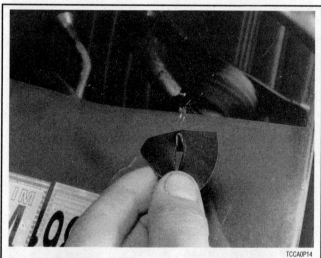

Fig. 39 The chip will still be slightly visible, but it should be filled with the hardened solution

adhesive. The syringe is mounted on the pedestal and is used to create a vacuum which pulls the plastic layer against the glass. This helps make the chip transparent. The adhesive is then injected which seals the chip and helps to prevent further stress cracks from developing. Refer to the sequence of photos to get a general idea of what windshield chip repair involves.

➡**Always follow the specific manufacturer's instructions.**

Inside Rear View Mirror

REPLACEMENT

◗ **See Figure 40**

1. Remove the mirror by pushing the deflecting spring with a screwdriver. Insert the screwdriver from the lower side of the spring and slide the mirror assembly off of the mounting plate.

➡**Should the mounting plate come loose from the windshield, repair kits are available.**

2. Install the mirror by sliding the assembly onto the mounting pad, so that the spring engages.

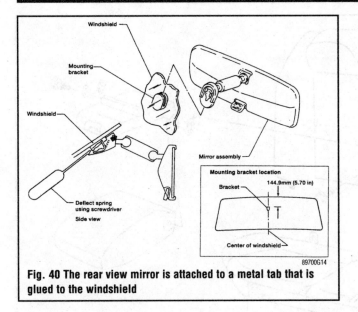

Fig. 40 The rear view mirror is attached to a metal tab that is glued to the windshield

Seats

REMOVAL & INSTALLATION

Front

▶ **See Figure 41**

1. Locate and remove the four seat mounting bolts.
2. Disconnect any electrical harnesses attached to the seat.
3. Carefully lift the seat from the vehicle.
4. Installation is the reverse of removal.
5. Tighten the seat mounting bolts to 32–41 ft. lbs. (43–55 Nm).

Rear

▶ **See Figures 42 thru 48**

1. Locate and remove the two mounting bolts under the bench portion of the rear seat.
2. Locate and remove the two mounting bolts at the bottom of the seat back.

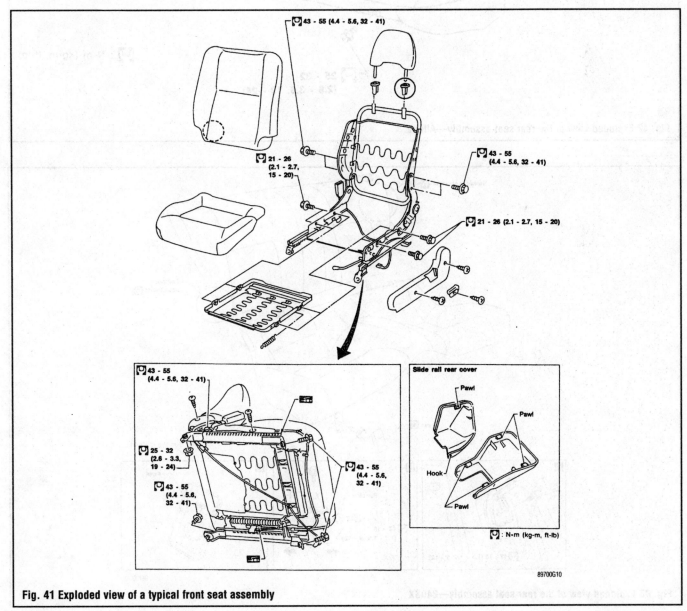

Fig. 41 Exploded view of a typical front seat assembly

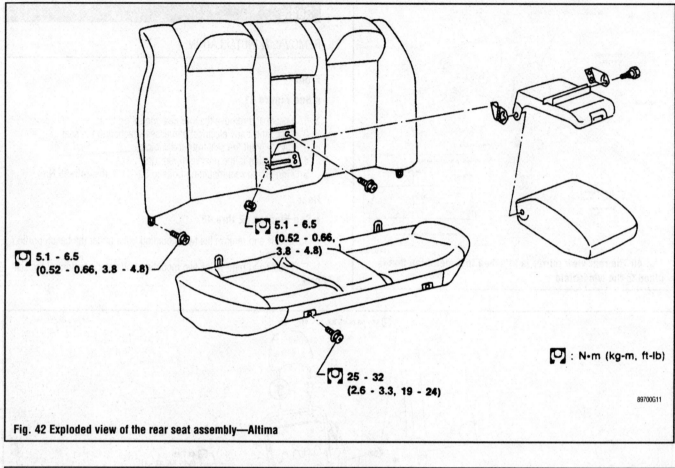

5.1 - 6.5
(0.52 - 0.66, 3.8 - 4.8)

5.1 - 6.5
(0.52 - 0.66,
3.8 - 4.8)

5.1 - 6.5
(0.52 - 0.66, 3.8 - 4.8)

25 - 32
(2.6 - 3.3, 19 - 24)

: N•m (kg-m, ft-lb)

89700G11

Fig. 42 Exploded view of the rear seat assembly—Altima

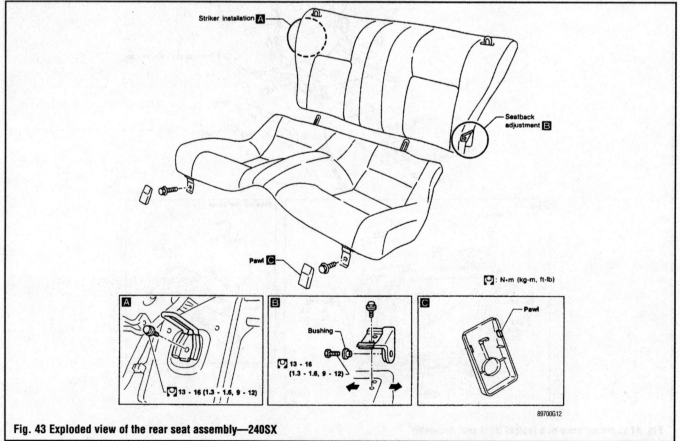

Striker installation A

Seatback adjustment B

Pawl C

: N•m (kg-m, ft-lb)

A

13 - 16 (1.3 - 1.6, 9 - 12)

B

Bushing

13 - 16
(1.3 - 1.6, 9 - 12)

C

Pawl

89700G12

Fig. 43 Exploded view of the rear seat assembly—240SX

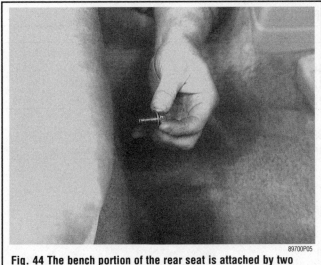

Fig. 44 The bench portion of the rear seat is attached by two bolts, one on each side of the vehicle

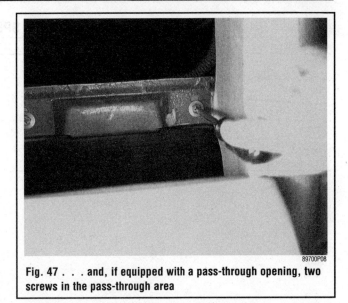

Fig. 47 . . . and, if equipped with a pass-through opening, two screws in the pass-through area

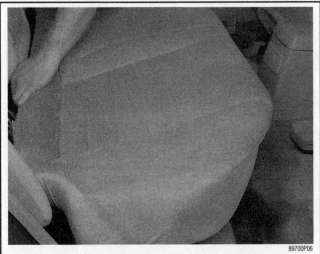

Fig. 45 After removing the fasteners, the bench portion of the rear seat should slide out easily

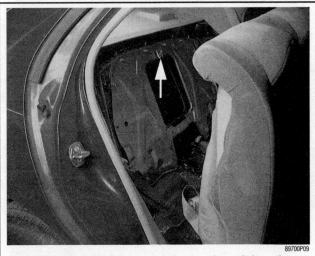

Fig. 48 Lift the back of the rear seat up to release it from the clips (arrow)

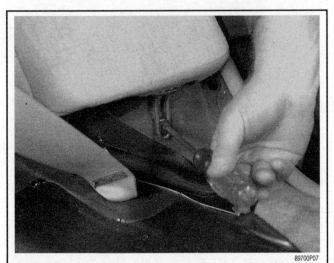

Fig. 46 The back portion of the rear seat is attached by two bolts, one on each side of the vehicle . . .

3. If equipped with a pass-through opening/center armrest, remove the two screws from the frame.

4. On Altima, lift the seat back straight up to release it from the clips which attach it to the package shelf.

5. On 240SX, disengage the seat back lock and fold the seat down.

6. Carefully remove the seat from the vehicle.

7. Installation is the reverse of removal.

8. Tighten the seat mounting bolts to 32–41 ft. lbs. (43–55 Nm).

Power Seat Motor

REMOVAL & INSTALLATION

1. Remove the seat.

2. Turn the seat upside down to access all seat adjusting motors.

3. Remove the seat trim panels.

4. Remove the seat motor mounting bolts.

5. Remove the seat motors.

6. Installation is the reverse of removal.

7. Tighten the seat mounting bolts to 15–20 ft. lbs. (21–26 Nm).

TORQUE SPECIFICATIONS

Components	Ft. Lbs.	Nm
Exterior		
Door	15–21 ft. lbs.	21–28 Nm
Hood	12–14 ft. lbs.	16–19 Nm
Trunk Lid	12–14 ft. lbs.	16–19 Nm
Interior		
Seats	32–41 ft. lbs.	43–55 Nm
Power Seat Motor	15–20 ft. lbs.	21–26 Nm

89700C01

GLOSSARY

AIR/FUEL RATIO: The ratio of air-to-gasoline by weight in the fuel mixture drawn into the engine.

AIR INJECTION: One method of reducing harmful exhaust emissions by injecting air into each of the exhaust ports of an engine. The fresh air entering the hot exhaust manifold causes any remaining fuel to be burned before it can exit the tailpipe.

ALTERNATOR: A device used for converting mechanical energy into electrical energy.

AMMETER: An instrument, calibrated in amperes, used to measure the flow of an electrical current in a circuit. Ammeters are always connected in series with the circuit being tested.

AMPERE: The rate of flow of electrical current present when one volt of electrical pressure is applied against one ohm of electrical resistance.

ANALOG COMPUTER: Any microprocessor that uses similar (analogous) electrical signals to make its calculations.

ARMATURE: A laminated, soft iron core wrapped by a wire that converts electrical energy to mechanical energy as in a motor or relay. When rotated in a magnetic field, it changes mechanical energy into electrical energy as in a generator.

ATMOSPHERIC PRESSURE: The pressure on the Earth's surface caused by the weight of the air in the atmosphere. At sea level, this pressure is 14.7 psi at 32°F (101 kPa at 0°C).

ATOMIZATION: The breaking down of a liquid into a fine mist that can be suspended in air.

AXIAL PLAY: Movement parallel to a shaft or bearing bore.

BACKFIRE: The sudden combustion of gases in the intake or exhaust system that results in a loud explosion.

BACKLASH: The clearance or play between two parts, such as meshed gears.

BACKPRESSURE: Restrictions in the exhaust system that slow the exit of exhaust gases from the combustion chamber.

BAKELITE: A heat resistant, plastic insulator material commonly used in printed circuit boards and transistorized components.

BALL BEARING: A bearing made up of hardened inner and outer races between which hardened steel balls roll.

BALLAST RESISTOR: A resistor in the primary ignition circuit that lowers voltage after the engine is started to reduce wear on ignition components.

BEARING: A friction reducing, supportive device usually located between a stationary part and a moving part.

BIMETAL TEMPERATURE SENSOR: Any sensor or switch made of two dissimilar types of metal that bend when heated or cooled due to the differ-ent expansion rates of the alloys. These types of sensors usually function as an on/off switch.

BLOWBY: Combustion gases, composed of water vapor and unburned fuel, that leak past the piston rings into the crankcase during normal engine operation. These gases are removed by the PCV system to prevent the buildup of harmful acids in the crankcase.

BRAKE PAD: A brake shoe and lining assembly used with disc brakes.

BRAKE SHOE: The backing for the brake lining. The term is, however, usually applied to the assembly of the brake backing and lining.

BUSHING: A liner, usually removable, for a bearing; an anti-friction liner used in place of a bearing.

CALIPER: A hydraulically activated device in a disc brake system, which is mounted straddling the brake rotor (disc). The caliper contains at least one piston and two brake pads. Hydraulic pressure on the piston(s) forces the pads against the rotor.

CAMSHAFT: A shaft in the engine on which are the lobes (cams) which operate the valves. The camshaft is driven by the crankshaft, via a belt, chain or gears, at one half the crankshaft speed.

CAPACITOR: A device which stores an electrical charge.

CARBON MONOXIDE (CO): A colorless, odorless gas given off as a normal byproduct of combustion. It is poisonous and extremely dangerous in confined areas, building up slowly to toxic levels without warning if adequate ventilation is not available.

CARBURETOR: A device, usually mounted on the intake manifold of an engine, which mixes the air and fuel in the proper proportion to allow even combustion.

CATALYTIC CONVERTER: A device installed in the exhaust system, like a muffler, that converts harmful byproducts of combustion into carbon dioxide and water vapor by means of a heat-producing chemical reaction.

CENTRIFUGAL ADVANCE: A mechanical method of advancing the spark timing by using flyweights in the distributor that react to centrifugal force generated by the distributor shaft rotation.

CHECK VALVE: Any one-way valve installed to permit the flow of air, fuel or vacuum in one direction only.

CHOKE: A device, usually a moveable valve, placed in the intake path of a carburetor to restrict the flow of air.

CIRCUIT: Any unbroken path through which an electrical current can flow. Also used to describe fuel flow in some instances.

CIRCUIT BREAKER: A switch which protects an electrical circuit from overload by opening the circuit when the current flow exceeds a predetermined level. Some circuit breakers must be reset manually, while most reset automatically.

COIL (IGNITION): A transformer in the ignition circuit which steps up the voltage provided to the spark plugs.

COMBINATION MANIFOLD: An assembly which includes both the intake and exhaust manifolds in one casting.

COMBINATION VALVE: A device used in some fuel systems that routes fuel vapors to a charcoal storage canister instead of venting them into the atmosphere. The valve relieves fuel tank pressure and allows fresh air into the tank as the fuel level drops to prevent a vapor lock situation.

COMPRESSION RATIO: The comparison of the total volume of the cylinder and combustion chamber with the piston at BDC and the piston at TDC.

CONDENSER: 1. An electrical device which acts to store an electrical charge, preventing voltage surges. 2. A radiator-like device in the air conditioning system in which refrigerant gas condenses into a liquid, giving off heat.

CONDUCTOR: Any material through which an electrical current can be transmitted easily.

CONTINUITY: Continuous or complete circuit. Can be checked with an ohmmeter.

COUNTERSHAFT: An intermediate shaft which is rotated by a mainshaft and transmits, in turn, that rotation to a working part.

CRANKCASE: The lower part of an engine in which the crankshaft and related parts operate.

CRANKSHAFT: The main driving shaft of an engine which receives reciprocating motion from the pistons and converts it to rotary motion.

CYLINDER: In an engine, the round hole in the engine block in which the piston(s) ride.

CYLINDER BLOCK: The main structural member of an engine in which is found the cylinders, crankshaft and other principal parts.

CYLINDER HEAD: The detachable portion of the engine, usually fastened to the top of the cylinder block and containing all or most of the combustion chambers. On overhead valve engines, it contains the valves and their operating parts. On overhead cam engines, it contains the camshaft as well.

DEAD CENTER: The extreme top or bottom of the piston stroke.

DETONATION: An unwanted explosion of the air/fuel mixture in the combustion chamber caused by excess heat and compression, advanced timing, or an overly lean mixture. Also referred to as "ping".

DIAPHRAGM: A thin, flexible wall separating two cavities, such as in a vacuum advance unit.

DIESELING: A condition in which hot spots in the combustion chamber cause the engine to run on after the key is turned off.

DIFFERENTIAL: A geared assembly which allows the transmission of motion between drive axles, giving one axle the ability to turn faster than the other.

DIODE: An electrical device that will allow current to flow in one direction only.

DISC BRAKE: A hydraulic braking assembly consisting of a brake disc, or rotor, mounted on an axle, and a caliper assembly containing, usually two brake pads which are activated by hydraulic pressure. The pads are forced against the sides of the disc, creating friction which slows the vehicle.

DISTRIBUTOR: A mechanically driven device on an engine which is responsible for electrically firing the spark plug at a predetermined point of the piston stroke.

DOWEL PIN: A pin, inserted in mating holes in two different parts allowing those parts to maintain a fixed relationship.

DRUM BRAKE: A braking system which consists of two brake shoes and one or two wheel cylinders, mounted on a fixed backing plate, and a brake drum, mounted on an axle, which revolves around the assembly.

DWELL: The rate, measured in degrees of shaft rotation, at which an electrical circuit cycles on and off.

ELECTRONIC CONTROL UNIT (ECU): Ignition module, module, amplifier or igniter. See Module for definition.

ELECTRONIC IGNITION: A system in which the timing and firing of the spark plugs is controlled by an electronic control unit, usually called a module. These systems have no points or condenser.

END-PLAY: The measured amount of axial movement in a shaft.

ENGINE: A device that converts heat into mechanical energy.

EXHAUST MANIFOLD: A set of cast passages or pipes which conduct exhaust gases from the engine.

FEELER GAUGE: A blade, usually metal, or precisely predetermined thickness, used to measure the clearance between two parts.

FIRING ORDER: The order in which combustion occurs in the cylinders of an engine. Also the order in which spark is distributed to the plugs by the distributor.

FLOODING: The presence of too much fuel in the intake manifold and combustion chamber which prevents the air/fuel mixture from firing, thereby causing a no-start situation.

FLYWHEEL: A disc shaped part bolted to the rear end of the crankshaft. Around the outer perimeter is affixed the ring gear. The starter drive engages the ring gear, turning the flywheel, which rotates the crankshaft, imparting the initial starting motion to the engine.

FOOT POUND (ft. lbs. or sometimes, ft.lb.): The amount of energy or work needed to raise an item weighing one pound, a distance of one foot.

FUSE: A protective device in a circuit which prevents circuit overload by breaking the circuit when a specific amperage is present. The device is constructed around a strip or wire of a lower amperage rating than the circuit it is designed to protect. When an amperage higher than that stamped on the fuse is present in the circuit, the strip or wire melts, opening the circuit.

GEAR RATIO: The ratio between the number of teeth on meshing gears.

GENERATOR: A device which converts mechanical energy into electrical energy.

HEAT RANGE: The measure of a spark plug's ability to dissipate heat from its firing end. The higher the heat range, the hotter the plug fires.

HUB: The center part of a wheel or gear.

HYDROCARBON (HC): Any chemical compound made up of hydrogen and carbon. A major pollutant formed by the engine as a byproduct of combustion.

HYDROMETER: An instrument used to measure the specific gravity of a solution.

INCH POUND (inch lbs.; sometimes in.lb. or in. lbs.): One twelfth of a foot pound.

INDUCTION: A means of transferring electrical energy in the form of a magnetic field. Principle used in the ignition coil to increase voltage.

INJECTOR: A device which receives metered fuel under relatively low pressure and is activated to inject the fuel into the engine under relatively high pressure at a predetermined time.

INPUT SHAFT: The shaft to which torque is applied, usually carrying the driving gear or gears.

INTAKE MANIFOLD: A casting of passages or pipes used to conduct air or a fuel/air mixture to the cylinders.

JOURNAL: The bearing surface within which a shaft operates.

KEY: A small block usually fitted in a notch between a shaft and a hub to prevent slippage of the two parts.

MANIFOLD: A casting of passages or set of pipes which connect the cylinders to an inlet or outlet source.

MANIFOLD VACUUM: Low pressure in an engine intake manifold formed just below the throttle plates. Manifold vacuum is highest at idle and drops under acceleration.

MASTER CYLINDER: The primary fluid pressurizing device in a hydraulic system. In automotive use, it is found in brake and hydraulic clutch systems and is pedal activated, either directly or, in a power brake system, through the power booster.

MODULE: Electronic control unit, amplifier or igniter of solid state or integrated design which controls the current flow in the ignition primary circuit based on input from the pick-up coil. When the module opens the primary circuit, high secondary voltage is induced in the coil.

NEEDLE BEARING: A bearing which consists of a number (usually a large number) of long, thin rollers.

OHM: (Ω) The unit used to measure the resistance of conductor-to-electrical flow. One ohm is the amount of resistance that limits current flow to one ampere in a circuit with one volt of pressure.

OHMMETER: An instrument used for measuring the resistance, in ohms, in an electrical circuit.

OUTPUT SHAFT: The shaft which transmits torque from a device, such as a transmission.

OVERDRIVE: A gear assembly which produces more shaft revolutions than that transmitted to it.

OVERHEAD CAMSHAFT (OHC): An engine configuration in which the camshaft is mounted on top of the cylinder head and operates the valve either directly or by means of rocker arms.

OVERHEAD VALVE (OHV): An engine configuration in which all of the valves are located in the cylinder head and the camshaft is located in the cylinder block. The camshaft operates the valves via lifters and pushrods.

OXIDES OF NITROGEN (NOx): Chemical compounds of nitrogen produced as a byproduct of combustion. They combine with hydrocarbons to produce smog.

OXYGEN SENSOR: Use with the feedback system to sense the presence of oxygen in the exhaust gas and signal the computer which can reference the voltage signal to an air/fuel ratio.

PINION: The smaller of two meshing gears.

PISTON RING: An open-ended ring with fits into a groove on the outer diameter of the piston. Its chief function is to form a seal between the piston and cylinder wall. Most automotive pistons have three rings: two for compression sealing; one for oil sealing.

PRELOAD: A predetermined load placed on a bearing during assembly or by adjustment.

PRIMARY CIRCUIT: the low voltage side of the ignition system which consists of the ignition switch, ballast resistor or resistance wire, bypass, coil, electronic control unit and pick-up coil as well as the connecting wires and harnesses.

PRESS FIT: The mating of two parts under pressure, due to the inner diameter of one being smaller than the outer diameter of the other, or vice versa; an interference fit.

RACE: The surface on the inner or outer ring of a bearing on which the balls, needles or rollers move.

REGULATOR: A device which maintains the amperage and/or voltage levels of a circuit at predetermined values.

RELAY: A switch which automatically opens and/or closes a circuit.

RESISTANCE: The opposition to the flow of current through a circuit or electrical device, and is measured in ohms. Resistance is equal to the voltage divided by the amperage.

RESISTOR: A device, usually made of wire, which offers a preset amount of resistance in an electrical circuit.

RING GEAR: The name given to a ring-shaped gear attached to a differential case, or affixed to a flywheel or as part of a planetary gear set.

ROLLER BEARING: A bearing made up of hardened inner and outer races between which hardened steel rollers move.

ROTOR: 1. The disc-shaped part of a disc brake assembly, upon which the brake pads bear; also called, brake disc. 2. The device mounted atop the distributor shaft, which passes current to the distributor cap tower contacts.

SECONDARY CIRCUIT: The high voltage side of the ignition system, usually above 20,000 volts. The secondary includes the ignition coil, coil wire, distributor cap and rotor, spark plug wires and spark plugs.

SENDING UNIT: A mechanical, electrical, hydraulic or electro-magnetic device which transmits information to a gauge.

SENSOR: Any device designed to measure engine operating conditions or ambient pressures and temperatures. Usually electronic in nature and designed to send a voltage signal to an on-board computer, some sensors may operate as a simple on/off switch or they may provide a variable voltage signal (like a potentiometer) as conditions or measured parameters change.

SHIM: Spacers of precise, predetermined thickness used between parts to establish a proper working relationship.

SLAVE CYLINDER: In automotive use, a device in the hydraulic clutch system which is activated by hydraulic force, disengaging the clutch.

SOLENOID: A coil used to produce a magnetic field, the effect of which is to produce work.

SPARK PLUG: A device screwed into the combustion chamber of a spark ignition engine. The basic construction is a conductive core inside of a ceramic insulator, mounted in an outer conductive base. An electrical charge from the spark plug wire travels along the conductive core and jumps a preset air gap to a grounding point or points at the end of the conductive base. The resultant spark ignites the fuel/air mixture in the combustion chamber.

SPLINES: Ridges machined or cast onto the outer diameter of a shaft or inner diameter of a bore to enable parts to mate without rotation.

TACHOMETER: A device used to measure the rotary speed of an engine, shaft, gear, etc., usually in rotations per minute.

THERMOSTAT: A valve, located in the cooling system of an engine, which is closed when cold and opens gradually in response to engine heating, controlling the temperature of the coolant and rate of coolant flow.

TOP DEAD CENTER (TDC): The point at which the piston reaches the top of its travel on the compression stroke.

TORQUE: The twisting force applied to an object.

TORQUE CONVERTER: A turbine used to transmit power from a driving member to a driven member via hydraulic action, providing changes in drive ratio and torque. In automotive use, it links the driveplate at the rear of the engine to the automatic transmission.

TRANSDUCER: A device used to change a force into an electrical signal.

TRANSISTOR: A semi-conductor component which can be actuated by a small voltage to perform an electrical switching function.

TUNE-UP: A regular maintenance function, usually associated with the replacement and adjustment of parts and components in the electrical and fuel systems of a vehicle for the purpose of attaining optimum performance.

TURBOCHARGER: An exhaust driven pump which compresses intake air and forces it into the combustion chambers at higher than atmospheric pressures. The increased air pressure allows more fuel to be burned and results in increased horsepower being produced.

VACUUM ADVANCE: A device which advances the ignition timing in response to increased engine vacuum.

VACUUM GAUGE: An instrument used to measure the presence of vacuum in a chamber.

VALVE: A device which control the pressure, direction of flow or rate of flow of a liquid or gas.

VALVE CLEARANCE: The measured gap between the end of the valve stem and the rocker arm, cam lobe or follower that activates the valve.

VISCOSITY: The rating of a liquid's internal resistance to flow.

VOLTMETER: An instrument used for measuring electrical force in units called volts. Voltmeters are always connected parallel with the circuit being tested.

WHEEL CYLINDER: Found in the automotive drum brake assembly, it is a device, actuated by hydraulic pressure, which, through internal pistons, pushes the brake shoes outward against the drums.

MASTER
INDEX